Endorsements

"*Swords and Plowshares* is full of surprises, overturning the standard conceptions and misconceptions about Evangelicals and war. Focusing on World War II, Korea, and Vietnam, author Timothy Padgett explores what Evangelical writers during these years said about America, America's enemies, war, and the end times. Highly recommended for Evangelicals and critics of Evangelicals."

—**Bruce Riley Ashford**, Provost and Professor, Southeastern Baptist Theological Seminary; author of *Letters to an American Christian*, *Every Square Inch*, and *One Nation under God*.

"Historians who correct false and damaging perceptions of individuals or groups engage in commendable acts of generosity. Timothy Padgett is one such historian. In the present work he successfully corrects the wide-spread historiography that Evangelical Christians from 1937 to 1973 were quite simply mindless military hawks. According to this claim Evangelicals uncritically accepted any military policy or action of the American government. With clear prose and a very impressive use of primary sources, Padgett demonstrates this contention is simply without merit. Padgett's well-crafted study, therefore, constitutes a marvelous contribution to any fair-minded quest to understand Twentieth-Century American Evangelicalism. For this reason as well as others the volume deserves a wide-readership."

—**John D. Woodbridge**, Research Professor of Church History and the History of Christian Thought, Trinity Evangelical Divinity School

"In many corners of the world, white American evangelicals are viewed as God-and-country hawks, blind supporters of their nation's military-industrial complex. But in this thought-provoking book, historian Timothy Padgett demonstrates that, from the time of World War II to Vietnam, the reality was rather more complicated. At their best, the most insightful evangelicals he features thought carefully and critically about their nation's wars and related foreign policy. They published support for the United States government. But they also criticized it— time and time again—based on teachings in the Bible. In their best-known magazines, they claimed allegiance more to God than to country."

—**Douglas A. Sweeney**, Distinguished Professor of Church History and the History of Christian Thought, Trinity Evangelical Divinity School

"This is a major new work in historical moral theology by an up-and-coming scholar sure to become a major contributor to Christian thought on the ethics of war. Timothy D. Padgett's *Swords and Plowshares: American Evangelicals on War, 1937–1973* is a first rate academic achievement. While narrow it is well written and very well researched. It is narrow because it concentrates on a single issue within the larger field of Christian ethics—the ethics of war; on a single faction within the larger Christian community—American evangelicals; and on a single aspect of analysis—the history of views expressed by American evangelicals on war over the span of a single generation: from 1937 to 1973. But while narrow this work deals with what it addresses in such depth, and documents all details so exhaustively, it is sure to be the standard reference for all future work touching on the subject, community, and time it addresses."

—**Daniel Heimbach**, Senior Professor of Christian Ethics, Southeastern Baptist Theological Seminary

"*Swords and Plowshares* combines a deep read of evangelical writings on war and global affairs with a deep understanding of the historical and theological contexts. The result is an important and engaging analysis of evangelicals' understanding of the United States and its role in the world. Scholars and general readers alike will learn much from Tim Padgett's fine work."

—**Craig A. Kaplowitz,** Professor of History and Director of The Honors Program, Judson University

SWORDS *and* PLOWSHARES

American Evangelicals on War, 1937–1973

SWORDS *and* PLOWSHARES

American Evangelicals on War, 1937–1973

TIMOTHY D. PADGETT

STUDIES IN HISTORICAL AND SYSTEMATIC THEOLOGY

LEXHAM PRESS

Swords and Plowshares: American Evangelicals on War, 1937–1973
Studies in Historical and Systematic Theology

Copyright 2018 Timothy D. Padgett

Lexham Press, 1313 Commercial St., Bellingham, WA 98225
LexhamPress.com

Print ISBN 9781683591061
Digital ISBN 9781683591078

Lexham Editorial Team: Todd Hains, Eric Bosell, Danielle Thevanez
Cover Design: Bryan Hintz
Typesetting: Kathy Curtis

Contents

Abbreviations xi

Acknowledgments xiii

1. Introduction 1
    Historical Overview 4
    Literature Review 8
    Contribution and Methodology 13
    Source Material 16
    Structure 19

2. The Road to War, 1937–1941 20
    Overview 20
    Enemies 21
    America 34
    War 40
    End Times 47

3. The Conflagration, 1942–1945 55
    Overview 55
    Enemies 56
    America 66
    War 77
    End Times 92

4. Plowshares into Swords, 1946–1949 100
    Overview 100
    Enemies 101
    America 111
    War 121
    End Times 132

5. Turning East, 1950–1953...142
    Overview 142
    Enemies 143
    America...153
    War 165
    End Times 176

6. A Tense Peace, 1954–1958 184
    Overview 184
    Enemies 186
    America...200
    War 215
    End Times 222

7. Battles Near and Far, 1959–1963 232
    Overview 232
    Enemies 233
    America...247
    War 264
    End Times 272

8. Almost Armageddon, 1964–1968 281
    Overview 281
    Enemies 281
    America...293
    War 306
    End Times 317

9. The End of War, 1969–1973...326
    Overview 326
    Enemies 327
    America...337
    War 352
    End Times 359

10. Conclusions...375
    Overview 375
    Enemies 376
    America..380
    War 383
    End Times..386
    Conclusion...389

Bibliography... 392

Author Index 422

Subject Index 424

Abbreviations

ACCC	American Council of Christian Churches
NAE	National Association of Evangelicals
MBI	Moody Bible Institute
CH	*Christian Herald*
CT	*Christianity Today*
ET	*Eternity*
MM	*Moody Monthly*
OH	*Our Hope*
PJ	*Presbyterian Journal*
SPJ	*Southern Presbyterian Journal*

Acknowledgments

This topic was a lifetime in coming. History in general and military history in particular had always been a passion of mine. What drew me in were the great tensions of war, the best and the worst of humanity on display in the same events and often the same individuals. It was not the excitement of explosions and battles which interested me but the reasons behind it all. The writings of Francis A. Schaeffer, John Keegan, and Victor Davis Hanson encouraged me to look beyond the "what" of history to the "why" of the ideas driving people to think and act in a given way. I wanted to know why people acted in the ways that they did, and what made one group more moral, successful, and memorable than another. Yet it was issues of the church which drove me into academic work. I wanted to know how servants of the Prince of Peace reacted to a time of total war.

Had it not been for the counsel of a great many along the way, I would have been left with nothing more than disparate passions of little value to anyone besides myself. It was Craig Kaplowitz who encouraged me to find a subject which I was passionate about. Only then, he warned, would I be able to push through the weeks and months of solitary research.

I would like to thank my doctoral committee and the church history department of Trinity Evangelical Divinity School: John Woodbridge, Douglas Sweeney, Richard Averbeck, and Scott Manetsch. Each in his own way took the interests and passions on my part and molded them into discipline, focus, procedure, and productivity. More than mere scholarly counsel, they drove home to me the priority that the work I did needed to serve God and his church in some way, to ask how the bride of Christ would be bettered by my efforts. I can only hope that I have lived up to that calling here, and that the church is both challenged and encouraged by this retelling.

I would also like to note the invaluable assistance of John Simons, Dan Hummel, Christina Loucks, and Todd Hains along with all the others who acted as my sounding board throughout this process, with Todd serving double-duty in this regard as also editor and exhorter in the transition from paper to book. Likewise, were it not for the teaching opportunities provided by Jay Simala at Trinity International University, John Fry at Trinity Christian College, and, again, Craig Kaplowitz at Judson University, the practice of translating academic data into meaningful facts would have been left immature. This book would have been a far poorer project without them.

Introduction

As the United States drew near to war with the Axis in the late 1930s, President Roosevelt and his officials could be excused if they paid evangelical Christians scant attention. With their dwindling influence and their uncontroversial support of the coming war, they would hardly have stood out from the crowd. Thirty-five years later, when President Nixon's administration was seeking peace with honor in Vietnam, they could count on finding staunch support, and a measure of opposition, from a movement that had defied expectations of a quiet retirement and had emerged as a growing force in the American socio-political landscape. In all the conflicts of that tortuous period, American evangelical leaders responded to their nation's martial endeavors with a remarkable consistency. The fervency of their faith and the stubbornness with which they held to their theological principles combined with a mandate to engage the watching world and led them to call on their followers and wider society to live out the ideals of the Bible in America's foreign policy. Whether it was a call to arms or an appeal to lay them down, US evangelical leaders rooted their counsel and criticism in the application of the moral law of God to the contemporary situation.[1]

---

1. Defining evangelicalism is a cottage industry all its own, and a definition adequate for the mid-twentieth century of this study would simply not be suitable for the situation of the early twenty-first century of this writing. Having influences as far back as the fourteenth-century theologian John Wycliffe, the fifteenth-century Czech reformer and martyr, Jon Hus, the Magisterial Reformers of the sixteenth century, and the seventeenth- and eighteenth-century renewal movements of the Puritans and Pietists, evangelicalism can be explained doctrinally as those animated by a passion for the Bible as the actual revelation of God to humanity, with all its themes of creation, humanity's divine image marred by a corrupted nature and condemned status before God, the miraculous, the deity of Jesus, the Trinity, the second coming, the priority of personal conversion and revival, and the call to evangelize and transform the world. As these criteria could well be applied to a great many Christians outside

In both the popular and academic imaginations, evangelicals are often portrayed in a less than complimentary manner. In many ways evangelicals can find their public image to be entirely unrecognizable to what they see in the people they rub elbows with at their local church. This is hardly a new phenomenon. In the 1920s we see Sinclair Lewis satirizing the gullibility of the religious populace and deriding the character of church leaders in his novel, *Elmer Gantry*. By the 1960s we have the fictionalized account of the Scopes "Monkey Trial" with Spencer Tracy boldly standing up against religious irrationality in the

---

the boundaries of evangelicalism, the movement may be further characterized historically, borrowing from Douglas Sweeney's definition, as Protestant orthodoxy accented by a "twist" from eighteenth-century revivalism. Douglas Sweeney, *The American Evangelical Story: The History of the Movement* (Grand Rapids, MI: Baker Academic, 2005), 24–25. David Bebbington has offered another clear set of criteria which act as boundary markers. With his famous "quadrilateral," he has centered evangelicalism around the four points of conversionism, crucicentrism, Biblicism, and activism. David W. Bebbington, *Evangelicals in Modern Britain: A History from the 1730s to the 1980s* (Grand Rapids, MI: Baker Book House, 1989), 2–4. George Marsden offered a half-humorous definition of evangelicalism, saying that, at least as of the 1950s and 1960s, an evangelical was someone who liked Billy Graham. George M. Mardsen, *Understanding Fundamentalism and Evangelicalism* (Grand Rapids, MI: Wm. B. Eerdmans, 1991), 6. As lighthearted as such a statement may be intended to be, it also carries with it a fair amount of truth. Someone who likes Rev. Graham will be someone who, like him, holds to Douglas Sweeney's "classical protestant orthodoxy with an eighteenth-century twist," the theological principles of the magisterial Reformers coupled with a revivalist emphasis on personal renewal and public manifestation of faith. Someone who likes Rev. Graham will also appreciate the conservative arguments of the Fundamentalist versus Modernist controversy, while maintaining the more open approach of the Neo-Evangelicals coming out of the 1940s and 1950s. The delineations for inclusion here are partly doctrinal, referring to the key beliefs noted above, partly historical, in keeping with Sweeney's definition, and partly self-definitional, taking people's application of the term to themselves. Although the above criteria make no mention of ethnicity or gender, nearly all the source material will come from white, male elites. In many ways it is unfortunate that the academic custom has been to portray theologically conservative white males as representative of evangelicalism while African Americans, in particular, who are just as conservative theologically, are lumped in with other African Americans who are in no way theologically conservative. Since much of the rest of the literature uses the term "evangelicals" to describe the white conservatives of American Protestantism, and to see their ideas as flowing partly from their societal status, this book will take this definition and examine whether the recent consensus on their beliefs about US foreign policy as Manichean, monolithic, and uncritical is borne out by their own words.

movie *Inherit the Wind*. Like some moustache-twisting ne'er-do-well of silent films, the image of the theologically conservative Christian leader has become a standardized villain in movies and on TV. Now, this sort of thing should never be taken very seriously. After all, the 1990s hit show *The X-Files* once manifested the depth of its research when one of the oh-so-educated special agents referred to the time in the Bible when St. Ignatius practiced teleportation.[2] Trying to get an accurate impression of religious reality from movies and TV is like picking up your understanding of physics from cartoons.

However, particularly when discussing their impact on national security, this caustic image of evangelicals has escaped from its confines on the silver screen and has made its way to the pages of books chronicling evangelicalism. Speaking specifically of the role of evangelicals in US foreign policy, some authors have suggested that American Christian conservatives are embarked upon a dangerous crusade to gain socio-political control of the United States and the world. *With God on Our Side: One Man's War against an Evangelical Coup in America's Military* suggests nothing short of a cabal threatening the very liberties of ordinary Americans and the peace of the world. The authors argue that evangelicals will embark on a crusade, using the US military to convert the globe by force.

Is it really such a stretch to extrapolate spiritual warfare into the realm of actual bullets and bloodshed? Are we at risk of arming and equipping an army of our own fanatics single-mindedly focused on ushering in the kingdom of God by converting, or killing, every last unbeliever? This isn't my formulation. The evangelical credo is clear on this point: the gospel must be preached to all the world. Every knee will bow and every tongue confess. That's a mission of conquest."[3]

---

2. Chris Carter and Kim Newton, "Revelations," *The X-Files*, Season 3, Episode 11.

3. Michael L. Weinstein and Davin Seay, *With God on Our Side: One Man's War against an Evangelical Coup in America's Military* (New York: Thomas Dunne Books, 2006), 207–8.

This is a characterization more likely to be found in the imaginations of evangelicalism's critics than among evangelicals themselves.

While mischaracterizations like this can and should be dismissed, even those projects which are more nuanced and well-researched can paint evangelicals with overly stark tones. Very often evangelicals are shown as reflexively hawkish on foreign policy, though allowance is sometimes given to the evangelical left as being reflectively dovish. Aside from strict pacifists there are few who would object to the support given by evangelical writers to the American war to defeat Nazism and Japanese militarism.[4] The same equanimity was not granted to evangelical advice given during the Vietnam War, even though the substance of their commentary was at the very least analogous during each conflict. The idea in this book is to examine evangelical comments about American wars from the so-called "Good War," World War II, beginning in the late 1930s up through the so-called "Bad War," the Vietnam Conflict, coming to an end in the early 1970s and to examine these responses as the manifestation of their ideas in all their complexity.

HISTORICAL OVERVIEW

During the Second World War theological conservatives in the United States were struggling to reconstitute their shattered place in society. As new leaders began to rise and new organizations began to take shape, some conservatives became more isolationist while others adopted a more interventionist attitude with the creation of institutions such as the National Association of Evangelicals (NAE) in 1942. Others still sought to remain on good terms with both those in the new denominations as well as with so-called mainline groups like the Federal (later, National) Council of Churches. Having lost the denominational battles of the previous decades, they could no longer rely upon institutions or access they once had as these had been largely appropriated by the mainline Protestants.[5]

---

4. Many have protested given tactics employed by the United States and the Allies, such as the intensity of the Anglo-American air campaigns against German and Japanese cities, but it would be quite unusual to single out theological conservatives for going along with these attacks, given their general support at the time.

5. Not every evangelical operated outside mainline organizations. Several of this book's significant subjects, such as L. Nelson Bell, Donald G. Barnhouse, and

While many mainline denominations opposed any kind of war on the principle that it was incompatible with a Christian view of the world,[6] many evangelicals supported America's entry into the Second World War. In fact part of the impetus toward the creation of the NAE came from the desire to counter the mainline monopoly on chaplaincy in the armed forces.[7] Evangelical periodicals sought to bring their readers around to their viewpoints on the building conflagration. Throughout the conflict both the Fascism of America's European enemies and the militarism of its Japanese foe were roundly condemned, even as qualifying remarks were made warning against overzealousness in Christians' support for the Allies or expectation of divine favor. For example, *Moody Monthly* warned against both a complacent attitude toward Allied sins and a hateful stance toward Axis people. The end of the war brought unambiguous relief and rejoicing which was, nonetheless, tempered by concern over the new potential of atomic warfare.[8]

Daniel A. Poling remained either within mainline denominations or even, in the case of Poling, went so far as to write approvingly of both mainline groups like the National Council of Churches and the efforts of Billy Graham.

6. Lyle W. Dorsett makes reference to this in his *Serving God and Country: US Military Chaplains in World War II* (New York: The Berkley Publishing Group, 2012), 22–24, and Andrew Preston provides details of the mainline struggle in the lead up to World War II in his book, *Sword of the Spirit, Shield of Faith* (New York: Alfred A. Knopf, 2012,) 301–3. This mainline opposition was not universal, and much of it did not outlast the events of Pearl Harbor or the discovery of Nazi atrocities. Further, as the books described below by Inboden and Herzog note, many of the leaders of the National Council of Churches, Reinhold Niebuhr and John Foster Dulles most notably, were among the earliest and strongest proponents of American intervention, both in World War II and in the Cold War. Preston goes so far as to say that the primary opponent of mainline pacifism in the first years of the Second World War was not political leaders but Reinhold Niebuhr. Preston, 303.

7. Carl F. H. Henry, *Confessions of a Theologian: An Autobiography* (Waco: Word Books, 1986), 105.

8. In 1945, just weeks after the first use of atomic weaponry, Wilbur Smith said, "The world will never be the same from that hour when the first atomic bomb to be used in war was dropped upon Hiroshima. We can never go back to that former age, and what the future holds, no one knows. Probably not one single day in all history, since the death and resurrection of our Lord, has witnessed any one event which has had and will continue to have such an enormous, transforming influence over the thinking of mankind." Wilbur Smith, *The Atomic Bomb and the Word of God* (Chicago: Moody Press, 1945), 5–6. As will be seen below, the possible devastation

For a brief period the United States seemed poised to revert to its prior isolationist stance as its massive wartime armed forces were scaled back rapidly, but this atavism came to an end in short order with the increased tensions of the Cold War. Having seen the greater part of the Western world gobbled up by Nazism before an effective response could be mounted, America and its allies went back to a wartime footing to challenge the perceived new threat posed by the Soviet Communism ruling from central Germany to the Bering Sea. Particularly after the Chinese Revolution of 1949 and its attendant loss of this longstanding Christian missions field, evangelicals supported the new US assertiveness, seeing in Communism the single greatest threat to human dignity and religious liberty in the world. And this support was no longer that of a voice crying in the cultural wilderness. With new inspiration, such as Carl Henry's *Uneasy Conscience*[9] and new prominence, coming off Billy Graham's Crusades, evangelicals were returning from exile and engaging the world with a renewed vigor.

Though not fans of one another, Presidents Truman and Eisenhower issued a uniform call highlighting the shared goals of the United States and religion in the early days of the Cold War.[10] In slightly different ways each president sought to unite the religious bodies of the nation and the world in a common cause against their common enemy, the Communist Bloc. At the same time many programs were introduced to the US military encouraging religious observance and ethical standards. Although these programs initially received a great deal of support from mainline denominations, evangelicals were less impressed with what they saw as syncretistic calls for general religion over against a genuine, conversion-centered biblical orthodoxy. They saw Communism as a deadly enemy, and preached and wrote accordingly, but they sometimes

---

brought with atomic weapons was a mortifying prospect for many evangelicals in the post-World War II era.

9. Carl F. H. Henry, *The Uneasy Conscience of Modern Fundamentalism* (Grand Rapids, MI: Wm. B. Eerdmans, 1947).

10. For an excellent discussion of the parallel yet dissonant approaches to the Cold War and religion, see Jonathan P. Herzog, *The Spiritual Industrial Complex: America's Religious Battle against Communism in the Early Cold War* (New York: Oxford University Press, 2011) and William Inboden, *Religion and American Foreign Policy, 1945–1960: The Soul of Containment* (New York: Cambridge University Press, 2008).

had little stomach for any nebulous Judeo-Christianity, devoid of the clear convictions which make political cooperation run less smoothly.

Throughout the 1950s evangelicals continued their backing of the American Cold War effort, but they occasionally rebuked the government, not for overly aggressive initiatives but for inadequate reactions to Communist moves. The prospect of an amicable truce in Korea and a passive response to the Soviet invasion of Hungary resulted in admonitions from evangelical leaders across the movement. The newly formed evangelical organ, *Christianity Today (CT)*, gave regular attention to the dangers of Communism, both nationally and internationally, with articles by theologians as well as by government officials such as FBI director J. Edgar Hoover and US Army General William K. Harrison. However, as the decade came to a close, changes began to emerge. The government began to move away from the religious emphases found in the addition of "under God" to the Pledge of Allegiance, while the mainline denominations tried to strike what they considered a "balanced" pose between the Communist East and Capitalist West, leaving evangelicals as an ever more important constituency in support of US policies. Perhaps most importantly for the future of evangelical responses to American moves, the United States was increasingly involved in reconstituting the Western response to the French defeat in Vietnam.

The decade of the 1960s was bracketed by two psychically scarring geopolitical events, with the US and USSR dancing on the edge of a nuclear apocalypse with 1962's Cuban Missile Crisis and pyrrhic American victory in 1968's Tet Offensive. The heady years of the Space Race brought with them the development of weapon systems capable of raining atomic devastation anywhere and anytime. While much of American elite culture and the mainline Protestant establishment seemingly looked with equanimity on the respective merits of Western liberal democracy and Eastern Communist dictatorships, evangelicals, on the whole, continued to look at the United States as a contingent good, not at all perfect, but certainly the better choice, given the totalitarian alternative. Seeing Communism as an imminent danger to humanity as a whole, evangelicals preached against any slackening of resolve in combating it.

The year 1973 was a time of great change, both for the US military and for evangelicalism. Though the war would continue for the next two years, it was at this time that came the official end of combat operations by American forces in Vietnam. This event would send the military and its supporters into a time of soul searching, and the "Vietnam Syndrome" would not be purged until the Gulf War nearly twenty years later. This time also saw the rise of both the evangelical left as well as the first stirrings of the religious right. Both sides saw themselves as calling their country to the priorities of the Bible, although for the one it was forward to principles so far ignored and for the other it was back to a righteousness which had been lost.

LITERATURE REVIEW

In the wake of the Cold War, there were those, such as Francis Fukuyama, who predicted an "end of history" now that the political and economic liberalism of the West had triumphed over its Communist foes. It seemed the issue had been settled, and now all that was left was to allow the unstoppable forces of secularization, democracy, and rationality to shake out the remaining difficult areas, as the world entered a new stage of cooperation and left competition in the past. Advocates of this idea were caught unawares at the dawn of the twenty-first century when the United States, now the world's reigning hyperpower, elected to its presidency, George W. Bush, a man expressing views of the world, morality, and spirituality with a vocabulary starkly different from post-religious lexicon many had come to expect. This event was followed hard upon by the traumatic 9/11 attacks on the centers of global economic and military power, an assault inflicted by Al-Qaeda, a radical Islamic group. Global conflict, it seemed, was not at an end, and it was being driven by religious motivations entirely unfamiliar to enlightened elites of the West. Into this context, and even before, many new works were produced at the popular and academic level seeking to explain, and sometimes explain away, the significance of theological conservatives in reference to the issues of national security and international relations.

In his work, *Spiritual Weapons: The Cold War and the Forging of an American National Religion*, T. Jeremy Gunn suggests that Christianity was commandeered by political and business leaders. Gunn sees the church leaders as willingly adopting a governmental theism, which allowed for no criticism of United States policy. Governmental theism is analogous in many ways to the more commonly used civil religion with the exception that Gunn here emphasizes the way the US government and many religious authorities encouraged a conflation of government and religion.[11]

In somewhat of a contrast Raymond Haberski argues that civil religion serves a generally constructive role in which the idea, "God," if not the actual person, stands over against any American pretension of omniscience or moral purity. This is an interesting idea in and of itself, standing, as it does, in opposition to Gunn's study in which civil religion or governmental theism connote a shallow faith created by the powerful. Haberski warns that a danger for evangelicals has to do with their failure to think critically. For example he uses the word "Manichean" repeatedly to describe the way evangelicals saw the global situation as a stark choice between the forces of good, the United States and its allies, and the forces of evil, the Soviet Union and its minions, using the term three times in two pages to describe the ideas of Billy Graham and his fellows.[12]

Similarly, in *Faith and War: How Christians Debated the Cold and Vietnam Wars*, David Settje applies the word "monolithic" to conservative evangelicals arguing that they failed to distinguish sufficiently the complexity of the Cold War's intricacies. Similar to the present book, Settje analyzed periodicals from the 1964–1975 era, managing to provide perspective from a wide variety of Christian groups, and his project bears the marks of this quite extensive research. At times he is quite fair to those with whom he disagrees, noting of *Christianity Today* that "it is clear from the material published that the editors, writers, and even readers studied the war and formulated opinions based on their

11. T. Jeremy Gunn, *Spiritual Weapons: The Cold War and the Forging of an American National Religion* (Westport, CT: Praeger Publishers, 2009).

12. Raymond Haberski, Jr., *God and War: American Civil Religion Since 1945* (New Brunswick, NJ: Rutgers University Press, 2012), 23–24.

perception of factual information, not visceral feelings."[13] However, at other times his modifiers give a greater benefit of doubt to mainline groups, saying things like, "the editors and writers understood the complexity of the situation,"[14] but of evangelicals that they "clung to traditional Cold War mentality."[15]

Considering the possibility of a fiery global cataclysm during the Cold War, it is understandable that some authors have approached the issue of eschatology and evangelicals. As Angela Lahr's title, *Millennial Dreams and Apocalyptic Nightmares: The Cold War Origins of Political Evangelicalism* might suggest, the author roots the later political activism of evangelicals in the fusion of Christ and country brought about by the intensity of Cold War tensions reverberating in premillennial theology.[16] Covering similar ground, Timothy Weber highlights the importance not just of premillennial thought but of dispensational eschatology in particular. In his book *On the Road to Armageddon: How Evangelicals Became Israel's Best Friend*, Weber discusses the way evangelicals encouraged a staunchly pro-Israeli stance by the United States in part because of the influence of Dispensationalist teaching. The book falls into three basic sections: a study of the history of Dispensationalism in the late 1800s and early 1900s, a study of evangelism directed toward Jews in America, and a study of Dispensationalist pro-Israeli political agitation.[17] His portrayal of evangelicals is largely positive even as it is critical. Weber treats his subjects as well-intentioned and willing to learn from mistakes. Although, this does not keep him from concluding that their influence upon American foreign

---

13. David Settje, *Faith and War: How Christians Debated the Cold and Vietnam Wars* (New York: New York University Press, 2011), 12.

14. Settje, 111.

15. Settje, 61.

16. Angela M. Lahr, *Millennial Dreams and Apocalyptic Nightmares: The Cold War Origins of Political Evangelicalism* (New York: Oxford University Press, 2007), 61–62.

17. One failing of Weber's book is that it is, in effect, three excellent short books discussing the topics noted above, all tied together under a single theme. Each subsection is informative and well-researched, but at times the whole is disjointed.

policy was very often negative, radicalizing both US and Israeli policy[18] and as turning a blind eye to the suffering of Palestinian Arabs.[19]

In his book *American Apocalypse: A History of Modern Evangelicalism*, Matthew Sutton shares with Lahr the contention that evangelicalism has been shaped significantly by premillennial eschatology. He does, however, with a stronger focus on the complexity of the movement, and his definition of evangelicalism is as thorough and clear as any.[20] He explained the basis for evangelical views on politics with a greater appreciation for their theology than some, but his focus on eschatology sometimes led him to oversimplify particular cases for the sake of coherence.[21]

Religion and American Foreign Policy, 1945–1960: The Soul of Containment by William Inboden and *The Spiritual Industrial Complex: America's Religious Battle against Communism in the Early Cold War* by

---

18. On page 260 Weber describes two Israeli right-wing groups which had received financial and moral support from American Dispensationalists, and on 262–66 he makes note of the attempt by American Dispensationalist cattle breeders to produce a pure red heifer, without which a new Temple of Jerusalem could not be fully consecrated.

19. Timothy P. Weber, *On the Road to Armageddon: How Evangelicals Became Israel's Best Friend* (Grand Rapids: Baker Academic, 2004). Interestingly, in his forthcoming book Dan Hummel argues that Weber puts too much emphasis on Dispensationalism and not enough on the role of interreligious cooperation between American Jews, Israelis, and evangelicals. He also questions how important Dispensationalism is to political support for Israel, which he sees as more a product of evangelicals following the biblical injunction to "bless those who bless" Israel (Gen 12:3). *A Covenant of the Mind: Evangelicals, Israel, and the Construction of a Special Relationship* (Philadelphia: University of Pennsylvania Press, 2018).

20. "I use the term 'evangelical' to refer to Christians situated broadly in the Reformed and Wesleyan traditions who over the last few centuries have emphasized the centrality of the Bible, the death and resurrection of Jesus, the necessity of individual conversion, and spreading the faith through missions." Matthew Avery Sutton, *American Apocalypse: A History of Modern Evangelicalism* (Cambridge, MA: Belknap Press, 2014), x.

21. For example, on page 296, when addressing a booklet by Wilbur Smith, Sutton argued that the author believed that atomic warfare would be the means of the end of the world, but all Smith had said was that it would be that kind of thing and went so far as to say that atomic weaponry would not be the means, saying, "I do not mean that the passage at which we are going to look is a *prediction* of the atomic bomb, because this passage speaks of something which God is to do, while the atomic bomb is something man has accomplished." Wilbur M. Smith, *The Atomic Bomb and the Word of God* (Chicago: Moody, 1945), 10, 17.

Jonathan Herzog both chronicle the relationships between various
Christian groups and American Cold War actions primarily in the period
of the Truman and Eisenhower administrations. Though covering the
same issue during the same time period, each author approaches his
subject from a different perspective and with slightly different conclusions. Herzog treats the period almost as a dramatic tragedy, with rising
and falling action. He suggests that the increase of religious thought
and practice in the wake of World War II, from Graham's crusades to the
film "The Ten Commandments," was a top-down contrivance, albeit a
sincere one. Instead of being the result of a move of the Holy Spirit or
even of human religious impulse, he portrays it as being the calculated
response by American elites to Soviet atheism.[22]

Inboden also had a thematic structure to his work, but he followed
his subject by focusing on four lead characters: Presidents Truman and
Eisenhower, and theologians Billy Graham and Reinhold Niebuhr. With
the two politicians Inboden suggests that the latter was able to succeed
for a time where the former failed because, while Truman sought to
have global religious leaders create a common "religious" answer to
Communism, Eisenhower merely asked them all to cooperate against
a common foe. In the end he shows that whatever consensus they were
able to share for a time, their differences were too great to last the test
of time and fell apart by the 1960s.[23]

Jason Stevens's book, *God Fearing and Free: A Spiritual History of
America's Cold War*, is a very broadly based book, examining both
standard historical sources as well as the efforts of novelists and play-
wrights as they argued and wrestled with the religious aspects of the
global conflict. Though works from Harvard English professors are not
the normal place one would go to find a defense of evangelicals, the
author challenges the assessment of evangelicals as posited by its critics
saying that, in many cases such a negative portrayal has less to do with

---

22. Herzog, *The Spiritual Industrial Complex*.
23. Inboden, *Religion and American Foreign Policy*.

what evangelicals actually think and more to do with a self-satisfying and self-justifying caricature foisted upon the Right by the Left.[24]

Andrew Preston's book, *Sword of the Spirit, Shield of Faith*, is one of the latest entrants into this discussion. Although his study begins in the seventeenth century and covers Christian as well as some Jewish discussions of American wars, his expansive and detailed work allows for greater analysis of evangelicals than many others on this list. Most interestingly he counters the argument put forward by Gunn and Settje that evangelicals wedded themselves to supporting their government, come what may. Even as he acknowledged that some of the Southern conservatives' opposition to the growth of the central government into state-level affairs was "often a fig leaf to disguise racism," he argued that, beneath this, was a genuine fear of the implications of expanding federal power.[25] He further stated that evangelical opposition to Communism was based on honest concerns and not mere nationalism.[26]

CONTRIBUTION AND METHODOLOGY

The role of evangelicals regarding American foreign policy is clearly something which has drawn a lot of attention of late, and this for good reason. During the mid-twentieth century, evangelical leaders played

---

24. Stevens, 68. He says there, "In the polemical battles of today's so-called Culture War, the association of the Christian Right with fascism, totalitarianism, or extreme, irrational regression from modern life has devolved into a rhetorical weapon of center Democrats and left-wing forums like the *Nation* just as bluntly driven as the terms 'secular humanism' and 'liberal-fascist' are wielded by those on the Right."

25. He argued that this opposition to government power was central to evangelical thought, and not a pretext for other motives, saying, "Evangelical and fundamentalist had always prized the separation of church and state because it prevented the government from regulating religious life. This meant everything to the eccentric, unconventional, and emotional churches of evangelicalism, to say nothing of even more radical offspring like Mormonism and Pentecostalism. By the 20th century anti-statism had become hardwired into the genes of conservative Protestants," Preston, 548.

26. "But there was more to the conservative worldview and simple old-time patriotism. Just as conservative opposition to civil rights legislation was not solely due to racism, Christian views on foreign policy were not entirely a product reactionary nationalism and anticommunism. Instead, as a civil right, the conservative worldview was shaped by a deep-rooted hostility the government interference and a fear of unrepresentative bureaucratic power." Preston, 548.

an increasingly prominent role in the shaping of public perceptions
of United States geopolitical affairs. Many of these studies have done
an admirable job of trying to understand what motivated evangelicals
during those tumultuous decades. Some have focused on evangelicals as
a part of the general religious scene in America. Others have centered
in on a particular idea within evangelicalism and how that concept
affected evangelical attitudes toward their nation and its wars. However,
this book intends to do something somewhat different, and, by doing so,
to correct a few of the conclusions of these other works, to fill in some
lacunae in the current research, and to provide a different perspective
by setting these evangelical comments in their historical context. What
we learn from this study is that evangelical leaders offered consistent
counsel to their followers during these difficult times and that this
counsel was rooted in a careful study of the geopolitical solution and
in a devoted adherence to longstanding Christian principles.

To see this we will be looking at evangelical discussions of American
foreign policy throughout the period from the popular Second World
War all the way to the protested Vietnam Conflict. Specifically, we will
be conducting an analysis of commentary and arguments by evangelicals found in evangelical magazines running from the late 1930s to the
early 1970s. In a sense this book is both narrower and broader than
similar studies. It is narrower in that it focuses solely on evangelicals
and what they said about American military conflicts, and it is broader
in that it looks at the entire period from the beginning moves of World
War II to the end game of US involvement in Vietnam. This will bring
in the context of the Second World War in which many later leaders of
evangelicalism came of age in a time when they had seen the threats
posed by expansionist totalitarian powers and the devastation of total
war with nuclear weapons. This dissertation addresses the question
by examining what, if any, common themes in evangelical arguments
continue throughout the entire period, but it will do so by focusing on
the way they responded to particular crises. It is quite easy for scholars
to look back upon the choices made in a given time and criticize them
with the advantage of hindsight. However, since the subjects of historical inquiry cannot have known how their counsel would play out,
they can hardly be blamed for such ignorance, in and of itself. When

examining evangelicals' view of US foreign policy, we may disagree
with them for their decisions at this or that point, but our analysis
must be rooted in what information was available to them at the time
coupled with an awareness of how their belief systems would have
led them to interpret the data in front of them. Therefore, this study
will be taken from comments by evangelicals as close to the conflict in
question as possible.

While some person-to-person communications and letters to the
editor will be included, news reports and editorials will provide the
primary source material. This is for several reasons. Periodicals are
written, in most cases, far closer to then-contemporary events than
book-length analyses, thereby opening a window to what people
thought at a specific time as opposed to only what they might want
others to see, edited with the benefit of hindsight.[27] Also, while formal
works of theology, political theory, and philosophy are often shared only
among fellow scholars, magazines formed a junction point between
the elites and the laity, as the former worked to sway the views of the
latter in a direct and nationwide fashion. Further, as publicly distrib-
uted documents, magazines display the direction evangelical leaders
wanted their followers to go in ways that do not necessarily fit with
the expectations of later historians. Through their choices about what
stories to emphasize and what to put in the background, through the
structure of their arguments, through their explicit statements, and
other such things evangelical elites provided a framework for their
readers to understand the tumultuous world around them. By shaping

27. Carefully researched books written long after the fact have a definite value,
but the distance does not always yield objectivity when people describe their own
past actions or beliefs. Memoirs are good, but they are too often colored by the
knowledge of what came later and are edited, honestly or not, by an awareness of
what turned out to be wise and what ended up being less so. One historian wrote
of the spate of accounts of the Second World War which had the unintended effect
of displaying as self-perceptions and projections as they did the reality underneath.
"In the decades after the war ended, with self-serving autobiographies and diaries,
admiring biographies and slanted histories being published en masse ... it was
difficult to arrive at an objective judgment about Allied strategy." Andrew Roberts,
Masters and Commanders: How Four Titans Won the War in the West, 1941-1945 (New
York: HarperCollins, 2009), xl.

their understanding, they hoped to affect the way their readers interacted with the world. In a unique way it is in periodicals that such a wide group of intellectual leaders regularly came together in a single forum, making magazines by their very nature to be consensus projects. Although editors and regular news columns will be the focus, since they can provide a consistent voice, the offerings of contributing writers will be included at times as well.[28]

Specifically, this book will evaluate the analysis by evangelical leaders concerning four basic subjects: American enemies, America itself, issues of war and peace, and eschatology. For the first the question, what are the ways in which evangelical leaders spoke about those nations or groups opposed to the United States as well as what reasons, if any, did they give for opposing those nations themselves? Second, since one of the criticisms centers on their relative approval of their nation, what was the nature of their evaluation of America? Third, what did these leaders think about war as such, the weapons and tactics involved, and the implications of the bloody strife? Finally, in keeping with the attention given to evangelical views on the end of the world, what role did the question of the relationship between then-contemporary events and their eschatological interpretations play in their analyses of those events?

SOURCE MATERIAL

The main periodicals included will be *Moody Monthly (MM)*, *Christianity Today (CT)*, *Christian Herald (CH)*, *Our Hope (OH)*, and *Southern*

---

28. In terms of citation, news reports will be ascribed either to "The Editors" of a given magazine or to the news editor by name if such a person is named on the masthead. Similarly, editorials will be ascribed to the editor in chief unless specifically noted as coming from another author. With CH all editorials were specifically attributed to Daniel Poling. Both MM and SPJ/PJ left the byline blank unless it was written by a member of the editors or regular contributors. At such times the author's initials were provided. With ET the editorials were left blank up through 1960 when Donald Barnhouse unexpectedly passed away. Until they settled on a new editor in the person of Russell Hitt, editorials came with the author specified. After Hitt was in place, these reverted to anonymous. Only CT maintained full anonymity of editorial authorship throughout.

Presbyterian Journal (SPJ).[29] Some additional individuals or institutional documents will be included to some degree, but not in a primary role. The point is not to create a hypothetical and monolithic evangelical mind but to examine how a sample of evangelicals, who have been prominent voices to and for the movement, have developed their responses to United States foreign policy during the period in question.[30]

At *Christian Herald* (*CH*) the primary voices are Daniel A. Poling (1884–1968) and "Gabriel Courier" who was actually no one at all but a pseudonym for various staff members of a *CH* standing column, usually entitled "Gabriel Courier Interprets the News." Poling was the long-time owner and editor of the magazine, a staunch prohibitionist, and sometime political candidate. While clearly in sympathy with more well-known evangelicals in terms of his theology, Poling was also quite friendly with more mainline Christians such as Harry Emerson Fosdick

---

29. The magazines studied here include those from a generally Dispensationalist perspective, such as *OH*, *MM*, and *ET*, those from a specifically Calvinistic/Presbyterian perspective, such as *SPJ*, and from a non-denominational viewpoint, such as *CH* and *CT*. This study will limit itself to those sharing a broadly Calvinistic anthropology and soteriology, entailing an emphasis on the enduring sinfulness of humanity. Although no specifically Baptist magazines are included, *CT* had the Baptists Carl F. H. Henry and Billy Graham as a part of its leadership. However, Wesleyan periodicals, such as *Pentecostal Evangel, The Wesleyan Methodist/ Advocate*, and *Christian Advocate*, which could also be a part of the general evangelical movement, will not be covered in this project. Research in Wesleyan magazines could prove instructive, indeed. All of those studied here, with the exception of *CH*, shared authors and editors quite extensively and formed a semi-unified constellation of forums acting from the same basic viewpoint. *CH* did not interact with the others, but it operated from the same general perspective about the nature of humanity and the role of the state.

30. Many of these periodicals underwent renaming and unification. *Southern Presbyterian Journal* (*SPJ*) was renamed simply *Presbyterian Journal* (*PJ*) after 1959, and in 1958 *Our Hope* (*OH*) was folded into *Eternity* (*ET*). Interestingly enough, all three of these were eventually folded into one, after a fashion. *ET* and *OH* were already united. *Presbyterian Journal* went into decline right after the period of this study since the 1973 creation of the conservative Presbyterian Church in America eliminated the need for a conservative voice in the mainline Southern denomination. However, it was restarted under the same charter in 1986 as *World*. After *ET* went out of business in 1988, its subscription list was purchased by *World*. *Christian Herald* would remain up to 1992, and *Moody Monthly* (*MM*) would last until 2003. *Christianity Today* (*CT*) continues as a major voice within evangelicalism, and *World*, as the descendant of many of these periodicals, does as well.

and Charles Sheldon, having the latter on the board of the magazine. Courier had a regular contribution where "he" offered his insights on events of the day, whether geopolitical or ecclesiastical. The editors at *CH* went to great lengths to avoid stating that there was no such person, even going to the effort to quote Courier's reaction to letters to the editor, defend Courier's supposed ideological errors, and even refer to him being overseas. They never disclosed the "real" identity until Poling retired in 1965 when the pseudonym was dropped.

Our Hope (OH) was run by Arno C. Gabelein (1861–1945), a biblical scholar, leading dispensational theologian, and strong advocate of doctrinal purity. Up to the mid-1940s, he wrote a regular series entitled "Current Events in Light of the Bible" where, as the title suggests, he tried to connect contemporary world events with eschatological themes in the Bible. This role was taken up by *OH*'s new editor, E. Schuyler English (1899–1981), a biblical scholar who worked on the influential Schofield Reference Bible. At the end of 1949, this series was written by Wilbur M. Smith (1894–1976), professor at the Moody Bible Institute (MBI), Fuller Theological Seminary, and Trinity Evangelical Divinity School. He was also a regular contributor to *Moody Monthly*, often in connection to eschatology.

Leadership at *Moody Monthly (MM)* was provided by the editors in chief, initially by William H. Houghton (1887–1947) in the first part of the period and then William Culbertson (1905–1971). Donald Grey Barnhouse (1895–1960) was a Presbyterian pastor in Philadelphia for many years as well as the editor of *Eternity (ET)* from its inception in 1931 to his death in 1960. After this time the editorship of the magazine passed to Russell Hitt (1905–1992). Although he was a layman, L. Nelson Bell (1894–1973) played a large role in the Reformed branch of evangelicalism and in the creation of two primary sources for this book, *SPJ*, where he was an associate editor, and *CT*, where he was the executive editor. He had been a missionary in China and later became father in law to the most famous evangelical of them all, Billy Graham (1918–2018). Carl F. H. Henry (1913–2003) had his hand in nearly every significant evangelical undertaking throughout this period and beyond. He was a founding faculty member of Fuller Seminary, which was founded explicitly to provide high quality education for evangelical ministers, and editor in chief at *CT* from its founding until 1968. Despite all this work, he still found time to collect two earned PhDs.

Despite being slightly older than Henry, Francis A. Schaeffer (1912–1984) came to evangelical prominence two decades later. Starting out in the fundamentalist world of Carl McIntire's American Council of Christian Churches (ACCC), Schaeffer broke from that group and founded L'Abri Fellowship in 1955, a group dedicated to providing orthodox Christian "honest answers to honest questions" coming from disenchanted Christians, hippies, and seekers of all sorts. William K. Harrison (1895–1987) was a career US Army officer, the American representative at the peace talks ending the Korean War, head of the Officers Christian Union, and a regular contributor to evangelical magazines. Given the nature of magazines, a great many of the articles studied below come from anonymous or otherwise unnamed sources.

STRUCTURE

The years from 1937 to 1973 were highly complex, with multiple interdependent and independent factors interacting simultaneously: empires rose and fell, social structures were challenged and altered, economic transformations were changed by and changed their host nations, and new technologies altered the way humanity related to the world and to one another. As a result there are any number of ways to break down the period chronologically. In this book we will look to times when there was a discernable change in America's relationship to the world at large, with each chapter looking at a handful of whole years corresponding to significant events in foreign affairs. For example, even though the United States entered World War II at the end 1941 and the conflict concluded before the end of 1945, the chapter covering the war itself will begin with January of 1942 and end with December of 1945. For the first several chapters this will mean four years to each chapter and five years to each of the last few chapters.

2

The Road to War, 1937–1941

In the midwinter's chill of New Year's Day 1937 in Bismarck, North Dakota, a middle-aged man's cold took a turn for the worse, taking his life through pneumonia. In his heyday J. Gresham Machen had been a professor at Princeton Seminary, one of the nation's premiere theological institutions. But that day was long past, and he was now an outcast from elite society, the most visible victim of the denominational battles of American Christianity in the early twentieth century. In that clash over the nature of the faith, the conservatives had fallen before their more liberally minded opponents and found themselves purged from office as a result. Half a year and half a world away, simmering tensions between the Empire of Japan and the Republic of China broke into open war at the Marco Polo Bridge in Beijing. By fits and starts this regional conflict would lead the United States out of comfortable isolationism and into reluctant interventionism, leaving America in the possession of the strongest military in the history of the world and as sole proprietor of warfare's most potent weapon, a weapon which would bring death in the midsummer's heat of August 1945 to Hiroshima, Japan.

As this era began, Americans watched the embers of war gather strength. The United States was not officially involved in the conflict until the very end of 1941, but the rest of the planet was hardly at peace. The Japanese continued to advance into China after 1937, and the Italians made moves toward a new empire. A reinvigorated Germany began assimilating territories into the Third Reich, even if the people therein did not consider themselves to be particularly German. The Russians and Finns fought in their Winter War, and the Spanish fought the Spanish for years on end.

By 1939 and 1940 many of these conflicts were absorbed into one by the German invasion of Poland. This act brought Britain and France in against Germany and, later, Italy. The following year saw the Axis in control of the bulk of Europe, with only Britain remaining both free and hostile. Spain was neutral, but friendly to the Axis, while the Soviets were not exactly chummy with their old rivals in Germany, they were willing to cooperate. This cooperation ended in June 1941 with the Axis invasion of Russia. Six months later the war expanded once more. Intent on pursuing its invasion of China without the threat of outside interference, Japan, now a full member of the Axis, attacked Western outposts across East Asia and the Pacific.

ENEMIES

THE SOVIET UNION

As American evangelical leaders reacted to these crises and counseled those looking to them for understanding, they did not have the advantage of hindsight to know how each issue would play out in the end.[1] While it is obvious that they would not have known whether the "good guys" or "bad guys" would emerge victorious, it is also true that they had no way of knowing just who the "good guys" and "bad guys" would turn out to be. With Stalin moving into Finland at the same time that Hitler was moving into Austria and Czechoslovakia, it would be hard for observers to differentiate the moral quality of Moscow and Berlin. In fact, evangelical magazine articles written prior to June 1941 were quite likely to portray the Soviet Union as humanity's primary nemesis. Writing in April 1937 William H. Hockman said, "The terrors of Russia are so commonly known as to be virtually a household word throughout the world. From the beginning of the Soviet regime the upper classes

---

1. One telling example of this came in November 1941 when *MM* shared an article about missionary opportunities on Wake Island and Midway Island, little knowing that within weeks the American garrison on Wake would be overrun by the Japanese and that in seven months Midway would be the site of a devastating American naval victory over the then-seemingly invincible Japanese navy. William H. Houghton, "American Missions Fields—Wake and Midway Islands," *MM*, November 1941, 140-41.

were 'liquidated' (exterminated), the middle classes deprived of possessions and personal liberty, and the Christians subjected to persecutions
almost too terrible to print."[2] As in this article many evangelicals called
attention to the acts of internal repression within the Soviet Union in
addition to the focus on Russia as an external military threat to world
peace. Nearly every issue of *Moody* of the period had either articles by
contributors or advertisements by outside organizations highlighting
the plight of Christians in particular or Russians in general. Perhaps
most common were calls to send Bibles behind this nascent Iron Curtain.

Similarly, Arno C. Gaebelein wrote, "You can trust a vicious dog, but
not the vicious Reds of Russia."[3] A year later he accurately predicted a
three-part alliance between Germany, Italy, and Japan, but he saw this
potential Axis not in opposition to the democratic West but solely as a
counterpoint to the Soviets.[4] Even advertisements for evangelical institutions carried this theme. One emphasized the eschatological implications of the events of late 1939. For its triumvirate of villains, the ad
included not only Adolf Hitler and Benito Mussolini but also Soviet
leader and soon-to-be American ally, Josef Stalin.[5] Although the traditional conservative disdain for Communism might be a factor in this
suggested unholy trinity, considering that these words were written
when Germans and Russians had signed a non-aggression pact, Soviet
forces were occupying eastern Poland, and Stalin was soon to annex
the Baltic states, it would not take great imagination to view Germany,
Italy, and Russia as three of a kind.

In the same way the pseudonymous Gabriel Courier gave a half-
hearted endorsement to an arrangement for the United States to sell
aircraft to the Soviets. He wrote, "This move does not mean that we
have handed Stalin a coat of moral whitewash, or declared the invaders
of Finland clean and sweet." He then went on to say, "Russia, if truth
be told, fears a German victory more than a British triumph. She will
be smart to play along with the US we [sic] will be smart in alienating

---

2. William H. Hockman, "No Escape from Terror," *MM*, April 1937, 417.
Parentheses in original.
3. Arno C. Gaebelein, "Diabolical Hypocrisy," *OH*, January 1937, 473.
4. Gaebelein, "The Coming World-Wide Anti-Red Pact," *OH*, January 1938, 476.
5. Advertisement for *The Sunday School Times, MM*, November 1939, 136.

what we can of her good will toward Adolf Hitler." This attitude did not extend to any acceptance of the Soviet state's foreign policy regarding Finland. "Nothing, not even a government action, can remove the moral stigma on Russia; nothing could wash the blood from the hands of Lady Macbeth!"[6] Even after the June 1941 German invasion ended the possibility of a Russo-German alliance, the evangelical animosity toward the Soviet regime endured. There were fewer articles denouncing Stalin, but these were not replaced by pieces supporting the democracies' new totalitarian ally.

THE JAPANESE EMPIRE

Japan gained some of the earliest and most consistent condemnation. Criticisms of the Japanese actions in China continued to be more common than complaints about Germany or Italy, even after the outbreak of war in Europe. Writing in January of 1938, Gaebelein complained about the loss of Chinese lives to Japanese air raids. After summarizing a news account from another source, he wrote, "Nothing like it happened in the world war. Over twenty thousand men, women and tender children were killed, so that the streets literally became rivers of blood. Systematically women were hunted down in all Chinese homes. If they resisted rape they were cut to pieces. Even sixty year old women and eleven year old girls were not immune." His rebuke extended to the watching world, saying, "The nations, as always, stand

---

6. Courier, "Moscow," *CH*, March 1941, 12. The editors and writers at *CH* were more open to change within Russia than were others. For instance, in reply to a reader's question about religious persecution in the Soviet Union, Daniel Poling admitted that Stalin had never allowed religious freedom, but pointed out that Russia was facing revolutionary changes once again and that these changes are "many believe, moving toward democracy." Poling, "Doctor Poling Answers," *CH*, November 1941, 4. Courier later suggested that the Russians had made a deal with the Japanese to encourage Chinese Communists to rise up against the Nationalist government in return for Japanese assurances against a war Russia was unready to fight. He continued, "That may not be true, but Russia is capable of it." Courier, "China," *CH*, April 1941, 8. This may seem a strange thing to suggest considering that the Soviets were Communists themselves. However, Stalin and Mao Zedong were not always the best of friends. See Harrison Salisbury, *The New Emperors: China in the Era of Mao and Deng* (Boston: Little, Brown and Company, 1992).

by, saying they are helpless, while Germany and Italy lend more or less help to this program and hell. How long, O Lord, how long?"[7]

William Houghton spoke in much the same way, suggesting that Japanese tactics were designed to conquer the Chinese "by terrorizing them."[8] Deflecting some of the blame toward the European crisis, Courier suggested that Adolf Hitler had induced the Japanese into pushing its war against China and that the reality was being hidden from the Japanese population. He held out hope that the Japan's citizens would not stand for their nation's actions, if only they could be told. However, since, as he put it, the government in Tokyo was under the control "of 100% extremists," he confessed that this was a false hope[9]

Raising awareness was only part of these writers' plans for the crisis. They hoped that their readers would do something about it, as their own nation's well-being could depend upon it. In an editorial from early 1939, Houghton urged his readers to contact their representatives in Washington to cut off war supplies from Japan, which he named "a bloodthirsty aggressor." He complained that by continuing its trade with the Empire of Japan, the United States was complicit in its evil. "One hates to think that a so-called Christian nation like America would deliberately supply oil, trucks, planes, and scrap iron to Japan, knowing that these things will be used for the looting of China." He also pointed out that cutting off supplies could be more than merely altruistic. "It is not impossible that the very scrap iron which America is selling to Japan today, will be the shells used on our own soldier boys not many months hence, as arrogant little Japan continues to dream of world conquest."[10] Courier echoed this call for an embargo, highlighting the very real effects of the loss of oil in particular. He then favorably quoted Chinese leader, Chiang Kai-shek, saying, "One drop of oil to Tokyo means gallons of blood in Chungking." Addressing a Japanese emissary who warned of a global conflagration, Courier concluded, "There is but one way to put out the fire, Ambassador. That is to withhold the

---

7. Gaebelein, "Japan's Vicious Warfare—China's Sufferings," *OH*, September 1938, 180.

8. Houghton, "Japanese Cruelty," *MM*, March 1938, 348.

9. Courier, "Japan," *CH*, January 1941, 11.

10. Houghton, "America Helping Japan?" *MM*, January 1939, 244.

material of aggression from the aggressors. Even from a Japan that now waits for Russia to collapse before Japan takes a few more inches of territory in Siberia!"[11] Opposition to Japanese actions in East Asia was rooted in both moral and pragmatic reasoning. The destruction of Chinese cities and lives offended their Christian ethics and demanded a response, and the Japanese forces now rampaging across China could, and indeed would, soon turn against the complaisant Americans. For these writers it was their duty to call their readers' attention to each of these dangers.

FASCIST ITALY

The Italians sometimes escape contemporary attention when thinking about the Axis in the Second World War. This is understandable given their decidedly underwhelming battle performance and switch to the Allied side midway through the war. However, for those observing world affairs in the early stage, it was Rome rather than Berlin which was the rising star of Europe. Much of evangelical commentary on Italy in the years before the war was neutral or even laudatory in nature, with particular attention to the possibility of a revived Roman Empire and Mussolini as a new Caesar. One *Moody* contributor argued that Mussolini was making good on his insistence of a new era for Rome. "The Italians have gained a strong footing in Libya, have taken over Ethiopia, have won the war for the Nationalists in Spain, are [*sic*] fomenting trouble by embittering the Moslems against the English." Noting that Il Duce referred to himself as "the defender of the Moslem faith," the author said,

> Remember the bitter conflict in Palestine and the Euphrates country, the riots in Egypt and Morocco, and the rising among the Moors, that Italian troops are being sent to these localities to assist the Mohammadans. Remember that the Fascists now hold both shores of the straits of Gibraltar, save for the great rock at

---

11. Courier, "Burned," *CH*, November 1941, 9. The allusion here to "a few more inches" is to a quote earlier in the article by a Japanese official who declared that his nation was not seeking "an inch of Chinese territory."

the entrance. Is the new Caesar getting ready for the crossing of the Rubicon?[12]

Speaking of Mussolini in 1937, Gaebelein wrote, "We could fill many of our pages with all the achievements of this man. He promised to put Rome back on the map some seven years ago and he has certainly kept his promises." Gaebelein pondered a revival of an empire centered on Rome, saying, "In Western Europe, the Spanish Revolution has arrested for the present developments in the line of the restoration of the Roman Empire, but inasmuch as Spain was a part of it and Il Duce Mussolini's hand is the guiding hand there, a victory for Fascism can be easily forseen [sic]."[13] Later, Gaebelein favorably compared the stated desire of the Italian ruler to include the Bible in children's education with the moves to have it removed from American schools.[14] The coming of actual combat would soon change this opinion, but, at least before 1940, many evangelical writers spoke of Italy with real if reluctant admiration.

This reluctance became more obvious quite soon as Italy's conquests in Africa and southeast Europe were indistinguishable from those of Russia and Japan. *Moody* readers found a firsthand account of Italy's initial moves into the Balkans in October 1939's issue. As Albania's parliament pondered a response to a set of Italian demands, Italian warships floated in their harbors and Fascist aircraft flew overhead. The author wrote, "Italy came in like a flood, displaying tremendous force but using only enough to beat down resistance." Faced with insurmountable odds, the king and his military leadership fled the country, leaving Albania to its fate. This author ended on a dismal note, saying, "Thus, in one day, Albania's hopes were shattered, and she became a part of the Great

---

12. Clarence H. Benson, "Restoring the Roman Empire," *MM*, August 1939, 673. This, like the articles in *MM* by Hockman, are part of a regular series, with these under the group heading of "Our Monthly Potpourri." Unlike the Hockman articles, these are noted as being drawn from other sources, in this case from *The United Presbyterian*. As it is unclear where the source ends and Benson begins, and Benson offers no further information other than the periodical's title, only Benson will be referenced in the citation.

13. Gaebelein, "Imperial Rome Reborn," *OH*, June 1937, 828.

14. Gaebelein, "Mussolini's Attitude Towards the New Testament," *OH*, June 1934, 829. His views of Mussolini were not as positive as these remarks might suggest, as will be seen below.

Roman Empire of the future. We knew the change was coming, but scarcely expected that it would come so quickly."[15]

After 1940 evangelicals no longer saw Rome as the seat of a new empire of the Caesars but as the hapless sidekick to the genuinely threatening power of Germany. By early 1941 the image of Italian invincibility had been fully replaced. Courier was able to write,

> Off and on again in this column we have said or hinted that whoever won Italy as an ally in this war got no bargain. We think the rout of the Fascists in Albania by the "despicable" Greeks bears that out. ... Mussolini has already lost his most important bases in Albania, and even his chest-thumping "Legion of Death" is running so fast that the poor Greeks can't keep up with them.

He also said, "[Italy is] doing its best to save its face; actually, there isn't much face left to be saved. Her navy is crippled; her record of 'battles at sea' is a record of running for refuge under shore batteries at first sight of the British fleet." He also suggested that the only hope Mussolini could hold would be assistance from Hitler's Germany.[16]

NAZI GERMANY

With good reason, Germany received a great deal of criticism from evangelical writers in this period. Although rebukes against outright military aggression had to wait until late 1939, commentators before this time found Germany's treatment of its own people to be despicable, this was particularly so when it came to German Jews. However, mirroring comments about Mussolini at the same time, there was some ambiguity from certain authors. Gaebelein wrote that an address by Hitler before the Reichstag had "brought new hopes for peace in Europe." In what was, in retrospect, an ironic series of points, given the events to occur just two years later, the author said that Hitler had promised neutrality to the Low Countries and "extended a friendly

---

15. Arthur Konrad, "Guns in Albania," *MM*, October 1939, 82–83. This article was a part of the regular series by Hockman, but, unlike most in his series, this one was entirely a quotation.

16. Courier, "Greeks," *CH*, January 1941, 10–11.

hand to France." [17] Gaebelein spoke of how "The recent declarations for peace, and the assurance from the Reich that no aggressions in North Africa were planned, had a great effect on all Europe." [18] Nonetheless, he was not hopeful for Europe's future, but, contrary to what postwar hindsight would suggest, he saw the danger coming from Germany's ancient rivals in France. [19]

Gaebelein continued with this largely positive evaluation of the Third Reich. Through a series of articles, starting in November 1937, he told of a speaking tour he had made throughout Germany. In the first installment he wrote glowingly of the new ability of ordinary workers to travel without much cost to themselves and of new construction projects popping up across the country and said of a march by thousands of uniformed members of labor service groups that it was "a great sight." He spoke of a vigorous Christian church, free to assemble and to preach. He concluded by promising to share the "dark side" in subsequent installments. [20] This he did the next month when he confessed to being "shocked" that Hitler could speak highly of someone like Alfred

---

17. Gaebelein, "Germany's Favorable Attitude," *OH*, April 1937, 687. Gaebelein's views on Jews and Zionism were somewhat complicated. He often condemned the Nazis for their anti-Semitism, but he did so with less vigor than what is found in *MM*. He was not a Zionist in any sense. In the same issue noted here he wrote of the increase in the Jewish population of Palestine and spoke of "the false national hope of Zionism." Gaebelein, "What is the Population of Palestine?" *OH*, April 1937, 689. At the same time he was amendable to certain forms of Zionism. After suggesting that Zionism had, up to then, been largely secular in orientation, he argued that the recent infusion of biblical language and principles into Zionist discussions was, "surely a better note in Zionism. They should now go a step further and consider the conditions which God himself has laid down for their return to the God given land, which is not to be bought or to be sold." Gaebelein, "The Bible is our Mandate. A Better Note in Zionism," *OH*, June 1937, 833. Further, Gaebelein, while he might have seen Hitler's Nazism as a lesser threat than Stalin's Communism, it did not follow that he considered the Germans to be the "good guys" in global affairs. Long before the Non-Aggression Pact of 1939, in a series of articles focusing heavily upon prophecy, Gaebelein wondered about a possible alliance between the Russians and the Germans in competition with Italy and France. "In a short time the world may witness the beginning of the two great confederacies, the North-Eastern terminating in Gog and Magog, and the Western, the Roman Empire." Gaebelein, "More Evidence as to Russia and Germany," *OH*, August 1937, 109.

18. Gaebelein, "A True Statement from Secretary Eden," *OH*, April 1937, 691.

19. Gaebelein, "Germany's Favorable Attitude," *OH*, April 1937, 687.

20. Gaebelein, "Observations and Experiences," *OH*, November 1937, 330–34.

Rosenberg who was "through and through an antisemite [sic] and also attacks the Lutheran State Church." He added that, according Germans he spoke to, arrest would be awaiting anyone quoting the Bible's "salvation is from the Jews."[21]

Gaebelein soon turned from this neutral attitude to Germany, but, for a time his, fierce anti-Communist stance led him to turn a blind eye toward the growing evil of Nazi Germany. This would end as his worry over anti-Semitism pushed his fear of Communism to the background. He was keen to distinguish the views of most Germans, and even the government as a whole, from radical ideas of certain Nazis. Yet, he did not see Nazism as an ideology in any way compatible with Christianity. He offered these words: "Our forthcoming articles will deal with the religious question in Germany and show that the complete domination of the German youth by the enemies of the cross of Christ, who attempt to end true, supernatural Christianity, differs but little from what has been done with the young in Sovietism."[22] The following month he showed concern over the growth of anti-Semitic laws affecting all of German society and warned against the call to purge Christianity of Jewish elements.[23]

By 1939 any element of patience present in Gaebelein's words for the new German regime had evaporated, though he kept his abiding opposition to the Soviet Union. In June of that year, he wrote, "The two world menaces are Communism and Naziism [sic]. One created the other. Each keeps the other alive. … The two forces—Communism and Nazism-Fascism—thrive on each other. If Communism were destroyed, Naziism and Fascism, the antidote, could not exist long."[24] In January of that year he wrote, "It is known that the Aryan maniacs Hitler, Goebbels, Goering, Streicher, and others are sworn enemies of Communism as it flourishes in the Soviet Republic. In the beginning of

21. Gaebelein, "Observations and Experiences," *OH*, December 1937, 386–87.

22. Gaebelein, "The End of German Capitalism," *OH*, December 1937, 391.

23. Gaebelein, "Observations and Experiences," *OH*, January 1938, 460–65.

24. Gaebelein, "Menaces," *OH*, June 1939, 838. This is apparently a quotation or a summary of a piece from *National Republic* from April of 1939, but there is no indication who the original author might have been nor any differentiation between the words of Gaebelein and another writer.

Nazism they denounced the religious persecutions of Russia and some of their blasphemies." He then went on to condemn them for their own profane decrees. "But it is still written in the Bible, 'Be not deceived, God is not mocked.' The day is coming when these infidel leaders with the modern Haman, Hitler, will find out that this is true, and then they will also know what it means, 'It is a fearful thing to fall into the hands of the living God.' "[25] In just a few short years Gaebelein had gone from giving Hitler the benefit of the doubt to comparing him to the worst villains of the Bible.

Moody's writers in particular expressed a great deal of concern over anti-Semitism. One piece on global Jewish migration noted that thousands of Jews had left Germany. While the author did not specify any reasons they might have had for emigrating, he also did not name any other nation which Jews were leaving en masse.[26] Another *Moody* contributor saw this as a worldwide problem but one which was centered in Germany and one which demanded that the church act in response: "Today the Jews and the Jewish Christians find themselves unwanted, robbed of their possessions, prohibited from earning their living, and free only to end it all by suicide, unless the Christian and freedom-loving portion of the world comes to their rescue."[27] An ad for The Friends of Israel Refugee Relief Committee highlighted both the material need of the Jews suffering in Europe as well as the spiritual opportunity to evangelize.[28] "If it is a time of trouble for the Jews, it is also a

---

25. Gaebelein, "The Hitler Regime Outdoes Red Blasphemies," *OH*, January 1939, 462–63.

26. Clarence H. Benson, "16,291,000 Jews," *MM*, May 1937, 475.

27. Joseph Taylor Britan, "An Appeal for Persecuted Israel," *MM*, February 1939, 316.

28. It is beyond the scope of this project to analyze this particular subject, but there was a great emphasis on evangelizing Jews found in articles and advertisements in American evangelical literature. The most common foci of evangelism in *MM*, for instance, during the 1930s and 1940s were Jews, Russians, and Chinese. This is pertinent to this study in that these three groups were integral to many of the conflicts the United States became involved in over the period in question. This adds a level of complexity to evangelical thinking about global affairs. Russians were more likely to be portrayed as those in need than as enemies to be destroyed. The Chinese were seen as victimized allies who were led by Christians. Jews were seen as suffering people who needed physical and spiritual salvation, leading the

time of testing for Christians. For it is by sympathy and kindness in a time like this that we can demonstrate to the Jewish people the reality of the faith we profess."[29] At a later point, when the war was on in earnest, Houghton continued this theme and warned that the Nazis would not stop with Jews, saying, "Let no one be mistaken about this. The forces at work for the destruction of the Jew will just as earnestly one day seek to destroy the believer."[30] This was a step beyond evangelical criticism of Japanese aggression. With Japan the danger had merely been the circumstantial threat of conquest; they were going to attack anyone in their way. With Germany the concern was of something deeper as the fear was that the totalitarianism of Nazism was an existential threat would seek out any who failed to fit in.

The advent of war in Europe did little to appease the dwindling evangelical impression of Germany. One *Moody* writer compared Hitler to the long-prophesied Antichrist,[31] and MBI president Houghton pointed to the Nazi leader's hypocrisy, saying, "Hitler banished religion and the Church, but in time of war called on God for help and victory. Then he threw his arms around the neck of the atheist Stalin and cried, 'Brother!' "[32] Praising those pastors who stood up against the regime, one *Moody* writer pointed to the nationalization of the German, Austrian, and Czech Christian churches, noting that this should have been easy to foresee from the Nazi stated goals. "This is a part of Hitler's plan as outlined in his *Mein Kampf*, in which he says, 'Christianity is to be destroyed by intolerance and terrorism.' "[33] Long before many Americans were willing to consider it their business, these evangelicals were comparing the Nazis to the worst villains of history and prophecy.

---

editors of *MM* to dedicate an entire issue, November 1940, to issues surrounding the suffering of and ministry to Jewish people around the world.

29. The Friends of Israel Refugee Relief Committee, Inc., Advertisement, *MM*, September 1940, 25. At the end of the advertisement, there is a list of some of the sponsors of the committee which contains some fairly prominent names in the world of evangelicalism such as Lewis Spencer Chafer, Will Houghton, Harry Ironside, Harry Rimmer, and Wilbur Smith.

30. Houghton, "The Plight of the Jews," *MM*, June 1941, 566.

31. Grant Stroh, "Hitler as the Antichrist," *MM*, August 1940, 680.

32. Houghton, "This Thing Called Civilization, No. 10," *MM*, November 1939, 116.

33. Clarence H. Benson, "The Nazi Church," *MM*, July 1940, 618.

The state of the world during this period was clearly quite dire, and evangelicals saw enemies on every side. As these events unfolded, there was no mistaking the sense of significance of what was before them. A *Moody* contributor wrote, "We are living in a day that will go down in history as being as significant as the fall of the Roman Empire, or as the day in which Charles Martel turned back the invading Moslems at the gates of Tours." Alluding to a Japanese official who had claimed that the purpose of the conflict was "to secure permanent world peace," he described the world envisioned by the Axis. "The method to be employed is to forcibly divide Europe, Africa, Asia, and the islands of the southern ocean between the three members of the present axis, Germany, Italy, and Japan, with the possible inclusion of Russia as a fourth member." The author then wryly noted that this Axis official suggested a role for America in this new world, if not as an ally the at least as a disinterested rival dominating the New World. "He considerately suggests that if the United States will keep her hands off, she will be permitted to conquer and rule the entire western continent."[34] Fortunately for the future of humanity, this hypothetical arrangement never saw the light of day. The following months would see the Soviets join the Allied cause halfway through the year and the Americans were thrust into the conflict in December.

Leaning Toward War

As 1941 ended and their nation switched from an observer to a participant in the global war, American evangelical writers had some very definite opinions about the nations of the world, and they had no qualms in sharing these opinions with their readers. For the Soviet Union these criticisms centered on two basic things: its internal oppression and its external expansionism. They did not root their arguments against the Soviets in them being foreign but for being immoral. They based them in the way the Communist rulers of Russia oppressed their people and had extended this oppression to other nations such as Finland. They spoke of Communism as something that was wrong because of what it had done to the Russians and what it threatened to do to others, not

---

34. Benson, "The Meaning of the Present War," *MM*, February 1941, 354.

as something which was wrong because it was Russian. Communism was a force to be feared and opposed, but Russians were its victims, not its embodiment.

It was the same for the Axis Powers. Soon-to-be American enemies were rebuked by these evangelicals for their immorality, not for their nationality. The Japanese, Italians, and Germans were condemned for their slaughter of civilians, expansionist policies, and oppressive treatment, not for being Japanese, Italians, and Germans. Courier's stereotype of the Italians in the wake of their dismal martial performance in and around their Mediterranean home was not the nicest thing to say, but teasing your enemy in wartime is hardly an extraordinary example of xenophobia.

Gaebelein's early praise for Mussolini and his seeming insensitivity to the evil of Hitler is problematic. How could he condemn the Japanese for their barbaric treatment of the Chinese yet give the Nazis and Fascists the benefit of the doubt? Part of this apparent contradiction came from the reality of confronting difficult circumstances. While he did praise Mussolini for his abilities, he also spoke of him as a tool of the devil. While this might seem like an inconsistency or even hypocrisy, he wrote these words within a few months' time of one another. This was not hypocrisy, but Gaebelein's albeit histrionic attempt to wrestle with the complexity of the issues. At one and the same time Mussolini was a man who had accomplished a great deal for his nation, and he was also a man who was personally responsible for great evil. However, there is another explanation which is somewhat more mundane. Since others far more notable, such as Joseph Kennedy Sr. and Charles Lindbergh, also failed to see the significance of what was happening in Nazi Germany, perhaps this is an instance where present-day retrospection grants a clarity unavailable to those in the moment. With Kennedy, Lindbergh, and Gabelein, it did not take long before they came to see the horrors of the Third Reich and to speak out accordingly. What is clear to people today also became clear to people in the past.

For many of these writers, this was not a question of Left-or-Right ideology or nationalism but a matter of the oppression inherent in all forms of totalitarianism, requiring the starkest of countermeasures.

Poling, for example, suggested that the freedom of speech could and should be limited when it came to democracy's totalitarian enemies. In July of 1941 he wrote, "The unrebuked 'boos' for Britain in certain great mass meetings are equally 'heils' for Hitler, and he hears them. Can those who speak, be speaking for the best interests of America? Let us be warned." He continued, "It would be a major tragedy for any man or group not to be allowed to speak, but it is hardly less a tragedy when in a time of national emergency free speech is invoked to attack the integrity of the nation's commander-in-chief. Surely we may disagree without sabotage of American unity."[35] At another time he argued that the Communist Party should be denied radio time as its totalitarian goals were at odds with those of American democracy.[36] Communists, Fascists, militarists, and Nazis may not have seen themselves as having much in common, but their expansionistic totalitarianism made them equal evils deserving a shared response.

AMERICA

Evangelical evaluations of these American foes were largely negative, much as might be expected from writers who were themselves American. However, these writers did not have a uniformly positive view of their own homeland. Certainly, each July saw magazine covers embroidered with Lady Liberty and fireworks, and every fall found Thanksgiving and Christmas scenes worthy of a Frank Capra feature, but nestled within these celebrations of all things Americana were indictments of the land of the free. There was no question that these commentators viewed the United States as far better than Fascists and Communists. However, it is equally clear that they held grievances against America that were far from merely superficial, and that their support of their homeland was of a highly contingent nature.

AMERICA THE BEAUTIFUL

That being said, there were occasions when these writers seemed to conflate following the Bible with being a good citizen. For example in

---

35. Poling, "Fourth of July Meditations," *CH*, July 1941, 12.
36. Poling, "Out of my Mail," *CH*, January 1941, 6.

November 1938, younger *Moody* readers were warned, "Be careful which clubs you join, affiliate with, or even compete against. Be sure they are religious, patriotic, and controlled by those who promote American interests rather than those of some foreign dictator."[37] Similarly, William Houghton proudly reported that the entire faculty, staff, and student body of MBI took a loyalty pledge, adding, "In a day when so many schools are shot through and through with un-Americanisms, it should be a source of satisfaction to multitudes that here is one school pledging itself with one voice to sacrificial devotion to the land we love."[38] In their own way, advertisements in these magazines called people to view the world in a certain way. Just in time for Fourth of July celebrations, readers were asked, "Is the youth of America ripe for Collectivism? Shall a pagan philosophy displace the Bible teaching that Christ died to save sinners ... hence every soul is sacred. The way youth turns will seal our fate." These words were under a banner of the "Spiritual Defense of the Nation" and accompanied by an image of children marching behind a flag bearing a prominently featured cross.[39]

By and large evangelical commentators held the US Presidents in high regard throughout this entire period. Courier, for example, spoke glowingly of bold words by President Roosevelt on the growing crisis, noting that even FDR's 1932 party nomination rival, Al Smith, found it great. Courier admitted that this speech would make war with Germany more likely, but he added, "And it will slap America awake. We know now exactly where we stand; we've heard it from the President's own lips."[40] Addressing the same speech, Poling added that the United States was the world's best hope. "Today, America is the only possible 'Good

---

37. Leonard Benedict, "Youth of America, Beware!" *MM*, November 1938, 135.

38. Houghton, "A Loyalty Pledge," *MM*, September 1940, 3.

39. Advertisement for "All Bible Graded Series," *CH*, July 1941, 1. The ellipsis is in the text of the ad and the sentence ending "hence every soul is sacred" lacks a question mark. Presumably, this comes from a quote, but it is not clear from the text what might be alluded to here.

40. Courier, "Washington," *CH*, February 1941, 7. Al Smith had been the Democratic candidate for President in 1928 and had lost the nomination four years later to Roosevelt. In his book, *American Apocalypse*, Matthew Sutton has entire chapter, "Seeking Salvation with the GOP" (179–206), based on theological conservatives' animosity towards Smith in his bid for the Presidency.

Samaritan.' ... Here we can go clear out with the President of the United States. He is right—right as an American, right as a Christian. Self-protection, and stark realism dictate this course. The Christian ethic dictates no other course." Yet he warned his readers that they needed to approach the conflict with caution. "We cannot see the end of the way to which our feet are planted. We do know that there are incredible dangers. But to live dangerously now is the only hope of the more abundant life for ourselves, for our children, and for all men—German, Italian, and Jap[41] as well as British and Chinese."[42]

AMERICA THE WAYWARD

Often evangelicals complained that Americans were unwilling to follow the Bible, and this unwillingness held evangelical support of their nation to conditional levels. With a patriotic sounding title, "Liberty," Houghton lamented his fellow citizens' shallow biblicism. "The freedom to read the Bible unhindered carries with it the freedom not to read it. Some who would shout for the right to read it, never embrace the privilege."[43] William Hockman bemoaned the fact that, unlike in previous administrations, there was no evidence of family prayers conducted at the White House of President Roosevelt.[44] Some were less subtle. Betty Bowlsby, for example, blasted America for its failure to live for God, saying, "Back to the Bible! Back to the faith of our fathers! Back to the daily reading of the Word and teaching it diligently to our children! Back to the Bible in our schools! Back to Jesus Christ, America! On your knees!"[45] America was indeed a force for good in the world, but this goodness could only exist so long as God's word was America's guide.

---

41. In the following issue of *CH*, Poling issued an apology for the use of the term "Jap." He wrote, "That is a mistake for which I apologize to every *Christian Herald* reader. As written it was, as it should be always, 'Japanese.' I never use the other word. I thoroughly despise that word and all its kind." Poling, "A Correction," *CH*, March 1941, 34.

42. Poling, "We Choose Our Alternative," *CH*, February 1941, 38.

43. Houghton, "Liberty," *MM*, July 1937, 555.

44. Hockman, "Family Prayers in the White House," *MM*, December 1938, 202.

45. Betty Burrell Bowlsby, "On Your Knees, America! Back to God!" *MM*, July 1937, 557.

In light of this many evangelicals worried that Americans might not have the stomach to stand up against the sorts of dictators which had come to power in Europe. Houghton wrote about "our American smugness" which made people in the US think they were immune to the dangers of demagoguery, but he saw the recent history of Europe as a warning to his homeland. Continuing with a pessimistic challenge to his readers, he wrote,

> Of course, no individual American will silently consent to forfeit his liberty. For his "blood bought freedom" he is willing to die—or at least to fight—well, let us say, shout. It may be another indication of history repeating itself, for it was long ago said of the Athenians that they were like sheep, of which a flock is more easily driven than a single one.[46]

One writer called the United States to return to God, writing, "We stand today on an exalted peak among the nations of the earth. But in all due respect to our position, there seem to be changes taking place rapidly that are changing the moral stamina of our nation. What is wrong with America?"[47] Gaebelein added his own strong words for the American people when he wrote, "Our youth is increasingly misguided, religious apostasy is seen everywhere in control. Crime conditions are worse than ever. Sexual crimes and murder connected with them show a decided increase. So do suicides. How will it all end?"[48] Speaking about the government, he said, "It beggars descriptions. We shall not defile our pages with the political corruption which is in evidence everywhere. Again we face the worst of all corruption, the attempted buying of votes to maintain a tottering administration in power. Lust for power of an insane character is only too evident."[49] In each of these cases, the

---

46. Houghton, "Pessimism and Despair," *MM*, May 1938, 451.

47. G. M. Van Arnam, "What is Wrong with America?" *MM*, July 1937, 570.

48. Gaebelein, "What About the United States?" *OH*, December 1938, 383.

49. Gaebelein, "The Internal Chaos of the United States," *OH*, July 1938, 47. Gaebelein's commentary was often of a conspiratorial nature. That is, where others saw America as drifting away from God, he suggested that it was being pushed by groups intent on eliminating Christianity. "The atheistic and anti-Christian, anti-Bible and anti-religious agitations increase in our country. Many educational institutions are hot beds of this propaganda. What a terrible seed they are sowing!

writers saw America as well along a road heading away from God and away from the success it so far had enjoyed in the world.

Nonetheless, they were not without hope. Echoing the language of the Old Testament prophets, these twentieth-century theologians wrote that if only the American people turned to God, then God would be with and for them. As 1938 neared its end, Houghton opined,

> But we are also a year nearer the dissolution—apart from revival—of the type of government established by our fathers at great personal cost. They believed in personal liberty within limitations of common good, and those limitations they outlined in the Constitution. ... A Bible reading, worshiping people will be sound in their thinking and safe in their living. As we close the old year and face the new, we say again, "Let's go back to the Bible."[50]

One contributor to *Moody* laid out many of the crises facing America at that time including domestic economic and, most pertinently, global military issues emanating from Europe and Asia. He then spoke of his own country's collapsing moral state, writing, "It is a moral and ethical

---

What will the harvest be? Increase of crime, of immoralities, and finally a frightful revolution." Gaebelein, "The Fight against Religion in the United States," *OH*, March 1937, 619. That same issue saw his revelation of a secret meeting in Ohio of what he termed "a left wing aggregation." He wrote, "The meeting of the United Christian Council for Democracy was held in secret and behind closed doors. The press and the public were for some unknown reason excluded. It is said that one of the radicals present took exception to the rule adopted which refused to commit the movement definitely to the use of the 'democratic method' in bringing about a change in our government." Gaebelein, "Left wing Religionists Organize in Ohio," *OH*, March 1937, 621. A few months later he spoke positively of most citizens when he declared that, "The American people are fed up for the most part with the radical preachments of these professional radicals, who are using their positions to promote their Marxian, pacifist and internationalist theories." Gaebelein, "Radical Preachers Fight Criticism of Radicalism," *OH*, July 1937, 28. However, he was concerned that Americans were not sufficiently aware of the danger they were in. "The American people do not realize that an organized attack is being launched at their liberty, their Constitution, their homes, all their possessions, since they are misinformed about Communism." Gaebelein, "Be Aware," *OH*, July 1938, 49. It is unclear from the article how much of it is from the pen of Gaebelein and how much is from *National Republic*, which is referenced at the close.

50. Houghton, "The Year Closes," *MM*, December 1938, 171.

crisis. Drunkenness now is increasing. Vice and crime are rampant and popular. Gambling is becoming a national pastime, and lottery an obsession of the federal government by which our national deficit should quickly and easily be wiped out and our empty treasuries be refilled." Asking whether God could be the hope for America in its difficult times, he replied, "We answer that question unhesitatingly in the affirmative. God can, and only God can meet America's need."[51]

GOD AND COUNTRY

Sometimes these writers expressed a genuine love for their country that was yet tempered by the awareness that America was not always what it ought to be. There were times for rallying around the flag, but, when the national drift led away from God, there were also times when opposition was what was needed. Houghton, for instance, challenged his readers to consider the nature of their support for their homeland. "Patriots are many and varied. In times of war and election, the rabble rousers and other home guard generals rush to the rescue of a threatened nation. Some of the patriotism is real, but much of it is a mere uniform put on for the occasion. There are too many who care little what happens to the nation so long as they can attain or retain power." He concluded by succinctly challenging any sense of governmental theism. "There is a patriotism that deifies the State. But the proper kind gives God His place and agrees with the Word of God that 'righteousness exalteth a nation but sin is a reproach to any people' (Prov. 14:34)."[52] Their nation was drifting dangerously far from the foundation of its success, but for many of these evangelicals, there was still the possibility of returning to a godlier path. If not, then there was precious little hope for the future.

Just as the other nations of the world came under evangelical scrutiny when they behaved aggressively toward neighbors or were tyrannical to their own people came in for particular condemnation, evangelicals rebuked America for its deep and abiding corruption and

---

51. Reginald Shepley, "Can God Meet America's Need in the Present Crisis?" *MM*, July 1938, 563.

52. Houghton, "Wanted—A New Americanism?" *MM*, July 1940, 591.

failure to follow the will of God. In this way these evangelical voices took their cue from the Old Testament prophets who challenged the nations around them for humanistic and universal failings and their own country for disloyalty to God. And, just as ancient Israel was given no hope of success apart from following the faith of the fathers, so too, the United States was dismissed as a vehicle of God's work in the world insofar as Americans diverged from the faithfulness of those who had gone before. It is an interesting question whether they spoke of the US in this way because they saw America as a new Israel in covenant with God as opposed to the rest of the world or whether they wrote in this way simply because they were consciously or unconsciously imitating the style found in the Bible. There is evidence of either option. While there were comments which highlighted special blessing given to America by God, there were also points when authors said that the US could not count on God's special favor in the face of continued sin.

WAR

While these evangelical commentators expressed a willingness and even an insistence to unleash the dogs of war, their views of war, as such, could be ambiguous. Sometimes they expressed little hope that real peace could be achieved in the face of humanity's nature, a fear reinforced by the then-recent devastations of the First World War, yet they maintained that there was "a time to kill." Their understanding that war was something which needed to happen, given the crises of the day, did not taken away from their feeling that it was also something to be avoided.

DEATH AND DESTRUCTION

Gaebelein, with his normal dramatic tone, spoke of the possibility of a new world war as nothing less than diabolical yet as entirely consistent with humanity's then-present state. "A great eruption threatens, and when it comes it will mean a world-conflagration that will not leave a shred of our Christ-less, God-less civilization. A conflagration which will enthrone Satan's power and Satan's man."[53] Making use of

---

53. Gaebelein, "What Will Happen in 1937?" *OH*, January 1937, 477.

the same fiendish imagery, he later wrote derisively of the glorification of warfare coming from the pens of Fascist elites. Referring words
written by Mussolini's son, he commented, "He describes his seven
months' vicious, diabolical service of bombing the Ethiopians as 'magnificent sport.' He says, 'everything was fun.'" Gaebelein's evaluation
was particularly harsh, given that he would offer a measure of praise
to Il Duce that same year. "This is more than inhuman, it is devilish.
He is a worthy offspring of an equally inhuman father. Old Mussolini
need not worry now. In case he dies the devil has already provided his
demon controlled son to carry out his destructive program."[54]

It was not only the prospect of war, in and of itself, which drew
concern but also that the nations of the world were racing to create
the means of their own destruction. Gaebelein chronicled the great
increase in Soviet military budget and then offered a dismal analysis.
He feared that such a strong force in the hands of a totalitarian regime
would mean "the end of our tottering civilization."[55] Even defensive
materials were cause for concern, since they hardly encouraged confidence that the years to come would be filled with pacific bliss. He wrote
of Britain's preparation of some nine million gas masks and plans for
millions more in case of an "emergency," and declared, "Europe keeps
on preparing and preparing for a great catastrophe—the coming world
war. How will it end?"[56] For Gaebelein these preparations had a very
specific destiny, a destiny which would lead to the eschaton: "It means
that the end of the age with its final great conflict is not far away."[57] As
we shall see, Gaebelein was never hesitant to connect the beginning of
a new world war with the end of the world, but, in this case, his great
fears of devastation were on point.

Gaebelein was not alone in fearing a conflagration, and many of
these fears found their basis in the then-recent past. The First World
War weighed heavily on the minds of those writing in the period. It

54. Gaebelein, "The Beastly Wholesale Murder, Called War, Glorified," *OH*,
January 1938, 478–79.

55. Gaebelein, "The Soviet Military Budget," *OH*, March 1937, 618–19.

56. Gaebelein, "Britain Has Turned Out Nine Million Gas Masks," *OH*,
September 1937, 190.

57. Gaebelein, "Mussolini Speaks of Peace," *OH*, February 1937, 549–50.

had been such a devastating conflict that they looked to any means
to keep it from happening again. In a short piece bearing the title,
"Who Wants War?" this same *Moody* writer listed the cost of the Great
War in lives and treasure and then wrote of aftershocks of that great
conflict which continued to reverberate in his own day. "It wiped out
the Hohenzollern, Hapsburg and Romanoff dynasties, turned Russia
Bolshevik, spread Communism over the earth, gave the world Hitler and
Mussolini, bankrupted nations, changed the boundaries of twenty-six
nations, ... and filled the whole world with the poison of hatred and
fear."[58] In November of 1938, Houghton shared a reflection upon the
twentieth anniversary of the end of that bloody conflict. In a fairly
prescient article he warned that the "seeds" of a greater war could
well be growing even in his day of peace.[59] An article in *Moody* also
pondered the ephemeral nature of peace in light of the "War to End
All Wars." The author argued, "The world thought on November 11, 1918,
that lasting peace had been made. We now know better. There is no real
peace even where technical peace exists, for the horrors of declared and
undeclared wars go on, and domestic persecutions are worse than the
punishments of wartime spies."[60] Another author remembered fondly
the joy everyone felt at the end of the war, reminding his readers of the
great joy that they had in November 1918 when the guns fell silent and
encouraging them to work for peace. "Both sides lost about everything
worth-while—almost everything, but not all. Hope remains. That is
universal, and the uniting link of all races." He admitted that this hope
was fleeting, as conflict returned and both victor and defeated faced
up to a devastated new world.[61]

A TIME TO KILL

Others saw the preparations for war in a better light. For some, their
American pride showed through in full color. Frankly, Courier's zeal for
the burgeoning arms race bordered on the ghoulish. After describing

---

58. Benson, "Who Wants War?" *MM*, March 1939, 290.
59. Houghton, "The New Armistice," *MM*, November 1938, 116.
60. Mortimer B. Lane, "The World's Richest Man," *MM*, November 1939, 127.
61. E. A. Hallen, "World Peace—When and How?" *MM*, June 1939, 547.

the US Navy's newest torpedo boats in the glowing terms of someone having bought a new sports car, saying, "They carry four torpedoes, have the smashing power of a 1500 ton destroyer, carry 5000 miles of cruising gasoline in their tanks, and could cross the Atlantic if they had to."[62] At the same time, this bellicose impression was undercut by an editorial cartoon on the very same pages showing a weary-looking Uncles Sam setting out with his snow shovel to tackle the wintery effects of "Debt, Relief to War Stricken Peoples, Unemployment, and Defense." Under this image ran the sardonic caption, "Happy New Year, Uncle!"[63]

Some looked at the arms race as a good thing, too, but they did so for a very different reason than did Courier. By getting ready now, the US might ensure a victory or even prevent a war happening in the first place. In an article entitled "Peace by Preparedness," a *Moody* contributor spoke of those who encouraged American war-readiness as those best seeking to avoid war. "He is a man of peace, opposed to war—till the day when he must choose between war and something worse; he then chooses war. Because it must be this way, the United States owes to itself and to the human race to maintain an unexcelled equipment to police the seas. It is poor logic to teach that unpreparedness makes for peace."[64] Calling on the age-old philosophy of peace through strength, the hope was that by being ready for any war, they might dissuade enemies from trying their luck.

A TIME FOR PEACE

The question of pacifism rarely came up in evangelical magazines in this period, and, when it did, it was the subject of tolerance at best and disdain at worst. Houghton argued that war was detestable, but that, nonetheless, it was sometimes necessary and even moral. Any attempt to live in the present sinful age without military action was a vain dream. In April of 1937, he wrote, "No one deplores war, with all its attendant and aftermath of evils, more than we do. Our country

---

62. Courier, "Defense," *CH*, January 1941, 9-10.
63. R. O. Berg, Editorial Cartoon, *CH*, January 1941, 10.
64. Benson, "Peace by Preparedness," *MM*, July 1938, 581.

should go to every extreme possible in order to avoid it. But for America to disarm in the presence of the godless nations of today, would be suicidal." His argument was both practical and biblical. First, he compared the need for the armed forces to the requirement of cities to employ firefighters and police officers. Then, he cited several Bible passages to support the legitimacy of war in certain cases. He acknowledged that the Bible looked to the hope for a future millennium without lethal strife, but this was not to come until Christ returned. For those who preached otherwise, he said that it was "well meant," but he also hinted that it was "inspired by Russia," and simply did not deal with the reality of the world as it is.[65]

This skepticism toward pacifism was a common event in such articles. Gaebelein's commentary focused on what he saw as hypocrisy among American leftists. To his mind they were opposed to war in general, but they supported it when it suited their goals. In August 1937 he condemned them for opposing a neutrality act only because they wanted arms to continue to flow to one side of the Spanish Civil War.[66] At a later point Gaebelein offered a more in-depth accusation against Western pacifist leaders, arguing that their policies would lead to a greater war in the future. He wrote, "It seems that pacifists are saying little in these troublous days. Those radicals and liberals who were the loudest in denunciation of war are now falling into the very delusion that led to the world war. As they contemplate the rise of fascism, which they hate, they are convinced that one more war is necessary—this time to save democracy from fascism." He then condemned them for their looking the other way when it came to the horrors of the Soviet dictatorship but being myopically focused on the dangers of Hitler and Mussolini.[67]

Even if they did not share Gaebelein's strident rhetoric, his fellow evangelicals had equally little use for pacifist arguments. For some of them, it was not so much that they disagreed with pacifism's goals

---

65. Houghton, "War," *MM*, April 1937, 430.

66. Gaebelein, "Pacifists and Radicals Oppose 'Neutrality' and Defense Acts," *OH*, August 1937, 110.

67. Gaebelein, "Where is Pacifism These Days?" *OH*, November 1937, 322.

but that they considered the thinking too limited. A common refrain was that slogans and treaties were of little use when human nature remained as flawed as it was. There would come a day when the hope of not studying war any more would become reality, but that day had to await the miraculous intervention of God at the end of time. Aware that this might appear to be only so much pie in the sky, one clarified this point, saying, "Apart from Jesus Christ there is no peace for the world. That may sound like a religious platitude, but it is one of those things we are compelled to repeat over and over again. He is the only guarantor of peace we have in this sorrowing, stricken and war-ridden world. He can give peace among the nations of the earth, but it has to be on his terms, not on ours."[68] A 1939 editorial cartoon in *Moody* reiterated this point. It portrayed scholars, soldiers, and other leaders attempting to buttress an incomplete arch named "World Peace" with uncertain supports entitled things like threats, brute force, appeasement, and diplomacy. Over this the caption read, "The rejected keystone to world peace," referring to the missing piece in the foreground inscribed with "Jesus Christ."[69] The fundamental obstacle to world peace was not lack of education or the presence of weapons but the essential form of human nature, damaged as it was by human sin.[70]

While these commentators certainly came down in favor of the United States entering the war, they were sympathetic to the uncertainty felt by many evangelical readers. In an editorial cartoon with the caption, "Which Way, Christian?" a man was shown standing on a bridge with signs on either side marked "Defense of America" and "Conscientious Objections to War." With question marks over his head, the man was looking back and forth between the two, even as the wooden planking under his feet cracked. A choice had to be made.[71]

---

68. Benson, "Seeking World Peace," *MM*, May 1937, 474.

69. A. Bell, Editorial Cartoon, *MM*, July 1939, 614.

70. Sometimes publications could be less subtle in their criticism of pacifism. Clarence Benson announced that "*Christians and Fighting*, by Reginald Wallis, a pamphlet full of arguments to use against the peace-at-any-price pacifist, may be obtained free for the asking by writing the Moody Bible Institute of Chicago." Benson, "Christians and Fighting," *MM*, August 1937, 630.

71. R. O. Berg, Editorial Cartoon, *CH*, March 1941, 10.

One writer also pointed to the moral complexity of warfare when he asked, "If God's love and power are unlimited, why does He permit war to ravage the earth, and plunge millions of people into an abyss of suffer and woe? In these grim days this question is perplexing many minds."[72] In another piece in that same issue of *Moody*, he risked losing friends around America when he offered a partial answer which said,

> We speak of the horrible Hitler, but we do not want to face up to the truth spoken by James that wars come from our human lusts. We do not want to face the issue that unregenerate human nature is as hopeless as it is in the man who swaggers his totalitarian power yonder in Germany in the butchery of multitude, hoping for selfish aggrandizement of his nation, and the glorification of his own person.[73]

All in all, these evangelical writers found the hopes of pacifists to be headed in the right direction, even if they were rather simplistic their view of human nature. There would come a day when "We ain't gonna study war no more," but that day could only arrive when Christ returned to Earth and made humanity new.

A Time for War

In their stance on war as such, these writers were remarkable only for their ordinary attitude. Even if some did betray some enthusiasm for military technology, there was nothing which could be called militaristic. Besides that, this was hardly unique in the late 1930s or in any other time for that matter. As we shall see below, they were quite willing to connect the present conflict with a future final war, but this did not drive their analysis. Rather than their intense religiosity and eschatological focus giving them a ghoulish zeal for the coming war, they bemoaned the fact that the war had come. While some spoke of a world-ending war as inevitable, they also spoke of it as an evil which must be endured, not relished. There was no talk of this conflict providing a way out of the world but instead of mourning for what it was

72. Benson, "Why Does God Allow War?" *MM*, September 1940, 30.
73. Benson, "War in the Plans of God," *MM*, September 1940, 30.

doing to the world. These authors disagreed with pacifism and even suggested a sense of naïveté for pacifist motivations, but they also spoke of pacifism as a principled if misguided philosophy. When the war finally did come, none of these commentators had any qualms about identifying the Allies with the cause of justice in the world, yet they did so without conflating this mission with cause of the church. Given the extremity of the evil coming from Berlin and Rome, this atrocious war had to go forward even with all the suffering which would inevitably flow from this. This would not be an unusual position to take in 1941 or today.

END TIMES

Selling the End

With such cataclysmic events occurring and the fate of the entire globe on the line, it is not surprising that many evangelicals wondered about the relationship between the beginning of this conflict and the end of the world. Interestingly, it was in advertisements within magazines that people were likely to highlight this potential connection, and they did this to an astonishing degree. In the accompanying text to one, the ad promised insights concerning, "Why Russia Had to Break with Britain and Join Germany; Why Italy Must Break with Germany and Join Britain; Why the Final War Must Head Up in Armageddon; Why the Rapture of the Church Must be Very Near,"[74] Another called for premillennialists to join "The American Prophetic League, Inc." Potential members were reminded, "Never has the world witnessed such rapid turning and overturning as we see in our day. The prophetic significance of these things is undeniable."[75] An ad for the American Board of Missions to the Jews spoke of "the welter of a world gone mad, of nation rising against nation," and warned, "The time is short. That is why we keep reminding you of the privilege of sharing Him in His

---

74. Advertisement for *The Sunday School Times*, *MM*, November 1939, 136.
75. Advertisement for The American Prophetic League, Inc., *MM*, November 1939, 139.

yearning over the lost sheep of Israel."[76] Under the banner of "War in Europe! Nation Shall Rise Against Nation, and Kingdom against Kingdom, Luke 21:10," an ad for the American-European Fellowship asked, "When England and France sign a pact with Mussolini will the Ten Kingdom Federation be complete? Germany, Austria, Spain and the Little Entente are apparently all ready, and the Promised Land lies within easy reach. The Jews are already there! Look at your Bible map of the Roman Empire."[77] An ad for the periodical *Prophecy Monthly* promised to help its readers understand the times, saying, "Swastika Marches Over Europe! What does it mean? How does it fit in with Mussolini's map of the Roman Empire? ... When will Ezek. 38–39 be fulfilled?"[78] On the very same page readers were asked, "Is this age rapidly drawing to its close according to prophecy? Hitler's persecution of the Jews and their return to Palestine set the stage for the return of Christ? Does Mussolini's declared purpose to revive the Roman Empire fulfill Daniel's prophecy?"[79]

FINDING THE PRESENT IN THE BIBLE

It was not only advertisers who wrote in this way but many commentators also were confident that the events of the day were the manifestation of long-held prophecies. In response to a reader's question concerning the identity of Gomer in Ezekiel 38, a writer suggested that this referred to contemporary events. He argued that it was reasonable to assume that Rosh and Gomer in the biblical book referred to Russia and Germany, respectively. These two, he averred, would usher in the end of the world with an invasion of a future Jewish Israel in Palestine. "This appears now to be more probable than ever by reason of the recent pact made between Germany and Russia."[80] This was

---

76. Advertisement for The American Board of Missions to the Jews, *MM*, June 1937, 501.

77. Advertisement for The American-European Fellowship, *MM*, April 1938, 419. Interestingly, according to the address contained at the end of the ad, this organization was headed by none other than Gaebelein, editor of *OH*.

78. Advertisement for *Prophecy Monthly*, *MM*, May 1938, 479.

79. Advertisement for Silver Publishing Society, *MM*, May 1938, 479.

80. Grant Stroh, "Practical *and* Perplexing Questions," *MM*, November 1939, 148. Italics in title in original.

echoed by Houghton in a February 1940 editorial which had the decidedly confident introductory line of "Here is further evidence that those who study and believe the Bible are better informed concerning the meaning of present-day events than those who merely read the news." The author quoted a past president of MBI who, in 1917, had said that his study of the Bible led him to believe that the newly Bolshevik Russia would one day align with Germany. That these words were originally written decades before Stalin and Hitler's 1939 non-aggression pact led to the title of "Russia and Prophecy."[81]

Gaebelein had long been expecting this alliance between the totalitarian states. He wrote, "Such a union is demanded by the great prophecy in the 38th and 39th chapters of the Prophet Ezekiel. ... In fact it is most interesting in these days to trace the final prophecies in the Book of Ezekiel. Many have written us what splendid help they got from our exposition."[82] The following month brought a greater sense of confirmation for Gaebelein's ideas enabling him to write, "Surely for us these should be waiting times."[83] Interestingly, one of Gaebelein's boldest claims about the present day being the fulfillment of prophecy came while debunking another supposed fulfillment. When word came that the Iraqi government was to rebuild the ruins of Babylon, he undermined any idea that this was the long-predicted rise of a new Babylon. He said,

> But our christless [sic] and godless civilization, with its God-defiance and God opposing schemes, is the Babylon of the end of our age. According to the Book of Revelation the final Babylon has a twofold aspect. The Babylon [in Revelation 17] is the papacy in her final domineering power. The Babylon in the chapter which follows is the political, commercial, economic combination in a godless way during the closing years of our age.[84]

81. Houghton, "Russia and Prophecy," *MM*, February 1940, 304.
82. Gaebelein, "Is the Final North-Eastern Confederacy Looming up on the Political Horizon?" *OH*, July 1937, 30–31.
83. Gaebelein, "More Evidence as to Russia and Germany," *OH*, August 1937, 109.
84. Gaebelein, "The Tower of Babel for the Paris Exposition," *OH*, April 1937, 690.

For Gaebelein it might have been quite clear that America's potential enemies were the servants of the enemies of God, but he had no qualms about including his own civilization as being among the "christless" and "godless" regimes of the world.

Overreaching the Future

There were ample portions of hubris among the prognosticators in these magazines as commentators were quite confident that they could discern the path of prophecy in current events. One author declared,

> We do not find today in the movements of the nations any great event that is not moving toward the great ultimate which God has revealed in His prophetic word. Even the very war which is taking place today is but a cog in the wheel of future events, which are outlined so clearly and unmistakably for the Bible lover to see.

Continuing, he offered specific examples of this, saying,

> When we look at southern Europe today, we are not at all surprised to find that Mussolini thus far has been neutral in this war. ... He will, in all probability, be neutral today because God said that there would be a complete break between southern and northern Europe. It is already approaching, and it will be clearer as the days go by."[85]

It likely did not enhance his reputation that these words were published in June of 1940, which was the very same time that Italy entered the war on the German side, contrasting with his expectation of a split between north and south.[86] Similarly, Gaebelein's predilection for connecting the prophetical dots led him to be overly sure of future events.

---

85. L. Sale-Harrison, "The Combination of Nations and God's Great Prophetic Word," *MM*, June 1940, 549.

86. A similar embarrassment may well have occurred for the leaders of the Biblical Research Society. In June 1941 they placed an ad in *MM* which asked "When the Russo-German allies invade Palestine, what then?" This would have been published the same month that a German alliance invaded not Palestine but Russia. Advertisement for the Biblical Research Society, *MM*, June 1941, 607.

As circumstances turned out, these interpretations were not the most accurate. Speaking of the alliance between Mussolini and Hitler, he wrote, "The Rome-Berlin-Axis is unnatural and not according to prophecy. It will not last long. Mussolini will over-tower Hitler."[87] This, of course, was not the reality of history as Il Duce ended his career as the puppet of his master in Berlin, with the former needing to be rescued by German forces when his own regime collapsed in 1943.

HESITATIONS

Perhaps for fear of such embarrassments, evangelicals could be skittish about specific predictions. In 1938 Gaebelein cautioned against a too-eager interpretation of Italian moves as a full confirmation of prophecy, but he did so out of his belief that the full criteria had not yet been met.[88] Another contributor to *Moody* wrote, "Not only our country, but the world as a whole is headed for another and greater war. The tidal waves of unrest and hatred are continuously rising, and subsequent suffering and sorrow." Yet, even this somber imagery was written against an overly optimistic expectation for a peaceful future and was not about naming this as necessarily the end of history.[89] Many evangelicals, indeed, expected that a disastrous war would come someday, and they wondered if that day might have arrived. However, while they may have thought God's will was certain, they were less certain about their own interpretation.

In an article discussing the role of the Mediterranean Sea in the Bible, Wilbur Smith came just shy of connecting the present-day situation with biblical prophecy, but he was careful to avoid suggesting anything concrete. He argued that the Mediterranean was key in biblical history as a metaphor, and he did end with some commentary on how such things fit with contemporary issues, but he did not say that current events were the fulfillment of any particular prophecy.[90]

---

87. Gaebelein, "The German Reich Takes over Austria," *OH*, May 1938, 761.

88. Gaebelein, "Is the Revival of the Great Roman Empire in Europe at Hand?" *OH*, April 1938, 689.

89. E. A. Hallen, "World Peace—When and How?" *MM*, June 1939, 547.

90. Wilbur M. Smith, "The Significance of the Mediterranean Sea in the Old and New Testaments," *MM*, May 1938, 453-54, 469.

Smith could be suggestive about prophetic implications to the news of the day. He noted that many biblical scholars of the previous decades had expected that "the end of this age would be characterized by a dual form of government." He then continued, making an oblique reference to Communism. "We today are actually beholding such a government functioning, and the ideology of such a form of government mastering the minds of men throughout the western hemisphere. One phrase ... perfectly incarnates that which Daniel predicted twenty-five hundred years ago, 'the dictatorship of the proletariat.' In these five words are iron and clay bound together." In the remainder of his article, Smith warned about the dangers implicit in revolutionary movements and the dictatorships which, according to him, inevitably result. However, he refrained from overtly claiming for any current leader or even political movement a starring role in such a final act of humanity.[91]

Perhaps the most striking example of such hesitation came in March of 1941 with one article on Revelation. On its surface it sounded as though the author would explain how the events found in newspapers were predicted long ago; however, this was not the case.

> We may feel instinctively that God and righteousness will triumph, but we can have no certain knowledge of how the end will come unless we study those parts of the Bible which have been written and preserved for the purpose of warning and information. In particular, the book of Revelation contains an important message for these dark and difficult days.

Rather than showing how Hitler's rise was predicted, this author used it to show that the Bible's final book was written as a comfort to suffering Christians of any era, even if it was not the end of the world.[92]

---

91. Smith, "World Government at the End of This Age: Part Iron and Part Clay," *MM*, February 1939, 312–13, 337. Italics in original.

92. Henry E. Anderson, "The Book of Revelation Has a Message of Comfort," *MM*, March 1941, 396.

THE SONS OF ABRAHAM

The dramatic events in the Middle East of 1947 and 1948 were still to come, but many evangelicals had their eyes on a future for the Jewish people. Jews were consistently shown in a favorable light. Granted, many Jewish people would not appreciate this attention as so much of it was directed toward evangelizing them into Christianity. However, the increased danger posed by Nazism led many to consider a return to the promised land. There were those who saw any return to be a matter of prophetic certainty, but not everyone saw it in this way. Gaebelein, for instance, challenged the prophetic nature of the return of Jews to Palestine in the late 1930s, saying, "Zionism as it is today will pass away under the judging hand of the God of Israel."[93] While this perspective on the Jewish aliyah would become rare after 1948, a decade earlier evangelicals were not as uniform in their support of Zionism.

Regarding Jews in general, evangelicals regularly voiced opposition to anti-Semitism and had little trouble linking it to the worst aspects of the end of the world. *Moody* was one of the most eager to condemn such things. One of their authors was willing to say that the rising tide of anti-Jewish rhetoric and activity was "the spirit of the Antichrist, and the battle is now joined between the forces of Satan and his hosts and the forces of Christ and His Church," and he praised President Roosevelt for his willingness to rebuke the Nazi regime.[94]

THE PIECES FALLING INTO PLACE

Evangelicals watching the rise of alliances and non-aggression pacts at the close of the 1930s and the start of World War II thought that this might be the end of all things. Frankly, it is somewhat understandable that they would, given their belief that the end was nigh. Sometimes they were willing to be bold in connecting a given news event with a particular prophecy from the Bible, even if this meant having to eat their words shortly thereafter. Yet, there were many times when they were hesitant to infer any eschatological significance to current events.

93. Gaebelein, "The Bible is our Mandate. A Better Note in Zionism," *OH*, June 1937, 834.
94. Britan, "An Appeal for Persecuted Israel," *MM*, February 1939, 416.

Perhaps the most pertinent point is the silent one. For all the articles addressing eschatology there were far more comments about the emerging global crisis which made no mention whatsoever of prophecies of any kind. The most that can be said is that sometimes their view of the end of the world affected their understanding of the present, but it was clearly not the single determining factor for any of them.

Within a few short months the end of the world seemed to have grown all that much closer. Soon everything would be different. It was one thing to ponder potential enemies of their nation from the safety of peacetime America. It was quite another to be sending their sons off to fight back the seemingly invincible Axis flood. By the middle of 1941, American and German sailors were openly at war in the Atlantic, even if their nations remained at peace. By the end of 1941, peaceful reflection was a thing of the past as Japanese forces stormed across the Pacific, driving the Stars and Stripes before the Rising Sun. In reaction to these events, evangelical writers continued to counsel their readers how to follow God in a world turned upside down.

3

The Conflagration, 1942–1945

OVERVIEW

With the Japanese assaults on Western targets launched as 1941 drew to a close, Americans could no longer look on the bloodshed as distant observers. The oceans might keep away many effects of the war, at least for a while, but this battle was something new. Instead of one conflict in Asia and another in Europe, there was a truly worldwide war. This was no longer a contest for the control of one part of the globe or for spheres of influence. Whichever side won could dominate the entirety of Europe, Asia, and possibly Africa.

The year 1942 was the period when the Axis Powers were at their apogee and the Allies were struggling simply to survive, let alone emerge victorious. But, as Winston Churchill noted after the British victory in the Battle of El Alamein in that year, this was the end of the beginning. In 1943 and 1944 the Germans and Italians would be driven from North Africa and Russia. The justly famous Normandy landings in northwest France would find the Germans confronted with two massive armies on either side: The Anglo-Saxons to the west and the Russians to the east. On the other side of the world, it seemed for a time that the Japanese would ride their rising tide to victory. Even after being smashed by the American navy at the battles of Coral Sea and Midway, it would not be until the years that followed that the Japanese would feel the effects of the war. It was then that their forces were driven from the field and their homes were destroyed by the devastation of firebombings and, eventually, atomic warfare.

The American entry into the war brought a new focus to evangelical commentary on the conflict. No longer could pundits speak of it in the abstract, as though it were a merely intellectual problem to consider.

It was now something which was claiming the lives of family members, and US support of Allied nations now meant American boys dropping American bombs on Axis cities. Calls for justice, for revenge, and for compassion all blended together as these evangelical thinkers attempted to apply biblical wisdom to a modern horror.

ENEMIES

America's Comrades

With the arrival of war in earnest, the way evangelical writers spoke about other nations changed. The most obvious change was that even if anti-Communism continued in the background, there a general absence of anti-Soviet articles.[1] Criticism was not absent entirely. L. Nelson Bell, for example, offered caution to his readers in their haste to join forces with the democracies' new eastern ally.

> We have profited by Russia's military genius and might. Russia has profited by our lend-Lease supplies and by our military pressure and air power in the West. Our relations with Russia should be realistic enough to avail ourselves of the friendship she will give but also realistic enough to face the fact that her totalitarianism and communism are incompatible with Christian democracy. Failure to see this could bring about compromises or commitments which would do America irreparable harm.[2]

This, however, was the exception as many commentators seemed content to let Communism's failings be left in the background during the current crisis. When a reader asked if the US were headed toward Marxism, Daniel Poling said that was not the case and then went on to heap praise upon the Communists: "We shall render our own freedom a sad disservice if we do not 'embrace' our courageous Russian comrades who thus far have been our most potent defense."[3] Likewise,

---

1. There were exceptions to this rule. In August of 1942, Alexander Stacey wrote a piece on the future postwar world entitled, "Will Russia Stay with the Allies?" *CH*, August 1942, 16.

2. L. Nelson Bell, "Russia," *SPJ*, June 1944, 7.

3. Daniel A. Poling, "Doctor Poling Answers," *CH*, April 1943, 5.

Arno C. Gaebelein, who had previously spoken of the Soviets as entirely untrustworthy and as the Nazi's equal, now showered them with praise for their martial prowess. "We do not need to rehearse the startling achievements of the Russian-Soviet armies during the last year, especially the Soviet victory at Stalingrad, their masterly strategy and fighting in defense of Leningrad and Moscow."[4] The Russians might still have been devils, but now, with the pressing threats of Japan and Germany, at least they were "our" devils.

FALTERING FASCISTS

The Italians were given short shrift during the war. As the conflict progressed they were often described in tragic or passive tones. They were losing, and everybody knew it. In contrast to Gaebelein's reticent respect to the nascent new Roman Empire, Courier declared the Fascist military to be incompetent. "Since Italy went to war at the side of Germany, she has lost 4,000 of her 6,000 planes, she has lost probably one-fourth of her vaunted submarine fleet, and what is left of her surface craft hug her harbors, fearful of venturing to sea; no one seems to know how many men she has lost. ... To put it briefly, Italy never had a chance."[5] Well into the war, a piece in *Moody* described the nation's plight, saying, "Italy stands today as one of the world's great battlefields, and Italians are paying for all the sins of Fascism against the world order."[6] Once Mussolini had been tossed from power in 1943, Gaebelein wrote of the man he had earlier lauded as a potential new Caesar, "It is true that the loud-mouthed Mussolini has been silenced. The Italian government gave him a big kick and, at our writing, it is unknown where that kick had landed him. Some say he is under lock and key, in the custody of Italy; others say he tried to escape to Nazi lands in order to find shelter under the protecting wings of his friend [Hitler]."[7]

---

4. Arno C. Gaebelein, "The New Great World Crisis XXIV," *OH*, July 1943, 19.
5. Gabriel Courier, "Italy," *CH*, January 1942, 9.
6. Frederick W. Christiansen, "A Report from Italy," *MM*, October 1944, 69.
7. Gaebelein, "The New Great World Crisis XXVI," *OH*, September 1943, 160. Without excusing his failings, E. Schuyler English pointed to the tragedy of Il Duce's career. "It is unfair to say that Mussolini never did anything for Italy. He took the country in hand when Italy was in the throes of revolution, corruption, poverty

THE RISING AND SETTING SUN

Perspectives on the Japanese were complex in many ways, alternatively displaying some of the worst stereotypes of the era and, concurrently, taking pains to understand the new enemy. Gaebelein's commentary on the Japanese was both expansive and offensive. On the one hand, he accurately predicted when the war would end and seemed fairly aware of its course, but, on the other, he described the Japanese with racialist terms. When speaking of the American advance in the Pacific, he said that this "bodes nothing good for the yellow criminals. Some of them begin to see things by this time, not victorious things but the very opposite, yet the disastrous defeat which will push the yellow heathen invaders to their hermit kingdom may not come till some time in 1945."[8] While the first instance of "yellow" could refer, hypothetically, to cowardice, the combination with the second "yellow heathen" makes a racial remark the only reasonable conclusion. This was confirmed the following month when he again spoke in this way of Japan, saying, "At last the Aleutian Islands seem to have been swept clean of this yellow pest."[9] E. Schuyler English, who had taken over for Gaebelein at OH in 1943, skirted the edge of this sort of characterization when, in 1944, he said, "More islands must be taken, and air bases established in China perhaps, before the uncomfortable little Orientals will know how mild was their present discomfort in comparison with what is to come."[10] This was a moral failure on their part, but in using such degrading language, these authors were entirely consistent with the sort of language of the day. That does not make it acceptable, but it also does not make them stand out as uniquely evil.

At first Courier had doubts about Japan's ability to wage the war it had started, suggesting that they were drastically ill-equipped and

---

and starvation and made her a self-respecting, cleanly, industrious and honored nation. We must give the devil his due, and Benito this much credit." He then explained Mussolini's fall from grace by saying the "power went to his head." E. Schuyler English, "Shrunken Caesar," OH, September 1943, 180. English had taken over from Gaebelein writing the "Current Events in Light of the Bible" article series.

    8. Gaebelein, "The New Great World Crisis XXIV," OH, July 1943, 20.

    9. Gaebelein, "The New Great World Crisis XXV," OH, August 1943, 96–97.

    10. English, "Little Change," OH, April 1944, 689.

on the run from the Allied military.[11] Just a few weeks later, he had to change his tune. As the Japanese were running British, American, and Dutch forces out of Southeast Asia, he admitted, "What's happened here is that we have completely underestimated Japan's striking power. We say, 'We,' including the United States as well as Britain. Remember Pearl Harbor? Unless tremendous reinforcements are piled into Malaysia, Malaysia is lost. If it is lost, heaven knows how long it will take to beat Japan—and her Axis master to the West."[12]

Evangelicals were of two minds when it came to "enemy aliens" within the United States. Like many in the nation during this time, Courier advocated the internment of Japanese Americans into what he called "concentration camps." While concentration camps gained a very specific connotation coming out of 1945 and the horrors of the likes of Auschwitz and Buchenwald, that definition was still in the future for Courier's comments here from 1942. Presumably, therefore, he does not have gas chambers in mind here when using this phrase. It was a certainty to his mind that some of the supposedly innocent Japanese fishermen haunting American waters were reporting back to Tokyo about US naval movements.[13] However, to his credit, Courier allowed that he might be wrong and went so far as to share statements by Christian groups on the West Coast who were strongly protesting the internments. He did not agree with them and said that it was hard to see it their way with American vessels falling to German U-Boats "every day," but he conceded that the West Coast Christians were in a better position to judge than he was.[14]

---

11. Courier, "The East," *CH*, February 1942, 8.

12. Courier, "East," *CH*, March 1942, 8–9.

13. Courier, "Aliens," *CH*, April 1942, 8.

14. Courier, "Internees," *CH*, August 1942, 10. Italics in original. Courier was not always this stark. After telling of an American girl born to Japanese parents who was elected president of her class at the University of Pennsylvania, he said, "And if [that] isn't the most hopeful item on the peace that is to come—you tell us!" By way of contrast to this story he also told of a parade where another girl wore a dress made from the parachute and scarf taken from a Japanese plane. When it had crashed in her yard in Hawaii, she salvaged the material. Courier called this "the grisliest, most barbarous, and disgusting piece of anti-Christianity yet to appear in the press." Courier, "Peace," *CH*, May 1942, 7. The seeming inconsistency could be

A more sympathetic tone was also in evidence in another *CH* article. A contributor wrote of efforts by the American authorities to identify which enemy aliens, German and Italian as well as Japanese, might pose an imminent threat and how German and Italian Americans who were not considered a menace were then permitted to go about their business. "But with the Japanese Americans in the West Coast areas, it was different. Most were given a very short time in which they must sell, at a forced sale for whatever price they could get, their homes and the businesses in which they had been usefully earning their livings." In contrast she asked whether German Americans, many of whom she claimed had been public with their support of the Nazis, had been "forced to sell their businesses and homes at any price they could get, move out of the city into a wild, unsettled tract in the Appalachian mountains and begin to earn their living with their hands?"[15]

Attitudes toward the Japanese nation and its people outside of America mixed attempts at analysis with calls for mercy, albeit a mercy accompanied by overwhelming force. A long-term missionary to Japan offered his commentary on why Japan fought with such intensity. While Americans tended to think of the conflict as a defensive war into which religion played no intrinsic part, this was not the thought of the Japanese. "It is out and out a religious war for them. The emperor of Japan is god and to many the only god." The author added that the Japanese did not consider themselves to be conquerors, per se, but that they were acting for the common good of the world. "Naturally, they think foreign peoples are dumb and dull as to these blessings. They do not understand. Therefore with 'great regret' the sword must be used to open their eyes at first, but in a few years under the imperial rule these benighted people will be singing the praises of Japan."[16] This analysis might not have led any readers to have any new affection for their enemy, but it might well have helped them to understand some of the reasoning involved in Japan's war of conquest in East Asia and the Pacific.

---

attributed to the stress of the time and also to the fact that there was no singular "Courier" that might be consistent with himself.

15. Dorothy Canfield Fisher, "Exiles in America," *CH*, April 1943, 37.
16. S. M. Erickson, "A Holy War," *SPJ*, November 1942, 22.

A 1944 article by a pastor who had been interned by the Japanese and released early in the war offered both a sharp-edged realism about the foe yet still did so with an emphasis on loving that same enemy. He suggested five points needed for the restoration of Japan and East Asia as a whole. First and foremost was the call for the elimination of Japanese militarism. Pointing to his five years of experience with their governance, he said that "the Japanese military and the military government of Japan are not fit to rule." He continued in this vein, saying, "Their trusteeship of power is being taken away from them. God uses human instrumentality. God is using the military might of America to crush the evil militarism of Japan." Despite these reasons for anger at the Japanese people as a whole, the author did not call for their destruction. "Some people say, 'Exterminate the whole Japanese race!' No! Such an attitude is unreasonable! We must **help** the common people of Japan." His fifth and final point was forgiveness. "After the above four steps have been taken, we should forgive the common people of Japan and treat them as equals. I do not make this statement lightly. I have seen the Chinese suffer under the Japanese. I have also suffered. But that is the Christian attitude to take."[17] This was not an easy thing for him to say. He knew that this forgiveness would be costly, as his eighteen-year-old son had been killed at the Battle of Bougainville. Nationalism and war frenzy may have taken hold in many parts of the country, but at least for this man, his desire to follow the pattern of Christ trumped even his natural desire for vengeance.

Facing the Devil

When evangelicals spoke of Germany during the war, they were somewhat less interested in understanding the enemy than they had been with the Japanese. One author wrote, "I am glad that I am not a German national today. From what I know of the Bible, I could have no hope of the blessings of God upon my country in this war. ... From God's book I am convinced that God is against Hitlerism, and therefore it

---

17. George A. Hudson, "Five Point Program for the Far East," *SPJ*, August 1944, 20-21. Boldface in original.

must finally fail."[18] This might not have been the most sophisticated argument ever made, but it is one which continued to ring true down through the ages. At another time a chaplain's sermon described Hitler's effect on his people in almost magical terms. He argued that in the pre-war years Hitler had bewitched the Germans' ability to think for themselves and replaced it with "his own diabolical will."[19] Houghton struck a different pose, placing the blame firmly on the Germans themselves. He argued that the Nazis had come to power expressly by the will of the people in contrast to the situation in Italy where Mussolini's "Blackshirts" had seized power through revolution. "It is plain silly to place all the blame for Hitler on Hitler. The German people voted him into being. He is the expression, visible and vocal, of the Germany of our day." He did not, by this, mean to excuse Hitler for his crimes but only to include his followers in the guilt.[20]

These evangelical commentators were not above making fun of their Teutonic foe if the opportunity presented itself. As 1943 came to its close, Courier mocked the Germans' attempts to hide their faltering war effort. "Falling back, back, back in Italy, losing Smolensk and Kiev in Russia and hurled back to the Polish border itself, Hitler's propaganda-men are having a tough time of it breaking the news of defeat after defeat to the war-weary Germans."[21] English taunted the Nazis in much the same way in early 1944, saying, "We wonder how Goering is able to face the people whom he promised 'Berlin will never be bombed'! But its citizens are still laboring under the delusion, reluctantly confessed by a number of Nazi prisoners on this Continent. 'We were told that New York had been lowered to the ground by German bombs.' "[22] Or, again, "It has been a long time since either Germany or Japan has been able to report a victory to the home folks."[23] Houghton warned Axis leaders to

---

18. J. E. Harris, "Hitler Will Fail—But When?" *MM*, July 1943, 619.

19. Ben L. Rose, "A Call to Humility," *SPJ*, June 1943, 9. This article was taken from a sermon given by Chaplain Rose to the General Assembly of the Presbyterian Church in the United States on May 27, 1943.

20. William H. Houghton, "The Spirit of Hitler," *MM*, January 1944, 255.

21. Courier, "End?" *CH*, November 1943, 9.

22. English, "Recapitulation," *OH*, March 1944, 605.

23. English, "The Great Enigma," *OH*, September 1944, 200.

pay attention to history, saying, "The dictators should be reminded that men have been crowned as victors one month and covered as corpses the next month. It is not far from being dined by the kings of the earth and dined upon by the worms of the earth. Newspapers of Tokyo, Berlin, and Rome please copy."[24] Given that he wrote this just six months after the American entry into the war, at a time when things were going quite badly for the US, this last comment could be written off as bluster or even a case of "whistling in the dark." Even so, there was never a time when a German victory was entertained as a real possibility in these magazines.

Yet, they knew that in Germany, the Allies were faced with a dangerous and still capable enemy. In a 1942 piece Courier discounted signs that Germany's endurance might be wearing thin, noting that the Nazis had had several years to consolidate their position on the Continent and to secure its resources for the fight ahead.[25] Just one year later, however, Gaebelein saw events as pushing toward an Axis collapse. Writing after the Allies were secure in North Africa, he commented, "The situation throughout Europe is changing and becoming unfavorable for Hitler and his fellow gangsters. The morale in Germany is greatly weakened and another victory like the one in North Africa may produce a big crash. Opposition to Hitler is on the increase."[26] The difference between Courier and Gaebelein can be explained by a string of strategic Allied victories in the time between their writings. At the time of Courier's piece, the Allies were on the run almost everywhere, but by the time of Gaebelein's, the Germans had endured the Russian onslaught at Stalingrad, the British victory at El Alamein, and the Anglo-American landings near Casablanca.

Much like his attitude toward Japanese Americans, Courier advocated a harsh response when faced with the prospect of German saboteurs operating in the United States. After recounting the capture of Nazi agents by the authorities, he counseled, "The other element is that from now on, every Bundist and ex-Bundist in this country should be

24. Houghton, "The Editors to Those Who Run," *MM*, June 1942, 571–72.
25. Courier, "Berlin," *CH*, March 1942, 10.
26. Gaebelein, "The New Great World Crisis XXIV," *OH*, July 1943, 18.

watched day and night, by FBI and civilian alike. They are more a more terrible threat because they are working from the inside out, as familiar with this country as any true American. ... Vigilance is the word for it!"[27] He made a similar appeal just two months later after recounting his observations of a trial of a captured German spy. After reminding his readers that the spy likely did not seek out his new profession, he still warned people to keep their eyes open, saying, "The German who has lived here, gone back to Nazi Germany for a visit however long, and then returned, is the man to watch, if you are spy conscious."[28] Talk of this sort did make an appearance in evangelical articles, but they were few and far between. Most of the time pieces in these magazines were aimed at counseling readers about how to face their fears, not to stoke them up to greater and greater fear.

LOVING THE ENEMY

For many, however, a harsh view of the Axis as the enemy was qualified by the biblical call to love one's neighbor. Occasionally, the ethnic nomenclature sometimes left much to be desired, but the sentiment would have been a strong rebuke to humanity's ordinary response to international conflict in any age. William Houghton several times used his position at *Moody* to cool war frenzy. In February 1942, in the issue published after Pearl Harbor, he reminded his readers that someone being an enemy had as much to do with chance of birth as it did a conscious choice. Further, as a Christian, it was his duty not only not to hate his enemy but he was called to pray for them.[29] At another time he argued against letting the passions of war go unchecked. "It is one thing to fight the enemy and it is another to hate the enemy. ... One can be maudlin in his sympathy for the enemy. On the other hand, one can be hellish in his dislike of the enemy." To make his point he recounted the story from one of the Japanese internment camps when some American-born Boy Scouts faced down a crowd of some of their fellow internees who were aiming to pull down the American flag. Houghton

---

27. Courier, "Closer," *CH*, August 1942, 7.
28. Courier, "Spies," *CH*, October 1942, 7.
29. Houghton, "Concerning the War," *MM*, February 1942, 327.

reminded his readers, "You cannot hate all the Japs unless you hate these young heroes who are just as American as you are."[30] The next year Houghton reminded readers that among the enemy were men who were themselves fellow Christians, but even if they were not believers, he called on people to pray for those they fought. "But above all, let us pray for foes as well as friends. Ask God to help us to show forth the compassion of Christ in this hour of testing."[31]

One of the most potent examples of this love for enemies came in what, on the surface, seemed like nothing of the sort. In the provocatively entitled, "We Encountered the Japs, *and Not a Shot Was Fired*," a US Army private wrote about what sounded rather ominous from the headline, but turned out to have been a rather beautiful story. This was the tale of a group of twenty-five American soldiers of whom all but six were African Americans, led by a Southern, white major, and who were all headed toward this encounter with Japanese civilians. The major was a chaplain and had gone to seminary with a Japanese-American pastor now locked away in the relocation camp inside the United States. The private wrote of the moment, saying, "As hearts were united in chorus and hymn, we knew that within we were of one color, and of one blood—the blood of Christ." The author was himself somewhat stunned that the multiracial event could occur, confessing, "Perhaps some of us could scarcely believe the emotions ... that moved within our hearts as we marveled to see North and South, black, white, and yellow, the latter our 'enemies,' enjoying this oneness through 'the Lamb of God, which taketh away the sin of the world.' "[32] This piece is

---

30. Houghton, "Fighting or Hating?" *MM*, February 1943, 352. Inexplicably, the original sentence ends with a question mark, presumably as a result of a typographical error.

31. Houghton, "Love Your Enemies," *MM*, August 1944, 655. He was not the only person to point to things in common with "the other." A contributor to *SPJ* informed her readers that many Japanese were fellow believers who had taken pains to act rightly. "Stories can be told of Japanese Christians. One group of Japanese finding a wounded American on the roadside in New Guinea, placed him out of danger, and said, 'We are Christians and hate war.' " Jane Smith Shields, "Our Soldiers and Foreign Missions," *SPJ*, February 1944, 12.

32. D. Glenn Chambers, "We Encountered the Japs, *and Not a Shot Was Fired*," *MM*, August 1943, 670, 681. All italics in original. In contrast to this nuanced approach was an advertisement in *CH* by a movie studio mocking the Japanese

remarkable for several reasons. As with the articles by Houghton, it is impressive that these authors were able to say this in the midst of a bloody war between different ethnicities. Perhaps more significant than this is the fact that this army private not only told his readers to love the enemy across the sea, but he not so subtly hinted that something was amiss with race relations at home.

AMERICA

God's Country

Some of the most commonly recognized images of the Second World War are of the propaganda-like posters and movies, urging citizens to do their part for the war effort. Some of this is nothing more than popular culture tapping into current events to reach their consumers, much as advertisers after 9/11 found a way to put the flag on nearly every product. Other parts are seen, perhaps correctly, as working to instill a war frenzy into the general population, a frenzy which would leave precious little room for critical thought. The association of America with all that is good and the induction of everyone from cartoon characters to God himself into the war effort created the impression that nuance was passé. Sometimes this came in imagery from the magazines

---

government for saying "American movies have had a terrible influence on Japanese thought!" There is nothing controversial about such a quotation, but along with this quote came an image of a bespectacled, bucktoothed, slit-eyed caricature of a Japanese man. This image did not originate from an evangelical source, but *CH* did agree to include it in its magazine. Advertisement for Warner Bros., *CH*, July 1944, 1. What can be held directly to the account of the staff of *CH* is the cartoon shared in their November 1945 issue which showed a Japanese hand reaching across the barbed wire with claw-like fingers towards an Uncle Sam standing with his arms crossed. From the Japanese hand comes the words, "So sorry, please," which is answered by the caption saying, "Too Late for Apologies." Lewis, Editorial Cartoon, *CH*, November 1945, 9. Also in tragic contrast to Chambers's article, Vernon Patterson included "Inter-racial Teachings" among his list of five dangerous ideas held by the non-evangelical Federal Council of Churches. "The position of the Council, as expressed by its leaders, is strongly for race equality, both social and political. ... Some of the Federal Council leaders have even gone so far as to advocate that serious consideration should be given to inter-marriage between the races." Vernon W. Patterson, "The Principles and Objectives of the Federal Council," *SPJ*, October 1944, 17.

themselves and sometimes it was from sponsors who sought to associate their cause or product with the global conflict in some way.

One example of this came on the table of contents of every issue of *Moody* during the period in question. In the top left corner was the Stars and Stripes by the title of one of conservative Christianity's flagship journals. One article, entitled "God and Country," portrayed "Old Glory" and the so-called "Christian Flag" flapping side-by-side in the wind. Beneath this was written a line from "The Star-Spangled Banner" and a quote saying, "The Son of God goes forth to war, A kingly crown to gain; His blood-red banner streams afar; Who follows in his train?"[33] A poem in *CH* entitled "America, My Country" lifted the United States high as an example to others.

> Climb higher, higher still that other lands
> May hear your challenge, see your valiant climb
> Take firm foothold and reach your strong young hands
> To the shackled nations of this darkened time,
> And draw them up with hands as yet unstained,
> Strike off their chains, and keep yourself unchained![34]

Another poem all but equated being a soldier of the United States and a soldier of Christ.

> Each star a soldier, brave and true,
> Resolved his best to give,
> That we who honor liberty,
> In freedom still may live,
> Each star a soldier of the Cross,
> A follower of the Lamb,
> Enlisted in the sacred cause,
> For which his Captain came.[35]

---

33. Anonymous, "For God and Country," *MM*, July 1942, 654.
34. Grace Noll Crowell, "America, my country," *CH*, February 1942, 2.
35. Avis B. Christiansen, "The Service Flag," *MM*, July 1942, 644.

Similarly, one mother recounted her thoughts about her son's enlistment. After saying that she had dreamed of her son as a pastor or a missionary, she later realized,

> [B]ut now it seems, A soldier boy I gave!
> But more than just a soldier boy
> In handsome khaki clad
> I give to Him with greatest joy
> A Christian soldier lad![36]

For this mother, and, by implication, for the staff at *Moody*, the role of her son as a warrior for America was just as righteous a calling as if he had gone into full-time ministry. The September 1942 issue of *Moody* had American military aircraft flying in formation gallantly across the skies. Next to this was the photo of a man in stylized pilot's gear, flying-scarf included, gazing beyond the reader with a steady confidence in the rightness of his cause. Beneath these pictures was the title, "Young America."[37]

THE GOOD GUYS

These evangelicals were not above uniting cause of Christ with that of the United States, with one important qualification. A recurring theme down through the decades was that America's blessing by God was entirely dependent on America's connection to Christianity, not the other way around. This nuance was not always easy to see, however. One writer called for American flags to find a prominent place in Christian churches. "The flag should be displayed in every church activity to remind all that Christian men and women are proud to be Americans. The task of the church will be to maintain the moral spirit of the nation, never to allow our citizens to forget that the American way of life is based upon well-defined principles of perspective and behavior."[38] When the war in Europe had ended, a writer in *SPJ* praised

---

36. Mary Helen Anderson, "A Mother's Gift," *MM*, October 1942, 82.
37. The Editors, *MM*, September 1942, front cover.
38. Ralph Sadler Meadowcroft, "What My Church is Doing to Maintain Morale," *CH*, September 1942, 28.

the American love of freedom. "It is inborn in the American, who left the Old Country for freedom for all to believe in this good thing for all men. And so when we won the war with Spain and took Cuba and the Philippines we promised them freedom. Cuba got hers long ago and the Philippines are to get theirs next year, and they believe us." Pertinently, he saw the uniqueness of America as flowing from the prevalence of Christianity in the land, pointing to the peace found along the US–Canadian border when compared to other similar frontiers around the world.[39]

The shock of Pearl Harbor led many to put aside past differences in order to be more ready to face the present crisis. A US Navy chaplain expressed his thoughts poetically in *CH*, saying,

> Blindly we waited on the brink of war
> Each busy with his ant-like, vast designs
> Nor cared what other men were fighting for
> We dwelt behind the sea's protecting lines
> Then in a Sabbath dawn the bombers spoke
> Over the palm trees of a peaceful land—
> Complaisance vanished in *Arizona's* smoke
> God knows we wanted peace, But now WE STAND[40]

In his initial word about American involvement after the Pearl Harbor attack, Houghton stated, "Our first thought is that America must be united as never before if this war is to be successfully prosecuted and terminated." After clarifying that any newfound unity could not allow "communistic" forces to take advantage of the situation, he went on to say, "We must forget our lesser differences and unite in the common task of defeating the enemy. It is right to pray for peace, but we believe it is right and wise to pray for victory."[41] At another time he said, "Men may differ on many things in days of peace, but the moment war is

---

39. J. Kelly Unger, "The Great Delusion," *SPJ*, August 1945, 8–9.

40. William W. Edel, "We Stand," *CH*, August 1942, 1. Emphasis in original.

41. Houghton, "Concerning the War," *MM*, February 1942, 327. As at many other times, the production schedules for magazines meant that there was a lag between an event and periodical commentary. Here, it was February 1942 before *MM* was able to comment upon the December 1941 Pearl Harbor attack.

declared many of those differences disappear. Men who wobbled or were uncertain before Pearl Harbor, are definite and committed now."[42] In and of itself, there was nothing remarkable about this attitude. The same can be seen at the beginning of nearly any war by nearly any subset of any nation. By and large the evangelicals never devolved into any kind of "my country, right or wrong," but the temptation to go down that path was as present for them as for any other group in the nation.

As the war continued beyond the initial passions of December 7th, evangelicals unambiguously identified the Allies with the right side. Again, it is hardly controversial that they took sides against the per-petrators of Auschwitz and Nanjing. What is worth noting is the way they justified their support of America and its cobelligerents. When compared to their Nazi and militarist opponents, the nations of the Allies were pure as the driven snow. As Houghton put it, the Allies represented everything which his readers prized about being American and being Christian. While he did not say that the Second World War was the final war of history, he did suggest that the principles of the present conflict were "the principles for which the final war of this earth are to be fought."[43] As he had during the lead-up to the war, Poling was adamant about the justness of the Allied cause. "At the heart of this Atlantic Charter is a promise that captures the imagination of free men. It is the promise of peace in our time. Not appeasement as of Munich, not peace in assent to the dictators' ultimatums, but peace with all the freedoms, peace with liberty and with justice for all."[44] After the hard days of 1941 and 1942 faded and the Axis forces were pushed back, E. Schuyler English's confidence in the ultimate outcome grew proportionately. After noting that there had been no big news from the war in the previous month, he wrote, "Nor is it necessary for us to mention miles gained or towns taken by the Allies—they are too many to enumerate and too difficult to spell."[45] The shock of Pearl Harbor had led to some serious soul searching, as will be seen below. However,

---

42. Houghton, "The Christian War," *MM*, October 1942, 64.

43. Joseph Britan, "God in a World at War," *MM*, April 1944, 500.

44. Poling, "The Atlantic Charter," *CH*, January 1942, 12.

45. English, "Review of the Month," *OH*, December 1943, 408.

the starkness of the moral contrast between the Axis and Allies and the relative swiftness of the war's turn against Germany and Japan led many to rest easily in their nation's just cause.

THE NOT-SO-GOOD GUYS

The zeal of war did not give these commentators an unconditional faith in the United States. They were quite willing to offer up some specific complaints about their country's policies and to provide a strong check against any divinizing of the nation. Sometimes their criticism was a matter of declaring that the state did not have the Christian's ultimate loyalty. For example L. Nelson Bell argued, "Caesar must have the things that are his. But by incomparably greater compulsion of duty and gratitude and love, so must the Lord Jesus Christ have the things that are His. We must not fail Him."[46] He offered a qualified support to the US.

> We boast of the actual and potential military might of America today, and our enemies are increasingly feeling this might. Thank God that He has seen fit to accord us this privilege of effectively meeting the attacks of our enemies. But stop! We hope for a cessation of hostilities some day. Are we as a nation capable of meeting the responsibilities which lie ahead?[47]

Christians were ordered by God to obey the state, but this obedience had its limits. Throughout this period, both the time of the Second World War and the extended era of the Cold War which followed, there was never a call by these writers for Christians to give the government or the nation absolute trust and fealty. This divinely ordained support was to be real, but it was to be contingent upon the conformity of America to God's will.

This was keenly demonstrated by regular comments aimed at puncturing Americans' confidence in supposedly being God's special people. One army chaplain warned Americans that a failure to turn to God would make the efforts of the war meaningless, saying, "We must, therefore, speed the work, we must work with an urgency, for mark this

---

46. W. Twyman Williams, "Christ And Caesar," *SPJ*, January 1943, 23.
47. Bell, "Making Democracy Safe For The World," *SPJ*, March 1944, 4.

word—if America wins her victory without first being humbled, she is doomed! But if she is brought to her knees before God, she shall rise to great service for God."[48] Houghton responded to those questioning the goodness of God in allowing the tragedy of the war to take place, saying, "People who have ignored God for twenty years are the first to expect divine intervention in their extremity. God is supposed to drop everything else in the universe and rush to straighten out their little or big affairs. ... If a nation ignores God and denies His Word, what right has it to expect God to at once get it out of a jam?"[49] At another point Houghton quoted a clergyman who seemed, at first, to argue that the nature of the Axis's evil meant that God had to be on "our side," then he qualified this. "It is all very, very, comforting, BUT—What right has America to brazenly presume that God just must be her ally in war, when America has driven God, to a very large extent, out of her national life?"[50] A year later Houghton argued in the same way, saying,

> In the early days of the war much was said concerning prayer for victory or peace. Now with war's increasing tempo we seem to take victory for granted. Hitler and Hirohito are entirely wrong, of course. But that doesn't mean that of necessity we are entirely righteous. We seem to think God is taking our side in this struggle. Certainly he is against our enemies. Then He must be for us! This is our reasoning. But is it true?[51]

English echoed this, saying, "In times of war we are inclined to magnify the sins of our enemies and look with pride upon our own righteousness, so-called. ... But while we are exclaiming about the evils of enemy governments and ideologies we need to examine our own household."[52] A *Moody* author warned that whatever glory or nobility the United States might possess could well be lost through its increasingly

---

48. Ben L. Rose, "A Call to Humility," *SPJ*, June 1943, 9.

49. Houghton, "A Question Often Asked," *MM*, September 1942, 22.

50. Houghton, "God, Time, and Russia Are on Our Side ... or Are They?" *MM*, March 1943, 396.

51. Houghton, "Prayer and Victory," *MM*, June 1944, 543.

52. English, "First Cast the Beam Out of Thine Own Eye," *OH*, September 1943, 182.

immoral behavior. Beginning positively, he pointed to the great benefit of being American, saying, "Contrast the slavery in the Nazi-occupied countries of the world, if you will, with the freedom of thought and expression we enjoy." However, this tone changed swiftly into negative. "America! America! You are not the first great civilization that has stood in pomp and glory. Others lie buried in the ruins of past centuries, and one of the main causes of ruin was immorality."[53] It was a good and godly thing for the United States to take up the Allied cause, but any suggestions that God's blessings were unconditional were rebuked in no uncertain terms.

At other times the criticism addressed specific sinful actions. Some of these sins were the sort that concerned mainly the more conservative elements of society, with drunkenness and lewd behavior earning top billing. Poling warned, "The question reflects a nationwide growing situation in America. If present trends continue, whatever the results of the war, there is disaster ahead for American freedom."[54] In a similar tone Houghton informed readers, "There are increasing signs of general moral decay. Drunkenness, gambling, immorality, the vices which accompany war, were having a happy holiday even before we got into the conflict, but now they are holding carnival. Some of the cities near army and naval training centers present sins as sordid and sensual as ever graced, or disgraced, cities of ancient infamy."[55] He also mourned the fact that "the great masses never darken the door of any church and are entirely pagan in ideas and character."[56] This was not merely a

---

53. Oscar C. Hanson, "Are They Dying in Vain?" *MM*, January 1945, 273–74.
54. Poling, "Doctor Poling Answers," *CH*, October 1942, 5.
55. Houghton, "Sinning Children," *MM*, March 1944, 372.
56. Houghton, "Pagan America," *MM*, February 1945, 318. American churches themselves were not immune such criticism. Harold Lundquist challenged his presumably evangelical readers to consider what sins their own religious communities might be practicing. "Today as we survey the religious life of America and behold unmistakable evidences of spiritual decay, disloyalty and destruction, the conviction forms itself upon us that the world needs another reformation." Lundquist's list included far more than the expected doctrinal or legalistic failings but included "the grasping of certain groups by which they hope to heap up property, money and influence," and those who wanted to "exercise force and assume a dominant role in national or world politics," as well as "the class and color discrimination that often flourishes in the name of the God whose Word tells us that He 'made of one blood

failure to live up to a fussy religious code but a threat to the war effort
as well. Houghton said, "The war news is favorable, and for this we
are grateful. But the story of day by day events is not pleasant to read.
Strikes, race riots, zoot suit riots, increase of sex crimes and of juvenile
delinquency—all are symptoms of America's moral disease." He ended
with the less than optimistic line "What shall it profit America if it win
the war and lose its soul?"[57] *SPJ* printed the text of a joint resolution
by Baptist and Presbyterian pastors calling for the US government to
ban alcohol throughout the nation as a matter of national defense.[58]
Despite the failure of the prohibitionist movement, this opposition to
alcohol would be an enduring aspect of evangelical social commentary
for another two decades. The focus in such passages had more to do with
its practical side effects than anything else. While they occasionally
threw some Scripture verses into their rhetoric, by and large, evangelicals criticized the social harm done by alcohol consumption, the waste
of financial resources, the siphoning off of agricultural products, and
the way its producers had politicians in their pay.

The Fallible State

The pre-war skepticism toward governmental systems continued into
the conflict itself. Even democracy itself was not immune to evangelical criticism. It may have been the best environment for God's intentions for human society, but it had its own dangerous predilections.
Houghton was particularly concerned about this. In October of 1943,
he challenged those who put their faith in democracy, as such, noting
that democracy had very different meanings even among the Allies of

---

all the nation.' " Harold L. Lundquist, "The Sins of the Church," *MM*, March 1945,
396. Poling specified American pastors as creating many of the problems facing the
nation. He wrote, "The trouble is in the soul of America; it is a spiritual sickness
and we the soul doctors have greatly failed. We have or will have the guns and
tanks, the ships of the sea and air, armies and their equipment to meet supreme
demands, but is 'not by might nor by power,' but by the spirit—or lack of it—that
finally we shall prevail or perish." Poling, "It is Not Too Late," *CH*, October 1942, 12.

57. Houghton, "What Shall It Profit a Nation?" *MM*, August 1943, 663.

58. J. P. McCallie, "Resolution in Behalf of America and Victory," *SPJ*, September
1942, 12.

the US and USSR.[59] A few months later he argued that America's only hope was in a continued adherence to the Constitution, although even that was a feeble hope. "Only a fool would claim that our Constitution has given us a political economy without fault or flaw. Representative government will not iron out all inequalities, but it will do more to reduce the number of them to a minimum than any other system ever devised, ancient or modern."[60] Houghton warned that American democracy was no sure antidote to totalitarianism. In January of 1944 he offered a stark assessment of America's future. "Hitler is the symbol of an age. In the last analysis, the difference between the various forms of totalitarianism is only a difference of degree. In essence, Communism and Nazism are the same. And the modified State Socialism, now evident in the United States and Great Britain, is rooted in the same evil." Continuing with this dire tone, he reminded their readers, "It has been said before, that every nation gets the kind of government to which it is entitled. Rulers are but the embodiment of the ideals of the ruled. The ideals of the day around the world are all in the direction of the deification of the state. It's a repetition of the tower of Babel, only this time the tower is a political philosophy."[61] Democracy was certainly seen as better than any form of totalitarianism, but a freely chosen ungodly path was potentially just as wicked as a tyranny directed at evil.

RACIAL SINS

Somewhat unexpectedly, complaints about racial injustice were to figure largely in many, but not all, evangelical magazines during this period. Poling strongly rebuked war industries, particularly those in the South, which refused to employ African Americans or Jews. "Such a condition is intolerable in face of the fact that there is a growing scarcity of skilled workers." He went on to praise the Republican Party for working to have such work-denials declared "wrongs under the

---

59. Houghton, "Government and Peace," *MM*, October 1943, 59.

60. Houghton, "Is America Facing Sunrise or Sunset?" *MM*, April 1944, 434.

61. Houghton, "The Spirit of Hitler," *MM*, January 1944, 255. The complexity of evangelical opinions in this matter was displayed in that immediately after these words was an editorial asking readers to conserve paper as a part of the war effort.

Constitution."[62] Courier offered backhanded praise to American society when he noted that lynchings were down from past levels,[63] while
English pointed to the "growing evidence of not-so-latent anti-Semitism in the United States" in many major cities and spoke of this as
a "dread scourge."[64] Despite the reluctance of the evangelical laity to
consider the issue, and the willful ignorance of society at large, notable
popular theologians were beginning to raise awareness about America's
treatment of African Americans long before it became the expected
thing to do.

The Americans may have been the good guys in the general evangelical estimation, but, as in the pre-war years, the United States was
hardly their image of a perfect nation. Its sins were varied and deeply
held. Its governmental system was certainly better than those of its
enemies, but there was no guarantee that democracy would not vote
itself into corruption. Like the rest of the country, or any country at
war, evangelicals did get carried away and conflated the well-being of
their nation with their higher loyalty to God, and this was unfortunate.
However, this impulse was checked by the same authors with warnings that the favor shown to America was not unconditional and that
fealty to the state or nation should always be contingent on the moral
behavior of their native land.

---

62. Poling, "Doctor Poling Answers," *CH*, June 1942, 4. Courier echoed these
concerns later that same year. An African American man told how infuriating it was
that he had been good enough to be drafted at the end of the First World War and
he was constantly hearing how every able body was needed in the defense plants,
but when he showed up at a munitions plant, he was told to leave his name and
they would get back to him if an opening came up. This treatment led him to the
point of saying that he did not care if America lost the war. To this Courier replied,
"Bitter, terrible words, these, for any American. The last thing we want right now is
this sort of racial feeling—and the last thing democracies can afford is to have is a
denial of democracy right at home which would lead a man to talk like this. We in
America have little reason to condemn the British in India when there are Negroes
in America feeling like this! If this is a war for democracy, then let democracy start
at home." Courier, "Democracy," *CH*, November 1942, 7.

63. Courier, "Lynchings Still Decreasing," *CH*, September 1942, 9.

64. English, "Anti-Anti-Semitism," *OH*, March 1944, 609.

WAR

THE DOGS OF WAR

"Now the madness is complete, now Mars has the whole world in the hollow of his hand." In this way did Courier begin his commentary on this new period of American history. "The moment the first Japanese airman pressed the first bomb-trigger over Pearl Harbor, the last chance for peace in our time was gone. The United States is 'in,' fighting it out in the Pacific sector. By the time these lines are set in type, we may also be at war with the other two members of the Axis." Courier challenged his readers to prepare for a long, hard struggle. "It will not be easy. This will be no short, quick victory. A year, two years, five years—who knows? It will be long, bloody, terrible. Thus shall we win, and thus alone."[65] There was no "gung-ho" attitude among these writers about an easy war. As early as mid-1942 a pastor could write in SPJ,

> This war has been described as the worst of all history. The assertion is true. It has involved more nations than any previous war. It has brought into use more destructive instruments of death than any former war. It will probably kill more people and destroy more property before it closes than any war of the past. It will probably cause more hatred and sorrow before the last gun has fired than any war on record.[66]

Not all of the destructiveness was seen as unjustified. Gaebelein invoked the biblical imagery of the Israelite conquest of Canaan as he called for judgment upon Japan for its crimes against the Chinese people. However, this judgment was not an end in itself but, hopefully, would be

---

65. Courier, "War!" *CH*, January 1942, 7. The impact of Courier's words here was somewhat counteracted by a later piece he wrote about the draft. "It will not take a huge army in the field to win the war; most of the selectees will serve miles behind the lines. ... Ninety per cent will be in the service of supply, ten per cent will be at the front. It's that kind of a war." Courier, "Draft," *CH*, February 1942, 7. As always in "his" case, contradictory statements may be the result of two different *CH* editors taking on his persona.

66. John R. Richardson, "The Fearful Night That Has Fallen on Our World," *SPJ*, August 1942, 10.

the means of leading the Japanese to change their ways.[67] At another point he mourned that the horrors of war had been so devastating to Germany, but he laid the blame for the destruction firmly at the feet of the Axis leadership. They had begun the war, and now they would reap what they had sown.[68]

Poling had this to say. "I do not pretend to make war lovely. It can never be that! Its leper spots can never be washed out. It is the sum of man's inhumanity to man and in our time it has refinements of torture that the darkest ages never knew. God pity the church and shame those of us who speak for the church if we ever glorify war."[69] At a later point he added, "We will not bless war, but we will not withhold our blessing from our sons who fight and from our country's cause in which they with the sons of the Allied Nations now engage."[70] A piece in *SPJ* spoke of war's ambiguity, saying,

> In a sinless world there would be no war, which is a dreadful manifestation of the corruption of human nature. ... War calls forth some of the worst traits of human nature—hatred, bitterness, and revenge. ... War, on the other hand, calls forth

---

67. Gaebelein, "The New Great World Crisis XXV," *OH*, August 1943, 97. "How China has suffered under the Japanese monsters is indescribable. If there is any nation which should share the fate of the Canaanitish nations of Bible times, that is, a complete extermination, Japan seems to be that nation. And yet we must also remember that we are Christians. We agree with many that only a disastrous visitation to the Japanese Empire is going to bring them to their knees." In this instance Gaebelein's predictions were quite accurate. Japanese cities would be reduced to ashes before surrendering. For a study of the air campaign against Japan, see Max Hastings's *Retribution: The Battle for Japan, 1944-1945* (New York: Alfred A. Knopf, 2008).

68. Gaebelein, "The New Great World Crisis XXV," *OH*, August 1943, 96. "What the bombings of the Ruhr and the great industrial centers have done can hardly be imagined. The Nazis themselves acknowledge it, and loud-mouthed Goebbels charge the United States and Great Britain with the most cruel acts of inhumanity recorded in history. But he forgets that he himself, with his boasted unconquerable Luftwaffe, started this awful campaign of destruction. They can only blame themselves for it."

69. Poling, "What Jesus Christ Has to Say," *CH*, February 1942, 13.

70. Poling, "The Peace," *CH*, July 1944, 12. At the close of this article was the following: "*(This is the Resolution written by Dr. Poling and adopted by the Northern Baptist Convention at Atlantic City, May 25, 1944, —Ed.)*" Parentheses and italics in original.

some of the noblest traits of human nature—courage, loyalty, self-sacrifice, readiness to endure hardship and to die for something outside the self, bigger and greater than the self.[71]

DEATH AND DESTRUCTION

Many spoke of the demoralizing effects of war upon the human psyche as people searched the gloom, wondering if there was reason for hope. After the war was over, one commentator looked back on what had transpired, saying, "Almost six years of war have left their indelible impression on the face of the world. In Europe, some cities that once were mighty strongholds have ceased to exist. Towers and forts have crumpled into dust. Blood has watered the ground that shells have plowed. Hate and greed and lust—the tares—have been sown in that soil along with bravery and courage and right. One wonders what will be the harvest of this seedtime."[72]

Houghton acknowledged that those looking for an optimistic view of humanity would have some hard work ahead of them, given the news of the day.[73] At another time he wrote of the despair induced by the calamity of the war. "What descriptive words are needed to picture our kind of civilization—'torn,' 'broken,' 'bruised,' 'tormented,' 'battle-scarred,' 'bleeding,' and a hundred others." He bemoaned the universal cost of war on human society, saying, "War touches us all. It reaches into most of our homes to demand our sons. Fortunate are those who have only the need of surrendering their coffee and their tires and their money."[74] When the war was in its last phases, he wrote, "When this war is over, several million young men will be released, some of them with broken bodies and some with disturbed minds, but multitudes with yearning hearts."[75] Despite having confidence in the rightness of their nation's

71. Robert F. Campbell, "Christ's Words on War and Peace," *SPJ*, May 1942, 13.

72. Egerton C. Long, "Some Things War Cannot Touch," *MM*, September 1945, 11.

73. Houghton, "Good News," *MM*, April 1944, 427.

74. Houghton, "An Afflicted World," *MM*, December 1942, 192.

75. Houghton, "In a World of Tragic Need," *MM*, May 1945, 472. One evangelical group urged people to have compassion on those displaced by the Nazi war machine, saying, "Hitler destroys three million Jews. We are living in the darkest hour of the world's history. Stark savagery and horror stalk naked over the earth. Never has there been there been so many refugees, and never has the word 'Refugee' had such

cause, they were fully aware it would cost to bring the war to a just conclusion. The devastation of the war was so intense that any peace which might result could hardly deserve the name.

Facing the horrors of war often required difficult answers to difficult questions. Where was God in all the chaos of blitzkrieg and saturation bombing? Commentators answered as best they could.[76] An

---

a tragic connotation as now. It is more than mere want and deprivation. It is more than physical suffering. *It has come to be stark terror, mental anguish, frenzied despair* [sic]." Advertisement for The Friends of Israel Missionary and Relief Society, Inc., *MM*, April 1944, 461. Italics in original.

76. One area which commentators addressed quite regularly was the pastoral care for military personnel. At times it comprised a plurality if not majority of the coverage. *MM* did this through a series running July 1942 and throughout the war. This longstanding series highlighted the ways that chaplains within the armed forces were reaching out to the service members. The magazine did this through articles featuring specific people as well as through photo-essays which showed the work in action. *SPJ* highlighted the work of chaplains throughout the war years in a series of articles, but, while it was a consistent element, its title varied somewhat from issue to issue. One stand-alone article by *SPJ* detailed the exploits of an American chaplain who stayed behind when his unit was cut off by a German advance in Africa. "The German officers expressed their admiration for the Chaplain who had stayed to care for their wounded. ... At his own request Chaplain Daniel was transferred to a camp for enlisted men where he teaches the Bible five days a week, preaches Sunday morning at the camp for war prisoners and Sunday afternoon at a work camp for American prisoners." William C. Robinson, "A Good Soldier Of Jesus Christ," *SPJ*, January 1944, 6. Although not with a standing article series, *CH* also paid regular attention to the work of chaplains, including one glowing report focusing on Chaplain William Arnold who was the first chaplain to achieve the rank of Brigadier General O. K. Armstrong, "But Don't Call Him General," *CH*, April 1942, 16. Another article pointed to the work of Lutheran chaplains in the wake of Pearl Harbor. Carl Solberg, "The Lutheran Church Ministers to its Men Under Arms," *CH*, August 1942, 28. Wilbur Smith wrote a short book for chaplains to use with their military charges. He admits that there is not much to it more than an outline of sermons drawn from the Gospel of Mark, but he chose that biblical book in particular after being asked by chaplains what he would share with soldiers knowing he had perhaps only four times to speak to them before heading out to a new unit. Wilbur M. Smith, *Studies in Faith and Hope: The Gospel of Mark for Men in Service* (Moody Press: Chicago, 1944), 5. Interestingly, this book was given a positive review in *SPJ* in their August 1944 issue, 32. According to Smith the book of Mark was uniquely suited to service members because of its terse language, action-oriented narrative, and prevalence of military terminology. Smith, 9–11. Although the book is not an analysis of war, as such, Smith scattered throughout his notes quotations from military and political leaders, emphasizing the importance of the Bible to their work. Finally, two

editor at *SPJ* counseled people not to give into hysteria about their loved ones in uniform, noting that the bulk of armies lived through even the worst battles.[77] In 1942 Bell offered a pastoral application of the words of Isa 25:4. He stated that "it is impossible for God's children to find themselves in situations shut off from His love. Seven hundred years before Christ the Holy Spirit directed Isaiah to describe accurately and minutely a bombing raid. Even in the horrors of modern warfare can we find in Him peace and strength." In this case Bell is making a claim about the prophetic nature of the Bible, but this is not, strictly speaking, about eschatology, as he is not here drawing conclusions about the end of the world.[78] Another writer gave a somewhat discomfiting answer to an age-old question of how a good God could allow such evil in the world. He admitted that the divine counsel permits evil to exist and to endure, but that God himself was not responsible for it. He did not leave his readers in this uncertain place but offered a clarification. "As we look over the world we are tempted to think that there is no limitation on evil today, no restraint from God on the diabolical plans and deeds of demon-inspired men. But just here we may greatly err." He then consoled his readers with the hope that the reason dictators have to take such drastic and devastating measures is that God is working so powerfully through the church in the world to oppose them.[79]

Peace in Our Time

Evangelical authors continued to express cynicism about humanity's ability to forge a lasting peace in the world. It was not only the presence of weapons or unjust governmental systems which were primarily responsible for the destruction of the war. These things had changed over time, but the ubiquity of war remained. The constant down through the ages was the corrupted nature of humanity. One writer said, "Man is naturally self-centered. ... Even the impulses of love and

---

of several appendices detail the use of soldiers and military imagery throughout Mark and the entire Bible. Smith, 82–88.

77. William C. Robinson, "Sparrow—Soldier—Sailor," *SPJ*, June 1943, 12.

78. Bell, "Bombing Raid Described in the Book of Isaiah," *SPJ*, May 1942, 23.

79. Joseph Britan, "God in a World at War," *MM*, May 1944, 500.

patriotism are forms of selfishness, centering in objectives in which we have a personal interest. All man's natural impulses are motivated by self-interest, and until he learns the way of sacrifice, no peace that he can devise can be either just or durable."[80] E. Schuyler English doubted that the idealistic pronouncements of the Allied leaders would ensure peace after the war. "Why? Because of sin. Selfishness, greed, lust for power, and the rest of the catalogue of that which lies in men's hearts will not die with the fall of Hitler and Tojo. ... And however perfect the peace plan, it cannot work until the Prince of Peace shall come. He alone gives peace today. He alone can bring peace to this sin-cursed world."[81] As 1945 dawned Bell wrote of the same concern, saying, "Do we realize the magnitude of the task and our utter inability to cope with it, unless we are guided by supernatural wisdom and endowed with supernatural power? Do we see the blackness of the picture? ... Sin in all its worst forms remains and these people in their despair and hatred are ripe for anything."[82] The *sine qua non* of a peaceful world was a fundamental reordering of the human condition through the work of God himself. Without that, the best laid plans would go quite expectedly awry.

THE SPOILS OF VICTORY

This problem endured in the commentary as writers began to look to a future after the war. Victory would soon be in the Allies' hands, but would the peace after the war be any better than the peace which had preceded and led to the war? In an article which fairly accurately fore-shadowed the postwar alignment of superpowers, Courier considered the prospects for peace, saying, "Certainly the aggressors should be so disarmed that they can never, never do this thing again. But, *how*, is that to be done? If we arm two or three powerful nations to the teeth and set them up as the military police over the whole race, what guarantee have we that one or more of these nations will not in time become aggressors?"[83] This was merely an extension of human corruption to

---

80. Stephen E. Slocum, "A Just and Durable Peace," *MM*, November 1943, 128.
81. English, "All Present and Accounted For," *OH*, September 1943, 186.
82. Bell, "Post-war Planning," *SPJ*, January 1945, 2.
83. Courier, "Peace," *CH*, April 1943, 7.

the national level, and no country could be exempt. A contributor to *Moody* intoned, "But if there is to be a just and enduring peace there must be a righteous judgment of all nations—not just the Axis Powers. Who is to judge Russia for her former invasion of Finland? Who is to judge the United States for supplying Japan with scrap iron and other war materials with which to devastate China?"[84] Just as all the nations of the world were participants in the war, so, too, all nations had played a role in bringing it about.

The war had inadvertently produced a tremendous amount of material benefits for humanity, but these could no more guarantee a future peace than the Munich Accords had kept Germany out of Prague. This was a regular concern from its earliest days through its near-apocalyptic conclusion. Given the way human ingenuity had been employed in the previous few years, one writer was not optimistic about this technological innovation. "We are hearing much about the new gadgets that will be developed in the postwar world, the new fields that science and the ingenuity of man will exploit, and the necessity of becoming internationalists. ... But new gadgets and new discoveries of science have never yet produced a warless world nor made men more moral in their dealings with each other."[85] Instead, this advancement had dramatically increased humanity's ability to wreak destruction on itself. War had always been bad, but now the killing seemed all too easy.

E. Schuyler English addressed this, too, by focusing on the dynamic nature of modern mechanized combat. "The pace of mobilized warfare is so speedy that before it is possible to analyze the current situation it has become no longer current. Within twenty-four hours territories are gained or lost that were bathed in blood for periods of weeks or months in the last great war."[86] At another time he looked toward the future of warfare in a September 1944 article with foreshadows of

---

84. Roy L. Aldrich, "A Just and Enduring Peace," *MM*, July 1944, 603. As can be seen from this title, the issue of the postwar world became an increasingly significant question for observers. There was little doubt that the Axis tide had crested and that the inexorable drift would lead to an Allied victory. Just what would come thereafter was less certain.

85. Erling C. Olsen, "The Gospel in the Postwar World," *MM*, February 1945, 321.

86. English, "Communism vs. Christendom?" *OH*, October 1944, 269.

twenty-first century drone war. "The robot planes which the Nazis are using so effectively against England ... may be the forerunners of great robot attacks in the next war. ... Among engineers now there is talk of the development of super-robots which can be controlled and directed hundreds, perhaps thousands of miles, to a set target." He concluded with, "In the 'buzz-bomb,' vistas of destruction have been opened beyond the imagination of men. Thus does civilization advance in a Christ-rejecting world."[87] The cleverness of the human mind was clearly bent toward its own destruction so long as the human heart remained unregenerate.

Houghton noted the gap between older weapons like swords and spears with the new weaponry of tanks and guns,[88] and wondered if humanity had a death wish: "How terribly destructive modern warfare can be, can only be realized when it is seen against the background of ancient warfare. When weapons were primitive, struggle was largely hand to hand, by the throwing of missiles." He went on to say, "But not so in modern warfare. ... In fact, it seems as if modern civilization in a strange blending of good and evil is seeking its own destruction."[89] That these words were written years before Hiroshima make them all the more compelling. Once atomic warfare entered the lexicon, evangelical concerns about humanity's self-destructive streak grew even more pronounced.

Finding Peace

This aversion to the destructiveness of war did not translate into an appreciation for nonviolence as a universal principle. Bell blamed pacifists of unintentionally exacerbating the carnage of the war. "Pacifists, sincere though they were in their desire for a warless world, must face the fact that sincerity cannot deliver from the effect of misguided purpose. In trying to save life, pacifists are **partially** responsible for the

---

87. English, "Weapons for World War III?" *OH*, September 1944, 205.
88. Houghton, "The Christian War," *MM*, October 1942, 64.
89. Houghton, "God and Human Folly," *MM*, November 1942, 124. "Missiles" here does not carry the contemporary definition of missile as a rocket powered device. Here it has the meaning of any object—rock, arrow, etc.—thrown through the air.

millions dead in Poland and Central Europe and China, for the destruction of billions of dollars' worth of property and the dark future for our nation."[90] As he had before Pearl Harbor, Poling opposed pacifism while supporting the rights of those who would refuse to fight for reasons of conscience. He did insist, however, that if the pacifists stood such a principled stand, then they had best be willing to pay the price in jail time or other penalties.[91]

A *Moody* writer argued that military service was as much within an ethical vocation as was being in law enforcement.

> The whole question of the place of human government is involved in your question, and the only *consistent* theory that works out with denial of the state's power over the lives of its people and their enemies is anarchy. There can be no middle ground; either human government is not of God or else it must have the right and power to preserve itself at any cost to the property and lives of men.[92]

One writer argued this same point when he wrote, "If we resist an intruding and dangerous marauder, a **police force**, to protect the community from such is certainly right and proper. If a **police force**, then a **State Militia** to disperse marauders on a wider scale such as riots and the like. If a **State Militia**, then a **National Army** to protect from International marauders and wrongdoers." To his mind the reality of corruption in America did not undercut the legitimacy America's war. "The fact that Nations and Governments are imperfect again 'begs the question.' They are imperfect, they **always have been**, and they **always will be** as long as fallible human beings provide that Government."[93] Such statements were not unique to evangelicals as this was the basic

90. Bell, "Some Fruits of Pacifism," *SPJ*, August 1942, 3. Emphasis in original.

91. Poling, "Doctor Poling Answers," *CH*, March 1942, 4.

92. Harold L. Lundquist, "Can a Soldier be a Christian?" *MM*, May 1944, 514.

93. Tom Glasgow, "The Bible—A Christian And War," *SPJ*, October 1942, 12. Emphasis in original.

argument put forward by many during that time and by most Christian leaders going back to the early centuries of the church.[94]

Sometimes evangelical looked on pacifists as amusingly naïve. When the editors at CH were informed by a hopeful reader that *all* that needed to be done to ensure peace in their time was for the US government to call for an armistice, after which "delegates from the aggressor nations will be urged, honourably, to make a general confession of their guilt," and that this would lead to the relief of starving masses and the development of a "United States of the World," the editors at CH replied with mild sarcasm. "We admire reader Smiley's optimism and hopefulness, but wonder where we can get hold of a man who will be able to get Hitler and Company to sit down honorably and confess their guilt. If there lives such a mighty one, will he please communicate with us immediately at 419 Fourth Avenue, N.Y.C."[95] An author at SPJ added his own satiric words, saying, "Imagine in a zoo the lamb, the deer, and the goat proposing to the lion, the leopard, and the bear that, since they are all brothers, and since bars and barriers create suspicion and ill feeling, these should be all removed and a community organization of brotherhood and cooperation set up." Of this proposed world he asked, "What would become of the lamb, deer, and goat, if such a plan were carried out? They, of course, would be quickly destroyed. It could not be otherwise so long as the nature of the lion, leopard, and bear is ferocious and bloodthirsty."[96] It was not merely that they had drawn an

---

94. Many early Christian leaders were pacifists, but the ideas of Augustine of Hippo later came to dominate official church teaching on war in the West. The debate between Christians holding to the Just War Doctrine and those claiming Christian pacifism centers significantly on whether Augustine's teachings were an innovation and accommodation to paganism or were representative of the beliefs of Jesus and the New Testament writers. Such is an important discussion, but it is also one beyond the scope of this book

95. The Editors, "We Open our Mail," CH, November 1942, 78.

96. Vernon W. Patterson, "Bases of a Just and Durable Peace: As Proposed by the Federal Council of Churches," SPJ, June 1942, 8. The author does not ascribe national identities to these animals, as though some nations are naturally vicious and others kind. He concluded, saying, "Little or no space in the imposing resolutions of these great churchmen is dedicated to the essential and inescapable fact of the necessity of the regeneration of mankind through the purging blood of Jesus Christ which the Christian world knows to be a condition precedent to the international justice and world peace."

incorrect conclusion about how to handle a given problem. It was that they had had a deeply flawed understanding of human nature. Where the pacifists saw it as a cognitive problem, that negotiations and mutual understandings would lead to greater peace, these evangelical writers saw war as a heart problem, that humanity's corrupted nature led to selfishness, greed, and aggression. It was humanity's fallen, sinful souls which led to war.[97]

THE BIRTH OF THE BOMB

The advent of atomic warfare was highly disconcerting for many commentators. While they did ponder the eschatological implications of this new weapon system, they seemed far more fearful what this meant for the present than they were hopeful for the future return of Christ. A writer for *SPJ* offered these grim words. "The power that was unleashed in the atomic bomb shocked us into numbed horror. ... Physically speaking, man has unlocked a power that may well destroy this planet which he calls his home—at least, may destroy man himself." Later, the writer's words became more visceral.

> In an orgy of blood and human misery one terrible weapon of destruction after another was turned upon flesh and blood. The world's best in mind and matter was flung with abandon into the struggle. And when we had reached the point where many were imagining that nothing further in the way of bigness or

---

97. Wilbur Smith wrote an article series from March through June 1942 entitled "What Christ Actually Taught about War." This was not so much a positive statement about Christian Just War thought as much as it was a negative critique of the Christian pacifist position which he thought of as sloppy theology. His primary indictment was that while Christ only spoke about war on a very few occasions, pacifists refused to address one of the most prominent examples. Smith argued that whatever else Jesus might have been teaching, he was clearly not suggesting that there could come a time when wars would cease before his second coming. To him for pacifists to ignore this passage was inconsistent with the word of God. He further argued that many of those who had most vociferously advocated Christian pacifism had been those who did not hold the Bible as high in their lives as they truly should. Wilbur Smith, "What Christ Actually Taught about War," *MM*, March 1942, 393; April 1942, 467; May 1942, 522; June 1942, 588.

badness could surprise them the curtain was raised on the horror of Hiroshimo [sic].[98]

Just weeks after Hiroshima and Nagasaki, Wilbur Smith preached on the significance of the atomic attacks, and in October 1945, this was published as a short booklet by Moody Press. With what had to be one of the earliest uses of a mushroom cloud for the cover of a book, this treatise was stark in its language about the impact of this new weapon. Smith declared, "The world will never be the same from that hour when the first atomic bomb to be used in war was dropped on Hiroshima. We can never go back to that former age, and what the future holds, no one knows."[99] He continued in this same tone throughout, saying, "In that one day the thinking of the world underwent a greater change in the realm of material things than the Reformation and the Renaissance together were able to accomplish in a hundred years."[100] He accurately predicted that the advent of this new weaponry would come to haunt political and military considerations for decades to come. "Exactly eight weeks have gone by ... since the bomb was dropped on Hiroshima. Instead of there being signs of a lessened interest in the atomic bomb, of a lessened concern, we should say, its enormous potentialities are looming up in an ever-increasing fear."[101] The dawn of the atomic age

---

98. T. A. Painter, "Helping Forward the Affliction?" *SPJ*, October 1, 1945, 11–12.

99. Wilbur M. Smith, *The Atomic Bomb and the Word of God* (Chicago: Moody Press, 1945), 5–6.

100. Smith, 7.

101. Smith, 8. Cartoons explored this issue as well. A November 1945 editorial cartoon expressed great concern over the bomb. It portrayed a gigantic and muscular baby sitting in a highchair. With a smile on his face, this infant was playing with a hammer in one hand and the globe in the other, and his bib read, "Young Atom Bomb." To the side were pictured tiny figures holding up their hands for him to stop or simply running for the danger. Above the cartoon was written "The Problem Child" while below was inscribed, "When he grows up, what?" A. Bell, "The Problem Child," *MM*, November 1945, 148. *CH* added its own cartoon, showing members of the newly minted UN seated at a table which was itself the base of a giant scale. On one side rested the globe which was being lifted by a tiny speck labeled "Atomic Power." Below this ran the words, "First Order of Business." Crawford, Editorial Cartoon, *CH*, October 1945, 9. The cartoon has the name Crawford as a signature and the editors at *CH* have noted, "Crawford in *The Newark Evening News*."

was a "game-changer" for humanity, and the pages of evangelical magazines were littered with commentary on this very point.

Houghton, too, was deeply worried about the ramifications of this new technology. He wrote of the reaction in America to the atomic attacks, "There seems to be great rejoicing and not much realization of the solemn implications. ... Perhaps someone had to discover how to release that power, but where do we go from here? It shortened the war, and something has been gained temporarily. But what will it do to the next war?"[102] Later, Houghton wrote, "Scientists and historians unite in saying that the explosion of the first atomic bomb in New Mexico was the beginning of a new age. Alas, it may prove to be a more terrible age than the awful period through which the world has just passed."[103] E. Schuyler English's ideas were in the same ambiguous direction. He called the news an "appalling announcement," and continued, saying, "The atom can be used for men's ennoblement, or for their destruction. We doubt not how it will be used—men's hearts have not changed, sin still reins on earth, and Satan remains still the prince of the power of the air."[104] Poling agreed, saying, "War has destroyed the dictators but in

---

102. Houghton, "The Atomic Bomb," *MM*, October 1945, 57. Houghton was not entirely opposed to this development. He even felt comfortable, in the very next article, pointing out the irony that one of the key physicists who laid the groundwork for the atom bomb, Lise Meitner, would have been working for Germany, except for the fact that, being Jewish, she was exiled from the Nazi state. Houghton, "A Joke on Hitler?" *MM*, October 1945, 57. Additionally, *MM* published an article which dealt with the positive implications of atomic theory. "The breaking of the atom to obtain energy is the scientific achievement of the century. How much greater is the work of God in making it in the first place!" Irving A. Cowperthwaite, "The Marvels of God's Atoms," *MM*, December 1945, 200.

103. Houghton, "Wonderful!" *MM*, December 1945, 189. This article was in the editorial notes section which had previously been unsigned. For this issue Houghton's name appears at the top of the page.

104. English, "Extra! Extra!" *OH*, September 1945, 190. The title is due to the news of the August 6 attacks coming just as they were preparing to go to press. The following month he continued, "Such is the fear of this dreadful weapon which contains the power of the universe harnessed for the destruction of mankind. ... The invention of the atomic bomb would seem to reduce war to an absurdity, so that no nation would wage war on another. But it actually does nothing of the kind, and already, we can be sure, the nations of the world have entered a race to see who can go there 'fastest and bestest.' " English, "What About the Atom Bomb?" *OH*, October 1945, 273-74.

doing so has unleashed the ultimate forces. Will the victors control and
direct these forces? Can we survive our triumph? Will we administer
our victory or have we but created a Frankenstein that will destroy us?"[105]
The evangelical response to the atomic attacks was nearly uniform:
great relief at the end of the war, but the means by which this peace
was secured brought with it its own troubling thoughts. Pandora's box
had been opened, and no one knew how it might be closed again.[106]

THE PRICE OF PEACE

When the war came to an end in late summer, 1945, along with the rest
of the world, many of these writers breathed freely for the first time
in years. Nonetheless, there were reasons for concern as the guns fell
silent. Would a new war erupt on the ashes of the one just finished?
Would the tyranny that was defeated be replaced by a new one? Would
prosperity return with the peace?[107] However, for the most part it was

---

105. Poling, "Epic Hour," *CH*, October 1945, 12.

106. Courier offered these words on the bomb's morality: "American Churchmen
are divided in their reaction to the use of the atomic bomb. We believe the majority
of the clergy were as shocked as the majority of laymen; many a face went white
when we realized what this thing really meant. There is no security for us now,
short of a tremendous development of Christian character." After sharing some
of the condemnations from religious leaders around the world, Courier offered
his own take. "We loathe the atomic bomb. We would have loathed it even more
in Axis hands—and the Axis was uncomfortably close to the secret. But the bomb
is *here*. Let's be sensible enough to admit that. If we can outlaw it, well and good,
we should do that. It is impossible that the United States can keep the secret; soon
every nation on earth will have it. The future isn't exactly rosy." Courier, "Bomb,"
CH, October 1945, 9. Italics in original. Contrary to Courier's claim, the Axis was not
close to developing atomic weapons. Some moves were made by German scientists
early on, but they never got as close to the Anglo-American Manhattan Project. See
Jim Baggot's *The First War of Physics: The Secret History of the Atom Bomb, 1939–1949*
(New York: Pegasus Books, 2010).

107. Courier wondered about the economic impact of millions of soldiers and
workers looking for jobs when their livelihoods suddenly lacked a purpose. He
said, "The war is over. Comes the depression! The depression is with us right now.
It may not be too noticeable, but it's here. There's no sense trying to say it isn't;
what we must do is to get ourselves out of it as soon as possible." Courier, "Out,"
CH, October 1945, 7. He continued after this with a more positive tone, suggesting
that, while painful for many, the depression would last less than a year. Another
author warned Americans, saying, "No one that reads the paper can fail to see that
while World War II is officially at an end, strife, unrest, confusion, hatred, misery,

the joy which took center stage. One piece asserted, "Thanks be unto God who giveth us the victory. This is the **Lord's** doing and it is marvelous in our eyes. ... Thanks be to those who have given their lives for the safety of the Republic, for the preservation of the liberties of the world."[108] *Moody* chose to note the moment by heading their editorial page with the Bible's Psalm 46.[109] A poetess offered reflection on the homecomings taking place across the nation. While overjoyed to have their sons safe at home, parents inevitably had to note,

> There is a gleam of sternness in his eye
> That does not belong and so we pray
> That our great love may cause him to forget
> And wipe some memories of war away
> Such horrors he did meet in foreign lands.[110]

English reminded his readers that even as they rejoice they needed to think of "the homes that have been broken by the death of loved ones, and others who have been mutilated as a toll of conflict."[111] The approach of the holiday season of 1945 led Houghton to quip, "At last we are to celebrate a Thanksgiving of peace! Praise the Lord! And no ammunition to be passed!"[112]

On the whole there was nothing particularly unique about the basic coverage of the war itself. The early days of 1942 saw some impassioned calls for victory and vengeance, and the years which followed witnessed some impatience mixed in with elation at the apparent slow pace of the war. Even so, there was also a great sensitivity shown to the pains brought on by wars in general and this new technologically advanced conflict in particular. Evangelicals wrote of the broken bodies of soldiers and civilians alike and reminded their readers that even those

---

and a score of minor wars are still with us." J. Kenton Parker, "Peace, Peace, When There Is No Peace," *SPJ*, December 15, 1945, 3.

108. William C. Robinson, "V-E: A Day For Thanksgiving," *SPJ*, June 1945, 2. Emphasis in original.

109. The Editors, "Victory! Peace!" *MM*, September 1945, 3.

110. Estelle Lovelle Welch, "He's Home Tonight," *MM*, September 1945, 20.

111. English, "Finis," *OH*, October 1945, 270.

112. Houghton, "Thanksgiving," *MM*, November 1945, 117.

who come marching home again do so only by leaving something of themselves on the battlefield.

What did stand out was the way these evangelicals reacted to the advent of the atomic age. They did speak of its use in warfare as a contingently positive thing in that it ended the conflict more swiftly than it otherwise might have done. They were not privy to the counsels of the Japanese government to know whether it was the bomb or the concurrent Soviet invasion of Manchuria which drove their surrender. What these writers did see was that immediately upon the detonation of these two weapons, the war came to a speedy end. However, such positive statements were dwarfed by an overwhelming fear of this radioactive Pandora's box. Within weeks of Hiroshima and Nagasaki, these pastors and theologians recognized that the world had changed in a way that would never allow it to go back again to the way it was before. Their relief at the war's end soon changed to the realization of what they had done and what could now happen to them, too.

These evangelicals watched as individual major wars became absorbed and then dwarfed by a monstrosity of a conflict raging in nearly every corner of the globe. They watched helplessly as nation after nation was gobbled up by some of the most nefarious villains imaginable. Then they watched with pride as their own nation's armed forces smashed with blow after blow until the world would finally be free of both war and tyranny. Yet, their joy was short-lived as they realized that their victory had come at a cost. The armies of liberty had marched in step with forces indistinguishable in effect from their now-defeated Fascist enemies, and these erstwhile allies had designs on the world which made the recent sacrifices seem futile. A war begun to free central Europe from German Fascism ended with those same nations under Russian Communism. The one trump card America possessed was a weapon many evangelicals feared almost as much as they did totalitarianism, but not quite as much.

END TIMES

For many evangelicalism watchers, there is nothing quite so definitive of the movement as its unusual fascination with the end of the world. While many stereotypes of evangelicals fail to live up to reality, the eschatological focus comes the closest to being true to life. It did not fail to occur to non-evangelical thinkers that the events of 1939 to 1945 foreshadowed a possible end to human history. With the entire world intent on destroying itself and a peace secured through the literal dissolution of matter, it would not take much imagination to see the end as nigh. For evangelicals, however, it was more. A great many of the events dovetailed all too well into their previously held beliefs about the fate of humanity and thereby enhanced the priority of eschatology, even if they very often missed the true nature of the trees in their fascination for the end-times forest.

A Future Perspective

Many evangelicals tried to see their current situation in light of the bigger story of humanity's end. They did not always see their time as the very end, but it was in the back of their minds and not far from their pens. One man wrote, "Germany is shouting, 'We will conquer the world.' England shouts back, 'Not while we and the United States stand together.' Russia declares, 'They shall not pass.' Japan insists, 'We must expand.' And so the tumult expands. And all the while the gentle but authoritative voice of Christ is saying, 'Can you not discern the signs of the times?' " He urged his readers to go back to what the Bible said and to realize that they could know the truth about the era. This was, so he thought, the final act of the human race.[113]

Moody's parent organization, MBI, offered readers the chance to answer their questions about world events and the end of time. "Who will stop Hitler? What will this war bring? Will civilization burn itself out? What about future world events? Learn to read your Bible with your newspaper and get the answers. Enroll in MOUTAIN PEAKS OF PROPHECY, a home study course from Moody Bible Institute."[114] *Moody* was particularly interested in any end-times connection. In an article reprinted from the First World War, then-MBI president, James Gray, offered hope to the Allied side that they would win because of the role,

---

113. C. I. Stacy, "The Other Side," *MM*, April 1942, 466.
114. Advertisement for MBI, *CH*, October 1942, 54. This institute is the parent organization for *MM*. Emphasis in original.

or, to be precise, the lack of a role which Germany played in biblical prophecy. He told his readers that Germany could not win the war for global domination since, never having been a part of the ancient Roman Empire, it could not end up being the ruler of the world. "Now the point is that Germany, if we except the southwestern corner of her land, was not represented in Nebuchadnezzar's image; in other words, she never became a part of the Roman Empire. Hence the impossibility that she should be finally and permanently victorious over those nations which are so represented."[115] This was more than noting that a contemporary event was described in ancient prophecies; this was a call to respond to that event in light of the ancient words.

BACKTRACKING THE END

The failure of these events to fit into their prophetic plans gave evangelicals cause for verbal gymnastics at times. After Gaebelein had spilled so much ink implying that the 1939 Nazi-Soviet pact was the mark of an end-times alliance, E. Schuyler English had to walk back the remarks once the Germans and Russians were at war. Since it seemed unlikely that Hitler and Stalin would make peace any time soon, he argued that a government in exile made up of German POWs captured by the Russians just might form the Northern Confederation expected earlier by Gaebelein.[116] He made a similar point responding to a suggestion that the postwar world would see two great confederations: one encompassing Russia and China and another Western Europe and the Western Hemisphere. He did not know if this would be the long-sought end-times alliance, but he expressed caution: "We do not know the exact times and seasons, we cannot set any dates. Whether what we see or what men anticipate is that which is written in God's Word cannot be known. We simply watch these changing frontiers with immense interest in the knowledge that the signs all about us point, unless we err, to the fact that the coming of the Lord draws nigh."[117] On the whole

---

115. James M. Gray, "Why Germany Cannot Rule the World," *MM*, September 1942, 5–6.

116. English, "And in the North," *OH*, September 1943, 180–81.

117. English, "An Interesting Prophecy," *OH*, January 1944, 487–88. As many times as he may have been wrong, in this case, with the exception of having

English was more hesitant than his predecessor to make specific claims about the future. This did not prevent him from speculations, but he was careful that qualifications were in place. In July of 1945 he continued his questions about the postwar world, saying,

> Comparing the present outlook with the prophecies of Scripture, it may be that the program will be as follows: Japan to fall to China by military victory of the United Nations; China to fall to Russia by war or by treaty; the peoples of Japan and China to compose the "many peoples with them" of Ezekiel's prophecy concerning the Northeastern Confederacy. ... We say this *may* be the setup. We cannot be sure.[118]

The experience of seeing several confident predictions come undone as events unfolded led him, and others, to be more careful in their proclamations.[119]

In fact there was often a great deal of hesitation in terms of eschatology. Sometimes this was only in terms of how things were phrased, but at other times there seemed to be more genuine reluctance to connect the dots. One article in *SPJ* in 1943 described the return of Jesus

---

both Germany and Japan included in the purported Sino-Soviet alliance, the expectation of a bipolar world was quite close to the reality after 1949 with the Chinese Revolution.

118. English, "On the Other Side of the World," *OH*, July 1944, 49–50. Italics in original.

119. In a rather ironic statement, given his predilection to do this very thing in his own way, Gaebelein rebuked those who were too keen to assign eschatological roles to contemporary characters. In the wake of Mussolini's fall, he wrote, "We advise the male and female pamphleteers who announced him to be the predicted final Antichrist ... to withdraw their productions and acknowledge their mistake, which they probably will not do." He continued with a broader application to others in the church. "Yet it ought to be a lesson to others who think they should write on Prophecy, *not* to attempt to be prophets themselves, thus avoiding becoming a laughing stock and the devil's tool in darkening the bright rays of the lamp of Prophecy and thus bringing Prophecy into disrepute." Gaebelein, "The New Great World Crisis XXVI," *OH*, September 1943, 160. Italics in original. This theme was echoed by English after Hitler and Mussolini were safely dead. "At least, we shall no longer need to answer the oft-received question, 'Is Mussolini the Beast?' 'Is Hitler the Anti-Christ?' Beasts they both were, and anti-Christ, but not *the* Beast or *the* Anti-Christ, as we so often stated." English, "All They That Take the Sword ... ," *OH*, June 1945, 848. Ellipses and italics in original.

without once mentioning anything about the raging conflict.[120] Some of the reticence on the author's part may stem from the tendency in Calvinistic circles to put eschatological questions in a secondary category of importance. He notes this in a comment that any of several doctrinal positions on the issue were accepted within Presbyterianism. While *SPJ* did not often comment on eschatological concerns, when its authors did so, their beliefs were largely in line with their Baptist and Dispensational brethren. However, the fact that they did not take the opportunity with as tempting a target as the Second World War is interesting in itself.

Others were less hesitant, but even they could be cautious. Houghton did not say that any current dictator was the Antichrist in any ultimate sense. Instead, he saw any given tyrant as the inevitable result of human rebellion which would find its final expression at the end of history. "Every dictator is an expression of the spirit of Antichrist and is a foreshadowing of that dreadful personage." In a section that was as much a pastoral admonition to the general human condition as it was an exploration of eschatological significance, he wrote to the people of their day, "so an age talks much about liberty and a strong leader seizes this characteristic—the desire for unrestrained freedom—and uses it to make himself master and the people his slaves."[121] Another *Moody* author countered any enthusiastic eschatology about the global crisis. When dealing with the morality of war, he added a note about end-times: "This war is certainly a war of evil against good, of pagan philosophy against Christian, of Antichrist against Christ." Left alone this might sound like prime eschatological overreach, but he did not leave it there. "In saying this we do not imply that any present-day despot is the Antichrist, but the final conflict between Christ and Antichrist will be fought along the lines outlined in the present war."[122] Carl Henry made much the same point when, in June 1942, he said, "When the Christian speaks of the present world conflict, he recognizes it as a part of an age-long conflict with its ultimate issue, despite earthly

---

120. J. E. Flow, "The Second Coming of Christ," *SPJ*, March 1943, 17.
121. Houghton, "How Slaves Are Made," *MM*, March 1945, 373.
122. Joseph Britan, "God in a World at War," *MM*, May 1944, 500.

appearances, in the triumph of righteousness. There is no struggle between good and evil, right and wrong, that is not a part of this great drama, in every act of which one is conscious of two mighty figures— the eternal God and the evil one."[123] Hitler and his ilk were anti-Christ, and should be opposed accordingly, but they were not *the* antichrist.

THE BOMB AND THE END

Despite the easy temptation to connect the bomb to the end of the world, Wilbur Smith, who elsewhere was keen to look to the end, refrained from such a facile argument and counseled others accordingly. In his booklet, *The Atomic Bomb and the Word of God*, he wrote,

> [I have always] shunned interpretations of biblical passages which claim to find ... predictions of almost any modern mechanical inventions, such as the airplane and automobile, or to find in the New Testament prophecies concerning antichrist, predictions of Hitler or Mussolini, or some other character soon after removed from the stage of history by death (and thereby condemning such nonsensical identifications).[124]

Later in this same work, when addressing the chance that a nuclear war could end humanity, he shared some of his sadness over the tendency of some to make specific statements about the end of the world. "More than once I have heard some saint of God ... publicly declare, 'I have the assurance I will never die—that Christ will come before death shall come to me.' But these dear people are now in heaven. Signs of the times, we all can see, but to be dogmatic about the time of the Lord's return is not becoming sober students of the Word."[125] The end of the world would come, and it would come in the way prophesied by the Bible, but people, both laity and scholars, needed to exercise restraint

---

123. Carl F. H. Henry, *Theology in the Present World Crisis*, Carl F. H. Henry Papers, Box 1964, Rolfing Library Archives, Trinity Evangelical Divinity School, Deerfield, Illinois. Although this pamphlet is filed in the box containing Henry's papers from 1964, there is a handwritten note on the first page indicating that this came from Henry's address to the Northern Baptist Theological Seminary in June 1942.

124. Smith, *The Atomic Bomb and the Word of God*, 9.

125. Smith, 23.

in their predictions. God's word was true; human interpretations were all too fallible.

In an article also addressing the implications of atomic warfare, a *Moody* contributor reported that many were now asking whether the bombs were mentioned in the Bible. His reply was, "The answer is, No, not as bombs. But the atomic bomb does give an accurate scientific picture of what will happen to the heavens and the earth when God descends to judge the wicked at the great white throne." He argued that the language in the Bible suggested that the world would end with a "whirring crash," a "break up," and a "glaring heat." This, he claimed, matched well the descriptions of eyewitnesses to the events in Japan that August.[126]

Falling into Place

With events like those which occurred through 1945, it would not take hyper-sensitivity to consider the end of the world. Not only was the Second World War the most cataclysmic event in the lifetimes of these commentators, but it was arguably the largest singular action ever taken by humanity. Some authors, like Gaebelein, were more prone than others to connecting both of these issues. He even went so far as to dismiss reasonable possibilities out of his conviction that this was humanity's final act, but even he could and did analyze current events without noting their relationship to the future. If the commentary by these writers on foreign policy and on the end of the world were each represented by circles, they would indeed overlap at points and a significant portion of the eschatological articles would have shared space with the foreign policy questions. However, the same could not be said of the foreign policy circle. Some of this circle would overlap with eschatology, but the vast majority of foreign policy questions were addressed without any connection to the end of the world.

Perhaps the key aspect of the future to flow from the Second World War had nothing to do with eschatology at all. These events would shape the counsel of evangelical pundits for decades to come. The specter of

---

126. Donald J. Holbrook, "What about the Atomic Bomb?" *MM*, November 1945, 124.

militant totalitarianism spreading out across the globe was not a mirage they imagined to justify their political beliefs, but a reality they had seen in the flesh. This was something they had seen grow before their very eyes. They had seen that it had taken force, and extreme force at that, to push the political ideology back and to destroy it. To their minds persuasive words and good intentions had done nothing but create a living space for a disease which had nearly taken humanity down with it. The intensity of the conflict and the way and the weapons it had developed would leave a deep and abiding impression on these men who were professionally coming of age during the war and who would lead evangelicalism over the next period of its life.

4

Plowshares into Swords, 1946–1949

OVERVIEW

When the war finally ended in 1945, Americans longed to have their sons and daughters returned home as swiftly as possible and to have their swords turned into plows by repurposing the now-idle munitions factories.[1] For a brief period it seemed as though this wish would come true. Millions of erstwhile soldiers, sailors, and airmen were demobilized at a rate far faster than anyone had expected, but this was not to last. Even as the hot war with the Axis powers was drawing toward its end, tensions within the Allies began to grow into rifts and then rivalries. American and Russian troops, who had once danced together when their armies met up in central Germany, now formed new lines across the globe, this time with deadly intent. The cooperation of former allies came to an end as the United States embarked upon a policy of containing the Soviet Union, now its de facto enemy.

By 1947 the American people had largely abandoned their hopes to remain behind their oceans and supported their new role as guarantor of security for Western Europe and Eastern Asia. In contrast to their longstanding policy of isolation from European conflicts, they were now willing to finance a dramatic increase to their standing, peacetime military power. The year 1949 saw the loss of China, and the United States was faced with the red flag of Communism flying from the Baltic to the Pacific. With Russian garrisons across Central Europe and Communist insurgencies throughout Asia, Americans began rebuilding their wartime prowess

---

1. For an excellent study of the building up and then redirecting of the American industrial system in the 1940s, see Arthur Herman's *Freedom's Forge: How American Business Produced Victory in World War II* (New York: Random House, 2012).

just two years after the close of the Second World War.[2] Conservative Christians, too, were becoming far more proactive in relation to the wider world. Champions like Machen were gone, but, in his place, new leaders were rising, and they were now speaking to the world around them and not merely about it.

Much of the concern in postwar America had been centered on the possibility of war in Europe. Would the former allies go to war over their shared conquest of Germany? Would Communism spread to Turkey and Greece even as it was being imposed on Poland and Hungary? Some of these fears could be soothed by the knowledge that the United States still had the upper hand. Russia might have more men under arms and more tanks along the newly christened Iron Curtain, but America was still the only nation with the bomb, a monopoly it had shown a willingness to use. All that changed in August 1949 as the Soviets developed their own atomic weapons. Already confronted with the possibility of a devastating conventional war, Americans now faced the real possibility of seeing in New York and Los Angeles what had visited Hiroshima and Nagasaki.

ENEMIES

As 1949 dawned E. Schuyler English described the uncertainty of the postwar era. Old friends were now enemies, and old rivals were now staunch allies. The irony of the shifting American intentions in Europe and Asia was apparently enough to make his editorial head spin. "Yesterday the United States was helping the Russians to defeat Germany; today the United States is helping the Germans to beat Russia. Yesterday the United States was helping China to destroy Japan; today the United States has forgotten China in her effort to save Japan."[3] The

---

2. The Truman Doctrine, which committed the US to aid any nation facing a Communist threat, came into play in 1947 as did the National Security Act which reorganized the American military. In 1950 the Truman administration issued NSC 68 which gave specific direction to the military in the already ongoing Cold War. For an introduction see, Ernest R. May, ed., *American Cold War Strategy: Interpreting NSC 68* (Boston: Bedford/St. Martin's, 1993).

3. E. Schuyler English, "Where Lies the Answer?" *OH*, February 1949, 475–76.

world had turned on its head as formerly isolationist America made alliances with those it had only recently firebombed.

THE PACIFIC RIM

Even though East Asia would soon become a hot zone of the Cold War, it was not always clear how things would play out. Long before Vietnam became a touchstone of the ideological battle within the United States over the conflict with Communism, editors at *Moody* criticized both camps fighting in Southeast Asia, noting that a Christian pastor had been killed by the Communists in Indochina for protesting their pillaging and that four Christian workers were executed by French forces without even a pretense of a trial.[4] Courier pointed ahead to the dangers in Korea which would break out into open war a year and a half later. "Things go badly for the forces of democracy in Korea: Communist sabotage is getting in a deadly work; revolutions and disturbances grow like mushrooms—carefully tended by the Russians."[5] A photo caption described the willingness of Korean Christians to defend South Korea even though there was a withdrawal of American forces.[6] According to a news blurb in *Moody*, refugees fleeing south in Korea were creating a population boom in the American protectorate. "The exodus of Koreans from the northern, or Russian, zone of Korea into the southern, or American, zone has been revealed. ... In a little over seven years the population of the southern zone has grown from less than fifteen millions to more than twenty millions, a net increase of more than a third. ... Many of the refugees from the north are Christians."[7] Whatever legitimacy there may be to his point, his claims need to be qualified somewhat. He speaks of the population growth as covering the previous seven years, meaning that this data goes back to 1942 at least. Therefore, the move south cannot have been entirely due to the Russians being

---

4. The Editors, "French Indo-China," *MM*, May 1948, 660. This was a part of a section with the overall heading "News Report." No author is given with the article or section, and the table of contents lists only "Editors."
5. Gabriel Courier, "The East," *CH*, January 1949, 12.
6. The Editors, Photo Caption, *CH*, September 1949, 14.
7. The Editors, "Korea," *MM*, February 1949, 420.

in the north and the Americans being in the south, as each had been there only since the end of 1945.

A Chinese Puzzle Box

Evangelical writers were not quite sure what to make of the Chinese Civil War, at least in the years immediately after World War II. Courier initially had a fairly neutral attitude toward the Communists, with his commentary focused more on the desire to end the fighting than on having any particular side emerge victorious. In April 1946 he hoped that the peaceful times could continue, as both Chiang Kai-shek[8] and the Communists seemed willing to negotiate peace. He was also keen to point out that the Communists in China were not cut from the same cloth as their co-ideologists to the north in the Soviet Union. "This Chinese 'Communist' is misnamed. He is not at all a Communist of the Russian pattern; he is not an international propagandist for Lenin's way but a national malcontent. He wants certain changes made, and while we do not at all champion him as the hope of China, we do see some good in his suggestions, something democratic and progressive."[9] This positive portrayal was not to last, however. Three years later he wrote, "We rise to admit that we've been mistaken about the Communists. We've been saying that they were a particular brand of Red, *not* of the Russian variety. But Mao Tse-Tung is reported to have made a speech in which he said for him the world was divided into two camps, and that he is definitely in the Red camp."[10] As will be seen with the Cuban Revolution in a subsequent chapter, evangelicals could give the benefit of the doubt to nationalist reformers in their goals to rectify social injustices. However, this allowance inevitably came to an end once it became clear that any revolutionary had thrown in the formal Communist movement from Moscow.

---

8. Here and elsewhere, quotations referring to Mao will keep the older variants of "Mao Tse-Tung" instead of the contemporary "Mao Zedong." Quotations and commentary will use the older "Chiang Kai-shek" rather than the contemporary but less common "Jiang Jieshi."

9. Courier, "China," *CH*, April 1946, 8.

10. Courier, "China," *CH*, October 1949, 11.

This early ambiguity about Mao was reflected in an uncertainty for his rival, Chiang. E. Schuyler English expressed doubts whether Chiang Kai-shek could defeat his Communist foes. After the Generalissimo broke off US-sponsored peace talks, confident in his ability to subdue Mao Zedong's army, English noted that Mao was successfully "playing on peasant demands for land reform" and was putting himself in a better military position.[11] Later he predicted that Manchuria would break away from Chiang's control and become a Russian puppet-state.[12] When, a few years later, it became clear that Communism would emerge victorious across the whole of China, he predicted that this event would lead to Russian domination of the world.[13] L. Nelson Bell offered a fairly nuanced critique of American policy in China, having spent many years living there and having seen Japanese, Nationalist, and Communist forces in control. He acknowledged that the Nationalist government of Chiang Kai-shek had not been the best caretaker of the Chinese republic, but he chided those in the West who made too much of these failings. Bell's ultimate counsel was that even if Chiang were ideal, he was far better than his Communist opponent. This meant that "for the sake of Christian missions, for the sake of China and for the sake of America herself," the US should do whatever was necessary to ensure Chiang's success.[14]

Bell's role as a missionary commenting on foreign policy was not unique in evangelical publications, and this made a great deal of sense. Despite their popular culture image as out of touch, missionaries have often been far more connected to local situations than government officials. Regarding China, many missionaries encouraged support for Chiang's government by telling readers of massacres by Communist forces and their persecution of Christians in China. One missionary

---

11. English, "No Peace in China," *OH*, September 1946, 169.

12. English, "Manchuria's Future," *OH*, February 1948, 497.

13. English, "The Collapse of China," *OH*, March 1949, 544. Specifically, he said, "China's fall shifts the balance of world-power from the nations of the West to Russia and the East. Without assuming the role of a prophet, we suggest that it is hardly likely that India and Japan (if and when US control is removed) will be able to stand long against Communist infiltration and a similar collapse."

14. L. Nelson Bell, "Our China Policy," *SPJ*, December 1, 1948, 4, 21.

asked readers for prayer as the area where he planned to work was reportedly now behind Communist lines in China, noting that when they had been there in the late 1920s, the Communists had been brutal.[15] Another piece quoted a missionary in China describing the advance of Communist forces, saying, "As reports come in from these places, we are shocked at the cruel treatment Chinese co-pastors and other Christians have suffered. Many were beaten, some burned, some shot, and a few in Laiyang city were actually crucified, suffering several days before death relieved them."[16] Bell reported on missionary properties which had been destroyed by the advancing Communist forces and of Chinese Christians, who "have been taken by the Communists and are being held for 'instruction.'" He then sharply criticized a US government policy which had allowed UN supplies to go to Communist groups. "The policy of our American government in this matter seems so tragically unwise as to beggar description. ... Every American citizen should make it clear to his representatives in Washington that our egregious mistake should be rectified immediately."[17] As American evangelicals read accounts such as these, their sympathy was aroused not because of the threat to US geopolitical posturing, but because their fellow Christians, Chinese and American alike, were being oppressed by totalitarian armies with few qualms about torture and mass execution. While they often underplayed the problems of pro-American governments, the support given by American evangelicals for anti-Communist regimes was rooted in their opposition to tyranny.

Eventually, what hopes evangelicals had for China changed to despair, and this despair extended to the entire global situation. Courier wrote, "If the Yellow Sea becomes a Red Lake, our position in Japan will have become impossible. And from latest reports, the Yellow Sea promises to become exactly that. ... While we hold the line in Europe, Red armies are gobbling up the East. Diplomacy, the weapon of peace, has failed to stop the octopus. What next?"[18] Saying that the US had

---

15. W. C. McLauchlin, "Sailing Back," *SPJ*, January 15, 1946, 18.
16. The Editors, "China," *MM*, June 1948, 746.
17. Bell, "Missions And Our China Policy," *SPJ*, February 15, 1946, 2.
18. Courier, "The East," *CH*, January 1949, 12.

fumbled badly, Courier argued that there was now an existential threat to the peace of the world and the safety of the United States.[19] As Mao marched closer to victory, Courier declared, "The fates are about to write 'finis' in China. The Nationalist regime under Chiang Kai-shek is about done. His army is a rabble and in retreat. The Communists win everywhere, closing like a mailed fist around one Nationalist 'stronghold' after another."[20] A few months before the end of the war, he admitted that there was nothing left to be done. "*How* can China be saved short of an American expeditionary force? And who wants that, aside from the Chinese? The day after that American expeditionary force arrived, there would be a Russian expeditionary force on the way. Who wants that?"[21] China was near and dear to evangelical hearts, but, for many, it was not worth starting a Third World War just four years after the Second had concluded.

YUGOSLAVIA

Evangelicals may have been solidly opposed to Communism, but they did not treat all Communists as a monolithic entity. Just as some did with Mao early on, many were willing and even hopeful that the Red Menace was not as monochrome as it might seem. The Communist Yugoslav leader, Marshal Tito, provided the occasion for hope here. Courier noted the tension between Tito and the dictates of the Soviet Union, wondered if the traditional Balkan, anti-foreign sentiment might undermine the entire Eastern Bloc. He even suggested that if the West were to "keep a cool head," Communism would implode of its own accord.[22] He may have been looking for it around forty years too soon, but this 1949 prediction showed a willingness to embrace a less confrontational method for ending Communism. In October of that same year he wondered at the Russian reticence to squash Tito for his independent streak and his calling on his fellow Balkans to seek independence from Moscow, and predicted that it would not be very long

---

19. Courier, "China," *CH*, January 1949, 12. Italics in original.
20. Courier, "Finis," *CH*, February 1949, 11.
21. Courier, "China," *CH*, March 1949, 11. Italics in original.
22. Courier, "Titoism," *CH*, June 1949, 12–13. Italics in original.

before the Balkans would explode into war with Russia facing a tough fight with its fellow Communists.[23] E. Schuyler English also expressed some interest in this potential internecine conflict, and suggested that Stalin might have few options if Tito continued to follow his own counsel. As the Germans had found out in World War II, the Balkan geography was simply too arduous and the people too obstinate to contemplate a Soviet invasion. This, he hoped, would lead to a lessening of Russian control and a general decentralization of the Communist movement.[24]

STALIN AND COMPANY

Communist leaders came in for their fair share of criticism, whether in a mocking or serious tone. *CH* pointed to the difficulty in negotiating with Russia's Josef Stalin with a cartoon in May 1946. A figure representing the world was shown looking quizzically at four Stalins. Under one face was written "Peace," another said "Bluff," a third said "Imperialism," and the final one said "Marxist Propaganda." Beneath the cartoon itself were the words, "The Big Question."[25] E. Schuyler English echoed this shifting image of Comrade Stalin in April 1946, saying, "It turns out that Marshall Stalin—the same Stalin that was pictured as first cousin to the devil when Russia and Germany had a common non-aggression pact, who was given wings and a beatific and angelic smile when he became US ally, but who is now, according to the cartoonists, assuming his earlier character."[26] It was not Stalin alone who received this attention. Soviet Foreign Minister Molotov was Courier's target in December 1946 when he wrote, "The peace conference in Paris was just about 90 percent failure. When Mr. Molotov goes to work on what's left of it, at the Big Four meeting in New York, he may whittle down the other 10

---

23. Courier, "Tito," *CH*, October 1949, 10–11.

24. English, "Stalin's Dilemma," *OH*, December 1949, 357–58. Italics in original. The staff at *MM* pointed to some concrete differences between the formal Soviet bloc and its Balkan cousins when they reported on the opening of a government-approved Protestant seminary within Yugoslavia. The Editors, "Yugoslavia to Have First Protestant Seminary," *MM*, June 1949, 699.

25. The Editors, Editorial Cartoon, *CH*, May 1946, 9. The cartoon is ascribed to Pease in The Newark Evening News.

26. English, "Strange Actions," *OH*, April 1946, 690.

percent."[27] English similarly wrote, "We are beginning to understand Russia's diplomatic peregrinations better than we did. Her obstinacy is her way of getting what she wants, and it has worked quite well for her, thank you. ... So why not try for more prizes, since the only cost is to 'walk out in a huff' or 'play very, very tough.' She can always change her mind if the going gets to be too bad."[28] Left like this, the problem could well have been nothing more than dealing with a fickle nation. However, the problem was deeper than that. It was not that the Communists could not make up their minds. It was that they had only one thing on their minds, the enhancement of their own power, and they were willing to make any temporary claim to get it and to dispense with that claim as soon as its usefulness had withered.

NEMESIS REBORN

Opposition to the Russians was not American jingoism but of global preservation. Evangelicals saw the Soviet Union as the primary obstacle to world peace. E. Schuyler English argued that other nations had demonstrated a willingness of compromise for the sake of peace, but the Soviets never found cause to yield on anything.[29] When coupled with atomic threats, the Russians, so thought English, were far more likely than the Americans to strike first. In May 1948 he averred, "Russia does not want war, but she is prepared to assimilate every minor power within the reach of her long arms, by every means available—short of war. From here on, however, the going is going to be rougher than it has been to date."[30] In another article, he compared the current geopolitical situation to the troubles of 1938.

> The only language that Russia understands is straightforward talk that can be backed up by an iron fist. We can be sure that Russia is no more anxious for war than is this country. But we can be equally sure from past experience that the Soviets are going to take everything they can get the easy way, that is, short

---

27. Courier, "Failure," CH, December 1946, 10.
28. English, "World Conflict, 1946 Variety," OH, July 1946, 23.
29. English, "And Speaking of Russia," OH, March 1946, 616–17.
30. English, "World War III?" OH, May 1948, 677–78.

of war. To appease the U. S. S. R. now can only bring disaster, another Munich.[31]

Just a few years after the world had plunged into a cataclysmic war, there was great fear that Western hesitation was setting the stage for a new and greater conflict.

This recent history was a significant reason evangelicals called on the US government to keep a hardline with the Soviets. Only a decade before they had watched as attempts at conciliation with Germany had led to a stronger Nazi position once hostilities began, and they had no intention of accepting a similar situation with the Communists. Courier explicitly compared the global situation immediately after World War II to that immediately before it. "The Munich of Chamberlain could have been avoided, had there been a firm and united front against Hitler when he threatened the Rhineland. The Munich of 1946 may still be avoided if there is a firm and united front against the new imperialism of this Soviet."[32] One great difference between the Nazis and Communists lay in the greater threat posed by Moscow than had been posed by Berlin. It was not simply that the Soviets were aggressive; English thought that their military infrastructure made them dangerous. "In Russia, the United States and other peace-loving nations have a foe more formidable, and with far greater resources than they had in Nazi Germany. In addition to her 4,000,000 men now under arms, she has a vast air-fleet, a pack of 250 radar-proof submarines, and is said to be making considerable progress toward solving the secret of atomic warfare."[33] It is not exactly clear what a "radar-proof submarine" might be, but his fears were founded on the perceived threat posed by the gargantuan Soviet military.

THE COMMUNIST FAITH

With the Soviet Union evangelicals saw more than a rival nation; they saw a government run by a rival religion. Christianity and Communism were mutually exclusive and could not exist in the same place. Speaking

---

31. English, "Building with Blocs," OH, May 1946, 756.
32. Courier, "Powers," CH, July 1946, 7.
33. English, "The Chief Menace to Peace in the World," OH, November 1948, 294.

about Communism in general, E. Schuyler English wrote, "We are unre-
servedly opposed to Communism on several counts, as every Christian
ought to be. In the first place, Communism is completely atheistic. In
the second place, Communism is totalitarian to the nth degree. In the
third place, Communism is incredibly cruel. And in the fourth place,
Communism is tirelessly aggressive for world power."[34] This antipathy between the cross and the hammer and sickle was a mutual one.
As *Moody's* editors described it in 1949, some of the reasons Eastern
Europeans were fleeing their homes. "Thus this May, exactly four years
after the end of World War II in Europe, it seems clear that Russia has
begun an all-out offensive against religious groups—Catholic and
Protestant, liberal and evangelical." The article noted that church
leaders in many European Communist nations had been arrested and
charged with various crimes such as corruption and treason, even as
the governments had been careful to avoid creating martyrs.[35]

This would be a consistent theme throughout the decades of the Cold
War; Christianity demanded opposition to Communism as a unique evil
in the world of the day. When some Christian leaders declared that it
was the duty of Christians to work for better relations between Moscow
and Washington, Bell blasted, "If Communism was solely a political
issue this editorial would not have been written. But, Communism
is a hell-inspired and directed ideology aimed at the destruction of
Christianity and the freedoms which have come from Christianity. ...
It is as impossible for Communism and free enterprise to cooperate as
it is for light and darkness." Bell rooted his intense opposition in the
tyrannical and expansionist behavior of the Soviet regime which had
"imposed despotic police states on the erstwhile free peoples of [Eastern
Europe and North Korea]." Never one to mince words, he wrote, "These

---

34. English, "The Menace of Moscow," *OH*, December 1946, 362. Again
appealing to the historical context, he added, "The totalitarianism of Fascism and
Naziism [sic], which America went to war to destroy, was no more absolute than
that of Russian Communism." Of the fate of those living under Communist rule:
"Banishment is nothing; sadistic beatings and tortures, slow starvation, and death
through malnutrition mixed with forced-labor, are the order of the day in the
U. S. S. R. Spying and false witness are practiced so universally as to make the
Gestapo seem insignificant."

35. The Editors, "Communist Move Against Church Groups," *MM*, May 1949, 618.

people are under a system as evil and as oppressive as anything Hitler ever dreamed of."[36] He later contended that America's past and potential cooperation with the Soviet state had been severely misguided. "It behooves every Christian to realize that Communism is the foe of everything we hold precious, including the right to worship God and preach His Christ. ... For expediency's sake we have made common cause with the most colossal reign of terror in the world's history."[37]

After the guns of World War II fell silent, these evangelical pundits returned to their prior open animosity toward global Communism. Despite their later reputation, these authors were not being paranoid to be concerned with the growth of their nemesis around the world. It really had grown dramatically and not merely in their imaginations. It is perhaps comparable to what people in the 2010s might have done were the whole of South America suddenly to declare its loyalty to ISIS. It matters little whether or not Communism was as bad as the theocrats of Iraq and Syria. The evangelicals of the late 1940s, along with much of the rest of America, thought that it was. They became intensely agitated when they saw what they considered to be an openly expansionist and inherently tyrannical force took control of a strategically significant part of the world. They might have been wrong about this or that fact, but they were not insane to react as they did.

AMERICA

YANKEE DOODLE

After the passions of war had faded, strong embers of patriotism remained, yet criticisms endured as well. On the positive side Courier noted the effect of Americans' affable nature on their erstwhile enemies. "Someone in Germany has said that the finest propaganda the United States ever used is the broad grin of the Yank G.I. The Yank is making friends, fast, in occupied territory. ... The attitude of democracy-bred G.I. Joe will work more wonders of understanding in [the Japanese]

---

36. Bell, "Christian Realism," *SPJ*, January 1, 1948, 4. Bell had a radical plan in this article to respond to the Soviet threat. This plan will be addressed below.

37. Bell, "While Men Slept," *SPJ*, August 16, 1948, 3.

than fifty years of propaganda leaflets."[38] Charles Woodbridge, a contributor to both *Moody* and *SPJ*, spoke of the joy to be had at the sight of the flag. "What truly American soul is there that has not thrilled at the sight of our flag floating in silent splendor in the breeze? Old Glory— every loyal citizen of our beloved nation revels in the beauty and historic grandeur of our banner spangled with stars."[39] Another author shared ten reasons to be grateful for living in the US. These focused on liberty of conscience issues such as the freedom of religion, movement, and speech as well as the right to join labor unions, political parties, and even secret fraternities without fear of government interference. His final statement was the most all-encompassing. "I am living in the best part of the best continent under the best government in the world."[40] In July 1947 a *Moody* writer said, "It is America for me! With all her faults I love my country! If there are communized Americans in our land who want Russia in America, instead of America in America, they ought to go to Russia and save themselves the trouble. Our forefathers fought to gain freedom from outside oppression. We do not want to fight to get outside oppression back."[41] There is no doubt that a positive view of the United States was common among many evangelicals in this period.

---

38. Courier, "Missionaries," *CH*, February 1946, 9.

39. Charles J. Woodbridge, "Half Mast," *SPJ*, February 15, 1946, 30. This article was not about the flag or America as such but only used this discussion as an introductory illustration for a theological point about preaching Christianity.

40. Samuel M. Lindsey, "Thank God for The United States Of America," *MM*, July 1946, 678. As this piece came immediately after and in the same format as a quotation from D. L. Moody, it is not clear whether this was a then-current article or a quotation from an exterior source.

41. Warren Filkin, "Allegiance," *MM*, July 1947, 743. This same editorial page made note of the sudden passing of longtime *MM* editor, Houghton, at the age of sixty. Harold Lundquist was equally affirmative when he said, "America rests upon four cornerstones: the English Bible, the English language, the common law, and the tradition of liberty. But liberty, language, and laws might have been drawn from the Bible alone. Had we brought nothing with us across the seas but this supreme Book, we might have still been great. Without this Book, America could not have become what she is; and when she loses its guidance and wisdom, she will be America no more." Harold L. Lundquist, "The Bible Made America," *MM*, July 1946, 689.

CALLING FOR REPENTANCE

Even so, for many evangelicals, this positive view was accompanied by very specific doubts. Many called upon Americans to come to the aid of the many starving people still suffering from the results of the war. William Houghton challenged his readers, saying, "It is time we in America stopped wasting food and took seriously our humane responsibilities toward the women and children of Great Britain, Western Europe, and the Far East."[42] With a photo of Italians at risk of starvation was written, "Hunger stalks in the bomb-gutted capitals of Europe. In Rome today, children sleep in the streets after a day spent begging for food. And unless we in America feed them out of our abundance, they will starve and die."[43] Another photo showed, on one side, the body of a man who starved to death in India and, on the other, wheat in Colorado being poured out on the ground for lack of storage.[44] An editorial cartoon challenged Americans harshly, showing three contented Americans about to say grace over an amply laden table, all the while looked upon by a wall of spectral, skeletal figures.[45]

Such moral failures reminded readers that their divine blessings were always conditional. One *Moody* author cautioned Christians that they did not have a privileged place in US society. He argued that, unless they wanted to share the fate of Germany's evangelicals during the rise of Hitler, they had best be more proactive in their relationship to the government. As "liberal and humanistic concepts become more and more important in the political thinking and activity of the American people," the comfort and even security of Christians in the United States could become increasingly at risk. The only hope, both for the nation and the Christians within it, was a revival of Christianity in the land. "There is no alternative for America in 1947 between totalitarianism and a return to the historic Christian view of government. The seriousness of the situation presents to the Church not only a great challenge, but

---

42. William H. Houghton, "Europe Starving," *MM*, July 1946, 658.

43. The Editors, Photo Caption, "War's Harvest," *CH*, May 1946, 7.

44. Courier, "To Have and to Have Not," *CH*, September 1946, 9.

45. The Editors, Editorial Cartoon, *CH*, August 1946, 39. The cartoon is ascribed to Herblock in the Washington Post and accompanied an article about providing food for those still devastated by the effects of war.

an inescapable obligation both to liberals and to fundamentalists to return to an acceptance and application of the whole counsel of God."[46] He did not see America's path as conjoined with Christianity, but he did see Christianity as America's best hope of avoiding its own tyrannical future.

This man was not alone in his Christian hope for the United States. With his title, "Christian America's Contribution to World Peace," a *Moody* author skated close to the edge of Christian nationalism. However, by "Christian America" he meant that portion of the US which was Christian rather than a conflation of the two. He spoke of the role "Christian America" had played in encouraging world peace, such as President Roosevelt's four freedoms. He argued that the US was trusted by many on account of the prevalence of Christianity in America. Yet, he did not give "Christian America" a clean slate. There were biases and bigotries to contend with in the land of the free, and he admitted that it was very hard for Americans to see people of other nations as their neighbors. He concluded that it was through evangelism that "Christian America" could best aid world peace: "If permanent peace is dependent on the establishment of unity among the nations, and if that unity has never been found on a racial, political, material or social level, is it not contingent upon us as Christian Americans to point the way to real unity through Christ?"[47] Francis Schaeffer argued that the failure of Christians to stand up for classical Christianity would imperil their traditional civil rights. He did not equate Christianity with America or even democracy, but he did suggest a connection.

> The English church has boasted that she is largely responsible for the growth of Socialism in Great Britain. All over the world the modernistic churches are pressing the socialistic economic system. Wherever these ideas have gone, human liberties have been snatched away. These things are a complete reversal from

---

46. C. Gregg Singer, "Are We Forgetting Our Government?" *MM*, July 1947, 745–47. In keeping with the fluidity of the terms at the time, Singer uses "evangelicals" and "fundamentalists" interchangeably in this article.

47. Luther J. Holcomb, "Christian America's Contribution to World Peace," *MM*, October 1946, 98–126.

those ideals for which historic Bible-believing Christianity has stood, that is, an ever-increasing liberty for the individual."[48]

While many suggested that Christianity was America's only hope, they were emphatic that it was not the other way around.

THE FAITH OF OUR FATHERS

The relationship between America and Christianity was and is a perennially debated issue, and this question arose during this time period, too. When a reader inquired whether America was "still" a Christian nation, one writer replied, "It can hardly be said of any nation that it is Christian. A distinction must be made between Christianity and Christendom. The nations of Christendom are those which have heard and lived under the influence of the gospel, but that does not necessarily make them Christian nations." He added that with the decreasing church attendance by Americans and crime and corruption on the increase, "we cannot be called a Christian nation."[49] Another author went much further than this, saying, "The present era is obviously a time of apostasy. It is a time of falling away and of indifference. It is a time when many profess and few possess, when real conversions are few and backsliders are many. Churches are half empty and people have given themselves over to the pursuit of pleasure. Unbelief is the order of the day." To be precise the author never stated that he was speaking of the United States in this article. However, neither did he ever suggest that his target lies overseas. Additionally, the illustrations accompanying the article included people in baseball and football uniforms. That he does not have America in mind here is a dubious proposition.[50] Instead of suggesting that American citizenship and political liberties were the highest goods of human life, William Culbertson said Americans had a very shallow view of the very freedom they so prized. He alluded to a speech by Wilbur Smith where he had said, "It would

---

48. Francis A. Schaeffer, Letter to George Smith, December 15, 1947, Francis A. Schaeffer Collection, Box 57, File 22, The Library, Southeastern Baptist Theological Seminary, Wake Forest, North Carolina.

49. Nathan J. Stone, "Practical and Perplexing Questions," *MM*, August 1946, 758.

50. Wesley W. Nelson, "Living in Apostate Days," *MM*, November 1949, 160.

be far better to be a slave in Russia and to know the Lord Jesus Christ, than to enjoy all the political liberties of America without Him."[51] None of these could count as a ringing endorsement of the United States as God's chosen land.[52]

Instead of being a sinless and holy land, evangelicals saw their nation on a moral precipice. Its refusal to follow the will of God as found in the Bible was more than one neutral choice among others; this was the way their homeland could and would be destroyed. One *Moody* author opined,

> We in America are imperiled by the growing forces of evil and the increasing disintegrations of the finer things of life. ... For a nation to forget God and wander into degrading sins is a thousand times worse than empty pockets and scanty food. Dens of vice, placed where strong drink is sold, obscene and suggestive shows, lurid books and magazines are far worse than bread lines.[53]

An author in *SPJ* sang a dirge over the Land of the Free, yet, he seemed to want to have it both ways. He, along with many like him, saw America as a tragedy, a once-noble nation that had been granted many blessings but which now was changing its course and leaving its liberty in its haste. "A country founded in Christian ideals, nourished on the bosom of Christianity, made great, made possible because of the Bible and its principles, now denies its paternity, divorces itself from its sure sustenance and sole guarantee."[54] Rather than being two separate issues, the questions of America's growing immorality and failing faithfulness

51. Culbertson, "Do You Want Real Freedom?" *MM*, July 1948, 793. Italics in original.

52. For some, America's cousins across the pond provided an omen of America's future. Bell wrote, "The tragedy which is England today is to be a preview of the tragedy which will be ours tomorrow unless we repent. God is a faithful God, one of infinite love and mercy, but he is also a consuming fire." Bell, "Britain's Tragedy," *SPJ*, May 1, 1947, 7. At the close of this article Dr. Bell refers to an evangelistic effort in the UK headed by Rev. Billy Graham, who had been Dr. Bell's son-in-law for the previous three years. This is two years before Graham vaulted to fame with his Los Angeles Crusade.

53. Horace F. Dean, "Revival Must Come," *MM*, March 1948, 498. Underlining in title in original.

54. Robert F. Gribble, "Column Left: March!" *SPJ*, July 15, 1948, 3–4.

were intertwined. The loss of biblical morality entailed the loss of any blessings from God the United States might contingently enjoy.

E. Schuyler English had some harsh words for his native land in his article entitled "Polygamous America." He wrote, "Man has enthroned himself in the center of the universe and has left God out of his calculations. Self-centeredness and self-will, abetted by self-expression, have united to capture that state of mind which is America's god even more than money—'happiness.' "[55] William Houghton expressed similar thoughts when he wrote, "The spirit of lawlessness is in the home. There is practically no discipline in the homes of America. Each child is a law unto himself. The modern rendering of Paul's familiar injunction might well be, 'Parents, obey your children ... for this is right' "[56] A cartoonist cast a shadow of doubt on America's future, asking, "How long can we stay on top?" and portraying a map of the United States standing above the globe. The supporting struts of "Sobriety," "Virtue," and "Christian Homes" were being knocked aside, leaving only the visibly shaky and thin buttresses of "Drunkenness," "Crime," "Loose Morals," "Greed," and "Divorce."[57]

PREMONITIONS ON RACE

Sexual immorality and crime were well-known topics for Christian jeremiads over the years. What was becoming a new focus, inside and outside of evangelicalism, was the issue of racial justice. This was most prominent during this era in the pages of *CH*, but it appeared in increasing frequency in other venues as well. Courier's view of America was attenuated by his view of race relations. After challenging white denominations with the question, "Is it Christian teaching to outlaw the Negro from pews where the white men sit?" he declared, "Being a Northerner, we shall certainly be reminded by our white brothers in the South that 'You Northerners don't understand the race question down here.' Maybe not. But this question of race and segregation

---

55. English, "Polygamous America," *OH*, November 1947, 281.
56. Houghton, "Revolution Everywhere," *MM*, May 1946, 545. Ellipsis in original.
57. Wendell Arnett, Editorial Cartoon, *CH*, April 1949, 12.

isn't confined to the South, we have it all over the country!"[58] In a later issue he reported the renaissance of the KKK within America. When a Southern pastor claimed that the Klan's presence had a "sobering influence" in the positive sense, Courier's sarcastic response was, "The Klan has a 'sobering influence'? Since when did men ashamed to have their faces seen accomplish anything but intolerance, bigotry and social cowardice?"[59] When he heard that the Klan's activities had diminished to the point that African Americans were laughing at its antics, he toasted, "Here's health to Alabama—and power to those riding down those yellow-backed night riders who dare not show their faces in decent company."[60] An editorial cartoon entitled "Lincoln's Legacy" in CH called for greater racial harmony, having the Civil War President tell a chastened looking Uncle Sam, "Without regard to race, creed, color, or national origin."[61] Another pushed against ethnic elitism with a quartet of prides. Four pictures with accompanying text rebuked "Pride of Race," "Pride of Face," and "Pride of Place"; "But the worst is 'Pride of Grace,' referring to spiritual elitism."[62] Moody's editors were not as apt to be overt in their complaints about racial issues. They did, however, offer an implicit criticism of American race relations in an article mentioning that an African American New Yorker had traveled to Nigeria to become a Muslim. They suggested that she might come back to the US as a Muslim missionary, saying, "Such a possibility, however, is far from remote. Many Negroes are attracted by the lack of race prejudice they believe they will find in Mohammedanism."[63]

---

58. Courier, "Separation," CH, January 1946, 10.

59. Courier, "Klan," CH, February 1949, 14.

60. Courier, "Klan," CH, September 1949, 11.

61. The Editors, "Lincoln's Legacy," CH, February 1949, 12. The cartoon is ascribed to the Institute for American Democracy.

62. The Editors, Editorial Cartoon, MM, July 1949, 796. The cartoonist's signature is illegible, but above the cartoon is printed, "Copyright by the Sunday School Times; used by permission."

63. The Editors, "Nigeria," MM, May 1948, 662. Evangelical voices were not uniformly raised in protest against racial injustice. SPJ published articles condemning attempts at desegregation. For example, see J. David Simpson, "Non-Segregation Means Eventual Inter-Marriage," SPJ, March 15, 1948, 6–7. Sadly, this is only one of several similar articles published by SPJ which argued for continued segregation and against racial intermarriage.

RED SCARE

The late 1940s was a time of great fear in American society concerning the possibility of Communist infiltration. Evangelicals were just as interested in the issue as others in their day, and their staunch moral and philosophical disdain for Communism made them ready to accuse those guilty of cooperation with the "red menace."[64] While they had no qualms about seeing their religious and civic duties dovetailing together, they did not equate the two. For example, in a paragraph putting the interests of the United States and its Christian citizens on a parallel path against Communism, E. Schuyler English argued that the United States could successfully rid itself of Marxist influence but still be morally corrupt itself. "We do not expect, if and when the Reds are thoroughly purged, that America will turn back to God. It has gone too far away from Him morally and socially for us to look for any such change of heart."[65] This distance between Christians' dual loyalties meant that evangelicals saw a basis to protest when nationalistic zeal got the

---

64. Several articles in multiple sources spoke of the danger posed by Communism in America. Bell worried that Americans' easygoing nature could blind them to the danger posed by Communist plots. "Americans are a tolerant, and a gullible people. It is perfectly possible, in the name of freedom, to permit forces to form and thrive which will in turn destroy that freedom. ... [W]e do earnestly believe that Christians in America should acquaint themselves with the infiltration which has already taken place in our vital economic, social and political life and take necessary steps to eliminate this Communistic fifth-column from our national life." Bell, "Tolerance and Communism," October 15, 1946, 3. He again spoke of Communist influence in America when he wrote of those members of the US government too friendly to Soviet ideals. "The degree of infiltration of those with Communistic leanings into our government in Washington during the years of the New Deal is just becoming known. Few of these men were actually members of the Communist party but they greatly aided spread [sic] doctrines and concepts of government foreign to our own." Bell, "Eternal Vigilance," *SPJ*, July 1, 1947, 3. Bell was one of the strongest anti-Communist voices in these magazines, but he was not the only one. Reacting to the exposure of Soviet espionage networks within the United States in the late 1940s, Courier wrote, "What we should be concerned with is the ease with which men in the top jobs of the American government were able to get this information out to Russia—if they got it out. There's something rotten in American Intelligence. It may be as many an expert has claimed, the poorest spy system in the civilized world. That, and not the fate of Mr. Hiss or Mr. Chambers, is about all that matters, for in it the fate of us all is involved." Courier, "Spies," *CH*, February 1949, 11.

65. English, "Blindfold Removed," *OH*, May 1947, 682.

better of investigators. When the House Committee on Un-American Activities accused some church groups of being either "tools" or "targets" of Communist agents, Courier was displeased. According to the article one of the organizations named as a Communist front had not even been in existence for nine years, leading Courier to quip, "The House Committee has blundered; if this be intelligent investigation of the Communist menace, down with it! We clearly understand that eternal vigilance is the price of freedom, but shouldn't the 'Vigilantes' be at least within nine years of the times?" His conclusion was, "If these politicians spent as much time making politics respectable as they do flinging (political) mud at the just and unjust alike, they'd be worth their pay. Ultimately, we'll whip the Communists not by one investigation after another, but by making Democracy so clean and wholesome that nobody will want to be a Communist."[66] Later he wondered if things were getting out of hand. "Once it seemed just a matter of a few crackpot Communists testifying ... and refusing to say whether or not they were Commies. Now it is including almost everybody in the country except possibly Charlie McCarthy and the Daughters of the American Revolution."[67] Communism was a dangerous threat to American society and to Christianity, and evangelicals found their loyalty to each to be very important, but they did not find them to be equally important.

---

66. Courier, "Un-American," *CH*, February 1949, 14. Parentheses in original.

67. Courier, "Loyalty," *CH*, August 1949, 12. Courier was specifically addressing the issue of so-called loyalty oaths being demanded of many Americans. He argued that although it was legitimate for the government to ferret out traitors and saboteurs, it was "stretching things a bit far to require everybody from Danbury to Santa Barbara to say like a well-trained parrot, 'Oh, yes, I'm loyal!' " His ultimate conclusion was to lean in favor of such oaths. "Sometimes the innocent have to suffer in order that the guilty may be punished; perhaps all of us should be ready to take an oath we just don't like in order to run down those who, in disloyalty, refuse to take it." In contrast to his view of this and of professional politicians, Courier thought quite highly of FBI chief J. Edgar Hoover. After summarizing the twenty-five years of his career to date, Courier praised Hoover for his pursuit of Communists. "He probably thinks less of the Reds than any other fifty men in the country—and so far as we're concerned, we hope he stays right where he is for another twenty-five years. He's in a good spot! We salute Mr. Hoover: cop extraordinary, and Christian gentleman." Courier, "FBI," *CH*, July 1949, 12. Hoover was later to appear several times as a contributor in the as-yet-to-be-created *Christianity Today*.

This typifies in many ways the evangelical attitude toward their nation. America was a good thing, and, by and large, was a net positive in its effect upon the world. Believing it to be rooted in some ways in the teachings of the Bible, they found that God had blessed America through its adherence to the Bible's principles. Sometimes they hinted that the United States had received particular blessing because of generally righteous behavior, but this was always seen as a contingent and, most of all, a fading factor in American life. As it moved further and further from biblical morality and the teachings of Christianity, the United States was becoming an increasingly immoral place and a place which could not count on divine support, general or particular.

WAR

DESPAIRING DAYS

"Whatever hope we ever had of a quick peace in China and the Far East is blasted now; there is a real civil war in Cathay. Nationalist troops have been hurried to the scene of battle with American aid; they carry American weapons and ammunition. Chinese Communists, thirsty for Manchurian spoils, object. American Marines have been wounded, probably killed. Peace, it's wonderful!"

In this way Courier lamented how quickly the hopes of peace faded as new wars broke out in the aftermath of the Second World War.[68] This was not an uncommon sentiment. How could the whole of the human race have gone through what it did, its single largest collective effort, and come out essentially the same as it had been going in? It was not only the formal articles which shared this perspective, but editorial cartoons pushed the same ideas, too. In July 1947 a cartoonist showed Uncle Sam manning his post by the shoreline, gun in hand, with darkness coming from over the sea in "War Clouds." Over this illustration ran the words, "Trust God ... and keep your powder dry."[69] As the following year arose, he looked to the uncertain future of the age with an illustration entitled, "1948—What?" Accompanying this was a

---

68. Courier, "Civil War," CH, January 1946, 8.
69. A. Bell, Editorial Cartoon, MM, July 1947, 766. Ellipses in original.

two-faced globe, with one side holding a dove of peace in the sunshine and another in military garb under dark clouds.[70]

E. Schuyler English mourned the lack of constructive change in the world. Rather than improvement he saw "more unrest, more confusion, more strikes, more crime, more intrigue, more immorality, more deceit, more fear, and more proposals as to the way to peace."[71] Or, as he put it in another article, "Contrary to that hope and expectation, world conditions are far from encouraging—the war seems to have settled very little, if anything; Europe remains in a mess, Asia remains in a mess, the Near East remains in a mess, and Russia is a continual irritation."[72] Or, again, "It was part and parcel of the nihilistic philosophy of Hitler and his followers that if Germany could not win the war and dominate Europe, in her defeat she should drag the world to destruction with her. Germany lost the war all right, but we cannot yet know whether anyone else won it."[73] If they could hardly call the victory peace, could they ever hope to avoid a similar war in the future?

PEACE THROUGH STRENGTH

Over the next few decades, this abiding fear of a future, greater war fought for preeminence with the fear that the very plans for peace were only setting the stage for the war they sought to forestall. When many mainline denominational leaders urged a conciliatory approach to global relations, many evangelicals looked to the failure of such an attitude in the lead-up to the war. Pacifism was, for many evangelicals, the best way to achieve its own failure. In 1948 Bell stated, "A pacifist and a peace-maker are not the same. In fact they are very different and

---

70. A. Bell, Editorial Cartoon, *MM*, January 1948, 382.
71. English, "Only More of the Same Things," *OH*, January 1946, 463.
72. English, "World Conflict, 1946 Variety," *OH*, July 1946, 22.
73. English, "Did Anyone Win the War?" *OH*, September 1946, 167. His dismal outlook only increased over the next few years. Towards the end of 1948 he wrote, "Even the most optimistic of men can hardly expect the present period of peace—such as it is!—to be lasting, when so much of the world's energy, ingenuity, and wealth are going into preparation for another war. Jerusalem is explosive, indeed. But so is the whole world!—or it is being filled with explosives." English, " 'The Peace' that Was Won by World War II," *OH*, November 1948, 292–93.

the effects of their work often are diametrically opposed."[74] While never questioning their good intentions, he rebuked those who suggested absolute nonviolence as a means to avoid a new conflict.

> Now we find certain church groups who again are sponsoring a pacifist movement which fits perfectly into the scheme of those who would destroy America as a land of freedom. We do not question the sincerity of Drs. Fosdick, Buttrick and those associated with them in the movement, but, we do question their wisdom and judgment and we insist that those who are misled and follow their plan will live to regret their follow.[75]

He then attacked a new proposal by the Federal Council of Churches, "that the United States renounce distant military bases; won at such a cost in blood and money, which might be distasteful to Soviet Russia." Bell declared that this was not the way to secure peace in their time. He compared their idea to the similar suggestions put forward in the wake of World War I which led to the devastation of the Second World War through unpreparedness.[76]

William Culbertson distinguished between being for peace and being realistic about how to secure it. He suggested that it had become trendy to say that the best way to avoid a war with Russia was to avoid confrontational language, and then he went on to say, "Now, any intelligent person will agree that another war will exceed in horror anything the human race has ever experienced. But this talk about Russia not wanting war, and the implication that war will not come unless we provoke, is ridiculous. Of course Russia doesn't want war. But Russia wants the world." Looking back a decade, he argued that there had been those who had said that the Germans did not want war a decade earlier. "We face the same situation today, and 'peace at any cost' only permits the aggressor nation to go right on with its plans while we throw up our hands in shocked dismay." After asserting that there are many issues revolving around lethal conflict where Christians may disagree, there

74. Bell, "Pacifists Versus Peace Makers," *SPJ*, February 16, 1948, 3.
75. Bell, "Pacifism Is Not Dead," November 1, 1946, 5.
76. Bell, "The Federal Council and National Policy," *SPJ*, November 15, 1946, 3.

was one principle which he thought towered about the rest: *"The most important factor is not to maintain peace, but to preserve justice. ...* It is still righteousness that exalts a nation, and as Christians it is up to us to demonstrate a moral leadership that may influence the actions of our nation in world affairs toward the promotion of justice, and thereby toward peace."[77] A peace which included collaboration or capitulation to tyranny was not worthy of the name.

Evangelicals might have generally been in favor of a more confrontational stance than their mainline fellow Christians, but they could also call on politicians to lower the temperature of the global debate. For example, Courier challenged the wisdom of Churchill's famous "Iron Curtain" speech.[78] He felt that the former and future Prime Minister was needlessly antagonistic to the Soviets. "Mr. Churchill's appeal is an appeal for the old disastrous balance-of-power political philosophy which has put us where we are today. To go back to that is to go back indeed—back to more disaster. It's high time we tried the collective way, and Mr. Churchill isn't helping us in that direction, a bit."[79] Similarly, E. Schuyler English was pleased that, so far, it was only a matter of speeches and accusations, but he was concerned about the direction such verbiage might take the world. "There is no heat of flying missiles, but words and pens are white-hot in the war of words that is now being pursued by the Russians, at home and in satellite countries, and by proponents of the Marshall Plan and opponents of Communism in

---

77. Culbertson, "More Important Than Peace," *MM*, June 1948, 713–14. Italics in original.

78. He nowhere makes mention of the famous phrase, "The Iron Curtain," but, writing in May 1946, he is commenting on a recent speech given by Winston Churchill in Missouri, making his target quite clear.

79. Courier, "Churchill," *CH*, May 1946, 7. Elsewhere, he was concerned that the bellicose rhetoric coming from the various national governments were preventing ordinary people from forming an accurate understanding of the geopolitical situation. "We need truthful information on a global scale. What we need is facts about *all* of us, not one-sided propaganda to boost the stock of a few of us. It may be that the Russians have *some* truth on their side: if they have, we never hear of it." He concluded with a jest. "It's been suggested before, and it may be good to suggest it again: if war comes, why not let the leaders fight it, with the common man sitting peacefully in the grandstand?" Courier, "Information," *CH*, May 1946, 9. Italics in original.

the United States and Britain." Speaking of the deadly gravity of conflict, he wrote, "More and more leaders of the United States are becoming conscious that it is absolutely impossible for the two countries to come to an understanding. It is, however, a war of words only. Neither country is ready for war, nor are any of the associated nations. Through words, alignments of powers are being drawn."[80] His hopes for salvation through the efforts of the diplomat class were not the highest. In October 1948 he wrote, "In such an inept way world-leadership bungles on and gets nowhere in particular, while discord, starvation, and threat of war hover over a mass of humanity."[81] There was precious little trust in the governments of the world to solve the world's problems. Being human themselves, politicians could never disentangle themselves from the very causes of war, and even with their sincere quest to do the right thing, the wrong word could touch off yet another planet-wide war.

WORKING FOR PEACE

Evangelical comments were not always as dire as this. There were wise politicians in the world, and some of their policies were headed in the right direction. However, even as they offered praise for given organizations and plans, evangelicals very often did so with a word of caution. English, for instance, was encouraged by the shift in US policy evidenced by the Truman Doctrine of Containment and the Marshall Plan for Europe's economic recovery. He was specifically in favor of Truman's new policy, writing, in July 1947, "The doctrine is, however, of great significance, inasmuch as it states the principle of American foreign policy—resistance to Communistic ideology."[82] And, of the Marshall Plan he added, "Whether designedly or not, the Marshall Plan seems to have been a stroke of political genius, for it forced the Soviets to show their true colors, their genuine aims. ... Russia has openly, if unwillingly, put herself on record as being opposed to Europe's attempts to work out her own salvation."[83] Even so, like many of his fellow evangelicals,

---

80. English, "Cold War," *OH*, January 1948, 404.
81. English, "The Moscow Menace," *OH*, October 1948, 227.
82. English, "The Truman Doctrine," *OH*, July 1947, 34.
83. English, "The Molotov Plan," *OH*, September 1947, 147.

his praise of political solutions applied only to limited goals. The larger and longer-lasting the organization, the less likely it was to receive evangelical backing.

Thus, while he was not a fan of the nascent United Nations, English was open to alliances on a smaller scale. When Western governments began to make moves toward NATO, he offered limited support. "Thus the policy laid down by George Washington 173 years ago, in his Farewell Address, when he warned against entangling alliances with European nations, has been abandoned. But there were no airplanes and guided missiles in Washington's day."[84] The ideas of even as greatly respected a figure as Washington could be trusted only so far. Bell was hopeful about NATO as a bulwark against Russia, but also this was only somewhat so. On the one hand he was in favor of the Atlantic treaty, stating, "Russia's heartless, calculated, tyrranical [sic] and lawless overrunning of her neighbor states is an open book. America has entered into a defensive alliance with nations seeking protection from further expansion on the part of Russia." Yet, this support was limited. "We are not optimistic over any alliance or grouping of nations which ignores God as the rightful object of individual and national worship."[85] Political solutions were always and inevitably contingent goods, and, owing to their human origin and leadership, could just as easily turn into instruments of evil.

Life with the Bomb

Human nature was the same as it ever was, but one new factor had entered the equation of war. Humanity now had a means to destroy itself. If anything the end of World War II increased the significance of the bomb to the point that many evangelicals spoke in despairing

---

84. English, "The Atlantic Pact," *OH*, May 1949, 623.

85. Bell, "Our 'Spokesman' Again," *SPJ*, May 16, 1949, 3. Even though he was very prone to make specific suggestions when it came to political affairs, he was displeased when a conference from the F.C.C. argued against the Atlantic Pact. They had said America should see Soviet hostility as they would feel were the Russians to establish a similar alliance with Latin America. Bell shot back, "For the Federal Council to place America and Russia on a comparable basis in international manouvering [sic] is an affront to the facts. ... [W]e do resent the intrusion into the realm of international politics of the Federal Council."

tones. One writer suggested that the advent of the atomic age was the beginning of new way of life for humanity, a new way of life for which collective death was the most likely outcome.

> A few months ago the world was confidently drawing up plans for a "just and durable peace" to follow the war, when its blueprint for the world of tomorrow was suddenly destroyed by the bomb that fell on Hiroshima. Since that eventful day, no more has been heard of the four freedoms, certainly not the freedom from fear, for the world is obsessed with the problem of how to escape total annihilation.[86]

This was not the only moment of despair. Fielding a question about the length of the days in Genesis 1, one author answered the question but then added the seemingly unrelated comment, "But why worry about it, now? We're all sitting on top of an atomic bomb that Genesis doesn't even mention. Adam can't help us now!"[87] This dark tone was echoed in an article where the author wrote,

> The prophets of despair are in the saddle, riding hard, they lay their whips of fear across the backs of all mankind. We sit atop the atom bomb, wondering how long it will be before the fearful thing goes off and blows us all to kingdom come. Having fought a war to rid mankind of fear, lust, piracy and Adolf Hitler, we find our hearts and mind again in shackles. Aye, we have won the war, and yet we hear the prophets say, "We haven't learned a thing!"[88]

For a group that had long been predicting a fiery end to the human race, evangelicals were quite discombobulated when faced with a mechanism capable of doing just that. Like many others in the world, it took them quite a while to figure out how to respond.

Some turned the crisis into an opportunity for reflection, with several suggesting that the time had come for international cooperation. A

---

86. Stephen E. Slocum, "While We Watch for the Sunrise," *MM*, February 1947, 338.

87. Frank Mead, "Adam Can't Help Us Now," *CH*, May 1946, 41.

88. Spencer Duryee, "Candles or Thunderbolts: An Interview with Congressman Charles A. Eaton," *CH*, March 1946, 13.

scientist writing in *Moody* likewise warned that humanity had turned a corner, saying, "It appears now that man has a possible means for his own extermination. Many doubt that that will ever come to pass, yet there can be no reasonable doubt that destruction would practically force all nations back again to a primitive stage in their histories." He continued, noting that this new age forced certain positions upon Christians. Since Scripture demanded that Christians love their neighbors, they had now to consider the implications of this love, even if it meant global efforts to secure peace.[89]

Looking to this dismal future, Courier similarly wondered if the new weapons of war required new measures, even if, in keeping with his pseudonymous nature, he could not quite make up his mind. In March 1946 he wrote, "There is no good reason why if the U. N. O. fails that atomic bombs may not reach us via Japanese balloon and German rocket. If they do, then we all perish!"[90] Later, he suggested a unilateral approach. Fearing that it was only a matter of time before the Russians or others got the bomb themselves, thereby opening America to this devastating danger, he suggested that "we," presumably the United States, "should have arsenals filled with the A-bomb so strategically located, all over the world, that no nation would dare to start anything."[91] In August of 1946 he said, "There can be no reservations in the interest of any purely national sovereignty. *Nothing less than a global patriotism can save us now.*"[92] The following month when he challenged

89. Robert B. Fischer, "The Message of the Atomic Bomb to the Church," *MM*, March 1946, 428.

90. Courier, "Balloons," *CH*, March 1946, 8. He is not here, necessarily, fearing an atomic attack by Japan or Germany. This quote comes from an article discussing the use of balloons by Japan during the recent war, and, at this time, only the Germans had made significant use of ballistic missiles. A few months later, he wrote despairingly of new delivery systems for atomic weaponry, which, in retrospect, seem quite quaint. "We learn that experiments are now in progress which if successful will hurl the atom bomb by rockets flying 175 miles high. These rockets could reach almost from anywhere to anywhere in our world. Second, naval men are talking of super-submarines atom-powered, which could discharge missiles from under the water and guide them to targets by remote control. And there are still some folks who think the US can control the A-bomb!" Courier, "Future," *CH*, June 1946, 9.

91. Courier, "U. N. O.," *CH*, March 1946, 8.

92. Courier, "Atom," *CH*, August, 1946, 8.

an early call for nuclear deterrence to make war impractical, Courier expressed his doubts. Instead of deterrence he proposed collective security.

> So long as we have war, any weapons available will be used; it is just too much to expect that all men are decent enough to reject a weapon, however horrible, if that weapon will win. But when the strength of nations are pooled against the aggressor, that aggressor will think twice before raising the mailed fist. It is the only way.[93]

That government-averse evangelicals could consider such international cooperation indicates how seriously the bomb had affected people's view of the world.

Others, too, were open to an international effort to reel in the threat of atomic warfare, but evangelicalism's distrust of the state remained intact. In February 1946 English made note of the tentative moves by the three major powers of America, Britain, and Russia, toward UN control of atomic knowledge, but he did nothing more than to report that agreements were in the works and offered no evaluation of these plans.[94] A few months later he gave a qualified appraisal of these moves in response to a publication by nuclear scientists. After recounting some of their horror stories of what a fully atomic war would mean to the world, he described their proposed solution of a single world government which could guarantee a world without such a fate. English was not critical of their fears, saying that they "are not hysterical, they are laconic, and they are frightening." Neither did he rebuke their desire for a world government. He affirmed their desire but challenged their expectations, suggesting that the scientists were calling on the UN or similar organization to prevent the danger, but they were forgetting a key ingredient to world peace. No human inspired effort could save the human race. Only by including the aid of God himself could

93. Courier, "Bomb," CH, September 1946, 10.
94. English, "Better Understanding at Moscow Conference," OH, February 1946, 560.

the world hope to survive.[95] It was for this reason that, in the end, he decided that deterrence would not preserve the peace, declaring that it was inevitable that the bomb would be used once war finally came. After the Soviets had secured their own atomic weaponry, he wrote, "The basic antagonisms between the USSR and the US are so great that no settlement is at all likely to be made. Therefore, there must be war in due course, and in that coming war the atom bomb will be used. No new instrument of war, no matter how frightful it may have been, has ever deterred men from killing each other."[96] Humanity was without hope without God. The advent of the atomic age had made human self-destruction more practical, but humanity's fundamental nature remained as corrupted as ever.

L. Nelson Bell entertained hope that the bomb could lead to a more peaceful world, but his ideas had less to do with disarmament than destruction. In response to the growing power and reach of Russian Communism, and its oppressive treatment of its own and conquered peoples, he suggested that America should deliver an ultimatum to its Cold War antagonist. The Soviet Union would have to begin withdrawing from "all territories into which she has expanded since 1942." Within one week of this demand, the US would drop a bomb onto uninhabited areas of European Russia and Siberia as a demonstration of American resolve. If the Russians were not headed home after this point, "at the end of five more days the next bomb will be dropped on the Kremlin with immediate and continued use of the bomb until the present Communist regime is replaced by men who are willing to comply with our demands." In defending this proposal, he said, "Either we now use the power we have to bring freedom to others and insure our own peace, or we will someday fight a desperate war for self-preservation itself."[97] This was a horrific option which would have been possible

95. English, "There Is No Defense," *OH*, June 1946, 803.

96. English, "September 23, 1949," *OH*, November 1949, 281–82. The date in the title refers to when President Truman announced that the Russians had acquired the bomb.

97. Bell, "Christian Realism," *SPJ*, January 1, 1948, 4. As a preface to this article, *SPJ* had written that the article had been written months before but had been held back because "we sincerely hoped that our position was wrong. However,

only for the short period between the end of World War II in 1945 and the Soviet development of the bomb, four years later.[98]

Having faced global war twice in their lifetimes certainly made these commentators prone to see the possibility of a third a realistic possibility. Now that the world was divided into planet-embracing alliances and the Americans and the Russians each possessed atomic weaponry, the dangers involved in war were greater than ever. For a few years in the late 1940s the United States, had it so desired, could have dealt out a hell on earth for any who opposed its will. However, once this genie was out of its bottle, there was precious little anyone could do to keep its secrets from spilling around the world. Not every nation could manage to secure the information or logistical requirements to create their own bombs. However, by 1949 the two strongest countries in the world could and did produce both the necessary weapons and delivery systems to enable them to share the experience of Hiroshima

---

subsequent events have convinced us that this is the only solution to an increasingly intolerable and dangerous situation in the world." Bell was not always so bellicose about the bomb. Two years earlier, less than a year after Hiroshima, he wrote, "The discovery of means to unlock atomic energy has brought about a situation never faced before—For the first time man realizes that not only is it possible for civilization to commit suicide, it is even possible to destroy the entire world, as we know it. Mortal fear has gripped man and certainly thinking statesmen and scientists realize that the potentialities for evil stagger the imagination." Bell, "Riding A Tiger," *SPJ*, August 1, 1946, 2.

98. Bell's proposed preemptive strikes on Russia did not underrate the power of the bomb as he thought the horror of the threat would compel the otherwise notoriously recalcitrant Kremlin to the negotiating table. This is not to suggest that this statement was wise. He was callously proposing that the goal of seeing that "the present Communist regime is replaced by men who are willing to comply with our demands" was worth the deaths of tens of millions of innocent Russians, Russians who had just lost twenty million souls in a war he supported. One thing to keep in mind, however, is that he proposed this in 1948, the year before the Soviets developed their own atomic weapons. He was not chancing the fate of the world on a roll of the nuclear dice. He was calling for America to press its advantage while it still retained the edge. As will be seen in the next chapter, Bell did not see atomic devices as a fundamental shift in military affairs. He saw them as merely bigger bombs. Nonetheless, when both his statements presented here are shown together, his 1946 comments about global suicide by nuclear weapons and his proposal for preemptive strikes, they demonstrate an uncertainty about the new systems. What is key is that Bell's idea was the bellicose exception to an otherwise terrified unanimity in evangelical commentary.

and Nagasaki with the wider world. This was a prospect that understandably frightened evangelical thinkers, and they were not quite sure what to do about it. Some appealed to the new United Nations, while others seemed to fall into despair. While there was some mention of these new devices playing a role in the end of the world, the bulk of the commentary was more akin to sheer terror at the new world they had helped to create.

END TIMES

Peace in 1945 brought in a new set of eschatological concerns. Nazis were no longer dominating evangelical end-times imaginations, but new world systems and organizations provided ample fodder for concern. Few minds were fundamentally changed by the new situations, but fears shifted from just nation states like Germany to include supranational entities and alliances. Russia and Communism resumed their prior places as the primary objects of eschatological concern, but even friendly powers like Western Europe earned attention regarding end-times alliances.[99]

Pausing the End

The practicality of finding the key to the future in present events continued to be an issue. Perhaps thinking of failed eschatological predictions in recent years, William Culbertson opposed both those who would make outlandish predictions for the future and the people who, in reaction, would discount the legitimacy of biblical prophecy on the whole. He admitted, "The subject of Bible prophecy is in a measure in disrepute because certain hasty and ill-advised prophets have gone beyond the bounds of Scripture in seeking to be sensational." However,

---

99. Not all evangelical commentary linking contemporary events to eschatological concerns dealt with deadly consequences. One author saw the possibility of the end of the world as a call to preach Christianity even more fervently. "We are living in significant days. The Church cannot stand idly by. It is the time for action, for heroic witnessing, for sacrifice, for missionary activity, for prayer and for loving service. God is giving the Church its greatest opportunity in all history to proclaim the gospel to every creature in its generation." Harold Lundquist, "Is the Stage Being Set?" *MM*, August 1946, 752.

he maintained the importance of eschatological work, arguing that, when done with care to stick to the Bible, many such prognosticators had not been embarrassed by their own overreach.[100] In a similar vein another *Moody* writer rebuked those who were too quick to connect the dots of biblical prophecy and contemporary events. "The tendency to look for signs and build conclusions on them has done incalculable damage to the cause of God. So many silly prophecies have been made in the past that myriads of unsaved people today ridicule the very thought of the Lord's coming." He recounted all the failed prophecies concerning Hitler and Mussolini and those of the previous generation about the Kaiser. "Do you remember when would-be prophets told us the German Emperor Wilhelm II was to be the Antichrist, because his right eye was blind and his right arm paralyzed? For didn't Zechariah testify that 'his army shall be clean dried up, and his right eye shall be utterly darkened?' " He was not trying to undermine any Christian's hope in Christ's return, but he did want to caution them not to pretend to have knowledge that they did not in fact have and thereby focus more on predictions than on serving God. "The simple fact is that we are not to be concerned with what He knows, but only with what He has told us. He told His own then—He tells them now—to expect Him at any moment. That is the blessed hope that will keep us clean, busy and happy."[101] Rather than trying to find out for themselves the day or the hour of Christ's return, this writer called on his readers to trust that God had it all under control. As it had been when the biblical prophecies had first been written, there was a strong pastoral emphasis in apocalyptic

---

100. Culbertson, "Prelude to Prophecy," *MM*, February 1948, 397. The ultimate conclusion of the article was to recommend the scholarship represented by the article in the same issue written by Wilbur Smith. Interestingly, not only would Smith's perspective be found in *MM*, but, starting in January 1950, he would take over the "Current Events in Light of the Bible" series in *OH* from Schuyler English even as Smith's work continued on in *MM*.

101. August Van Ryn, "Is Jesus Coming Soon?" MM, April 1949, 610. Underlining in title in original. Later, Smith poked fun at this same issue, saying, "During World War I, Kaiser Wilhelm was said to be the Anti-Christ—they had him all worked out on 666, only it didn't add up. They were six short so they added six to 660!" Smith, "The Testimony of Bible Prophecy," MM, September 1949, 14.

writing. The goal was to help people best endure the ups and downs of world history and not to figure it out as a puzzle.

E. Schuyler English's comments provided a study in contrasts. On the one hand he seemed more and more prone to believe that the end was nigh, but he was also quite capable of discussing geopolitics without recourse to biblical connections, even to the point of denying any such connection. Speaking of a Moscow conference in December 1945, "There is nothing unusually significant in all this—that is, in respect to Bible prophecy. We watch Russia with interest, of course. But in the short view nothing occurred at Moscow to cause us to see the scroll of predictive Scripture unfolding."[102] Yet, just one month later he wrote, "If what we are seeing in the world news of today does not resemble that which is to occur 'in the last days,' then we have not read our Bible aright." He was careful to distance himself from any overly specific claim about the future, but he had little trouble seeing current events as harbingers of the end.[103]

---

102. English, "Better Understanding at Moscow Conference," *OH*, February 1946, 561-62. He was not precluding the possibility of eschatological significance, but he was saying that he did not think, at present, that the current events pointed to a future significance. After these last words he wrote, "These matters are reported simply that we may be up-to-date on the news and ready to understand events yet in the future—but perhaps not very distant." In his articles written since taking over the series "Current Events in the Light of the Bible" from Gaebelein, English displayed somewhat less enthusiasm for specific prophetic connections than his predecessor. This could qualify the perception of Gaebelein created by his own words previously. While it was in this same issue of February 1946 that *OH* reported the Christmas Day 1945 death of Gaebelein and the subsequent promotion of English to Editor, there would have been a period when both men were writing for *OH* with Gaebelein as editor.

103. English, "A Hook in the Jaws of the Bear," *OH*, September 1949, 162. In a move that both confirmed his interest in the end of the world and took a swipe at governmental pretensions, he suggested that President Truman's hopes for peace through the new organization were built on false grounds. His cautious support of the NATO was encouraged by his belief that it was an integral move towards the return of Jesus to establish his kingdom. "In a way, the Atlantic Pact is a step toward a world of peace, but not in the way Mr. Truman expects; for it may easily be an instrument in bringing about the aggression on the part of the East which will precede the coming of the Lord. Actually, then, the Atlantic Pact may be, first of all, the first step toward war!"

FINDING AMERICA

As events unfolded they did not always do so in ways which evangelicals had expected, and many had to alter the nature of their predictions to fit the new circumstances. In what was to become a recurring, if minor, theme among American evangelicals, English was somewhat unclear what role his own nation would play in the final story. Initially, he looked to an East vs. West demarcation in the world but with Britain assuming leadership of the West while the US sat on the sidelines.[104] This potential British leadership was in great contrast to the Italian focus in Gaebelein's articles of decade earlier. Later, English seemed open to the idea of an American inclusion in a revived Roman Empire, suggesting that the new empire need not be constrained within the borders of the original Pax Romana and might well extend to the Western Hemisphere.[105] By the middle of 1947, he had shifted from a simple American inclusion to overt US leadership. When President Truman announced his policy of containment, English commented, "And it becomes more and more evident that two camps are forming— those mentioned so often in these pages. Russia and the satellites to the northeast; democratic agencies south and west. That the United States will be the moving and most powerful factor in the latter alliance *seems* every day to be more obvious."[106] That this was the end was, seemingly, confirmed to English by the continued connection of geopolitical events with his own understanding of eschatology. "A decade ago such alignments as those of Bible prophecy seemed, to human eyes, unlikely if not impossible, in *our* generation. Today we see them taking shape in precise and spectacular fashion. 'Blessed is he that watcheth.' "[107] At

---

104. English, "Only More of the Same Things," *OH*, January 1946, 463.

105. English, "Building with Blocs," *OH*, May 1946, 757.

106. English, "A Date with Destiny," *OH*, May 1947, 681. Italics in original. The following January he noted with interest that the Soviets had sent a large delegation to their embassy in Siam. This, along with other diplomatic moves by Moscow, suggested to English the possibility that Southeast Asia would make up many of the nations mentioned in Ezekiel 38. English, "Looking Eastward," *OH*, January 1949, 404.

107. English, "The Collapse of China," *OH*, March 1949, 544-45. Italics in original. At one point in June 1949 he counterintuitively used the failure of certain predictions as the basis for encouraging the idea of others. After reciting several

one and the same time, the news reports from around the world had shaken the confidence of eschatologically-minded writers to the point that they included more qualifications than they had done earlier, but they managed to find new material to buttress their old beliefs and created new formulations to accommodate them.

BUILDING THE END

The years of the war and the events surrounding it had undone many expected landmarks in eschatology, but they had also set in motion other events which confirmed to many evangelicals that the end of all things was closer than ever. One of these things was the development of atomic weapons. Wilbur Smith looked to these devices as a key element in the creation of an end-times superstate with power over the entire world. He argued that before this time there had been no mechanism so significant to lead the nations of the world to put their trust in a single entity, but the terror induced by the bomb would induce the world's nations to "yield their sovereignty to this one supreme organization."[108] Not every evangelical saw the bomb as quite so significant. Robert Fischer, who had been a part of the Manhattan Project and was an occasional contributor to *Moody*, gave a pointed criticism of any connection between the bomb and eschatology. He gave no names, but he rebuked those who had spoken publically about the prophetic implications of the new weapon. Carefully skirting any science vs. faith condescension, he cautioned preachers to be wary of offering technical information when they did not have the necessary education to do so.

---

rumors of wars which had not come to pass in the early days of that year, he wrote, "Of course, all of these things are not going to happen all at once. As a matter of fact, it is highly probable that none of them may occur at this time. They are but rumors, and nothing more. But *rumors* of wars is but one of the signs that the Church's part in this age is almost played out. ... The persistency and universality of these rumors ... is but another indication that the coming of the Lord Jesus Christ ... is imminent indeed." English, " ... But the End Is Not Yet," *OH*, June 1949, 745. Italics in original. Ellipses in title in original.

108. Smith, "How Antichrist Will Rule," *MM*, February 1948, 400.

He asked them to have someone check over any technological jargon before putting it into their sermons.[109]

RETURN FROM THE EXILE

Few events in that era had so crystalized end-times thinking as the return of the Jews to the Promised Land. The establishment of the State of Israel in the wake of World War II grabbed the attention of many evangelical commentators, and it did so for very understandable reasons. Many evangelicals had long expected that this would happen, even as many others doubted its feasibility. However, neither evangelical opinions nor their reasons for those opinions were uniform throughout. Some argued for Israeli independence without recourse to eschatological thinking, some argued against the new regime specifically because of their end-times beliefs, and some were either of two minds or downright disinterested.

CH offered the unique perspective of strongly pro-Israeli articles while being completely disinterested in eschatology. Regular articles appeared which encouraged sympathy for the Jewish refugees and argued for the justness of their cause and the legitimacy of the new state. However, none of these pieces suggested that this was a matter of prophetic fulfillment. Even before the outbreak of war, Courier was quite clear where his sympathies lay. "The Arab League is not yet one year old. A mere baby. And an *enfant terrible*. The council of this Arab League is now in session in Cairo. And there have been deadly Arab-Jew riots in Cairo. Is there any connection?" Referring to the issue of the Holy Land itself, he said, "The Jews want a ridiculously small section of land on which to build their state; the Arab could grant it and never miss it. We wonder why he doesn't, and then end this slaughter."[110] This pro-Jewish sentiment was enhanced with a photo of Jews arriving in Palestine, bearing the caption, "In spite of unrest and riot, Palestine still spells hope for the world's desperate Jewry. Above: European Jews

---

109. Robert B. Fischer, "The Message of the Atomic Bomb to the Church," *MM*, March 1946, 427. Fischer's article cannot have been referring to the Smith article as it predates it by two years.

110. Courier, "League," *CH*, January 1946, 8–9.

arrive in the land of their fathers."[111] Courier was skeptical of the Arabs' willingness to stand by a negotiated settlement, saying, "The Arabs call for the UN to step in. If the UN did step in, would the Arabs abide by the UN decision? We think not. Is there, then, any peaceful solution for the Palestine problem? As things stand now, we think not. It is time for the UN to take over, *and to enforce its decisions with arms*."[112] Similarly, Poling came to the defense of Jewish immigrants to the Middle East, saying that it was the Arabs and not the Jews who were at fault for the poverty among their people. "[Senator Owen Brewster] affirmed that if Arab rulers had devoted ... even a fraction of one percent [of oil revenues] to bettering the physical conditions of their poverty stricken subjects, the standard of living in Arabian lands could have been shifted toward the high level enjoyed by the Jews."[113] Whether or not Courier or Poling rooted their pro-Israeli stance in eschatology, neither of them found it important enough a consideration to include in their arguments before their readers.

Even though they were very interested in end times when it came to seemingly everything else, E. Schuyler English and his fellow writers at *OH* found little of eschatological relevance to the return of Jews to Palestine. English made regular mention of the steps toward Israeli statehood, but he continued to reject the premise of Zionism or any idea that the State of Israel was a manifestation of biblical prophecy. When violence in the region continued to fester, English laid the blame at the feet of not the Arabs but those he called Jewish terrorists.[114] As opposed to the words of Courier, a contributor to *OH* expressed a more positive view of the Arabs. In contrast to the Jews who had "been scattered among the nations, the Arab has not left his land ... he lives and dies in the presence of all his brethren. The Arabs continue a distinct people and inhabit the country of their progenitors in adjoining lands even to this day." Oddly enough, he based his opposition to Zionism in his own eschatological understanding. For example, when writing of

---

111. The Editors, Photo Caption, *CH*, January 1946, 10.
112. Courier, "Without Hamlet," *CH*, November 1946, 10. Italics in original.
113. Poling, "Open Palestine Immediately," *CH*, January 1946, 12.
114. English, "Operation Crossroads," *OH*, August 1946, 90.

those Jews going toward Jerusalem, "Every right-thinking Jew as well as every right-thinking Christian will say that no group of communistic, atheistic people can ever rehabilitate the land of Palestine with any success. We are told that there are far too many of the communistic and atheistic variety there at the present time." He concluded with a warning for those Jews going to the Promised Land that they ought to be careful, considering that there were millions of Arabs and Muslims living in the lands around Jerusalem.[115] These writers emphatically discounted any end-times significance to the Zionist enterprise, even though they were dedicated to the idea that the end of human history was upon them.

SPJ articles generally stayed away from eschatological issues. When they did touch on such things, they were in basic alignment with what was found in Moody, but these were quite rare. One which did deal with the Israeli situation was one by a contributor who wrote an extensive piece in which he challenged the assessment of a British diplomat who had argued that the Jews had no right to the land of Palestine. In response the author retorted that this betrayed either a lack of belief or simple "ignorance" regarding the Bible. The bulk of his article went through the Old Testament and cited times when the land was promised to the Jews and when it was promised that they would return after exile. While he made little mention of current events regarding the State of Israel or whether such things meant the end of the world was at hand, he did refer to the events of 1947 and 1948 as "the final restoration."[116]

This occasional indifference did not hold true for writers at Moody. The emigration of Jews out of Europe to the land was the fulfillment

---

115. William Ward Ayer, "Should the Jew or the Arab Have the Land of Palestine?" OH, April 1946, 663-73.

116. Aaron J. Kligerman, "Palestine—Jewish Homeland," SPJ, June 1, 1948, 17-20. Despite this clearly pro-Israeli statement based in Scriptural texts, articles of this sort in SPJ were few and far between. This very same issue of SPJ had another article delving into how Christ would return and what would happen at the Eschaton, but, unlike articles in other magazines, this one by Willis Thompson said nothing about when this would happen or whether anything of the then-contemporary world events had anything to do with the end of the world. Tellingly, his title asks how Jesus will return, and not when. Willis Thompson, "How Will Jesus Return?" SPJ, June 1, 1949, 16-17.

of ancient prophecy, and while this would be opposed by many, it could be stopped by no one.[117] When discussing America's role in the beginnings of the State of Israel, William Culbertson was careful in his comments. On the one hand he noted that the previous year's machinations at the UN appeared to be one more link in the inevitable chain of events leading to the end. When the United States withdrew its support for an internationally backed Palestinian security, he neither supported the American move nor particularly criticized it. The US had acted for its own reasons, and the final role of Israel would come into existence whatever any American administration might desire. "We watch the happenings in Palestine with particular interest, though they have been temporarily reversed. We go right on believing the biblical prediction that God will someday regather the people of Israel out of the nations to their homeland in Palestine. We do not believe the prophecies because of current events but because of God's unalterable Word."[118] He and others had a great deal of confidence that the Jewish state would be established and would succeed, whether it received any aid from America or not. That things played out so closely to the way they had predicted could not but have boosted their confidence in the midst of a chaotic age. However, at least at this stage, this confidence was in what they perceived to be the testimony of the Bible and not their own cleverness or the virtue of their nation.

THE OBVIOUS CONCLUSION

The years after World War II seemed tailor-made for eschatological speculation. For centuries Christians had spoken of the world as ending

---

117. Frederick Erdman, "Jewish and Gentile Paradoxes," *MM*, September 1946, 16. "Just as the nations today are united in their efforts to prevent the harassed Jews from becoming a nation in the Promised Land, in the future when they have become a nation this same anti-Semitism will be the cause of the final futile attempt of Gentile nations to destroy the Jewish nation, as described in Joel 3 and Zechariah 14."

118. Culbertson, "Backtrack in Palestine," *MM*, May 1948, 634. A few months later he stated, "Palestine becomes more and more the ring to watch. We have no question that the cradle of history is undergoing preparation for its significant place in the final fulfillment of prophecy." Culbertson, "Communism in Israel," *MM*, August 1948, 858.

in an all-consuming fire. Now just such a fire was in place, but not in the supernatural or mythical but in the hands of two warring factions. For decades premillennial evangelicals had predicted the rise of a revived Roman Empire facing off against a Northern Confederation led by Russia and bringing in Asia's vast numbers. Now this exact situation seemed to be playing itself out as Western Europe and America faced off against "the Reds" from Central Europe to Southeast Asia. And finally, after nearly two thousand years scattered among the goyim, the Jews were back in Palestine. With that being said, evangelicals were not of one accord about the birth of the State of Israel, and there was some uncertainty about where the United States would fit in the new world order.

Everything that many had said would happen had, in fact, come to pass more suddenly than any human could have predicted or planned. The question in retrospect is not how they could have thought the end was nigh but how any could have considered otherwise. Yet, for all that, many evangelicals either discounted the signs which others saw to be clear as not yet completed or never even thought to consider them. Nations were rising and nations were falling, but the task ahead seemed unchanged in a rapidly changing world. Germans and Japanese switched from hated enemies to promising mission fields and potential allies in the great new conflict. Russians moved from uncertain allies to definite enemies who had to be stopped. China lost its place as the next great Christian civilization and became a country that had been simply "lost." America secured its place as the best hope of a bright future for the world, even if that corrupted American future seemed bright only in comparison to the darkness of the surrounding world. The bomb terrified any who paid attention, yet it was the hope for many of preserving human liberty and dignity. Throughout it all the one thing held in common by all evangelicals, whether eschatologically obsessed or indifferent, was that it was only through the preaching of God's word and the conversion of the nations that any hope for tomorrow could safely be entertained.

5

Turning East, 1950–1953

OVERVIEW

In the waning months of 1949, American evangelicalism vaulted into the public consciousness in a way unseen in decades. With his Los Angeles Crusades Billy Graham found his place in the world, and evangelicals found a spokesman to bring their message to any who would listen. Thousands of Angelenos converted to this new, yet old, conversion-centered Christianity, and the American media found a poster boy useful enough to "puff."[1] At the same time in China, Mao Tse-Tung was proclaiming a very different message, yet one that equally promised a blessed destiny to the faithful and harsh judgment for the outsiders. On October 1 of that year he declared the founding of the People's Republic of China, bringing the largest nation on earth into the Communist camp. The country which had once been a favorite missionary destination for American Christians had been converted to another faith, a faith hostile to both Christianity and the United States.

Nine months later America would find itself at war once more. Korea, the spoils of victory over Japan, was divided into Russian and American protectorates. Months of mutual haranguing between Seoul and Pyongyang led to open war in June 1950. Whether the Communists thought the West would not react or simply hoped to present the world with a fait accompli, the US responded in force just in time. An American-led UN army pushed from the Pusan perimeter in the south to the banks of the Yalu River in the north, leading the Chinese People's Liberation Army to send volunteers to aid their fellow Communists. Until 1953 the

---

1. In a widely reported anecdote, William Randolph Hearst is said to have instructed his media empire to "puff Graham."

Korean peninsula was a bloody stalemate as Communist forces could not break the UN lines and the US could act only so far for fear of a Russian response. With the threat and reality of war on every front page, evangelical pundits continued to argue their case before the world. Now, however, their new prominence in the public consciousness meant that their words were reaching wider audiences than ever.

ENEMIES

Throughout this period evangelicals' attitude toward America's enemies was fairly clear. The United States was a flawed nation, but its rivals and opponents were worse in some specific ways. However, in many ways it was not the nations, as such, which were the true enemy. Russia and China were not innately worse than America but they became so by their behavior and this behavior was driven by their ideology. By the early 1950s evangelicals were as likely to speak of Communism as a self-existent enemy as they were to so describe any particular nation-state in the world.

THE COMMUNIST RIVAL

Evangelicals consistently portrayed Communism as a clear and present danger to humanity in general and to religious people in particular. They opposed Communism for many reasons, but one of the keenest was the way in which this political group used its power against religious entities around the world. Communism was a jealous god who would tolerate no rival deities in its presence, and many evangelicals discussed Cold War issues through the lens of religious tolerance.[2]

---

2. This emphasis on religious tolerance extended beyond Communism to the point that many evangelicals found it unpalatable to make common cause with Roman Catholics in opposition to Moscow. Donald Barnhouse went so far as to equate supposedly conservative tyrannies with those of Communism, calling them both "Satanic." Donald G. Barnhouse, "Right or Left," *ET*, July 1951, 25. In another editorial on the same page, he wrote, "There are iron curtains against the Gospel in Latin America as well as in Soviet Russia." Barnhouse, "How Evangelize the World?" *ET*, July 1951, 25. Francis Schaeffer viewed both Communism and Roman Catholicism as two forms of tyranny and saw no virtue in aligning with the one to defeat the other. Writing to President Truman in 1951, he said, "From my knowledge of Europe, it has seemed to me that the United States made a serious mistake

Moody's writers kept their readers well-informed about the subtle and not so subtle anti-Christian activities of Eastern European governments. They told of the frustration of East German clergy facing the implacable hostility of the state. Churches were still in operation, and were, in some cases, adding new construction, but they had to combat the increasingly atheistic orthodoxy in the educational system.[3] By 1953 *Moody* was reporting on the new requirements that all Polish church positions had to be approved by the Communist state and all new appointees were required to swear loyalty to the government.[4] The editors at *ET* cited a report out of the Vatican saying that well over 10,000 "priests and members of religious orders" had been killed in the postwar years alone.[5] In articles such as these, evangelicals were more incensed at the affront to their fellow citizens of the kingdom of God than the threat posed to their fellow citizens of the United States.

The danger posed by Communism was greater than a mere rival nation as though Russia in itself was the problem. It was far deeper than this. It was a belief system which was determined to refashion

---

in uniting fully with totalitarian Russia in order to defeat totalitarian Germany. ... Roman Catholicism is totalitarian in those places where it is in control and surely the United States should be able to find some means of standing against one totalitarian system without joining with another to do so." Francis A. Schaeffer, Letter to President Harry S. Truman, November 19, 1951, Francis A. Schaeffer Collection, Box 57, File 23, The Library, Southeastern Baptist Theological Seminary, Wake Forest, North Carolina. Carl F. H. Henry chided the Truman administration for its moves to appoint an envoy to the Vatican. In a letter to the editor of a local paper he wrote, "The alternatives clearly are not Communism or an ambassador to the Vatican, are not the doom of the American way of life or a Vatican ambassador. ... The real issue, as Protestants see it, is religious liberty or a Vatican ambassador." Carl F. H. Henry, Letter to the Editor of *Pasadena Star-News*, November 7, 1951, Carl F. H. Henry Papers, Box 1951 1, File Protestants and other Americans for the Separation of Church and State, Rolfing Library Archives, Trinity Evangelical Divinity School, Deerfield, IL. Underlining in original.

3. The Editors, "World News in Brief," *MM*, July 1950, 769. Throughout the period *MM* editors included numerous accounts of this sort in their "World News in Brief" each month. They highlighted the travails of religious groups as they adjusted to the new regimes. This attention extended to Jews and Muslims as well, as seen in another *MM* piece later that year. The Editors, "Behind the Iron Curtain," *MM*, December 1950, 257.

4. Sam Paxton, "News Report," *MM*, April 1953, 594.

5. The Editors, "A Window on the World," *ET*, February 1951, 23.

the image of humanity and the world at large. The rabid loyalty which it inspired meant that there was little hope of meaningful compromise for peace. Distrust was the only reasonable response to an expansionist ideology willing to use any and all methods to enhance the cause. As Culbertson wrote, "A little group of men who one short generation ago controlled nothing and had nothing but a burning idea has gained control over lives of more than 700 million people, and is determined on world power. Fanaticism, skill, intrigue, ruthlessness and murder have carried their program far."[6] Later, Culbertson would condemn Communism further, noting that even with its power and oppression, it had failed in its primary goal, the remaking of humanity. He wrote, "Particularly is it clear that corruption, greed and lust for power have played bloody but major roles in recent years. The point to note is that Communism has failed completely to make good its promise in bringing forth a perfect society where equality, justice and human kindness prevail." Continuing, he said,

> For thirty years [Communism] has had opportunity to produce a breed of man without greed and lust for power. This it has failed to do, and their godlessness has given rise instead to corruption, bloodshed and misery. Communism as an evil expanding force is still to be reckoned with, but it has already shown its failure to deliver the essential good which it has promised.[7]

Evangelicals had such animosity toward Communism partly because they saw it as Christianity's opposite number. The United States may have found its enemy in the Soviet Union, but Christianity and Communism were one another's evil twin.[8]

---

6. Culbertson, "Call for Mobilization," *MM*, September 1950, 7. In the context of the article, mobilization was not a military issue. Rather, using the start of the Korean War as a backdrop and inspiration, Culbertson was calling on his readers to mobilize for prayer and Christian living. These alone, he averred, would save the nation in its time of need.

7. Culbertson, "Where Communism Has Failed," *MM*, June 1953, 719–20.

8. Culbertson, "Communism Chooses Weapons," *MM*, December 1950, 224. In the first of a series offering a fairly detailed history of the Communist movement, another *MM* writer, Jimmie Johnson, began saying, "If you are a Christian, Communism has declared war on you and your God." Jimmie Johnson, "What Is

For Carl F. H. Henry, too, the cold conflict with Russia was not merely the same old game of international power plays and rivalries. He told his radio audience that the combination of new technologies and ideologies made for a devastatingly potent mix in the Soviet Union. To him Russians had been

> indoctrinated in the belief ... that the Russian people are a superior race destined to bring in a new world order, that there are no changeless moral principles, that might makes right and that whoever gets there first with the strongest fist has the privilege of erecting the rules from the game of human life, and it is no wonder a chill of horror begins to creep up and down the spine of Americans a few thousand miles away.[9]

Henry saw Communism's rejection of religion as the basis for its tyrannical nature, saying, "Communism sees this relation between God and human rights far more clearly than most Americans see it. Communism has dismissed God as an enemy of the state, and the dismissal of God has meant a dismissal also of human rights against the state."[10] This was

---

Behind That Curtain?" *MM*, August 1951, 832. The next month he provided a chilling anecdote about the effect of Communist propaganda on youth. "There was a fanatical gleam in the young Communist's eyes as he answered the American's question about his faith in the party. 'Why, if my leaders told me to kill my own mother, I would do it without batting an eye!' ... That is fanatical Communism as it works in the mind of the blinded follower. It is more than a conviction; it is an obsession, and it is absolutely contrary and opposite to all that is Christian." Johnson's conclusion worked to embolden his readers to the intense days before them, saying, "Whatever lies ahead, whether judgment with death and destruction, or the dawn of a great spiritual awakening, let us as young people be in the midst with a ringing determination to give our all for our Lord with a conviction that is more than the fanatical enthusiasm of the Communist." Jimmie Johnson, "What Is Behind That Curtain?" *MM*, September 1951, 61. The term "young people" is present since this article was a part of *MM*'s "Youth Supplement."

9. Henry, November 9, 1952, Carl F. H. Henry Papers, Box "Let the Chips Fall," Rolfing Library Archives, Trinity Evangelical Divinity School, Deerfield, Illinois.

10. Henry, November 17, 1952, Carl F. H. Henry Papers, Box "Let the Chips Fall," Rolfing Library Archives, Trinity Evangelical Divinity School, Deerfield, Illinois. Here and elsewhere, the date for this broadcast is unclear. There are two manuscripts which appear to be marked by Henry as from November 17, 1952. However, in each case the date is crossed out and replaced. In this case the original date typed was the 16th, but it has been written over making it likely into a 17.

a consistent theme for Henry and others. Communism was not evil by accident, nor was its opposition to religion an optional characteristic. Oppression and hostility to religion were innate to Communist theory and practice.[11]

General William K. Harrison, who had represented the United Nations at the peace talks ending the Korean War, said of the Communists, "None of us had any doubt that there is simply no basis for assuming that any real Communist is trustworthy in the slightest degree. Admittedly they may carry out some commitment correctly but, if so, it will be a matter of expediency to gain their own ends rather than faithfulness to moral principle." At another point in the article, he was explicit in his condemnation of his foes. "Communism as a system is incredibly evil, and real Communists are necessarily criminals." Even so, Harrison did not think this duplicity was unique to Communism, even if they might be particularly good at it. In this same article he added,

> As a Christian, what interests me is the manner in which Communists illustrate the first three chapters of the epistle to the

---

11. Henry's soon-to-be coworker with *Christianity Today*, L. Nelson Bell, had a similar view. His account of Communism combined a rejection of the ideology and a rebuke of any accommodation which well-meaning but ill-informed people might make with it. When people spoke of the "great concern" Communists had for lifting up the world's poor, Bell retorted that this was nothing more than a ruse to conceal Communism's intrinsically oppressive nature. "Such 'concern' is **bait** to quiet the individual while his most precious possession, his freedom, is taken from him and he becomes a serf and an automaton to fulfil the plans and desires of the State which becomes his master and tyrant." L. Nelson Bell, "Challenge to What?" *SPJ*, February 15, 1950, 4. Boldface in original. Bell showed particular frustration for his fellow Christians who had been taken in by Communism, saying in this article, "We become weary of hearing again and again that Communism challenges Christianity because it has a concern for the material welfare of the individual and the Church does not." He then rattled off a litany of comparisons: "Christianity leads to personal freedom, Communism to enslavement. Christianity produces love and service, Communism hate and regimentation. Christianity spreads the message of eternal salvation to those who will accept the Saviour, Communism preaches materialism and atheism." He urged people to seek a better understanding of Communism's true nature. With little subtlety he defined it as "a hell-inspired conspiracy to take over world control, never changing in its objective and never stopping in its course unless forced to do so. ... Their own books proclaim this policy and their actions prove by every move how relentless is the determination for world domination." Bell, "Communist China and the U.N." *SPJ*, September 2, 1953, 4.

Romans. The evil which is so apparent in the Communists, and which is prevalent in the entire human race, is there because God has given mankind over to just those things. Men reject God's sovereignty, refuse to recognize that He is the source of all that they have and are in a permanent state of rebellion in their efforts to live independently of Him.

Although it was quite literally his job to fight Communists, Harrison conditioned his opposition by a bigger, religious backdrop, saying, "Finally, while seeing Communists realistically, we should not hate them. They are human beings, dead in sin and alienated from God. Except for the grace of God, we who are 'in Christ' would be as they. Christ died for all men, and John 3:16 is for Communists also."[12] The conflict with Communism was greater than nation vs. nation, and its solution and its hope had to be higher still.

A STICH IN TIME

Evangelicals were fearful about more material concerns as well. The events of recent history understandably colored the way current events came across in the minds of commentators. When they looked at the size of the Soviet and Chinese militaries, they saw reason to believe that the emerging Eastern Bloc was walking on a path already traveled by Nazis, Fascists, and militarists quite recently. European nations gobbling up their neighbors as a prelude to further aggression was no hypothetical possibility for people in the early 1950s; they had seen it with their own eyes just a short time ago. Donald Grey Barnhouse made this connection explicit. In his retrospective on the year of 1950, he argued that "Russia has studied history well," and that by alternating between demands for expansion and protestations of innocence, Moscow hoped to take as much ground without open war.[13] Similarly, Culbertson paralleled the Russian moves toward Turkey and Iran with events just over a decade before, saying, "Anyone whose memory goes back to the late thirties and the Nazi occupation of the countries surrounding Germany,

---

12. William K. Harrison, "I Faced the Communists at Panmunjon," *ET*, December 1953, 10–11, 44.

13. Barnhouse, "1950," *ET*, January 1951, 8.

cannot help but see the counterpart in what the Soviet Union has done during and since World War II."[14] Bell forecasted a similar expansionist future for the Soviets, suggesting that they were acting according to a thought-out strategy, saying, "Russia has a master plan for world domination. Strings controlling the puppets are pulled in Moscow and these strings reach into many corners of the world." He felt that the options open to Soviet advances were nearly limitless with expected incursions into the Middle East, Southeast Asia, and Western Europe.[15]

It would have taken no great bout of paranoia to convince people who had lived through the Fascist buildup in the late 1930s to be somewhat bothered by the Communist order of battle in the early 1950s. Henry warned, "The State department [sic] has warned that the Kremlin and her satellite states have stationed 491 divisions of troops in Europe and Asia, that Russia is channeling her national production to war, and that the policy which motivates Soviet leaders is directed toward wiping from the world all democratic institutions of the free world." With some greater detail, he added, "Stationed in Europe are 129 Soviet and 60 satellite divisions; in East Asia are 35 Soviet divisions and 250 Chinese Communist divisions; in central Russia are 17 Soviet divisions. Secretary of State Dean Acheson has estimated that the Communists have 9,000,000 men under arms, 4,000,000 of the Russian and 3,500,000 Chinese."[16] Whether or not these estimates were correct or merely the result of Russian and American propaganda, it was in these perceived circumstances that the likes of Culbertson and Henry framed their response to the Cold War. Culbertson warned,

---

14. Culbertson, "Two Years to Work?" *MM*, March 1950, 455.

15. Bell, " 'Knowest Thou Not Yet' (Exodus 10:7)," *SPJ*, August 15, 1950, 11. Three years later he wrote, "With every act of Russia proving her avowed policy of disruption, conquest and domination of the world, it makes one both heart-sick and frankly disgusted to hear of those who wishfully hope that we can do business with Russia and who see in some modification or temporary change in policy, an indication that Russia is changing her basic philosophy so that the Western world can hope to live in peace and harmony with her." Bell, "Pollyanna in the U.N.," *SPJ*, October 7, 1953, 2.

16. Henry, December 1, 1952, Carl F. H. Henry Papers, Box "Let the Chips Fall," file dated Sep–Apr alphabetical by first word A–F, Rolfing Library Archives, Trinity Evangelical Divinity School, Deerfield, Illinois.

The maritime vulnerability of the United States is apparent. Russia already has a fleet of submarines. In fact, the US *New and World Report* for December 23, 1949, tells us that while Germany had 132 submarines as an average during the war, Russia now has 300—the world's largest submarine navy. ... [R]ocket-firing submarines fifty miles off our coast could paralyze our eastern shores up to 150 miles inland.[17]

Further, he was concerned that time might well be running out for a peaceful solution to the world's crises. He wrote, "While it is probably true that Soviet Russia is not yet ready to engage in a shooting war there seems to be less and less of an attitude of forbearance and the desire to refrain from activities which might be regarded as belligerent and provocative of conflict." This fear was magnified by his perception that the Russians had the Americans outclassed in several key areas such as "man power, technological potential and supplies."[18] At the very time when Soviet power was increasing, it seemed to many evangelicals that American power was lagging further behind.

China Bleeding Red

Oddly enough, this opposition to Russian power was not equaled at all times by criticism of newly Communist China. Barnhouse had some downright positive comments for the new regime. While he was not pleased with the Marxist ideology now dominating China's educational system, he noted that roads were being built and officials were taking in taxes instead of the bribes of recent years. He even credited the Communists for bringing a level of peace not known in the country for decades. "China has known civil war, and before that the world war, and before that the Japanese local war, and before that pillage and banditry. The latter exists in some places, but reports from every part of China indicate that the government is establishing control with a speed that

---

17. Culbertson, "Two Years to Work?" *MM*, March 1950, 454.
18. Culbertson, "1952: A Sequel," *MM*, March 1951, 442. The sequel aspect of the title is due to this article being an intentional follow-up work to his March 1950 piece, "Two Years to Work?"

had not been dreamed possible."[19] As shall be seen, Barnhouse was fairly unique in this approach to China. He was consistently more open to Beijing than others were and drastically more so than he himself was to Moscow.

More common were the reports of persecution by Mao's administration. *Moody's* staff told readers that Chinese Communists did not always use overt force to counter Christian activities under the new regime. For example Christian hospitals were pressured to buy Communist bonds through the imposition of high business taxes or demands.[20] A few months later a missionary returning from China suggested that some of the limited public tolerance offered by the Beijing government was a matter of public relations, noting that it was only in places like Shanghai that such tolerance was practiced as this center of commerce had a high number of foreigners, and Mao wished to cultivate a good impression among them. The reality was somewhat different. "Behind this façade they carry on their persecution of the Church in inland China."[21] This was yet another common theme of evangelical evaluations of Communism, even the best of reports were treated as likely propaganda.

Not everyone's account of the new government in China was even this sunny. Given his personal history with the country, L. Nelson Bell was particularly interested in its fate and wrote about it quite often. In what is, in retrospect, a naïve expectation, he argued that

---

19. Barnhouse, "1950," *ET*, January 1951, 45. He later suggested that part of the reason Mao had been so successful in creating stability was that he had tapped into longstanding Chinese customs. "The new hierarchy has replaced the Mandarinate of the old Empire; they are the same people who have governed China for the past two thousand years." Barnhouse, "China and the Western Powers," *ET*, September 1952, 7. Another author in the same issue of *ET* gave a neutral description of Beijing's directives to Christian groups, saying, "The Government has suggested to Christian organizations that they gradually dispense with foreign funds and foreign personnel." Arthur T. F. Reynolds, "The Missionary in China Looks Ahead," *ET*, January 1951, 14.

20. The Editors, "World News in Brief," *MM*, July 1950, 796.

21. J. Herbert Kane, "The Future of Missions in Red China," *MM*, January 1951, 313. This expectation of persecution became more pronounced when Harold Cook reported on the false suicide of a Western missionary at the hands of Chinese Communists. Harold R. Cook, "From the Fields," *MM*, May 1951, 598.

the Communist experiment could not last long in the face of growing indigenous opposition. Rather than being "cowed into submission" by the terror, the people of China were becoming "completely disillusioned by the benevolent claims of Communism."[22] Supporting this idea, he reported that there were five hundred thousand anti-Communist troops on Formosa and another one million six hundred thousand guerillas in China proper ready to fight Beijing.[23] Decades after the fact such a

---

22. Bell, "We *Must* Change Our China Policy—And Quickly," *SPJ*, February 14, 1951, 5.

23. Bell, "While Rome Burns," *SPJ*, April 4, 1951, 2. He also critiqued American naïveté about Communist intention. On the one hand he asserted, as he had earlier, that, contrary to popular opinion, it had been the Nationalists and not the Communists who had fought with greater dedication against the Japanese invasion. Bell, "Our China Policy," *SPJ*, May 1, 1950, 6–7. He also said, on the other hand, that the US had been naïve about the trustworthiness of its Nationalist allies. "None of that which has been written can in any way ignore the fact that the post-war Nationalist government gradually became more and more corrupt. Nor can it be ignored that this corruption was fostered and furthered by pouring in of American equipment and money **without the American supervision down to the point of ultimate use**." Boldface in original. Bell ultimately blamed the US for the loss of China and described the fall of China in stark terms, saying, "One of the great tragedies of our generation is that China today is listed as a potential enemy and is under the domination of a government which is actively and openly anti-American. Such a situation need not and should not have occurred. It is the worst single diplomatic defeat in the history of the United States and it has, potentially, changed the balance of world power. That those who are responsible for this debacle should continue in positions of power within our government is hard to understand." Bell, "Shall We Recognize Communist China?" *SPJ*, October 11, 1950, 3. Bell also attacked the American government for what he considered "double dealing" by granting the Soviets, who had fought the Japanese for six days, a seat at the negotiating table ending the Pacific War, while excluding the Nationalist Chinese, who had fought Tokyo for eight years. Bell, "Seeing Jesus," *SPJ*, September 12, 1951, 3. *SPJ* printed an article by Congressman Walter Judd which spoke sharply against underestimating the goals of Mao's regime. "The first requirement of a policy is that we wake up to the real nature of the Communistic movement in China and to the fact that its real target is ourselves. ... [M]any of us maintained that there was some hope in the Chinese Government and none in the Communists, because they are committed to dictatorship and to world conquest." He went on to call for isolation for the new government and increased aid to the old regime now exiled on Formosa. "In short, what China has most needed all along and needs now is not more aid but proper aid, which is what we have not given since 1945. Munitions without American advice and assistance in their use cannot succeed any more than advice without munitions could succeed." Walter H. Judd, "What Should United States Policy in China Be?" *SPJ*, July 1, 1950, 4–5. Much of the commentary on China in *SPJ* spoke of

position can seem baffling, but it points to the uncertainty of the times. China had only just turned red, and it was not inconceivable to even experienced observers that it might not change once more.

THE ENEMY WITHIN

Evangelicals are often critiqued for getting carried away with the Red Scare. The fact that these evangelical magazines would publish several articles either about or by J. Edgar Hoover does not help with this reputation. However, to write off all concerns about Soviet infiltration as the product of a Cold War fantasy, present only in the imaginations of right-wing extremists, is a rather Manichean understanding of the times. It was hardly paranoia to think that Russians were working to undermine their American opponents in all sorts of ways, no more than it would be fanciful to suggest that the Americans were seeking to do the same to their rivals. At the same time it is fascinating that, far from letting these fears deprive them of their senses entirely, several magazines published articles critiquing the excesses of the anti-Communist movement. They did not lessen their insistence to root out Communists wherever they might be found, but they did call upon those doing the rooting to take care as they did their work. After all, it would hardly stop Communism to ban those who were not Communist. Getting carried away in the heat of the moment is fairly ordinary. Taking steps to keep from getting carried away is worth remembering.

AMERICA

AMERICA THE BEAUTIFUL

The Eisenhower years have been sometimes seen as defined by naïve optimism and absolute patriotism, but this does not quite fit the reality of evangelicals' commentary on the United States. As the calendar turned to the 1950s, the place of America in the words of evangelical observers underwent a shift to the negative. Paeans to "Old Glory" were dropped by the wayside and replaced with warning flags all around.

---

the Chinese themselves passively. They had fallen on hard times because of what others had or had not done.

It is not that they suddenly started speaking only negatively about America, but they spoke of the positives primarily in terms of being threatened with disappearance or destruction. A writer in *SPJ* pointed to this hesitancy with his words, "We think in America, and our hearts say, 'America the Beautiful,' and then our minds think of some other things about America and there is a question mark in our minds and in our hearts, and we say: 'America the Beautiful?' "[24] Another author with the same magazine added, "Our nation has now rebuilt its armed forces so that we are once again the dominant power in the world today. With this action, the American people have bought an insurance policy against aggression. Have we likewise rebuilt our spiritual forces up to be a dominant power for righteousness in the world today?"[25] An advertisement connected the endurance of American liberties with the preservation of Christianity in academia.

> Our flag is the sign of freedom around the world. We are justly proud of our emblem and what it stands for in lives, in loyalty and sacrifice, in the promise of liberty and justice for all. But pride is not enough! Freedom so dearly won must be greatly cherished. Where are those who will do in the future what our fathers did in the past? ... Let us keep our freedom by keeping Christ in all education.[26]

---

24. W. G. Foster, "America the Beautiful?" *SPJ*, June 20, 1951, 11. These lines were part of a regular sample devotional program for readers. Immediately after these words Foster said, "This program is designed to remind us why there is a question mark and how it can be removed and become an exclamation point." Some of what followed praised America for its glories, but other parts were more critical. For example, after describing some of the technological marvels created by America, Foster added, "Today our dreams have come tumbling down around our ears and science has led us to become captive to the fear of the atomic bomb and the H-bomb."

25. Roy LeCraw, "A Message for Presbyterians," *SPJ*, July 4, 1951, 1–2. The byline indicates that LeCraw had been the commander of an American Air Force bomber wing. His overall message was a call for repentance as the only hope for the nation. He said, "History holds no record of a nation on its knees being destroyed from within or without."

26. Advertisement for the Presbyterian Educational Association of the South, *SPJ*, July 1, 1953, 16. In a rather more dramatic fashion another message to the country came with the warning, "America Beware the *rage* of the *godless* THREATENS OUR LAND!" With equal parts sensationalism and vagueness, an advertisement for Scripture Press warned readers of the dangers posed to the republic. "Beware,

The nation at large may have been thinking "In God We Trust," but evangelicals were doubtful that this was true.

WE LIKE IKE

President Eisenhower presented evangelicals with a fascinating prospect. Here was a war hero and now supreme political leader in America who was quite open about his personal Christian faith in ways that seemed to go beyond mere posturing. Barnhouse said of him, "Eisenhower has well expressed his simple faith on several occasions. It is not a very well-informed faith, from the point of view of a Bible-taught Christian, but is in line with Christian principles."[27] A writer for *SPJ* also called attention to the new president's immature faith, but challenged readers to be patient with Eisenhower's faltering steps as they were "headed in the right direction."[28] A piece in *Moody* described the statements by Eisenhower about the relationship between religion and the state favorably, noting that the new president was very keen to connect a strong faith and a strong nation.[29] Wilbur Smith reiterated this theme, saying, "At no ceremonies relating to the inauguration of a President of this country in the twentieth century ... have there been

---

America. ... The awful beast lunges toward us! Look before it destroys, and brings death to what we hold so dear. The rage of the godless threatens our very lives. Unbelief and compromise have weakened our defense. *For this national tragedy the churches must bear a full share of blame.*" Parents were urged to see if their children's Sunday School materials had "degenerated into places of social learning and [had] failed to mold God-fearing men and women to teach and to lead this hour of national crisis." While the ad did not specify just who the external, godless foe might be, it did picture this "beast" in the form of a bear, which could plausibly be seen then as a stand-in for Russia. However, other versions of this same basic ad portrayed a claw-like hand reaching for children in a church. Advertisement for Scripture Press, *MM*, August 1951, 825. Capitalization and italics in original.

27. Barnhouse, "For Whom to Vote," *ET*, November 1952, 42.

28. Anonymous, "Quench Not the Smoking Flax," *SPJ*, February 4, 1953, 3. Given Bell's predilection for political commentary, it seems likely that Bell was the writer. The article itself was unsigned which might suggest that the editor, Henry Dendy, was the author rather than Bell, the associate editor. However, a poetic editorial later said that Bell had not gone away despite the absence of his signed article. "He's just hiding—he hopes with grace, behind anonymity." The Editors, "Where is 'L.N.B'?" *SPJ*, March 11, 1953, 2.

29. Paxton, "Faith, Government and Sense," *MM*, April 1953, 594.

as many references to the need for faith in God, and reports of such frequent attendance of church, as in the recent one of President Dwight D. Eisenhower."[30]

Courier was a bit skeptical at first, saying that there was some uncertainty about the erstwhile general. Not long before Eisenhower announced his entry into the 1952 race, Courier wrote, " 'I Like Ike,' blossoming celluloid buttons are trumpeting, but nobody is quite sure what Ike likes. Ike himself hasn't had too much to say—not even when he hurried home in November." Courier then cynically suggested that Eisenhower was keeping quiet about his intentions as a political ploy.[31] By the following year Courier had come around. With Eisenhower now inaugurated as president, he wrote glowingly, "In contrast to the festive spirit of Washington's Inauguration Day crowds, was the spiritual note introduced by the new president. ... Ike rested his left hand on two Bibles and took the oath of office. His first act as President was the offering of a prayer in which he asked the audience to join him." After quoting

<hr />

30. Smith, "Religion in the White House," *MM*, May 1953, 655. Henry was hesitant regarding Ike. Immediately after the 1952 election, he asked his listeners what sort of standard the president-elect would show for America "in the matter of church membership and attendance, prayer meeting attendance, devotion to prayer, and concerning the place of the Word of God in modern life?" and he critiqued Eisenhower for not belonging to any church. This was no minor fear for Henry. Right after these words he rebuked Eisenhower's predecessor, saying this was "a question which, had Harry Truman answered it differently, might have assigned him the destiny of lifting the world out of moral apathy and chaos and restoring it to spiritual health instead of leaving it to the indecision of neo-paganism." Generally speaking, evangelical writers of the time had little use for Truman. Henry, November 5, 1952, Box "Let the Chips Fall," Rolfing Library Archives, Trinity Evangelical Divinity School, Deerfield, Illinois. There are two manuscripts dated November 5, 1952. Schaeffer thought Truman had accelerated the slide towards socialism as seen below in footnote 412. In the lead-up to the 1952 election, Barnhouse wrote, "The nation has never perhaps been governed by such a babe as Harry S. Truman. Beyond question his political naïveté, coupled with his narrow outlook ... has brought us to a very low place in the eyes of the world. ... The fact that we fight China today is the direct responsibility of Mr. Truman, Mr. Acheson, and their helpers. Any change from this leadership must be for the better. It is fortunate that the two candidates, General Eisenhower and Governor Stevenson are both men of very high caliber, tried and proven. Either of them would make a good president, and Americans can hold their heads higher after the little politician has gone back to Missouri." Barnhouse, "For Whom to Vote," *ET*, November 1952, 13.
31. Gabriel Courier, "Ike," *CH*, January 1952, 10.

the prayer, Courier concluded, "Thus President Dwight D. Eisenhower shouldered the tremendous burdens of his office."[32] On the one hand it is odd that evangelicals fell so much in love with the card-playing occasionally foul-mouthed career soldier, but, on the other hand, they were able to point to times when their new hero had gone above and beyond in his association with their own movement.

Some, however, were more extreme in their support, but this had more to do with America as a whole than the individual president. The analysis of Russian-born Hyman Appleman on the role of the United States and Eisenhower in world affairs was quite stark. "Behind the tensions which are ever drawing tighter, Satan is on one side, but God is on the other." Thus far his summary was within the norms of evangelical pronouncements, but his commentary then went beyond this and named national representatives of this cosmic war.

> [Soviet leader] Malenkov is not Satan, but in a very terrible way he is for all that for which Satan has been campaigning. Eisenhower is not God, but in some measure he stands for that which is pleasing to Him. By Eisenhower, of course, I mean the United States, the United Nations after a fashion. By Malenkov, I mean Russian ideologies, Communism and the Communistic countries as a whole.

While he did qualify this extreme statement by saying that America had to make sure that God was on its side, he did double-down by saying that were the US to get right with God, he would fight the Russians for America.[33]

The Godless Nation

Not everyone agreed with this assessment. Carl F. H. Henry, for example, saw America as a country in danger, but it was in danger from its own inadequacies. It was not tanks and bombs which most threatened his homeland but a false religion prevalent at home as well as

---

32. Courier, "Invocation," *CH*, March 1953, 11.
33. Hyman J. Appelman, "Can Eisenhower Stop Malenkov?" *MM*, August 1953, 863-64, 888-89.

abroad. Writing in *The Watchman Examiner*, Henry said, "The extent to which Americans think that naturalistic Communism can be adequately met and refuted by some other species of naturalism is mute evidence of the declension which has befallen our culture." From his viewpoint all the efforts put forward by Americans to fight their tyrannical rival were doing little more than establishing its mirror image at home. Continuing, he said, "The hour of peril for a nation established on Christian bases has arrived when a substantial block of its citizens think they are resisting an enemy philosophy while actually they are promoting another variety of the same species of thought."[34] He reiterated this a year later on his radio show, saying, "American policy and Communistic policy agree in the rejection of Christ and Christianity as the relevant solution of the critical problems of our age; they disagree as to what the solution is, but they agree in seeking a solution other than the Christian solution."[35] Rather than seeing the United States as "God's Country" or advocating any kind of governmental theism, Henry had grave doubts about even the semblance of Christian faith in the land. To him, America was a nation which had completely lost its way.

This uncertainty about American holiness was a common refrain from Henry. In a letter to Senator Nelson Dilworth, he wrote, "The founding fathers of our nation knew that it was Christianity which rescued the western world from paganism; we have forgotten it in the west, simply because we are gliding back into paganism again."[36] In response to a 1952 poll suggesting that 99% of Americans believed in God, Henry replied cynically,

> The vast majority of Americans today may believe in a ghost god, in a phantom god, in a god who makes very little difference in the great decisions of life and even less in the cares of everyday existence. ... These must be non-Christian gods, non-biblical gods,

---

34. Henry, "Modern Education and the Secularistic Tide," *The Watchman Examiner*, October 11, 1951, 965–66.

35. Henry, November 9, 1952, Carl F. H. Henry Papers, Box "Let the Chips Fall," Rolfing Library Archives, Trinity Evangelical Divinity School, Deerfield, Illinois.

36. Henry, Letter to Nelson Dilworth, Carl F. H. Henry Papers, Box 1953, File Correspondence to Senator Nelson Dilworth, Rofling Library Archives, Trinity Evangelical Divinity School, Deerfield, IL.

gods who have little in common with the gods of our fathers which many of these 99% of the Americans worship.[37]

Even political action by Christians would be of little merit unless Americans drastically changed their trajectory. On Election Day, 1952, Henry told his listeners, "We are doomed in America—and no majority ballot at the polls will ever be able to find a way around that doom—unless there is a rebirth of conscience, unless there is a reaffirmation of great conviction and ideals, which hold the line against a materialistic view of life, unless there is a return to God and to the churches."[38] In a dramatic rebuke to any form of Christian nationalism or American moral superiority, Henry wrote,

> God is not above a righteous use of one degenerate segment of humanity to destroy another degenerate segment; he can loose the fanatic hordes of Russian Communism against us, before he deals with the Communists another way. God does not need an unmoral answer to Communism, for an unmoral answer is no answer, but only needs to be answered itself.[39]

Henry, a lifelong conservative, was as staunch an opponent of Communism as could be found among American evangelicals, but he still found room to rebuke his homeland for its many flaws.

Henry was not alone in this foreboding view of America's future. Some of L. Nelson Bell's declarations about the United States and its government were even more stark. He acknowledged that his homeland

37. Henry, October 17, 1952, Carl F. H. Henry Papers, Box "Let the Chips Fall," Rolfing Library Archives, Trinity Evangelical Divinity School, Deerfield, Illinois.

38. Henry, November 4, 1952, Carl F. H. Henry Papers, Box "Let the Chips Fall," Rolfing Library Archives, Trinity Evangelical Divinity School, Deerfield, Illinois. A failure to seek God was not just a failure for Henry's particular form of spiritual expression; failure here would mean a failure for human dignity. "The real center of reference for the American resistance of totalitarian statism is what the American people do with God. Indifference to God will mean indifference to human rights also, and no redefinition of human rights without God can amount to anything more than a disguised preparation for totalitarianism." Henry, November 17, 1952, Carl F. H. Henry Papers, Box "Let the Chips Fall," Rolfing Library Archives, Trinity Evangelical Divinity School, Deerfield, Illinois.

39. Henry, November 4, 1952, Carl F. H. Henry Papers, Box "Let the Chips Fall," Rolfing Library Archives, Trinity Evangelical Divinity School, Deerfield, Illinois.

was particularly lucky when it came to things like geography and cultural ability, but it lacked the "spiritual and moral leadership" needed to keep it from defeat and destruction. His solution was not to turn to the American leadership in increasing fealty to the state but for Christians to "humble themselves and pray and confess their sins and the sins of the nation."[40] Shortly thereafter he grimly stated that the US was more in danger from its own immorality than Russian malevolence.[41] At another time he concluded that "the low standards of morality and honesty brought to light in various Washington investigations are not peculiar to Washington but are a reflection of the conditions which are general all over America." This was no idle fear of moral contamination for Bell. He concluded this article, saying, "Judgment may be close, God offers us a choice as He offered to Judah of old—if we are willing and obedient to Him and His Word we can continue to eat the good of the land. But, if we refuse and rebel—JUDGEMENT IS CERTAIN!"[42] Whatever blessings America had received from God, and evangelical writers were keen to note those, all could be lost were the nation to stray too far. Unlike "Judah of old," America had no Abrahamic promise that it would endure.

Donald Grey Barnhouse was quite obviously a patriot who regularly spoke of American forces as "ours" and certainly hoped for a UN victory in Korea. Yet, at the same time, he saw a way in which victory might not be what America needed just then. "Every time I think about the

---

40. Bell, "The Way Out," *SPJ*, May 30, 1951, 2–3.

41. Bell, "Forward—On Our Knees," *SPJ*, June 6, 1951, 1.

42. Bell, "Before America There Lies a Choice and It Must Be Made Soon," *SPJ*, October 24, 1951, 3. Capitalization in original. In the same article Bell spelled the one word both as "judgment" and "judgement." Despite this negativity, Bell did not think this meant that America was equal to its Cold War rivals in depravity. In response to a statement by his denomination which had, to his mind, equated American and Soviet moral failings, Bell granted that the US was in dire need of confession and repentance but stated, "We refuse to have the record of American idealism and world-wide philanthropy compared with the ruthless invasion and exploitation of Poland, Esthonia [sic], Lithuania, Latvia, East Germany, Hungary, Czechoslovakia, North Korea, China, etc. etc. etc., and the carefully planned infiltration of other nations which is going on today, with the same ultimate view of destruction and exploitation." Bell, "A Strange Pronouncement," *SPJ*, November 18, 1953, 2.

situation in Korea, and every time I pray for our Armies there, there is the temptation to pray for victory, and I find that the Holy Spirit … puts a block in my mind that makes it impossible for me to pray for victory." He then said that he felt quite comfortable praying for conversion and Christian growth of those in the American forces, "but I am unable to pray for a national victory. I believe it would be very bad for us as a nation." After describing the decision to pursue Communist forces into North Korea and the subsequent Chinese counteroffensive, he said, "This action, however, is leading to crushing defeat, and great humiliation for this country. This, at least is an affirmative answer to our prayers, public and private, that God shall do to this country that which we most need."[43]

Schaeffer, likewise, had doubts about the future of liberty in the Land of the Free. In a theme that would run throughout his professional life, he argued that true human freedom could only grow in the soil of biblical Christianity. In 1951 he wrote, "I have been thinking a lot about these things, and for me the crux of the matter is this question of human liberty, which I do believe only comes in its full form when Christianity has been preached and received by an appreciable number of people in a society."[44] He further held that liberty could not exist without Christianity as a basis. "After a nation increases in personal liberty and then through unbelief loses Christianity which provided the basis for it, what then happens to individual liberty? … I wonder if it is possible for a democracy to be maintained after the Christianity which has produced it has passed." He then argued that the recent history of the UK and US proved his point as the power of the state had grown dramatically.[45] The following year he wrote of the irony of recent American history,

---

43. Barnhouse, "National Predicament," *ET*, February 1951, 12.

44. Schaeffer, Letter to J.O. Buswell, April 16, 1952, Francis A. Schaeffer Collection, Box 57, File 22, The Library, Southeastern Baptist Theological Seminary, Wake Forest, North Carolina. The original document indicates that this letter was written to "J.C. Buswell." This is likely a typographical error and should read "J.O. Buswell." The Schaeffer collection has several other letters to J.O. Buswell, a prominent Presbyterian theologian of the day.

45. Schaeffer, Letter to Robert G. Rayburn, July 16, 1951, Francis A. Schaeffer Collection, Box 57, File 22, The Library, Southeastern Baptist Theological Seminary, Wake Forest, North Carolina.

saying, "This is surely another step in our country's deficiencies. It is an interesting thing that our day is a time when men would kill democracy under the name of democracy, Christianity under the name of religion and freedom under the name of freedom."[46] Rather than seeing America as the protector of Christianity, Schaeffer saw Christianity as the only thing which could save the nation, but the chances of such a salvation seemed to be slipping further away each day.

AMERICAN PREJUDICE

As had been the case during World War II, there were glimmers from evangelical commentators where they complained of their nation's treatment of ethnic minorities. With the trajectory of history moving toward the Civil Rights movement, this conversation became more focused on the place of African Americans. Some of the strongest words came from *ET* magazine. For example, an editorial rebuked America for its racial prejudice and segregation, with Christians coming in for particular condemnation. The author tacitly rebuked the state of race relations in US churches by stating, "Statistics show that politics, sports, education, trade unions, and industry have more strides in breaking down racial barriers than have the church. It would appear that less than 1 per cent of all the churches in the USA have members of more than one race."[47] The following year he wrote again of this state of affairs, saying,

---

46. Schaeffer, Letter to J.O. Buswell, July 7, 1952, Francis A. Schaeffer Collection, Box 57, File 22, The Library, Southeastern Baptist Theological Seminary, Wake Forest, North Carolina. In another letter to Buswell a few weeks earlier, Schaeffer wondered about what he considered the slide of America into Socialism. "From a practical viewpoint, I wonder about the following: If I am correct about what I said in the previous paragraph, should we then who are Bible-believing Christians in the States, consider it a religious responsibility to preach aloud and speak against the Democratic Party as Christians from the pulpits, etc.—not because the President happens to try to send an Ambassador to the Vatican but on these socialistic tendencies. My own impression is that most of our Bible-believing Christians in the States would not be willing for this. And yet, as I say, there is no question in my mind that the Democratic Party, since Roosevelt, has actually taken further steps along this line than some of the socialistic parties on the continent." Schaeffer, Letter to J.O. Buswell, May 30, 1952, Francis A. Schaeffer Collection, Southeastern Baptist Theological Seminary, Wake Forest, North Carolina.

47. Barnhouse, "Racial Barriers," *ET*, February 1952, 32.

If that [situation] does not bring a deep sense of sorrow to your heart, and a poignant desire that the grief of the Holy Spirit should be stopped in this great *sin* against the Lord who shed His blood for black, white, brown, yellow, and red, then I have a right to wonder if you have really understood the nature of the sacrifice of Calvary and the wonder of your own personal salvation through grace.

Concluding, he added, "May the blessing of the Father, Son and Holy Spirit be upon any and upon all who do anything to change 11 o'clock Sunday morning from the most segregated hour to the time of common worship from all the hearts for whom Christ died."[48] Saying this at the dawn of the twenty-first century would still sting many readers' ears; to say it in 1953 was more than a little bold.

ET also published another article which blasted American Christians for their racism. The author wrote, "But there is one sin that evangelical Christians seldom write about, for someone might be offended—or could it be that we ourselves might be convicted? Most of us do not even pray about it. Either we do not see this sin, or we think it too large a problem even for God." As to why the church had not dealt with it, she had this to say: "It's not even a sin, only human nature, some think. Or

---

48. Barnhouse, "The Most Segregated Hour," *ET*, July 1953, 8. Italics in original. In another piece he quoted extensively from a Congressional speech made by a Representative from Illinois, William L. Dawson. Barnhouse noted that the congressman was a combat veteran who had volunteered to fight in the First World War and been gassed and wounded in battle with the Germans. After Dawson said, "I would give up my life of mine to preserve this country and every American in it, white or black," he demanded of the other representatives, "Deny to me, if you will, all that American citizenship stands for. I will still fight for you, hoping that under the Constitution of the United States all these restrictions will be removed and that we will move before the world as one people, American people joined in a democracy toward all the world." Speaking to the vital concern of the day, Dawson said, "I say to you who claim to love America in this hour of distress that the greatest argument the Soviet Union is using among the black peoples of the world to turn them against us is your treatment of me, me an American citizen." Barnhouse, "Segregation," *ET*, August 1951, 35. His concern about racism extended beyond the United States. He rebuked South Africa for its refusal to grant visas to two American bishops on account of their African race. As he put it, "It is rather startling to see a headline 'Negroes Are Refused Entrance into Africa.' " Barnhouse, "Negroes Unwelcome in Africa," *ET*, June 1953, 9.

it may lift up its head and claim to be a virtue. For this sin is that form of pride that is called prejudice. Because each man's prejudice is the dear child of his own natural heart he nourishes it and protects it as long as he can from the searching light of God's Spirit." She challenged those who gave to the Christian work of others overseas but showed no Christian love themselves at home.

> If we are really burdened by the love of the lost in far away countries, would any of us hesitate to sit beside the same kind of people in America? If our hearts bleed for the eternal welfare of men and women and children in the Congo, how would we react when worldly people organize to force out of our neighborhood a family of another race who had been trying to bring their children away from the foul air and more foul moral atmosphere of the slums?"[49]

49. Helen Sigrist, "Prejudice: The Respectable Sin," ET October 1953, 14–15. As in years before, SPJ was less exemplary in its understanding of race relations. In June 1950 Bell wrote favorably of the decision to segregate a youth conference along racial lines. "Intermingling on a social basis has been a serious problem at the Young People's Conference. Many young people have been led to feel that, 'one is not Christian,' unless he or she enters into these social contacts. The Board has looked deeply and frankly into the implications of this situation and has acted realistically and courageously. It has decided that in the future the Young People's Conference will not be on an inter-racial basis, so far as Montreat is concerned. ... [W]e believe an honest, a realistic and a Christian position has been taken, a position which may do much to clear our thinking and also guard against more serious problems in the future." Bell, "Race Relations and Montreat," SPJ, June 15, 1950, 2–3. Bell then followed up this article a month later expanding on these points in response to criticism. Bell, "Race Relations at Montreat," SPJ, July 15, 1950, 5–6. Also that same month, SPJ printed an article strongly defending segregation. The writer's main point in this case was that God had ordained that the races be kept separate socially and sexually. He backed up this mandate by appealing to a medical doctor who had indicated the mixing of racing produced "hybrids" which were not as strong as those of either race in its purity. William H. Frazer, "The Social Separation of the Races," SPJ, July 15, 1950, 6–7. Interestingly, SPJ printed an article in their "Young People's Department" condemning prejudice and saying, "One of the most tragic fruits of prejudice is neglect. God made us our brothers' keeper, and charged us with the responsibility of caring not only for our brothers, but of sharing with all men the unsearchable riches of His grace. If we entertain prejudice in our hearts, holding some in contempt while serving others, we are not fulfilling our Lord's commands, and many will suffer loss by reason of our neglect. Sometimes we turn aside from needs because of racial prejudice. Then we often neglect those whom

Such condemnations moved beyond the expected evangelical denunciations of "wine, women, and song," and, like the complaints of Henry and Schaeffer, pointed to a deeper sickness in American life. Evangelicals continued to back their nation in its opposition to the Soviet Union and its Communist ideology, but many times this support was closer to the mere co-belligerency of the enemy of an enemy than support for the nation's virtues.

WAR

Same Tune, Different Verse

The world of the early 1950s seemed designed to induce despair for the prospects of peace. The victory of the Allies in the 1940s had not changed human nature, and the events of the years which followed gave only further evidence to evangelicals that their pessimistic anthropology was built on a strong foundation. In 1951 Culbertson began an article positively, saying, "For a score of years November 11 seemed very meaningful. A terrible war had been fought and won. ... Though there were clouds and revolutions, in local wars, in the indecision and inactivity of international authority, the passing of years seemed to revive the shattered sanguine hopes for a warless world." However, his tone shifted downwards immediately, saying, "But with a second World War [sic] on the pages of history, with the conflict in Korea, with a third world conflict an ominous possibility, can we celebrate Armistice Day?" He thought the future was indeed hopeless, if humanity banked on the abilities of "unregenerate men," but there was a place for working for peace with prayer and an expectation of God's plan for the world.[50] Henry said much the same thing, arguing, "There is no precedent in all history for the avoidance of war. I do not think we should take a pessimistic attitude about it, as if war is inevitable, but we had better

---

we consider 'socially incompatible' as far as our own church groups are concerned ... if we feel that certain races and classes of men are beneath our consideration, or are beyond reach, we will turn aside in our neglect; neglect born of prejudice, and because of us they may never know the way of salvation through the blood of Jesus Christ." H. Lawrence Love, "Roots of Prejudice," *SPJ*, July 8, 1953, 15.

50. Culbertson, "Thoughts for Armistice Day, 1951," *MM*, November 1951, 147.

take a realistic attitude. ... The Bible knows no answer to the problem of war other than the answer to the problem of man, the answer to the problem of sin, and that answer is Jesus Christ."[51] Any attempt at peacemaking through human means was pointless if not downright harmful in and of itself. Only Christianity offered a solution to humanity's violence-prone nature.

Schaeffer also looked to a theological hope for humanity's present troubles, and put little stock in peace conferences and treaties. To him the external conflicts which oppressed people down through the ages were merely the manifestations of humanity's endemic and intrinsic corrupted nature. Responding to a letter from a woman inquiring about the Christian response to war, he wrote,

> As far as the question about why God allows war and so on. The first part of this answer is that after all the world is not as God made it. He made it perfect and then man deliberately sinned and because of this sin the whole universe is different from what God made. Thus, in this sense we can say we live in an abnormal universe, i.e., it is different from the perfect world God made. Wars, and in fact all the sorrows of life spring from this.

Continuing, Schaeffer looked to the return of Jesus as the ultimate hope for peace, but he also included hope for the meantime in the efforts of believers to convert their neighbors to Christianity. In keeping with his Reformed theology, Schaeffer saw evangelism as a means to restore the present world and not just a means of escape from the final judgment.

> Therefore, I have the feeling that if we are going to be any help in this vicious circle that leads to wars, etc., we can not just deal with the external things but must get to the heart of the matter. That is that those who spend their lives leading others to the Lord Jesus as Saviour, though their work may seem small, yet

---

51. Henry, November 9, 1952, Carl F. H. Henry Papers, Box "Let the Chips Fall," Rolfing Library Archives, Trinity Evangelical Divinity School, Deerfield, Illinois. Likewise, Bell said, "The solution of our problem does not lie in money or in armaments. God alone can help and we do not believe He will do so until we return to Him." Bell, "Peace Cannot Be Bought," *SPJ*, August 1, 1950, 2.

nevertheless are really doing more than all the great plans the world can make to overcome war and these other things.[52]

Human society could be transformed, but only after a sufficient number of human beings were first transformed and then worked to change the habits and structures making human corruption manifest.

This sort of thinking was the root of evangelical opposition to pacifism. It was not that they did not want peace. It was that they thought pacifism would bring anything but peace. Pacifism was more than ineffective; it was counterproductive. Bell critiqued the attempts by American pacifists to achieve peace through an absolute principle of nonviolence. "Pacifists and propaganda for pacifism are permissible within the rights of a free people, but the only way pacifism can continue is *for others to fight* to preserve the way of freedom which makes such propaganda possible. Appeasement of evil has never resulted in the triumph of right." He conceded the good intentions of such Christians but even so pointed to the danger posed by their positions, saying, "Given their own way, they would inadvertently, but none the less surely, deliver America and all we hold dear, into the hands of the most diabolical system the world has ever seen."[53] When flawed human nature was coupled to a tyrannical ideology like Communism, a dedication to pacifism could yield only surrender and enslavement.

PLACING THE BOMB

The bomb presented a challenge to evangelical commentators, as it did to any who spoke into society. It was a weapon, but, for most of them, it was more than a weapon, and they struggled to know how to relate to it. Despite later working together for several years at *CT*, Henry and Bell discussed atomic war in very different ways. Henry was at pains to tell his listeners what was at stake in the atomic contest. "On every hand leaders are reminding us that war is 'a loathsome and useless relic of barbarism', that the next great war cannot escape the dimensions of

---

52. Schaeffer, Letter to Molly Holt, February 23, 1952, Francis A. Schaeffer Collection, Southeastern Baptist Theological Seminary, Wake Forest, North Carolina.

53. Bell, "No Time for Pacifism," *SPJ*, September 13, 1950, 6.

a conflict more deadly and devastating than any in previous history."
Referring to a recent book on a post-nuclear world, he said,

> Drop the next bomb ... let it go over New York or Moscow, over
> Los Angeles or Korea, and the game is on, that great game with
> the nations of the world for the stakes, with millions of lives
> gambled on the turn of hydrogen or atomic dice, that big game
> which takes us all in, and after which, if there are any of us
> left ... [we can] agree that here is one past civilization that the
> archaeologist's spade will never be able to turn up.

He feared modern civilization was rushing toward its destruction,
driven by its own advancement. "We are devoting the genius of our age
to the development of weapons so destructive that they have no value
for defense, but can serve only an offensive and destructive purpose."[54]
He reminded his listeners that America alone had used such weapons
in warfare. "They dropped the bomb, and if there was any guilt in the
dropping of that bomb, in the sudden erasure of those Japanese lives,
in the distorted features and ugly scars and suffering bodies which
we bequeathed to a multitude of blistered survivors, we share in that
guilt." He said that most Americans agreed that the lives saved through
this act was worth the cost to Japan, but he offered a warning about
what doing so may have meant for the US: "Our political and military
leaders did so without preparing the inhabitants of our great land to
think through the ethical implications of the use of the bomb, and as a
consequence ... there is the greatest moral uncertainty and indefinite-
ness in the minds of great masses of people about the ethical legitimacy
or illegitimacy of such a weapon in modern warfare." He then held the
American government to a high moral standard, saying,

> If our leaders know some moral and spiritual justification for
> the use of the atomic and hydrogen bomb in international war-
> fare, they had better implant these convictions in the conscience
> of the nation; if they know no such rationale, and contemplate

---

54. Henry, November 9, 1952, Carl F. H. Henry Papers, Box "Let the Chips Fall,"
Rolfing Library Archives, Trinity Evangelical Divinity School, Deerfield, Illinois.

the use of the bomb, they had better stop prattling to the world about our concern for ethical and spiritual realties. What is needed urgently in the United States is a frank presentation by our statesmen and military leaders of the ethical implications surrounding the use of the bomb."[55]

Yet, even as he considered the horrors of a nuclear exchange, Henry did not rule out the possibility of an ethical use of such devastation. He suggested that there may be a time when circumstances called for the destruction which was part and parcel of such methods. He was emphatic that the US must make its moral case clear to both itself and the watching world. Failure to do so would risk "dulling what sense of moral alertness survives in the [western world], by precipitating us unexpectedly over the precipice of ethical chaos."[56] An America with so many fundamental moral failings was hardly one which he trusted always to make the right decision.

Bell, on the other hand, again saw no particularly new ethical implications arising from the bomb, but this was not from a lack of concern over the devastation. He knew what the bomb could do, but declared that he could "see no difference in wiping out a city in a moment of time and in taking two days to do it. Both are horrible to contemplate." He found it inconsistent to take a stand on atomic warfare while ignoring the results of conventional bombings such as the Anglo-American air raids which had just as thoroughly destroyed German cities, even if such destruction took days rather than seconds.[57] Late in 1952 he

---

55. Henry, November 17, 1952, Carl F. H. Henry Papers, Box "Let the Chips Fall."

56. Henry, November 17, 1952, Carl F. H. Henry Papers, Box "Let the Chips Fall." The full quote is, "We had better not let the world overhear us speaking about the use of atom bombs and hydrogen bombs, against a Communist 'might makes right' philosophy, without making it abundantly clear that in our case this superior might is being used because right requires it, and indeed makes its use unavoidable, and even makes a failure to discharge atom and hydrogen bombs over certain cities a wicked and immoral thing. We had better exhibit the ethical compulsion of such an act to the world and to our own people, or the dropping of these bombs, even it should succeed in bringing us peace in our time, may do so by dulling what sense of moral alertness survives in the [western world], by precipitating us unexpectedly over the precipice of ethical chaos."

57. Bell, "The Atom Bomb," SPJ, December 13, 1950, 4.

challenged the hesitation of the United States to use its atomic stockpile to end hostilities in Korea. He argued that just as it would be sheer folly to refuse to use anything but ordinary rifles while having machine guns in the US arsenal, so, too, it continued to be pointless to refrain from using atomic bombs when their raw power could break the stalemate and bring victory. Then, admitting it could more complicated than that, he went on, "There are, of course, the strategic and military problems involved and these should be the final and determining factor. If atomic warfare will end the war in Korea then the sooner it is started the better for all concerned."[58] The following year he articulated a version of what would later become known as Mutually Assured Destruction. When it became known that the Soviets would shortly be able to reach the United States with hydrogen bombs, he argued that America should accumulate sufficient stockpiles of atomic weapons that the "sheer fear of consequences" would keep Russia from using the bomb itself.[59]

Courier challenged some of the basis of disarmament talks and treaties. After discussing some ongoing peace talks, he pointed to the uselessness of such meetings, saying, "Let's face it, speeches notwithstanding. You don't get peace by laying down your cudgels. We've had disarmament conferences before. They all did the same thing." He then moved on to ask whether such endeavors missed the point. Acknowledging that the efforts of diplomats helped to diffuse tensions in some respects, he went on to ask, "But do *weapons* cause war? Granted, we have the A-bomb and we're working on the H-bomb—but do you feel like using either of them on England? Of course not. ... Weapons aren't the basic cause of tensions; tension produce the weapons. Take away Russia's bombs and our bombs—but nothing else—and all you'd have is a new atomic race." He did have hope, but his hope lay in another

---

58. Bell, "Paralyzed," *SPJ*, November 26, 1952, 3. This was one of the first political articles Bell had contributed to *SPJ* for quite some time, though previously such pieces by Bell had appeared regularly. Apparently, there had been some complaints about the appropriateness of political commentary in a religious periodical. Towards that end this article, along with another political piece preceding it, was prefaced by a note from Henry Dendy, editor of *SPJ*, acknowledging these complaints yet maintaining the importance of engaging the culture and claiming the precedent of biblical prophets who regularly challenged the government of their day.

59. Bell, "Not If But When?" *SPJ*, October 28, 1953, 2.

direction. "Disarmament has to begin at Something Else: a change of heart. Do we know how to bring that about? We are smart enough to build a bomb. Are we smart enough to build a friend?"[60] For the staff at *CH* who were giving voice to Courier, negotiations might be the most effective tactic toward world peace as a means to keep the nations talking, even if the ostensible purpose of such talks, the elimination of physical weapons, was a fool's errand. Ultimately, as with many other evangelical discussions on human conflict, the only way to ensure peace was for the people involved to be transformed by Christianity.

THE FORGOTTEN WAR

It took some time for reactions to the Korean War, as such, to appear in print. In October 1950, several months after the outbreak of hostilities, *Moody* editors pointed young men to an upcoming series in the magazine. "Young Men 18 to 26! So you're being drafted and you don't want to go. You can't work up any enthusiasm about fighting a war you don't understand. Are you bitter? Rebellious? Afraid? Dr. Robert G. Lee, president of the Southern Baptist Convention, has the answer for you in *MM*'s new Youth Supplement ... for November."[61] In initial installment of that series, Robert Lee alliteratively intoned, "Again, our country is at war. Upon us is war with its cruelties and crimson terrors—its battles, bursting bombs, bullets, blood—building to the world's folly and man's inhumanity to man that makes millions mourn, a monument of skulls and skeletons." In short order Lee summarized the tension in the classical Christian view of war. "War, the quintessence of all horrors the human heart has ever known, is upon us—with antagonists against all that is Christian making inexcusable aggression. And still we face the possibility of a third word war or surrender of our liberty-loving lives and blood-bequeathed liberties to the ideology of Communism."[62]

---

60. Courier, "Disarmament," *CH*, January 1952, 11. Italics and capitalization in original. His capitalization of "Something Else" likely means that he was referring to Christian conversion here.

61. The Editors, Announcement, *MM*, October 1950, 72.

62. Robert G. Lee, "Weighed and Found Worthy," *MM*, November 1950, 212. Presumably the author's affinity for alliteration likely came from the practices of his day job as a pastor.

Here was no Manichean view of the world. Certainly, the democracies of the West were vastly to be preferred over the tyranny of Moscow, but the author nowhere entertained a call for heedless violence against a faceless "them." War may have been justified in this case, but war was always horrible.

The longtime association of American missionaries with East Asia made this new conflict a personal affair. A former missionary to Korea brought an eyewitness's perspective to the Korean War. Eleanor Soltau wrote, "Those of us who love the country and its people are still dazed by Korea's sudden emergence into the full glare of worldwide attention. We can hardly believe that the military objectives mentioned in communiques are the picturesque towns and villages we remember so well." The author echoed many of the questions and concerns ringing in the minds of Americans who might have had trouble finding Korea on a map and were asking why Americans had to die for these strangers instead of simply using a few atomic bombs to clarify the situation. However, her affection for the Korean people led her to encourage Americans to support the war effort as worthy and even vital. "As we back up our government and our boys to the hilt, prayerfully watching for the outcome, let us never forget to pray for the Koreans of like precious faith ... in the north as well as in the south."[63] Support for the

---

63. Eleanor Soltau, "Spotlight on Koreans," *MM*, November 1950, 213, 216. Ellipses in original. The place of evangelism in the Korean War was an obvious area of interest for evangelicals. In a brief article on missionary work, *MM* readers were told of civilian massacres by North Korean troops as they retreated north. According to this report some thirty Christian leaders had been called to a meeting with the Communist representatives, and none of those thirty had been heard from since. The Editors, "From the Fields," *MM*, December 1950, 246. But there was also hope that Christian evangelism of enemy forces would bring some good out of the horrors of war. While Chinese forces in Korea were ostensibly volunteers, reports from prisoners indicated otherwise. According to a missionary working with Chinese POWs quoted in a *MM* news blurb, "nearly all reported they had been either captured while fighting in the Nationalist Army or drafted outright. Many were only sixteen or seventeen years old and most were badly wounded." The Editors, "News Report," *MM*, September 1951, 33. Barnhouse echoed this claim almost exactly: "Many of the prisoners captured among Northern troops were young men who had been rounded up and forced against their wills to carry arms." Barnhouse, "Postscript on Korea," *ET*, March 1951, 17. Whether this anecdote was representative of the general situation of Chinese troops, such stories helped to

American intervention was centered on the justness of the cause and not simply the fervor of nationalism in wartime.

Interestingly, Bell placed blame for the conflict and attendant suffering of the Koreans squarely on the leadership of the United States, saying, "America has probably never sinned against another nation as we have Korea. Our own plight in Korea today may prove our belated judgment on our own perfidity [sic]." He would not even grant to the United States the assumption that it now acted for the good of others but allowed only that this was about "saving face" before the rest of the world. He did not seem to expect a quick end to the fighting and called on Christians to pray for the forces sent into battle, noting that many of these young men had gone from the easy life of garrison duty in Japan to the front lines in Korea in a very short period of time.[64] Six months later he was to write of his despair that the now-retreating American

---

shape evangelical impressions of the Beijing government as tyrannical. North Korean troops who had been captured by UN forces were so grateful for the Bibles they had received from the American Bible Society that they sent a thank-you plaque "made of discarded dried-egg and fish cans, carefully flattened out, nailed together and decorated with a design in purple and white." According to the same article, hundreds of North Korean POWs had enrolled in a Bible correspondence course. The Editors, "News Report," *MM*, October 1951, 102. MBI proclaimed the effectiveness of one of its gospel films in leading several hundred Chinese POWs to convert: "The power of the Word was very evident recently at a showing of a Moody Bible Institute gospel-science film to Communist soldiers. ... Several hundred prisoners-of-war had come to see the Mandarin version of 'God of Creation,' shown by a Chinese evangelist. At the conclusion of the film, an invitation to receive Christ was given. *Three hundred Communists professed to accept Christ and prayed with the evangelist!*" Advertisement for MBI, *MM*, November 1951, 171.

64. Bell, "Korea," *SPJ*, July 15, 1950, 4–5. Bell found it frustrating that President Truman had dismissed Douglas MacArthur when the general was advocating what was to Bell only a common-sense approach to the war. "We have studied General MacArthur's statements and nowhere found even a suggestion that America become involved in a full-scale war in China. He has asked permission to bomb air bases in Manchuria from which American planes are being attacked—a reasonable request." Tying the Korean War to larger issues in East Asia, he hoped support of anti-Communist Chinese forces would enable peace to return to Korea. "Why should the financing and supplying with ammunition of the Nationalists in an invasion of China—an invasion which will be welcomed by 90 percent of the people—be considered such a grave threat to our own involvement in World War III? *How else can we hope to extricate ourselves from Korea?*" Bell, "Policies—Not Personalities," *SPJ*, April 25, 1951, 3.

forces were evidence that this conflict was far from over and was in fact merely one in a line of battles yet to be fought across the world.[65] The combination of America's failures before the war were being compounded by its many mistakes during the conflict.

Despite his regular condemnations of American morality, Henry was adamant that the United States should not come to terms with the Communists. When a group of clergy declared that war was the worst of all possible tragedies and called for an immediate end to the Korean War, Henry replied that war was not the worst thing possible and that a half-hearted peace would do nothing but ignore the sacrifices already made by American soldiers and encourage the Communists to attempt further aggressions. To him this was yet another example of American moral failure as his nation had demonstrated its unwillingness to "stand for the right."[66]

In contrast to its conciliatory approach to the new government in Beijing, articles in *ET* spoke very strongly against Russia's involvement in the Korean War, even if this would affect China. One called for an ultimatum to be sent to the Soviets, threatening an escalation by the United States if the Communist forces did not stand down.

> We must issue a flat ultimatum ordering Russia to give the word to her satellite Koreans to withdraw immediately, and that if she will not do so, we shall consider her an aggressor by her failure to keep her children in order. The ultimatum should say that we know that we are being fought in Korea by Russian war materiel, and that we consider it the act of an aggressor which will have to be dealt with directly.

---

65. Bell, "Blood, Sweat, and Tears," *SPJ*, December 27, 1950, 2. His disdain for America's wartime leadership continued into 1953, when he said, "In the Summer of 1951, when we had the Communist armies of Korea on the verge of complete defeat—this confirmed by the highest military authority—we joyously jumped at Moscow's offer of truce talks. By our act of stupidity we gained nothing—Communism gains it all. Today we are again faced by apparent offers of a reasonable solution. *This is a deadly peril.*" Bell, "A Deadly Peril," *SPJ*, April 8, 1953, 5. Italics in original.

66. Henry, November 5, 1952, Carl F. H. Henry Papers, Box "Let the Chips Fall," Rolfing Library Archives, Trinity Evangelical Divinity School, Deerfield, Illinois.

It had some specifics in mind were the Soviets to refuse to comply. "The Yalu River bridge, connecting Korea with the railroad line from Mukden, should be destroyed, and we should proceed to bomb all the arteries that link Korea with Russia. In any future aggression, we should follow the same policy."[67] Two years later an author had become quite frustrated with the bloody quagmire and said it was high time for a change of tactics. "If the United Nations are not ready to use the full strength of their force, including atomic weapons, and bombing the cities of China, there is no possible chance of breaking the deadlock."[68] That same year ET said that the message to the Communists should explicitly include the threat of atomic attacks on Chinese cities.[69]

Atomic weapons continued to horrify many evangelicals, but, in the midst of the Korean War, there were many, like Barnhouse above, who found their use to be acceptable in some way. Bell, for example, spoke of the advent of the weapons as nothing more than an acceleration of already existing destructive technology, and he argued that not to use them in the present context made no more sense than only to use rifles when machine guns were on hand. He was not so much underestimating the destructiveness of the bomb but highlighting the devastation which conventional war could inflict upon humanity. Others called for the use of the bomb against Communist targets out of frustration over the stalemate on the Korean peninsula. Therefore, this sort of appeal was not seen as increasing death and pain in the world. Death and pain were ongoing, and they saw nuclear weapons as a means to end the violence in one very fell swoop. There is a sense in which they had a point. The 100,000 and more people of Tokyo killed by American incendiary

---

67. Barnhouse, "A Window on the World," ET, January 1951, 36-37. Beginning this section of the article, he wrote, "For the sake of the record, I put down here what should be done, but which undoubtedly will not be done. Five years from now, however, if we are still permitted to publish a magazine, we believe we will quote this paragraph at a time when the rest of the nation will be saying it."

68. Barnhouse, "1952," ET, January 1953, 8.

69. Barnhouse, "Korean Debacle," ET, August 1953, 14. This is quite harsh, and it is hard to reconcile this with Barnhouse's earlier positive statements about the new China, but it is likely borne of his antipathy for Russia. While China played no great role in his eschatological views, Russia was a dominant actor. This will be discussed below.

bombs on the night of March 9–10, 1945, were not somehow less dead
than their fellow 100,000 and more people of Hiroshima five months
later. Yet, what Bell missed was that there was indeed something new
and utterly terrifying about this new product that was "Made in the
USA." The conventional destruction that he cited had taken hundreds
of thousands of soldiers or thousands of airmen flying hundreds of aircraft over the course of hours if not days or weeks. The atomic attacks
that Bell relativized had taken a crew of ten flying their single B-29 to
annihilate a goodly sized city in seconds. What these others missed was
what would happen were the atom bombs to start falling. Did they have
enough confidence in Comrade Stalin's humanitarianism to think that
he would not respond in kind against Western cities if US forces started
taking out targets in Manchuria? He might not have been able to reach
continental America, but he certainly could have reached continental
Europe. This was a new world.

END TIMES

The End is Nigh

"For the world at large, the fact that the nation of Israel intends to
strengthen its hold on Jerusalem by making it the seat of its national
government is not earth-shaking news. But for Christians in this day
of rapidly moving events, this decision is of more than surface importance. It should cause us to consider God's eternal plan: For Jerusalem
is destined for great things." Culbertson here made a clear connection
between global events in his day and the final events of human history.
He wondered if what he could see in the papers was what he read in his
Bible, but he was careful to couch it in hesitant language. "Here is not
the fulfillment of prophecy itself, but the shaping of events which may
well lead to the fulfillment of prophecy. Meanwhile other prophecies
are being fulfilled before our eyes. Though no man knoweth the day or
the hour, the age in which we live is fast drawing to a close."[70] To his way
of thinking the careful student of Scripture could see in the events of
the day a pattern emerging. It was not a matter of specific connections

---

70. Culbertson, "The Night is Far Spent," *MM*, February 1950, 380.

but of general trends. The world seemed to be drifting ever closer to the pattern he observed in the Bible. In March 1951 he argued that the combination of fear of war, the ineptitude of deliberative bodies like the United Nations, and the increasing power of "militant Communism" were preparing people to long for "strong-man leadership." This was no ordinary fear of dictatorship; this was a prediction that the ground was being readied for the end-times Antichrist.[71]

The eschatological interest seemed to be rising. A 1950 advertisement for MBI offered correspondence classes in prophecy which centered on Wilbur Smith's work. With a background photo of an atomic blast, the text read, "A magnificent study of the world of 1950 in light of the Word of God! Twelve fascinating chapter lessons, including such subjects as: 'The Increasing Demand for World Government,' 'The Re-establishment of Israel,' 'Russia's Prophetic Place in the Last Days,' 'At The Center of the Earth,' etc."[72] Speaking for himself a month later, Smith observed that the phrase "apocalypse," which even secular writers used more than any other to encompass the terror of the present age, came not from general literature but from the Bible: "As one moves through the vast literature created by the atomic bomb, it is significant that writers draw their phrases from a volume finished eighteen hundred years ago, parts of which were composed more than three thousand years ago."[73] Smith's writings made it clear that he believed that he was living in the last days of humanity, and he quite often argued his point from the Bible. However, he only rarely connected the dots of then-current events to scriptural passages with any specificity. His confidence in his conclusions was profound, but his assertions remained largely in generalities.

CLEAR SIGNS

While articles in *Moody* leaned heavily in a pro-Israeli direction, not all of its readers and writers were in favor of this stance. One letter to the editor in August 1950 rebuked the magazine for an article which

71. Culbertson, "Preparation for Last Things," *MM*, March 1951, 439.

72. Advertisement for MBI, *MM*, May 1950, 627.

73. Smith, "World Crises and the Prophetic Scriptures, Part I," *MM*, June 1950, 680.

he considered "sentimental whitewash." In response to the article's suggestion that the Arabs had left their home without compulsion, the reader said, "As if out of the clear sky, these people whose ancestors for centuries had populated the land should suddenly flee to the hills." After recounting Israeli atrocities, he concluded, "One wonders how soon and in what way the Almighty will deal with this ungodly Zionist aggression, which by all the many so-called Christians is being encouraged and sponsored."[74] The editors provided a counterpoint, of sorts, to this way of thinking with an article a few months later, which claimed that the Arab homes destroyed were those who had been vacated by people joining in the fight against the Israelis or who had fled to the Kingdom of Transjordan. The author did, however, express sympathy with the suffering of the Arabs, even if this sympathy would only go so far. "An Arab official in Hebron asked us if the people of the United States knew that there are Arabs in Palestine. They feel that everything has been and is being done for the Jews and nothing for them." The author suggested that anyone in their situation would feel as they did had they been "driven from their homes, either forcibly or by the fear of what might happen." Nonetheless, in what was far less comforting than he perhaps intended, he said that a better understanding of Israel's place in the Bible would ameliorate some of their sense of suffering.[75] It is unlikely that this would have made anyone feel better about exile.

Barnhouse was nearly as confident about end-times predictions as Gaebelein and English had been. While his Presbyterianism would ordinarily mean a lower emphasis on eschatology, he was also a Dispensationalist, which would lead him to grant the end of the world a higher prominence.[76] Sometimes he only made a tentative connection between contemporary events and biblical prophecy. Reacting to fears that the Israelis were becoming increasingly Marxist politically, he used end-times beliefs to calm his readers, saying,

---

74. G. Eric Matson, "Whitewash for Zionism?" *MM*, August 1950, 804–5.

75. Coulson Shepherd, "The Unholy Holy Land," *MM*, July 1951, 718–19, 762.

76. In one of the few times when his fellow Calvinists at *SPJ* made mention of eschatology during this period, Bell merely critiqued the World Council of Churches for undermining confidence in the second coming. Yet, in the same piece,

We need not be concerned about the situation in Israel, for we are convinced that it will remain conservative and attached to Western Europe. The situation as exists in Arabia, however, is very different. We have constantly affirmed that, in our opinion, and according to Bible prophecy, Russia would possess Persia and Arabia, and all the oil lands thereof. This is but a tendency that we are seeing today.[77]

At other times, however, he was more explicit. For example, in 1951 he suggested that the assassination of King Abdullah of Jordan and the intra-Arab conflict which followed was possibly an early step toward the Israeli capture of the whole of Jerusalem.[78] Then, in 1952, he connected the expected end-times revival of the Roman Empire with the early moves toward what would become the European Union, saying they were "undoubtedly a great step in that direction."[79] Likewise, in 1953 he saw a reported alliance between Greece, Turkey, and Yugoslavia as a move toward the new Roman Empire, too.[80] Probably more than anyone else aside from Gaebelein, Barnhouse saw the geopolitical conflicts of his day first and foremost through the lens of his eschatological presuppositions. He did not merely find parallels between contemporary events and ancient prophecies but determined his analysis of the present based on his expectations for the future.

---

he criticized those who would pay too much attention to eschatology and noted dispensationalists as regularly guilty of this latter offense. "The writer is just as aware as any that the certain coming of Christ has been preached by some almost to the exclusion of all other doctrines. He is also aware of the vagaries of extremists and of those who have accepted the dispensationalists' teaching, a position from which he most vigorously dissents. But, if the Bible teaches anything, it teaches that Christ is to return in person. Too often and too long this glorious truth has been played down. What the Church needs is a new emphasis on this Blessed Hope." Bell, "Evanston and the Lord's Return," *SPJ*, December 16, 1953, 3.

77. Barnhouse, "Window on the World," *ET*, January 1951, 36. Interestingly, although Barnhouse was deeply interested in eschatology, most of his comments about the State of Israel during this period focused on Israel's economic viability, demographic growth, and military capabilities. While these things certainly had implications for end times study, his eschatological attention was most often centered on nations outside of the State of Israel.

78. Barnhouse, "Arab Against Arab," *ET*, October 1951, 8.

79. Barnhouse, "Western European Unity," *ET*, May 1952, 15.

80. Barnhouse, "The Roman Empire Again," *ET*, June 1953, 34.

One of Barnhouse's common themes was that the Bible had pre-dicted the place of Russia in humanity's endgame.

> The word of God [gives] us no possible alternative. The powers of
> the North are to dominate all the territory outside the Old Roman
> Empire, and Russia is to reach down and dominate Germany. On
> several occasions I have pointed out that the empire of Russia is
> to extend over Persia and Arabia, and to penetrate into Africa.
> Today I am concerned with the advance of Russia into Persia,
> first step in the accomplishment of her plans in the Middle East.

He then described these as "plans which are following along the lines of prophecy, which is history written in advance." Concluding, he wrote that he had arrived at this opinion from both biblical study and ordinary observation. "I believe Persia is lost to us. It is merely a question of time. I believe it is not only because of Ezekiel 38 shows Persia as an ally of Russia in the time of the end, but because the tendency of today's history shows that the surging powers in that land have passed beyond the bounds of control by a selfish nation that lies across the world."[81] When addressing the report that an oracle from the Fatima Shrine in Portugal had instructed children to pray for Russia, Barnhouse responded to this hope for Russia with extreme skepticism. "We do not know what may happen in the intervening years to give the Devil credit for any improvements in Russian relationships, but we do know that the curse of God is upon Russia and that ultimately she is to be destroyed."[82] For Barnhouse eschatological concerns came first. Like all of his fellow evangelicals, he had great confidence in the word of God as supreme over human understanding. However, what made him and Gaebelein different is that this confidence extended to his eschatological perspective.

Henry, on the other hand, did not often make reference to the end of the world. He did use the advent of atomic weapons to chide those who doubted the reliability of the Bible and doubted that God would ever send judgment on the world. "And, by the way, do you remember

81. Barnhouse, "Russia Moves to Take Persia," ET, August, 1951, 11, 45.
82. Barnhouse, "Fatima and Russia," ET, August 1951, 36.

how this picture of the end of the world was ridiculed ten or fifteen years ago—this idea of the elements being destroyed by a great noise, fervent heat—back in the days when people didn't see the atom bomb and the hydrogen bomb around the corner of modern science felt it just couldn't be?"[83] His overall point was about the need to turn to God and not the end of the world, as such, but he did connect this present-day event with the Eschaton.

RECALIBRATING

For all the fears aroused by atomic warfare and Communist advances, the world did not end. The great charts and tables created to demonstrate the exactness of biblical prophecy all came to nothing. The stage was set, but the actors went off script. American-led alliances failed to keep China in the fold, but Russian advances in Europe, the Middle East, and East Asia were blunted or turned back. There was no more talk of a great Russo-German alliance slouching toward Bethlehem as at least the greater part of Germany was firmly allied to the West. All in all, the expansionist and oppressive nature of the Soviet-led regimes was enough to elicit evangelical fears without aid from eschatological sources. For example, throughout their articles and broadcasts on the Korean War, evangelicals gave clear pronouncements about what was right and what was wrong, yet they generally refrained from

---

83. Henry, November 7, 1952, Carl F. H. Henry Papers, Box "Let the Chips Fall." Eschatology was not Henry's ulterior motive here. The bulk of the broadcast dealt with the failure of analysts to predict the outcome of the 1948 presidential election or significant details about the 1952 vote. Similarly, just two few days later he said that "[the Bible] speaks of a horrible war which will bring down the curtain on human history." Here, too, eschatology was not his focus but merely a motivation to consider the claims of Christianity. Henry, November 9, 1952, Carl F. H. Henry Papers, Box "Let the Chips Fall." *ET*'s editors made a similar use of the bomb as an illustration of biblical principles. They described the devastation of a volcanic eruption in New Guinea and compared it to the relatively weak effects of atomic bombs and then said, "When the Great Tribulation finally comes to this earth and God begins to pour out his judgments it will make all of man's furies seem as picnics. Yet the world today is in stark fear of its own wars, and this is because it has abandoned any thought of God's judgment." The Editors, "A Window on the World," *ET*, April 1951, 7.

connecting Pusan, Inchon, and Seoul with anything from Ezekiel, Daniel, or Revelation.

That being said, as noted above there were those, like Barnhouse, who saw his as the last days of humanity and connected current events with eschatological themes. Even more than this, while some of his fellows seemed have let their end-times ideas influence their understanding of contemporary events, with Barnhouse, such ideas seemed to be taking the lead. He suggested that Persia was "lost" to the West because the Bible said so. Granted, Iran did part ways from the West, but not when or how Barnhouse would likely have ever expected it. In the same way for all his openness to positive elements of Mao's regime, he could not countenance anything good to be said about Russia. While he shared the general evangelical disdain for Soviet tyranny, he rejected Russia, in part at least, not for its Communism or oppressiveness but because his eschatological formulation dictated it. Since he was convinced that God would destroy Russia in the endgame of the world, and he was also sure that this was the end of the world, he said that the Soviets must be opposed. Similarly, he counseled people not to fear the Israelis siding with the Soviets not so much because of statements out of Tel Aviv but because he believed that they were to stay allied to the revived Roman Empire. However, Barnhouse and Gaebelein before him were the exceptions in this trend. Many evangelical writers, most notably Smith and English, were as convinced that the end was nigh as was Barnhouse. Yet, within their pronouncements was a level of hesitation. Even if some or even all of this caution were merely a front, this entails the awareness on their part that they could be shown wrong by future events. After all, those who cannot conceive of being wrong do not normally put escape clauses in their statements. They might be absolutely convinced of the accuracy of their understanding, but they had also seen many others before them be just as sure about things.

The rise of the State of Israel was one of those things in eschatological study where the nations of the world had not gone off script. End-times writers had for many years predicted that the Jews would go back to the land, and now they were there. For all intents and purposes, evangelical comments on the Jewish state were positive, yet there were a few murmurings that not everything was right with the behavior of the new nation. For example, despite their staunch pro-Israeli stance, the editors of *Moody* published a letter to the editor challenging some of their own pro-Israeli commentary. In the future, as will be seen in later chapters, they and others went further than this and provided formal articles taking up the Arab cause even as they continued their overall support of the Israelis. The events of their day excited the eschatological interest of nearly all evangelicals, but they were not of one mind as for how to respond.

6

A Tense Peace, 1954–1958

OVERVIEW

By the mid-1950s Americans had settled into the new normal of the Cold War. With the end of the Korean Conflict in 1953, the immediate threat of open war between the superpowers had receded from imminent to merely likely. The world certainly was not calm. Americans, Russians, and various Europeans intervened all over the world according to their national strategic agendas.[1] Nonetheless, for the time being it seemed that the shared terror of a nuclear contest kept Washington and Moscow from pressing advantages too closely or from making moves likely to elicit a direct response from their rivals. The policy of containment inherited from Truman meant that America focused on halting Soviet

---

1. In a strange moment of unanimity in the midst of a tense time, the United States and the Soviet Union both opposed the Anglo-French-Israeli invasion of Egypt in 1956. Eisenhower went so far as to have an American fleet shadow the combined British and French fleet near Egypt and tacitly threaten to cut off Britain's supplies of oil if it did not withdraw. Evan Thomas, *Ike's Bluff: President Eisenhower's Secret Battle to Save the World* (New York: Little, Brown, and Company, 2012), 224. Henry was baffled at the united front presented by the US and USSR at this point, saying, "Of the two positions [surrounding the Anglo-French-Israeli invasion], that of the United States carries with it the major force of world opinion, including not only United Nations support, but that of Soviet Russia (for whatever reason)." Henry, "International Crisis on the Sandy Wastes of Sinai," *CT*, November 12, 1956, 24. American involvement in Iran and Guatemala received scant attention in evangelical conversations. Barnhouse mentioned Iran only in passing and only then to praise Herbert Hoover Jr. for his role in orchestrating peace between the Iranian and British governments. He made a similarly superficial comment about Guatemala, saying only that the Russians had given supplies to the central government while the US had provided weapons to revolutionary forces which had then pulled off the revolution. Barnhouse, "A Survey of 1954," *ET*, January 1955, 4–5. He also suggested that one bright point to troubles in Hungary was that the Russians were in no position to take advantage of the crisis since they were too occupied putting down a revolt in their own empire. Barnhouse, "The Tragic Year," *ET*, January 1957, 41.

advances rather than launching any major offensives of their own, and Eisenhower's reputation as a wartime leader meant that the Russians could not count on his folding under pressure.[2]

As the 1950s moved toward their end, the world seemed closer to war than it had been a generation earlier, yet a general conflict did not come. In the late 1930s people wondered if national rivalries would lead to conflict. Twenty years later people wondered not if but when war would break out. In addition to the fear of political enslavement to hostile powers they shared with their parents' era, people now had to worry whether a nuclear holocaust would incinerate them as they slept. The United States had never been stronger than it was at this point, yet for many Americans they had never felt more exposed to danger. The avuncular persona of President Eisenhower reassured many that all would be well, even as the man who would soon decry the military-industrial complex provided the US with an extensive arsenal. Communism consolidated its hold over several new nations, and America's closest allies went down to defeat in unplanned offensives. The supposed happy-go-lucky 1950s were in fact filled with feelings of self-doubt and preparations for self-defense.

American evangelicals faced a changing situation. The refusal of the world to go down in apocalyptic flames dampened some of the fervor for eschatological certainties. Those prone to see the end as nigh did not suddenly stop thinking it would be so soon, but they became somewhat less likely to talk about it. Far from becoming a land of increasing ungodliness, the US saw church membership rising to record levels, biblical epics gracing the silver screen, and God's place in civic life becoming enshrined in the Pledge of Allegiance.[3] Perhaps

---

2. In President Eisenhower, Soviet leader Nikita Khrushchev was faced with someone who had already demonstrated the ability to win a war for the control of Western Europe and who had made bold statements about the willingness to use atomic weapons. Despite his genial and grandfatherly public persona, Eisenhower was keenly aware of the power he possessed and the impression America's wealth and military could have on rivals. For a study of this aspect of his political practice, see Thomas's *Ike's Bluff* (noted in the footnote above).

3. This development of the public place of God in America of the 1950s had begun earlier. See Robert S. Ellwood, *1950: Crossroads of American Religious Life* (Louisville, KY: Westminster John Knox, 2000). This is also a major concern of

more importantly, evangelicals were no longer the country cousins of American Christianity. Elite religious bodies may not have liked them any more than a generation earlier, but evangelicals were now moving in powerful circles and moving up in their proportion of American churches. They could no longer be ignored.

ENEMIES

OPPOSING THE RED SCARE

Communism as a worldview was still despised, but there was also a concern to curtail the rush to judgment found in the so-called Red Scares. Francis Schaeffer had no qualms about attacking Communism as a diabolical danger, but he was self-critical about the way he and others had been quick to form opinions based on false information.

> Of course there are frightful modernists, and that is of the Devil, and there are compromisers, and there are communists; but it seems to me that we no longer can believe that any man is a modernist, a compromiser or a communist JUST because [Carl] McIntire etc. have said they are. And it seems to me we have a moral responsibility which we must discharge if we are to know God's blessing for the future, to consider if we have acted in the past on misinformation in a way that has violated truth, or has violated an exhibition of the love of God.[4]

Herzog in *Spiritual Industrial Complex* where he goes into great detail about the machinations regarding the Pledge of Allegiance and other cultural artifacts of the 1950s.

4. Francis A. Schaeffer, Letter to Robert Rayburn, January 9, 1956, Francis A. Schaeffer Collection, Box 57, File 22, The Library, Southeastern Baptist Theological Seminary, Wake Forest, North Carolina. This criticism of Carl McIntire was not isolated to this moment but was part of Schaeffer's move away from the Fundamentalist ACCC towards a broader evangelicalism. In this same letter he wrote, "Of course, Carl is a liar ['a liar' is scratched out and replaced with some words difficult to decipher. Perhaps 'not care about the truth'] and I feel that the knowledge that he and the men around him deal in untruth and fabricating things to their convenience does lay a solemn responsibility upon us to rethink and re-evaluate all that they have told us about other men in the past. That they have so blatantly said about us that which we know is not true, we must question if what they told us about others is true." The previous summer he had written Rayburn, saying of McIntire's

In the same way and period, Billy Graham wrote to Carl Henry insisting that their nascent periodical, *CT*, should not conform to the pattern set by the anti-Communist heralds, saying, "Carl, this magazine cannot be another fundamentalist publication, taking hair-splitting views and narrow positions. Instead of attacking liberalism altogether from without, with McCarthy tactics, we must use strategy and bore from within, leading these ministers step-by-step."[5] G. Aiken Taylor, soon to be the new editor in chief at *SPJ*, noted that Americans had become rather paranoid about Communism, noting that,

To most Americans today the word "communism" suggests all manner of evil. You need but whisper, "He's a Communist," and,

---

group, "You've heard of the formal announcement of the new National (Home, I should say) Missions Board. Actually, I consider it a disgrace that Carl should have undertaken such a thing, but the list of board members—I think there are 45—certainly displays the poverty of their personnel. They really haven't any men of real force, just yes-men." Francis A. Schaeffer, Letter to Robert Rayburn, July 17, 1955, Francis A. Schaeffer Collection, Box 57, File 22. Another letter read, "At the present moment we understand, that McIntire is broadcasting on the radio around Phila, that Joe Bayly is a Communist! McIntire has also said that I am a Communist. Ted, the Bible says that we are not to vindicate ourselves, but always to rather suffer wrong, and I think this is always the way if we really want spiritual ... [sic]." Francis A. Schaeffer, Letter to Ted Noe, December, 1957, Francis A. Schaeffer Collection, Box 57, File 22. The day of the month is indecipherable. This frustration with McIntire was not limited to those, like Schaeffer, who had once worked closely with him but had later parted ways. Bell came to Billy Graham's defense in 1955, making strange bedfellows of some of Graham's critics. "During his ministry, it is inevitable that Mr. Graham should have made some mistakes. He has also made some enemies. Among his bitterest opponents are to be found the Communists, the extreme Liberals, and those Fundamentalists associated with Dr. Carl McIntire and the *Christian Beacon*." Bell, "The *Christian Beacon* and the Communists Attack Billy Graham," *SPJ*, April 6, 1955, 3. Bell's attack on Graham's went further than defending his son-in-law. In a letter to Carl Henry, Bell wrote, "Re Calr [sic] McIntire—ignore him. He thrives on mentioning and he and his organization do not deserve recognition. He stands for some good things but he is 'crazy'." Bell, Letter to Carl Henry, May 9, 1958, Box 1958 1, File Correspondence, L. Nelson Bell, Carl F. H. Henry Collection.

5. Billy Graham, Letter to Carl Henry, December 22, 1955, Box 1956, File 1956 Correspondence—Graham, Billy, Carl F. H. Henry Collection. Graham's father-in-law, Bell, shared this concern about the direction of *CT*, saying, "I have been particularly concerned that we not be led off to be a right-wing CHRISTIAN CENTURY, more concerned with the right attitudes to modern problems than we are with the Christian faith, it's [sic] statement and defense." Bell, Letter to Carl Henry, May 9, 1958, Box 1958 1, File Correspondence, L. Nelson Bell, Carl F. H. Henry Collection.

if your neighbor believes you, the alleged Communist could next
be charged with almost any crime whatever and your neighbor
would not be surprised. The Communist has the role of international villain once held by Fascist, except that the Communist
enjoys an even worse reputation.

He also reported that one anti-Communist group had blasted a Sunday
School curriculum as communistic for nothing more than having
advocated sharing.[6]

------

6. G. Aiken Taylor, "Why Communism Is Godless," *CT*, December 22, 1958, 13. As
his title makes clear, despite his desire to avoid overreaction, Taylor was not interested in any accommodation with Communism. Taylor would take over the editorship of *SPJ* in 1959, then renamed as *Presbyterian Journal*. This concern over excessive
anti-Communist zeal was partially rooted in evangelicalism's anti-Roman Catholic
stance. Barnhouse was concerned that anti-Communism was not enough to save
American liberties. He wrote that the US was not in danger merely from Communist
absolutism but from all sorts of tyrannical pretensions. "We must awaken our discernment, and love God so much that we will hate the false gods of absolutism, and
learn to hate it *in any form*. For the absolutism that is most to be feared is not that
which is the most talked about, but that which prepares in the shadows." He feared
that the greater danger to the US was not flowing from Moscow but from Rome.
Relying on an article in the *Christian Science Monitor*, he suggested that, thanks to
the anti-Communist efforts of Senator McCarthy, Roman Catholics were increasing
their proportion of American office holders and that some of the Senator's efforts
were focused on Protestantism rather than just Communism. "Not all who fly the
anti-Communist flag are working for liberty. Some are aiming their ultimate attack
against freedom of religion. What makes this particularly dangerous is that few
Americans see this camouflaged attack, and fewer dare speak out against it for
fear of being called pro-Communist." Continuing, he added, "In many circles in
our country a man can get away with anything if he shouts anti-Communist slogans. He may be a liar, immoral or a fascist; everything is condoned so long as he
vociferates against Communism. Men who recognize and expose this dangerous
brand of anti-Communist are doing America a service." Donald G. Barnhouse, "The
Nature of Our Danger," *ET*, March 1954, 8–9. Italics in original. Barnhouse would
later center his opposition to a constitutional amendment declaring America to
be a Christian nation in his fear that this would become the basis of oppression,
specifically a Roman Catholic tyranny within the United States. Barnhouse, "Perils
of Christian Amendment," *ET*, July 1954, 10. An advertisement for *The Converted
Catholic Magazine* offered a similar message of American Protestantism under
Roman siege with the headline, "Defend Our American Heritage" and promised
to inform readers about "the plans, purposes and program of the Roman Catholic
Church in this country." Advertisement for Christ's Mission, Inc., *ET*, May 1954,

Opposing the Reds

Deep and abiding concerns remained, however. When some argued
that the best way forward to world peace was through negotiations
with the Soviet Union, Bell gave a litany of the purges enacted under
Stalin, and said, "*That* is the government we are being urged to 'negotiate' with. Have we forgotten the stories of our own captives in Korea?
Are we blind to the national rape of the countries of central Europe?
Are we oblivious to the infiltration and intrigue taking place in every
nation, including our own, today?"[7] Touching on a common theme in
these magazines, he reminded readers that, "The avowed program of
Communism is world dominion," and that they would do anything—lie,

---

32. Another short piece told of the hardening of the Ecuadorian government
against Protestantism because they had been convinced by McCarthy's hearings
that most American Protestant pastors were actually Communists. Barnhouse,
"Repercussions Against Christianity," *ET*, December 1954, 51. Later, he was able to
report with some glee that Senator McCarthy had fallen from grace. "In the United
States the news was dominated in the first part of the year by the Cohn-Shine-
McCarthy fiasco, and at the end of the year by the McCarthy censure. He had shot
up only to fizzle out like a sky-rocket. This was a bitter pill for some, especially the
Roman Catholics who had seen him as a rising star. ... At all events, McCarthyism
seemed mortally wounded. Its idealism will undoubtedly find a further reincarnation, but the successor had not yet appear on the horizon." Barnhouse, "A Survey of
1954," *ET*, January 1954, 5. By 1958 an unsigned article was alerting evangelicals to the
possibility of a Presidential run by a relatively unknown Roman Catholic senator,
John F. Kennedy. Anonymous, "What About Kennedy?" *ET*, February 1958, 31. Bell
was keen to draw distinctions between genuine anti-Communism from others
claiming the title, saying, "There have been pseudo patriots whose patriotism has
consisted in flag waving, loud speeches and words of criticism and denunciation
against those of other nations." However, even though he thought they had erred,
and erred greatly at times, he did not wish to throw the baby out with the bathwater.
"But, their chauvinism in no way vitiates true patriotism, nor does it lessen one's
responsibility to love, honor, and defend his country against her real enemies." Bell,
"The Evangelical Faith vs. 'Fundamentalism,' " *SPJ*, July 27, 1955, 2. Bell's overall point
was to say that just as these obnoxious patriots did not negate the importance of
healthy patriotism, so too, the inelegant nature of Fundamentalism did not mean
that its doctrinal stances were invalid. Later, he repeated this concern, saying, "No
one would defend the flag-waving of those 'patriots' whose chief aim seems to be
the glorification of self, or the grinding of some particular axe. Such is shallow
and even obnoxious. On the other hand, every American citizen should be proud
of this land in which we live and a zealous guardian of those things for which she
stands." L. Nelson Bell, "Is Patriotism Wrong?" *SPJ*, August 1, 1956, 2.

7. Bell, "It Is Not 'Cynical' to Face the Facts," *SPJ*, January 20, 1954, 5. Italics
in original.

cheat, and steal—to achieve this goal. He found it nothing less than fool-ishly naïve to think otherwise.[8] The rapid expansion of Communism in a short time coupled with its human rights record was enough to make evangelicals uneasy. "Can the Communists wipe out the church behind the curtain? In less than my lifetime they have swept across more than one-fifth of the surface of the globe and shut off from freedom one-third of the world's population. ... Can they destroy the church as easily as they have blotted out all other institutions that have stood against them?"[9] Billy Graham had much the same to say:

> Communism is sweeping across the world like fire. In 1917 Lenin went across to Russia with 40,000 men. Today Communists con-trol about 800 million people. They are penetrating every part of the world; they are challenging the Christian Church as it has never been challenged before. They are teaching us some lessons, and I pray that we will learn them before it's too late.[10]

It was no trick of self-deluding paranoia for evangelicals to think that Communists wanted to take over the world; they had said as much themselves and, by the 1950s, they were well on their way toward this goal.

In keeping with his academic mind, Henry's comments on Communism were often philosophical. He admitted that there was something appealing to workers about its rhetoric, but he also argued that its imagery of dignified labor had been stolen from the Christian view of humanity. Therefore, Communism could not long sustain the illusion it had crafted to hide its reality. "The glory of the worker turns out really to be the glory of the state-god. The fundamental dignity of the worker, as human being bearing the image of God, bearing the supernatural significance and in everlasting destiny, is obscured, and

---

8. Bell, " 'Peaceful Co-Existence' The Road to Ultimate Tragedy," *SPJ*, December 22, 1954, 7.

9. Samuel H. Moffett, "Can Communism Kill the Church," *ET*, May 1954, 8.

10. Billy Graham, "Christ Demands No Less," *ET*, June 1958, 7. In reality, Graham's overall point here had less to do with Communism than with using it as an example. If the Communists could be so dedicated, why could not the Christians?

he is sacrificed to the myth of the eternal state."[11] Similarly, he wrote, "Just as Communism ignores the tragic and sinful side of human life, so it ignores man's created dignity and assigns him an inferior status. Since it excludes God and the supernatural, from whom the writers of the Bible derive the concepts of man's dignity, freedom, and rights. Communism suspends all of man's economic dignity and rights upon the tolerance of the state."[12] The accusation that Communism is a deeply flawed Christian heresy has been fairly common in evangelical circles, but for men like Henry it was more than a shorthand invective. For him the ideology holding a third of the world in its embrace was a worldview with all the trappings of a religion, a religion which had stolen and warped its goals from his own.

KOREAN COMMUNISTS

The place of Korea in the evangelical mind had, in some ways, lessened with the fragile peace of 1953. Yet, owing to its large Christian population and substantial American military garrison, it continued to hover on the outskirts of commentary. General William K. Harrison wrote of the Korean War as bringing into focus the ongoing global conflict.

> In that war, men of the United States and fifteen other countries fought Chinese and Korean communists who were goaded and supported by the communist rulers of Soviet Russia. The immediate issue was the question of who would control Korea. The real issue was communist imperialism and lawless aggression. The war was localized in Korea but the issues and consequences were worldwide.[13]

Barnhouse wondered that the recent ceasefire was being used by the Soviet and Communist Chinese to reinforce their position in Korea for a resumption of hostilities,[14] while Bell mourned the suffering inflicted by the Communists after the Second World War, saying,

---

11. Carl F. H. Henry, "The Dignity of Work: The Christian Concept," *Vital Speeches of the Day*, August 15, 1954, 666.

12. Henry, "Christianity and the Economic Crisis," *ET*, June 1955, 43.

13. William K. Harrison, "Reminiscences and a Prophecy," *CT*, March 4, 1957, 13.

14. Barnhouse, "Nineteen Fifty-Three," *ET*, January 1954, 4.

"Later even greater and more universal atrocities were perpetuated by the Communists who rightly considered the church and Christians their greatest source of opposition. At least five hundred pastors were martyred by the red invaders and tens of thousands of other Christians died because of their allegiance to Christ." Interestingly enough, he did not lay primary blame on the Communists. Certainly, they were the ones committing the atrocities, but they were doing so because of a failure of "American leadership" and an American church which had become far too comfortable in its own "peace and plenty." Only be working to support and not hinder South Korea, could true peace be found in the land.[15]

MAO'S CHINA

By the mid-1950s China had long been "lost," but its role in the world and in evangelical discussions continued apace. Henry rejected calls for the US to offer diplomatic recognition to Beijing, arguing that it was nonsense to give the respect of UN legitimacy to a nation which so repudiated everything which the United Nations claimed to stand for.[16]

---

15. Bell, "Korean Missions: Triumph and Shadow," *CT*, February 18, 1957, 16–17, 25.

16. Henry, "Red China and World Morality," *CT*, December 10, 1956, 21. Another *CT* piece affirmed this, saying, "No more critical issue faces American leaders in the days ahead than the one of admission of Communist China into the United Nations. As in all major phases of international relationships, Christianity itself has a deep interest in the moral overtones of this issue." Another writer's point was rooted in the pragmatics of geopolitics and the relative morality of the regimes in question. He suggested that acceptance of Mao's government was tantamount to moving America's defensive line back to California and the Pacific Northwest. To those who hoped that the UN could be a better source of global peace once Beijing was admitted, he responded, "Americans will not, I believe, soon forget that the present Chinese Communist regime is the same regime that committed aggression in Korea in violation of a United Nations indictment and was responsible for inflicting 140,000 casualties on us, including 35,000 dead." He then added that the UN fight was almost entirely an American affair in terms of actual military participation. He saw the current situation as being of utmost importance and as one which could hardly be overestimated. "We must not forget that Communism is a world-wide conspiracy against freedom and independence and that the objective of the men in the Kremlin was pointed out many years ago in Lenin's statement that 'the Road to Paris is through Peking.'" William F. Knowland, "Admit Red China?" *CT*, October 29, 1956, 10–11.

Bell saw recognition of Mao's government as a betrayal of the Chinese people. "The greatest single ally America has in the world is that great host of people in the Communist countries who are oppressed by that monstrous evil which has enslaved them. Recognition of a Communist government goes far to destroy confidence and hope, confidence in our essential goodness, and hope of future deliverance."[17] This was a regular emphasis of his regarding China; America was failing not its own self-interest but that of the Chinese people. Bell was not alone in

---

17. Bell, "Shall We Recognize Communist China?" *SPJ*, February 24, 1954, 4. The next year he spoke again of the Chinese people's hopes for liberation, saying, "The writer has been told by a Chinese leader who escaped from Communist China that, 'If [Chiang Kai Shek] ... should lead the Nationalists back to the mainland it would be the most joyous day China has ever known.'" Bell, "Chiang—Hated by Whom?" *SPJ*, February 23, 1955, 2. Reports from China did not encourage evangelicals to look fondly on the Communist regime. The Taiwanese ambassador to the US repudiated the view that Mao's National Christian Council was tolerant of Christianity. One commentator told *MM*'s readers, "[Beijing] has instituted a government bureau for the control of religious affairs, under which the 'Council' operates. The fanatical Communists who compose this bureau make all the decisions in regard to the status of the Christian churches in China." Hollington K. Tong, "Christians Are Still Being Martyred in Red China," *MM*, October 1957, 16. Charles Lampman told his readers that a young man in Hong Kong had been driven to steal from a missions organization to pay a ransom demanded by Chinese Communists for the lives of his family still in the People's Republic. Charles T. Lampman, "Chinese Youth Steals Mission Funds for Reds," *MM*, January 1954, 5. Culbertson reacted to Communist claims about the freedom of religion by saying, "Such reports as filter through the Bamboo Curtain indicate that Communists have not changed their attitude toward the Christian faith, but only their methods of opposing it. Pressure—slow, steady and relentless—has largely replaced the open opposition of earlier days." Culbertson, "A New Coat for the Wall," *MM*, March 1954, 10. Later, Lampman even asserted that persecution had not lessened but increased recently, citing a report that twenty-eight Chinese pastors had been shot when they refused to say they would not cease preaching. Lampman, "Christian Persecution in China Increasing," *MM*, June 1954, 5. Barnhouse chided observers from the UK for being taken in by Chinese Potemkin villages and ignoring the persecution of Christians all around them. He also erroneously reported that a major Chinese Christian leader had been executed. Barnhouse, "Survey of 1954," *ET*, January 1955, 5. He declared that "Wang Ming Tao" was the "martyr of the year," but Wang Ming Dao lived for many years thereafter. See David Aikman's *Jesus in Beijing: How Christianity is Transforming China* (Washington, DC: Regnery, 2003). Barnhouse later implicitly admitted his error when he wrote of Wang in the present tense and as still undergoing persecution. Barnhouse, "Persecution in China," *ET*, October 1956, 16. The following February he made this correction explicit. Barnhouse, "Wang Ming Tao in Peking," *ET*, February 1957, 17.

this. A contributing writer told *CT's* readers, "With the revolution came the awful innovations of which the people told me. The Communist Party set groups and instigated 'study classes for self-criticism' if there was opposition. It was actually 'brain washing.' It is still in progress." It was not only this such reeducation which concerned the author but the more absolute methods the Communists employed as well. "Anti-revolutionists were quickly liquidated. Suicides occurred in such large numbers that it was dangerous to walk near high buildings. *Mao Tse-Tung* admitted 800,000 'liquidated,' exclusive of suicides. Reports varied, however, for Hongkong [sic] hear it was 4,000,000 and Formosa, 12,000,000."[18] The accuracy of such figures may have been open to question, but it was hardly irrational for evangelicals to oppose China given this perception. While there was an argument to be made that opposing the Mao regime served American interests, this was not the primary focus of these writers during this time. In their commentary on China, they justified opposing Beijing as support for China.

---

18. Toshio Suekane, "Report on Red China," *CT*, November 25, 1957, 31–32. Italics in original. Not everything evangelicals said about China was negative. When some pointed to the great material advances made since the Communists took over, evangelicals had mixed responses. David Adeney admitted they had had experienced success. "China is rapidly becoming a great power in the world. Currency has been stabilized and means of communication throughout the country have greatly improved Health services and educational facilities are being made available to more people, and there is a great campaign toward literacy." Adeney was not complimenting Communism, as such, but he was rather warning Christians to be aware of the strength of their rival. He listed out the many points which drew different people to Communism, and he presented it as a potent rival to the Christian faith, one which made use of many of the same methodologies and incentives. David H. Adeney, "Communism and Christianity," *ET*, September 1955, 18–19. Henry, on the other hand, responded that this could not all be attributed to the skill of the new rulers. He said that the combination of China's earlier low level of technological advancement meant that dramatic looking improvements would be possible, regardless of who was in charge. Further, he argued, had the Japanese not invaded and the US not prevaricated, the Nationalists would have been able to do just as well if not better, all without "cost of personal freedoms and national enslavement" which had been the price of Communist rule. Henry, "The Church and Red China," *CT*, March 17, 1958, 23–24.

Hungarian Revolt

The short-lived revolution in Hungary in 1956 was, until its end, everything these evangelicals hoped for in Europe as a previously free people
threw off their foreign and tyrannical rulers and called for political
and religious freedom.[19] Culbertson rebuked the church behind the
Iron Curtain for its silence regarding the Soviet invasion, accusing
pastors there of cowardice. "It would have taken real bravery to have

---

19. The religious aspect of the abortive revolution held an obvious appeal for
many evangelical writers. One report highlighted the religious connections of one
of the rebel leaders, saying that, while a longstanding Communist, he had been
raised in a Christian home and had not objected to his son-in-law's profession as
a Protestant pastor. The Editors, "Hate in Hungary," CT, November 12, 1956, 28. An
article by Eugene Osterhaven traced the history of Protestantism in the land, and
these Reformed Christians were no strangers to oppression by state or church. The
writer noted some of the leadership of the anti-Communist factions had come from
these Calvinists. Osterhaven then blasted the Soviets for their oppression, saying,
"Again it has been Russia the Communist rulers of which, by their own admission,
have liquidated millions of their own countrymen to consolidate their power
which has steam-rolled the heroic, and pathetic, Hungarian quest for freedom."
He wrote these somber words even as he lifted up the Hungarians as an example
to follow. Responding to a call for the West to listen to their plight, he concluded,
"That request has become a cry. It is a cry from a Hungary which today is in the
throes of death. The free world has heard it. May God give us the courage and
strength to respond." M. Eugene Osterhaven, "Pathos of Hungarian Protestantism,"
CT, November 26, 1956, 11–12. Another CT piece, this one by a Hungarian-born
theologian, reached for American sympathy. The author wrote that Hungary's
plea was for two simple things, "bread and freedom." He said that the things his
people had wanted were not extraordinary but the most commonplace in the world.
"They wanted for themselves things which we in America simply take for granted:
national independence and full sovereignty, free elections and a representative
government, free press and free communication with all the countries of the world,
a readjustment of wages and the assurance of the possibility of a decent human
living; finally, the withdrawal of Soviet troops from Hungary in accordance with
peace treaty and 'neutrality' in foreign politics. If these demands were the prompt-
ings of a 'reactionary spirit' (as now charged by the Soviet Union and its puppet
Hungarian government) then the signers of the Declaration of Independence, and
all of us who believe in the promotion of basic human rights must be, indeed,
nothing more than narrow-minded reactionaries." He then described the fate of
those who had stood up for their liberty now that the Russians had squashed the
revolt, saying, "And now, those who survived are facing starvation, the freezing
cold of winter and, perhaps worst of all, the possibility of deportation to Siberia.
Many thousands, whole families, but especially young men and women, sought
their refuge in the West. Once again the Hungarian nation is torn to pieces." Bela
Vassady, "Marginal Notes on the Tragedy of Hungary," CT, December 10, 1956, 28.

spoken out against Russian in Hungary, more bravery than they evidently had." He concluded with a warning to Christians around the
world, saying, "The lesson—which Bible-believing Christians should
never forget, however attractive the offers of appeasement—is clear.
The church cannot compromise in its battle against enemies of God
unless it wants the tragic world 'Ichabod' written over its portals."[20]
Barnhouse mourned the crushing of revolt, saying, "Man of the Year
might have been some unknown Hungarian who ran out from hiding
to die but who first succeeded in throwing a home-made bomb into a
Russian tank and destroying it." He then critiqued the American refusal
to intervene, saying, "A nation that is not willing to go to war to destroy
a power capable of destroying a liberty-loving people may itself be
destroyed."[21] A CT article said, "The growing surge to be free came to
a climax a year ago last fall in Hungary. Foolish? Yes, just as foolish as
the country farmers on a green at Lexington who stood up against the
finest professional soldiers of the eighteenth century."[22] These writers
were, arguably, a bit naïve as they hoped that pressure from religious
leaders or complaints from foreign politicians would dampen the Soviet
expansionist spirit, but, as with China, it was the plight of those under
Communist rule which provided the focus for their complaint.

Others, while sharing this emphasis, were more cynical, both about
the likelihood of a positive outcome and the role Western powers
might play. Henry asked his readers about the implications of the
nascent revolt,

> How are the demands of an enlightened Christian conscience
> to be met when confronted by the situation in Hungary? When

20. Culbertson, "Whose Face is Red?" *MM*, February 1957, 11. Specifically he
was criticizing Eastern European clerics who had been invited to come to the US
for World Council of Churches meeting in 1954. "Ichabod" is likely a reference to
1 Samuel 4:21, suggesting that God would depart from churches that did not stand
up when called to it. The following month he noted the irony that Bibles were
arriving in the West having been printed by the Hungarian government during
the brief revolution. Culbertson, "Communist Printed Bibles Reach Canada and
US," *MM*, March 1957, 6.

21. Barnhouse, "The Tragic Year," *ET*, January 1957, 41.

22. Walter H. Judd, "World Issues and the Christian," *CT*, June 23, 1958, 6.

men are dying in their desire for freedom; when God-given aspirations for self-determination are being brutally crushed; when a reign of terror unexceeded in rigor is being perpetuated even as these lines are being written, what should be the reaction of Christians living in freedom and peace?

He condemned the Soviets in the most visceral terms, and he blasted his own land for its inaction. "The rape of Hungary may be the desperate act of a tottering regime which was born in terror and which has continued to exist in the same manner. But America and other free nations share the blame insofar as they have sustained that regime by recognition and given it a forum of respectability in which to operate."[23] He may have been naïve to think that the Soviet regime was, at that point, tottering, but his cynicism about the Western response was palpable.

Bell had a similar approach to Henry here. His response to the Hungarian revolution was to rebuke the US for its passivity. "For all our vaunted morality America has stood by through the years and watched regretfully but inactively while the nations of Central Europe have been enslaved by a godless tyranny. ... Polite expressions of regret have not saved these nations from slavery, nor have they helped Poland, Hungary, or Czecho-Slovakia." Looking to the biblical parable of the

---

23. Henry, "Christian Responsibility and Communist Brutality," CT, November 26, 1956, 24. The Hungarian revolt had a deep and longstanding impact on Francis Schaeffer, who featured it prominently in his 1976 book and movie series, How Should We Then Live? Of particular focus was a young student tried and executed by the Communists for her part in the revolt. This was something which apparently stuck with him up to the time of his death. In 1982 he wrote Kenneth Kantzer, comparing her fate to a young woman who had recently mounted a protest in Russia, "Another mistake that I do not think can be overlooked, is our not knowing what has happened to that poor girl who hung up that banner in the church service and was arrested immediately. Where is she today and tonight? ... She gave away her freedom, and maybe her life, to speak for freedom against tyranny and persecution. ... If I only had her picture I would place it side by side in my office with the picture of the girl Ilond Troth that has hung there ever since the Hungarian revolt and which I used in How Should We Then Live?, opposite page 215. ... I have not been able to forget her in all these years, and quite frankly, when I am going to bed at night at this moment I cannot forget that girl who tried valiantly in Moscow." Schaeffer, Letter to Kenneth A. Kantzer, June 5, 1982, Francis A. Schaeffer Collection, Box 78, File 14, The Library, Southeastern Baptist Theological Seminary, Wake Forest, North Carolina.

Good Samaritan for inspiration, he said, "Now we see these people making a desperate struggle against their Communist masters and our hearts bleed for them. Are they not like the wounded man on the road to Jericho? Have we forgotten our moral and spiritual principles?" Bell's heroes were the Hungarians, leaving the Americans to a far lesser role. "The high hopes of Hungary of a few days ago seem shattered at this writing. Blood, suffering and death has come to thousands who had the courage to stand for freedom, even more than death. ... Here in America too many want peace so that they may continue to serve the Devil in luxury and quiet."[24] The driving force of the evangelical complaint against Communism was a Christian humanism which saw loyalty to fellow Christians and people created in God's image as of greater import than the realpolitik interests of their own nation.

The Soviets

When it came to the Soviet Union, there was slightly less commentary by evangelicals than in earlier years, but the overall opinion remained the same.[25] Barnhouse granted that the newly ascendant Khrushchev

---

24. Bell, "A World in Agony and Some Things We Forget," *SPJ*, November 14, 1956, 3.

25. Its actions in foreign lands were roundly condemned, but most commentary on the Soviet Union related to the state of the church in Russia. One writer was able to report, "The invincible nature of the Church is dramatically demonstrated in Communist Russia today. The powers in the Kremlin have not succeeded in stamping out the Christian faith. Not only is the Church surviving in Communist dominated countries, it is growing in strength." Henlee H. Barnette, "The Church in Soviet Russia," *CT*, December 23, 1957, 3. A photo in *ET* showed a Baptist church in Moscow with standing room only as American Baptists met with their Russian counterparts. The Editors, Photo Caption, *ET*, September 1954, 40. Lampman reinforced this idea with a report out of London from a Russian Baptist leader who claimed that there were a half million Baptists in the USSR, and that they had full freedom to preach and to proselytize. Lampman, "Baptists in Russia Said to Enjoy Full Freedom," *MM*, October 1955, 7. Barnhouse noted with quiet pleasure that the Soviet authorities were taking a harder line on this growth, critiquing it on Russian radio for distracting workers from Communist glory. Barnhouse, "Reds Push Anti-God Campaign," *ET*, October 1954, 16. A brief piece a year later indicated that the claims to freedom of religion by Russian Baptists in front of the delegation of their American coreligionists were more symbolic than substantial. "A confidential source" had informed Barnhouse that the Russian Baptists could not evangelize outside their church building and they were forbidden to baptize anyone under

had shown great skill in securing his position and that of the Soviet Union, saying that even the bad press flowing from the crushing of Hungary were not enough to prevent Russia and its ruler from dominating world news." Later in the same piece he made clear what this meant for the US. "Remember that one year ago there were parades in a hundred cities against Russia's actions in Hungary. The crimes of Stalin had been freshly revealed. Now, in spite of the ruthless rejection of all other major leaders and the entrenchment of a stolid Russian peasant as ruler of 200 million people and the mentor of 500 million more, Russia stands at a very high peak."[26] Bell also looked with trepidation at the forces the Soviets could marshal, suggesting that in addition to having the largest submarine and land forces in the world, it was likely equal to or greater than the United States in air power.[27] Of Soviet expansion in the previous decade he wrote that while Russia gobbled up nation after nation of Eastern and Central Europe in the wake of World War II that American interests seemed never to rise above their own self-interest.[28]

---

eighteen years. Barnhouse, "Russian Liberty," *ET*, October 1955, 17. A contributor to *ET* informed his readers that even when allowing for superficial or false Christians, there were far more Russians convinced of Christianity than were members of the Communist Party. John Lawrence, "Here are the Facts about Russian Protestants," *ET*, November 1955, 8. In 1957 an author wrote about the week he had spent in Russia, getting to know the situation firsthand. He enjoyed his trip immensely and was pleasantly surprised to find that no attempt was being made to suppress radio signals coming in from Christian stations in the West. He was overjoyed to be able to share Christianity with a young man in his hotel who had been listening to one of these stations with him in the lobby. Not everything comported with a free faith, however. "I had been told; 'Be sure to just preach about Christ and don't talk about anything else.' Now, of course, as an evangelical Christian I agreed completely that my message should be Christ-centered. But there was more in this statement than that. I got the strong impression that the Christian leaders in Russia, in spite of their claim to religious liberty, had to be very careful not to speak about other matters and issues. And wherever I went and wherever I spoke there was always a guide, so-called, in the meeting." Nonetheless, his overall impression was quite positive, even if he saw a deeper concern as well. When speaking of his time in a Russian church, he said, "Never in my life have I seen such love and devotion to Christ as was written on the faces before me. There was no question but that Christ was real to them. One tragic note marred the whole. I saw almost no young people there." Paul E. Freed, "Seven Days Behind the Iron Curtain," *MM*, May 1957, 19.

26. Barnhouse, "Sputnik's Year," *ET*, January 1958, 16.
27. Bell, "Can It Be? America, a Second-Rate Power!!" *SPJ*, May 16, 1956, 3.
28. Bell, "The Year Ahead," *SPJ*, January 1, 1958, 2.

AMERICA

WE STILL LIKE IKE

Eisenhower continued to fascinate many evangelical writers. Unlike his predecessor, whom many found wanting in one way or another, here was a leader who claimed to be, if not one of them, at least friendly to them.[29] The editors of *ET* went so far as to have the president declared their "Man of the Year," in 1956,[30] and Barnhouse praised the president's handling the Suez Conflict, calling his speech on the subject "magnificent."[31] At the beginning of 1958, one of *SPJ*'s editors pushed back against the "Sunday editors" who were, by his account, seeking to undermine the President's authority by saying that he was no longer fit to lead. Pointing to the biblical example of David's respect for King Saul as the Lord's anointed, Robinson said, "We respectfully suggest to these editors that they accept the act of Divine Providence in providing Dwight David Eisenhower as the President of these United States for this term, or until such an act of Providence to his health or strength makes his retirement mandatory."[32] Billy Graham was quoted as saying that Eisenhower "was very earnest about spiritual matters." Even his

---

29. This is in contrast to some attitudes towards Eisenhower's opponent. When addressing the question of the religious background of perennial Democratic Presidential nominee, Adlai Stevenson, Barnhouse was clear where his sympathies lay, but he also distinguished between America and the kingdom of God. "The present Editor does not claim that the United States is a Christian nation. The day may come when a godless majority, or even a thoughtless majority will put an anti-Christian in the White House." But he then pulled back from this distinction somewhat, saying, "What we do say, however is that no true Christian should have any part in it. As good Christians we must be good citizens and seek to put only qualified men in office; and we reserve the right to believe that being a Christian is one of the most important of the qualifications." Barnhouse, "Adlai's Religion," *ET*, March 1956, 10. Stevenson was, according to a quote in the article, a Unitarian, something which would place him out of bounds by most traditional Christian organizations.

30. The Editors, Cover, *ET*, January 1956.

31. Barnhouse, "The President's Speech," *ET*, April 1957, 8.

32. Robinson, "From King David to President David," *SPJ*, January 29, 1958, 3. Robinson was not overtly endorsing Eisenhower's policies here, and he was careful to distinguish that here, saying, "In recognizing God's hand in the choice of a President we are not setting up an infallible ruler. Not only Saul, but later King David, was by no means infallible. The Bible accounts the sins and mistakes of both but it did not encourage lifting up hands for the removal of either."

pastor, Edward Elson, received the benefit of being the subject of an article in ET. Asking what sort of man had such a powerful post as spiritual adviser to the most powerful man in the world, the writer concluded, "Ike, it appears, is in pretty good hands."[33] After some wondered if Eisenhower's Christian statements were little more than the posturing of a politician, an article related the story of one of the President's aides coming into the Oval Office unannounced and finding Ike alone and on his knees in prayer. The author also quoted a White House staffer as saying "the President has a deep religious conviction" which he did not want to advertise for fear of giving offense.[34] Even as they retained

---

33. Russell T. Hitt, "What Ike's Pastor Believes," ET, February 1954, 44. Both the quote from Graham and the commentary on Elson came from this same article. Lampman also gave information about the president's pastor, noting that Ike had heard a sermon attacking American Christians for their shallow sense of giving. Elson was quoted in the article as saying, "The Christian Church is the most telling antagonist of Communism today, yet many Christians spend more on one night's entertainment than they give in a whole year to Christ's Church." Lampman, "President's Pastor Scores Inadequate Giving," MM, January 1954, 3. Elson was himself one of the most prominent and unabashed patriots among theological conservatives of the era. He said, "America has become great and strong not simply by vast natural resources made secure from all enemies by wide oceans and friendly neighbors. Other nations have had all that and for longer periods. America has become great and strong principally because of a creative spirit emanating from her religious faith, chiefly and dominantly evangelical Christian faith." While he acknowledged that there could be no nation which could be called a Christian nation, he did believe that some countries could "become less obstructed conductors of the Christian evangel and more direct conveyors of God's truth to the world." He encouraged his readers to work to see that their nation would become such a channel of divine favor to the world. "When America is most faithful to its origin, to its truest self and to its God, it is that kind of nation. In humility and fullness of dedication, it may well be that in this epoch when America carries such a heavy international responsibility, God can use her as an instrument of His purposes on the earth. Should that be true, as I believe it is true, the leaders and the people of this land must keep close to God, seek to discover His will and resolutely perform this providentially bestowed role of world leader." His counsel, therefore, contained a high degree of contingency. If Americans acted in accordance with God's will, then the United States could participate in the divine plan. Edward L. R. Elson, "Worship in the Life of the Nation," CT, November 12, 1956, 10-11.

34. Lampman, "Seaton's Statement as Later Related for Publication," MM, August 1955, 5. While extensive essays were rare, there were, however, many regular new reports on Ike's connection to Christianity. Lampman shared with his readers the news that Eisenhower had received Bibles in seventy-eight languages, so any visitor to the White House could read it. Lampman, "President Accepts Bibles for

the willingness to critique the President as the situation warranted, many evangelical thinkers found they could support Eisenhower in a way they had not either of his immediate predecessors.[35]

White House," *MM*, January 1954, 3. This event was also recorded with an unsigned photo caption in *ET*. The Editors, "White House Gets Bibles in 78 Tongues," *ET*, January 1954, 19. Lampman also recorded the President's message encouraging businessmen to live out their Christianity in their work. Lampman, "President Praises Ministry of Christian Businessmen," *MM*, January 1957, 5. The cover of a 1954 issue of *SPJ* showed the President laying the cornerstone at a church in Georgia. The Editors, Cover, *SPJ*, May 12,1954. The cover just shy of two years later showed Bell, his daughter Ruth, and her husband Billy Graham posing with Vice President Richard Nixon when the Grahams were in Washington to be the guests at the White House. The Editors, Cover, *SPJ*, April 4, 1956. Many *SPJ* editorials criticized the government's stance towards Communism but such rebukes were general and never specifically addressing the President or even his administration.

35. Eisenhower was not the only high government official to receive a positive hearing among evangelicals during this time. Another who did was the controversial director of the FBI. J. Edgar Hoover was clearly not a pastor, but his analysis of the nation's problems fit in well with those provided by fully fledged evangelicals. In a 1955 piece in *MM*, he praised America's abilities and, most of all, its liberties, but he warned that these ought not be taken for granted. "To maintain this liberty, every citizen must be willing to do his share to protect law and order. American freedom over the years has been based on fair play, justice and the orderly operation of the law. Not to obey the law creates anarchy. A citizenry, alert to its responsibilities, is the best defense of American Freedom. There can be no alternative." J. Edgar Hoover, "We Must Defend America," *MM*, July 1955, 13–14. A few years later he contributed to *CT*, saying, "In this year of 1958, when the world is so rent by divisive forces, America stands in great need of spiritual guidance. The country as a whole must draw from its great heritage of religious freedom, justice and liberty to meet the challenge of the future." Just as did many of the more theologically credentialed writers, Hoover looked to the clergy to support this effort. "Ministers in America are truly on the front lines of the battle for freedom. On their shoulders, in large measure, depends the future of our nation." When faced with the increase of juvenile delinquency in postwar America, Hoover looked to the nation's failure to train young people in the proper way. "That is one of our great challenges today—to make American youth into productive citizens of tomorrow. Young people are full of energy, initiative and talent. They are looking for something to do. They need guidance. The key lies here." In no small part he blamed families who were more interested in their busy schedules and presenting an image of a good family than in actually being one. As much as any preacher would, Hoover looked to a religious solution to America's problems. However, unlike many evangelical commentators, he spoke of the positive influence of a general religiosity rather than a specific set of doctrinal principles and spiritual regeneration. "This nation was founded on religious freedom. Religions have guided us in years past. They must continue to be our guide in the future. An America faithful to God will be an America free and strong." Hoover, "The Challenge of the Future," *CT*, May 26, 1958, 3–4. Immediately

KEEPING THE FAITH

Henry looked to evangelical pastors to do some of the heavy lifting
in encouraging their hearers to consider the religious background of
the United States. In an address to the NAE, he said, "Your pastors
will fail you and the nation if they do not bend before its responsibilities, with special emphasis on our Christian heritage, special prayer
for our nation, conferences with governmental leaders of evangelical
spiritual conviction, and letters to our elected officials assuring them
of our prayerful interest and moral concern."[36] He admitted that some
of America's Founding Fathers were not ideal Christians, but he maintained that most of them had been evangelical Christians.[37] Henry
saw America's place in the world as the product of God's will, and he
viewed this as a mighty responsibility not for its own glory but for the
common good of humanity. "In the midst of the totalitarian suppres-
sion of human rights and the totalitarian discard of human dignity,
our nation, our beloved land, with its vast economic resources and
its productive military efficiency, and even more basic, its regard for
a democratic way of life, has become a guardian of men's souls." Yet,
he did not see the land of the free as the land of the pure. Against
the temptation to see America as completely innocent in creating the

---

after Hoover's article, Henry wrote a follow-up piece praising the FBI Director for
his insight and influence in American society. Lampman, too, wrote a piece which
gave Hoover credit for providing a Protestant vespers service for FBI employees at
Elson's National Presbyterian Church. Lampman, "FBI Employees Attend Special
Vespers Service," *MM*, August 1954, 3.

36. Henry, Address to the National Association of Evangelicals, November
27, 1954, Box 1954, File Public Education and Catholicism, Variety—Paper by
Henry, Newspaper clippings and other misc., Rolfing Library Archives, Trinity
International University, Deerfield, Illinois. This copy is from an NAE press release
from November 28, 1954, of Henry's talk given the previous day. While Communism
was a definite target of this talk, a greater portion was devoted to condemnation
of political moves by the Roman Catholic Church.

37. Henry, "Human Rights in an Age of Tyranny," *CT*, February 4, 1957, 20.
A later article in *CT* discussed differences between the somewhat Christian-
influenced Continental Congress and the Constitutional Convention a decade
later. The author noted that much had been made of Benjamin Franklin's appeal
for prayer to start the proceedings, but little notice had been given to the fact that
Franklin's motion did not pass and the prayer was not given. Delber H. Elliot, "God
in the Constitutional Convention," *CT*, July 8, 1957, 12.

world's plight, he said, "The real crisis is that so many persons, in the free world as well as behind the iron curtain, hold a perspective on life and existence which makes our cultural downfall inevitable." He went on explicitly to state that no one could say that there was such a thing as a Christian Europe, Britain, or America.[38]

The 1950s saw a great many "pro-God" statements and actions by the US government, but these did not convince everyone that this was truly a nation under God. There were those who looked on increasing formal claim of God's blessing on America in a positive manner. A *Moody* writer gave a generally favorable portrayal of the move to add "In God We Trust" to US currency, quoting the treasury secretary's claim that this would broadcast the nation's allegiance before the watching world.[39] When it came to including God in the pledge, he was even more optimistic, saying "Multiplied millions of Americans will have to revise a quotation which they have been repeating with assurance and pride since early childhood. Because of the worldwide spread of Communism, which denies the very existence of God, the pledge of allegiance to the American flag is being altered."[40] On the other hand, in the very same issue of *Moody*, Culbertson looked at these things as far too shallow and too general. "But conceding that we are 'under God' does not make us a godly nation or give right standing in His sight. How quickly we forget that man by his own choose has placed himself at enmity with God. No mere acknowledgement of His Person or His power can wipe out this one great fact." He concluded with joy wrapped in a warning, saying, "America under God! Let us be thankful indeed that we live in a nation that is in the sense pointed out under his rule and the recipient of many blessings. But even an America under God, if it is without the Christ He sent, can in the long run be only an America under judgment."[41] Barnhouse was similarly unimpressed as he pondered American priorities, saying, "Our frenzied increase in living standards may well cause some people in the world to wonder

38. Henry, "Christianity and the American Heritage," *United Evangelical Action*, July 1, 1954, 263.
39. Lampman, "US Currency Motto to Honor God Urged," *MM*, February 1954, 3.
40. Lampman, "God to be Honored in Flag Pledge Change," *MM*, July 1954, 3.
41. Culbertson, "Nation Under God," *MM*, July 1954, 9.

if we did not make a mistake when we put 'In God We Trust' on our postage stamps and got the name of God into the pledge of allegiance to the flag."[42] Words on coins, it seems, were not enough.

The perennial issue of Christian America continued in the 1950s. An article in *SPJ*'s "Young People's Department" in 1956 challenged readers to consider just how Christian America actually was. The author acknowledged there was some basis in fact to this common assertion, noting the prominence of religious books and pronouncements by government officials. He did not downplay the reality of such things, but he did offer a new perspective. "All of these are hopeful signs. Our nation is probably more religious than it has ever been before, but there is still reason for raising the question of how 'Christian' we are. There is a great deal of difference between being religious and being Christian."[43] Henry pushed this same line with his analysis of the passing year of 1955. He granted that the year had seen a great upswing in religious activity, but he questioned its substance, as American spending on "the sordid things of life" grew apace with the growth of church membership.[44] As might be expected, he called for a return to a robust and lived-out Christianity as the solution to the crisis in the West, saying, "In a world which has lost its way spiritually and morally, it will require a coherent and consistent exhibition of the Christian world and life view, and no mere series of hit-and-run attacks of its materialistic competitors, to convince the multitudes who waver intellectually in the valley of indecision."[45] He warned his readers not to assume their past prosperity was a divine promise of future blessing, saying that its relative safety during the horrors of the world wars would not be guaranteed in any similar future conflict. He went so far as to say that American immorality demanded God's retributive judgment and that

---

42. Barnhouse, "The Tragic Year," *ET*, January 1957, 43.

43. B. Hoyt Evans, " 'But We are a Christian Nation,' " *SPJ*, October 3, 1956, 16. Italics and capitalization in original. Quotation marks in title in original.

44. Henry, "Religion in Review: Outstanding Events in the Religious World During 1955," *Evangelical Beacon and Evangelist*, December 27, 1955, 4.

45. Henry, "Christian Education and Our American Schools," *United Evangelical Action*, December 1, 1955, 564. The first page of this article has an illustration of the American and so-called Christian flags.

only by "ordering their affairs in line with God's holy and righteous will" could the nation avoid that fate.[46]

ONE NATION UNDER SIN

Society's moral corruption continued to bother many evangelicals with particular emphasis on the practical implications of cultural trends. Culbertson wondered how effective censoring in movies had been, comparing it to "plugging a hole in a dyke with a strainer," but he still accused Hollywood of putting money ahead of morality and even safety. "Like it or not, we live in communities which movies help to shape. New headlines every week make it all clear that women and children as well as men are only as safe as the level of decency and morality in the communities where they live."[47] This was about more than having

---

46. Henry, "Joint Moscow-Peking Threat Calls for Christian Realism," *CT*, March 4, 1957, 24. If some of Henry's comments made him sound particularly glum, he was in good company. "Pronouncing judgment on America is no longer an exclusive franchise of a few weeping Jeremiah. Nor is it peculiar to evangelists constantly reminding the nation of its spiritual decline, its neglect of a great Christian heritage, its whoring after false gods of money and ease." To those who pushed back against this by looking to the supposed revival, he said, "Many pulpiteers are indeed swift to show that despite America's religiosity no sweeping repentance and faith, no decisive change of heart and life, places social forces in our great cities in the service of the living God. ... Religious analysts are finding America spiritually and morally second-rate." Henry, "Can We Salvage the Republic?" *CT*, March 3, 1958, 3. His fellow *CT* editor, Bell, shared this dismal view of the nation. "A candid study of contemporary American life reveals the sobering facts that we have flourishing within our midst those seeds of decay which, if left unchecked, will lead to national destruction. That the incidence of immorality and crime is greater and that it is increasing at an alarming rate certainly adds to the urgency for remedial means." Bell, "Lest We Forget," *CT*, June 23, 1958, 19.

47. Culbertson, "Movies Unlimited," *MM*, March 1954, 9. Culbertson did not see popular culture as a contagion before which its consumers were mere passive observers. He held that people were responsible to use discernment about what they exposed themselves and their children to through TV. He later was to say, "It goes without saying that many TV 'westerns' and crime stories are doing irreparable harm to the moral life of our young people. Everybody knows that. But there is one virtue—if it can be called that—about most of these lessons in brutality. You at least know them for what they are, and you can refuse to let them into your home. It means learning to discriminate between the evil and the good and making the right choices, but that's a principle which holds in every area of life." Culbertson, "TV and Christian Ethics," *MM*, April 1957, 13. Movies and TV were not the only cultural factors to elicit evangelical angst. Even a seemingly innocuous thing as comic

what would later be called "family friendly" movies. Certainly he was worried about decency and the rule-breaking aspect of immorality, but he spent as much if not more attention to the harm done to and through the rule-breakers. He, and others like him, saw biblical morality as tied to the well-being of the human race and not as a mere arbitrary set of laws or ecclesial whims. The following year he said that many had claimed that the US was a Christian nation, and he admitted that they had some reason for doing so. But, whatever principles might have been built into its foundation, the country was clearly in moral decline. "The moral tone and the standards of life in this great nation seem to be at an all time [sic] low. Evil is apparent on every hand and those who have access to statistical reports make it crystal clear that vice in every form is on the increase." Like many others, he believed that something was wrong in the land at its core, and its people seemed interested only in libertinism. Rather than seeing America as inevitably secure in God's hands, he thought it more likely that God's hands would

---

books could come under skeptical scrutiny. The problem for one pundit was that while the formal declarations and messages of such literature focused on fighting crime, the upshot of the focus on crime was to glamorize criminals and their activities. He noted the irony that the comics shown in newspapers for adults and the like tended to be relatively tame compared to what could be found in those comic books designed for children's consumption. "The world recoils at the thought of warfare by means of germs which attack the body. The American public, however, is blithely permitting the distribution of far more deadly germs in exchange for the nickels and dimes of children. Meanwhile the juvenile courts are seeing their sad procession of six and eight and ten year olds who 'learned how' through the comics." Ernest D. Christie, "Those Un-comic Comic Books," *MM*, January 1954, 10. Lampman revisited this theme in early 1955, noting that a new self-imposed code of ethics by comic book producers would not do much good. Lampman, "New Clean Comic Book Code Seen to Lack Teeth," *MM*, January 1955, 5. Similarly, Bell told his readers, "Even a casual examination of the so-called 'funnies' which flood our newsstands and which are so popular will show that they are in no sense 'funny' and that many of them are vicious in the extreme, portraying crime and vice, even to revolting details. Also, many of the television programs for young people need to be checked as many of them are based entirely on the portrayal of violence and death." Bell did not see his analysis as leading to a passive response by Christians, comfortable in the knowledge that their hands were clean, but he called upon his fellow believers to get to know the basics of juvenile delinquency and to provide care themselves. "To make this very practical: are there boys and girls in your own community who need such help? Is it available? Are you helping?" Bell, "Juvenile Delinquency," *SPJ*, February 17, 1954, 3.

come down against the US. "Except for the grace and long suffering of God, one might well wonder why His blessing has not long since been withdrawn from our country. We dare not assume that God will continue to bless our land in spite of its wickedness. If we continue indifferent to His Word and persist in our disobedience, judgment is inevitable."[48] America's hope was in God's mercy in spite of its sins and not in its innate goodness.

In many ways both Henry and Schaeffer were quite skeptical about the future prospects of the entire democratic experiment in the West. Frankly, they did not think that there was sufficient character among its people to persevere in the face of the determined opposition flowing from Moscow and Beijing.[49] This is not to say that they found the Cold War rivalry to be a matter of indifference. Henry saw it in explicitly moral terms, saying that the West was the "champion of

---

48. Culbertson, "The Downward Path," *MM*, September 1955, 12.

49. At another point Henry wrote of the military implications of American cultural failings. The following year Henry cited a government report on why some American service members succumbed to Communist brainwashing while prisoners of war, saying "The majority of these men seem to have lacked (a) Spiritual and moral convictions; (b) Understanding and appreciation of the American heritage; (c) Discipline in the sense of a basic concept of right and wrong; (d) An understanding of Communism and its propaganda methods. Many of these men came from broken homes while few of them had Church training or religious ties." Henry, "What of Tomorrow?" *CT*, March 3, 1958, 20. Culbertson also addressed this brainwashing, but his point was more to make a spiritual point using the Communist activity as an illustration of temptation. "Satan, it would seem, uses much the same methods and techniques in accomplishing his ends in our material world that he uses in spiritual combat. How quick he is to suggest that our situation is hopeless, that a life which will count for Christ in an active, aggressive way is beyond our reach or that the difficulties we face are overwhelming." Culbertson, "That Same Subtle Weapon," *MM*, January 1957, 11. A year later he revisited this issue when a new report came out suggesting that American forces' collaboration with the Communists and high death rate had less to do with enemy action than many had at first believed. Though he admitted that any conclusions must be tentative, he posited that they had been coddled in the US. "Too much of our national, community and private life fosters such questions as What is there in it for me? Who will take care of me? In our quest for security, we are in danger of failing to grasp opportunity. We tend to sacrifice challenge for comfort, work for welfare, duty for dole. Important as humanitarian actions are, they can be carried so far as to crush incentive, initiative, and resourcefulness." Culbertson, "The Spirit of the Age," *MM*, January 1958, 11.

human freedoms" as opposed to the totalitarian slavery practiced by its Eastern rivals. Nonetheless, he couched this praise in the context of grave doubts as to whether the American-led West even knew what their prized freedom actually was. Compared to the viewpoint of the Communist faction, which he described as formidable, he said that his own side had a "lack of a positive philosophy of freedom" and that this failing was endangering its ability to convince the neutral nations to join it.[50] Just a few months later he reiterated this with, if anything, an even more dismal tone. "The real question before us is not whether Europe and America will be cut to the Soviet pattern, or Russia to the Anglo-Saxon; rather, it is whether the whole world in our day will go down in nihilism. We are face to face not merely with one of the great divides of history, but with the divide of divides in the sphere of human decision."[51] To him it was only in conformity to the revelation of God that human flourishing could actually exist.[52] As he had earlier, Schaeffer remained concerned about America's direction, seeing his homeland moving away from the very belief system which had granted

---

50. Henry, "The Fragility of Freedom in the West," *CT*, October 15, 1956, 8.

51. Henry, "Is Modernity Worth Saving?" *CT*, January 7, 1957, 20. Henry rebuked the attempt by diplomats to fashion a human-centered basis for liberty and dignity, suggesting that this would leave the strivings of the Cold War as nothing more than two versions of the same materialistic and tyrannical product. "For if the U.N. is the source and sanction of human rights, there can be no appeal to a source and sanction higher than the U.N. ... In that event the conflict between the Soviet orbit and the United Nations reduces to a conflict between superstates." Henry did not call for advocacy of the American position simply because it was his side. Instead, he called upon America and its allies in the UN to root their fight "in the fact that man bears by divine creation a unique dignity, and that the state and the citizen alike are bound in a responsible way to the Living God." Henry, "Human Rights in an Age of Tyranny," *CT*, February 4, 1957, 22. A few years earlier Henry had an article published in *ET* which argued in the same way about the UN, saying, "If the United Nations are the ultimate sanction for rights, then we have no rights against the United Nations, since the United Nations define our rights. If that is the case, then we seem to be faced with the threat of totalitarianism on an almost global basis. For it makes little difference whether it is a state, or a league of nations, or the United Nations, which claims for itself the right to legislate what rights belong and what rights do not belong to mankind; as long as such a superstate is defined as the source of rights there remains no other reference point in the name of which to challenge the superstate, since the superstate defines his rights." Henry, "Moral Values in Public Education," *ET*, September 1954, 42.

52. Henry, "A Firm Reliance on Providence," *CT*, June 23, 1958, 20.

it liberty in the first place and toward the philosophical basis of its
Cold War enemy.

> Speaking of the United States, and I think that it would apply
> also to certain other countries, it seems to me that we have for-
> gotten that the basis of our country was historic Christianity—a
> complete antithesis to the base of the French Revolution. ... The
> fact that each individual had a God who was a greater King than
> any earthly king for He could read the hearts. Nothing could be a
> greater contrast to this than the base for the French Revolution
> and later the Russian one which were built on the cult of man ...
> yet it is unhappily not a mistake to largely equate the base at the
> present moment in the US etc. with the base originally and at the
> present moment of the French Revolution and the Russian one.[53]

The success of the West in the Cold War depended upon philosophical and religious issues, far deeper than mere loyalty to the Stars and
Stripes. If America continued in its present declining path, only failure
and defeat lay before it.

Proclaiming the Unpopular

Racial issues in America rose in prominence during this period, and
evangelicals continued to offer sometimes mutually exclusive criticism
for the nation.[54] A news editor at *Moody* rejoiced that, according to its

---

53. Schaeffer, Letter to Kenneth de Courcy, September 15, 1956, Francis A.
Schaeffer Collection, Box 57, File 22, The Library, Southeastern Baptist Theological
Seminary, Wake Forest, North Carolina.

54. South African racism was also used as a means to critique the American
version. Another article, this time addressing South Africa, led off with a quote
from the Anglican Archbishop of Cape Town, saying, "It is a sad commentary on
the work of the Dutch Reformed Church of South Africa that it spends a great deal
of money on missionary work but believes in keeping African and white congregations apart. It has a warped and inaccurate Calvinistic outlook." Later the author
critiqued the South African church for attempting to buttress apartheid by appeal
to the separateness of ancient Israel from the nations. He wrote, "Apartheid has
been 'proven' to be scriptural by politicians and as well as theologians." As many
of the arguments by South Africans for apartheid echoed in detail the convictions
of those in the American South arguing for segregation, the implicit point to an
American audience in 1958 would be hard to miss. The Editors, "South Africa Race
Tensions," CT, September 1, 1958, 31. Barnhouse was also to condemn South Africa's

own report, a group dedicated to ending segregation in Washington, DC
had been so successful that it had "worked itself out of a job." He went
on to quote a government official who declared that "more progress has
been made toward ending racial discrimination in the last few years
than in a similar period since 1865."[55] Barnhouse offered tacit criticism
of a church in Georgia that had fired its pastor for his desire to integrate.
He offered no commentary but ended with the ex-pastor's statement,
saying, "You should withdraw yourself from the Southern Baptist
Convention, call yourselves a community club instead of a Christian
church, and elect a president instead of a pastor."[56] In the increasing
tension of the period, it was apparently an easier tactic for editors
simply to state the facts about the crisis, leaving the reader to glean
the obvious implications. This passive aggressive approach appeared in

---

racial policies. In January 1956 he wrote, "The Union of South Africa pursued its
devilish and foolish policy of *apartheid*, and near the end of the year its delegates
walked out of a United Nations session when that body ... voted disapproval of the
racial discrimination practiced in that country." Barnhouse, "A Survey of 1955," *ET*,
January 1956, 9.

55. Lampman, "Desegregation in Capital Seen as Most Dramatic Success," *MM*,
December 1955, 5.

56. Barnhouse, "Pastor Fired on Segregation Issue," *ET*, February 1955, 34. The
pastor providing the actual quote was Henry A. Buchanan. In contrast, when speaking about a church group affirming segregation, Barnhouse simply stated the fact
starkly. Barnhouse, "Methodists For Segregation," *ET*, July 1955, 37. The group in
question was some two hundred Methodists in Mississippi. The following year
he gave a similarly tacit rebuke to segregationists when he spent all but the final
sentence of a short piece reporting that the three-hundred-thousand-member
American Baptist Association had quoted the Bible to support their strong segre-
gationist stance. His concluding comment was, "Meanwhile, in St. Paul, Minn., the
Lutheran Church-Missouri Synod called on its two million members to work to
eliminate racial discrimination 'where-ever it may exist.' " Barnhouse, "Integration
and Segregation," *ET*, September 1956, 17. Barnhouse was in some ways the most
open about his opposition to segregation. He shared the account of African
Americans who had challenged their fellow theological conservatives. Why was
it, they inquired, that the hated Communists and Roman Catholics were quite open
to their place in their movements, but they were kept out of their own? They said
that this was true in the North even more so than in Dixie. Barnhouse's rhetorical
question to his readers was, "Who can tell why those whose faith should move them
faster to right wrongs are the slowest when it comes to practical understanding of
the basic problems of the compassion of Christ put into effect? Does the Devil have
more love than Christians who boast of their doctrinal faithfulness?" Barnhouse,
"Race," *ET*, August 1956, 10.

other places. A *CT* news article in 1958 did not expressly condemn segregation, but the author's tone made it clear that his sympathies were
with the move to integrate. Proponents of segregation were described
as "hard-shell" and a "determined minority," while those favoring integration "displayed a solid front." The writer's concluding plea was that
peace would prevail, an unlikely request were he seeing state-enforced
integration as an injustice.[57]

At other times these magazines could be more explicit. Addressing
the problem of segregation and its near-universal acceptance in the
South as intrinsic, Henry attacked churches that aided and abetted
racism. "Whereas one might have expected Christian churches to lead
the way to an era of improved relations, not a few were invoking the
Bible in circumvention of its emphasis on the equal dignity of men and
on transcending racial distinctions in the body of Christ, to justify the
status quo." For Henry, the quest for racial justice in the American scene
was not an optional one. "Nonetheless, the Church is obliged to proclaim
a divinely revealed ethic of universal validity. She is not precluded from,
nor can she be justified for failure to seek social justice for the Negro.
The Church has no license to make conversion a precondition of her
support of right and decency in the world at large." While he insisted
that there needed to be an understanding that disagreement over meth-
odology did not entail disagreement over substance, he believed that the
church had provided a self-inflicted wound to its standing in the world
through its hesitance in this matter. "If the Church had taken a vigorous
and courageous initiative in deploring the evils of segregation, even
with a special eye on the Negro in her own fellowship, her hesitancy

---

57. David E. Kucharsky, "Race Showdown—An Unlikely Site," *CT*, July 21,
1958, 29. *CT* was in an awkward position. As part of its senior leadership was the
northerner, Carl Henry and the southerner, L. Nelson Bell. Henry would later
place the American denial of civil rights right along with Nazi atrocities and South
African apartheid. Henry, *God, Revelation and Authority Volume VI: God Who Stands
and Stays Part Two* (Wheaton, IL: Crossway Books, 1999), 444. This book, Henry's
magnum opus, was originally published between 1976 and 1983. Bell, on the other
hand, was a strong opponent of segregation, as seen in his own comments and those
of his fellow writers at *SPJ*. However, as noted below, Bell's views on segregation
were either more complex than some of his previous articles might suggest or show
that he was open to correction.

in approving some specific 'program of integration' as *the* Christian solution would not give rise to misunderstanding."[58] Harold Lindsell penned an article for *ET* in 1956 challenging Americans on their racial views with these strong words:

> Whatever the outcome of this struggle, Christians all over America must approach the problem penitently, aware that the existence of the problem is the fault, not of the Negro, but of the white man who brought him to America against his will and as chattel property. Amends for the wrongs done the Negro in the first place should loom large in the thinking of Christians who believe in justice and righteousness.[59]

---

58. Henry, "Desegregation and Regeneration," *CT*, September 29, 1958, 20–21. In this same article Henry referenced a statement prepared by Bell for a conference of southern Christian leaders. In it Bell offered no defense of segregation, but, in fact, stated that "it can be safely affirmed that that segregation of races enforced by law is both un-Christian and un-American," and "Church membership should be open to all without discrimination or restriction." However, the same document allowed for self-segregation. That is he spoke against the "segregation of races enforced by law," and that "in most areas and under normal conditions this will not result in an integrated church, since various races will prefer separate churches for social, educational and many other reasons." In essence Bell was opposed to both government-mandated segregation and state-imposed integration. He had expressed this explicitly a few years earlier in *SPJ* where he said, "Therefore, segregation by law cannot be legally defended. This in no way precludes the expediency wisdom and right of voluntary alignments along racial or other social lines (and it should not be forgotten for one minute that it is the Christian thing at times to be expedient). In like manner, *forced integration* cannot be defended, either on legal or moral grounds. Both forced segregation and forced integration infringe on the legal right of the individual." Bell, "Christian Race Relations Must Be Natural, Not Forced," *SPJ*, August 17, 1955, 3–4.

59. Harold Lindsell, "The Bible and Race Relations," *ET*, August 1956, 12. Lindsell would later succeed Carl Henry as editor of *CT*. This article received an angry letter to the editor in October 1956 where the soon-to-be-former subscriber said, "As of now, you will please cancel the unexpired subscription of your filthy magazine, *Eternity*. ... It's disgraceful that under the name of 'Christian Truth,' you are permitted to use the mails and the term Christianity to propagandize your Socialist filth and ill-political football, namely the article, 'The Bible and Race Relations.'" Ralph Roberts, Letter to the Editor, *ET*, October 1956, 2. Despite this remonstrance, in this and subsequent issues, *ET* kept up the pressure on segregationists. A piece in this same issue had the challenging subtitle, "A penetrating evaluation of our imperfect Christian witness," and offered a lengthy argument filled with biblical allusions. Joseph T. Bayly, "A Northern Christian Looks at the Race Question," *ET*,

One of the most poignant pieces condemning segregation was an article by an African American pastor accusing American evangelicals of
being a big part of the problem. It would have been no small thing for
a largely white evangelical magazine to feature an African American
lecturing his largely white evangelical audience in 1957.[60]

October 1956, 8. This was followed up a few months later by a counterpoint by a
southerner offering Dixie's response in defense of segregation. Guy T. Gillespie,
"A Southerner Looks at the Race Question," ET, July 1957, 22. This same article had
appeared a month earlier in SPJ. Gillespie, "A Southern Christian Looks at the
Race Problem, SPJ, June 5, 1957, 7–12. Prefacing the article in ET, the editors wrote,
"Eternity is not trying to ride the fence in publishing Dr. Gillespie's viewpoint. All
of the members of our editorial staff have pronounced views on various aspects
of the issue. Yet it is extremely complex, and thus far strongminded proponents
of the divergent views have not found a solid meeting-ground." However, on the
facing page to this article, the editors placed another piece with the heading, "The
last word about man is not that he is different in race, but that he belongs to that
one human race that God loves and desires to save." Martin H. Scharlemann, "The
Church Must Be Color-Blind," ET, July 1957, 23.
    60. B. M. Nottage, "You've Neglected My People," ET, December 1957, 12.
Barnhouse's fellow Presbyterian theologians at SPJ did not take the same approach.
They, too, included comments by an African American thinker, Davis Lee, publisher
of The Newark Telegram, but his words, if not in favor of segregation, were at least
highly critical of many integration activists. He granted that a color-blind society
was "a laudable objective," but he was skeptical about its present implementation.
"Integration in the schools in the North and East is not a howling success. A Negro
can attend most of the schools up here and get an education, but few of the states
that educate him will hire him as a teacher. The State of Connecticut doesn't have
twenty-five Negro teachers." He continued his rebuke of northern conceit by pointing out that despite the common impression, African Americans were more likely
to be in positions of authority over institutions in Dixie than in the North. Davis
Lee, "Segregation," SPJ, July 7, 1954, 7. Ellipsis in original. This was not an article by
Lee. The editors of SPJ printed extended quotations from a source which they did
not identify. Interestingly, this piece was reprinted exactly and in its entirety just
three weeks later to accommodate the influx of requests for copies. The Editors,
"Segregation," SPJ, July 28, 1954, 7. In the same issue the editors provided two other
comments on segregation. The first merely reported that a Mississippi church had
voted unanimously to reject the suggestion of the wider Southern Presbyterian
denomination to end segregation, although, to be precise, they rejected the move
on procedural grounds. The Editors, "First Church of Jackson, Miss. Declares Itself
on Segregation," SPJ, July 7, 1954, 8. The second summarized a letter to the editor
by a white woman in Mississippi who recounted the frustrations of her African
American housekeeper who feared that desegregation would mean the loss of
independent privileges for African American schools. The white woman then
concluded, "You see, there are two sides to this question, and they do not want us
in their schools." Anonymous, "They Don't Want It," SPJ, July 7, 1954, 8. No name is

WAR

"The problem of war is as old as man. War with its accompanying passions, destruction, and suffering, is one of the greatest evils in human society. In fact, wars have been so frequent throughout history that, in spite of the general desire for peace, we may say that peace is only a temporary condition." [61] These mournful words by General Harrison,

---

given for the letter to the editor. A later article offered the following analysis: "In aiding the NAACP the Presbyterian Church, North, whether it so intends or not, is aiding the advance of Communism. If the old law of mathematics still holds true that 'things equal to the same thing are equal to each other,' then the NAACP is equal to the Communists by reason of accomplishing the Communist objective of division, strife, hatred, enmity, chaos, [and] confusion." Joseph S. Jones, "The Ku Klux Klan, the NAACP, and the Presbyterian Church," *SPJ*, July 31, 1957, 7. In contrast, while Barnhouse did print a criticism of the NAACP in *ET*, Barnhouse, "NAACP," *ET*, June 1958, 4-5, not only did he also print that organization's reply in defense, John A. Morsell, "NAACP Answers Charge," *ET*, November 1958, 3, but he attached a note to this rebuttal stating that he partly wished he had not written the article in the first place as it had turned out to have been unhelpful.

61. William K. Harrison, "Christianity and Peace in Our Day," *CT*, October 29, 1956, 13-15. Part of his reasoning focused on the fallibility of national leaders. "By understanding this responsibility of the head of state we can see why it is impossible to prevent war. It is impossible to prevent some men from becoming criminals. It is also impossible to prevent some criminals from becoming the rulers of states." Since, according to him and general evangelical anthropology, there was no human being without the corruption which made war a reality, there was no way to set up a form of government which precluded aggression. "At bottom, the problem of war is a moral problem. ... An international organization, with or without an authoritative head, cannot solve this moral problem. ... Any organization, no matter how worthy its purpose or how stringent its rules, will succumb to ineffectiveness, corruption disruption, and destruction unless prevented by the moral integrity of the men in it." He even went so far as to say that Christian morality, as an external, philosophical principle, held out no hope for peace in any time. After all, it had failed so miserably in the twentieth century. "Only a regenerate mankind is enabled to tame the lusts and passions which make for war. That is why the preaching of the Gospel of redemption and regeneration is urgently needed and vitally relevant to each generation of fallen man. What Marx, Lenin, and Stalin needed was not simply exposure to the 'Christian ethic' but to be 'born again.' " Harrison put precious little faith in humanity's ability to avoid such a fate despite a general desire to avoid that end. He acknowledged that method after method had been put forward as certain means of achieving peace, but all had failed. Some were able to make progress for a given time or place, "but on the balance sheet of history, none of these efforts have been profitable, and nothing indicates that they ever can be." He blamed these failures on the failure to ask the right questions. "Why do wars occur? Too often consideration of the matter starts with another question, What is the cause of war?

a man who had seen war more closely than many of his readers, typ-
ified much of evangelicals' thought on war. It was awful. It was inevitable. It was not inevitable in a way which excused its presence, but
it was unavoidable given certain ubiquitous human characteristics.
Until humanity's very nature was altered, conflict and strife would be
endemic to human society.

OPPOSING PACIFISM, ENFORCING PEACE

While the reality of war's horrors led many mainline Protestants to
oppose war entirely, evangelicals tended to stay within the classical
Just War tradition of Christianity. War was indeed awful, but it was
preferable to select alternatives. Further, the mainline insistence of
peace in the present could lead to even more devastating wars in the
future. As L. Nelson Bell argued, "It is our opinion that at a time when
America can and should wield the greatest influence in international
affairs we are in grave danger of desiring 'peace' so much that we will
lose our perspective and look for peace through compromise with that
which is basically wrong." He feared that many Christians calling for
negotiations with the Russians were actually paving the way toward
oppression and devastation through an unhelpful humility. He was
quite willing to admit America's failings, but he refused to accept any
moral equivalency with the Soviets, who he described as "the very
incarnation of evil." It was not that he found modern warfare palatable
but that it might well be preferable to the alternative. Complicity with
Communist tyranny would yield a far worse fate in God's judgment than
confronting the danger from Moscow.[62] In contrast to this approach,

---

But the real question is, Who causes war? War is a human activity. No matter what
the incentives or secondary causes, men do not have to fight. They choose to do so."
    62. Bell, "Not Peace but a Sword," *SPJ*, January 6, 1954, 2-3. He was disdain-
ful of those within Christianity who called for too close an association with the
Communists, believing that they were aiding the perpetrators of oppression. "That
radical and left-wing groups and individuals, along with the parlor pinks and
fellow travelers, should advocate this line of action is not surprising. A dedicated
Communist, placed in a strategic position (and there are many such), can pull the
strings and secure the vocal support of many who are stupid and easily led. But,
when respected and influential representatives of the Protestant Church begin
to advocate doing business with the Communists it is high time that Churchmen

Bell argued for the legitimacy of a limited war now to forestall a greater war later. In reaction to Beijing's raids on Taipei-controlled islands, he counseled that the US should attack China since the Russians were not in the mood for a general war.[63] Bell was certainly the most vocal advocate of this "stitch-in-time-saves-nine" policy, but it undergirded much of evangelical military counsel during the period.

Henry may have feared the results of modern war, but he, like Bell, worried that American leaders did not fully appreciate other dangers in the world. Reacting to the Suez Crisis of 1956, he was largely complimentary of Eisenhower's response, but he held out some strong criticisms as well. "An air of unrealism, however, clings to the President's announced policy. That the United States will not intervene in the present hostilities is doubtless reassuring to all who dread the perils of war in an atomic age. But recent American pronouncements suggest at times the notion that war must always be avoided as the worst of

---

everywhere take notice and also action." Bell, "It Is Not 'Cynical' to Face the Facts," *SPJ*, January 20, 1954, 5. By early 1956 Bell emphatically stated that the US was losing the Cold War to the Soviets out of its continued misguided attempts at peaceful negotiation. Bell, "Needed—A New Policy!" *SPJ*, January 11, 1956, 3. Culbertson also critiqued much of the Christian peace movement. Without naming any particular pacifists, he pushed back against those who saw war as intrinsically incompatible with Christianity. "There is extant these days a great deal of talk about the evil of war, as though war were inherently wrong. But this is not the mind of God nor the teaching of His Word." He argued that conflict was endemic to the human condition because there was an eternal tension within all human hearts flowing from the sin of Adam. "Within, without and all around is war. For this same trial of strength engaging individual men is found in the larger sphere of man's contacts with his fellows. Frustrated by his failure to rule himself, he would rule other men, and given power, would oppress. It has always been so—the constant clash of men with men, each man or group of men, determined he—or they—shall rule." He did not see himself as compromising with evil but as standing up to it. "We long for peace. We yearn to keep our sons at home. We know the bleakness of bereavement and of loss. But no man worthy of the name would want to let the terror rage, the tyrant rule, the criminal have his way." Culbertson, "War is Not Always Evil," *MM*, November 1954, 11.

63. Bell, "Quemoy—A Principle," *SPJ*, October 8, 1958, 5. Ironically, his confidence that the Soviets would not go to war over Taiwan flowed from his expectation that the Russians were winning the Cold War. "Her philosophy is—why should we fight when we are already winning by infiltration, subversion, intrigue and through the moral and spiritual degeneration of Western society—and that without the use of a single Russian soldier, or the firing of a single shot."

all evils." Henry believed that such a policy encouraged aggression by implicitly telling other nations that the US would not become involved militarily unless directly attacked, leaving the watching world to its own resources.[64] A US failure to be realistic could have dire consequences in a nuclear-armed age. Even recent apparent setbacks by Communism in Europe did not suggest to Henry a time of peace ahead but the increased likelihood of war in Asia, with Korea, Taiwan, and, almost prophetically, Southeast Asia as possible new theaters of conflict. He wondered if a Chinese incursion to one of these areas would enable the Soviets to move into the Middle East, freed to do so by the distraction of the Western powers in Asia.[65]

LIVING WITH THE BOMB

In the midst of such dour concerns, Courier was encouraged by the simple absence of a nuclear war. "What is the chance of H- and A-bombs being used? The former, nil. The latter slim. Why? Because scientists have finally convinced top officials of US (and Russia, too; they're as much interested in self-preservation as we are) of the dangers of 'fallout' to civilian populations over wide areas." Much as had Bell a few years before, Courier concluded that the shared terror of atomic weaponry would keep them unused. "So we have in effect an H- and A-bomb stalemate. Neither side will use them, because of the retaliation potential of the other fellow, and because they might figuratively go off in the face of the side shooting them. Does this mean no war in the future? Not at all. It simply means 'little' rather than 'big' wars—a return to 'primitive' weapons."[66] On the surface this sounds naïve, but it was also what occurred in reality: America and Russia avoided overt direct confrontation with one another throughout the entire Cold War period, keeping even proxy wars in Vietnam and Afghanistan small.

Atomic warfare had been a part of evangelical discussions for a decade, but not only had the threat endured, but advancements in the

---

64. Henry, "International Crisis on the Sandy Wastes of Sinai," *CT*, November 12, 1956, 24.

65. Henry, "Joint Moscow-Peking Threat Calls for Christian Realism," *CT*, March 4, 1957, 23.

66. Gabriel Courier, "The Bombs," *CH*, January 1956, 10–11.

weapons and their delivery made it more of an issue than ever before. Barnhouse maintained that such new technology was necessary, given the nature of the Russian threat, but the military must take precautions to ensure the safety of those near these experiments and confess it when a new bomb exceeds expectations and causes harm.[67] Culbertson, on the other hand, emphasized the negative implications, saying,

> The H-bomb tests that blasted an island out of existence and resulted in radio activity [sic] which affected fishermen scores of miles away present an ominous preview of what tomorrow may bring. Even this fearful weapon, however, is not the end. Russian scientists, we are told, by-passing the ordinary H-bomb, are concentrating on inventing the C-bomb. The plan is to have the first tests of this far more powerful bomb in the second half of 1955. What a dark picture!"[68]

In contrast to this hesitation, Bell saw the existence of the bomb as a net-positive development, at least in the sense that it was the US and not the Soviets who had the advantage. He further argued that there was little doubt that were it not for American nuclear weapons, the Russians would have overrun Western Europe long before.[69]

The weapons themselves were dangerous enough, but with the late 1950s advent of the Space Age, the situation became even graver. Writing in *CT*, a contributor discussed the implications of the October 1957 launch of Sputnik. "Scientists tell us that it is the most significant event since the splitting of the atom. Military strategists inform us that

---

67. Barnhouse, "National Lying," *ET*, August 1956, 11. He said of the Soviets, "In fact, as long as there are mad dogs in Russia we must study every possible method of dealing with mad dogs and with their hydrophobia of ideas and actions." Culbertson was later to note, without comment, that several church groups around the world had called for an end to atomic testing. Culbertson, "A-Bomb Tests Opposed by National Churches," *MM*, June 1957, 7.

68. Culbertson, "The Christian and His Times," *MM*, June 1954, 9. Culbertson offers no explanation of what a "C-bomb" might be. It is possibly a bomb made with cobalt, which was discussed in the time period as a particularly destructive variant but was also never said to have been constructed. Less likely is the possibility that he was speaking of a "Tsar/Czar bomb," which the Soviets did construct just a few years later as the largest nuclear device ever built.

69. Bell, "The Church and Nuclear Weapons," *SPJ*, September 15, 1954, 2.

it will change the face of future warfare. Were a rocket with an H-bomb warhead to be launched in Moscow, they say, it would destroy New York or Washington twelve minutes later." He warned against what he called a "Maginot Line temperament," which placed confidence in America's military power, saying that Sputnik had shown that even the mighty US could be outclassed.[70] Bell agreed, saying, "The launching of the earth satellite by Russia is potentially the most significant event since the explosion of the first A-bomb over Hiroshima. That this should have been effected by Russia carries with it implications which are sobering and revealing for it indicates a technological advancement not previously suspected."[71] Culbertson included some gallows humor with his thoughts on Sputnik with the suggestion that all this new technology simply gave people something else to worry about.[72]

This was no hypothetical threat. Henry argued that America was in a great danger when it came to its Russian rival and its expanding nuclear stockpiles.

> Scientists no less than religionists are doom-conscious. Pointing to Soviet superiority in the satellite sphere, they question America's capacity to reverse the balances of strategy to overtake and outdistance the Soviet program. ... By late 1959, they warn, the United States will be less than 15 minutes from 75 ICBMs capable of wiping out the Strategic Air Command's existing bases.[73]

Henry saw the situation as putting new pressures on the church and said that the church needed to speak out, because, if it did not, the conversation would be dominated by those hostile to Christianity in one way or another. He was not, however, saying that the church needed to speak out against nuclear weapons, as such. When some Christians argued that there was a fundamental difference between atomic and conventional war, Henry retorted, "No clear case has been made for a

70. Richard W. Gray, "God, America and Sputnik," *CT*, December 9, 1957, 15–17.

71. Bell "A Rude Awakening … It Is *Much* Later Than We Thought," *SPJ*, October 16, 1957, 2.

72. Culbertson, "Sputnik and Perspective," *MM*, December 1957, 11.

73. Henry, "Can We Salvage the Republic?" *CT*, March 3, 1958, 3.

qualitative difference between nuclear bombs and other weapons of warfare; the difference, however great, remains quantitative. Eliminate the bombs, and terrible though more conventional weapons of war remain." The only hope he offered in avoiding the fate humanity had created for itself lay in looking outside of humanity. As he often did, he pointed to "the lordship of Christ in the reaffirmation of the Judeo-Christian view of life" as the only hope for humanity in the face of atomic warfare and any other threat.[74]

Atomic weapons in the evangelical imagination continued to be largely fear-inducing, but not what one could call fear-mongering. Even Bell, with his continued advocacy of their use, highlighted their danger as one of the reasons that the American government needed to change its foolish ways. General Harrison, who had seen war up and close, spoke of a nuclear contest in a third world war as unimaginably more horrible than even the devastation of the previous two, and Carl Henry spoke of the fear of them as one of the very few things uniting a very disunited world. With the rise of ICBMs during this period, a nuclear attack on the American homeland became an unstoppable threat were war to break out. Rather than reacting with a careless "Nuke 'em all and let God sort them out" or a ghoulish glee that the means of the end of the world had finally been revealed, these writers seemed genuinely terrified about what humanity had created.

---

74. Henry, "Christ and the Atom Bomb," *CT*, September 2, 1957, 20–22. Carlos Fuller also thought the UN was no ultimate solution to the atomic crisis. He said that the only things commentators ever seemed to put forward as impediments to a nuclear holocaust were overwhelming military force and the United Nations. "However necessary fearful military equipment may be, it is at best but a negative restraint upon the passions of potential dictators. It cannot transform a warmonger into a lover of peace. The United Nations is a useful public forum for the focus of world opinion. But again it is fundamentally an organization of external pressure." This was, however, not a commentary on atomic warfare, as such, but on the failure of the church to live up to its true power. Carlos Greenleaf Fuller, "A Church Powered for an Atomic Age," *CT*, January 6, 1958, 3.

END TIMES

ISRAEL BY THE RED SEA

The reality of a war in the Middle East involving Western powers and Israel was a scene made for eschatological excitement. Yet, the Suez Crisis of 1956 elicited relatively little commentary by evangelical writers, and much of that spoke against any end-times certitude or Israeli sanctity.[75] While evangelicals would, with good reason, be later associated as among the most strident pro-Israeli factions of American life, much of this would await the dramatic events of the Six Day War in 1967. For example, in keeping with CH's customary eschatological disinterest, Courier's response was calm but critical of America's best allies. "Aggressors: It's a hard name. But what other name can be applied with correctness to Britain and France, not to say Israel? ... In this time of stress, Israel and especially Britain and France (who ought to know better) have reacted lamentably, not to say tragically."[76] Henry wrote an editorial as the conflict was ongoing, but he spoke of it only in terms of its geopolitical and moral implications. He wrote of the creation of the State of Israel flowing not from eschatological necessity but from the horrors and suffering of the previous twenty years, and he was quite willing to critique the Israelis for being "ruthless and aggressive, as the tragic camps of 900,000 displaced Arabs can attest."[77] Another article in the same issue did discuss the end of the world, but it did so only to check the rush to connect the prophetical dots.

> Undoubtedly, there are prophetic enthusiasts who will see in the new crisis specific fulfillment of prophecy. Such may be the case, but many observers feel that Christians will be wise to refrain

---

75. Interestingly, Smith predicted trouble around the Suez Canal two years before the conflict broke out. Smith, "This Serious Hour," MM, November 1954, 28.

76. Courier, "Aggressors," CH, December 1956, 11.

77. Henry, "International Crisis on the Sandy Wastes of Sinai," CT, November 12, 1956, 24. The article was printed after the war had ended on November 7, but, given the nature of periodicals, he would have written it before this time. Interestingly, although his reference to the recent suffering of the Jews clearly included that enacted by the Nazis, Henry does not mention them by name but broadens his condemnation to "totalitarian states."

from hasty judgments while centering their energies more on praying for all concerned ... that God's restraining hand may be in evidence and that even in this conflict the wrath of man may please Him.[78]

This hesitation was in great contrast to what had been seen in *OH* twenty years earlier and to the renewed enthusiasm found in evangelical commentary a decade later. For the moment, many evangelicals seemed content to wait and see. One exception came in June 1958 with an article in *SPJ* which declared forthrightly that the end times were at hand. After detailing some of the signs given in the Bible for when the end had arrived, the author said, "Every one of these signs has happened and one additional one besides during the past 40 years since 1917 when Allenby took over Palestine from the Turks as Grattan Guinness long before 1917 said would happen from Daniel's prophecies."[79] More

---

78. The Editors, "Mechanized March by Children of Israel," *CT*, November 12, 1956, 28. *CT* did publish an interview on the following page which pointed to the founding of Israel as the fulfilment of prophecy, but the interviewee was not an American evangelical but an Israeli Zionist. Don C. Odell, "Answers from Israel," *CT*, November 12, 1956, 29. George Burnham saw the fighting as a chance to right certain wrongs, but, as had Henry, he did so without recourse to eschatology. "Israel must help in the resettlement of Arab refugees and compensate those Arabs whose lands have been expropriated. The Arabs, likewise, must cease their undeclared war and establish an era of peace and cooperation with Israel through which all their peoples might have an abundant life—heretofore unknown in this part of the world." George Burnham, "Report from Israel," *CT*, December 10, 1956, 29. To close out a tumultuous 1956 *CT* provided dueling articles on the place of Israel in the evangelical worldview. Oswald Allis spoke for those who did not see the biblical promise to the Jews to live in Palestine as applying to the modern State of Israel. Going through the narrative of biblical history and prophecy, he argued that the present nation owed its existence to American Jews and British imperialism. He strongly condemned Israeli actions of recent years, saying, "The persecution of the Jews in Europe was a grievous act of injustice. But allowing the Jews to take possession of a large part of Palestine and force hundreds of thousands of Arabs out of it is an equally grievous wrong." His counsel for his evangelical readers was quite stark. "Does the Israeli cause deserve to succeed? Should Christians be willing to plunge the nations into a third world conflict just to restore unbelieving Jews to, and maintain them in, a land from which they were driven nearly two thousand years ago? We believe the verdict of history will be, No! May God grant that this verdict will not be written in rivers of blood!" Oswald T. Allis, "Israel's Transgression in Palestine," *CT*, December 24, 1956, 6, 8-9.

79. J. Park McCallie, "The Signs of the Times," *SPJ*, June 4, 1958, 9.

common at this juncture was to examine the Middle East conflict in
terms of its mundane geopolitical implications.[80]

THE CHOSEN PEOPLE

Another way that evangelicals in the 1950s differed from their later
impression was their openness to rebuke the Israelis. Despite his

---

80. The normally eschatologically averse Bell gave his own opinion of the Arab-
Israeli tension just a few weeks before the Suez Crisis. Offering a brief survey of the
situation, he noted a hardening of attitudes by the Arab nations, flowing from the
combined effects of a growing sense of nationalism and the mistreatment of their
fellow Arabs by Israeli forces. Bell spoke of Egyptian president Nasser as "probably
the most dangerous man in that part of the world" and expressed concern about
his connection to the Soviet bloc. The bulk of his attention was focused on the
practical geopolitical implications of the place and future of the State of Israel, but
he included two points with end-times significance. He tacitly pushed back against
any eschatological role in the conflict, saying, "Many Christians feel that there is a
prophetic significance in this emergence of Israel as a nation. Others discount this
aspect of the situation but all students of the Middle-East agree that is potentially
the most dangerous spot on the globe." However, he did not squelch the possibility.
"History, both Biblical and secular, would indicate that none have ever prospered
who have mistreated the Jews. Regardless of the future role Israel may be destined
to play in world history it is certainly worthy of note that this small, virile and
struggling national entity has again become the center of controversy, hated (and
possibly of destiny) in the affairs of the entire world." Bell, "The Arab Nations and
Israel," *SPJ*, July 11, 1956, 3–4. A year and a half later he focused his readers' attention
on the Middle East once more with the same basic thrust. "Because our Christian
faith has its geographical origins in that part of the world, all Christians are concerned. Because many believe that prophetic history will have its denouement in
this same region there is also keen interest and anticipation from that standpoint.
… Regardless of the basis of interest, the world is confronted with a situation of
the gravest importance. Just how and when the tensions may be resolved no one
knows. But one thing is certainly indicated: Watch the Middle East." Bell, "Syria
and Egypt," *SPJ*, February 12, 1958, 5. The ambivalent attitude of the editors of *SPJ*
was demonstrated again with its "Young People's Department" a few months later
which encouraged American Christian youth to help Arab refugees. "It is not our
purpose in this program to fix the blame for the serious problem which exists in
the Holy Land today. Our concern is for almost a million suffering Arab refugees
who have had little or nothing to do with the situation which has brought them
into their dire plight." B. Hoyt Evans, "Scholarships for Arab Refugees," *SPJ*, March
26, 1958, 14. In his book, *American Apocalypse*, Sutton argues that eschatology was a
significant factor in Bell's thinking, even saying that his family was known among
other missionaries in China for this interest. However, whatever role it may have
played in private, such concerns only rarely broke through the surface of his public
writings in either *SPJ* or *CT*.

fascination with eschatology, Barnhouse was not above criticizing the Jewish nation. "[The State of Israel] managed to live though practically bankrupt, by the continued dole from the United States. Near the end of the year the troops of Israel went across the border into an Arab town and murdered every inhabitant in what was said to be a reprisal for a violation of the borders by the enemy." After a reference to the biblical account when two sons of the biblical Patriarch, Jacob, slaughtered the men of an entire town as vengeance, he wrote, "Now, in 1953, they had done it again. The cup of their abominations was slowing filling, and their great tribulation, when it comes upon them under the rule of the Antichrist, will be seen as well-deserved." His Israeli comments ended with an allusion to the Arab refugees who "still festered in the rotten camps that had been set up for them by the United Nations."[81] He spoke out against Israel after the Suez Conflict, stating that, "Much as the sympathies of Christians lie with Israel, we must realize that Israel is committing a great wrong and must be condemned."[82] That being said, he also rebuked America for its willingness to be led by its interest in Arabian oil to take the Arab side against the Israelis. This seemingly contradictory set of counsel was, for Barnhouse, a matter of national security. He argued that the only way America could successfully defend itself against Soviet aggression was if God prevented it. This was all tied up in the American response to Israel. "If we take a definite position in defense of the ancient people of God, the Almighty will be forced to bless us and protect us." He continued with this radical line of thinking with the suggestion that if the US took sides against the Israelis that God would, in turn, be forced to destroy America.[83]

---

81. Barnhouse, "Nineteen Fifty-Three," ET, January 1954, 4.

82. Barnhouse, "The President's Speech, ET, April 1957, 8.

83. Barnhouse, "Policy Toward Israel," ET, November 1954, 8. He followed this piece up two months later with a condemnation of the US for its apparent siding with Arab oil interests rather than backing the Israelis. He recounted the nations in history, including Rome and Spain, which had once been powerful before persecuting the Jews. His final example was that of the British, who, according to him, had broken their promise to establish a Jewish homeland in Palestine and lost their great empire within years. His ending comment on this subject was, "I put this in a paragraph by itself for emphasis: If the United States favors Israel against the Arab States, God cannot allow Russia to strike us. If the United States takes the

The Israelis could act in a wicked way and ought to be condemned accordingly, but the United States was still compelled to protect it or find itself in need of protection from God himself.

Not everyone was quite this stark. As might be expected given his previous commentary and emphasis on eschatology, Wilbur Smith called on his readers to see the State of Israel as the definite realization of prophecy. On the one hand, Smith argued that the land of Palestine had, indeed, been promised to the Jews as an eternal possession, even saying that it was only by studying the Bible that Israel's reincarnation made sense. Of the Arabs Smith asserted, "Anyone who saw the pitiful bareness and poverty of that land even thirty years ago, and has seen the land more recently, recognizes that the Arab was a curse to the land, showing no advancement in agricultural methods for two thousand years." On the other hand, he never here appealed to America to be Israel's protector. Such an arrangement would go against his main argument: "This will be God's victory for that portion of the earth which He has called His own land. No anti-Semitism, no wars, no unbelief, no pogroms, not Antichrist himself will be able to prevent the fulfillment of these divinely given promises."[84] Despite its gentler tone, this was the same sort of argument as put forward by Barnhouse: Israel would and must endure simply because of the grace of God and regardless of international opinion, American or otherwise.

One particularly sharp contrast within evangelical attitudes toward the Israelis came in May 1955 when nearly the entire issue of *MM* was devoted to articles on conditions in the State of Israel, including photographic essays, glowing descriptions of the Jews as enduring and triumphing over adversities, and reports on evangelistic opportunities. While little of it made explicit reference to eschatological concerns,

part of the Arabs against Israel we will have removed the last divine barrier and our protection will be gone." Barnhouse, "A Survey of 1954," *ET*, January 1955, 4.

84. Smith, "Israel in Her Promised Land," *CT*, December 24, 1956, 7, 9–11. Despite his sense of certainty about such things, he was able to discuss eschatology without appeal to current events. He wrote an extensive piece for *MM* in 1957 offering a strong defense of his end times view without any mention of any contemporary situation or correlating nations or individuals of the day with those of Scripture. Smith, "The Church, the Tribulation and the Rapture," *MM*, March 1957, 26–28, 30–32.

the impression of the State of Israel as blessed and a blessing would be hard to miss.[85] However, to this themed edition there were those who took issue. A contributor, Fayez Sayegh, challenged some of the articles as being an idealized presentation of the Israelis as morally upright in every way. In contrast this writer referred to the Israeli actions as terrorism. As one of the articles had suggested that the Arabs had fled Palestine of their own accord, Sayegh countered, "Anyone familiar with the Arabs of Palestine will realize that it is *inconceivable* for people of their temperament to abandon land and home and property for any reason short of the pursuit of *survival*. Only self-preservation could outweigh in their minds their keen attachment to fatherland and the soil!"[86] *Moody's* emphasis was clearly in the Israeli's favor, but their willingness to share such pro-Arab statements cuts against a monolithic view of the crises.

Moody was not the only place to demonstrate such latitude. The pages of *CT* were more likely to be the place of prophetical restraint than advocacy. Henry wrote an editorial praising the fact that some of the passion for date-setting had died down in the previous few years, even as he acknowledged that there were "some fundamentalist Bible conferences and churches (perhaps a few Bible institutes also) would have to shut their doors were they to cease from eschatological polemics, their main stock in trade."[87] Again, another article pondered the tenth anniversary of the State of Israel and its possible eschatological significance.

Does the current influx of Jews into a new Israel truly represent a scriptural preliminary to the second coming of Jesus Christ? Many dispensationalists think so. Others feel that the promise to Abraham concerning the land was conditioned upon obedience

---

85. The Editors, *MM*, May 1955.

86. Fayez Sayegh, "The Arab View," *MM*, July 1955, 8. Immediately opposite this article was a parallel piece providing the Israeli perspective.

87. Henry, "The Trumpet of the Lord," *CT*, June 10, 1957, 21. Parentheses in original. His reference to "Bible institutes" may not have been exclusively about *MM*, but it would be hard for it not to be included.

and that the Jews were oppressed in the land or driven out of it because of disobedience.

However, the author refused to take a side in any debate. "Whatever appraisal is accurate, Israel still needs her Messiah. ... At last count, there were only 45,000 Christians in Israel and almost all of them were Arabs. Some Hebrews profess Christ secretly, but only a handful publically proclaim him as Saviour."[88] At least in this instance, Christianity

---

88. The Editors, "Israel—The Fulfillment of Prophecy?" *CT*, May 26, 1958, 28. Theologians were not the only ones to offer up eschatological thoughts in *CT*. Two former military officers contributed their perspectives, but, somewhat understandably, they focused on geopolitical trends rather than Scriptural motifs. A retired navy chaplain discussed events with potential eschatological implications but either did not consider the connections or decided an indirect approach was more efficient. He told his readers that democracy seemed to be losing its enthusiasm for the contest at hand. "Whether we like it or not, the whip of despotism cracks like rifle fire in the modern world. These despotisms are the frightening forces that today are making all of earth's millions dance to their tunes. The principles of democracy seem like fading fires. Leaders, not people glamorized." He then detailed the dangers of a possibly emerging world government and the attendant tendency towards dictatorship. This would be easy fodder for end times speculations, but, aside from saying that this would be a bad arrangement for Christians, he rooted his objections in the oppression of such a superstate and its likelihood of being largely anti-Christian. His conclusion was, "The idea of World Government is a hypnotizing and a fabulously fascinating thing. It is easy to see why millions succumb. But Christianity should comprehend the immense and terrifying implications." H. H. Lippincott, "World Government and Christianity," *CT*, February 3, 1958, 3–5. General Harrison, though not a theologian, parleyed his wartime experience fighting Communists into a forum to comment on the eschatological implications of current events. Eyeing broad trajectories of recent events, Harrison hinted that the end of the world might be sooner than many might want to think. "It does not take a seer to see something of the possible future effect of such God-rejecting rulers on a society which is daily becoming more complex in its relationships." He suggested that the chaos and uncertainty of the past few decades stripped away from most people the ability to think that they could handle their own lives, making them all the more susceptible to the influence of demagogues. "As such helplessness becomes more apparent to men, they will discover the need for someone to save them from themselves. They must turn to someone, either to God or to some human leader. They reject God; therefore, they will welcome a Man, putting security above freedom." He ended with cautious expectation, clarifying that there was no way to know if this was indeed the end of all things but admitting that the sensation in that direction was strong. "Nevertheless, one cannot help feeling as though he were in a dimly lit theater watching the preparation of the stage for the play that will shortly begin." Harrison, "Reminiscences and a Prophecy," *CT*, March 4, 1957, 13–15. At the end of that year, Henry wrote of Harrison's views in an editorial on

of many Arabs in the region was of equal importance to the potential prophetical significance of the Jewish state.

DEFENDING THE END

ET could be of two minds about the end of the world. Its pages were often home to end-times speculations, but even writers there could analyze issues about the return of Christ apart from connections to the present. John Walvoord offered an extensive piece asking if the end was nigh, yet he did not find it necessary to make any notes about the world of his day.[89] To those who wanted to make specific predictions, Barnhouse said, "Anyone attempting to set a date for the second coming of Christ tries to make himself bigger than Christ and bigger than the Word of God. The Lord said flatly that no one knows the day or the hour ... the times or the seasons ... and said that He Himself, in His humanity, did not know."[90] Another time *ET* appealed to the eminent C.S. Lewis to rebuke both those who were overly interested in end times as well as those who, in reaction, dismiss eschatology entirely. "I am convinced that those who find in Christ apocalyptic the whole of His message are mistaken. But a thing does not vanish—it is not even discredited—because someone has spoken of it with exaggeration. It remains exactly what it was. The only difference is that if it has been recently been exaggerated, we must now take special care

---

evangelical advances. "Lt. General William K. Harrison, U.N. truce delegate at Pan-mun-jom, finds prophetic significance particularly in four major developments: nations preparing for war with weapons capable of worldwide destruction, Israel as a nation inhabiting the Holy Land after eighteen centuries of dispersion; Russia with the ability for the first time to invade the Near East and Middle East in power equal to that depicted in Ezekiel 38 and 39; and nations situated in the territory of the old Roman Empire progressing ... toward the 'ten state federation' reminiscent of Daniel 2, 7 and Revelation 13." Henry, "Signs of Vitality," *CT*, December 23, 1957, 21. Similarly, G. C. Berkouwer focused expressly on eschatology, yet he did not mention anything about current events aside from the fact that eschatology was "demanding the energetic attention of both the Church and its theology." Even the subheading "The Crisis of the Present" had nothing to do with any connection to the end of the world but with the tension between eternity and the present. G. C. Berkouwer, "The Church in the Last Days," *CT*, April 14, 1958, 3-5.

89. John F. Walvoord, "Is the Lord's Coming Imminent?" *ET*, January 1954, 10-11, 47-48.

90. Barnhouse, "British Israel Discredited," *ET*, January 1954, 12.

not to overlook it."[91] At other times, however, *ET*'s articles were keen
to highlight the end-times angle. Barnhouse very often overtly read
the current news in light of biblical prophecy. In 1954 he stated plainly
that he had rooted his understanding of the spread of Communism in
Europe in his eschatological interpretation that Western Europe would
not turn Red.[92] Walvoord offered similar hope to his readers that the
Soviets would not win and cited biblical prophecy for proof. At least
as far as securing global domination, Russia could not achieve its goals
since the Bible did not have a place for this eventuality. "These simple
facts, quite familiar to many Christians, point to the truth that the
Scriptures allow for no other world empire than those already mentioned. Russia as a military power can never gain control of the whole
world." He assured his readers that, whatever they might fear after
hearing the latest news, the Soviets were headed toward a military
defeat as predicted in Ezekiel 38 and 39.[93]

The events of this era did little to halt the evangelical interest in
the end of the world. No, the Americans and Russians had not gone to
war as swiftly as many had previously thought. There was no strong-
man emerging in Europe to be a latter-day Caesar to revive the Roman
Empire, and freedoms did not seem to be diminishing overtly in the
United States. The Western world in general had settled into a kind
of stasis. At the same time, however, the progress toward the end
seemed quite pronounced in the Middle East. Events there appeared
to following the script which the likes of Smith and Barnhouse had
been predicting for years. In this way, the State of Israel became an

---

91. C. S. Lewis, "The Christian Hope," *ET*, March 1954, 10. Bell also made this
point in 1955 when he wrote of eschatology as a neglected part of Christian thought.
"It is no excuse to discard this truth because there have been extremists who have
emphasized it to the exclusion of other doctrines: or others who have distorted
its message to something not taught in the Bible." Bell, "A Neglected Doctrine," *SPJ*,
August 3, 1955, 2.

92. Barnhouse, "The Nature of Our Danger," *ET*, March 1954, 8. This promise of
a limit to Communist expansion had limits of its own, as he believed that Germany
would eventually join in with Russia as a major ally. He arrived at this conclusion
not from a study of current events but from his understanding of biblical prophecy.
Barnhouse, "A Survey of 1955," *ET*, January 1956, 43.

93. John F. Walvoord, "What is the Future of Communism?" *ET*, March 1955,
15, 43.

increasingly important touchstone for evangelical commentary on eschatology. Twenty years earlier evangelicals writing about a Jewish presence in the land of Palestine could only speak about possibilities. Ten years earlier these same evangelicals could discuss the reality of a restored Israel settling in the land of its ancestors. By the late 1950s they could point to a new nation which had not only held its own but had pushed back against its ancient enemies of Egypt and Syria. The future held the promise of even greater victories as long-held expectations seemed to be coming to their fulfillment with each passing year. There were those like Barnhouse who fulfilled, in part, the general stereotype of evangelicals as heedlessly supportive of any Israeli move and who explicitly stated that the United States' place in the world was intrinsically tied to its support of the State of Israel. Others like Smith could be at least passively dismissive of Arab concerns, pointing to the better stewardship of the lands under Jewish control than under their previous population. There was no question that the majority view among American evangelicals was solidly pro-Israeli, but there was also a notable place for either strong criticism or even outright rejection of the State of Israel.

7

Battles Near and Far, 1959–1963

OVERVIEW

As the 1950s came to their close, Americans found themselves faced with the possibility and reality of battles they had not expected. The Armageddon between Communist and democratic forces in northern Europe had, thus far, failed to materialize. Along that part of the Iron Curtain the lines had indeed hardened as American and Russian troops dug in deeper and, soon enough, actual walls would be erected. Even with these threats of war, Americans and their Western European allies lived in peace. Yet it was to unforeseen places that Americans soon found their military attention drawn. Following the French defeat in 1954 in Indochina, the United States began to take up greater responsibilities in supporting the newly created South Vietnamese regime. Large-scale involvement would need to await the post-Tonkin Gulf world of President Johnson, but American advisers trickled into Southeast Asia in the waning years of President Eisenhower's tenure. The US also felt the stress of the Cold War much closer to home. In 1959 the Cuban Revolution broke out and, for a time, befuddled many as to how to react. The increasing tempo of the nascent Space Race meant that the danger was no longer safely "over there," but potentially bringing atomic destruction to their own cities and homes. Evangelical leaders responded to these various crises according to the same patterns which had governed their thought for the previous twenty years and more: opposition to any totalitarian rule, support of an assertive foreign policy, distrust of state control, and a patriotism tempered by an expectation of divine judgment for the nation's many besetting sins. America was their country, and sometimes it was right. It could also be very, very wrong.

ENEMIES

ENEMY INFIDELS

The general opposition to Communism continued apace, with its perceived degradation of human dignity and religious intolerance being high on the list of complaints. Also continuing was the tendency of evangelicals to see Communism as Christianity's evil twin. Carl Henry, for example, had some morbid sarcasm for Communism's goal for the world in an editorial about the testing of the largest atomic weapon to date. "Though its methods differ, Communism no less than Christianity seeks the salvation of the world. On October 30 Soviet communism so loved the world that it presented us with the greatest demonstration of physical power ever put on by man."[1] Henry argued that Christianity, instead of inducing a pie-in-the-sky predisposition regarding world events, provided the best motivation for vigorously opposing Communism. He further suggested that it was even more than a civic duty to America; it was the religious duty to God for Christians to oppose Communism. Since Christians had a hope of a future beyond the immediate moment, he said they could look at death not as the end of all things. He suggested that while the more materialistically minded might call for an appeasing accommodation with the Soviets to save the present physical order, "we must bring the holy judgments of God to bear against the present fear, appeasement and confusion which threaten to destroy Western unity and open the gates to atheistic communism."[2] At another point Henry spoke hopefully of hardening opposition in some parts of the world, suggesting that East Asia was "stiffening" its antagonism to Communism, and even offered hope that the need for a stronger philosophical base to defend against Communism could lead many in East Asia to embrace Christianity.[3] Rather than seeing Cold War activism as subsuming the Christian message within the limitations of Americanism, Henry saw the call to

---

1. Carl F. H. Henry, "Megaton or Manger?" *CT*, December 8, 1961, 20.
2. Henry, "The Christian's Duty in the Present Crisis," *CT*, January 5, 1959, 22.
3. Henry, "The Gospel in Modern Asia," *CT*, September 28, 1959, 20–21.

challenge Communism as a Christian goal, in and of itself and as the only hope of ending this spreading totalitarianism.[4]

CHINA AND MAO

As the largest Communist nation in the world, China loomed large in evangelical commentary. In 1959 Bell bemoaned the fact that state hostility had forced the closing of the vast majority of churches in Shanghai and Beijing and that pastors were being told what to say in their sermons. As to the supposed legal freedom of religion promised under Communism, he said this state tolerance of faith depended on capitulation to the powers that be. "The Christians of China need our prayers as never before. As has long since been predicted, the Communist Government will tolerate the Church only to the extent that it becomes an active and willing agent of Communism."[5] A few weeks later he revisited this theme, noting that all church government offices had been integrated into state organizations and that "hymn books and all other literature are now being carefully examined and

---

4. Henry was not the only person associated with *CT* to speak in this way. J. Edgar Hoover also wrote in magazine about the ideological nature of Communism. He wrote, "Just 100 years ago communism was a mere scratch on the face of international affairs. In a dingy London apartment, a garrulous, haughty, and intolerant atheist, Karl Marx, callous to the physical sufferings and poverty of his family, was busy mixing ideological acids of this evil philosophy. ... Communism is today literally a violent hurricane, rocking not only the chanceries of the world but seeking to capture the bodies, minds, and souls of men and women everywhere." He looked again to Christianity to be the philosophical basis for opposition to Communism. "If communism is to be defeated, the task must rest largely upon the theologians and the ministers of the Gospel. Communism is a false secular religion with pseudo-theological explanations of the great verities of life, such as the creation, life on earth and the world to come. Communism is an all-encompassing system with explanations—though wrong ones—for this great universe of God. The Party offers answers—though perverted ones—for the hopes, joys, and fears of mankind. In the final analysis, the Communist world view must be met and defeated by the Christian world view. The Christian view of God as the Creator, Sustainer, and Lord of the universe is majestically superior to the *ersatz* approach of dialectical materialism concocted by Marx and Lenin." J. Edgar Hoover, "The Communist Menace: Red Goals and Christian Ideals," *CT*, October 10, 1960, 3, 5. Hoover wrote an article for *CH* two years later, urging American clergy to be aware of the threat posed by Communism and not to be taken advantage of for Communist propaganda. J. Edgar Hoover, "Let's Fight Communism Sanely!" *CH*, January 1962, 33, 62–63.

5. L. Nelson Bell, "The Church in China," *SPJ*, January 28, 1959, 2.

all with 'poisonous' thoughts or ideas are being rejected. 'Only teaching favoring union and socialism shall be used.' "[6] Freedom of religion extended only to the point of being free to agree.

Going in a drastically different direction, in 1959 ET made the unorthodox choice of making Mao Zedong its man of the year, saying, "Our choice of General Mao as Man of the year is strictly from the criteria of worldly history. The man who can bring Khrushchev across Asia to his doorstep and cause him to reverse his policy before the whole world must be admitted to have unbelievably great power." They even went on to heap praise upon Mao. "In the last year he has done more than any other man to shape the course of world events in the months, perhaps years, that lie before us. ... There can be little doubt that Mao brought the best government to China that this ancient nation has ever had. Under no dynasty has there been such progress as in the last decade."[7] That being said, Barnhouse and his fellows were not supporters of Beijing. Describing the situation of Christianity in China, Barnhouse wrote, "Red Chinese leaders have subjected church workers to a compulsory three-months course in politics. This course goes on all day long, five days a week. ... In churches, no hymns are to be sung or sermons to be preached with what they call 'depressing' subjects, such as sin, judgment, etc." At the same time he held out hope that the Christians in China were continuing to work even under this pressure and cited several examples of Christian teaching enduring in its new illegal capacity.[8]

Criticism of Communist China was more normal in evangelical magazines. Courier gleefully informed his readers of setbacks in the road

---

6. Bell, "The Church in China Further Developments," February 25, 1959, 2. Bell did not specify whether his quotations came from Chinese government documents or from some other group's summary.

7. Donald G. Barnhouse, "Survey of the Year," ET, January 1959, 46–47.

8. Barnhouse, "Red China Increases Pressures," ET, January 1959, 28. He was later to suggest that China was stoking the tension between the US and USSR in the hopes that it would emerge as the global hegemon in the wake of such a clash. To discourage such activity, Barnhouse suggested that America make it clear that in the event of a war, China would be seen as one with the Soviets and could expect to have its cities attacked by American bombs. Barnhouse, "After the Summit—What?" ET, July 1960, 3.

to full Communism in the new China. "Bit by bit evidence comes out of Red China that the Chinese Communists may have gone too far in their efforts to out-Communize Russia." Noting that the Russians had given up on rural communes thirty years before, Courier said that the Chinese, too, were increasingly abandoning this policy in which, as he described it, "the people in rural areas were in effect made employees of the state, 24 hours a day, seven days a week." After the communes had failed to produce Communism, Courier reported that people were being allowed to go back to eat as families and even to plant their own gardens. The elderly and infants, who had been in communal care centers, were now being tended to by their loved ones instead. Since the reason given by Beijing for this reversion to individualism was a temporary food shortage, Courier worried that this little liberty might be taken away if conditions improved.[9]

KOREAN COMMUNISM

As he and others had done before, Henry compared the actions of the Communist regimes to that of the archetypal tyrannies of the twentieth century. In the preface to an interview with a South Korean pastor, he wrote, "The West is keenly aware of the terrible Nazi persecution of the Jews, but the story of the Communist persecution of the Christians in Korea and mainland China remains to be told." In the interview which followed, *CT* readers were told that despite the early hopes of Koreans in 1945, who saw the Russians as liberators, they were soon disenchanted as Soviet forces pushed Christians out of positions of influence and replaced them with Communists. When the newly christened North Koreans tried to organize political opposition to Communist dominance, they found their meetings disrupted and their leaders arrested. The Korean pastor told Henry that violence against Christians began as early as the end of 1945 and that, when the Communists occupied Seoul

---

9. Gabriel Courier, "Family," *CH*, September 1959, 14. These events would have been in the middle of the famine in China which would claim millions of lives. Jasper Becker argued that rather than the communes only being abandoned in reaction to the famine, the communes were largely responsible for the famine. He gives a possible number of deaths in the famine as forty million. See *Hungry Ghosts: Mao's Secret Famine* (New York: Henry Hold and Company, 1996).

briefly in 1950, some five hundred pastors were taken away, never to be heard from again. He also noted that, ironically, one of the greatest source of Christian growth in South Korea had been from North Korean Christians fleeing Communist oppression.[10]

VIETNAMESE UNCERTAINTY

American involvement in the Vietnam War was only just beginning at this period, but some evangelicals were paying attention to the goings-on in Southeast Asia. It was not clear, however, just how good the good guys actually were. One early comment came from *Presbyterian Journal*, and was critical of the South Vietnamese government's religious persecution conducted by the Roman Catholic leadership,[11] a concern that was echoed by Courier two years later.[12] *ET* reported that the South Vietnamese government had ended a fifty-year long policy of allowing free access to the country by Christian missionaries, although the author was uncertain as to why this new policy was put in place.[13] Some attention was given to the recently established Communist regime in the north, as Russell Hitt told his readers of the martyrdom of two Vietnamese Christians, one a pastor and one a recent convert.[14]

---

10. Henry, "Plight of the Korean Christians," CT, September 25, 1961, 34–36. The interviewee was Dr. Kyung Chik Han who had apparently studied at Princeton under J. Gresham Machen.

11. The Editors, "Stronger Stand Urged Against Vietnam Bias," August 21, 1963, 4.

12. Courier, "Viet-Nam," CH, August 1963, 7. To be precise Courier was highlighting the anti-Buddhist measures of the Roman Catholic leadership of South Vietnam.

13. Russell T. Hitt, "Vietnam Closes Doors," June 1961, 34. Hitt had taken over as editor of ET following the death of Donald Barnhouse. Another ET article was later to suggest that this was based in "security reasons" and was lifted shortly thereafter. Louis L. King, "Report from Viet Nam," ET, February 1962, 30.

14. Russell T. Hitt, "Martyred for Their Faith by Communists," ET, February 1961, 31. Hitt reported another martyrdom in 1963; this time the dead included an American and a Filipino translator as well as the latter's four-month-old son. They were stopped at a Viet Cong roadblock, and, according to the wife of the American killed, the insurgents fired on them unexpectedly and without provocation. Hitt, "Translators Slain in Viet Nam," ET, April 1963, 32. MM also reported on this incident. Phil Landrum, "Martyrdom in Vietnam," MM, May 1963, 22–23.

By early 1963 a writer in *ET* felt comfortable speaking with some
confidence about the situation as anti-Communist efforts by South
Vietnam increased and as "10,000 US military men with substantial
military equipment has greatly restricted the movements of the guerrillas."[15] Yet, Courier at *CH* maintained a focus on the moral ambiguity
of the situation. "There is a humiliation in [Vietnam] where freedom is
clashing with Communism. The humiliation lies in the fact that the man
we are backing, simply because 'he is there,' is a dictator. The government of President Ngo Dinh Diem is doing its best to suppress freedom,
at least as far as Buddhist protesters are concerned." Even after noting
that the US now had a force of twelve thousand in the country, Courier
was pessimistic about the options open to Americans, as all were less
than ideal. "All of which indicates that not always nor even often in
international politics do you have a clearcut [sic] choice between right
and wrong. More often it is a choice among two or more courses, each
of which is partly right and partly wrong."[16] Two months later he would
make his opposition more explicit. Referring to comments made by the
sister-in-law to the South Vietnamese president, he wrote, "When an
aid cut was suggested by some Washington lawmakers, Madame Nhu
reacted immediately and accusingly. A cut, she declared, would be the
equivalent of offering help to the Communists. It appears from where
we sit that continued support of Diem (and in-laws) is providing even
greater help to the Communists."[17] The Red Menace might have been
real, but not everyone was convinced that any and all alternatives were
necessarily better.

DIVIDED EUROPE

Berlin was a hotspot of Cold War rivalry during this period, even before
the infamous wall was erected. Courier compared the vigorous life of
West Berlin with its decrepit eastern counterpart, saying, "The trouble:
it's an island of freedom, initiative and glowing economic rehabilitation

---

15. Douglas Jackson, "Communism: Will the China-Russia Rift Grow Bigger?"
ET, January 1963, 29.

16. Courier, "Viet Nam," *CH*, September 1963, 6.

17. Courier, "Viet Nam," *CH*, November 1963, 6.

deep within shabby Communist Eastern Germany. On one side of the Brandenburg Gate you have a bustling, healthy, rebuilt, neon-lighted city. On the other you have unhealed bomb scars, deserted streets, darkened shop windows."[18] When Henry traveled to Germany in 1960 for a Graham Crusade, he praised the efforts of East Berliners to attend the meetings and belittled the opposition posed by the Communist government. He noted that the intense interest displayed by East Berliners in Graham's Crusade had led to crackdowns by the Communist leaders there. While such persecutions were clearly wicked, Henry argued that their efforts had a positive side effect since Communist leaders could hardly act as the hero of the masses around the world when they had to take such measures against their people at home.[19]

Castro's Briefly Open Door

As with the early stages of the Chinese Revolution a decade earlier, the Cuban Revolution provided many commentators with a chance to wait and see and even to change their minds. At first it was unclear just which way the revolutionary winds would eventually blow. An early *ET* news report was circumspect, saying only that the new regime had not been as friendly to Roman Catholicism as some in that denomination had hoped and that one Catholic editor had gone to Cuba lauding the Castro state but left accusing it of being wholly Communist.[20] A news report from *CT* in early 1960 was more enthusiastic and quoted a

18. Courier, "Berlin," *CH*, January 1959, 11.

19. Henry, Manuscript, Carl F. H. Henry Papers, Box 1960, File Correspondence, Writings, Rolfing Library Archives, Trinity Evangelical Divinity School, Deerfield, IL. Nevertheless, it was not all good news. In early 1961 a *CT* news report told readers that Christianity was losing the battle for the hearts of East Germans. "Church leaders are particularly distressed, according to recent reports, over the steady decline in baptisms in the Evangelical churches of East Germany. In some urban areas the number is said to have dropped to one-tenth the figure for previous years." The author noted that East German parents were having their children dedicated in a Communist name-giving ceremony rather than Christian baptism, to the point that this accounted to two-thirds of new infants by 1959. He attributed the failure of the church in this area to the hostility of the state, the weak response of the church, and the flight of many Christians into West Germany. David Kucharsky, "East Germany: Church Losing Ground to Reds," *CT*, February 13, 1961, 33.

20. Barnhouse, "Religion in Cuba," *ET*, July 1959, 33.

Protestant pastor as affirming the recent Cuban Revolution. After a ten-
day tour of the island, he declared that the Cuban people were entirely
behind the Castro government, and that there were no Communists
in the new state. He said, "A few of its members may have associated
with Communists or said kind things about their ideas. ... But calling
these people Communists is simply inaccurate."[21] Courier praised the
new government in 1959, even to the point of offering a half-defense of
political executions. After dramatically describing Castro's rise from

21. Kucharsky, "Report from Cuba," *CT*, January 4, 1960, 27. Given that the
pastor quoted was the moderator of the mainline United Presbyterian Church in
the USA, Kucharsky could have written this report off as yet another accommo-
dating stance by a liberal-leaning cleric. However, he did not offer any critique,
suggesting he may have been at least open to the veracity of Miller's impression.
Other commentators gave even more positive portrayals than this. *ET* provided
its readers with a glowing presentation of a Cuban pastor, Carlos Herrera, who
had given up his church to serve as a chaplain for the rebels seeking to oust the
previous ruler, Batista. Noting that he adopted the military fatigues and unkept
style of Castro's forces, the author spoke of Herrera's role in exclusively positive
terms. "That was Herrera's main job with this rebel army—to bring men to know
Jesus Christ as their personal Savior. He had joined the guerrillas in early 1958 ... to
show the men fighting for political freedom that they also needed spiritual freedom."
Homer Dowdy, "Chaplain for Cuba's Army," *ET*, June 1960, 19. *MM* also provided a
highly positive article of this same man, saying, "As Chief Protestant Chaplain of
Cuba's revolutionary army, Carlos Herrera is said to be the chaplain most highly
valued by Castro himself. Only days before I interviewed the chaplain in Cuba he
had attempted to resign in order to return to the pastorate. But he was immediately
informed by Castro himself that it was vital to Cuba's future that he remain Chief
Protestant Chaplain." The article's author concluded with mildly hesitant praise for
Herrera and the new Cuba. "Though some might disagree with the chaplain on such
political matters, his own sincerity and sense of dedication cannot be questioned. I
was impressed that it is as a true soldier of Christ that he is ministering to the new
Cuban army of twenty thousand men. And because of him and others like him a
new day has dawned in Cuba for the preaching of the gospel." Herbert J. Pugmire,
"Chaplain to a Revolution," *MM*, June 1959, 15, 17. Similarly, Barnhouse went so far as
to use Che Guevara as an example of Christian ethics, even if this recommendation
was couched in condemnation for the rebel's overall impact. After telling of a time
when Guevara stole fruit to feed starving children, Barnhouse added, "Much as I
hate, abhor and abominate Guevara's Communism, even as much as I would rage
against a condition that can allow small children to starve to death. To attempt to
alleviate any condition of misery is a Christian thing to do. ... If missionaries in the
lands where Guevara traveled had, in addition to their preaching, done something
about the conditions that could let children starve, perhaps he would not be in
Cuba today as the great enemy of our way of life." Barnhouse, "Che Guevara and
the Social Gospel," *ET*, October 1960, 6.

failed rebel to recognized ruler, he said, "When [Castro] began execut-
ing his former foes by the scores and then by the hundreds, there were
some second thoughts north of the border. But we would do well to
remember that this was not simply a quarrel between political parties.
This was war, no holds barred." Courier then pointed out that the previous government had made regular use of torture and executions and
added, "Although that does not absolve, it does help to explain." At no
point did he mention any Communist influence in Castro's camp. This
was, for now, seen as an example of a perhaps needed socio-political
revolution against a corrupt dictatorship.[22]

This semi-positive stance would change just a few months later.
Courier admitted that it was no longer clear what the revolutionaries
stood for. "For what [Castro] *will* do, the cheers give way to a bit of head-
shaking. Nobody is sure of the Castro future tense. Perhaps he himself
does not know. His first job was winning a revolution. His aim was to
better the lot of his people. It was a hard fight. It didn't allow much
time for planning what to do after the victory." Courier then threw in
his own reasons for doubt about the erstwhile rebel hero. He said that
Castro had claimed that he would pursue the democratic process, but
gave no indication when that might happen. Courier was becoming
skeptical of the claims of agrarian reform, since the same claims had
been made in China not too long before and had yielded to tyranny of
the worst form.[23]

Eventually Castro's regime wore out its evangelical welcome. By 1961
Courier's portrayal of Castro had definitively soured.

> The trouble with Mr. Castro—and with Communism—is that
> he and it can't stand to have everything. Theirs is a have-not
> philosophy. They've got to have scapegoats. They've got to get
> their people mad at somebody. Take away the scapegoats and
> their people will have no one to look at but their own leaders.
> *That* could be disastrous for the Castros and all they stand for."[24]

22. Courier, "Winner Castro," *CH*, March 1959, 13.
23. Courier, "Castro," *CH*, June 1959, 13-14.
24. Courier, "Cuba," *CH*, March 1961, 4.

By 1962 Russell Hitt was telling his readers, "There's no doubt about it. The Cuban situation has taken a turn for the worse, as far as freedom of religion is concerned. Until a few months ago, there was comparative freedom for Cubans to evangelize. Then as Cuba was increasingly communized, this freedom was restricted."[25] Culbertson warned his readers, "In Cuba, a mere ninety miles from our shores, a Red dictatorship is now in full control. ... The welcome mat is out in Cuba for a projected visit by Nikita Khrushchev, and an invitation is also on the agenda for Chou En Lai, Red China's premier. Meanwhile Cuban communists are frantically spreading an [sic] 'hate America' campaign."[26] Henry said, "While American foreign policy pursues its Antaean role of seeking strength by falling on its face, a little man who 'plays the rumba on his tuba down in Cuba' has whipped up a Grade-A threat to our national security. Fidel Castro is now threatening to turn the Caribbean sea [sic] into a red lake." He had some hope that someday the Cuban people would rise up against their new leader, but he insisted that this was a matter for more than Cuba. If the Cubans could be "mesmerized by an Animal Farm Napoleon" and come to see the US as the villain, then how many more in Latin America could come to the same unfortunate conclusion?"[27]

SINO-SOVIET SPLIT

Despite these real dangers, it was not a matter of Communism being an inexorably rising and united red tide. Many evangelical commentators made note of the split between Moscow and Beijing, yet they were unsure of the best way to react. Some doubted its reality while others wondered if fissure among America's biggest enemies would be in America's best interest. In 1962 Billy Graham offered his thoughts on the passing year, something he saw as of mixed value. While he saw some reason for hope found in the possibility of daylight between the Russians and Chinese, he also, citing an unnamed Kennedy aide,

---

25. Hitt, "Cuba's Christians Need Prayer," *ET*, April 1962, 32.

26. Culbertson, "A Look at the World," *MM*, August 1963, 10.

27. Henry, "Cuba Situation Becomes a Battle for the Hemisphere," *CT*, August 1, 1960, 24.

wondered if this could be a ruse. On the whole he acknowledged the reality of the Sino-Soviet split, but he did not think it a permanent arrangement. "While there may be a vast difference between the Soviet and Chinese brands of Communism, yet when the chips are down they will probably be united. The thing that unites them in their ultimate goal of building a kingdom on earth without God."[28] An *ET* contributor saw the tension between Russia and China as more substantial. Suggesting that the US and the Soviets had come to a tacit understanding where each side permitted the other to make demonstrations of its strength and resolve in public while actively working to undermine tensions behind the scenes, he added that as much as this might be amendable to the White House and Kremlin, Mao was less comfortable with this hard-edged peace. The author believed that China was frustrated with the continued Western presence in Berlin and was working to establish its own international Communist network that was independent of Moscow.[29] Courier, on the other hand, looked at a possible rift with trepidation, as he saw Khrushchev as something of a brake on Mao's China. "At best, its conduct would be unpredictable. A China with bridges burned behind it would be a China to whom war is no inconceivable option. Indeed ... it is not impossible to imagine that some day the US and Russia might find themselves on one side, Red China on the other."[30] The principle of divide-and-conquer might be a good idea in theory, but the subsequent instability could make for a more treacherous reality.

---

28. Graham, "Facing the Anti-God Colossus," *CT*, December 21, 1962, 6. Graham had a fairly dismal view of the basic world situation. In this same article he wrote, "Who would have thought three years ago that Russian generals would command a well-armed and well-disciplined army only 90 miles from American shores? Who would have thought that the four-power government of Berlin would be split by a wall, or that American troops would be fighting in a Southeast Asian war, or that China would dare to attack neutralist India?"

29. Douglas Jackson, "Communism: Will the China-Russia Rift Grow Bigger?" *ET*, January 1963, 29.

30. Courier, "Rift?" *CH*, March 1962, 6.

244 SWORDS AND PLOWSHARES

Dealing with the Devil

A fundamental reason that many evangelicals were disinclined to trust the peace process is that they found the Communists in general and Soviets in particular to be almost innately untrustworthy. Responding to calls that American policy ought to prioritize inviting the Soviets to negotiate and creating a mutually tolerant world, L. Nelson Bell retorted that with the Russians, broken promises were more common than kept ones. "Let us repeat—at these 'Summit' conferences Russia has made a total of 24 definite commitments and broken 23 of the 24. At Foreign Minister conferences Russia has made 15 definite commitments and *violated 14 of the* 15." He then suggested that negotiating with the Soviets was as foolish as the police making deals with the likes of Al Capone. Despite this skeptical attitude, he was optimistic in some ways. In the same article he declared his great hope that the common people of the world shared with him the great disdain for Communism. He challenged the Soviets to allow free and open elections and asserted that the primary reason this would never happen was because the Communists knew full well that they would lose and lose badly. Bell went on to emphasize that he had no animosity for the Russian or Chinese people but that they were governed by people he termed "criminals."[31]

---

31. Bell, "There Is But One Road From the Summit—Down!" *SPJ*, April 15, 1959, 3. Bell simply did not trust the Soviets. Bell was greatly concerned that the push for peace could lead to disaster if this was not tempered by a realism when it came to Soviet intentions. He lauded the American desire for a peace without imperial goals of its own, but he said this had its own downside. "Because of this attitude we are willing to grasp at any suggestion which Russia may offer hoping that a relaxation of tension and the cessation of the cold war may thereby be hastened. However, if we fail to appreciate Russia's real motives and her avowed plans for world domination, we will continue to play directly into her hands." He spoke approvingly of West German Chancellor, Konrad Adenauer, who spoke against the US making any premature deals concerning Berlin. "Pointedly he showed how world tensions are the direct result of Russia's actions and that if she is sincere let Russia make the necessary concessions. Otherwise, he pointed out, we are playing right into the long-range plans of this nation which has already brought so much suffering and sorrow to the world." Bell, "The Kremlin Smiles," *PJ*, April 13, 1960, 9. Henry echoed this distrust of Soviet intentions rooted in past failed promises. After the Russians suggested joint space activities in 1962, Henry argued, "Is this a gesture of good will? We fear not. Rather it suggests the strong probability that we have discovered some techniques the Russians are desperately anxious to acquire for themselves. History should have warned us by now. Up to 1948 Russia had entered

Similarly, Barnhouse spoke out against the efforts of the Eisenhower administration to ban all nuclear tests. Arguing that "the best informed scientists" asserted that such testing could be conducted illicitly, Barnhouse found that the Soviets' record of breaking deals meant that there was no reason to believe that they would abide by any ban, however noble in intention. "The Russians may say they are making no tests, but the Russians are liars; they cannot be believed in anything. In dealing with Communists, we should always assume that anything they do is from a bad motive. ... Have people not read the words of Stalin, 'peace is the period of time in which a nation gets ready for the next war'?"[32] Courier was also skeptical about the prospect for a negotiated agreement with the Russians, but he was less antagonistic than Barnhouse. He said, "The US has learned to its sorrow that in solemn undertakings of Russia, somebody usually gets buried." Even though he was, by and large, more sympathetic with the American position, he simply reported that while the Russians wanted a stop to nuclear testing followed by mechanisms to prevent further tests, the US wished it the other way around.[33]

---

into 40 major agreements with us and violated 38 of them. Since then the record is equally dismal." Henry, "Space Cooperation May Prove to Be an Earthly Trap," *CT*, April 27, 1962, 28.

32. Barnhouse, "Nuclear Tests," *ET*, April 1959, 4.

33. Courier, "Test," *CH*, January 1959, 12. William Harrison likewise had little trust in Soviet promises. He said that the danger of war in that day flowed from the "mutual antagonism and arms race" between the US and the USSR, and that, barring the actions of a rogue subordinate, the decision for conflict lay in the hands of the respective leaders of the nations. However, he argued that it was not from the Americans that such hostilities were likely to begin. He stated explicitly that "the danger of nuclear war results from the possibility that Soviet leaders will some day launch their armed forces either directly against the United States or against some object wish the United States wishes to defend. To these Soviet rulers, war, when favorable to them, is a legitimate and necessary means of action." He considered that this was the fairly obvious conclusion to be drawn from the observation of "all who read newspapers," and that to think otherwise was merely wishful. "The pages of history are full of tyrants and conquerors. Soviet leaders are no different. Communism is the ideology or propaganda that motivates these men, and by it they justify their actions. Their actions, acceptable by Communist standards, have been violent, deceitful, and ruthless. Any American policy that views Khrushchev and his kind as other than the most treacherous of criminals is endangering not only

The Soviet leader, Khrushchev, came under particular evangelical scrutiny as well. Carl Henry was rather less than diplomatic when he had this to say: "The sight of an insolent shouting Slavic bully is never attractive, whether fictionally in Dostoievsky [sic] or in the flesh in Paris; and the deliberate twisting of the spy plane incident into a cause for international misbehavior is a piece of 'brinksmanship' that Satan alone could have devised. The Communist world strains at a gnat while it asks the Free World to swallow a camel." Henry did surmise that the Premier's histrionics may have been other than simple propaganda. "Khrushchev's rage and his subsequent scuttling of the summit seem to spring from two facts: Soviet humiliation from the world's discovery that at least 50 flights of the U-2 had taken place over Russia before mechanical failure intervened May Day to bring down one of the planes," and a now weakened position in Moscow "which may have sent Khrushchev to the summit a virtual prisoner of those he had dominated up to that time."[34] He was later to take another swipe at Khrushchev by citing a report of a religious community that was discovered in remote Siberia whose members had never heard of the Soviet Premier.[35]

Courier also made an attack on the Soviet leader. "Why is Mr. Khrushchev so desirous of a summit meeting? Because he needs it. Not only has his health been something less than the best, but in another five years he will be 70. There's nothing much on the record now that would give him an enduring place in the Russian Hall of Fame or its equivalent. Matter of fact, he's turned out some sour ones." Courier conceded that Khrushchev was likely worried about his reputation for more than mere vanity. "And it's more than immortality in the history books. There's the matter of mortality now. In Russia, nothing fails like failure. You do your crow-eating in Siberia."[36] A few months later

---

the United States but the whole noncommunist world." Harrison, "The Search for Peace on Earth," *CT*, April 13, 1963, 7.

34. Henry, "God's Judgment on the Summit," *CT*, June 6, 1960, 20. Barnhouse was to make the same point in *ET*, suggesting that Khrushchev had seemed afraid of his own ministers even as he sent his verbal blast against the United States. Barnhouse, "After the Summit—What?" *ET*, July 1960, 3.

35. Henry, "Footnote on Glory: Who is Mr. K?" *CT*, March 29, 1963, 22.

36. Courier, "Khrushchev," *CH*, July 1959, 13.

he chided the Russian leader, saying, "It's hard to take seriously a plan for total world disarmament from a man who pouts when he can't go to Disneyland and clowns when he's feeling good."[37]

Evangelicals felt themselves on solid ground in their strong denunciations of Communist tyranny. It was oppressive and expansionistic, and evangelicals were insistent on spreading this news to all who would listen. There was a real danger, to Christians in particular and to the world at large. America's enemies were formidable, and these commentators saw it as both their Christian and civic duty to warn their fellow citizens accordingly.

AMERICA

The Lesser of Two Evils?

The ambiguity that evangelicals had felt toward their nation was not lessened by the long Eisenhower years. Many expressed great love for America and admiration for many of its leaders, yet these same voices were regularly raised in protest over US policies and general societal trends. Frankly, on the question of the lesser of two evils, many were decreasingly confident that their nation was less than its Soviet rival. One author was greatly concerned that America was on the brink of disaster. "We are engaged in a life-and-death struggle with Russia. We head up the free world, and Russia heads up the world of Communism. ... Which side should win? Is it not evident that the scales will be tipped by some outside power? The power that will decide is God, for he has promised the victory to those who serve him." Continuing with a focus on the perennial debate over the First Amendment, he added, "But if the secular view of the first amendment wins, this will no longer be so. The issue then will be between Russia, which is hostile to God but permits worship, and the United States, which officially is indifferent to God but allows liberty. How much difference is there between hostility

---

37. Courier, "Soapbox," *CH*, November 1959, 14. Courier then went on to say that Khrushchev needed to be taken seriously as he was absolutely determined to bring the world under his sway.

and indifference?"[38] It would be little comfort to be the second worst option when it came to divine judgment.

Billy Graham offered a favorable portrait of Russia, which was, by implication, a criticism of his own native land. In 1959 he wrote of his brief trip to the Soviet Union, and noted that this was one of the few places in the world where he could walk about unrecognized. Even so, he could share that a young woman inspecting his passport upon arrival quickly glanced around then looked back and pointed upwards. "This was my first experience among the silent believers that are in the Soviet Union today." On a trip to Gorky Park, he wrote in better terms than most evangelicals could muster for American equivalents. "Another impression of mine in this famous park was how disciplined the crowds were. One saw no trash about little drinking no unruliness. There were young people by the thousands but never once did I see doing more than walking arm in arm or holding hands. There is little emphasis on sex on the newsstands, in parks or in films on television."[39] Graham continued to see the drama of the Cold War in relatively stark terms, with the Americans clearly as the good guys, but he was willing to highlight the places where the bad guys were better. The liberty of his native land allowed for levels of immorality which deserved to be condemned.

Graham was not the only one to use the Communist "other" as a foil to highlight American corruption. A news report in *CT* took a swipe at

---

38. A. Culver Gordon, "Theistic or Secular Government?" *CT*, April 26, 1963, 12–13. Culbertson suggested that Americans were not becoming less religious; they just were choosing to believe in a far more comfortable god. "There is a soft streak in America. And no wonder. Having turned our backs on the God of the Scriptures, we have manufactured a god who has given no absolute standards in his revelation and who must perforce never condemn anyone to eternal death. Luxury, self-indulgence, avarice and lack of discipline are graphically illustrated in every level of our society. We are reaping the harvest in dissolute, selfish, secular, foolish, flagrantly sinful living." Culbertson, "In Wake of the TV Hearings," *MM*, January 1960, 15.

39. These positive impressions did not mean he had changed his mind about Soviet intentions. After applauding the work ethic and focus of the students at the University of Moscow, he added, "One thing I did find out at the University, and that is that 10 million Russian youth are studying English, while less than 10,000 Americans are studying Russian. These people mean business! They are getting ready for the day when … " Graham, "Impressions of Moscow," *CT*, July 20, 1959, 14–15. Ellipses in original.

American morals via an unexpected agent: Nikita Khrushchev. He noted that when touring the US in 1959, the Soviet delegation was presented with a "skirt-flipping" dance scene by Hollywood producers looking to access the Russian cinema. In response Khrushchev was said to have described the act as pornographic and that such things would be unwelcome in the Soviet Union.[40] Henry added his own appeal to Communist morality when it came to the growing reach of movies and television in the early 1960s. "Even the Communists are complaining about the moral listlessness of our movies. But think of the Americans fixed night after night to the almost vacant stare of TV." Quoting another author, Henry wondered if "mushrooms" of nuclear destruction were all that the future held for the United States.[41]

American Glory

Others were more prone to see the bright side of American society and government, often with far less nuance than Graham had demonstrated. As he had many times before, Daniel Poling was quite open in his support of the American way of life. After bemoaning the fact that the Communists had managed to turn capitalism into a dirty word in the minds of so many in the world, he offered his own alternative definition which turned the epithet into a principle of liberty. "But this capitalism is freedom—all the freedoms. Capitalism—under the Stars and Stripes, is yours and mine. By it, under God and by His grace, we live and move and have our economic, our social, our industrial, our religious, our political freedoms." Adding a modifier to distinguish it from what he thought a Soviet caricature, he referred to "People's Capitalism" as the place of "free trade unions" and "free industry and free commerce."[42] A year and a half later the cover of *CH* was emblazoned with one of the most overt connections between the US and Christianity as the American and so-called Christian flags were paired, flowing in front of a majestic ocean view.[43]

---

40. Kucharsky, "Did Khrushchev See America?" *CT*, October 12, 1959, 32.
41. Henry, "God Makes Us Great," *CT*, June 22, 1962, 20–21.
42. Daniel A. Poling, " 'People's Capitalism,' " *CH*, January 1959, 17.
43. The Editors, Cover, *CH*, July 1960.

Communist Purge

When it came to the famous and infamous congressional hunt for Communists in the US government and media, evangelicals were of two minds. On the one hand they tended to see such activities as both necessary and well within the purview of state action. At the same time they continued to be uneasy with the zeal expressed by its agents and supporters. G. Aiken Taylor at *Presbyterian Journal* warned his readers against letting down their guard. Responding to an American bishop who had accused the political right of attacking American institutions in their zeal to combat Communism, he admitted that a few might have gone too far, but he gave some measure of cover to these attacks which were intended to protect those institutions from the "termites" seeking to undermine them. Taylor then accelerated his criticism of his more liberal opponents, suggesting that the only reason to deny that such undermining was going on was to protect the termites going about their destruction.[44]

---

44. G. Aiken Taylor, "Not Attacking 'Institutions,'" *PJ*, February 14, 1962, 10. Another *PJ* piece connected America and Christianity, but it did so in a complex way. Hoyt Evans wrote to young readers of the magazine, asking them about the American way of life. He did not say that America was Christian, but he did argue that America, at its best, was drawn from Christianity. "In America we have been accustomed to telling people of other nations, 'Our American way of life is best because we have more material possessions than anyone else'. The time seems to be coming when this will no longer be true. When and if that time comes, what can we say? Perhaps we need to ask ourselves again, 'What is the *real* American way of life?'" Evans rooted America's glory in its God-centered origins. "The constitution is based on Biblical teaching about God, and on the Biblical teaching about the nature of man, and on the Biblical teaching with regard to right and wrong. ... The American way is good because it reverences God, because it has a high regard for man, and because it respects right instead of wrong. Here is the real difference between Americanism and Communism. Communism says there is no God, says that man has no soul, and ignores morality." His concluding challenge was to have his readers see the connection between their faith and their citizenship. "What can a Christian young person do to preserve and promote the real American way of life? The first thing he can do is to appreciate it. We need a fuller understanding of our heritage. ... The best thing a Christian young person can do for his country is to be sure that he is a Christian." After listing some of the basic requirements for Christian faith, Evans added, "If we can say an honest 'yes' to all of these, we have passed the basic tests of Christian citizenship and we can make our contribution to the real American way of life." B. Hoyt Evans, "The American Way of Life," *PJ*, January 20, 1960, 16–17.

Similarly, Carl Henry showed little patience for those doubting the overall effects of the FBI and Congressional committees regarding Communism. When a congressman called for an end to the committee pursuing Communism, he admitted that the FBI was flawed and that the stench of McCarthyism was hindering its efforts, but he insisted that its failings were more than made up for by the good it was doing. He thought that disbanding it would be a fool's errand as this would only allow "radical left-wing forces" to make gains in American society. Even so, Henry could be wary about rallying the citizenry against any and all perceived threats. He exhorted his readers to consider their role in supporting anti-Communist efforts and to be alert to the danger and supportive of those like J. Edgar Hoover who were charged with protecting the US.[45] However, he had an issue with those "who alertly but crudely warn against the Communist menace." He was not interested in either joining in with disreputable allies in the fight against Communism or in unduly attacking them. Further, he had no qualms about naming names, even if those names were prominent evangelical stalwarts.

---

45. Henry, "Left Wing Attacks on FBI and House Un-American Activities Group," *CT*, March 30, 1959, 21. Poling also came to Hoover's defense, this time against a reader saying that the FBI was 90% Roman Catholic. Poling responded, "This charge is completely false. There are, of course, many splendid Roman Catholics in the FBI personnel. J. Edgar Hoover himself is a Protestant and has been a trustee of the National Presbyterian Church in Washington." Poling, "Catholic F.B.I.?" *CH*, September 1959, 8. Bell came out against those who wished to abolish the House Committee on Un-American Activities in 1959. He granted that the infamous committee had, at times, gone beyond what was prudent, saying that it "may have exhibited more zeal than judgment." However, he maintained that it had done more good than harm and asserted that it had been reformed to the point where the abuses of the past were now absent. Arguing that this committee had been greatly feared by Communist supporters because of its ability to expose their connections to Communist and affiliated groups, Bell accused its critics of foolishness, at best. "This forthright demand for the abolition of the Un-American Activities Committee indicates that some of our leaders are extremely naive or extremely dangerous." Bell, "Shall We Promote Freedom, etc.," *SPJ*, January 21, 1959, 3. He was later to change his metaphor for Americans' desire to treat Communism with mutual respect from negotiating with criminals to a patient being unwilling to accept a cancer diagnosis. "Just as untreated cancer continues to grow and its cells to spread and infiltrate the entire body, so Communism, unrecognized, unrestrained, and untreated spreads through infiltration, indoctrination and subversion and the end result is not a converted Communism but a thoroughly invaded democracy." Bell, "You Don't Temporize with Cancer—Or Do You?" *PJ*, December 16, 1959, 11.

We have no sympathy with wild generalizations, whether made
by [Carl] McIntires or [Billy James] Hargises or others. The best
way to handle those who spend half-time denouncing churchmen and half-time denouncing Communism is hardly to major
in denouncing anti-Communism. While eschewing objection-
able methods, there is always the temptation to use those same
methods (more subtly) in the condemnatory process. Let's get
on with the Christian challenge to Communism.[46]

---

46. Henry, "What is the Target: Communism or Anti-Communism," CT, May
22, 1961, 23. ET provided an article attacking the John Birch Society, a staunchly
anti-Communist organization which attracted a great deal of support among religious and political conservatism during this period. Nonetheless, the author of this
piece gave no place to the Society in Christian morality or political liberty. Speaking
of its head, Robert Welch, he said, "The new leader of many of America's religious
and economic conservatives takes a dim view of liberalism of any kind, and especially of *democracy*, a term he goes to great lengths to castigate." The author went
to criticize the Society for its false appropriation of Christian identity, monolithic
leadership style, and fascination with Fascism. David M. Baxter, "What About the
John Birch Society?" ET, December 1961, 18–20. Courier also attacked the group
saying that it was ridiculous to suggest that President Eisenhower and his brother
were secret Communists. "You can go so *far right* that you come full-sphere around
to where the leftists are working equally hard to smash US unity and destroy confidence in church as well as state! ... Democracy can be killed as dead by extreme
rightists as by extreme leftists—and vice versa." Courier, "John Birch," CH, July 1961,
6. Italics in original. One author writing in CT was skeptical about the prospects
of a simplistic Christianity to counter the Communist threat. " 'Christianity is
the answer to Communism.' Few slogans are more certain to gain an enthusiastic
response from any typical gathering in America than this one. ... Using the term
Christianity in its widest and loosest connotation, the claim that it is the answer
is extremely difficult to substantiate." He then noted that the Communists had
managed to gain control over more people in a few decades than Christians had
managed present with the gospel. Of these new Communists, he said, "Many of
them can articulate the doctrines of communism more articulately than the majority of youth living in so-called Christian countries can articulate the doctrines of
Christianity." He spoke of a time when a fellow evangelical had confidently asked
if he agreed that a born again experience was the best answer to Communism. The
writer replied, "I fear I could not have hurt him more had I lashed him across the
face. 'No, I wouldn't. A born again experience is the answer to the question of the
possession of eternal life. It is not the answer to the question of safety on the high-
way. You need to know the rules of the road and to obey them.' " Seeing a shallow
understanding of the situation as the primary impediment a robust defense, he
argued, "Ignorance is dangerous, and frequently sinful. The ignorance of leaders,
even Christian leaders of the true nature of communism is appalling. Superficial
observation of local Communist behavior is no substitute for a knowledge of the

It was not enough merely to fight Communism as a real and dangerous enemy; Christians had to fight it for the right reasons, and mere patriotism and xenophobia were not enough.

DIVINE PRIORITIES

Russell Hitt went even beyond Henry here. In 1961 he blasted American Christians for being, as he put it in his title, "Americans First and Christians Second." He described how a group working on outreach to Cuba found their coffers coming up empty after the Bay of Pigs because many erstwhile contributors could not see why they should be funding an enemy country. Hitt's response was harsh to those of whom he said, "Their loyalty to Uncle Sam preceded their loyalty to Jesus Christ." He sarcastically asked, "Should the gospel be preached only to friendly nations? Should we ask our missions boards to determine if another nation agrees with US foreign policy before they support Christian work there? How ridiculous! The gospel of Jesus Christ knows no bounds. There are no Iron Curtains, Bamboo Curtains, or Sugar Cane Curtains in the Great Commission." He concluded with the suggestion that this nationalism would yield a counterproductive result. "If the gospel is thwarted in Cuba right now, it will not be because of Castro's Communism, but rather because of Christian's [sic] Americanism."[47] Two years later another *ET* article made a similar point, asking readers, "Do you pray for Christians in Communist China and other countries under Communist rule as you once did when missionaries were serving there, bringing back glowing reports? Do we identify with the Church of Jesus Christ, or only with American missionaries of Jesus Christ?"[48] Another *ET* writer argued that even if the goals of the American government regarding world Communism might align in many ways with that of evangelical Christianity, it would be a significant mistake to assume that the two were identical. "This is extremely hazardous. It is

---

philosophy, motives, morals, and organization of this evil enemy." Frederick G. Schwarz, "Can We Meet the Red Challenge?" *CT*, April 13, 1959, 12–13. Schwartz was a prominent anti-Communist activist out of Australia. *CT* here incorrectly lists his middle initial as G where it should read C for "Charles."

47. Hitt, "Americans First and Christians Second," *ET*, August 1961, 4.
48. Joseph T. Bayly, "We Have Blundered Badly," *ET*, March 1963, 35.

dangerous to think of American foreign policy as 'Christian' or to think of it as a simple, direct expression of Christian ethics. It is also dangerous to suppose that by a supporting American foreign policy a person can help accomplish a 'Christian' mission in the world." Rather than supposing that even the good intentions of American leaders ensured a divine blessing and open-ended support, he argued that, owing to human nature, things begun well often end up capitulating to the worst of the temptations of power. "Convince rulers that they are carrying out God's policies, and they may show an inclination to march out to end the reign of evil the world over. If such be the case, it is possible that the high aims of the originally worthy mission may be lost to the crass ambitions of personal glory."[49] Support of American foreign policy which veered beyond the contingent was not only bad theology; it was inherently dangerous.

Francis Schaeffer had some mixed words for the prospects of America's side in the Cold War. Writing in *CT*, he wrote that he did not foresee a Red future for the world, but neither was he sure the US would end up on top. "I doubt communism will win, for it seems to me that it contains even greater divisions in itself. But that is the secondary point. Communism does not have to win for us to lose. We are losing to ourselves." Ultimately, he saw little difference between what the materialist and capitalist American-led world and the materialist and Communist Russian-led bloc. "In the race of fission versus fission, fusion versus fusion, missile versus missile, what reason is there to think that those conceiving and engineering these things on 'our side' believe anything basically different concerning the personal versus the impersonal view of the universe from those on the 'other side,' the Communists?"[50] It was not enough to be better than the bad guys; America had to do good to be the good guys.

---

49. Walfred Peterson, "Is Anti-Communist Foreign Policy Christian?" *ET*, August 1962, 8, 10, 40.

50. Francis A. Schaeffer, "The Modern Drift: Is Nobody Home in this World?" *CT*, June 20, 1960, 3.

Our President

When it came to President Eisenhower, evangelical commentators were almost uniform in their support, even if that support allowed for criticism at times. Courier offered quiet criticism of Eisenhower's approach to international crises. Quoting extensively from Truman's Secretary of State, Dean Acheson, Courier encouraged the former diplomat's characterization of Eisenhower's strategy as "diplomacy by locomotion," with the idea being that rather than dealing with problems, the administration sent the President traveling.[51] However, even this mildly negative view was in the definite minority. For example, Barnhouse added to his earlier award to Ike as "man of the year" to declare the President the "man of the decade" for the 1950s.[52]

L. Nelson Bell's analysis was little short of hagiography, saying, "Our President is a man of great good will. He is a man who honestly tries to give God a rightful place in his life. Few indeed have been the world leaders who have persistently and obviously taken the time to attend church at times when the eyes of the whole world were focused on him and when some particular international problem was facing him."[53] Even the normally circumspect Henry spoke quote boldly about the President's role in the world. He said that the Soviet Union "confronts President Eisenhower with herculean tasks" with the twofold threat of duplicitous peace overtures and the new threat of Russian rocket power. He continued his praise for Eisenhower with an admonition to his fellow believers, saying, "But the President's responsibility—and he merits the prayers of all Christians—is larger still. In this effort to thaw

---

51. Courier, "Tour," *CH*, January 1960, 12. The following month he pulled back from this critical stance with a nearly identically entitled article. In this latter incarnation Courier picked at those who first found Eisenhower to be too aloof only later to accuse him of "trying to run the world singlehandedly." Courier, "Tours," *CH*, February 1960, 12.

52. The Editors, *ET*, January 1960, Cover.

53. Bell, "There Is but One Road from the Summit—Down!" *SPJ*, April 15, 1959, 3-4. Later, Bell favorably contrasted Eisenhower with his Russian counterpart, saying that the American had "conducted himself like a gentleman, as the great head of a great nation would be expected to do, he, and our entire nation, were subjected to abuse by a murderer, purgerer—a man who epitomizes evil in the world." Bell, "Destiny at Stake," *PJ*, July 27, 1960, 11. Presumably, this neologism is to say that Khrushchev was one who conducted purges, not one who committed perjury.

the 'cold war,' he stands—chief representative of a nation professedly 'under God'—as a mirror of men who champion unchanging truth, fixed moral principles, and the dignity of all men as creatures answerable to a divine Creator." While he was generally hopeful concerning the President's intentions and abilities, he insisted that America had only a contingent moral superiority to its Cold War foe.[54]

Henry was not uniformly supportive of Eisenhower's policies. After the United States was caught lying when one of its U-2 pilots was shot down over Soviet territory, he took his government, and its president by implication, to task for its duplicity. "We are now forced by events to take stock also of the fact that America stands morally humiliated before God. Not before Russia, not before the world, but before God. We have been trapped in attempting refuge in a lie. We have even encouraged men in our armed forces when facing torture to commit the act of self-destruction." He saw this, in turn, as an act of national self-destruction. "The high moral principles upon which our government was founded and the righteousness and justice which have been the invisible structure of our foreign policy, are being sabotaged by the relativistic and utilitarian ethics of a cynical age."[55] This is an important reiteration of a consistent point in evangelical commentary.

---

54. Henry, "Eisenhower, Khurshchev Talks Shadowed By a Red Moon," *CT*, September 28, 1959, 22.

55. Henry, "God's Judgment on the Summit," *CT*, June 6, 1960, 20. Courier, on the other hand, came to Eisenhower's defense about these matters, if only in a halfhearted way. In an article describing the British sense of shock when it was discovered that the US had been overflying Soviet territory despite repeated previous denials, Courier said, "No one here seems to be self-righteously arguing that the US should not spy as it can. Perhaps what has upset Britain is that we finally and fumblingly admitted we were spying. Espionage is a secret affair over here. There is something almost indecent about admitting it, even if one is caught with one's hand (or head) in the cookie jar." Courier, "U-2, Brutus," *CH*, July 1960, 6. The "over here" reference is alluding to the statement that, according to a preface to his column, Courier was traveling in Europe at the time. Granted, as there was no real Courier, there is no clear answer as to just who was where. Similarly, he spoke approvingly of the entire affair and suggested that the turmoil had less to do with American guilt than Russian shame. "For all the gee-ing and hawing, don't forget that the reason U-2 struck a nerve was that it proved the Iron Curtain to be made of cheesecloth. ... For once, the US grasp has exceeded its reach—a new, and to a degree, refreshing state of affairs." Courier, "U-2," *CH*, August 1960, 6.

They could very often be quite supportive of the United States and, in this case, of its leaders. However, this support could be taken away if moral behavior was not forthcoming.

JFK

President Kennedy was approached with a mixture of skepticism and hope. Many evangelicals were openly distrustful of his Roman Catholicism and what that might entail for religious liberty.[56] At the same time, many were willing to praise him when the situation seemed to warrant it. After the President's famous Berlin speech, Culbertson commented, "The spiritual implications of the speech, however, override by far the material ones. What really happened was this: Against

---

56. This was a common concern among many of these commentators. As noted in previous chapters, many evangelicals saw Roman Catholicism as just as much of a tyrannical force in the world as was Communism. Without mentioning Kennedy by name, Culbertson said, "The history, past and present of Rome's dealings in Catholic-dominated countries does not elicit confidence. Furthermore, Rome's opposition to the doctrine of the separation of church and state, with its related and supporting tenets, inspires suspicion and uneasiness lest basic American concepts ultimately be altered. Many a Protestant believes that the best protection is to prevent the first crack in the wall." Culbertson, "A Roman Catholic for President?" *MM*, March 1960, 9. This was not a uniform opinion, however. One *ET* article suggested that Kennedy's election was actually a great boon for religious liberty in the US. David Moberg argued that, on the whole, the election of a Roman Catholic to the American presidency further distanced the political office from any denominational standard. David O. Moberg, "A Victory for Religious Liberty," *ET*, February 1961, 18–20. A contributor to *ET* found it necessary to assure his readers that God had not abandoned his people solely on the basis of Kennedy's election. For both reasons of reputation and pragmatism, he implored evangelicals to offer the new leader the respect due his office. "God's standards for His people's behavior have not changed. As President of the United States, John F. Kennedy ought to find his most loyal and faithful citizens among his most obstinate religious opponents—the evangelical Christians. He is entitled to the fullest measure of patriotic respect." D. Bruce Lockerbie, "Now That Kennedy is President," *ET*, January 1961, 13, 29. Poling, who had often spoke against the potential danger posed by Roman Catholics in power, found himself complimenting the most powerful Catholic in the land. He thanked the President for standing by his pledge to continue to support the separation of church and state, saying, "Specifically, President Kennedy underlines and lifts up 'the clear prohibition of the Constitution' against allocating funds to 'church schools or church school teachers' salaries.' ... *CH* also applauds a President who, standing firmly on the Constitution of the United States, is the chief executive of all the people without regard." Poling, "Well Done, Mr. President," *CH*, April 1961, 19.

a godless—rather, a God-hating—regime and philosophy a nation philosophically dedicated to the worship of God said, in effect: 'Here we take our stand against you, though the man-made hell of nuclear warfare rain upon us. Thus you may go, and no farther.' "[57] In a distinctly more light-hearted piece *CT* published a photo of Billy Graham meeting with the President. As both men were soon to travel to Latin America, Kennedy joked that he would go first and be Graham's John the Baptist.[58] A contributor to *ET* described Kennedy in this way: "In January [1960] John Kennedy was an 'unknown quantity' except in his home state. By June he was unknown except in the United States. But by December, he was a 'known quantity' around the world. 1960 had proven him as a quantity; 1961 would test his quality."[59] Poignantly, after the President's death *CT* eulogized Kennedy in an editorial.

> America lost a man of great intellectual gifts, a President of strong courage and of great political imagination. Kennedy had kept his promise to the nation and had held the line on the church-state issue. And whatever one may feel about his civil rights stand, he held it with integrity and undeviating moral conviction, even when it threatened to be politically disadvantageous. Men of good will long will pay him tribute and the nation long will sorrow for such a man, cut down in the strength of his years and the height of his service.[60]

---

57. Culbertson, "The Time and the Place," *MM*, September 1961, 10.

58. Kucharsky, "Southern Travellers," *CT*, January 5, 1962, 32. According to the article this meeting occurred by accident. Graham was at the White House to meet with an old friend. Seeing the preacher in the hallway, the President sent an aide to bring him into the Oval Office where the two met for twenty minutes alone.

59. Petersen, "Dueling with Gigantic Windmills: United States," *ET*, January 1961, 22. This was part of the replacement for Barnhouse's annual "Survey of the Year," as Barnhouse had died of a brain tumor in late 1960. He was replaced as editor by Russell T. Hitt.

60. Henry, "The Assassination of the President," *CT*, December 6, 1963, 24. With horrifying accuracy, Courier accidently predicted the future concerning the upcoming 1964 presidential election. "You can say this for the Democrats—they don't have to wonder where their next candidate's coming from. Barring some unforeseen catastrophe, he's John Fitzgerald Kennedy." Courier, "Coming Candidates," *CH*, September 1963, 6.

While some of this could be written off as a refusal to speak ill of the dead, the specifics of this praise moves beyond mere politeness.

DECEITFUL AMERICANS

Nonetheless, the young President received his own share of critiques from evangelicals. After the Cuban Missile Crisis, some rebuked what they saw as the administration's use of deception for strategic and political ends. *CT*'s news editor noted that some theologians had allowed that there was a place for deception in warfare, but, thus far, situations like the Cuban Missile Crisis had not warranted what Kennedy's spokespeople had done. He quoted Poling of *CH* as being in favor of secrecy but critical of both parties' role in deceiving the American people. His conclusion was somewhat ambiguous, saying, "The ethical question probably focuses upon *when* deception is justifiable. Some maintain that it should be limited to military warfare. Others contend that the present cold war is as real an international conflict as any military operation ever was, and that deception is therefore justifiable."[61] Russell Hitt also commented on the media manipulation by the Kennedy administration, noting that the President "defended the actions of his staff on the grounds that secrecy was necessary for the operation, proper to a democratically elected government and beneficial to the people." However, he was stark about the morality of the actions, concluding that "it doesn't matter whether the foe is Communism, Khrushchev, or Satan himself, lying is never justifiable"; lying was always an absolute evil.[62]

DEPRAVED AMERICANS

Evangelical opinion regarding American society continued its downward spiral. Not unsurprisingly, many found their nation to be sinking beneath the weight of its own debauchery. Hitt, for example, found his contemporary culture to be sickening in its immorality and greed.

Meanwhile, Hollywood's film menu becomes increasingly nauseating. Competing with foreign films, the Hollywood film moguls

---

61. Kucharsky, "Special Report: Is 'News Management' Ethical?" *CT*, April 12, 1963, 33.

62. Hitt, "The Government's Right to Lie," *ET*, May 1963, 4.

have dropped any semblance of morality. They have learned that decent films—unless they can produce a "Ben-Hur"—don't make any money. And since the Almighty Dollar rules, they choose the easy course—immorality. Success is spelled with a capital SEX.[63]

Bell also found fault in America's sex-obsessed entertainment industry. Rather than speaking of Marilyn Monroe's death as her own fault or solely of a wicked cabal in Hollywood, he portrayed the actress as a victim of the corruption of the nation as a whole. "The poor girl never had a chance, either as a child or later when she was exploited by lustful men, greedy producers and a public who cared for nothing but cheap exposures. ... We wonder if some day this whole generation will not stand condemned for what it did to Marilyn Monroe?"[64] Henry accused newspapers of encouraging a greater acceptance of pornography in American society. He noted that there had been some success in getting outright suggestive material removed from such periodicals, but, he added, some illicit imagery had slipped in not as features but as advertisements for movies. "Whatever evil influence this type of advertising has on the adult mind, it is double-fold on the impressionable youth whose mind is extremely active and highly imaginative. Film ads exaggerate lurid features that may not appear in the actual showing of the picture but this nonetheless exerts an insidious influence on the mind of the reader." He ended by calling for concerned citizens to write letters to the editors of their local papers to make their displeasure known.[65] Four years later he compared America to the biblical archetype of immorality of Sodom and Gomorrah, suggesting that books and movies of his day would have fit in quite well with the mores of Lot's day.[66]

When US forces entered Thailand, Courier worried about the impact of American culture on a culture he admired. He was certain that Thailand was worth saving, describing it as "a pin-neat nation, its

63. Hitt, "Is Government Control Next for Hollywood?" *ET*, June 1961, 4.

64. Bell, "A Tragic Victim," *PJ*, August 22, 1962, 9.

65. Henry, "Newspaper Contribution to Modern Pornography," *CT*, March 16, 1959, 22.

66. Henry, "The Sins of Sodom—1963," *CT*, September 13, 1963, 26.

people industrious, clean, utterly charming." However, he wondered about the effect its new protectors might have on this wonderful nation. "One cannot help noticing the degree to which American 'occupation' of Eastern nations, be it Japan, Korea, Vietnam (and now Thailand) Americanizes the country involved, for worse as well as for better." This was more than a question of Yankee crassness for Courier; it was about the entire point of the effort. "If Americans were always sensitive to human personality, there would be no problem. But when we get carried away with causes to the point that people do not count, or are a secondary consideration, we've lost the only thing worth fighting for."[67]

America's Shame

Far from being uniformly uninterested in the growing Civil Rights movement, many evangelicals were using their positions to prod their followers into action. For Henry, the situation could not be more clear, at least in terms of the principles involved. "From the humanitarian standpoint the issue hardly exists. The Negro is one of those endowed by their Creator, as a Southerner put it, with certain 'inalienable rights.' He is a human being, and in a land founded on Christian principles he deserves the more to be treated as such." He then offered a strong rebuke to way America treated this one group of its citizens. After arguing that there was also no legal argument as African Americans were granted these rights by the Constitution, he said there was, indeed, a factor impeding the reality of these rights. "There remains the cultural issue, and it is serious enough to affect all the others and to keep the present debate in a turmoil that jeopardizes any healthy settlement. The North is dexterously avoiding the issue by its white flight to the suburbs. The South has lived with it for decades and intends to keep doing so—in its own way." Avoiding any confusion about what he was referring to, he added, "Compounding the issue is the fact that the badge of culture in the South (and increasingly in the North) is the color of one's skin."[68]

---

67. Courier, "Laos," CH, July 1962, 7.
68. Henry, "The White Conscience and the Negro Vote," CT, March 28, 1960, 22–23. At another time he commended President Kennedy's characterization of

Not all discussions were as dour as this. Courier mocked the state
of Arkansas for a new piece of legislation which required blood banks
to specify whether donated blood had come from Anglos or African
Americans. He noted that the medical community had said the policy
was "ridiculous" as there was no distinguishing characteristic between
these supposedly two types of blood, and pointed readers to a passage
from the biblical book of Acts, indicating that God had made all people
from one original ancestor.[69] He later took aim at Alabama libraries
which had removed a children's book where a white rabbit married a
black one. He was pleased that Florida had not chosen to ban an edition
of *The Three Little Pigs* which portrayed the two foolish pigs as white
and black-and-white, respectively, while the wise brick-builder was
fully black.[70]

ET gave a platform for an African American pastor to express his
views of America's race problem. He argued, "The struggle of the
Negro for justice in this country is built upon Christian foundations.

---

anti-Civil Rights actions, saying, "The President has described Birmingham as 'an
ugly situation.' And it is. As ugly as the arrest and jailing of a seven-year old girl;
as ugly as the use of water pressure strong enough to strip bark from trees, and
the use of dogs against human beings. For what? For wanting such simple rights
as eating in a cafeteria, attending a school." Henry viewed this current crisis as a
fundamental problem with American society and one which did not comport well
with the view of the United States as God's special land. Americans, he asserted,
were here distinguished not by their godliness unique from others but by their
sinfulness which they held in common with all humanity. "And any man not blinded
by twisted prejudice could see that the Nazi Germans were not special sinners,
for morally nothing distinguishes anti-Semitism from Birmingham's racism. In
the ugly clash of American against American, one could see the common human
nature we all share, and the common judgment under which we all stand. He who
looked hard the social ugliness in Birmingham saw not special sinners who fight
for state's rights but trample on human rights; he saw the human nature we all
share. He saw a time to weep, to repent, to remember—'inasmuch as ye have done
it unto these ye have done it to me.'" Henry, "Color is Skin Deep, Evil as Deep as the
Heart," *CT*, May 24, 1963, 22–23. Courier also looked to the imagery at Birmingham,
noting, "If both whites and Negroes had started out deliberately to antagonize
the other, they could hardly have done a better job of it than has been exhibited
in Birmingham. The photographs of police dogs ripping the trousers from Negro
men ... should give Kremlin propagandists quite a few gleeful chuckles." Courier,
"Birmingham," *CH*, July 1963, 5.

69. Courier, "Blood," *CH*, June 1959, 12–13.
70. Courier, "Pigs is Pigs," *CH*, August 1959, 11.

His concept of justice is not based upon the premise that what is right for the State is right for the individual. It is Judeo-Christian to the core in that it conceives of the right and justice as above the State and the individual, and as conformity to the law of God." He looked at many American churches as places where either African Americans were overtly persecuted or where their problems might be politely and prayerfully ignored. Yet, he had hope that success in the sight of God would come, even if that success was never found in the present. He said of African Americans who would seek to live as God had called them as human beings,

> He will be accused of violating providential arrangements, of seeking to do the impossible, of trying to be what he is not. His desire for a Christianity free from the hypocritical shackles of racism will be dismissed as an aberration unworthy of serious consideration. He will be labeled an agitator, and perhaps even a Communist. None of these things should move him, however, for his role under God could be that of demonstrating forever the glorious truth that in God's sight no flesh shall glory.[71]

This was far more than a mere token offering. This was an express condemnation of a pet sin of the America of the day.

---

71. C. Herbert Oliver, "The Christian Negro," *ET*, November 1960, 15–16, 58, 60. In a posthumously published article in *ET*, Barnhouse had a wide-ranging condemnation for many in the US and their willful ignorance of the place they had in past slavery. "Let us face the situation in the United States. Northerners must recognize that they are descendants of the slave-traders who built up great fortunes by traffic in human flesh. Southerners must admit that their early culture was based on the toil and washed in the tears of the kidnapped children of Africa." He even went so far as to compare American racism with the sins of the Soviet Union. He was grateful for what he had in his nation, but he asked his readers how they were any better than their counterparts in Russia. "We thank God that we do not have to contend with an arbitrary, Christ-denying government. We thank God that our nation has men of high principle and Christian conviction in many place of leadership. ... The godlessness of many of our national attitudes is no better than the godlessness of Moscow. How can racial discrimination be less sinful than class warfare between proletariat and bourgeoisie?" Barnhouse, "Race Relations and the Church," *ET*, November 1961, 33.

WAR

Despairing of Peace

The absence of open war in the period did not alleviate the deep sense
of unease felt by many during this time. With tensions high all over the
world, and particular crises threatening to spark a wider conflagration,
this time of peace was consumed with fears of war. One writer suggested that, rather than being a potential future to be avoided, World
War III was a realized present. "The Third World War began with the
Communist uprising in Greece in December, 1944. It continues down to
the present time, its intensity varying with the degree of Freed World
resistance encountered. ... We are living in an era of permanent wars
and revolutions."[72] Hitt described the world of 1963, saying, "In the
Pentagon, officers freely talk of how long total annihilation of the earth
will take. Best guess—12 or 15 minutes. What could trigger off a devastating nuclear warfare? Anything could. Cuba, Berlin, Taiwan, even
an insignificant incident in the Himalayas." Expressing some grim satisfaction that many evangelicals had been seemingly proven right, he
added, "A few years ago, only raving evangelists could be heard talking
about destruction. Nobody listened to them. Now military experts
are saying the same words. Nobody listens to them either."[73] Rather
than the happy-go-lucky view found in the popular imagination, the
late 1950s and early 1960s were, for evangelicals anyway, a period of
dark expectations.

Henry put the overwhelming nature of the crisis this way: "The
whole civilized world this morning is troubled by the swift tempo of
events. Dag Hammarskjold's death moves up the uncertainties about the
United Nations. And the perplexities in Laos, in Cuba, in Latin America,
in East Germany, and in West Berlin strike anxiety in these days even
more into the hearts of many Christians."[74] One of Henry's editorials

72. Anthony T. Bouscaren, "The War We Are In," *PJ*, July 3, 1963, 7. Ellipses in
original. The postscript to this piece says, "Adapted from an article in 'News and
Views.'"

73. Hitt, "Fifteen Minutes Over the Brink," *ET*, January 1963, 6.

74. Henry, Sermon at Southwestern Baptist Theological Seminary, September
19, 1961, Carl F. H. Henry Papers, Box 1961 2, File Speech "The Legacy of Christ,"

combined his concern over danger posed by both Communism and the possibility of nuclear war. He lamented what he called "the world's mad arms race," and the decision by Khrushchev to restart nuclear weapons testing. He warned that, with new "super bombs," the Russians could "rain death upon any spot in the globe." He was dismissive of those in the West who downplayed the threat:

> The only language the power-hungry naturalists have ever understood is the language of more power. The fact that Khrushchev's rocket-rattling surprised and shocked Western leaders only indicates their naïve understanding of the history of thought and the nature of man. Khrushchev made it clear that strongly-worded phrases with Harvard artiness hold no terror for him.

Henry here called for a vigorous response, but he couched it in terms encompassing the moral complexity of the situation. "Christianity is a religion of peace. The Church has no mandate to fuel the arms race. It must nourish the believer's aspiration toward constructive thought and life, and guard against sweeping man's energies into the service of irrational impulses and resentments." Yet this was followed hard upon by a more bellicose and eschatological corollary.

> No century in history provides clearer evidence than ours that the virtues of peace and justice cannot be superimposed upon unregenerate human nature. The answer to the problem of the human race is a new society of regenerate men and women. If the Church must remind the power that be, as indeed she must, that the only deterrent to slavery is the use of force in the service of justice, it must also remind the children of our age, as the biblical writers do, that enduring peace has Messianic roots, and that it deals not merely with political tensions but with the grip of sin and the stench of death upon our spirits. [75]

Rolfing Library Archives, Trinity Evangelical Divinity School, Deerfield, IL.

75. Henry, "World Arms Race and the Moralizing of Power," *CT*, September 11, 1961, 27.

Henry here spoke mournfully of the possible necessity of nuclear war while adamantly declaring that no war or political process can fix humanity's ultimate need. No human system, capitalist American or Soviet Russian, would solve the dilemma facing the world of his day.

Peace Through Strength

With this in mind, Henry found the American approach to engagement with the Soviet Union to be flawed at its heart. "Some US diplomats apparently retain grandiose faith in the power of words and dollars. ... For instead of exhibiting moral conviction and spiritual truth as the West's great armor, it largely moves within the context of economic benefits. We are in danger therefore of dying in our own materialistic sins even before the disease of communism smites us." According to Henry, this attempt at moderation and pragmatism would only render a self-induced defeat to the American cause.

> When momentary political expediency shapes and reshapes foreign policy in reaction to Communist aggression, and this is dignified as *real*-politics, and when long-range principles become more a matter of precept than practice, the inevitable vacillation in foreign affairs will gratify those who seek the decline of the republic, and it will disappoint and discourage allies.[76]

The situation was far too grim and treacherous to allow any place for policies based on an idealized view of humanity.

In 1961 Poling called for a "crusade" to spread freedom to every part of the world, with a goal of succeeding by 1976 to coincide with the 200th anniversary of the Declaration of Independence. This was not as naïve and imperialistic as it might at first have seemed. He did not mean this as a call to martial arms, per se, but rather a dedicated effort to spread liberty and roll back tyranny. He rebuked what he saw as an overzealous attempt to secure peace through the sacrifice of intrinsic human and American liberties. "Today, the supreme world issue is not 'peace.' The supreme world issue is not 'disarmament.' Here and now the

---

76. Henry, "The U.N. Falters in Debate While Dagger Diplomacy Widens," *CT*, October 13, 1961, 34–35. Italics in original.

supreme issue is FREEDOM. Men have the right to be free! When this fact comes into focus, not only is our determination to achieve it immeasurably strengthened, but other lesser objectives fall into their proper places." Moving specifically to those calling for compromise with the Soviets, he added, "They would have us mutilate American freedom in the interest of a world authority that in the expressed opinion of these mistaken ones would guarantee 'peace,' 'peace,' where there is and as of now can be no peace."[77] Although he stated his goals differently than Henry, they both saw their nation's approach to foreign policy to be rooted in more hope than reality.

Pacifists, particularly those in mainline denominations, again bore the brunt of many evangelical criticisms. Taylor was pleased to report that according to a group he described as a "left-wing pacifist group," the vast majority of American Protestant ministers were not pacifists. He was particularly happy to see that his own Presbyterians were among those least likely to advocate nonviolence as a universal principle, and he questioned the interpretation of the survey's sponsors that the only reason many of the pastors did not agree with them was that they did not wish to upset their congregations. Part of his joy flowed from his low expectations, as only fifteen percent would advocate surrender and nonviolence in the face of war. "We are encouraged. We thought the proportion was much higher."[78] A contributor to CT argued that Christian pacifists were entirely misguided. When some mainline groups looked to the success of Gandhi's nonviolent efforts to oust UK forces from India and the American civil rights movement, the author retorted, "Without minimizing the achievements of either of these, we would point out that there is simply no proper parallel between the British administration in India on the one hand, and what would occur if the Soviet Union or Red China were allowed to occupy the United States on the other." After describing the imperial rule by London as the lesser of two evils when compared to that practiced by Moscow, he said that anyone wanting to see the reality of pacifism in

---

77. Poling, "World Freedom is Our Real Objective," CH, June 1961, 25. Capitalization in original.

78. Taylor, "Clergy Not Pacifists—Fellowship Finds," PJ, October 30, 1963, 11.

the face of tyranny need only look to the recent experience of Hungary as the Communists crushed the peaceful revolt there.[79] Pacifism only worked, according to these commentators, when the ruling powers were self-constrained by an ideology hemming in the more natural violence of human power.

POTENTIAL CONFLICTS FAR AND NEAR

When the Communists began construction of the Berlin Wall, many writers did not know quite how to respond. It was portrayed as one among many recent Western defeats at the hands of the East, yet little blame was laid at the feet of American or Allied leaders. Henry accused Khrushchev of fomenting the crisis and offered praise to Kennedy's strong response, yet he wrote of the event as merely a spectacular example of the general downward trend of Western fortunes of the last few years.[80] Others found the wall to be of far greater import. An article reprinted in *ET* described the new situation as one where the wall was the central fact of life in the former German capital. "The wall dominates Berlin today. It is the epitome of her tragedy. Recent news has highlighted the 28 miles of concrete slabs which separate more than two million West Berliners from one million of their friends and relatives in the East. They cannot meet one another, all telephone lines between them are closed and the postal services are liable to interception."[81] The Editors at *Presbyterian Journal* simply recorded that, in accordance with the wishes of President Kennedy, one of the major Presbyterian denominations had sent out an appeal for prayer over the crisis.[82] Another brief notice informed readers that, counterintuitively, one East German pastor was denied reentry to the Communist zone,

---

79. Harold Kuhn, "Christian Surrender to Communism," *CT*, March 2, 1959, 9–10.

80. Henry, "Western Tension Mounts as Reds Seal East Berlin Border," *CT*, August 28, 1961, 34.

81. Alan Gibson, "Behind the Berlin Barrier," *ET*, March 1963, 32. According to the byline, this article was originally published in the British periodical, *The Evangelical Magazine.*

82. The Editors, "Berlin Prayers Asked," *PJ*, August 30, 1961, 3.

and others of his East Berlin colleagues were prevented from attending planned meetings in the Western sector.[83]

The failed Bay of Pigs invasion of Cuba by US-backed rebels was roundly condemned by many evangelical voices. It was condemned, not for the attempt but for inadequate effort. Reporting that there were some conspiracy-theory-minded Americans who doubted the reality of Yuri Gagarin's April 1961 spaceflight, Henry opined that there was no question about the Bay of Pigs. "Nobody doubted the US failure to give effective support to the counter-thrust for Cuban freedom only 90 miles offshore. A faint radio signal spoke volumes: 'This is Cuba calling the Free World. We need help in Cuba.' US prestige sagged not simply in outer space but in its own back yard."[84] He would later argue that despite the odious implication of financially backing the Castro state, America should pay the $62 million to free the nearly twelve hundred men captured after the Bay of Pigs since to do otherwise would deny the cardinal Western principle of the supreme value of human lives.[85] Courier was nearly sarcastic and said, "The 'invasion' was a tragedy of errors. Not the least of the errors (or the tragedy) was the denial of our government that it was involved when it was in fact involved."[86] A news report in CT warned readers that many of the newly immigrated Cubans in the US were openly calling for war to liberate their homeland, and that many of these two hundred thousand refugees were patient, in 1963, to wait it out in Miami until Castro was toppled. The author of this piece feared this promised that American involvement in the Cuba crisis was far from over.[87] Little would that author or the thousands of Cubans hiding temporarily in south Florida know that generations would pass with them still in exile.

83. The Editors, "Reds Block Church Official's Re-Entry," *PJ*, September 27, 1961, 3.

84. Henry, "The Fiasco in Cuba and Freedom's Supports," *CT*, May 8, 1961, 26. Henry went on to wonder if the Russian space victory and American Cuban failure were signs that America was inexorably failing. "More and more the question arose: had political democracy lost the spiritual convictions essential to its own survival?"

85. Henry, "Moral Dilemmas, Dual Standards Widen in a Self-Righteous Age," *CT*, April 27, 1962, 28.

86. Courier, "Cuba," *CH*, June 1961, 11.

87. Kucharsky, "Compassion for the Cubans," *CT*, January 18, 1963, 30.

THE BOMB

As it had been for nearly twenty years, atomic war was an ever-present possibility. While Russian bombers flying over the North Pole had been a worry for a decade and more, now Soviet missiles could be launched without any way to stop them. Nuclear devastation could visit American cities with a few minutes' warning. That such a horrible day would never come in their day was an unknown hope for the people living then. The Editors at *CT* gave their readers a stark reminder of the dangers implicit in atomic war with a pair of extended quotations from other works in early 1962. After noting that it would take a three hundred megaton assault to take out a US missile base in Arizona, they added, "By contrast, a single 20-megaton bomb, burst in the air over Chicago, would suffice to destroy the entire metropolis." This harsh possible future was presented as though it were an increasingly likely outcome of current events. "When the capacity for mutual annihilation mounts beyond the 30,000-megaton stage and as the number of contestants increases, the danger of war by miscalculation and accident must rise. At some point in the ever-less-distant future is the point of no return."[88] Russell Hitt offered his readers some

---

88. The Editors, "Conceded to Be Lost," *CT*, March 30, 1962, 47. This was a quotation from an article by Gerald Piel published in *Science*. Henry offered a nuanced reaction to the nuclear fears stoked by the Cuban Missile Crisis. He laid out in detail the arguments of a pacifist Christian leader, A. J. Muste, who saw the atomic brinksmanship of the crisis as pushing the world into a new level all too close to the reality of nuclear conflict and not just their use as deterrence. Henry was clear that his support of atomic weapons was not a position he took lightly. "One may not discount the agony of personal decision, pacifist or non-pacifist, to be made in a nuclear age. Muste obviously is not optimistic concerning chances for unilateral disarmament by the United States." His sympathy, however, had its limits. "Cuba has not put to flight those who yet see the necessity of the deterrence afforded by atomic arms. To deny the necessity, they say, is to fly in the face of history. And in this, we think they are right; our arena of discourse is a sinful world. We say this even while realizing that we risk a Hiroshima as we turn away from the abject servitude of Buchenwald or Siberia." His final word on the subject was to accuse Christian pacifism of wishing more than understanding. "From here it looks like a fanciful hope for Utopia which spells bad politics and bad theology." Henry, "The Cuban Crisis and Pacifist Reaction," *CT*, March 1, 1963, 30–31. Not all of Henry's descriptions of pacifism were this confrontational. He wrote of a conference where prominent Just War and Pacifist theologians gathered to discuss war and peace. Henry summarized the basic positions of each side and concluded with a fairly

dark humor in early 1962 with an article entitled, "How to Perish in a Nuclear Attack." He explained, "There are two ways of facing certain death in the event of a nuclear attack in America. The first is to remain in the open, unsheltered to encounter radiation. The other is to try to get into your neighbor's fallout shelter." He added that there were many Americans who had indicated that any stray human beings attempting to gain entrance to their shelters would be shot, and some had accumulated firearms in preparation. He wondered whether these shelter-owners were taking things too far. "Can a person become so calloused as to refuse entry to another human being caught in the open during an attack? This is a problem a great many people have begun to wrestle with recently. And there are no simple answers."[89] Appealing to the same set of concerns, the editors of *MM* designed the cover of their February 1962 issue with an illustration of a young girl and her father outfitting their bomb shelter.[90] The danger facing America through nuclear weapons was one of which these commentators were keenly

---

positive reflection of the events. "Although the discussion waxed long and sometimes loud, the conference reached no unanimous conclusion. The Anabaptist and Reformed traditions remained as far apart as they were four centuries ago. On the other hand, both groups felt that they had obtained a new understanding of each other's position and a new appreciation of each other as Christian brethren." Henry, "War and Peace at Winona," *CT*, September 27, 1963, 33-34.

89. Hitt, "How to Perish in a Nuclear Attack," *ET*, March 1962, 6.

90. The Editors, Cover, *MM*, February 1962. In this same issue *MM* provided an article which discussed the Christian reaction to bomb shelters and whether there was any moral basis for building them and if there would be anything left after the bombs fell. The author warned his readers not to consider that their nation was somehow special and therefore immune to the wrath of God. "America is no different from any other nation in the eyes of a just God. ... Some have said that Communism may well be God's scourge of judgment upon an indulgent, God-forsaking so-called Christian culture. If so, it would not be the first time He has used a savage invader to call His people back to their knees." After describing some of the horrors to be expected in the days after an atomic war, the author encouraged people to learn for the present from this fear of the future. "Decide what you are living for—or dying for. For a Christian, the question is not, 'Do you want to live through a nuclear attack?' but 'Why do you want to live?' " Robert A. Cook, "Why Do You Want to Live Through?" *MM*, February 1962, 20-22. Cook had a follow-up article in April of that same year where he offered descriptions in greater detail of what the world would be like immediately after a nuclear attack. Cook, "Twenty Minutes After," *MM*, April 1962, 18.

aware and one which they wished their readers to share in through this new, horrible understanding.

END TIMES

Eschatologically speaking, there was little in this period which altered the previous dynamic. Nothing happened which threatened anyone's confidence that the end was still nigh, but neither did anything occur which they could point to as proof of their beliefs. For example, one of the more interesting discussions dealt not with a new perceived fulfillment but with a non-event as several writers tried to find the place of the United States in the Bible. The capture of Jerusalem was predicted, but its reality would need to wait a few years until the Six Day War. The emerging Common Market in Europe elicited some attention but only so much as a tentative confirmation of the way many observers thought the world was already headed. The downward trend in American morals was noted, again, but this was nothing beyond what had been observed for a long time. Even articles about the normally exciting happenings surrounding the State of Israel leveled off into a fairly mundane discussion, with some evangelicals speaking in favor of the Israelis and others against. Rather than being able to discuss specific prophecies, those inclined to focus on the end spoke of the general climate of the world.

American Failure

In the wake of a tumultuous 1962, Billy Graham pondered the eschatological implications of recent events. "The question that many students of the Bible are asking is simply this: Are the present crises prophesied in Scripture? Even a casual investigation would seem to indicate that the Bible warns of a time of turmoil and trouble such as the world has never known. A predicted period of crisis was the burden of Christ's prophetic ministry." However, rather than seeing such possible signs in contemporary events as a reason to put America in the place of God's agent for world salvation, Graham thought the more logical conclusion was that the US was headed for judgment. After suggesting that the American-led Free World was numb to the reality of things or, perhaps, even under a divine curse drawing it to destruction, he asked,

Could it be that Communism is some vast judgment that God will allow to fall on the West for the deep moral rot that has infected almost every country? ... The English-speaking world and Western Europe have had far more spiritual light than any other nations in the world's history. Except for a dedicated minority, we are rejecting that light intellectually and morally."

He had much the same critique for Western Christians as he had for Western Civilization—that they had lost their focus on God and turned to materialistic false hopes—and his hope was in divine provision of judgment on Communism, even if that judgment came after the Soviets had won the day.[91] His end-times focus was centered not so much on eschatologically helping his readers peer into the future as it was pastorally aiding them in facing the dangers of the present crises in light of the final victory of God.

The place of the US in any end-times scheme had presented a problem to many eschatologists, given that that was no clear reference to America in the Bible. John Walvoord responded to this concern as had others by including it as part of the revived Roman Empire.

There is no specific word in the Bible stating this conclusion, but it is a reasonable conclusion based on the extent of the ancient Roman Empire which included Great Britain, France, and Southern Europe. The United States, originally a colony of Great Britain and racially related to Europe, would naturally be grouped with Europe rather than with Russia, the Orient or Africa.

However, he sublimated the role of America and its place in a new empire to the ways these nations would fight for, or against, the State of Israel. After reminding his readers that the US, among others, was supportive of the Israelis' independence, he declared, "The real stake for World War III is not the United States or Russia. The real stake is the Middle East, for the nation that controls the Middle East will control

---

91. Graham, "Facing the Anti-God Colossus," *CT*, December 21, 1962, 6–8.

the world."[92] This represented an increasing trend in evangelical eschatological focus. Twenty years before it was more often the interactions of Germany, Italy, Russia, and Britain which determined the pace of end-times expectations with the Middle East waiting in the background. However, by the 1960s the activities of Middle Eastern nations had become the center of eschatology. The great powers mattered, but it was first and foremost increasingly only insofar as they affected the Arab-Israeli conflict.

ELEMENTAL FIRES

The world-ending potential of atomic bombs again elicited comments on a possible connection between nuclear weapons and the end of the world, even if writers seemed more interested in their heuristic force than their destructive power. A contributor to *CT* primarily used the danger as a metaphor to help people prepare for the end of the world. Beyond this he admitted that the language of the Bible echoed descriptions of the August 1945 attacks on Japan, comparing the imagery of melted steel at Hiroshima and melted elements in the prophecies of Peter.[93] He did, however, cast doubt on the possibility that the Eschaton prophesied in the Bible would come as a result of a US/USSR nuclear exchange. Such a conflict might be in the offing, but this would not be the final conflict. "It *could* happen! However, I do not believe that men will bring about the end of the world. The Bible tells us that it is God who will one day wind up the earth's bankrupt affairs." For the bulk of this article, the author was more interested in using the possibility of a nuclear holocaust as a horribly effective illustration and example for the way people should approach the final end of the world.[94]

In a similar way others suggested that the constant fear of a nuclear holocaust made contemporary people more sensitive to biblical prophecies than people in the past had been. Although the bulk of the article was rather innocuous when it came to specific connections between

---

92. John F. Walvoord, "Russia and the Middle East in Prophecy," *MM*, December 1959, 24–25.

93. The author gives no citation for these quotes.

94. Manfred E. Reinke, "Christ is Coming! ... Soon!" *CT*, November 10, 1961, 17.

contemporary events and biblical prophecy, one *SPJ* piece pointed out that "it would not take much to turn our modern world into a 'hell on earth,' with all our modern inventions of nuclear weapons and H-bombs, etc." Even so, the writer cut against reading too much into such things. First, he declared that there were always parallels between prophecy and any given period. Then, as he concluded definitively, he added, "No one knows the time. It is useless to try to set dates, but we are to read the signs of the times and be ready." He was less interested in letting his readers be in the know when it came to the end than in extending a pastoral call to live holy lives.[95]

Pastoring through the End

As they had in the past, many authors writing on eschatology used their articles to give comfort to their readers. One *Moody* writer pointed to the great hope instilled by Christians who studied end times and found their fulfillments in the present. He argued that news of recent events of history with the European Common Market, the Russian domination of central Europe, and the establishment of Israel gave to the Christian great hope because the ancient words of the Bible were being confirmed.[96] Another writer made the same point by suggesting that Russia's current rise to superpower status had been long prophesied in the Bible, and for proof of this he pointed to the early mention of the name "Rosh" for a great nation in the north cited in biblical prophecies long before anyone had heard of Russia. In fact this author cited Wilbur Smith as an authority for the suggestion that, rather than being a coincidence, the modern name Russia was directly derived from the biblical term, Rosh, when the Patriarch of Constantinople applied the ancient word to the new group of Slavic raiders causing devastation.[97]

---

95. J. Kenton Parker, "Jesus Teaches About The End Of The Age," *SPJ*, February 4, 1959, 15.

96. Woodbridge, "The Second Coming of Christ," *MM*, May 1962, 54. This was the second in a series by Woodbridge on this subject.

97. S. Maxwell Coder, "The Future of Russia," *MM*, September 1963, 73-74. The "students" here presumably refers to students of the Bible and not pupils in a classroom.

Culbertson, too, highlighted the impact of realized prophecy on the world of his day and sheds light on how many evangelicals could sound so confident about their eschatology.

> [I]t would have taken a bold thinker indeed, fifty years ago, to dream that a half century later Israel would be established in her own land as a virile and vigorous nation. She is back, however, and doing quite well for herself. To an unbeliever, back in 1910, the concept of a war that would engage the whole world would have been classed as the vision of a dreamer—or a psychotic. Two world wars have occurred since then, however, and today the world is waiting on tiptoe, in momentary dread of a third.[98]

He later urged his readers to consider the times. He called on them to pay attention to the signs around them and to live as though the end could well be nigh. "What rebuke will be ours if we have indeed been chosen to live and minister in times of unusual need and opportunity, but we have lived as those who slept? May God help us to discern the times; to live with vision and with purpose!"[99] He was not certain that this was the end, but he did think that there were enough indications along those lines that prudence would warrant some thought on the matter.[100]

Culbertson's colleague at *Moody*, Wilbur Smith, was somewhat hesitant about looking for biblical events in contemporary headlines. "Personally, I do not believe there are any prophecies, either in the Old or New Testament, that predict some *specific event* that must be experienced by the city of Jerusalem between the fall of that city in A.D. 70 and the end of the age." He went on to point out that many significant events concerning Jerusalem, such as its infamous sacking in the Crusades or

---

98. Culbertson, "Historical Perspective," *MM*, May 1960, 11.

99. Culbertson, "Is It Later Than We Think?" *MM*, November 1961, 9.

100. Culbertson, "Prophetic Trends," *MM*, January 1963, 57. Culbertson was, however, willing to consider that these seemingly prophetic events could be innocuous, even if he thought the coincidences were too many. Speaking of the rise of the proposed union between Egypt, Syria, and Iraq, he first portrayed this as the likely fulfilment of eschatology. Then, however, he gave several reasons why there could well be a positive result of this unification, if the new government would actually benefit the people of these nations and keep the peace in the Middle East. Culbertson, "The United Arab Republic," *MM*, June 1963, 12.

its capture by the British in World War I, had no biblical connection whatsoever. He, however, thought that there were general conditions which would suggest that the end had come, such as an increase in warfare, an international concern for Jerusalem, and an occupation of that city by the Gentiles. These three he believed were in place. To this he concluded a final condition to be met before he would say the end had come. "If some morning we should open our newspapers and read that Israel has taken the old city of Jerusalem, and is able to hold it we shall know that the words of our Lord have been fulfilled—and when this takes place, we are at the end of the age of the Gentiles."[101] When this event took place just a few short years after this time, it became very hard for many evangelicals to suppress their expectation that the end was indeed nigh.

PROPHECIES COMING TRUE

The State of Israel occupied an ever-strengthening position in the evangelical imagination, but even at this late date, there was room for criticism. The Jewish state was portrayed in *Presbyterian Journal* in a largely, but not harshly, negative light. Specifically, the editors pointed to a trend by Israeli officials to curtail activity by Christian missionaries. It was clear that some in the Tel Aviv government saw proselytizing as a threat to Jewish identity. However, in what would be an increasing trend, there was a keen interest among Israelis in keeping the good will of Christian groups throughout the world.[102] Henry had a fairly positive view of the Jewish state and wrote several articles in 1961 for *CT* which shared his reflections after a trip there. As to its eschatological implications he had little to say. "The tiny state of Israel is one of today's most remarkable albeit controversial nations. Its resurrection from the dust of history is without parallel. Whether Israel's sovereignty is an act of political ingenuity, one of divine providence, or a strange mixture of both, neither Jewish nor Gentiles historians seem able to decide."[103]

101. Smith, "Jerusalem in Prophecy, Part VI: Prophecies That Relate to This Age," *MM*, October 1960, 37–39, 42.

102. The Editors, "Israelis Organize to Combat Missions," *PJ*, February 6, 1963, 3.

103. Henry, "Israel: Marvel Among the Nations," *CT*, September 11, 1961, 13.

There were enough reasons to wonder if something special might be going on, but also enough uncertainty to lead him to hedge his bets.

As expected given Barnhouse's eschatological predilections, *ET* did the opposite, showing the State of Israel in a largely, but not exclusively, positive light. For Barnhouse the presence of the Jews in Palestine was a matter of certain prophecy, and he looked forward to the time when they would make further gains in the region. He counseled his readers not to judge the future solely in terms of the present. "Right now we see that the Jews are back in half of Palestine, with Jerusalem split across the middle, the Jews possessing the suburbs, but not the whole city. The day is coming when Israel shall possess the whole land." While this part of his interpretation would come through in a few short years after the Six Day War, he expected that Israeli territory would extend "from Egypt to the Black Sea including Lebanon, Jordan, Syria and Asia Minor." This Greater Israel would one day, according to Barnhouse, find even greater power through an alliance with a "United States of Europe."[104]

When addressing this new Roman Empire, Barnhouse's eschatology again affected his political counsel. To his way of thinking, his beliefs had been strongly justified as world events had come more and more into alignment with his theological expectations. After discussing the ways Europe was coming together in the Common Market, he said, "During the last 30 years, I have pointed out again and again in this magazine ... that these nations will be reunited and that the final war will be between Russia and its allies and United Europe fighting in Palestine. And once we understand this basic principle of prophecy we can understand better the developments in our newspapers." As proof of this, Barnhouse argued that the West had nothing to fear from Belgrade, even though it seemed to many that Tito's Yugoslavia was far friendlier to Moscow than to Washington. Since the Balkans had been a part of the old Roman Empire, it was inevitable that it would be a part of its new incarnation, and this meant NATO and Western Europe. He had much the same advice for his readers concerning the Middle East

---

104. Barnhouse, "Israel Returns to Her Land," *ET*, March 1959, 8, 47.

where he predicted that Egypt and Syria would find themselves in the anti-Russia camp.[105]

While Henry was largely averse to specifics about the end of the world, he offered some preliminary thoughts. As 1959 ended he wrote of the years since the end of World War II, saying, "Whatever purging or cleansing effects war may have, they lack enough potency to accomplish the desirable end. Social evils are such that some evangelicals find themselves wondering whether there yet remains on earth the equivalent of 'ten righteous in Sodom.'" Following this he summarized the impressions for the future of several regular contributors to *CT*, including many comments which addressed the end of the world. He quoted General Harrison as suggesting that the corrupted lives of many supposed Christians was such that it was likely the final step in bringing down God's wrath and the great tribulation. He also quoted author Cary Weisger, who suggested that the tumultuous world events were endurable "if we keep looking for that blessed hope, the glorious appearing of Jesus Christ." However, neither his quoted contributors nor Henry himself offered geopolitical advice based on eschatological expectations. Instead, Henry called his readers to keep to their tasks at hand even as he acknowledged the power of end-times feelings.

> When a man stands in the arid Kidron Valley, he is on apocalyptic ground. Both Jews and Moslems believe this to be the site of the Last Judgment. … In one direction the observer looks up to see the tawny wall of Jerusalem, city of history most horrifying event. But happily he may turn and lift his eyes to the Mount of Olives, scene of the Ascension with its steeling words: "Go ye therefore, and teach all nations. … I am with you alway [sic], even unto the end of the world." And the white-robed men said,

---

105. Barnhouse, "The Roman Empire is Revived," *ET*, April 1959, 14–15. He repeated this claim about Egyptian intentions in a later issue, explicitly identifying present geopolitical machinations with biblical prophecy. "It has been interesting to observe how President Nasser of Egypt has flirted with Russia and has obtained some aid from her in the past few years. But the Bible says that eventually Egypt will openly oppose Russia. Then Russia will seek to take that nation and will be destroyed in the attempt." Barnhouse, "When Russia Descends on Israel," *ET*, June 1959, 20.

"This same Jesus ... shall so come in like manner as ye have seen
him go into heaven."

Henry's concluding words spoke for living in the present and not waiting on the future. "Whatever the hour on God's clock, the ultimate triumph is secure. But the countdown is not yet ended ... and there is yet
work."[106]

106. Henry, "God's Countdown: 1960," *CT*, December 21, 1959, 20–23.

8

Almost Armageddon, 1964–1968

OVERVIEW

In the 1960s the world droned on as it had before, only seemingly more
so. Within a single year's time both superpowers unexpectedly underwent a change of leadership, as Lyndon Johnson took over in the wake
of President Kennedy's assassination and Premier Khrushchev fell to an
internal coup orchestrated by his underlings. The United States and the
Soviet Union continued to build their atomic arsenals, and heated conflicts around the world enlarged the chances that these weapons might
come into play. The Soviets crushed yet another liberalizing regime in
central Europe, while the US was wracked by riots and assassinations
of prominent leaders. The Russians extended their reach into Middle
Eastern and South Asian affairs with their support of the Egyptian and
Indian militaries, while the Americans became involved in a full-scale
yet still unofficial war in Southeast Asia after the Tonkin Gulf incident.
All these strains threatened to come together in June 1967 as two of their
respective client states fought a sharp and remarkably short war, nearly
allowing East and West to meet at last not far from the actual Armageddon.
Evangelicals noted these events with a grimness unlike the zeal of World
War II or even the fear of later years. For decades now the world had
seemed headed toward a cataclysm, a danger that was never quite reached
but never really evaded.

ENEMIES

This was not an era for optimism. With war, assassinations, and riots
in every newspaper, it seemed that the bad guys just might win. In the
middle of the 1960s, with Communism still growing in power and extent,
it could have been difficult for its opponents to see the light at the end

281

of the Red tunnel. At a 1966 conference in Berlin, Carl Henry acknowledged those fears when he spoke of the current world climate. "We hear of a globe wholly in the grip of Communist tyrants; or of a few lone survivors of atomic holocaust pitching nomadic tents on a scorched earth; or of burgeoning populations that will automatically reduce the Christian community to a negligible remnant." In truth it would be another generation before the Cold War would end in a Western victory, yet Henry looked at the future with hope. To his understanding Communism was "a surface philosophy superimposed on the realities of history" and that its shallowness was even then been displayed. In its place he hoped would grow a renewed understanding "that the biblical religion strikes to the true depths of the human situation." His great hope was that the seeming might of the Soviet regime could not overcome the truth about human nature and the God who had created all things.[1] Communism was a real and dreaded enemy, but it would

---

1. Carl F. H. Henry, "It is Not Too Late," Remarks given at Berlin Conference, Box 1966, File Berlin Conference Background, Carl F. H. Henry Collection. At another time Henry pointed to the irony that in American universities, while the teaching of anything Christian was considered a dangerous violation of the First Amendment, "educators insist boldly that Communism be taught to preserve the liberal arts character of their campus." In this case to dismiss Christianity from academic discussion because of its religiousness but to include Communism was inconsistent at best. Henry, Remarks given at a luncheon sponsored by Campus Crusade, July 30, 1965, Box 1965 2, Loose, Carl F. H. Henry Collection. Schaeffer spoke of a similar issue in a letter concerning an East Bloc academic with whom he had had some communication. Explaining this to a magazine editor, he wrote, "The Polish political theorist is Adam Schaff. He was a teacher in Warsaw University until he was just put out a few weeks ago in the political disturbances in Poland. It is not so much that he is seeking a different answer than the communist dialectic but rather that he is seeking a 'socialistic humanistic' answer for the meaning of man in contrast to the orthodox communist doctrine that the individual has meaning in reference to the State. We exchanged a couple of letters when I was expecting to go to Poland in the beginning of May, but all the visas were cancelled because of the political disturbances, and I am not writing to him now because I fear it would not be helpful to him. There is no sign he is interested in Christianity, but the interest is because of his being the first one who has spoken out that the communist answer to the meaning of man was not adequate. Naturally, It [sic] would be my hope eventually to give him the Christian answer." Francis A. Schaeffer, Letter to Derek Sangster, June 13, 1968, Francis A. Schaeffer Collection, Box 49, File 26, The Library, Southeastern Baptist Theological Seminary, Wake Forest, North Carolina.

fall in the end.[2]

THE RED FAITH

As they had before, many evangelical writers spoke of Communism as being more than simply a rival political system in place in certain nations. Rather, it was a rival religious movement. Addressing what the writer termed Moscow's "Cold War on Christians," readers of one article were asked, "Why should the Soviet government with its armies, rockets, and atomic weapons be willing to spend millions of rubles and print millions of pages of atheistic propaganda to fight Christianity along with other religions? The basic reason is that Communism is itself a religion." Elaborating how the famously atheistic Soviet ideology could be religious, the author wrote, "Except for the fact that it recognizes no supernatural deity, Soviet communism has most of the characteristics of a religious faith. It claims to have the truth about life, man and the world; therefore it can tolerate no spiritual rivals. ... Before communism can dominate the world, it must eliminate other faiths."[3] Similarly, in the March 1964 issue of *Moody*, the "Teen Focus" section greeted its adolescent readers with the image of the quiet glare of a Communist solider, little older than themselves. The article accompanying the photo was entitled, "How to Stop Communism." As harsh and Manichean as this might seem, the proposed solution was far more constructive than simply finding a way to beat the enemy. The author told of being engaged in conversation with a Communist Party member

---

2. Another line of attack against Communism was the way defections were largely one way, East to West. Henry wrote of Soviet Olympians who had taken advantage of their time in Innsbruck, Austria to run to freedom and of a KGB officer who had switched sides in the midst of a disarmament conference in Geneva. After the Soviets pressed the Swiss to take measures to ensure their agent's return, Henry said that "Western governments do not ask similar favors. And the fact that East-West defection traffic is so largely one way bears striking witness to the enduring desire for freedom God has implanted in the human heart." Henry, "The Road to Freedom," *CT*, February 28, 1964, 27.

3. Anonymous, "Russia's Cold War on Christians," *MM*, December 1964, 16–17. The editors prefaced this article with a note saying that the author was well-known to the *MM* staff and they were confident of his reputation and familiarity with the issues. However, for the sake of his continued work, they were holding back his name from publication.

who claimed that the Red tide was certain to rise to dominate the world. The writer said he had his doubts about that, but the Communist then gave him an unexpected gift. "*And then he said it!* Neatly, wrapped up in the nutshell of a single sentence, he gave me the answer that could beat him at his own game, stem the sweeping tide of Communism and diminish the possibility of a nightmare world in the future. He said: '*The best way to combat Communism is to come up with something better.*' " He then encouraged his readers not to merely study up on the best answers to debate Communists or to become the best American patriots they could manage but to take up the challenge by living lives which demonstrated the superiority of Christianity over its Marxist rival.[4]

CUBA

Cuba received notably less attention during these years than those immediately after its revolution. Persecutions of Christians were noted, but only occasionally were there articles of any depth. One brief news report mocked the new government for an unusual order given to its people. "From Communist Cuba comes a new type of governmental order. The people of this country—which has oppressed religion consistently since the Castro regime took control—apparently aren't smiling enough. So Che Guevara has issued an order to the youth of Cuba: organize happiness and be a part of it. In other words—be happy or else."[5] One author pointed the mass emigration of 4,000 a month from Cuba to the United States as proof of the revolutionary state's malaise. The writer argued that those taking flight were more than mere malcontents but represented a wide swath of Cuban society. The reasonable question being, if Cuba's socialist paradise was so wonderful, why were so many risking their lives to flee?[6]

---

4. Dave Foster, "How to Stop Communism," *MM*, March 1964, 91–93. Italics in original.

5. The Editors, "But Why?" *MM*, July-August 1964, 7.

6. The Editors, "Flight to Freedom," *PJ*, May 24, 1967, 13.

The Hanoi Regime

The burgeoning war in Southeast Asia did not fall into a neat pattern of good vs. bad for several evangelicals. The Communists were certainly bad, but it seemed like their opponents were not always much better. It was a place where two of evangelicalism's bête noires, Communism and Roman Catholicism, created a situation where the enemy of their enemy was still their enemy. One news report in *CT* told readers of the dangers faced by Christian workers operating near Communist forces in Vietnam. The author wrote of a South Vietnamese town which "was 'turned over' to the Viet Cong as too difficult to defend. The pastor, unwilling to leave his flock, was slain by Red terrorists." Yet, the same article looked hopefully at the success of other Protestant efforts since, according to the piece, many Vietnamese saw both Roman Catholicism and Buddhism as "political movements" and steered clear as a result.[7] According to an article in *ET*, South Vietnam had been well on its way to peace and prosperity in the early 1960s before this progress was halted by the combined efforts of Communist insurgent attacks and internal conflicts within the new republic. The author asserted that economic conditions had improved dramatically, when "[the Viet Cong] pillaged and burned villages, committed atrocities, and rule much of the country by night and some of it by day. By early 1963 both the Vietnamese and United States governments optimistically announced that military success was assured." Nonetheless, this same writer said that it was in this year that the pro-Roman Catholic policies of the Vietnamese elites elicited resistance among the Buddhist population and that this and other issues led to the ouster of the Vietnamese president.[8]

Increasingly, however, they saw the danger from Hanoi as far more pressing than that from Rome. Evangelicals paid specific attention to the tactics employed by each side of the conflict. Henry, for example, described the US bombing in the area as very "measured," but when speaking of their foes he added, "The Communist Viet Cong are also selective, in their way. They aim their terrorism with particular force at native officials loyal to Saigon who attempt to establish some order

---

7. Kucharsky, "The Unsettling War," *CT*, August 27, 1965, 47.
8. Louis L. King, "Asia," *ET*, January 1964, 18–19.

and consensus in that bewildered and un-democratic land. These loy-
alists have been decapitated, their skin peeled off, their wives' bodies
disemboweled and slung atop fence posts."[9] The editors at *Moody* made
use of the term "terror" to describe Communist actions in Vietnam as
well. Calling them "victims of Communist terrorism," they told of a missionary family whose dwelling was destroyed.[10] Once news of the Tet
Offensive began to trickle back into the US, evangelical condemnation
was pronounced. The editors at *Presbyterian Journal* shared an article
which painted the action by Communist forces as a betrayal. "Vietcong
and the North Vietnamese Army were supposed to be observing a cease
fire to celebrate their Lunar New Year (Tet) on January 30, 1968. Instead,
5,000 Vietcong launched an attack on Saigon at 3:00 a.m. on that day,
with others coordinated throughout Vietnam in most of the provincial

---

9. Henry, "Viet Nam: Where Do We Go from Here?" *CT*, January 7, 1966, 30.
Kucharsky noted that America's South Vietnamese allies were not always the easiest
to support. He reported on an incident when an evangelical group, World Vision,
was prevented from establishing an orphanage for 2,000 of the many orphans in the
nations through the efforts of Roman Catholics in the area. Kucharsky, "Compassion
Gap in Viet Nam," *CT*, April 14, 1967, 40.

10. The Editors, "Getting Hotter," *MM*, April 1964, 4. The article was not only
about Vietnam but about the travails of missionaries all throughout the world. *ET*
also had a news report about this same incident and even used the same phrase
"a deafening roar" to describe the initial attack, suggesting a common source. The
Editors, "Missionaries Bombed in Viet Nam," *ET*, April 1964, 32. Kucharsky wrote of
the plight of American missionaries tending to the killed and wounded in the initial
assault. "The Rev. Robert Ziemer and the Rev. C. Edward Thompson realized they
were vulnerable to more attacks, even though their concrete buildings were virtually in earshot of American military outposts. The dug a trench out of a garbage
pit, just big enough for the whole staff to huddle down for the night. As expected
the Viet Cong blew up the other two homes. When daylight broke, the two men
decided they would appeal to the Viet Cong to get Carolyn to a hospital. They were
shot dead on the spot. Then the guerillas strafed the trench, killing Thompson's wife
and 42-year-old Ruth Wilting, a nurse from Cleveland." Kucharsky, "Viet Nam: The
Vulnerable Ones," *CT*, March 1, 1968, 16. Not all accounts of the fighting involved
chronicling atrocities. At another time readers were told of a Vietnamese pastor
who went to visit a sick church member, only to find himself in the midst of a Viet
Cong outpost which was itself soon under attack by American forces. Once one
of the Communist troops "vouched for him," he made his way through the fighting until out of the combat zone. The same article reported that US troops called
off an attack on a Viet Cong-held village after seeing a small church in the town.
Kucharsky, "Viet Nam Circuit Riders," December 3, 1965, 47.

capitals."[11] The accusation of cruelty and duplicitousness had been a regular fixture of evangelical criticism, but the 1960s brought it into a new focus as oftentimes the victims of Communist activities were their fellow Americans.

CHINA

Even though China was significantly cut off from the rest of the world during this period, news reports did filter out into evangelical commentary concerning the actions of Communist cadres during the Cultural Revolution. One contributor to *CT* spoke of the infamous Red Guards in this way:

> From all corners of the country these militant teen-agers are on the move with unsurpassed excitement and revolutionary enthusiasm. In the current political power struggle waged as a "cultural revolution," the Party hierarchy in Peking has succeeded in molding "youth for Mao" into a monolithic unity that seems certain—providing the present Mao-Lin axis remains intact—to prolong the Mao line for at least another generation.

This author went on to describe the fanatical loyalty of the Red Guards for their leader and his little red book, answering questions about who created the universe with, "Chairman Mao and the 'thoughts' of Chairman Mao!"[12] Bell shared tales of Red Guard atrocities with his readers. "According to this reporter he witnessed the beating to death of old people by these teen-age 'Red Guards.' Because of their advanced age they were associated with the former regime. Their belongings were

---

11. Anonymous, "Miracle at Hue," *PJ*, April 17, 1968, 7. Aside from the initial four paragraphs, for which no author is provided, the remainder of the article was compiled from missionary reports from the World Relief Commission of the NAE.

12. Michael Browne, "Red Guards: China's Mini-Mao Revivalists," *CT*, February 3, 1967, 48. The "Lin" referred to here is likely Lin Biao, one of Mao's inner circle. Contrary to the expectations of this author, the Mao-Lin axis did not last as Lin and his family were killed in an airplane crash just four years later after a purported failed coup against Mao. Likewise, Mao's legacy in China was mixed. In the years after his death in 1976, the remainder of his coterie was purged with the ascension of Deng Xiaoping, and many of his policies were overturned. See Salisbury's *The New Emperors* and Meisner's *Mao's China and After*.

piled in the streets and burned. Some had their faces pressed into the fire."[13] This was no mere political conflict. This was, for evangelicals watching from the outside, a great manifestation of evil in the world. Failing to oppose this was not an option.

Some commentators thought, or perhaps merely hoped, that China's experiment with Communism was fading. A news report in *Moody* reported on a defeat for Chinese Communist interests in Indonesia after a violent purge of Communist activists in the archipelago. The author suggested this action, along with several other international fumbles by China, indicated that the Beijing regime was experiencing some "confusion."[14] By 1968 one author referred to China's troubles as a civil war. He wrote of mutilated bodies floating into Hong Kong and of some eight thousand more which had been collected by Chinese authorities before they could make their way to the British colony. He quoted a missionary who hoped that these were a sign that the Communist tyranny in China was headed toward its final, violent end.[15] Chinese Communism would endure, after a fashion, but the scars of the Cultural Revolution would not heal quickly.

Fragile Hopes in Europe

Henry warned his readers not to be taken in by the more benevolent face put forward by Communists in Eastern Europe. Quoting a defector from Hungary, he wrote, "The ruthless Communists have been replaced by the smiling Communists and they are more dangerous." Henry then suggested that the state pushed friendly clerics into positions of

---

13. L. Nelson Bell, "The Red Guards," *PJ*, November 2, 1966, 13. After comparing the actions of the Red Guards to the Nazi-era Hitler Youth, a writer told *CT* readers that the ongoing turbulence had the potential to rework global relations. "China is now in the throes of a major crisis after which she will never be the same again. If a more militant regime emerges, there will be increasing trouble in the border areas of Russia, India, Viet Nam, and Thailand, with the classic maneuver of using a supposed external threat in order to unite an increasingly restless people." Then, somewhat predicting the diplomatic maneuvering with the Nixon administration a few years in the future, he argued that a more moderate Chinese elite could shift the relationship between the countries in a positive direction. Henry, "Red Guards Spur Attack on Christian Remnant in Communist China," *CT*, September 16, 1966, 29.

14. The Editors, "Confusion in Red China," *MM*, September 1966, 6.

15. The Editors, "China's Massacre," *MM*, October 1968, 7.

power within denominations who then obligingly censured pastors who grew too popular or too prone to evangelism or challenging the Party line. Concluding, he wrote that the "new congeniality" was just a shallow front hiding an "implacable opposition to Jesus Christ and his Church."[16] Somewhat in contrast, one contributor to *Moody* said that, whatever the attitude of the Communist leadership, the people and even soldiers of Eastern Bloc nations were open and eager to hear the Christian message, noting that he never found anyone reluctant to accept Christian literature, even among military forces in the East. He encouraged his Christian readers to see themselves in the plight of their coreligionists on the other side of the Iron Curtain, saying, "Most of the churches never see a visitor from abroad and they feel alienated from the rest of the world and discouraged. Over and over again I have been welcomed with tears as they proclaimed, 'You are the first to visit us since the outbreak of war (1938).'"[17] The people of Europe were oppressed by a tyrannical superstructure, and it was this fact, and not a short-sighted American nationalism, that drove evangelical opposition to Communism.

There was a flickering glimmer of hope for Europe even in this dark time as Czechoslovakia in 1968 experienced an echo of 1956 in Hungary. In May of 1968 the editors at *Presbyterian Journal* reported that Czech clergy were becoming more vocal and that the nation was experiencing a "nonviolent revolution."[18] In August Harold Lindsell reported that something was brewing as Czechs toppled their Stalinist leader in favor of a more liberal, but still Communist, head of state. Small liberties began to emerge. He then hoped that changes there could yield fruit across Communist Europe. "The problem is more than ideological for the Soviets. Loss of Czechoslovakia would crack the geographical buffer zone around the borders of the USSR. It would open a corridor from free Europe into the Ukraine, the most populous, the most restive, and the most nationalistic of the fourteen non-Russian 'republics' in the

---

16. Henry, "Beware That Smile," *CT*, December 3, 1965, 31.

17. The Editors, " 'Closed Door' Countries—Are They Really Open?" *MM*, May 1965, 22, 56. Parentheses in original.

18. The Editors, "Czech Churchmen Start Speaking Out," *PJ*, May 22, 1968, 4.

Soviet Union."[19] A news report in *CT*'s subsequent issue told of increasing religious tolerance from the Czech authorities and offered hope that similar freedoms could spread to Romania and Hungary.[20] These hopes were twenty years too early, but they pointed in the direction things would eventually go.

Once the Soviets had had enough and sent tanks into Prague, evangelicals had no qualms about comparing this incursion with similar events thirty years before. Lindsell's optimism collapsed with an allusion to Munich in 1938. "The Soviet-led invasion of Czechoslovakia will take memories back thirty years, when the same small country became the victim of another aggressor. That aggressor's emblem was the crooked cross. Britain and France stood by consenting, and Chamberlain's infamous treaty with Hitler made a pretense of ensuring 'peace in our time.' "[21] The editors at *Presbyterian Journal* chided their more liberal fellows for their supposed hypocritical hesitation, saying that those who complained so loudly about supposed American atrocities could only muster highly nuanced statements when it came to this clear Communist oppression.[22]

The end of the Prague Spring was also the end of a time of hope evangelicals had for the Czech people. An eyewitness to the invasion noted that the Czechs had somehow managed to scrawl a swastika on every Russian military vehicle in Bratislava. Czech police, unable to do anything to stop the Russian forces moving into their country, also did nothing to clear the civilian mobs surrounding the Soviets even as they made paths for Czech cars to get through. The writer noted that the Czechs now hated the Russians if anything more than they had the Germans of thirty years before. He quoted a local as saying, "The

---

19. Harold Lindsell, "The Czech Caterpillar Keeps Stirring," *CT*, August 16, 1968, 27–28. This was the first issue for which Lindsell was the chief editor in place of the recently retired Carl Henry.

20. Richard N. Otling, "Czech Church Thaw," *CT*, August 30, 1968, 41.

21. Lindsell, "Refining Czech Communism," *CT*, September 13, 1968, 33. He was not saying that the West should have responded in 1968 with guns blazing. In fact, he questioned whether that would have been practical with a nuclear-armed Soviet Union.

22. The Editors, "Czech Invasion Prompts Measured Statements," *PJ*, September 4, 1968, 5.

Germans weren't as bad as this. ... We knew at least that they were our enemies, but these people pretended to be our friends."[23] One of *ET*'s editors made her opinion clear when she gave her piece the challenging preface, "Unless the people of the free West react quickly and firmly, the Church in the land of Hus will find democracy crushed for the third time in thirty years."[24] The land from which evangelicals could trace their theological ancestry had been crushed under the boot of tyranny yet again. As much as this added to their early hopes, it also added to their pain when it ended.

The events in Czechoslovakia merely reconfirmed for many thinkers just what sort of a nation the Soviet Union was and what sort of ideology animated it. As the Communist Stalin had oppressed the Finns in 1937, so too did the Communist Khrushchev with the Hungarians in 1956, and now the Communist Brezhnev to the Czechs in 1968. Different leaders under different situations had reacted in the same way. Communist Russia continued to be an oppressive and expansionistic state which had demonstrated that it could only be dissuaded through the threat of overwhelming force. In that sense, even though many evangelicals used the rhetoric of calling them faithless, it was not that the Soviets could not be trusted but that they could be eternally trusted to continue their tyrannical policies until doing so became too costly. Whatever qualms they might have had about the United States at home or abroad, these overseas dangers warranted the continued contingent support of the policies of containing Russian influence in Europe and elsewhere.

---

23. Jaroslav Vajda, " 'We Will Not Give Up,' Czech People Vow," *ET*, October 1968, 32–33.

24. Nancy Hardesty, "Are We Selling Out Czechoslovakia," *ET*, November 1968, 38. There was reason for hope, at least in the eyes of some evangelicals. One writer pointed to the connection between Christian faith and the erstwhile revolutionaries. Speaking of a rebel leader in Prague, he wrote, "In this critical time, he brought with him his own Bible. At the end of the day it was impossible to leave the building, as it was surrounded by Russian tanks. There was nothing to do but sleep on the floor. As they got ready to do so, he took out his Bible and for himself read Psalm 68. When he had done so, one of his now quasi-Communist leaders asked him to read out loud so he could hear. Soon others appealed for the same, and an impromptu Bible study began in the besieged Czech parliament." Brother Andrew, "Behind the Czech Curtain," *MM*, December 1968, 18. "Brother Andrew" was the pseudonym for a Dutch Christian activist who regularly made trips behind the Iron Curtain to smuggle Bibles and Christian literature into Communist areas.

They were not reacting to imaginary policies the Soviets might enact if they got into Western Europe. They were reacting to realized actions the Russians had implemented in Central Europe with some regularity.

There were a few glimmers of hope for evangelical commentators as the turbulent late 1960s began. Communism was still a growing and going concern, but there were a few points where the tensions of the Cold War seemed to thaw. One point of hope came from the increasingly evident tensions within the Communist world. An author writing in *ET* wondered what such news would mean for the global relationships and Soviet leadership, saying, "Mr. K[hrushchev] will be counted among the faithless unless he can demonstrate by some dexterity that tactics rather than strategy motivates his shrewd antics."[25] As things turned out, the Russian Premier proved lacking in this very dexterity, and he was driven from power. The reaction to the fall of Khrushchev was fairly muted. There had been no love lost between evangelicals and the Soviet premier over the years, but no one expressed either much concern or hope when he was removed by his own people. The fall of the irascible Khrushchev did not improve anyone's impression of the Soviets. Henry said that the post-Khrushchev Soviet Union was neither kinder nor gentler than its predecessor and recounted instances of anti-Christian activity by the new regime. Nonetheless, Henry kept his hope that those who oppressed Christians would get their comeuppance in the end. "That those who so defy God are held in derision by him and will ultimately be brought to judgment is a scriptural and historical fact. Christians should be concerned that so many of their brothers are being repressed and imprisoned in this so-called enlightened age. When one part of the Body of Christ suffers, the whole Body is involved."[26] For

---

25. Lester DeKoster, "Communism," *ET*, January 1964, 20–21. Another *ET* contributor pointed to the India-Pakistan conflict as one where the split came into the open quite plainly. According to the author, after the Americans decided to stay neutral, the Soviets stepped in to aid them against the Chinese-backed Pakistanis. "The significant point is that Russia had decided that the defeat or humiliation of India by Pakistan would strengthen Red China's drive in Southeast Asia and would be in *Russia's national interest*." The author did say that this played out poorly for the US as democratic India now looked to Communist Russia as a protector. John Goodwin, "Survey of the Year," *ET*, January 1966, 14.

26. Henry, "Persecution in Russia," *CT*, January 1, 1965, 25. As might be expected, these evangelical writers' international concern manifested itself most poignantly

Henry and others like him, the center of their objection to America's enemies was not jingoism but the way these nation's rulers oppressed their own people and threatened evangelicals' fellow Christians.

AMERICA

AMERICAN EXCEPTIONALISM

One of the reasons for why many evangelicals supported the United States to a unique degree, and, conversely, were so very disappointed with it at times, was that they saw its founding as distinct from that of other nations. Rarely at this time were there suggestions of a special covenant between God and America, but there was the understanding that the Founding Fathers had drawn on implications of the Bible, even if the Founders had not been necessarily Christian themselves.

Writing in *CT*, a faculty member from Wheaton College wrote that the American Revolution was a different breed than its French or Russian equivalents. Arguing that the US revolution had its roots in the "rich subsoil of political Calvinism," he said that this meant that, unlike their Continental counterparts, any Anglo-Saxon thinker had to

---

when discussing their fellow Christians. Another article in *CT* was able to condemn the Russians as well as pick at mainline denominations for their silence in the face of Soviet Bloc oppression. The author cited a Russian church leader as suggesting that the World Council of Churches had not said enough about the continued religious persecution by the Moscow regime even as he warned them not to believe the "showcases" put forward by the state. The writer continued and referenced reports of two thousand shuttered churches and tens of thousands of Christians imprisoned at a single site. Kucharsky, "A Plea for Soviet Churches," *CT*, September 25, 1964, 58. Readers of *MM* heard of the struggles of their Russian fellow evangelicals. Noting that a number of Christians had left the state-sanctioned churches for non-registered bodies because of government interference in the official churches, the *Moody* article explained, "Evangelicals have been forbidden to preach evangelistic sermons, and pastors and church leaders have been instructed not to strengthen the faith of believers, but rather to quench it. The directive ... was issued by the top Protestants in Moscow by order of the government." The article went on to say there were only so many options open to Russian believers. "Unrest is increasing among religious leaders because a new law in the Soviet Criminal Code makes oral criticism of existing religious policies punishable by prison, forced labor or a fine of 100 rubles. Churches continue to be closed and demolished. More than 400 historic religious buildings in Moscow have now been destroyed." The Editors, "Report from Russia," *MM*, March 1967, 14.

look beyond the community for authority. "It must be external, always, whether grounded in the biblically revealed God or in the rationally conceived law of nature. There is a vast difference between this vision of a new order and in the visions that motivated the French and the Russian revolutions."[27] Henry, too, was to argue for a dual origin for much of the American government. He suggested, "Our national independence has two chief sources: on the one hand, the deism of men like Jefferson and Paine, who were strongly influenced by the French enlightenment [sic] and the philosophy of John Locke; on the other hand, the Calvinism of our Puritan, Scotch-Irish, French-Huguenot, and Dutch forbearers."[28] Henry looked to Christianity for the inspiration and maintenance of the American republic. While he was interested in the way freedom had come to the country through religious thought, he was more focused on its preserving power for the future. Instead of saying that the freedom-granting founding leaders or documents were

---

27. S. Richey Kamm, "The American Revolution: Revolutionary or Liberative?" *CT*, July 3, 1964, 3-5.

28. Henry, "Christian Faith and National Power," *CT*, July 2, 1965, 20. He then favorably quoted Leopold von Ranke as saying, "John Calvin was the virtual founder of America." Henry's successor at *CT*, Lindsell, had similar thoughts after the turbulent 1968 Presidential election. He acknowledged that the nation faced some tough crises, many of which had no observable solution, but his hope for the future lay in learning from the past. "The problems that confront this nation and the challenges that await us demand a well-disciplined citizenry dedicated to Christian ideals. It was only in the tight-beltedness, rugged optimism, and biblical rationale of the American Puritan fathers that enabled them to overcome great obstacles and settle in the New World. We in the last third of the twentieth century will get by with no less." Lindsell, "A Sobering Outlook for President-elect Nixon," *CT*, November 22, 1968, 26. With a similar theme, one contributor to *PJ* wrote, "Calvinist doctrine, Presbyterian government, Puritan virtues—these influenced early Americans and brought forth a great nation under God. The sickness and death of these as effective influences in American life have brought the nation to the point of impotency—without the spiritual and moral backbone necessary to resist the enemy which is out to conquer the world." Robert M. Metcalf, "Is the Night Inevitable?" *PJ*, September 1, 1965, 10. Interestingly, just a few months later, another *PJ* article challenged part of Metcalf's argument. The later piece said, "Representative democracy is neither a Presbyterian nor an American invention, but it is considered the best government system by most Americans, and presumably by most Presbyterians." Dallas Herring, "Democracy and the Church," *PJ*, April 20, 1966, 9.

Christian in some way, Henry asserted no freedom could come about without the prior foundation made by Christianity.[29]

This promise of a Godward-leaning America did not seem to be coming to its full fruition, and this failure angered evangelicals even more. A contributing writer at *Moody* found the US more the servant of mammon than of God. "Can we Americans stand such prosperity? There is evidence that we cannot. We are intoxicated with things. ... It is not that being well-fed, prosperous and comfortable is wrong. But there is a very real danger that we may give undue importance to things; that we may make the material side of things supremely important."[30] With his customary dramatic tone, Bell asserted that "America is doomed—heading for the certain judgment of a holy God," since they had forsaken the guidance of the Bible and substituted for it the fickle opinions of humanity.[31] Later he was to say, "Here in the US, with some exceptions, the 'news stands' of our cities and the books they sell are, morally speaking, an open sewer in our society. Filth is being spewed out and bought by tens of thousands of Americans every day."[32] Similarly, Culbertson opined, "For the most part, civilizations die because of inward moral decay. And that decay is upon us."[33] As the 1960s drew to their close with fraternal assassinations bookending the decade, Henry wrote, "The shooting of Senator Robert F. Kennedy, in a land that earlier witnessed the assassination of his brother ... and then of the Negro crusader, Dr. Martin Luther King, is further evidence that the American dream is turning into a nightmare."[34] America was sitting happily in Hell's handbasket, and there seemed little to stop it from continuing on its merry way.

Henry said, "It is possible that future historians looking back upon our times will evaluate the sex obsession that grips so many in our nation as even more far-reaching than the current race revolution." He went on to lay a large portion of blame upon the unending consumption

---

29. Henry, "The Ground of Freedom," *CT*, July 3, 1964, 20-21.
30. Norman Lewis, "America's Creeping Peril of Plenty," *MM*, November 1964, 22.
31. Bell, "Watching a Nation Die," *PJ*, February 12, 1964, 11.
32. Bell, "Open Sewers," *PJ*, January 26, 1966, 13.
33. William Culbertson, "Lest We Forget," *MM*, December 1965, 14.
34. Henry, "Where is America Going?" *CT*, June 21, 1968, 23.

and worship by the American people of tabloid stories of "Hollywood idols."[35] Later he was to say, "Dangle the impersonal, emptied sex symbol before the modern sex-ridden mentality and it is pursued like a tin rabbit on a dog track."[36] One *CH* writer began his article on pornography with words of despair and hope. "The tidal wave of smut and filth sweeping America is equaled only by a growing counter wave of revulsion and indignation. Even sophisticates and strong-stomached have just about had it."[37]

During this period Carl Henry had some of strongest words of denunciation for his native land. In 1964 he wrote, "Gone is the dream that America can lead the world. Today her very existence depends on her ability now to sail ahead, and now to tack into the storms of the revolutionary century. Gone is the dream that the United States can make the world safe for democracy; gone too the illusion that an

---

35. Henry, "Another Exposure of US Morals," CT, February 14, 1964, 27.

36. Henry, "A Time for Moral Indignation," CT, March 12, 1965, 28. Rather than seeing the government in general or military as somehow a representative of Christianity, Henry took the armed forces to task for their careless attitude towards the morality of American forces overseas. "Recourse to a prostitute by a lonely boy is a lapse soon regretted. But for some it has become a way of life." He went on to share the reports of one service member who spoke of American troops in Korea taking in a local woman for the duration of his garrison duty, only to sell her to replacement soldiers or even renting her out to make ends meet. Henry's source said, "A young boy may be horrified the first time this happens to him, but he is kidded out of his shock, and often becomes a repeater who never learns and ceases to care." He looked beyond governmental action or failure to the inadequacies of the American church. "Yet the over-all picture is depressing and frightening, not only for the 'American image,' but also for the 'Christian image.' ... If the American churches consider their image in Korea or Thailand, they must surely ask themselves what they once taught these members, and what they are doing for them now." Henry, "Shattering the American Image," CT, October 23, 1964, 26.

37. Fred R. Zepp, "Filth Threatens Your Home," *CH*, May 1965, 8. With a far more lighthearted tone, Henry gave America backhanded praise for its openness to allowing the Beatles to enact their British Invasion. "Take England's Beatles (the verb is in the imperative mood). The United States State Department could not readily claim that these hirsute young men were subversive of American tastes, for there was obviously a certain adolescent taste ready and waiting on these shores." He then said that the enthusiasm of American youth for these musical imports betrayed "the emptiness of youthful heads and hearts. But since America has already plagued Britain with many such exports, perhaps there is in the latest exchange a certain poetic justice." Henry, "The Road to Freedom," CT, February 28, 1964, 27.

increase of affluence can create a great moral humanitarian society." Whatever hopes Henry might have for the United States were not found in the nation itself as its own course was all too prone to wander. His hope for his country was in his God. "There is hope. There is a hope that cannot be shaken. In the death and resurrection of Jesus Christ, God has conquered every evil that man has devised and fulfilled every legitimate hope. The world's king-size problems have met their Lord and King in Jesus Christ."[38] In an editorial about America's role in Vietnam, Henry was to disabuse observers of any suggestion of Christian nationalism when he wrote,

> The Bible nowhere encourages the notion that the United States is the crux of God's purpose in history. The course of world history is downward, and for all its glorious heritage, the United States is not exempt from that decline. The Christian Church, which is the strategic minority in an alien environment, ought not to give a blank check to any government in the exercise of its power; rather, it ought to insist that the government to which it owes loyalties judge itself continually by criteria of justice. The course of human history is such that one might assume that wars are likely to be unjust, rather than just, and that Christian conscience, in respect to war, is called upon to justify involvement in terms of loyalty to Christ and the revealed will of God.[39]

Even the heightened emotions of wartime and the threat posed by Communism were not enough to overwhelm America's sins or to impose theocratic principles on the nation.

CIVIL RELIGION

Henry was not alone in this. After a TV special had featured a musical performance praising America and traditional morality, Culbertson pointed out that this production was not as beneficial or amenable to evangelicalism as some might have thought, as American nationalism

---

38. Henry, "A Future Big with Hope," CT, November 20, 1964, 28–29. Italics in original.
39. Henry, "Viet Nam: A Moral Dilemma," CT, January 20, 1967, 28.

and vague moralism were not Christian virtues. "The one-hour patriotic performance, aired no less than six times in Chicago alone, featured a group of 130 vibrant high school and college students who sang out against a soft, self-indulgent America. Fresh from a highly successful tour of Germany, they called for dedication, sacrifice, love of God and mankind." At first he praised these singers, saying, "In many respects we can admire the initiative of these clean-cut young Americans of 'Sing-Out '66' who set aside a year of their lives, without pay, to put feet to their convictions and spread their message around the world," but he soon changed his tune. "What has been missing in their message, of course, is the most basic of all ingredients for a world moral revolution: acknowledgement of sin and faith in Jesus Christ as Saviour." He said that evangelicals could learn something from this failing, and that was that a Christianity-lite was no Christianity at all.[40]

Christians were still to have loyalty to their earthly citizenship, but they had to do so with an eye to their heavenly citizenship. With the telling title "Must We Obey Our Country," a professor of political science writing in *ET* summarized the contingent support for the state common among evangelicals. Rather than being the unquestionable hand of God in the world, the state, including the American one, was an ad hoc measure to stem the worst elements of human nature. The state did not have absolute authority for the time being or could demand or deserve the total loyalty of Christians in its policies. "Even if the state were administered by the wisest and most just men it could not

---

40. Culbertson, "The Significance of 'Sing-Out'—'66," *MM*, September 1966, 15. In a similar quest to distinguish evangelicalism from sheer patriotism, Bell came to the defense of *CT*'s main financial backer, J. Howard Pew, after he was accused by a National Council of Churches publication of being a supporter of the stridently anti-Communist group, the John Birch Society. Bell insisted that, rather than a supporter of the Society, Pew had helped to sponsor the publication of the life story of John Birch whose martyr-like death inspired the later group but Pew had had no association with eponymous Society. Bell, Letter to Carl F. H. Henry, February 11, 1964, Box 1964 2, File Pew Correspondence 1964–1965, Carl F. H. Henry Collection. Henry later wrote in response to this or a similar letter, saying that, to his understanding, Pew had indeed supported the publication of the life of Birch, but he had differed greatly with Birch Society leader Welch on significant points. Henry, Letter to unknown recipient, February 1965, Box 1964 2, File Pew Correspondence 1964–1965, Carl F. H. Henry Collection. There is no addressee on the letter in question. Henry wrote that "you" had written him about Pew and the Birch Society, but he never says who the "you" is.

be totalitarian in the Christian view, for another and greater state, the kingdom of God, also presently exists. 'Render under Caesar the things that are Caesar's' means that there are some things which Caesar cannot control."[41] There was no place in evangelical understanding of Scripture, the state, or basic anthropology which allowed for an unquestioning loyalty to the government, even the United States.

LBJ

Of the man in the White House during this period, many evangelicals were quite favorable. Poling offered praise for Johnson at his unexpected rise to power after the death of Kennedy: "For so vast an ordeal in so tragic a time when the world rocks, perhaps no man has been so well trained and prepared as has Lyndon Johnson. First in his own state then in the House of Representatives and in the Senate of the United State and as Vice President, he has been made ready for his country's present crisis."[42] Culbertson applauded Johnson's handling of the national crisis after Kennedy's assassination, saying, "President Johnson did well in calling for a day of mourning to urge the people to assemble themselves in a new submission to God's will. May God help us to do just this as our country picks up the strands of national life."[43] Taylor, too, praised Johnson for his example of prayer. Describing the President's actions at a prayer breakfast, he said, "President Johnson responded and earnestly asked for the prayers of God's people, not only for himself

---

41. Walford Peterson, "Must We Obey Our Country," *ET*, March 1964, 28. General Harrison opened the door to the possibility of overt disobedience to the US government, even if he thought it an unlikely scenario. In an article discussing the legitimacy of warfare and service to the state in the military, he said, "It is possible that our duty to obey our government conflicts with our duty to God. The Christian must choose to obey God, being willing to suffer such man-inflicted penalties as may occur." After giving some examples from recent times when such a disobedience would be moral he added the qualification, "Certainly in the United States Army nothing like this is likely to occur. Before he disobeys orders the Christian soldier should be sure that his military orders are actually in conflict with the commands of God as given in the Bible and not the result of his personal or denominational prejudice." Harrison, "The Christian in Military Service," *PJ*, May 18, 1966, 11.

42. Daniel Poling, "Lyndon B. Johnson, 36th President of the United States," *CH*, January 1964, 27.

43. Culbertson, "The President's Death," *MM*, January 1964, 16.

but for all in positions of leadership. He frankly stated that without the prayers of Christians they could not solve the problems which press in on every hand and every day."[44] In late 1966 Henry sympathetically wrote, "Lyndon B. Johnson is now feeling strong vibrations on the tightrope of American politics he nimbly treads as President of the United States. Cautiously seeking to maintain his balance—to follow high principles as he leads the nation and yet retain the broad-based popular appeal necessary for continuing in high office—he finds himself in peril of falling on either side." Continuing with the same imagery, he offered hope that the President would find his way through. "Lyndon B. Johnson's political tightrope may feel shakier these days. But let us hope it will not send a shiver up his spine. Only a President with courage, wisdom, and perseverance can provide the leadership the nation needs in these critical days."[45] This was long before evangelicals became associated with one particular party, so it this would not have been incongruous. They did not see Johnson as a perfect man, nor would they feel it necessary to await perfection before offering praise if it was due.

FRUSTRATION ON RACE

This was a time of high tension in the nation over the question of Civil Rights and race relations, and these commentators were well aware of this fact. Several evangelicals saw the place of African Americans in US society as a keystone of the nation's morality. In January 1964 the editors at *Moody* reported the results of a poll they had taken among evangelical magazine editors, asking about the biggest stories of the previous year. For the third most important part of 1963, they said, "To most editors the race question was synonymous with 'the weakness of evangelicals to face up to the race issue.' ... And nearly all ballots

---

44. G. Aiken Taylor, "Prayer Breakfast Most Impressive Ever," *PJ*, February 19, 1964, 11.

45. Henry, "The Political Tightrope," *CT*, September 30, 1966, 34. After the election of 1968, President-elect Nixon received generally favorable reviews from evangelical sources, yet, despite his longstanding friendship with Billy Graham, there was yet no repeat of the paeans granted to Nixon's former boss, Eisenhower. Commentators wrote several pieces in the last weeks of the year which spoke highly of Nixon's potential, but they refrained from addressing his reality until he actually took office.

had some mention of the tragic Birmingham bombing ... that took the lives of four girls while attending Sunday School."[46] Hitt made much the same point when he argued,

> Let's face it. Most evangelicals, whether they are from the North, South, East or West, are supporters of the *status quo*, and consequently tend to be segregationists. They would rather not discuss the matter at all, but if you press them, they will spout almost the same defensive arguments as the most reactionary Southerner, whose white-dominated world really is threatened. They speak bitterly against the liberals who, they say, substitute social action for the gospel of personal redemption. ... Actually, most evangelicals take on the coloration of white suburbia; they hold virtually the same views as their neighbors who may be identified with nominal Protestant churchianity.[47]

------

46. The Editors, "These Were the Big Stories in 1963," *MM*, January 1964, 9. An article in *MM* four years later echoed this theme, saying, "Unfortunately, many Negroes in the United States today are beginning to feel that evangelical Christianity is unworkable. The Negro cannot understand why some Christians who proclaim the love of Christ have been so slow to accept him as a human being, slow to allow him into their churches, slow to see injustices. He cannot understand why the white evangelical church is often the first to pick up and run when the community changes (sometimes selling to the liberal church it so decries). He cannot understand how churches can raise millions for missions in Africa, yet seemingly have little or no burden for the Negroes in their own communities—where there is no ocean to cross, relatively little cultural problem and no language barrier." Tom Skinner, "Why We Must Win the American Negro," *MM*, April 1968, 35. A different perspective came from a letter to the editor in *ET*. In it a pastor wrote of his great love for African Americans and the joy he had in preaching in "their churches" and in leading them to Christ. Following this up he added, "But are we going to act the fool and be instruments in the hands of the devil and bring spotted babies into the world? Evidently you think that spotted babies bring honor and glory to our Lord Jesus? Even the animals and fowls do not integrate and so called intelligent people push integration. If you Yankees lived down south for a few years, you would get your eyes open." The writer neglected to point to any Scriptural passage which supported his contention that Jesus, whose ancestry included occasional multiethnic components, would object to "spotted babies." J. A. Atkinson, Letter to the Editor, *ET*, June 1964, 2.

47. Hitt, "Wrongs Do Not Make Civil Rights," *ET*, June 1964, 4. As the title suggests, Hitt's targets here were not limited to white evangelicals' failure to live out their faith as they should. He also attacked those supporters of the Civil Rights movement who used the righteousness of their cause for what he considered

Carl Henry could be just as bold. When speaking of the nascent Civil Rights Act of 1964, Henry wrote, "History will evaluate 1964 with its decision on the civil rights bill as one of the critical years in our national annals. The issue now before the country is more than one of integration versus segregation; it has to do with the integrity of our democracy."[48] Later, after quoting a German thinker who argued that

---

unrighteous methodologies. "What about the steps being taken by church leaders who encourage willful violation of existing laws? A case can be made for passive resistance and peaceful picketing, but many Protestant leaders, in their zeal for social justice, are encouraging lawbreaking and violence on the ground of the righteousness of a greater cause. This smacks of the ancient heresy that the end justifies the means." Interestingly, Hitt in 1966 chided some of his fellow conservative evangelicals who seemed to oppose political commentary by Christians leaders, but only if comments disagreed with their politics. "Many say that the church has no business making pronouncements in these areas. We have pondered that one for some time. As evangelical Christians we believe that the primary mission of the church is communicating the redemptive message of the gospel. Yet many orthodox groups regularly make pronouncements about the machinations of world Communism. Several groups which boast most strongly of their biblical position have issued statements supporting the government in the pursuance of the war in Vietnam. Unless our radar has gone dead, we recollect hearing again and again from conservative groups that Red China should *not* be admitted to the UN. Indeed quite a number have favored abolishing the UN itself. Thus, it would appear that it is not completely a question of whether the church should make pronouncements, but rather *what* pronouncements." Hitt, "Who Hears Ecclesiastical Pronouncements?" *ET*, January 1966, 5–6. The overall point of his editorial was to question the value of any such proclamations by church leaders as such, not to critique only his fellow conservatives. Another article in *ET* made the same point, saying, "Our problem is not in agreeing that Communism is a threat or is diabolic. Our problem is to look at Communism with the right philosophy. Do we look at Communism with the eyes of faith or the eyes of unbelief? Communism is not what gives life purpose and meaning. Christ does. Since when are Communists in control of history? To see a Communist behind every pulpit and to suspect every liberal politician of being a Communist sympathizer because he doesn't agree with our economic philosophy is to have the wrong perspective. Conspiracy doesn't fill all of time and space. God does." Eugene Madeira, "God is Still in Charge," *ET*, January 1967, 15.

48. Henry, "Civil Rights and Christian Concern," *CT*, May 8, 1964, 28. As was often the case, *PJ* failed to live up to its fellow magazines' call for justice. Throughout this era, whenever an article addressed civil rights, *PJ* printed the term in quotation marks as, 'civil rights' or 'Civil Rights,' subtly casting doubt as to the legitimacy of the endeavor. While most of *PJ*'s comments on racial issues centered on condemnation of those whom they saw as dragging the church into a state issue or to critique the perceived excesses of the movement, there were a few times when they spoke out explicitly in favor of fundamental racial equality as based in the Bible as well as a challenge to white superiority. In January 1968 the editors shared a quote which

this was in this day for America as important an issue as the place of the Jews in German society years before, Henry added,

> Are we not driven to the wall on these insistent issues of human dignity and social justice, of love for neighbor and reconciliation? Of what use are all the noble visions of a world of law and order if, in our own small province, we lack the passion for the equality of human beings before the law—God's law and ours? Is not the question of the dignity of the human race implied in the truth of the dignity and depravity of every race and not in the total dignity of some, or of one, and of the total depravity of others?[49]

Again, these were no token phrases to mollify critics; these were accusations against many of the readers and subscribers of their own magazines. That their readers did not heed their warning takes nothing away from the starkness of their complaint.

---

read, "My skin is white because I was born that way. I was not responsible for it, and had nothing to do with it. So with those who are colored, whether black, or brown, or red, or yellow. They are not responsible for the color of their skin; they were born that way. (By-the-way they are in the large majority.) *But* Jesus said (who was of brownish skin to a man of brownish skin), regardless of your color, 'You must be born again.' (Jno. [sic] 3:3). Repent, and make Jesus your own personal Lord and personal Saviour. Enter into Life Eternal *now*. Have heaven in your heart here and go to heaven hereafter." George W. Arms, "Born That Way," *PJ*, January 31, 1968, 17.

49. Henry, "Christ and the Human Dilemma," *Lebanon Valley College Bulletin*, July 1965, 8. A contributing writer at *CH* had some harsh words for whites concerning their attitudes towards their fellow Americans. When polls indicated that whites were afraid that if segregation laws were revoked, then African Americans would want to intermarry, he replied, "Some scientists, however, claim the reverse is true: whites ban intermarriages because such unions would tend to bring about racial equality. In any case, fear causes prejudice; prejudice brings restrictions; restrictions add to Negro resentment and widen the gap between races." Similarly, to claims that African Americans were intrinsically inferior students, this author argued, "With the passage of time, academic records have improved. Washington's Negro students now are scoring the same as pupils across the nation. This, educators say, proves Negro children have the same capacity to learn as whites if they are given an equal chance. At the same time, Negro teachers have ... done 'a magnificent and dedicated' job with pupils of both races." Fred R. Zepp, "Integration and You," *CH*, November 1964, 15-16.

At the same time there was an increasing hesitation regarding some of the methods employed for civil rights. Courier challenged those who wanted civil rights for African Americans but disapproved of the means used to secure them, saying, "Whatever one feels about demonstrations, marches, taking to the streets and highways—there wouldn't have been any Civil Rights Law without them,"[50] yet he also expressed concern that not every action intended to advance Civil Rights was the best course to this goal he shared. He was bothered by some of the tactics employed by some African Americans to call attention to their not-yet-finished quest, such as intentionally running out of gas on busy highways or a plan to drain New York of fresh water by perpetual toilet flushing. He did not think, however, that the Civil Rights movement had run its course. In fact, he was concerned that many whites thought it had reached its goal, any later reluctance to embrace reforms could be disastrous. Overreach or overreaction could push genuine reformers aside and set race relations and the progress of civil rights back by decades.[51]

By 1967 even Henry called less for reform than he did for peace. "With the steaming month of August ahead, all citizens, Negro and white alike, must work unrelentingly to build good will in urban communities so that other racial fires of Watts intensity will not ignite in any of a

---

50. Courier, "Corroded Conscience," *CH*, May 1965, 19. Courier took GOP Presidential candidate, Barry Goldwater, to task for the Senator's misunderstanding of the Civil Rights Act. When Goldwater argued that no law will make one person like another simply by its passing, Courier retorted, "That's entirely right. It's also beside the point. The Civil Rights Bill, or, for that matter, laws pertaining to murder, thievery or any other social injustice, aren't legislated to get people to like each other, [but] simply to see to it that they don't go around killing, robbing or otherwise clobbering each other." He said that liking others required "another rule more golden." Then, in keeping with evangelicalism's emphasis on the importance of an internal change by God as the prerequisite of genuine moral reform, he added, "Which brings us to this fact: where we go from here with the civil rights laws, beyond *merely* obeying them, depends upon us and our motivation as Americans and as Christians. The law's requirement is one mile. The second mile is yours." Courier, "Civil Rights," *CH*, August 1964, 10. The editors at *PJ*, on the other hand, favorably cited the Senator with the quote, "Mark this well—the day we permit anyone to equate protest with hate, we will set the stage for one-party tyranny and the end of open debate. To anyone who says that honest opposition breeds hatred, I say you lie—that you pervert the very basis of government." Barry Goldwater, "Hate and Debate," *PJ*, June 3, 1964, 15.

51. Courier, "Race," *CH*, June 1964, 6–7.

dozen tinderbox cities across the nation." His emphasis on the crisis may have shifted, but his solution remained the same. "Racial unrest is the most serious internal problem America has faced since the Civil War. It must be resolved if the nation is to prosper ... the Church of Jesus Christ must assume a major role in the struggle if racial peace is to be realized. It alone can provide the ultimate means of achieving real harmony between whites and Negroes."[52] As with anything involving

---

52. Henry, "Summer of Racial Discontent," *CT*, July 21, 1967, 27. In July 1964 Henry wrote of troubles afflicting the Deep South, saying, "Though Mississippi has made real efforts to improve itself in such fields as industrialization, agricultural reform, and education, it remains the state most closely related in the public mind to diehard segregation. Overt coercion and disrespect for law are evident daily." He then looked to other parts of the nation where the security situation had devolved to the point that calls for a revival of Reconstruction era occupation. He mourned that in the land of the free, the fact that "armed vigilantes have sprung up in the nation's greatest city and that parks and streets not only in New York but in other great cities are no longer safe shows the extent to which violence has invaded our society." He saw America's distance from the Christian ideal as the problem. "More federal action in Mississippi may regrettably prove necessary. But a Samaritan somehow haunts the scene. What might have been, had the white Christian tried to love his Negro neighbor just as much as he loved himself. And not only the Mississippi Christian but all of us." Henry, "Troubled Waters," *CT*, July 17, 1964, 23. Henry also expressed interest in the situation of Native Americans when he condemned the "callousness" of the US Congress dramatically cutting reparations payments by more than half. "Economy in governance is exemplary, but not when it is at the expense of justice. The Indian vote is not a large one, and this has bred a certain callousness in handling the affairs of the 'forgotten American.'" Henry, "The Forgotten American," *CT*, May 22, 1964, 22. Not all of his comments on race relations were negative. He looked hopefully at a recent Billy Graham evangelistic meeting, saying, "The many thousands of Negroes and whites who sat side by side in a stadium in Birmingham on Easter Sunday represented a remarkable and hopeful development in racial relations there. ... We feel it is especially significant that it was the preaching of the Gospel that brought these people together. For Alabama it was a first in terms of such numbers and such a wide cross section of society." Henry, "Hopeful Developments in Birmingham," *CT*, April 24, 1964, 26. He was willing to criticize many of those who shared his desire to end racial injustice. He found many programs intended to end racism to be problematic themselves since they proposed to address only surface issues and not the deeper failings of human nature which he felt could only be dealt with by God. Specifically, he spoke against Robert Kennedy's expectation that racial violence would continue so long as social injustice persisted. "We deplore social injustice, but we simply do not think one kind of social injustice excuses another. Nor do we share Mr. Kennedy's expectation of utopian erasure of all social injustice (upon which he apparently predicated the end of violence). Least of all is such a utopia to be expected from the

morality, all the government action in the world would do nothing to improve the human condition unless a thoroughgoing Christian faith animated the process and the people. Christianity was not a pie in the sky to keep America from progress but was in fact the only means by which any progress might be made.

WAR

THERE IS NO PEACE

The late 1960s saw concerns not that a war would break out, but that the fear that of it would never end. Culbertson pointed to the uncertainty of the day when he wrote, "By the time this issue reaches you the Viet Nam crisis may be over, or (and who knows), as you are reading this,

---

compulsory political manipulation of man's social environment." Henry, "Murder is Murder—Anywhere," *CT*, August 28, 1964, 31. Later, upon the death of Martin Luther King Jr., Henry cited an unexpected authority about what such a thing meant about America. "King's murder reinforced Ho Chi Minh's claim that the United States is a nation of violence and special privilege." Henry credited King as the sine qua non of the Civil Rights movement. "He helped them develop a sense of racial pride. As that pride quickened, black men's hearts and consciences burned indignantly over social inequality in the South and economic inequalities in the North. The American Negro became impatient for change. Had he not been impatient, he probably would still be discriminated against in public places and unwelcome in restaurants and hotels simply because of his pigment." Unlike what he said of several civil rights activists, Henry praised King's role in encouraging human rights in America. "Avowedly as an apostle of nonviolence, King courageously led the struggle against racism. He disowned arrogant concepts of black power but encouraged nonviolent civil disobedience in the name of 'higher moral law.' " Henry, "Johnson, King, and Ho Chi Minh," *CT*, April 26, 1968, 24. In an article with a rather complex orientation, Taylor eulogized King even as he strongly critiqued him and offered support for the goals of the Civil Rights movement while partially blaming even peaceful civil disobedience for their violent co-agitators. "Martin Luther King was not a man we admired. ... On the other hand, we do subscribe wholeheartedly to the basic principles of justice and equal opportunity for all men, regardless of race, color or creed. And we acknowledge that Dr. King was a most effective champion of the principles that he stood for. We greatly deplore the manner he died, which was reminiscent of the death of John F. Kennedy." He closed by saying that the justice Dr. King sought would never be achieved apart from law and order. Taylor, "This is Not the Way to Justice," *PJ*, April 17, 1968, 12.

the newspaper on your coffee table may have glaring headlines of full scale war."[53] Courier offered a poetic image of war throughout time.

> The shooting will stop. It always does. That's the supreme certainty of war, any war: it eventually comes to an end. The guns fall silent. The bombers are earthbound. The armies demobilize. Swords are beaten into plowshares. Lines are drawn on a map, fences are constructed across open fields and through houses and families and lives. All resumes—except the dead.[54]

War had continued and even intensified in this era, and evangelical commentators continued their previous emphases but with a twist. They were not all quite so sure that the given conflict was not doing more harm than good.

---

53. Culbertson, "No Room for Frustration," *MM*, April 1965, 16.

54. Courier, "War," *CH*, June 1965, 8. One intriguing aspect of the discussions during this period is the near-absence of articles about the bomb. After twenty years of fearing atomic devastation, the evangelical commentators had reached the point where such weaponry was no longer a talking point. Whether this was out of some terrible ennui, or simply that other concerns were far more pressing, nuclear arms generally came up only peripherally. While it was not about nuclear weapons in the then-present world, an article by an American missionary to Japan addressed the impact of atomic warfare. The author recalled the events of the first atomic attack on Hiroshima and celebrated the work of those who had rebuilt the city and the growth of the church. The missionary wrote with a fairly neutral tone, neither condemning the attack nor downplaying the suffering implicit in it. Winton Enloe, "Twenty Years Later," *PJ*, August 4, 1965, 10-11. Henry reported on an agreement between the US, UK, and USSR to limit their production of uranium. He admitted that this would not reduce weapons in any real sense as only the surplus was being trimmed, but he said this was reason for hope in the agreement, regardless. "Its significance is rather to be seen in the hope that mutual confidence may grow to the point where one day the Soviet Union may agree to disarmament steps *with* the essential condition of inspection." Rather than seeing any compromise with the Soviets in this arena as moral complicity, Henry asserted that, even as the West must maintain safeguards, peace was the goal of the godly. "The Christian's ultimate hope is God's intervention. But in the meantime God is interested in man's activity in this area, and Christians cannot but welcome even a small step toward mitigation of the nuclear threat." Henry, "A Hopeful Sign," *CT*, May 8, 1964, 31-32. In 1968 he dismally wrote, "For over twenty years the world had been haunted by the fear of a holocaust far worse than Hiroshima that would shatter the civilized world. Profound awareness of this horrible possibility has led to restraint in the use of American military power in Viet Nam and elsewhere." Henry, "Seven Minutes to Midnight?" *CT*, February 2, 1968, 31.

Even with this ambiguity, pacifism earned evangelicals' continued and longstanding criticism. Essentially, they saw pacifism as a good-natured error, the product of those who truly wanted to create a better world and who drew inspiration from the Bible, but who failed to understand either the world or Scripture. Henry, for example, granted that pacifists were not making things about the terrors of war, but he still did not agree with their solution since no treaty could undo the damage of sin to human hearts.[55] At another time he declared that "a vocal and uniformed piety is worse than silence," when a group of anti-war clergy had written President Johnson calling on him to withdraw US forces from Vietnam. With half-sarcasm he asked them what qualifications they had for offering military counsel.[56]

---

55. Henry, Letter to T. W. Wilson, September 2, 1965, Box 1965 2, File Correspondence, Billy Graham, Carl F. H. Henry Collection.

56. Henry, "Ignorance Often Has a Loud Voice," *CT*, February 12, 1965, 35. This was not a one-off complaint for Henry. Two months later he questioned the journalistic integrity of reports describing the success of a Christian peace conference in Prague. Henry, "The Price of Peace," *CT*, April 23, 1965, 30. In the same issue he rebuked a Christian group for producing a biased poll of clergy, saying, "Anybody seeking evidence of ecclesiastical objectivity would find little in its obviously weighted alternatives. Significantly, neither option gave any hint that Communist aggression is wrong, nor that America's defense of self-determination by small nations should be commended." He suggested that it was ironic that "many clergymen who in this poll registered opposition to America's military involvement in Viet Nam were the same ones who recently urged force, and lots of it, in Alabama." Henry, "Like a Russian Ballot," *CT*, April 23, 1965, 32. In late 1967 he heaped scorn on a militant anti-war demonstration at the Pentagon in which the novelist Norman Mailer had been arrested. "There is no excuse for lawlessness. Shortly after his arrest Mailer argued that the war in Viet Nam 'will destroy the foundation of this republic.' If it is destroyed, the cause will more likely be mob action. If it is preserved, as all good men desire, it will be preserved by the grace of God through the exercise of spiritual leadership, moderation, law, justice, and responsible dissent." Henry, "Dissent by Violence," *CT*, November 10, 1967, 33. The following month he directed his ire against certain mainline denominational pronouncements. "The secular theologians of social revolution who shaped the National Council of Churches' Church and Society strategy conference in Detroit sang a strange song: US force in Viet Nam is deplorable; ecumenical violence for socio-political goals is justifiable." Henry, "The Violent New Breed," *CT*, November 24, 1967, 25. The cover illustration for this same issue was tied to this article. It was a cartoon of a man in clerical garb declaring, "The Christian social-action material has arrived!" while unpacking rifles. A contributing writer for *MM* critiqued pacifism in 1967. Taking several common religiously-based objections to US involvement in Vietnam, he used biblical passages to argue that each was incorrect in

Sometimes criticism of pacifist thought was indirect. A CT news report offered muted commentary on some of the activities of religious leaders regarding the Vietnam War. At the beginning and end of his piece, the author cited the statements and movements of several groups who were largely anti-war. Between these two presentations was a description of the activities of evangelical missionaries operating in the midst of the combat zones. Although the writer offered no explicit opinion, the end result was a portrayal of one group of people risking their lives to preach Christianity and another group practicing politics while far from any danger.[57]

Others, however, were more strident in their opposition to pacifism. After briefly praising a recent book extolling pacifism, Poling then blasted a visit to Vietnam and advertisement published by The Fellowship of Reconciliation, a group of American clergy dedicated to peace in Vietnam. Poling complained that these were not pacifists but earnest supporters of the Communist cause. Poling was not through with his pacifist opponents. "For me at least, the Fellowship of Reconciliation and the mission of the clergymen and laymen of three faiths to Vietnam offers comfort only to those aggressors who are committed to the enslavement of their neighbors, who cross frontiers with violence and who would make of a free world struggling to be born a bloody and atheistic shambles of totalitarianism."[58] Taylor reiterated a

---

some way. Gary G. Cohen, "The Bible and The War in Viet Nam," *MM*, May 1967, 30, 61-65. Interestingly, in the following issue (July-August, 1967) the editors provided several pages worthy of letters to the editor which, for the most part, expressed opposition to the author's argument.

57. Kucharsky, "Viet Nam: Bullets and Brickbats," *CT*, July 30, 1965, 49. In another passive criticism, the author cited Martin Luther King, Jr. as saying that he was considering abandoning the emphasis on civil rights, a movement *CT* supported, to support the anti-war movement, a group *CT* opposed.

58. Poling, "Does Pacifism Become Activism?" *CH*, October 1965, 90. The "three faiths" comment refers to the composition of the Fellowship from Roman Catholic, Protestant, and Jewish clergy. Poling was to retire at the end of 1965, and then he passed away in 1968. After this happened Henry wrote an obituary in *CT* honoring him for his efforts on behalf of evangelicalism. He wrote that Poling was "an outstanding leader in an age of mediocre Protestantism. ... He argued that 'the Gospel is first, personal and always social.' But he added, 'The place of the Church is not to change society, but to change men and women who will then do the changing of society.' Poling himself was a changed man. He lived to see others changed and

common complaint, saying that pacifist Christians were not preserving the peace but making war more likely. Quoting a TV presentation, he asserted that attempts in the early days of World Wars I and II to avoid confrontation actually encouraged German and Japanese aggression.[59] A quote on the cover of an issue of *Presbyterian Journal* in December 1967 blasted anti-war workers within Christianity. "There are clergymen in America who evidently think that Communist commanders are humane, that their forces in Viet Nam didn't violate the Christmas truce this year, or last year and that they never kill any civilians in their raids, skirmishes and midnight assaults in South Viet Nam."[60] In this way of thinking, what had begun as a well-intentioned, if ill-informed, attempt to bring peace to a warring world had become instead advocacy for the worse of the two factions.

Vietnamese Ambiguity

The war in Vietnam dominated thought on war throughout this period, yet evangelicals tended to be of two minds about it. On the one hand there was the steady support for the effort to push back against what they saw as the oppressive, expansionist ideology of Communism. Some were more confident about the issues than others. A pastor writing to the editors of *Presbyterian Journal* declared, "The issue is freedom against tyranny, the living God against atheistic Communism. Are we so infected with the death-of-God theory that we cannot lift our voices in prayer that the Most High bare His almighty arm and intervene with a victory in Viet Nam that shall halt Communist aggression in Southeast Asia?"[61] On the other hand others were less inclined to see the American effort as quite so holy an affair. In mid-1968 Mark Hatfield, then a US senator from Oregon, told readers of *ET* that he had been told by a Vietnam veteran "that his unit cut the heads off the Vietcong they killed and spiked them up in conspicuous places with First Cavalry patches

to labor for the transformation of society." Henry, "Daniel A. Poling," CT, March 1, 1968, 29.

59. Taylor, "The Real War-Mongers," PJ, June 2, 1965, 12.

60. David Lawrence, "No Longer Treason?" PJ, December 6, 1967, Cover. This was not an article but a quote with no citation apart from the name.

61. William C. Robinson, "Pray for Victory!" PJ, August 17, 1966, 3.

stuffed in their mouths. This was to discourage the Vietcong from muti-
lating and disemboweling Americans." Answering a likely rejoinder, he
added, "Some people say, 'Oh, but you must fight fire with fire. War is
hell. So what can you expect?' But are we abdicating our standards of
moral conduct? Are we letting the enemy set the standards?"[62] It would
do little good to defeat the enemy only to find that they had become
indistinguishable from their opponents.

During this period there was an open uncertainty about the proper
way forward in Southeast Asia. Some thought a more assertive stance
would be the most beneficial while others began to question the enterprise. Of these periodicals, *ET* showed the most overt concern over
America's involvement in Vietnam. It is not that the editors came out
against the war, but they did include a greater number of articles in
opposition than their fellows at other magazines. A contributor to *ET*
pointed to the moral ambiguity of the war. As many had before, he
noted that the Saigon government was not an ideal ally in its treatment
of its own people. "*Four-fifths* of South Vietnam is still in Viet Cong
hands, and in these areas as in the rest, the farmers try to carry on
as usual. The Viet Cong takes half of their rice crop, and drafts their
sons at gun point. The Saigon government, when it 'liberates' an area,
collects back taxes, a good chunk of the remaining rice crop, and drafts
remaining sons at gunpoint." He had a few choice words for the impact
of American actions in the war.

> In the meantime, and in between time, the immense air power
> of the United States Air Force methodically rains death and dev-
> astation day after day. Three South Vietnamese civilians die for
> every Viet Cong killed by American bombs. America has yet to
> face the moral implications of this grisly arithmetic. If this goes
> on for several more years, what will be left to save or "protect"?[63]

Another article in *ET* echoed this when the author characterized one
side of the debate as saying, "What is there to debate? For many evangelicals, the question is simply, 'Shall we stand up to atheistic Communism,

---

62. Mark Hatfield, "What Has Happened to Our Values?" *ET* August 1968, 20.
63. John Goodwin, "Survey of the Year," *ET*, January 1966, 15.

or give in?' ... However, it is quite obvious to most thinking Americans that the issue isn't quite that clear-cut. It almost seems we are trying to save Viet Nam from tyranny by the euthanasia of bombs and napalm." Yet, he did not believe that the US was primarily in the wrong. As bad as America might be, its failings did not compare to the tyrannical wickedness of the Communists.[64]

In keeping with his pseudonymous nature, Courier was of two minds about Vietnam. On the one hand he could be skeptical about the American intervention. At one point he mused, "We don't mind, it

---

64. Robert J. St. Clair, "The Muddle of Viet Nam," *ET*, September 1965, 10. At other times *ET* would go further than this. One author, responding to his own question about the legitimacy of opposing any American war, said, "It is grossly chauvinistic to imply that one must stand by his country right or wrong," and then pointed to America's founding conflict, the Revolutionary War, which was, by its very definition, an anti-state conflict. Answering the question of Americans being always right, he said, "There has been a tendency in American history for its people to place themselves above the other nations of the world. Many citizens have felt that Americans are 'God's people' and possess the right to intervene in the affairs of other nations, especially if they are located in the Western Hemisphere." The author went so far as to challenge what he saw as the basis of American involvement in Vietnam. After saying that these assumptions "need to be challenged and re-evaluated in view of a changing world, principles on which our republic was established, and Christian standards," he offered new principles which he thought would do the nation and the church better in the quest for a moral foreign policy. Emery J. Cummings, "My Country: Right or Wrong?" *ET*, June 1967, 28–30. That these ideas would contested in the normally conservative readership of an evangelical magazine was acknowledged by editors who printed a blocked-off section saying, "We invite your reactions ... to this controversial article. Responses will be published in our 'Letters' column." They then summarized Cummings's main points and ended with "What do you think?" This same author, Emery Cummings, had his work appear in *ET* again the following year as a part of pairing of articles, each of which took either the "hawk" side or the "dove" side. In contrast to the stance taken by Cummings, as seen above, his conversation partner, Carroll Stegall, argued that the American involvement was moral and biblical. Further, he argued that the anti-war movement was benefiting from the predilection of the media to focus on the controversial as oppose to the war's supporters who "pay their taxes, accept their draft notices, fight and die." Also in contrast to Cummings's arguments, this author asserted that US policy was not the reckless example of American pride. Pointing to the agreement of such diverse figures as the previous three Presidents and their respective election opponents, he argued, "There have been no rash, hasty decisions made about Vietnam; nor has there been any ignorant drifting. There has been no manifestation to support the strange and false tale that 'America is arrogantly assuming the guardianship of the world.'" Rather than seeing Ho Chi Minh as the choice of the Vietnamese people, Stegall argued that the people had spoken after the division of the country when one million moved south. Carroll R. Stegall, "God and the USA in Vietnam," *ET*, March 1968, 12, 15.

would seem, a neat little war where only a few get killed (except for the people who live there, and they don't count, apparently). But let one of our bases be ambushed, shells explode, blood flow, and we exclaimed, 'Hey, that's not fair!' " He continued with his disdain, saying, "Is it a war or isn't it? Do we want to win it at all costs, or only if the price doesn't exceed a certain figure—and if so, what is the figure?" Then, critiquing the relative silence from the administration about the purpose of the war, he said, "Forgetting the war a minute, if the US could have precisely its own way in Southeast Asia, what would we want? Nobody has told us even that much. Maybe, of course, nobody knows. And has it occurred to anybody to ask what the South Vietnamese want?"[65] He later pointed out an uncomfortable fact.

> There is one interesting angle in all this that hasn't had much attention—the South Vietnamese government. We make much of the fact that we are there because we were invited by the government. But the government that invited us has long since disappeared. Other governments have come and gone. Suppose a government comes to power that invites us to leave?[66]

When the war continued without sign of an end, he wrote, "However, we have to keep fighting, the theory goes, fight harder, with more men and equipment, until we make the other side realize they can't win. The problem is that the other side very possibly has exactly the same intention."[67] Evangelical support of American wars had its limits, it seems.

---

65. Courier, "Viet Nam," CH, April 1965, 6.

66. Courier "Viet Nam," CH, July 1965, 6.

67. Courier, "Negotiations," CH, September 1965, 6. Culbertson wrote an article the following year which pushed back against a similar sort of reasoning. He wrote, "There are those who say that it is just the wise thing to do—sue for peace. The pitch is either you cannot win or the enemy is not so bad. Indeed, the whole story gets so perverted that the Communist aggressor is identified with the fighter for freedom. We heard one young man say that the Viet Cong and the American fighters in the Revolutionary War were one and the same in objective. How foolish can we become? Do not the captive nations say anything at all?" Culbertson, "Peace at any Price?" MM, June 1966, 17. Courier could also speak quite highly of the efforts and intentions of the US military. "They say that young men fight old men's wars. It seems to me that this time around the hawks are younger than the doves, and with impressive idealism. He then quoted the words of two young men, one, a civilian of draft age, and the other, a Marine already in Vietnam. The first said that

Henry was also skeptical about the American strategy, but his solution called for a redoubled effort, saying that a US withdrawal would only encourage the Communists to make even more grabs for power and territory, and, in keeping with his common refrain, that peace could only come through the spreading of the gospel.[68] At another point he said, "It is hard to see how the United States can avoid more direct intervention in the prolonged, bloody struggle for South Viet Nam. ... Unfortunately, the current strategy for ridding South Viet Nam of Communist guerrilla forces seems inadequate." While he was in favor of a more robust response by the US, he was worried about the singular role America was taking in the conflict, noting that traditional allies were keeping their distance, with the result that "the United States is again left holding the bag."[69] He came to President Johnson's defense for his determination to stay in Vietnam with the argument that the only moral response to the "naked aggression" of the North Vietnamese regime was to reply with significant force.[70] The following year Henry had come to praise the new boldness manifested in the more assertive American policy in Southeast Asia as seen in the air raids by US forces

---

he was not looking forward to the prospect of being sent off to war, but he added that he saw that the US had to hold the line against Communism somewhere. The marine, who Courier quoted more extensively, said, "All too often we read and hear in the news reports that people believe we are doing wrong in aiding Viet Nam. If we do not meet aggression with strong counter-measures, we can never show Communists that their efforts will be costly. If we do not meet aggression in Viet Nam, we will only have to fight on another soil, a soil that may well be closer to home." Courier closed out his summary with a mild qualification, but he also pointed out that reverence must be attached to this Marine's words. "[The Marine's] words raise some qualifications as well as answer some. For example, can America always expect to fight its battles on the soil of other nations? But his words have been hallowed. Within two weeks after his words were published, he had died for them." Courier, "Viet Nam," *CH*, October 1965, 12.

68. Henry, Letter to T. W. Wilson, September 10, 1965, Box 1965 2, File Correspondence, Billy Graham, Carl F. H. Henry Collection. Towards this hoped-for Christian transformation of human nature in Vietnam, David Kucharsky offered a cautionary tale of the troubles to be encountered. He said, "A dedicated coterie of American evangelical missionaries and Vietnamese Christians are pressing the claims of the Gospel in the face of numerous adverse circumstances such as Communist hostility, Roman Catholic influence, pagan culture, and sheer indifference." Kucharsky, "Viet Nam: The Spiritual War," *CT*, September 25, 1964, 53.

69. Henry, "The Last Battle in Asia?" *CT*, June 19, 1964, 23.

70. Henry, "Halting Red Aggression in Viet Nam," *CT*, April 23, 1965, 32.

outside South Vietnam.[71] He saw this as a "watershed" moment in the course of the war, even if this mean that "it is now more an American war than a South Vietnamese war." Significantly, he emphatically framed this hot war within the wider efforts of the Cold War across the world. American resolution in Southeast Asia would have positive ramifications all across the frontier between East and West.[72]

---

71. Kucharsky was to revisit this theme shortly in a news report about renewed peace talks. He noted the disappointment among many anti-war groups when, after US forces had held off on air raids for over a month, Communist forces had not sought a peaceful solution. "The churchmen were plainly disappointed that the bombing lull had not drawn Hanoi to the conference table. A number of pacifist-oriented clergymen had contended last year that a bombing lull would demonstrate the peaceful intentions of the United States and would induce the Vietnamese Communists to negotiate. The failure of the Reds to respond to the US and Vatican peace initiatives may have left some clergy a bit disillusioned, but others have indicated that they will press their dissent. Some new suggestions appear to be a virtual lobbying campaign in behalf of the Viet Cong politicians." Kucharsky, "Clergy Press Role in Peace Talks," CT, February 18, 1966, 51.

72. Henry, "Viet Nam: Where Do We Go from Here?" CT, January 7, 1966, 30. Henry's concerns over American grand strategy extended beyond Vietnam. To his manner of thinking, it was not an overly assertive tendency by the US which was causing its enemies to rise up and its allies and citizens to question its moral integrity. It was a lack of American resolve which had drawn out these problems. After North Koreans seized the USS Pueblo and interned its crew, Henry argued that the US reaction epitomized a general malaise afflicting the nation's foreign policy. Along with some questions specifically about the Pueblo incident, he asserted, "If an effective foreign policy is not indirectly to encourage injustice, it must provide effective restraint and swift reprisal. In the absence of this, we can see why America's allies are increasingly uneasy over inhibited fulfilment of our treaty commitments. We can also see why American criticism mounts over conduct of the Viet Nam war." Yet, even as he was displeased with the present status quo, he was not advocating a strategy that military force was the end of all diplomacy, but neither did he seek to give up and be "Better Red than dead." As he put it, "The alternative to stalemating cannot, assuredly, be annihilation of an announced enemy by the irresponsible use of total power, nor an advance abandonment of conventional for nonconventional weapons. But some alternative there needs to be to restrain aggression swiftly and retaliate injustice [sic]. The United States seems not yet to have found it." Henry, "All the King's Horses," CT, February 16, 1968, 28. William Harrison dismissed the idea that since they were openly terroristic, the US air raids on North Vietnam were obviously immoral. "Many people think that the purpose of the bombing cities is to terrorize civilians, causing them to surrender. This is not so. Experience shows instead that bombings infuriate people and increase their will to fight. Neither are bombs intended to overcome ideological Communism; ideas cannot be destroyed militarily." Likewise, he countered the contention that the US conducted these raids because it did not wish to negotiate but because its rival had chosen force

Henry allowed that the Vietnam War, like all lethal strife, presented the church with an ethical problem. He admitted that there were reasons to be concerned about the progress and plan of the war, even as he maintained his overall support. Specifically, he critiqued the disingenuous statements by government spokespeople that American bombs had done negligible damage to civilian areas in the war, stating that this had created a "credibility gap" in the minds of US citizens. He went on to note that there had been a shift in the way Americans approached their government. "Something significant has been happening in American religious life in our decade. Past generations of American Christians tended to tolerate national self-image and were reluctant to speak words of judgment. Now the tide of criticism is rising, sometimes from quite diverse parts of the church." He went on to say to those like him who supported the conflict and opposed the anti-war elements within the church that they needed to bolster their intellectual engagement with the debate on the war.[73]

In a letter to a prominent pastor, he gave a highly nuanced view of the war. It was a complex problem and one which suggested no easy solutions. "I agree too that the morality of the war is a matter of private conscience, that is, that every individual must justify to himself active

---

first. Rather, he argued, it was the Communists who had taken the role of aggressor and would seek a military solution until such a forced decision proved pointless. "Under these circumstances, for the other side to seek to negotiate will be futile; indeed, taken as an unwillingness to fight, it will only encourage the aggressor to strive harder for military victory. That the constantly expressed willingness to negotiate is answered with immediate scorn by the Communists is evidence of this." Echoing his own words in previous articles, he concluded, "Men who are willing to resort to military aggression and crime to gain their ends are for peace only on their own terms or when under external compulsion. No one has found a way to prevent such men from becoming heads of states. Their victims, having no alternatives but to fight or to surrender, usually fight, if victory seems reasonably probable." His call to his Christian readers was, "In the meantime, Christians who do not subscribe to pacifism can only look to God in faith for guidance and wisdom for their government and for themselves, that they may follow a path of integrity and justice, seeking peace but not afraid to fight if necessary, and withal not hating their enemies." Harrison, "Is the United States Right in Bombing North Viet Nam?" *CT*, January 7, 1966, 25–26.

73. Henry, "Viet Nam: A Moral Dilemma," *CT*, January 20, 1967, 27.

support or nonsupport, in view of the criteria of a just war." Looking back on the recently passed 1967, Henry wrote,

> The Viet Nam war fatality list continued to rise as intense fighting and bombing raged along jungle trails and in urban centers. But there was little evidence that the world's most powerful nation, unable to wrest a victory over North Vietnamese expansiveness, was any nearer a recognition that peace is a gift of God and not a product of military might alone.[74]

Moving on to questions of application, he added,

> What falls within the prerogative of authentic Christian witness? How do we place ourselves on the side of peace, which ought to be the church's first concern, and not place ourselves on the side of the promulgators of injustice? ... And where does your solution leave us predictably with regard to unilateral withdrawal from Vietnam (which I would consider wrong) or predictable resistance to aggression by tyrants?

Looking to two key biblical passages addressing the role of the state, he argued, "In other words, I'd like to identify myself with your emphases, and then try to find standing room within Romans 13, so as not to abandon the state onesidedly [sic] (as did the fanatical Anabaptists) to Revelation 13."[75] The war in Vietnam was a microcosm of all wars. It was awful and no one denied this, but it was, at least possibly, the only right thing to do.

END TIMES

THE CULMINATION

The capture of the site of the ancient Israelite temple by Israeli forces had been something long awaited by them more eschatologically

---

74. Henry, "Human Tragedy at Year-End," *CT*, January 5, 1968, 27.
75. Henry, Letter to Stephen Olford, May 15, 1968, Box 1963 2, File Correspondence, Olford, Carl F. H. Henry Collection. The letter indicates it was written in 1968, while it is filed in one of the 1963 boxes.

oriented evangelicals. Again, the very thing which so many evangelicals had predicted would happen, had happened. The world was aligned into two massive camps, with the nations of the old Roman Empire largely in one and a great northern confederation centered on Russia in the other. The Jews had returned and were in possession of the Old City of Jerusalem, worshiping where their ancestors had millennia before. The ingredients for the end were all in place.

It was not only the events of the Six Day War which elicited prophetic concerns, but other worldwide events seemed to push in that direction. Even those normally reticent about such matters found it hard not to say something. For example, *Presbyterian Journal* published a handful of articles dealing with the second coming, most of which avoided bringing the present into the discussion. One, however, did discuss current events. "One-third of mankind is under the domination of atheistic Communism. What better matrix for producing the antichrist has ever been offered to history? It does not seem idle speculation to wonder if the antichrist will prove to be a Red dictator who out-Stalins Stalin." The increasing prevalence of atomic weapons and the increase of atheism added to the author's sense of foreboding. Nonetheless, despite several more allusions to current or recent events, the author's focus was entirely on the pastoral implications of knowing the Christ would return to rescue his church and to judge the wicked. Among these wicked he included the United States, stating, "God will not be mocked. The flaming fire that attends Christ in His coming will find dross in plenty in Western lands. Must we not admit that Christ will of right judge our people too, should He in our lifetime come?"[76] The question was not how people may become a part of the elite few who knew what was coming but how they might change their ways and, possibly, avoid what was coming.

Also departing from a normal silence on eschatology was Henry. Although he was not making a specific end-times prediction, Henry suggested the modern age might have been better to listen to the warnings of the ancient world regarding its new military situation. "The distance from Moscow to Washington is shorter, much shorter, by

---

76. Robert Strong, "The Second Coming of Christ," *PJ*, November 30, 1966, 9.

missile or rocket, and all of us at times wonder whether the ancient prophets may not have taken the pulse of history more accurately when they warned of terrible judgment and desolation to come."[77] In another oblique reference to eschatological issues, Henry praised the US Senate for its vote to condemn Soviet anti-Semitism. He wrote, "Christians sometimes wonder why God continues to bless America in view of its widespread secularism and immorality." Given the way he often spoke of his country himself, this was a reasonable question. However, he added a potential explanation. "But on the deep religious level, our nation is sometimes better than it knows. When the government of the United States rises before the world to bless the Jewish people and to ward off the human curses that often fall upon them, it is putting itself in a position to receive the promised blessing of the Almighty, and not his curse." He was far less concrete in this expectation than Barnhouse had been a decade before, and he made no mention of the State of Israel, but he was nonetheless tying America's success to its treatment of the Jews.[78]

In 1965 Culbertson suggested that the end could be near by highlighting an unexpected line of evidence. Rather than looking primarily to the normal religio-political circumstances, he pointed to the growing agricultural developments within the State of Israel. "What is going on in Israel today may well be the preamble to the ringing down of the curtain on the times of the Gentiles and the triumphant revelation of the Son of God in His victorious return. We set no dates. But we are aware that tremendous things are happening in the Holy Land." He then proceeded to speaking of increased forestation, rainfall, irrigation, renewed habitation in cities abandoned since ancient times. As he went through each of these facts, he listed corresponding Scripture passages which prophesied that just such things would occur. Demonstrating why many evangelicals had such confidence that their long-held beliefs were being vindicated by contemporary events, he added,

---

77. Henry, "Christ and the Human Dilemma," *Lebanon Valley College Bulletin*, July 1965, 7.

78. Henry, "On the Lord's Side," *CT*, June 4, 1965, 28.

When apostasy within the Church, and moral breakdown and decay in western civilization, and the pieces of Roman Empire all seem about to come together, and anti-Semitism spreads despite the liberals' cry for brotherhood, then it is entirely possible that what is going on in Israel is part of this picture. All this may well say to us, "The coming of the Lord draweth nigh."[79]

For what turned out to have been a very brief moment in time, eschatologically-minded evangelicals could look at the news of the day with growing confidence as seemingly every one of their long-expected prophesied events were falling into place.

JUNE 1967

However, it was clearly the Six Day War itself which drew out the most commentary. On a purely geopolitical level, Henry noted that the Israeli victory had created a bit of a headache for the US, as the Israelis gave indications that they would never cede the city back to the Jordanians, much to the chagrin of the Johnson administration. However, this mundaneness was not his only comment on the issue. Glowingly, he wrote of the conquest, saying, "Israel, hedged in on three sides by Arab foes and outnumbered twenty to one, began fighting to ensure its survival as a nation. After mounting swift air strikes against Egyptian forces, Israeli troops in three short days circled and captured the old city of Jerusalem, controlled the Gaza strip, reopened the Gulf of Aqaba and reached the Suez Canal." Then, appealing to the great cry of Jews down through the years, he added, "But the popular Israeli toast 'next year in

---

79. Culbertson, "Israel and Prophecy—1964," *MM*, May 1965, 17. A writer at *ET* made a similar point in 1966. He asked his readers what would happen were he to make three outlandish predictions to come true over the next few years, and, one by one, they came true. After the first, he surmised, people would think he had been lucky. However, after the next two came to pass, "People would beat a pathway to my door to ask me to predict everything from the stock market to world conditions to horse races. My words would have been proved true by prophetic fulfillment." He then pointed to the prophecies of the Bible which he asserted had come true in history and in recent years as proof that the Bible's prophecies were a worthy and constructive area of study. He was not making any application to any current events but warding off attempts to discount the prophetic as irrelevant. Herbert Henry Ehrenstein, "Fulfilled Prophecy," *ET*, July 1966, 24.

Jerusalem!' was crowned last week by anticipatory fulfillment when a rabbi in soldier's garb blew a ram's horn at the Wailing Wall."[80]

Moody's editors provided a great many articles in this and subsequent issues concerning the implications of the conquest of Jerusalem by Israeli forces. Pieces by John Walvoord, Hal Lindsey, Wilbur Smith, and many others argued, with greater or lesser degrees of confidence, that the Six Day War had either brought in the actual circumstances of the end of the world in the short term or had at least done enough to make people consider the claims of the Bible and to lead Christians to revive their faith. A *Moody* editor, Robert Little, cautioned against any overzealous connections to the end and the Six Day War, saying, "We should like to reiterate here that we believe it wrong to consider any current happening a *direct* fulfillment of biblical prophecy, although many aspects of the political situation are strikingly similar to what the Bible says about conditions in the last days."[81] In this same *Moody* issue, scholars from MBI were interviewed on *MM*'s radio station about the Six Day War. One of these asserted that "though we may not be seeing direct fulfillment, we are seeing at least indications of the very real possibility of the return of Jesus Christ into this world in our lifetime."[82] The editors at *ET*, in contrast, were more hesitant, remarkably so given how prone to eschatological emphases the magazine had been in the past. One article, written in the wake of the Six Day War, spelled out the biblical promises of land to the ancient Israelites, a land which he

---

80. Henry, "War Sweeps the Bible Lands," *CT*, June 23, 1967, 20.

81. Robert J. Little, "The Mid-East Crisis," *MM*, July-August 1967, 18. Italics in original.

82. Todd Seelye, Robert J. Little, Louis Goldberg, and Alan Johnson, "Bible Prophecy and The Mid-East Crisis," *MM*, July-August 1967, 22. This was an extensive interview in which the panel suggested, but did not overtly assert, that the Six Day War could be a key development in eschatology. However, while they did maintain that the Russians, Egyptians, and Chinese were almost certain players in the final drama, they did not make mention of the place of the US in any such scheme. Louis Goldberg was the author of a subsequent article series in *MM* starting in September 1968 entitled "The Goldbergs Discover Israel," and the subheading, "Join this Hebrew Christian family in their nine-week visit famous for its past and its prophetic future." As might be expected, the series presented a highly favorable view of the State of Israel as Goldberg and his family toured the land. Louis Goldberg, "The Goldbergs Discover Israel: I. Around the Land in Eight Days," *MM*, September 1968, 9.

said could be as vast as from the Nile to the Euphrates. The author then gave a significant qualification, saying, "Now let's do some hard and clear thinking. This was God's promise to Abraham and his descendants. *That does not automatically mean, and I do not intend in any way to imply, that this is God's promise to the modern State of Israel.*" What he did intend to imply was somewhat more vague. He said he did not "concede that the State of Israel is to be identified as the Israel described in Holy Scripture." However, he also said, "I am willing to admit that it seems quite likely that the regathering of the Jews to Palestine, the establishment of the State of Israel, and the almost incredible military success of Israeli armies against what appeared to be overwhelming odds, are somehow to be related to God's promises." Ultimately, he came to no conclusion in this article, going so far as plainly to say, "I do not know." He halfway came down against these events being a sign of the end by noting what was missing. He looked for a real future conversion of Jews to Christianity preceding the return of Christ, yet he confessed he had seen no indications of any turning to Jesus among Israelis.[83]

Ishmael and Isaac

Culbertson made an appearance not in his own *MM* but in *CT* as one part of a pairing of articles discussing biblical implications of the Arab-Israeli conflict. As expected, he argued that the modern State of Israel was, indeed, the fulfillment of biblical prophecy, and he wondered if the capture of Jerusalem by Israeli forces meant that the end was finally nigh.

> Can it be that the beginning of these things is upon us? If Israel keeps Jerusalem, will that mean that Luke 21:24 is about to be fulfilled? I do not attempt to give a final answer. The times and seasons are in the Father's hands. But may I suggest that, in view of the signs of the times, it would be foolish to live as though the end of the age could not possibly be upon us.

---

83. William Sanford LaSor, "Have the 'Times of the Gentiles' Been Fulfilled?" *ET*, August 1967, 32–33.

Toward the end of his piece, he made note of the plight of Arab refugees cast out of their homes. While he declared his sympathy, he
put the blame for their condition on their fellow Arab neighbors. He
asked why such oil-rich countries could not take in the thousands of
Arabs pushed out of Israel just as the relatively poor Israel had taken
in the thousands of Jews exiled from their previous homes around
the Middle East.[84]

His conversation partner, James Kelso, a former professor of Old
Testament, also dealt with the situation of the Arab refugees, but
he made this the centerpiece of his argument. Part of his complaint
was that only a miniscule portion of Americans he spoke to about the
Middle East had even the basic understanding about the reality of the
crisis. He argued that the State of Israel was not the result of divine prediction or indigenous Jewish self-protection but was created "militarily
by European Jews who had fled from persecution in Christian Europe."
While some might have questioned just how Christian Europe had been
in the 1940s, he allowed for no religious blessing on the leadership of
the Israeli founders. "The Irgun and Stern gangs of Zionism had introduced the same murder techniques that the Viet Cong are now using
in Viet Nam." He continued this connection to Cold War issues toward
the end of his article, saying that, as a result of American support of
the State of Israel, suggesting that the Soviets were not the "dominant
power" in the Middle East to the loss of American power and prestige.[85]

Not every comment focused on the victorious Israelis. While it
certainly was not the primary focus, there was a minor theme within
these article which dealt with the impact of the war on the Arabs of

---

84. Culbertson, "Perspective of Arab-Israeli Tension," CT, June 7, 1968, 8.

85. James L. Kelso, "Perspective of Arab-Israeli Tension," CT, June 7, 1968, 7,
9. Writing in ET one contributor told his readers that their support of the State
of Israel had implications for American foreign policy. "The American evangelical Christian cannot understand what the Arab thinks, what he says and what
he does until he understands how complete and profound is this Arab hatred of
Zionism. The Arab is willing to suffer all kinds of economic loss if by doing so he
strikes at Zionism. He is also willing to strike at Zionism even though the effort
is completely empty of any force or power. The Arab is dedicated not to rest until
Zionism is ended, no matter how many reverses it may entail or decades it might
take. If the Arab believes that in any way America or Americans support Zionism,

the region. A *Moody* news blurb focused on the suffering of now land-less Arabs after the Six Day War, saying, "Thousands of Arab refugees settled in the open fields of Syria face the coming winter with no idea of where they will find protection from the sweeping cold air. Their only shelter: light summer tents. ... Observers predict that because of the Israeli government's attitude toward the Syrian refugees, they will never get back to their homes." His concluding paragraphs tied this problem to eschatology, saying, "The refugee problem ... is so tightly entwined with the whole Middle East political situation that a political settlement of Israeli-Arab differences is impossible without progress on the refugee problem. So Bible believers with an eye on the prophetic teachings about Israel continue to watch such Middle East developments."[86] A similar article in *ET* made the same point, saying, "Harsh winter winds are sweeping across the Judean hills and fluffy snow blankets the rolling countryside of the Middle East. It does not camouflage the squalor, it only heightens the misery of the estimated 1.5 million refugees in the Holy Land and surrounding countries."[87] The implications of the, apparently, realized prophecies were dizzying, but this enthusiasm was checked enough for many to take notice of the unpleasant side effects of these fulfillments.

THE BIG PICTURE

A year after the war Henry offered his own perspective on the post-Six Day War Middle East in one of his final editorials at *CT*. His only mention of eschatology here was to note that "a Christian has reason to believe that the ultimate crisis will center, not in Viet Nam ... but in Palestine," but the bulk of his argument was that the events them-selves suggested that "a bigger showdown" was in the offing. He pointed to indications that the Israelis were not content with their conquest of the West Bank and Sinai[88] but looked to the Nile and Euphrates as

---

he will extend his hatred to them and become violently anti-American even though in the past America might have done his country some enormous favor." Bernard Ramm, "Behind the Turmoil and Terror in the Mideast," *ET*, September 1967, 33.

86. The Editors, "Problem in the Middle East," *MM*, December 1967, 6.

87. The Editors, "No Room for Them," *ET*, February 1968, 30.

88. During the 1956 Suez War and the 1967 Six Day War, the Israelis secured control not only of the Golan Heights from Syria, the parts of the Kingdom of Jordan

ultimate goals and to the Arab desire "to see the Jews pushed into the sea." Further, with the American determination to preserve the State of Israel and the Russian desire to expand its influence, any regional conflict could quickly embrace all major powers.[89]

The potential of eschatology in this period could hardly be overstated. Its reality, on the other hand, was less dramatic, as this era was one of the most anti-climactic of recent experience. The year 1968 ended with the Middle East crisis failing to bring in the end of the world and with America failing to bring home its troops from Vietnam. The conquest of Jerusalem and the ancient Jewish homeland in the West Bank by the State of Israel seemed the perfect next step in an eschatological hope building for decades. While these events did stir the imaginations of many evangelicals, there still was no indication, beyond ever-present rumors, that a new temple would be built in the Holy City. With the Americans focused on Tet and the Russians on Prague, there was no immediate prospect of a superpower battle in the valley beneath Har Megiddo. Armageddon had not yet come. A half century later, it would be easy for critics and even friends to laugh at the great confidence which so many of these writers expressed. But, again, given the way in which things had continued to fall out exactly as they had been saying they would when all those around them were losing their confidence in any future hope, eschatologically-minded evangelicals had good reason to believe that their vindication was on the way.

now known as the West Bank, and the Gaza Strip from the Egyptians, but they also took over the entirety of the Sinai Peninsula from Egypt. This was returned to Egypt as a part of the 1979 treaty between the two longtime enemies.

89. Henry, "Is There Hope for Palestine?" *CT*, June 7, 1968, 26. In this same article he gave his own critique of Israeli policies, stating, "Israel seems uninterested both in the tragic plight of the Arab refugees and in the U.N. insistence that nothing be done unilaterally to change the status of Jerusalem. If considerations of social justice are not to be ignored, both these problems must be faced—and perhaps together."

9

The End of War, 1969–1973

OVERVIEW

As the 1970s began America's position in the world had remained the same for some time. The Soviets and the Chinese formed the largest potential foes, while the smaller nations of Eastern Europe and East Asia were alternatively the victims of or battlegrounds against these Cold War rivals from Beijing and Moscow. However, in some ways the situation had begun to shift. The Soviets had been boxed in on the European frontier since VE Day, and the Chinese were suddenly a nation that the staunchly anti-Communist Nixon could make deals with. Vietnam remained a place where battles were always being fought, but none seemed ever to be won or lost. The most likely place for the great powers to come into conflict appeared to be not Europe or East Asia but the Middle East. The capture of Jerusalem had been promised as the final sign of the final days, yet the world drifted on as before. Over several years open war was avoided, even as peace never really came. Even this false security ended in the unexpected Yom Kippur War over Palestine which pulled Soviet and American forces into the logistical chain, supplying their respective client states of the Egyptians and Israelis.

For evangelical leaders trying to explain all these events to their constituents, the answers remained much the same as they always had. Totalitarianism was a real danger to people around the world, particularly to Christians in all nations. America was the world's best earthly hope, but it was also the likely object of heavenly judgment for its many, deep sins. War was an awful thing to behold, and it was not always clear whether the outcome was worth the cost. The end might well be nigh, but Christians ought to live for God in the present.

ENEMIES

WHENCE CHINA?

The place of China in world affairs moved somewhat in this era. After decades of isolation, Mao's government reemerged into the community of nations, both through its inclusion in the UN and by the now proverbial Nixon outreach to China. There was a great deal of confusion by evangelical commentators as to what the right course was and what to make of China's own motivations. A missionary based in Hong Kong wrote of the "ping pong diplomacy," saying, "What does it all mean? Is this a sincere gesture of friendship to the United States, or is it a defiant move calculated to agitate the leaders in the Kremlin? Is it the start of a long and painful process of cementing cracks in international relations? Or is simply a knee-jerk reaction to the American government's relaxation of certain travel and trade restrictions?"[1] In December 1971 Hitt wrote approvingly of the UN decision to replace Taipei's Republic of China on Taiwan with Beijing's People's Republic of China on the mainland as the official delegation representing the nation.[2] The next month another writer said that Christians ought to "rejoice" over the new possibilities and that China was too significant a nation to be excluded from the family of nations.[3]

Not everyone saw it quite this way. A former missionary and member of Congress was quoted in news report in *Presbyterian Journal*, suggesting that the American recognition would have dire results in East Asia. He predicted that at the cost of only "a few smiles" Mao would collect the Pacific Rim into his sphere of influence if the West offered him an open hand.[4] Interestingly, despite his normally hardline stance, L. Nelson Bell offered a fairly complex reaction. When asked for his opinion of the new outreach to Beijing, he said, "Because we did live in China for so many years and feel that we know just a little of Chinese psychology, we are forced to reply, 'We don't know.'" He spent most of

---

1. Robert Larson, "China: Open Door to What?" *CT*, August 27, 1971, 3.

2. Russell T. Hitt, "World Peace, and Drama at the U.N.," *ET*, December 1971, 8.

3. Arthur F. Glasser, "Red China," *ET*, January 1972, 12.

4. Anonymous, "Reaction to President's Trip Varies," *PJ*, August 4, 1971, 4. No author is given.

the article highlighting the tyranny of the Maoist state and critiquing the American government for potentially abandoning its longtime and longsuffering ally, Chiang Kai-shek, but he ended with an openness to a peace that could be, provided that Mao could be held to any potential agreement with the West. As always, his hope for renewed missionary activity was central to his thinking.[5]

Lindsell saw little of any bright side to this new situation. When Senator McGovern said that China should be treated better because Communism was not ever the threat which its American detractors suggested, Lindsell responded, "But world events continue to refute the thesis that Communism is a peaceful political system, that it is not working for the death of democracy and the overthrow of non-Communist governments."[6] Later, however, he argued that recognition may be a

---

5. L. Nelson Bell, "China Today," *PJ*, August 4, 1971, 13. Bell was not the only person to look to these events with an evangelistic eye. An editorial in *MM* told readers that the church in China was thriving despite decades of overt hostility from the Communist state, saying, "Reliable sources out of China report that in one traditionally Christian area near a coastal city, out of a population of more than 30,000, there are now an estimated 3,000 Christians. These are said to meet together in small home congregations or church cells," and even that some of these underground churches were large enough to support a pastor. The writer quoted another source who said that the tendency of the Mao government to keep Christian leaders in prison, long after their terms had expired, spoke to their ineffectiveness at curtailing Christianity. R. J. L, "Good News from China," *MM*, May 1969, 14. No one with the initials "R. J. L." is listed on the masthead, but a Robert J. Little did write for *MM* during this time, suggesting that this is the correct identity.

6. Harold Lindsell, "Radicals on the Rampage," *CT*, November 6, 1970, 33. Another example of evangelical condemnation for Chinese Communism came in their treatment of the people of a fellow Communist nation. While Czechs and Germans struggled with Russian Communist intervention, according to one writer, the small nation of Albania had come under the sway of Chinese Communist influence. Even though this switch of allegiance had ostensibly come about in protest of the Soviet oppressions in Prague, the Albanian capital of Tirana was now the scene of an exported Cultural Revolution. Chinese infantry, ironically housed in infrastructure built by the Italian occupation forces of a generation earlier, encouraged Albanian Red Guards in the sacking of Christian sites and those of other dissident groups. Speaking of one of these destructions, he wrote, "Several hundred Red Guards marched on the church of Fier. The resident priests barricaded themselves inside—to no avail. The church was stormed, the main gate broken down, crucifixes torn down and trampled upon, priceless paintings ripped to shreds, the altar turned over and dragged to the main entrance, most of the priceless sixteenth century pews chopped to pieces." David Bligh, "Red Guards Sweep Albania," *ET*, August 1969, 27.

bitter pill to swallow, but it might do the world some good, nonetheless. Besides, he noted, the US could hardly keep out Communist China when it had embraced Communist Russia. One potential bright point for him was that Sino-American relations could prove a useful counterpoint to Russian interests in the world.[7]

Whatever hope there might have been on a pragmatic level for the renewed relations with Beijing, there remained a heavy dose of distrust and doubt for the future of China's government. A contributing writer in *Presbyterian Journal* warned of the danger of Maoism, a movement which he described more as a large-scale cult than a political system.

> The cult of Maoism maintains its strength by a constant barrage of ideological teaching. Chairman Mao says he believes in God, but God is the State. Marx, Engels, Lenin and Stalin are the prophets of Maoism. The saviour of the Chinese people is Chairman Mao. His teachings take the place of the Christian Scripture, while the ever-present branch of the revolutionary committee pervades every commune, every village and every home. There is no getting away from the eye of the party's spirit.[8]

One author, writing about the future of missionaries to China, wondered whether a new regime could come to Beijing, but he cast that hope aside quickly. As he pointed out, the only Chinese opponent to Mao was Chiang in Taiwan, and he could never invade the mainland.

7. Lindsell, "The Peking Gambit," CT, August 6, 1971, 24. He was not without his qualms about the whole affair. When it came to a UN vote on whether to accept the Communists from Beijing and expel the Nationalists from Taipei, he said, "The Nationalist government on Formosa was one of the original signatories of the United Nations Charter. It has stood by its commitments to that organization as loyally as virtually any other country. It had every right to continued membership. One of the ironies of the ouster was that many of the countries that supported the move had themselves been voted into the organization with Taiwan's help. ... We will be willfully blind if we ignore the fact that Communism is still grimly determined to dominate the world. The vote against two Chinas was a political victory for Communism. But the Communists also continue to work through aggression, infiltration, and subversion." Lindsell, "The China Vote," CT, November 19, 1971, 27.

8. Robert N. Thompson, "Mao's China," PJ, September 5, 1973, 8.

He further pointed out that an American military victory in China was "unthinkable" in light of its ineptitude in Vietnam.[9]

NORTH VIETNAM

Even as the debates over the morality of the war continued, evangelical commentators had nothing positive to say about the Communist Vietnamese. Questions about American strategy and ethics intensified, but these paled to the concerns over Communist practices. A contributor to *MM* rooted his support for the war in the behavior of Communist forces.

> I feel that both morally and ethically, the highest interest of the church of Jesus Christ are being served by American participants in Vietnam. Why? Because of the nature and tactics of the enemy. I am aware of the great controversy in America regarding the identity of this enemy. In Vietnam as in other southeast Asian countries there is no question. We are fighting communism!

After detailing some the horrors of what he termed "enemy terrorism," he concluded that the US needed to be there for the sake of the gospel and the sake of the Vietnamese. "Southeast Asia's right to hear of spiritual salvation is being threatened by a cruel, relentless foe. Naturally speaking, the one obstacle to Communist takeover is US intervention." He hoped that American forces could withdraw someday, but, until then, it was important for the Vietnamese that US troops remained.[10]

While he could be vocal in casting doubt on the wisdom of the war, Russell Hitt spared no love for the Communist regime in Vietnam. In a report from one of the returning American POWs, Hitt told his readers, "The cruel pattern of torture, threats and indoctrination was applied for several reasons. Sometimes it was to extract military information. Sometimes it was to break the prisoners' chain of command. More often it was to force the men to make statements or public appearances useful to the North Vietnamese." The same article described one of the common torture tactics, saying, "Imagine yourself sitting on the floor,

---

9. Herbert Kane, "Will China Re-Open to Missions?" *MM*, November 1971, 37.
10. Glenn Johnson, "The Face of the Enemy," *MM*, June 1969, 14.

knees up under your chin. With your wrists manacled behind your back, your tormentors loop rope around each upper arm and tighten until all circulation stops. More rope is used to draw your elbows together and then your shoulder blades as well, until they are touching and locked together." The ex-POW's tale continued,

> But the torturers do not stop until your feet are also shackled to an iron bar, with rope looped around it and your neck in such a way as to draw your head down between your legs until your toes are virtually in your mouth. Prisoner after prisoner endured all or part of the "rope trick," sometimes being abandoned for hours, their screams muffled by a towel being jammed down their throat.[11]

---

11. Hitt, "The POW Story: Seven Years of Prison and Prayer," *ET*, June 1973, 15-16. Hitt was the author of this piece which told the story of an American Air Force Colonel, James Risner. A piece in *MM* also cited the travails of Colonel Risner, telling readers that he had been "vice commander of the POWs" at the infamous "Hanoi Hilton." James C. Hefley, "Facing Their New World of Freedom," *MM*, September 1973, 25. At least one reader of *MM* did not feel that these POWs should be treated as heroes in any way. After the September 1973 issue noted above which had painted the returning Americans in a largely positive light, the reader wrote the editors, saying, "We tend to look upon them as if they were some kind of patron saint of the American dream, and as if the kingdom of God were at least temporarily (if not permanently) in some kind of alliance with the United States government. We act as if they were on some type of holy mission when they were in Vietnam. Let us be sure that we know exactly what they were doing in Vietnam: they were destroy-ing and making pillage of the Vietnamese countryside, bombing hospitals and homes, and killing innocent people. To be sure, the North Vietnamese were wrong in torturing them. (Just to keep it in proper perspective, though, the US and South Vietnamese were doing the same things, and no one seemed to be too upset about it)." J. Huffman, "About Those POW's," *MM*, November 1973, 4-5. In contrast, a pastor writing a letter to the editor at *PJ* contested what he saw as a false impression many people in the country had about the war in Southeast Asia. Rather than seeing the Americans as having stirred up the trouble, he argued, "The United States did not start the war. It was in full swing for several years before our country intervened." He also challenged the idea that this was an internal matter of a single country. "It is a conflict between two independent states in Southeast Asia, not a civil war, and was begun by North Vietnam by its invasion of South Vietnamese territory. ... This was done in violation of solemn agreements internationally witnessed, in alliance with subversive elements within South Vietnam itself, and with the con-nivance of China and Russia." He further asserted that this conflict should not be seen only as affecting Indochina. "The struggle, while localized in Southeast Asia, has implications for the freedom of millions of people in wide areas of the world,

As so often had been the case, the central thought regarding an American conflict was not the holiness of the US but the depravity of its foe.

This principle came up again when Harold Lindsell challenged pro-Communist activism on college campuses. When a university chapel held a memorial service in honor of the recently deceased Ho Chi Minh, Lindsell put forward a few questions for them about their praises for the policies of the Communist leader. "We must ask, however, whether this included freedom for the North Vietnamese who disagreed with some of the policies of the Ho regime. In America there is considerable freedom to disagree publically with our government's policies regarding South Viet Nam. Is there comparable freedom in North Viet Nam?" Then, observing that the memorial organizers condemned those in the US who had contributed to the deaths of people in Southeast Asia, Lindsell asked, "Was there any protest against Ho for having caused the deaths of tens of thousands—probably hundreds of thousands—of his countrymen? ... Would it not have been more fitting to hold a memorial service for the victims of Ho rather than for their murderer?" He ended his critique of Ho by being grateful his fellow Americans did not have the power to emulate their late hero.[12]

G. Aiken Taylor was much bolder in his support. After a 1972 trip to the war zone, he had a photo of himself alongside a South Vietnamese official,[13] and described her as "the spirit of Vietnam" and as "Vietnam's Florence Nightingale." As to the war itself he rebuked America for its callousness to Vietnamese casualties but called for increased support. Quoting "a top US official," Taylor wrote the Americans were using the Vietnamese as cannon fodder in a proxy war with the Soviets. "I am sick to death of the way both Russia and my country are making these beautiful people do their fighting for them. *We* are at war with *Russia*

---

wherever men are threatened with enslavement by totalitarian power. Had it not been for the brave resistance of South Vietnam and the help she has had from our country, it is likely that not only Vietnam, but Cambodia, Laos, Thailand, Malaysia, Burma and possibly India and Indonesia would by this time have been brought under the heel of a ruthless Communism." C. Darby Fulton, "A Deceitful 'Peace,'" *PJ*, June 21, 1972, 2.

12. Lindsell, "Hooray for Ho?" *CT*, October 10, 1969, 33.

13. The Editors, Cover, *PJ*, May 17, 1972, 1.

for the freedom of the world, but we are unwilling to pay the price for freedom. Instead, we are making these people pay that fearful price while we go about business as usual on the side. That is immoral." To this comment, Taylor replied, "Amen."[14] In an editorial written upon his return to the United States, Taylor said, "America has been sold a monstrous lie concerning the Vietnam War. From now on I intend to let my pride show, when the subject of our national involvement in Southeast Asia comes up. I am not proud of some of the Americans I saw in Vietnam, but as a country we need apologize to no one." This was not exactly a case of "My country, right or wrong." It was more a matter of "My country is wrong a lot, but theirs is more so."

CUBA

A decade after the revolution and the missile crisis, Cuba had faded from attention to a large extent, with much of the attention devoted to the ordeals of Christian workers and exiles. An *ET* news blurb in 1969 reported that two Southern Baptist missionaries in Cuba had been released from prison and allowed to return, first to Havana and then to the US. Not much was said about their previous activities, but they were apparently imprisoned for illegal currency exchange.[15] An extensive article in early 1970 reported on the same set of events for *Moody* where readers were told that some fifty-two Baptist church workers had been arrested during the same period in Cuba two years before, with one elderly pastor being sentenced to ten years in a Cuban prison, although this was later reduced to house arrest.[16] One piece in 1971 highlighted the problems faced by dissidents in Cuba. "They tell of suffering, deprivations, shortage of food and clothing, and opposition and harassment. Occasionally, they report the arrest of pastors and the destruction of church buildings." However, he also wanted to inform his readers that just because Cuba was a closed country when it came to foreign missionary activities, the local Cuban church was still quite active. He reported on Christians holding "island-wide conventions"

---

14. G. Aiken Taylor, "Across the Editor's Desk," *PJ*, May 17, 1972, 3.
15. The Editors, "Cubans Release Two Baptist Missionaries," *ET*, March 1969, 39.
16. Zeda Thornton, "Appeal to Castro," *MM*, January 1970, 36.

and vacation Bible schools as well as the conversion of many younger Cubans. Whatever troubles it might be having and whatever tensions existed between its government and the Americans, Christians on the island nation were still secure as part of the kingdom of God.[17]

PRAGUE'S AFTEREFFECTS

The Prague revolt of 1968 was still a sore subject for many evangelical commentators a year later. Lindsell wrote, "The Soviet Union's invasion of Czechoslovakia has neither extinguished the Czech desire for liberty nor produced the abject capitulation the invaders hoped for. The self-immolation of Jan Palach in protest against the military rape of his country speaks dramatically of the depth of his feeling and that of his fellow countrymen." In the remainder of his article he condemned what he saw as the hypocrisy of mainline church groups who could rally together to protest American military actions and support but were nowhere to be found when the Soviets took action. "In regard to Czechoslovakia, the WCC now has the duty and obligation to speak just as clearly and to work with equal urgency. If it does not, everyone has the right to ask why it operates selectively—and seemingly in favor of the Soviet Union."[18] One writer told his readers of the life of the Czechs now under occupation.

> Original promises for the removal of Soviet troops were never kept—in fact the Russians are making it obvious that a certain number of their troops are there to stay. Censorship was re-imposed immediately, worked only partially for a time, but was felt with full force again when new Party Leader Gustav Husak appeared on the scene. Arrests have been made, and 'disappearances' are no longer talked of in the past tense.

He was able to report that the recent travails had not only made many Czech people more open to Christianity but even some of their Soviet occupiers showed interest in getting Bibles to send home to their families. Interestingly, this author wrote sympathetically of the Russian

---

17. Wolfe Hansen, "What's Going on in Cuba?" *ET*, March 1971, 52–53.
18. Lindsell, "The Czech Quest for Freedom," *CT*, February 14, 1969, 25.

troops on garrison duty in Czechoslovakia, saying that they were so naïve about Moscow's actions that they did not understand why the Czechs seemed so angry with them.[19]

COMMUNIST COMPLEXITY

Many shared this emphasis on the Communist world as being a mixed bag, filled with some malicious and some merely misguided. Communists were still the bad guys, but not all of the Communists were as bad as others. Carl Henry, no friend to Communism, reported on his trip to Yugoslavia for a theological conference of Eastern European Christians. He said that the meeting "could signal new vitality for Christians in Soviet lands," and that the people coming to the meeting "could not but be impressed by the larger freedom and initiative of Christians in Yugoslavia in contrast with other East European lands."[20] A news blurb in *Moody* noted without comment that Yugoslavia had resumed full diplomatic relations with the Vatican.[21] One author of Russian origin visited his relatives behind the Iron Curtain and reported on what he had seen. He wrote, "When Soviet Cosmonaut Yuri Gagarin returned from space to say he didn't see God out there, most Christian Americans probably just shrugged and felt smug. Most of us have just written off Cosmonaut Gagarin and 250 million other Soviets as 'atheists' and without God. But recently my wife and I visited Russia and found God there."[22] Another writer laid part of the blame for such false impressions about East Berlin essentially on Western laziness. "The Communist East German regime is not recognized in the West, journalists report on affairs there through the hostile lens of the Cold War, academic specialists on Communism or German affairs tend to overlook the area and Western travelers seldom avail themselves of the opportunity to see it firsthand."[23] Hitt

---

19. Dave Foster, "Czechoslovakia, One Year Later," *ET*, August 1969, 17–18.

20. Carl F. H. Henry, "Eastern Europe's 'Congress on Evangelism,'" *ET*, November 1969, 56, 58.

21. The Editors, "Around The World," *MM*, November 1970, 16.

22. Ken Semenchuck, "We Toured the Ukraine … and Found God," *ET*, August 1969, 19. Italics in title in original.

23. Richard V. Pierard, "New Look Over The Wall," *ET*, August 1969, 22.

encouraged his readers to avoid lumping all those behind the Iron Curtain into one simplistic pot. Speaking of the place of Christians in Eastern Europe, he argued that despite the all-too-human desire for monolithic preconceptions, the situation behind the Iron Curtain was not uniform. Different countries varied from others, and different times altered the conditions even within single nations. He wanted them to consider that the choices before the citizens of Communist nations were not as black and white as cooperation with an evil state or standing for justice. He said, "It is easy to judge those Christians in Communist lands who don't do things as we would do them. Some we would label as compromisers; some we could label as underhanded smugglers who practice civil disobedience." For support he pointed to the biblical example of the prophet Elijah, who stood against the state as an outlaw, and his contemporary, Obadiah, who used his position within the government to protect God's prophets.[24]

This emphasis on complexity did not evolve into any sort of relativism about Communism in Russia, particularly as this touched on the place of Christians under this tyranny. Discussing the travails of a Soviet dissident, Lindsell lumped Communism in with the universally condemned Nazism. "Totalitarianism, whether to the left, or, as in the case of Hitler, to the right, always means the death of freedom. It always uses force and torture. It always dehumanizes men. Totalitarianism is antithetical to freedom, to love and to brotherhood. Real freedom can never exist in Communist-controlled societies, for real freedom allows for dissent, and Communism cannot permit dissent."[25] A commentator in *ET* reported that evangelical publications in Russia had to be "printed in a clandestine manner," and that the church leaders did their best to keep their meetings secret from the state. He hoped that something could eventually come of the efforts of these underground Christians, even if the nature of Russian society presented its own problems apart from Communist oppression. "If all three resisting groups—the evangelicals, the Orthodox and the intellectuals—were to survive and even gather momentum, the combined

---

24. Hitt, "Who Is The True Servant of God?" *ET*, August 1969, 9.
25. Lindsell, "The Options of Modern Man," *CT*, November 6, 1969, 30.

ferment could change the face of Russia." However, he found this hope to be a feeble one as the Russians had never known political freedom in their entire history.[26]

AMERICA

AMERICAN GLORY

The attitude of these commentators toward the United States continued to be that their nation had been given many blessings like freedom and prosperity, but the country also had become selfish and corrupt to a disgusting degree. It was not that some had a high view and some held a low opinion. That would be simple enough. The very same individuals wrote of the US as both a positive and a negative force in the world.

On the positive side, readers of *Moody* read of the "Honor America Day" in Washington, DC, an event headed up by the entertainer Bob Hope and the evangelist Billy Graham.

> The day's theme was set in a sermon during a morning interreligious service in front of the Lincoln Memorial by Graham, who said the event was designed "to renew allegiance to this nation's principles and institutions." His text was I Peter 2:17—"Honor all men, Fear God, Honor the king," the latter re-translated by the evangelist to apply more aptly to this country's government by reading "honor the nation."[27]

---

26. Robert Coote, "Russian Evangelicals: American Dilemma," *ET*, August 1969, 13.

27. Bob Hill, "Graham Leads 'Honor America Day,'" *MM*, September 1970, 10. Apparently, Carl McIntire held this event in derision. In a news blurb the following month, McIntire was quoted as comparing his planned "March for Victory in Vietnam" with the Graham event, saying that it would be "our united answer to both the New Mobe continual agitation and the Graham-Hope neutralism." Bob Hill, "From the Nation's Capital," *MM*, October 1970, 13. The MOBE was a group of anti-war protesters, The National Mobilization Committee to End the War in Vietnam. Although he nowhere named either McIntire or his fundamentalist denomination, the ACCC, Bell did challenge what he thought to be the false versions of patriotism flowing out of fundamentalism. These he blamed for supplying theologically liberal commentators with ample ammunition to denigrate conservatives of all stripes. "There have been pseudo patriots whose patriotism has consisted of flag waving, loud speeches and words of criticism and denunciation against those of

A pastor who wrote in *Presbyterian Journal* also praised his native land, saying, "There is something beautiful about the Stars and Stripes snapping in the breeze. It has a way of sending the blood surging through our bodies just a bit more rapidly. There is an emotion generated by the sight of our flag that is present on no other occasion. Our spines stiffen a bit. We stand just a little taller. We feel just a little bit better." Yet, at the same time he admitted that America was not all that he could wish it could be and called for his people to turn back to God. "We could be properly patriotic if our nation would, as one man, turn its back on the cesspools of iniquity within it, wipe them from off its face and turn its eyes on the God who alone is able to give glory to men. There is new glory for Old Glory if the people of God will put God's program into action."[28] In contrast to other times where authors distinguished carefully between the American people and the people of God, this writer is, at the very least, not making such a distinction a priority, and, quite possibly, speaking of the two as though they were one.

Lindsell was frustrated with some of his fellow Americans for what he saw as an uncritical disregard for patriotism in any form. In a Fourth of July issue of *CT*, he wrote that while many would be filled with national pride on the country's birthday, others could only think of tearing down their own nation. "For them patriotism is dead; love of country is archaic. Far from echoing Stephen Decatur, 'Our country, right or wrong,' they will even refuse to say, 'My country when it is right.'" He asked his readers to compare their condition with the plight of people in other lands where death or imprisonment awaited those who dared to defy the state. His conclusion was that just as the Apostle Paul could take pride in his citizenship in the corrupt Roman state which eventually killed him, so, too, Christians in America could rejoice in the good of their land even as they worked to rid it of the bad.[29]

---

other nations. But their chauvinism in no way vitiates true patriotism, nor does it lessen one's responsibility to love, honor and defend against her real enemies." Bell, "Thoughts About Fundamentalism," *PJ*, March 31, 1971, 13.

28. David H. Kennedy, "New Glory for Old Glory," *PJ*, July 1, 1970, 9, 22.

29. Lindsell, "Is Patriotism Dead?" *CT*, July 4, 1969, 20–21. "Patriotism is not dead; our nation is not finished. Let us rally behind our flag; let us love our country with all its faults; let us work to improve it with all our strength; let us defend it

At the same time he could ask just a few months later whether America would "soon need a new Gibbon to write *The Decline and Fall of the United States of America?*" He told his readers, "The signs of decay are not hard to find. The showy façade of affluence, technological advance, great knowledge, military might, and a high standard of living cannot hide the internal rot." His only hope was for the Christians in the nation to take up repentance. Echoing earlier calls by Henry, Lindsell declared that unless Christians in America repented of their sins, their nation would "be forced to its knees in judgment and dissolution by God." There was no confidence that the United States would be saved by its supposed special status. The great blessings America had been given could and would turn to curses if its sinful behavior continued.[30]

George Sweeting, *Moody's* new editor after the death of Culbertson, reminded his readers that America had been greatly blessed by God. "Thanksgiving is upon us—a national holiday, and American tradition, a time to count our blessings as a country and as individuals. Despite the gigantic ills of our nation and our world, we see much cause for thanksgiving these days. May we suggest, from a Christian viewpoint, some reasons for encouragement." He then described a greater readiness of Americans to hear the Christian gospel and the hope that the years-long conflict in Southeast Asia seemed to be drawing to its end. He also praised his nation's great wealth and what it meant for its people. "Despite pockets of poverty—especially in the cities and in Appalachia—Americans have more than enough to eat and enjoy a level of prosperity unparalleled elsewhere in the world." However, he also warned that the very blessings given to the US could be its undoing were its citizens to fail to respond to them properly. "But ironically our very blessings—particularly the material ones—could be our greatest stumbling block to revival. Prosperity doesn't usually mold the strongest type of Christian. One need only compare the dedication of

---

with all our resources; let us hand it on to generations unborn better than when we received it; let us instill in our children the hope of our forefathers for the ultimate fulfillment of their dreams. But above all, let us tell them that the greatness of America lies not simply in the achievement of the ideal but in the unrelenting pursuit of it."

30. Lindsell, "America on Its Knees?" *CT*, June 19, 1970, 20–21.

the average Christian in America to some of those in countries abroad where living conditions are the most severe."[31] In line with Lindsell, far from seeing America's wealth as the gift for its people's righteousness, Sweeting suggested it could be a curse.

These were not isolated cases. One writer said, "Freedom is a great word. The very sound of the word causes our blood to tingle. It is that for which the heart longs, the hands fight, the lips cry out and the soldier dies. ... We who live in America know what freedom is. But we have taken it for granted and are in danger of losing it." The author contended that in place of freedom, Americans were now living only for themselves. "It has come to mean, 'I can do as I please.' This is not freedom, this is license; license leads to anarchy and to bondage."[32] Two years later, another author leveled intense accusations against the US, saying that America had greatly benefited from having God in a central place in its life, but now it was trying to keep the "fruits of faith without the root." Needless to say, he did not think this was a viable hope. The inertia of faith might keep the nation safe, but only for a time.[33]

NIXON

By and large these commentators were approving of the administration of President Nixon, or at the very least they were willing to take a wait-and-see approach. Culbertson said that the new president faced an uphill climb. "Already flush of victory will have faded before the crush of oncoming responsibility—Vietnam, other foreign relations

---

31. George Sweeting, "Thanksgiving: More Than a Holiday," *MM*, November 1972, 20. One *MM* author said, "Throughout much of American history, Christianity has had a strong influence on the national life. Certain biblical truths, certain Christian standards, had a relatively solid hold on the populace and so, to a certain degree, righteousness was reflected in our national life." Yet, this was not the end of his analysis. "This is no longer the case. We can no longer count of a residual influence to be effective in keeping the national from moral, spiritual and civil corruption. This influence has waned virtually to the vanishing point, and in the last few decades—at an ever accelerating pace—standards of righteousness that once had broad popular acceptance in America have been spectacularly overthrown." John McCandlish Phillips, "Will The Christian Please Stand Up!" *MM*, April 1971, 20.

32. David S. Gotaas, "If You Want to Save Your Freedom," *MM*, July-August 1969, 26.

33. Oliver Price, "America There is an Absolute!" *MM*, July-August 1971, 19.

crucial decisions here at home. Though Mr. Nixon faced most of these questions in the heat and fervor of the campaign, then he had only the task of convincing voters that he knows the answers. Now he must supply solutions and make them work." He went on to give tentative praise to the President-elect, saying that Nixon "appreciates the magnitude of the responsibility he is facing" and the importance of seeking God's aid.[34] A few months later a news report in *Moody* spoke highly of the President's apparent embrace of Christian practices when discussing the Presidential Prayer Breakfast. "Mr. Nixon said that he and his administration are dedicated to faith in God and to the spiritual principles upon which the nation was established. For the first time in the history of the prayer breakfast, the entire cabinet attended; each member with his wife sat at the head table."[35] Another piece in *Moody* praised the President's attendance at a Billy Graham Crusade at the University of Tennessee. Accompanied by a photo of the smiling pair of Nixon and Graham, the author wrote,

> President Nixon shared the platform with evangelist Graham and in speaking thirteen minutes declared that "I can tell you America would not be what it is today, the greatest nation in the world, if this were not a nation which has made progress under God." The President also cited spiritual needs for young people today and exhorted them with the words, "If our young people today are going to have fulfillment beyond those material things, they must turn to those great spiritual resources that have made America the great country it is."[36]

Somewhat in contrast, *CT* readers were treated to some humor about Nixon's religiosity. "The inauguration was covered with religious trappings. Quipped Religious News Service's Elliot Wright; 'That was one of the finest church services I ever witnessed. Billy Graham prayed, Terry Cooke pronounced the benediction, and Dick Nixon preached

---

34. William Culbertson, "After the Inauguration—What?" *MM*, January 1969, 19.
35. The Editors, "President Inspired by Prayers," *MM*, May 1969, 7.
36. Hill, "Nixon Visits Graham Crusade," *MM*, July-August 1970, 12.

the sermon. Certainly, that message had the preacher's art to it.' "[37] The identification of evangelicals with one political party had not yet come into force, and evangelicals were content to offer roughly the same stance to Nixon as they had to his predecessor. They wanted to be convinced, but they were willing to be hopeful and supportive.

However, this basic support could come at times in terms of supporting an ally and not in fully identifying the administration with evangelical ideals. Henry was insistent on this point and wrote, "There is always the risk of seeming to confer approval on Nixon politics, and thus equating evangelical political action as such with a particular program which in essence—although it [illegible] the errors of leftist politics—is simply secular right, and lacks evangelical ingredients no less than its alternatives." Henry's concerns were more than the passive objection to Nixon not being an evangelical, but he had some overt theological criticisms to add. "I heard Mr. Nixon's comments to the Tennessee crusade and they were disappointing. I did not expect from him ... driving statements of a christological kind. ... But I did have every right to expect from him theistic statements of the kind our great presidents have given, and most recently Eisenhower among them." Going on, he argued that the President had given paltry remarks across the board. When the nation needed "intellectual leadership" its president was giving them "empty" remarks with little in common with emphases of evangelicalism.[38]

Ironically, given the later stereotype of evangelical political alliances, Hitt described a pro-McGovern group as the beginnings of overt political involvement by evangelicals as such. He admitted that evangelicals were "like the rest of the country" solidly behind Nixon, but this was the first time to his knowledge that evangelicals had explicitly organized behind a given Presidential candidate. He suggested that it was in reaction to this pro-McGovern move that evangelical luminary Harold Ockenga called for others to stand with him in support of Nixon. While

37. Richard N. Ostling, "Inauguration Amid Religious Trappings," *CT*, February 14, 1969, 30.

38. Henry, Letter to Billy Graham, August 1, 1970, Box 1970 3, File Correspondence, Graham, Billy, Carl F. H. Henry Collection. The illegible word is possibly "avoid."

Hitt offered general, non-partisan support for evangelical actions in the political realm, he was squeamish about having evangelicalism become connected to either party. He had some qualms about being too connected to Nixon in general and, as he put it, the "unanswered questions of Watergate," but had hope that the President would prove worthy of the trust that many evangelicals had placed in him. In what would sound naïve in retrospect, he placed his hope in Nixon's friendship with Graham and the fact that he had been raised in a Quaker home.[39]

WATERGATE

Early reactions to Watergate had less criticism for President Nixon, as such, than they did for the entire edifice of American politics. Taylor took the opportunity to attack his more liberal-leaning fellow Presbyterians. He pointed out that President Nixon and his assistants had done a wrong thing because they thought it was in service of a good cause. "No one has suggested that the leaders of Watergate did their deed for money. It was rather that they were so convinced that they were right that they felt anything could be done to guarantee the success of it." Taylor then suggested that this was hypocritical as this was the very same sort of logic put forward by many mainline denominational leaders who called for left-wing political militancy by church members.[40]

Specific condemnation for Watergate did come, but it often included a general complaint about the state of the nation rather than being focused on the President alone. After a poll indicated that most citizens found the scandal to be nothing more than politics as usual, Hitt argued that this was in fact something worth getting upset about. "Nobody denies that 'everybody does it.' What we have to face up to is that when corruption goes unchecked, its effects on a people are ruinous. That's why a society makes laws—to catch at least some of the 'everybodies' that threaten its very survival." As to the particular scandal, he said, "Well, it matters to citizens who counted on the Nixon administration to deal with crime in the streets and to restore integrity and responsiveness to government. It matters to the original defendants in the

---

39. Hitt, "Politics," *ET*, January 1973, 7.
40. Taylor, "See 'Watergate,' " *PJ*, June 6, 1973, 24.

Watergate trial whose lives are ruined and who were being made to bear
the full blame for a crime directed by some of the highest authorities
of the land." [41] Another author had even darker words. "Watergate. The
name has become odious. It conveys a one-dimensional political and
social view of the world, and naked use of power to enforce this view.
Now we face our greatest constitutional and moral crisis. We must deal
with the brute fact of national sins and national judgments. What conditions and values allowed this noxious political cancer to grow?" Yet,
even this author did not relegate his accusation simply to Nixon and
his fellows but enlarged it to the moral failing of the entire nation. "In
this value vacuum Americans have erected another god, the myth of an
all-knowing, all-righteous, all-powerful presidency."[42] The corruption
in Washington was simply further proof for evangelicals' longstanding
distrust of the growing power of the state.

　　Thus, for some the crisis merely highlighted the failings of any absolute trust in government. A former political operative had this to say in
the wake of Watergate: "Whenever we give any aspect of national life a
quasi-divine status we lose perspective. We forget that all our institutions are simply creatures of our own making and that sooner or later
they will reflect our own limitations."[43] One evangelical commentator
echoed Henry's early 1950s radio commentary as he condemned civil
religion as unchristian and woefully inadequate. Speaking about the
politically sponsored prayer breakfasts and enshrining of religious
language from the Eisenhower era, he described it in terms closer to
mainline ecumenism than his own evangelicalism.

　　Doesn't this promote religion? And isn't the promotion of religion
　　good? The answer is "No"—not from the viewpoint of concerned

---

　　41. Hitt, "Does Corruption Matter," June 1973, *ET*, 8. Interestingly enough, while
some evangelicals were not quite sure how they should react to Watergate politically,
some enterprising evangelicals found a way to react economically. The publisher
for *Baker's Dictionary of Christian Ethics*, edited by Carl Henry, placed an ad with the
title, "As Up-To-Date as Watergate!" Baker Book House-Publishers, "Advertisement,"
ET, November 1973, 62.

　　42. Calvin S. Malefyt, "Watergate: A Question of Values," *ET*, July 1973, 6–8.

　　43. Wallace B. Henley, "The Danger of Messianic Politics," *ET*, September
1973, 25.

Christians. For this is civil religion. It is not biblical religion at all. ... The god of this religion is, as must be the case for national purposes, a least-common denominator god—a god acceptable to all the people. That god is never defined in ways that fit the portrait of the biblical God. Rather, the definition is crafted to maximize social and political unity. Harmony of diverse people, not truth, is its end.[44]

At least in 1973, it was not enough for evangelicals to create a coalition of like-minded people for the good of the nation. The truth of Christianity trumped any moral reforms founded on mere religiosity.

God's Country

Another writer challenged preconceptions when he asked whether much of the despair felt by Christians in America was misplaced. He wondered if they found present conditions so very bad because they had an inflated view of the righteousness of the past. "Some Christians wonder today if America may be on the verge of *returning* to God. The thought implies that our nation's [sic] once swarmed with devout, Godly people. But I believe the past was at times more like the present than one might think. We face today not an altogether new experience in American life." He then went through a series of parallels between cultural traits which were mourned in his day but were also common in the past such as Americans' propensity to geographic mobility, aversion to institutions, movement away from biblical Christianity, the breakdown of families, and general alienation. He did not think any of these things were good, but he did suggest that their ubiquity in the past could give Americans perspective on their own flawed history.[45]

---

44. Walfred Peterson, "The Case Against Civil Religion," *ET*, October 1973, 23.

45. Howard Whaley, "The America of Today and Yesteryear," *MM*, July-August 1972, 34. Working in the same general theme, Hitt highlighted the rising crime rate as something his readers should be concerned with, but he did more than merely mourn that times were hard. He called upon his evangelical readers to take constructive steps not merely to stop crime but to keep those either likely to become criminals or those who had already crossed that line. "Since one out of every six teenage boys will be referred to a juvenile court before they are 18, the church faces a tremendous challenge. Yet, youth groups are seldom geared to

Similarly, a minister writing in *ET* challenged his readers to ask themselves how much they had conflated their Americanism with Christianity. "Are the principles of the American way of life necessarily Christian? Even to raise this question may seem like heresy. But, in fact, there are certain emphases of the American way of life today that conflict with Christian teaching." Among these points were the absolute devotion to democracy as an end in itself, the selfish results of American individualism, an obsession with freedom without the corresponding emphasis on responsibility, and an acceptance of the legitimacy of the profit motive in business coupled with a lack of generosity with accumulated wealth. Added to these was a critique of any sort of Christian nationalism. "Perhaps the most glaring heresy is the idea that America is special in the eyes of God, that our nation and the kingdom of God are one and the same. ... Patriotism has become more than just loyalty to country; it is religion. To be unpatriotic is almost the same as being atheistic. If we don't see America's enemies as God's

interest potential delinquents, and when disruptive young people drop out of the church, youth leaders often breathe a sigh of relief." With a direct challenge to his often-conservative readers, he asked, "If you are a citizen who has bemoaned the rising crime rate, complained about the Supreme Court decisions and supported the present administration in its campaign promise to do something about the rapidly spreading crime epidemic, what are you going to do about the situation?" Hitt, "Crime: What Are You Doing About It?" *ET*, March 1969, 9. He later wondered whether the US had a predilection towards violence. "If violence is a world-wide problem, it is also, in a very real sense, an American problem. Totalitarian countries use violence as an ideological weapon, but in America violence is part and parcel of the national psyche." Then, alluding to the work of Arthur Schlesinger Jr.'s work, he said that as much as Americans like to see themselves as advocates of law and order, there are parts to their history that they would rather pretend never happened. "In the beginning of our history, as a people, we killed red men and enslaved black men. The fact that we did this with the Bible in our hand hardly mitigates but rather compounds the enormity of our offense. One might wonder, with some justification, whether this initial experience did not fix a primal curse on this nation." Hitt, "Why Do We Have a Propensity for Violence?" *ET*, September 1969, 10. A few months later, in response to a new spate of statistics describing America's continued slide into violence, he added, "In the past we have expected God to bless our nation because of our goodness, because we were God-fearing people, because the biblical ethic was nationally acclaimed. Maybe now we should seek God's face humbly, without our characteristic America pride, maybe now we should seek God's mercy instead of His smile of approval." Hitt, "Our Epidemic of Violence: Is There A Cure?" *ET*, January 1970, 11.

enemies, we are unpatriotic." His goal was not to inculcate the opposite error, to conflate anti-Americanism with Christianity, but to offer
support where support was warranted and condemnation when that
was needed. Insisting that "the American way of life emphasizes some
aspects of Christian truth, but only some," he challenged Christians to
"stand against such selective perversion" and remember the difference
between their American and divine citizenships.[46]

---

46. George A. Harcus, "Some Very American Heresies," ET, July 1970, 12-13.
In an unusual move the editors at ET decided to print a previously unpublished
article on China by the magazine's late editor, Donald Barnhouse. He had written
it in 1959 around the same time as he had named Mao as "Man of the Year." At
that time the response from readers was so very negative that, despite Barnhouse
offering numerous strong criticisms of the chairman, he and the other editors
thought it prudent to withhold anything which might elicit a similar response.
In their summary before the article itself, the editors wrote, "In the mood of the
times, the present editors felt that the second editorial would accomplish nothing,
and so exercised a 'pocket veto' on it, stashing it away in our China file. Last month,
when we blew the dust off our China file, we discovered that the old Barnhouse
editorial was still there, and just as relevant (and as controversial) as it was 12 years
ago." In this piece which was mostly about China, Barnhouse put forward some
fairly substantial criticisms of his own nation. "We love our country. Along with
most other Americans, we personally abhor the ruthlessness of Communism. We
believe that our administration in Washington is seeking honestly and truly to
preserve our national interests as best it can. But we are not convinced that we are
being honest with *ourselves*. We fear our attitude of nationalistic pride is leading
us to eventual destruction." For those who saw no disjunction between American
foreign policy and Christian missionary interests, he had some challenging words.
"Furthermore, these men of Africa and Asia are the men we are trying to win to
Christ. We tell them that Christ loves them and that they need to know His love. But
they see this offer coming from a warmongering nation. Not only that, but we are
aligned with nations which have for generations held these emerging nations in
colonial subjugation. Consequently, when we offer them love and peace in Christ,
they don't believe us. Should they? Have we as Christians raised our voices in the
midst of this involved issue on the side of righteousness?" In the end he broke with
most of his fellow evangelical pundits by calling for the US to recognize the Mao
regime, arguing that there was greater opportunity for a good end through communicating with Beijing than through the then-current plan of isolating China. "Our
policy of brinksmanship and hatred (deserved though the latter may be, humanly
speaking) can never bring us to anything but destruction. Understanding may find
a minimum of common ground. We can choose our course, but we must accept the
responsibility for the results no matter which course we take." The Editors and
Barnhouse, "Should We Acknowledge Red China?" ET, September 1971, 6, 9. Italics
and parentheses in original.

THE DEATH OF THE INNOCENT

Abortion began to rise in importance as the focus of evangelical concern in the years before Roe vs. Wade. It was not the beginning of their disdain for American morality, but it brought a new urgency to their nascent political action. A contributor to *ET* compared the present US culture's disdain for children with the biblical example of pharaoh's murderous tyranny and the recent historical reality of Nazi genocide. When a contributor for *Atlantic* wrote that she hoped people with more than two children would soon be seen as being as in bad taste as "wearing mink in a starving village," Bayly said, "Pharaoh in Egypt and Hitler in Germany had more advanced persuaders to achieve population control. I know that we couldn't conceive of our present or future good American rulers using such means. Or could we? Is the American human less corrupt than his ancient Egyptian or recent German counterpart?" He then suggested the US was following the same pattern of childrearing set by the Soviets and would likely soon follow that set by the Nazis when it came to use genetic engineering to weed out those considered defective.[47]

Henry made a similar historical analogy about abortion. He wrote that while the Romans left unwanted children in trash dumps, "today in sophisticated America, many clergymen and others routinely approve of the destruction of life by abortion. Are these modern exponents of abortion-on-request any less barbaric than their Roman counterparts?" When a mainline denominations argued that the right response to abortion was to liberalize the pertinent laws, Henry replied, "To blame the stringency of existing laws for the increased incidence of abortions is much like blaming the principle of monogamous marriage for the rise of adultery." Henry allowed for some times when abortion might be a morally permissible action, such as to save the life of the mother, but the thrust of his arguments was to see the nascent pro-life movement as being about Christian love and mercy for the disadvantaged. "The right of weak and the helpless to protection and mercy has always been a distinctive emphasis of Christian morality; reverence for

---

47. Bayly, "God or Caesar? Caesar is Posing New Threats," *ET*, May 1970, 39.

life even at its despised frontiers and not merely at its most cherished horizons was an apostolic virtue."[48]

AMERICA'S PECULIAR INSTITUTIONAL SIN

Even with the progress made in previous years regarding race relations, there was still much to criticize. Lindsell praised the Supreme Court's decision to push states to speed up desegregation even as he mourned the need for such measures, noting that many areas had been trying to desegregate but would not be inconvenienced by the haste. This inconvenience, he noted, did not outweigh pains of African Americans who had waited long enough.[49] Later, he pointed to the recent time two African American college students had been arrested, fined, and sentenced to a month in jail for trying to enter a church in South Carolina. When the church denied that their race was the basis for obstructing their entrance but only for the risk of an "emotional disturbance," Lindsell retorted, "However, one senses the fear of an

---

48. Henry, "Is Life Ever Cheap?" *ET*, February 1971, 20-21. One writer tied the abortion debate into current issues of war crimes, connecting fetal deaths to the Vietnamese killed in American massacres. "Another dubious plea used by pro-abortionists is that every child should be a wanted child. But this argument assumes that the value of a human life is subjective. The child's value depends upon his parents' emotional reaction to him; it has no objective value of itself. This is My Lai morality." In place of this sort of thinking, she called for a return to biblical morality. "Acceptance of abortion is nothing less than a complete discarding of the whole Judeo-Christian belief—deeply ingrained into Western law, medicine, and culture—that life is inherently sacred and that it is the responsibility of the strong to protect the weak. In contrast the new ethic means that life is to be determined on a scale of social desirability." Joan K. Ostling, "Abortion: Time for a Hard, New Look," *ET*, May 1972, 19. When Roe vs. Wade finally came down in favor of a more liberal abortion precedent, the reaction of these commentators was understandably negative, even if at first there was some confusion as to how best to respond. Hitt tried to find some daylight between the position at *CT*, which he described as being "black-and-white," and the Court's decision, which he termed "strictly humanistic." He acknowledged that there was a precedent in Western jurisprudence for appealing to privacy from government interference, but he worried about the implications of such a trend. "One cannot help but wonder, if the overriding principle of all future judicial actions is to be that good government stays out of its citizens' 'private' lives, whether legalized homosexuality, marijuana, pornography, wide-open gambling and prostitution is just around the corner." Hitt, "The Abortion Ruling: Christian Citizen's Dilemma," *ET*, April 1973, 15-16.

49. Lindsell, "Speeding Up Desegregation," *CT*, November 21, 1969, 27.

'emotional disturbance' was not totally unrelated to the fact that the two students happened to have black skin." He then noted that the two students were released on appeal and even allowed to attend the church services. Lindsell concluded with a challenge. "In many churches the barrier of race has been broken down, and this is honoring to God. But as incidents like these—and the attitudes that lurk behind them—are allowed to continue, the Gospel of Christ is blasphemed."[50] America's tolerance of racism was not an abstract political of indifference. It dealt with core truths of Christianity itself.

A contributor to *ET* offered readers a satirical argument concerning the role of race in American society. He asked what they would think were the racial breakdown of US society reversed, with a majority

---

50. Lindsell, "A Cordial Welcome—If You're White," *CT*, February 27, 1970, 28. Taylor also spoke of such matters, but he took a rather different tone. He wrote of the attempts of an African American man to attend various Presbyterian churches in St. Louis and also of another African man who disrupted another worship service at a retreat center in North Carolina. His description of the first was almost entirely negative, noting that he was known "as a leader of the militants" and had a criminal record prior to these actions. The other man came across in Taylor's description as something of a hero who interrupted the service not because of segregation but because he found the youth-oriented service to be "psychedelic" rather than Christian. Speaking of the latter man, Taylor wrote, "Maybe seizing the microphone from the majority in control is not such a bad idea after all. It's a sort of insanity, we believe, that has swept over the high echelons of the Church in our time. Even the simplest souls with the most untried faith can see it." Taylor, "Two Black Men Went to Montreat," *PJ*, August 27, 1969, 13. He later praised a group of African American pastors who had taken up the theologically conservative line in denominational debates. "It frequently is charged that the root of the difference between 'liberal' and 'conservative' in the Church is *race*, that conservatives simply are reactionaries in racial matters. That myth was pretty effectively exploded during the recent Montreat, NC, conference season. In more than one instance powerful and dramatic pitches were made on behalf of evangelical Christianity and against pagan liberalism *by black men*." Taylor, "It's a Sort of Insanity," *PJ*, September 10, 1969, 12. Italics in original. Bell, too, offered complaints about the sufferings of African Americans. However, as might be expected from his previous comments, his ire was directed at those who would push for social change too fast and too far. Speaking of those in duress and their victimizers, he said, "These are all the victims of a selfish, vicious, even crazed minority—white and black who either for self-interest, willful delusion or calculated determination to destroy society, engage in any and all kinds of disruptive and destructive activities." He then reported that several African American pastors said they feared for their lives if they spoke out against those Bell termed "militants." Bell, "The Forgotten Ones," *PJ*, July 16, 1969, 13.

African American and minority Anglo populations, with "all the concomitants would be present, including a history of second-rate education of white people, edge-of-poverty living conditions, a lot of public assistance for whites." The bulk of his critique fell at the feet of his fellow evangelicals, but his overall goal was to have his readers see what he argued were hypocrisies and insufficiencies in their treatment of their fellow human beings.[51] A few months later the same writer pointed to American Christians' inconsistency. He argued that while they were generous to Africans in Africa, Americans did little for African Americans.[52] Another ET author pointed out that Americans in his day wondered how German Christians could have tolerated the Nazis, but they seldom asked how their "good Christian forefathers" could have brutally enslaved millions of African Americans.[53]

Schaeffer had been a longtime advocate of racial reconciliation, and he had hope for the future of the American situation given the progress of the previous years. "I have seen white evangelicals sit up and clap their heads off when black evangelicals get up to talk at conference times. How they clap! I must say that's an improvement, because six years ago they would not have been clapping at all." However, even his praise was couched with a sharp question. "But I want to ask you something if you are white. In the past year how many blacks have you fed at your table? How many blacks have felt at home in your home? ... And if you are a black Christian, it cuts equally the other way: how many whites have you invited to your home in the last year? How many have eaten at your table?"[54] Formal rejection of racism was one thing; moving

---

51. Bayly, "If Whites Were Blacks and ..., "ET, February 1969, 43. Ellipsis in title in original.

52. Bayly, "Resolutions, But Never Any Revolutions," ET, July 1969, 5. A news blurb in MM highlighted the role played by Billy Graham in promoting racial equality even outside the US. When he was headed to South Africa for one of his Crusades, he had arranged that these events would be completely integrated, leading to "the largest multi-racial crowd ever assembled in South Africa—almost doubled the attendance record for the sports arena where the services were held." Kay Oliver, "Graham Meetings Challenge Apartheid," MM, June 1973, 9.

53. James W. English, "Could Racism Be Hereditary ... ?" ET, September 1970, 21. Ellipses in title in original.

54. Schaeffer, "Christian Compassion: Have We Lost Our Touch?" ET, December 1970, 17. According to a short note accompanying the article, this piece was reprinted

forward to the place of seeing other races as fellow image bearers of
God and brothers and sisters in Christ was quite another.

Regarding the United States, these evangelicals seemed to position
themselves at the tipping point between the strong patriotism of the
likes of Carl McIntire and the strong national skepticism of the mainline denominations. Given their concurrent support of the US and
explicit rejection of what would later be called governmental theism,
this seems to have been more than a pretense of moderation to cover
an ulterior nationalism. They did not hold to "My country, right or
wrong," but they also stood apart from Lindsell's caricature of refusing
to say "My country, when it is right." As noted above this likely flowed
from their understanding of America as a deeply flawed nation that
was yet far better than its Communist rivals. Many of these writers
were quite willing to express their love for their native land even as
they chronicled what they saw as its ever-deeper slide into moral obliv-
ion. For example, Lindsell could bewail the lessening patriotism of his
fellow Americans even as he condemned them for their acceptance of
grave sins.

WAR

HUMANITY'S ENDURING PROBLEM

"For two generations statesmen have been dangling before a war-weary
world the slogans of 'warless world,' 'a just and durable peace,' 'peace
in our time,' and other phrases calculated to bring a sense of hope and
promised security. As we face the year 1971 we are confronted with
two conflicting ideologies, vying one with the other, for world power
and control."[55] These words by Bell showed the weariness of the time.

---

from Schaeffer's book, *The Church at the End of the 20th Century*.

55. Bell, "Peace in 1971," *PJ*, December 30, 1970, 13. His overall point here was
not really about geopolitics but about faith. Humanity's efforts led to the constant
tension and conflict which he had described, but Christ offered true peace despite
the failures of the world. Two issues later he took up the same theme, saying, "The
possibility of war looms before us. Shall we pray for peace and stop there? It is
our conviction that such prayers will be answered only in so far as we confess our
personal and national sins, repent of those sins, and, by the grace and supernatural
power of the indwelling Christ in our hearts, turn from our evil ways. Only in that

Despite decades of promises of peace being around the corner, the world was as on edge as the 1960s ended as it had been a generation earlier.

The 1972 Munich Olympic Games, which had been held out as a symbol of a peaceful world that could be, turned instead into an example of the continuing contentiousness of human nature in general as well as the manifestation of a particular enduring conflict. In a preview of what would dominate much thinking about war in years to come, Middle Eastern tensions broke into the Western consciousness as hostages were killed in a European city.[56] In reaction to this tragedy, Sweeting pointed to the horrible irony of it all, suggesting that peace might be the stated goal of all humanity, but the very nature of humanity makes any such endeavor futile without the participation of God. "The Olympic games closed in Munich, Germany surrounded by police and under an artificial rainbow which was intended to symbolize peace and understanding among nations. The Olympics symbolize man's best efforts for peace, and yet Munich 1972 was tragically scarred by the murder of eleven Israeli sportsmen and five Arab civilians." He then looked to another time in Munich's recent past when peace was proclaimed, this time by Neville Chamberlain on the eve of history's greatest war, and argued that the peace efforts of 1939, 1972, or any other time were built on far too shallow ground. "Today our world is desperately shouting 'peace, peace' when there is no peace. Man's best efforts, like Chamberlain's are artificial and false." God truly wanted "peace, good will toward men," but this peace could only come by the conversion of people to Christianity and the power of Jesus working in society.[57]

---

way is there real peace. Peace with God. The peace of God in our hearts. Peace with our fellow man." Bell, "Praying for Peace," *PJ*, January 13, 1971, 13.

56. Admittedly, the motivations of early twenty-first century groups like Al-Qaeda and ISIS are far more omnivorous than the relatively narrow goals of the Munich attackers. Yet, this was one of the first of an increasing series of attacks which shared similar goals with those which would a generation later be the focus of American foreign policy actions as well as evangelical concern.

57. Sweeting, "Peace for All Time," *MM*, November 1972, 5.

ENDLESS WAR

Vietnam was heading toward its denouement as the new policy of "Vietnamization" took effect. However, the intense suffering, both American and Southeast Asian, with no end in sight was looking more and more pointless to more and more people. For some the pain was real, but the goal was worth it. For others, the pain was too real for any goal to be worth the continued bloodshed.

As the death toll mounted in the ever-lengthening war, Lindsell mourned the losses and the numbness that seemed to go along with it. He said that even with 30,000 US dead, most Americans were now too calloused to such news, even if it made the news. The one exception to this, he noted, were those to whom the dead were not strangers but friends and family. After expressing his grief for those left behind, he suggested a pathway for those not directly affected, calling on the rest of the nation and church to "show the love of Christ to those whose lives have been touch by the terror of war."[58] Regarding the length of the conflict, Lindsell was later to offer some cover to the recently-former President Johnson, saying that people should cut him some slack. He could only act on the information he received, and no one could have expected the Communists to keep fighting as long as they did.[59]

One pastor writing in *Moody* spoke of the intrinsic sadness of war as manifested in Vietnam. After a trip to a military hospital containing thousands of US casualties, he cried, "Never, however, have I been so moved, so filled with compassion, as at the sight of this mass of suffering humanity." Yet, this suffering did not dissuade him from supporting the American involvement. The destruction, however bad, was worth the cost, an opinion he claimed to share in common with every soldier he met. "America may be confused; other nations may have little idea of why we are in Vietnam, but let me say that I did not find one soldier, from the ranks of generals, nor did I find a single chaplain or missionary, who was not solidly convinced of our enemy and our cause."[60] Hitt's view of the ongoing war in Vietnam was more

---

58. Lindsell, "30,000 Dead," *CT*, January 3, 1969, 21.
59. Lindsell, "Farewell to Mr. Johnson," *CT*, January 31, 1969, 26.
60. Olford, "A Communist War," *MM*, February 1969, 20, 22.

dour. After a litany of things gone wrong in the previous year, he stated that even with the de-escalation enacted by President Nixon, there was every indication that large numbers of American forces would remain in-theater indefinitely.[61]

---

61. Hitt, "Hope for the '70s," ET, January 1971, 6. There were several comments which did not directly address the war in Vietnam specifically but did deal with implications of being a nation at war and what wars like this were doing to the nation. A contributor wrote a lengthy piece for MM describing his feelings as his son had just taken off for duty in Vietnam. This article was more pastoral than didactic, as this was more an exploration of the feelings and spiritual ponderings of a father than the polemic of a pundit. "Our son left for military service in Vietnam today. His plane was due out of San Francisco less than thirty minutes ago ... the big military transport will jet toward Anchorage, then on to Tokyo, to Okinawa and finally—approximately twenty-four hours from now—the pilot will touch down at Saigon." He had mixed feelings about how he wanted his neighbors to react. "The last thing any of us wants ... is for people to make a big noise about our son's going to Vietnam. Even so, I find myself waiting for just one person to say, 'I hear your son's been called for duty in Vietnam. Sure sorry to hear that.' Or, better, for a warm hand to clasp mine as someone says, 'We're joining you in prayer for that boy.' It never happened. Not once." If there was any message in this article, it was simply for the families of those sent off to war to put their trust in God in their time of fear. Ken Anderson, "My Son Went to Vietnam," MM, October 1969, 48. This was in keeping with MM's emphasis a generation earlier on caring for the families of the armed forces as well as for the service members themselves. One piece from November 1969 highlighted the work of "Christian servicemen centers." The author pointed to the way these centers could act as moral supports for soldiers and sailors away from home as well as become vehicles for evangelism. William Needham, "On Duty for Christ," MM, November 1969, 32-33. Another article in that same issue praised the Christian faith of General William Harrison, arguing that it was his regular Bible reading which enabled him to face down the Communists at the Panmunjom negotiating tables. Tom Watson Jr., "Three-Star General Under Higher Orders," MM, November 1969, 34. Three years later MM printed a similar article praising another US officer, this time General Ralph Haines who had served in Vietnam. The author quoted him as saying, "I am proud to be a general in the United States Army, but I am prouder to be a private in the Lord's army." Wesley G. Pippert, "The Four-Star General Who Calls Men to the Lord," MM, November 1972, 22. While it was not exactly a pacifist article, one piece in ET suggested that a militarism had crept into American culture. Speaking of a group of small boys playing war, he said, "They had all the needed weapons—machine guns, pistols, hand grenades, war helmets and war uniforms. These boys knew how to stab the vitals of the enemy and how to react and fall dead when hit. They were instilled with the spirit of war. And they learned to delight in the game of killing." He then described some of the games marketed to American boys, such as one which the "players wage war for world domination" through a nuclear contest with cards denoting the megaton levels of their bombs. "Doesn't it seem strange that we talk

For one writer, the infamous My Lai Massacre of 1968 became the paradigm of problems with the Vietnam War. He said that the "Calley Affair," so-named for the American officer who oversaw the operation, "brought a vast number of issues to the surface." While he did not document any particular incident, he claimed that this event spoke to "the alleged frequency" of massacres by American troops. Further, he argued that this event called into question everything from the legality of the US involvement, the wisdom of its tactics, and the frustrations of combat in Vietnam, to the morality of its napalm and saturation bombing and the training of US forces which could allow troops to obey orders to fire on unarmed civilians.[62]

A writer in *Presbyterian Journal* took something of a broader view of the massacre, taking this tragedy as a symptom of a general human problem. "If the people of the world were good, wars wouldn't happen. North Vietnam would not have invaded South Vietnam. America would not have a commitment to protect South Vietnam. The Viet Cong would not have murdered thousands of South Vietnamese villagers." When speaking of My Lai itself, he saw it as the result of humanity's flawed nature. When he described Communist evil actions, he did so in terms of what they actively did and, in contrast, wrote of Calley passively, in terms of the position he was in. While this did distance Lt. Calley from any active guilt for the massacre, as the author emphasized the general horror of war, he did end the article by grouping Calley and the infamous Manson Family among those capable of receiving, and therefore requiring, the grace of God.[63]

Lindsell also looked to the message of Christianity for hope in reaction to this tragedy, but he focused on Calley's willful participation in this horror directly. While he admitted there might be something to

---

of peace while we pile war toys high in nearly all our stores?—that we claim to follow the Prince of Peace and yet scatter 'kill toys' over the living room floor at Christmas? What does it mean to teach children in church 'Thou shall not kill' and 'love others' while we buy toys which put them through all the paces of war?" John Drescher, "Is This How to Teach the Christmas Message?" *ET*, December 1969, 20–21.

62. Henry Stob, "Calley Affair," *ET*, January 1972, 13, 54.

63. Ed Ross, "The Real Lesson of the Calley Trial," *PJ*, May 19, 1971, 13, 19. An accompanying note indicates that this piece was originally from the periodical *For Real*.

the argument that Calley was a scapegoat and that civilians had been used in the past to kill American forces, he did not let this excuse the officer. "The conclusion that Calley is guilty as charged, as would be any others who ordered him to do what he did, seems unavoidable. But war is a brutal and dehumanizing business, and Calley appears to have been unable to rise above a sordid situation. We hope that justice will be tempered with mercy for this one whom we cannot admire."[64] Circumstances, no matter how terrible, were never enough to justify what this American officer had done.

A guest editorialist in *Presbyterian Journal* wanted his readers to see no war had ever been as clean as Vietnam protesters demanded that the conflict be. Rather than the pro-war camp being Manichean, he argued that it was the opponents of the conflict who were seeing things too starkly in black and white. Critics of the war were acting as though any war in history had been morally untainted. This was something which he found ridiculous. "But we need only transport ourselves backward to the moment of involvement to see that America has never fought an unambiguous war. If we want a clean war, that is, an unambiguous one, we shall not find one in time, and if only those are truly heroic who give themselves to a clean war, there are no heroes on this side of heaven." To those who accused US forces of being immoral to a unique degree, he said, "If there is all this grayness about human actions, how do we know that the grave we decorate with flowers does not belong to someone who died for a fuzzy cause? We don't know and we won't know. We do know, however that the keepers of peace died in devotion to a community which has enlisted their allegiance."[65] Another writer pushed back against conscientious objectors by suggesting that simply avoiding active participation in a war did not make someone guiltless of the killing. If the troops "over there" were guilty, then so were those back home, even if they did not participate themselves.[66]

64. Lindsell, "The Calley Verdict," CT, April 23, 1971, 27.
65. Karl A. Olsson, "We Remember Brave Men," PJ, July 2, 1969, 12. Accompanying the article is a note indicating "From an article by Karl A. Olsson, syndicated by Associated Church Press."
66. Klahr Raney, "Of War and Such," PJ, September 30, 1970, 10. There is a note attached indicating that this was originally published in *The Cumberland*

Peace with Honor?

As the American involvement in the Vietnam War ended, there were some mixed feelings about what might come next. Lindsell was concerned at the President's plan to withdraw US forces, but he seemed content to see it as the best option. "For good or ill we are left with what the President has decided to do and has the responsibility to do under the Constitution." With ambiguous words he urged his readers to back the President. "Whether or not Mr. Nixon's decision is the ideal one, we think that the welfare of the nation will best be served if its people rally behind him and give his plan a bit more time to succeed." He then noted that if his plan did not work as planned, then the results of the 1972 election would surely work against him.[67] In 1971 Lindsell continued this hesitant support of the President's plan. "More and more it appears that Mr. Nixon's Vietnamization program, though far from ideal, is the best of the available alternatives. Perhaps this move toward establishing diplomatic relations with [China] will do more to bring an end to the war than anything done in Paris so far." In the same article he overtly called for as early an end to the war as was practically possible, hoping that US forces could withdraw in peace with South Vietnam strong enough to endure on its own.[68]

One writer saw the tentative peace of 1973 as a new hope for the region with missionaries being able to return to their work. Most interestingly, he betrayed little expectation that the end of the war meant defeat for America.[69] Similarly, Taylor spoke of the ceasefire in a broadly positive manner. "The time has come for restrained rejoicing and profound thanksgiving that the agonizing struggle in Vietnam seems halted. At such a time, the nation's gratitude is extended to those who have made possible the potential of a peace with honor." He then praised an unnamed past US president, presumably Johnson or even Kennedy, who resolved to take a stand against Communism in Southeast Asia and the also unnamed but current president, Nixon, "for never

---

Presbyterian, although no further citation is given.

67. Lindsell, "The President's Viet Nam Policy," *CT*, November 21, 1969, 25.

68. Lindsell, "Viet Nam—Continuing Impasse," *CT*, August 6, 1971, 25.

69. Ted W. Engstrom, "A New Wind Blowing in Vietnam: Missions, Servant to a Growing Church," *MM*, February 1973, 24.

wavering in his purpose." Then he gave thanks to "those hundreds of thousands of young Americans, who performed their distasteful duty with courage, honor and integrity, despite the discouraging effects of the swelling tide of subversion at home, where a campaign of lies produced a faltering effort and even corrupted the original high purpose for which many died."[70] Somewhat unexpectedly, this was no wail for a war ending in defeat, but a sigh of relief that a battle had been won, if only just barely. It might not have been a clear-cut victory along the lines of World War II, but neither had Korea ended with parades. After nearly a decade of war far away from home, many American evangelicals were content with this passive peace without victory.

END TIMES

FADING HOPE

As the human race continued to endure despite regular evangelical expectations to the contrary, commentators worked to help their readers understand a world that rambled on, even as it seemed to teeter ever closer to the edge. Henry offered a dark judgment of his era, saying, "We live in the twilight of a great civilization, amid the deepening decline of modern culture. Those strange beast-empires of the books of Daniel and Revelation seem already to be stalking and sprawling over the surface of the earth. Only the experimental success of modern science hides from us the dread terminal illness of our increasingly technological civilization." While he was not making an overt connection between his day and the last days, he found the literary resonance evocative. He noted that worry about humanity's final act was no longer solely in the possession of wild-eyed prophets. "The warnings of where this is leading are voiced by secular scholars and echoed by the secular media. ... The end-of-the-world theme is not a concern only of sidewalkmen [sic] with unpalatable sandwich boards, nor of evangelists' reminders of an apocalyptic finale of history." Then, citing the work of Harvard professors, he said the likelihood of a world-ending catastrophe was dangerously high. "We are talking here of the destruction of the human

---

70. Taylor, "In the Wake of the Cease Fire," *PJ*, February 7, 1973, 12.

race by human violence." His appeal was not for his readers to fall into despair, but to take up the task put to them in the Bible. "In the twilight traffic snarl of a great civilization, the Church needs as ever before to be a light to the world and to shelter the moral fortunes of human history from crippling collision [sic]. ... The barbarians are coming; the Lord Jesus Christ is coming; let the Church that is here come *now*, with good news, with the only durable good news, and come in time!"[71] Here was

---

71. Henry, "What's Next?" *ET*, January 1970. 13-15, 48-50. Italics in original. As is clear from the context of the article, the "barbarians" he speaks of here were not outsiders coming in to crush Western civilization but a revival of what he called "pagan man," Westerners who had lost their genuine Christianity. After a fashion he did not blame the "barbarians." He wrote, "Institutional Christianity has dropped the last barricade to the return of the pagan man; preoccupied with the changing of social structures, it muffles the call for a new humanity, and in doing so forfeits a mighty spiritual opportunity to be at the crossroads of modern history. The organized Church that ought to have been burdened for the evangelization of the earth has been too busy either powdering her nose to preserve an attractive public image, or powdering the revolutionaries and reactionaries who need rather to be remade in Christ's image." Henry was later to declare that the world had reached the last days, but this pronouncement bore less significance than it might at first appear. By his title "We Are in the Last Days," Henry meant not that current events proved that the end was nigh but that all of human history since the time of Christ was the last days. "The tension between the present and the future is altered; no longer does it presuppose that the historical redemptive revelation decisive for all human destiny is still to occur. ... The prophetic timeclock thereby strikes a new age and moves salvation-history forward to a new and critically central stage." Instead of advocating that Christians wait until the signs were finally in place, he encouraged his readers to consider that "then" was in fact "now." As he put it, "The scales of prophecy are no longer imbalanced by predictions awaiting future fulfillment, by anticipations as yet unfulfilled. The 'not yet' has been so crowded by the 'already' that the New Testament events forge the turning-point for a prescribed outcome." Henry, "We Are in the Last Days," *ET*, July 1971, 9, 11. At the same time, he did hold that there was a great climax yet to appear on the historical stage. In a follow-up article the next month, he wrote, "What has already transpired ... does not diminish one bit the importance of the coming future, for the fullest manifestation of the Kingdom of God awaits Jesus' return. All that has gone before, and all that now already is, stands correlated with and inseparable from the remarkable events of world scope that are yet to come in conjunction with Jesus' return." He put the Christian's hope for the future not in contemporary prognostications but in the abiding testimony of the Bible. "Our world and every last man in it has been placed on emergency alert; the coming Judge of our race is at hand, and soon all eyes shall behold the sent Son of God. While we no more know the precise instant than did the Apostle Paul, we also know no less." Henry, "His Coming Draws Near," *ET*, August 1971, 23-25.

no hope of a great victory of godly Americans over godless Russians. The barbarians at the gates were from within as much as without and the only hope was in Christ.

The long history of prophetic expectation may have begun to weigh heavily on some. In some cases, this was a continued reiteration of prior calls for readers to curb their enthusiasm, but other times the concern was more pastoral. If Christians' eyes were always on a possible tomorrow, then they might have precious little time for today. In 1971 Hitt cautioned evangelicals who might be too prone to see with relish the prospect of the end of the world. After all, this was not the first time that historical events led believers to think the end was nigh. It might well be true that God was coming to save his people from this dark world, but, if his people became too eager, this would be to abandon the commands he had given them for this world. Now was not the time to give up but to keep spreading the word and loving the world.[72] The following year, one of *ET*'s regular writers told of a conference which he and Hitt had attended. While there one of the speakers declared with great confidence that his listeners would not have face the troubles rising in the world since Christ would come back too soon. Hitt then turned to the writer and said, "Do you have the feeling that we went through this once before, 30 or 40 years ago?" He then noted that a great many people had become increasingly interested in prophetic issues yet evinced little concern with present-day problems in society. He saw this as a "self-centered isolationism," which was leading evangelicals away from racial and economic concerns which had only just begun to be a priority. He was not opposed to thoughts of the end, but he thought the prophecies should be seen in their intended perspective. "My ultimate hope, both personal and social—my only hope—is the return of Jesus Christ. But what if His return isn't in the next five years, what if He doesn't return for 75 years, 500 years? The Second Coming was never intended to be a copout."[73] It was hardly a wise plan for Christians to

72. Hitt, "Hope for the '70s," *ET*, January 1971, 6.

73. Bayly, "Who Cares About Tomorrow?" *ET*, October 1972, 59. Even after decades of unfulfilled predictions, many evangelicals continued to see the end of history in the course of world events. Foreshadowing the success of his book sales of his *Left Behind* series a generation later, Tim LaHaye called people to look carefully

be so concerned about the return of the Lord that they could not be about the Lord's business.

Continuing Confidence

This critical stance was, all in all, the exception to the rule. Evangelicals continued to expect the end to come and to come soon. An editorial in 1970 reminded *Moody* readers that the final pieces for the end seemed to be coming into place. Reminding readers that articles in *Moody* had long argued that a revived Roman Empire of ten nations would arise at the end, the author noted ominously, "The European Economic Community now has a membership of six nations, France, West Germany, Italy, Belgium, the Netherlands and Luxembourg. Seeking to join the Common Market at this time are Britain, Ireland, Norway and Denmark." Although he admitted that many had turned away from belief in prophecy on account of notable false predictions in recent years, he nonetheless maintained that the eschatological study was still valuable, if done with proper qualifications. "But the misinterpretations and misapplications of prophecy should not constitute deterrents to its study. Rather, they should prompt one to be more careful in examining a given text and its context and to view it in the light of what is revealed elsewhere in Scripture."[74] Sweeting pointed to a great increase of interest in eschatological concerns from many segments of society not normally fascinated by such things. "Why is this so? Perhaps in part because we can look around us today and see not just one prophetic sign—but many of them ... not only the rise of Israel, but the alignment of China, Russia, the Arab bloc and the European Common Market. Not only lawlessness and hedonism in many forms, but the ominous rise of Satanism and the occult." Given that things such as these had been predicted for years by eschatologically-minded thinkers, it was not remarkable that interest in the end began to rise. As he put it, "One has to take note of the total

---

at the times. An advertisement for his book *The Beginning of the End* declared, "The events of Biblical prophecy are being fulfilled completely and rapidly today." Readers were assured that LaHaye "feels conclusively that we are living in the last generation." Tyndale House Publishers, "Advertisement," *MM*, September 1972, 11.

74. R. J. L. "Current Events and The Blessed Hope," *MM*, February 1970, 16.

picture: the convergence of events simultaneously which spell out ever more clearly the direction of world history."[75]

Similarly, just two years before his cynical comment quoted above, Hitt had looked back forty years to the words of his predecessor concerning some twenty "prophetic trends" which Barnhouse had expected to come about when the end times were finally upon them. With little commentary aside from saying that it was "interesting to look again at these 20 trends that Dr. Barnhouse noted four decades ago," Hitt listed these points, all with the presumed expectation that the readers would see how these had, indeed, come about. These trends embraced several types of expectation, some technological advances and things like what he termed the "infectious spread of immorality," but others were geopolitical in nature, such as the creation of the State of Israel, the spread of militarism and increasing effectiveness of military technology, and the prioritizing of ecumenical movements involving the Roman Catholic Church. Hitt challenged his readers, in effect, to consider how reliable they saw biblical prophecies in light of their apparent fulfillment over the past few years.[76]

---

75. Sweeting, "A New Surge in Prophecy," *MM*, March 1973, 19. Ellipses in original.

76. Hitt, "Twenty Trends," *ET*, January 1970, 11–12. Aside from saying that he was alluding to Barnhouse's words in *Revelation* magazine, Hitt did not specify his source or clarify how much of what he quoted here was from the words of Barnhouse or simply his own summary. Under Hitt *ET* continued its founder's emphasis on eschatological concerns, but it did so less often in its general commentary than he had and focused on it in occasional and special features. For example, James M. Boice, who had taken over the pulpit in Philadelphia once held by Barnhouse, wrote a series of four articles for *ET* which considered the role of biblical prophecy in current events. In the first he wrote of the human hope of a perfect world to come at the end of time. "Even though men dream of a Golden Age and even have some idea of what it should be like, nothing in actual history gives us any ground to hope that a utopian age or anything like it is forthcoming. ... We dream of a Golden Age. But if there is ever to be such an age, it seems that God Himself must establish it." James M. Boice, "Will There Really Be a Golden Age?" *ET*, September 1972, 13. The following month he pondered some parallels between his day in America and that of the Bible's description of the time of Noah before the flood. Even as he cited common features like increased population, greater technical knowledge, and rampant immorality, he cautioned against drawing conclusions too quickly. "Again, we dare not make the error of arguing that because these crimes and perversions are appearing to such alarming degrees in our age,

In an interview with *Moody*, a MBI professor offered his perspective on the situation in the Middle East. One of his observations was
that the Soviet Union was growing in influence throughout the Arab
portions of the region, as young Arab men were increasingly looking
to the Russians for protection against the American-backed Israelis, as
a source of education, and a guiding light for a better future. In what
was, in retrospect, an untenable observation, he said, "The Islamic faith
seems to be having less and less influence on Arab young people," and
that this partly explained why they were open to Russian influence
and even domination. As to the specific prophetical implications of
these moves, he said, "It seems to me we may well be moving toward
fulfillment of the conditions set out in Ezekiel 38. Speaking of the latter
days, the prophet describes a coming thrust at the land of Israel by a
power bloc from the north. ... In Ezekiel we read that Persia, Ethiopia
and Libya are confederate with the northern power." To him this was

---

the coming of Jesus Christ must occur immediately. We have no warrant for that."
With that qualification in place he then asked, "Are the alarming moral and economic conditions of our age not more than adequate fulfillment of the conditions
Jess taught must prevail in these areas before His return?" To this he added the
suggestion that the return of Christ could come within forty years of either the
1948 establishment of the State of Israel or the 1967 capture of Jerusalem by Israeli
forces. Like many others, his conclusion was the pastoral call for his readers to
consider their faith and to preach the gospel to their neighbors. Boice, "Are We Back
in the Days of Noah?" *ET*, October 1972, 16–18, 74. Boice later tentatively predicted
that the Bible's message included a promise that the Jews would one day rebuild
the temple in Jerusalem and pointed to the general expectation among Israelis that
it would be rebuilt within a few decades at the latest. Boice offered no counsel for
American foreign policy but merely again called on his readers to reorient their
lives in light of the message of the Bible. In the final part of the series, he gave some
clarity for the great final battle of the future. "We cannot precisely predict when
the events themselves will take place, but we can say with more certainty who
the combatants will be. In brief, the Bible speaks of four world powers— united
Europe, a Russian confederacy, a confederacy of the South (meaning the Arab and
African states), and a great Eastern power. Moreover, we can find current world
events tending to this precise alignment of world powers." His only mention of
the US in all this was that he believed that Ezekiel 39's reference to fire being sent
to "the coastlands" involved a nuclear attack on several areas, including America.
Therefore, he provided no appeal to his government towards any course of action
but suggested that the final battle would involve a conflict between the Chinese
and the Europeans. Boice, "Are We Nearing the Last Holocaust?" *ET*, December
1972, 19–20, 59–61.

semi-clear proof that the burgeoning geopolitical alliances of his day
were aligning perfectly with the expected final factions of the last days.[77]

THE STATE OF ISRAEL

The place of the Israelis continued to climb in eschatological plans. The
ambivalence of the 1930s and 1940s was now long gone. Criticism and
occasional doubts remained, but for a great many evangelicals, the State
of Israel was the Israel of biblical prophecy. As a part of an issue largely
devoted to eschatological concerns, a *Moody* contributor was later to
declare, "The fact that the nation of Israel has been raised up and still
survives today, though surrounded by implacable enemies, is striking
evidence that history is moving in the very direction long indicated
by Bible prophecy."[78] At the twenty-fifth anniversary of the formation
of the State of Israel, Hitt penned a highly positive article celebrating
not only its birthday but its survival. "Sometimes the expression 'the
miracle of birth' applies to nations as well as babies, and no modern
nation warrants the adjective 'miracle' more than Israel." Citing the
success of the new nation and the accuracy of the predictions to that
end made by Barnhouse long before 1948, Hitt took Christian skeptics
to task for refusing to believe what he found obvious; that the State of
Israel was the fulfillment of biblical prophecy. Nonetheless, he offered
two points of caution. First, he warned against "excessive dogmatism"
regarding eschatological predictions, saying, "History is littered with
the torn-up pages of prophetic scholars who have linked antichrists,
wars and other biblical elements with specific historical events." Second,
he reminded his fellow supporters of the Israelis not to be naïve about
the Jewish state. "There is a danger that we simplistically and ideal-
istically glorify the state of Israel. Politically Israel is no purer than
Washington, D.C. Its leaders are not inerrantly inspired. The need to
be rebuffed and rebuked at times, as all political chieftains do."[79] The

---

77. Anonymous, "What Will Happen in The Mid-East?" *MM*, November 1970,
19. No name is given for the interviewer.

78. Louis Goldberg, "Religious Thought in Israel," *MM*, October 1971, 21.

79. Hitt, "Reflections on Israel's Birthday," *ET*, May 1973, 10, 12. Around the same
time *MM* published a very similar article, praising the State of Israel and calling
it the "Land of Return." The author wrote, "Just twenty-five years ago the ancient

Israelis may have been the ancient people of God, but they were still sinners and capable of great failings.

Therefore, while evangelical authors were pro-Israeli by a sizable majority, they were not always keen on the behavior of the State of Israel or its supporters. Henry cautioned a Christian leader to take care not to let his support of the State of Israel be perceived as unthinking support. "While I am convinced that the return of Jewry to Palestine (and that in unbelief) fulfills the prophetic Scriptures, and also support the Israeli right to national autonomy, I am not thereby committed to endorsement of all the political aspirations of Israel as a nation." This caution was not in a vacuum but had everything to do with the treatment of Arabs caught up in the conflicts. "Old Testament Jewry had a special sensitivity to the stranger and needy in the midst, and I have an uneasy feeling that the failure to find creative solutions to the Arab refugee problem may have run its course almost to the point of no return."[80] A prominent dispensational theologian writing in *CT*

---

village of Beersheba in Israel's Negev desert served as an outpost of two thousand people for Bedouin sheepherders—about as remote, perhaps, as it was four thousand years ago when Abraham headquartered there en route to the Promised Land. Today Beersheba has suddenly grown into a city of 100,000 people." He saw this as no ordinary population growth but as due solely to the land coming to life again under its returned Israeli caretakers. "A short distance away to the west, hundreds of square miles of once arid wasteland has turned into rolling hills of green as Israeli farmers bring water to the land. The desert continues to recede slowly but surely, mile by mile." This paean did hold its own constraints, as the author admitted that his recent tour of the nation was entirely through Israeli eyes. "But in all this it is easy to disregard completely the Arab point of view. As a party of journalists, we were guests of the Israeli government, and, of course, our hosts could hardly be expected to show us negatives, or interpret events from an unbiased stance." He went on to praise the Christian faith of an Arab he had encountered and placed at least partial blame on the Israelis for the condition of Arab refugees. He even quoted criticism of a Billy Graham film for its overly pro-Israeli perspective. Robert Flood, "Israel: Land of Return," *MM*, March 1973, 22, 25.

80. Henry, Letter to Franklin Littrell, December 10, 1970, Box 1971 1, File Arab Israeli, Carl F. H. Henry Collection. Henry was not alone in this ambiguity. In 1969 the editors at *ET* provided a pair of dueling articles concerning the role of America in the perpetually simmering conflict in the Middle East. One author, taking up the cause of the Arabs, pointed to the material, present-world concerns that his readers might have. Specifically, he used the American fear of Communist advance to appeal for his them to reconsider their support of the State of Israel. "When America announces more Phantom jets for the Israeli army, the Arabs feel forced to turn to Russia for weapons.

highlighted the ambiguity of the Christian response to the tension in the Levant. In his piece he wrote, "Another aspect is the choosing of sides by missionaries and Christian leaders who let their pro-Arab or pro-Israel feelings be known. After a recent border incident one Protestant missionary who worked in Arab lands asked for a suspension of all aid to Israel, while another Christian leader who works in Israel openly justified and defended the nation's actions."[81] This willingness to

---

Oil men know that whoever controls Mideast oil has a hand at the throat of Europe. Whoever is the military ally of the Arabs has a foot in the door of Africa." To those who appealed to prophecy to base their support of the Jewish state, he said, "However you cut out the cloth, whatever analysis you make of the whole matter, however you interpret the prophecies of Scripture, this is an inescapable fact: great numbers of innocent people are suffering. Great numbers innocent people have lost the homes where their fathers have lived for over 13 centuries." A. C. Forrest, "The Arabs," ET, April 1969, 31, 35. On the other hand, his partner looked to the connection to the Old Testament felt by many American evangelicals, now that the Jews were again living in the same cities found in the Bible. "The biblical records as well as uninterrupted Jewish traditions have created the Israeli feeling of deep roots in the land of the Bible and its history. These roots they justifiably see as eternal since the Prophets from Moses to Jeremiah and Ezekiel reiterate it." To his understanding the problem of peace in the Middle East was exacerbated not by the Israelis but by their Arab neighbors. "Contrary to the policy of the Arab countries, we do not find opposition here to ideas of peace. Attempts to physically destroy civilians by border incidents or by planting of bombs in schools and theaters, to use women and children for political ends, are ideas abhorrent to the people of Israel. To them, the basic question is coexistence, not destruction." G. Douglas Young, "At East in Zion," ET, April 1969, 33–34.

81. Charles C. Ryrie, "Perspective on Palestine," CT, May 23, 1969, 8. For many Christians the presence of the Muslim Al-Asqa Mosque on the site of Solomon's Temple was an obstacle to Christ's return. When someone attempted to remove this block to the end of the world, many evangelical pundits reacted negatively. Perhaps the most telling thing about one piece concerning contemporary fulfillment of eschatology was the title, which read, "Arson in Jerusalem: No Way to Fulfill Prophecy." When a member of an apparently heretical group tried to start a fire on the Temple Mount to clear the way for an eschatological temple in Jerusalem, an article in ET described both the act and his group as beyond the pale of evangelical thought. The author noted that while some Jewish rabbis had declared that the temple ought to be built now that the site was in their hands, a ranking rabbi argued that any future temple would be built by God himself. The Editors, "Arson in Jerusalem: No Way to Fulfill Prophecy," ET, December 1969, 32, 34. Lindsell also rebuked the attempt to raze the Temple Mount, saying, "Whatever may be their merit for the eschatological view that the temple must be rebuilt before Messiah comes, surely God doesn't want arsonists to take it upon themselves to fulfill His plan." In the course of his argument, Lindsell also critiqued the high expectation of many that the temple was soon to be reborn. "By now most Christians have heard, via the grapevine, a 'fact' for which there is no support: that all the stones for the new Temple have been cut and are ready

see the Israelis as both the object of God's intentions and as the subject of strong denunciations is not as incongruous as it might at first seem. After all, the same biblical prophets who these modern-day seers read did the same thing. Ezekiel, Daniel, Isaiah, Jeremiah, et al., each spoke of their ancient nation in the same way.

Not everyone spoke with this sense of perspective. The leader of an organization dedicated to the evangelization of the Jewish people made a statement in *Presbyterian Journal* which at first hedged his bets about the eschatological significance of the Israeli state but then expressed incredulity that anyone could come to a differing conclusion. He began, saying, "I have been a student of prophecy for about fifty years. I have spoken and written on the subject; I have tried not to be dogmatic concerning the order of events; I have always granted anyone the right to differ with me. My mind has not been closed to helpful suggestions." However, this qualification was followed up by a sterner statement of belief. "But of this one thing I am certain: events which we are witnessing today are like those of biblical times. A land is being reborn and a spiritual revival is on the way. During my recent visit to Israel I saw prophecies of centuries being rapidly and literally fulfilled. Only the willfully blind fail to see God's hand in it all."[82] The editors at the same magazine made a similar point with the choice of their cover a year later. Citing the words of UN diplomat, Charles Malik, they proclaimed,

---

for assembly on the site of the mosque once it is destroyed." Rather than support what he considered a dubious proposition or stir the embers of eschatological hope, his focus was on encouraging both Arabs and Israelis to come to the negotiating table and make a long-term peace. Lindsell, "Arson in Jerusalem," *CT*, September 12, 1969, 33. One writer at *MM* was not so sure that the Israelis would not make the attempt, divine inaction notwithstanding. After building his credibility by describing his recent work on a documentary in the area, he wrote, "What I saw there, plus our research of the past months, convinces me that within the next ten years Israel could move to rebuild the temple. For those alert to the fulfillment of Bible prophecy, such an event would be electrifying." He immediately added the qualifying remark, "This of course is only an opinion." As to the problem of Arab intransigence over Israeli occupation of the Al-Asqa Mosque, he suggested a solution expressing an American's hope in the power of cash. "I personally believe that the Arabs will eventually lose interest in holding on to this ground. At this point it is only pure speculation, but the government of Israel could someday offer a substantial sum of money to have the mosque dismantled and moved to Mecca." Malcom Crouch, "When Will the Jews Rebuild Their Temple?" *MM*, December 1973, 34, 86.

82. Jacob Gartenhaus, "The Resurrection of Israel," *PJ*, November 19, 1969, 10.

"To dismiss the present conflict in the Middle East between the children of Isaac and the children of Ishmael as just another political struggle is to have no sense of the prophetic ultimate in history."[83] This was a doubly unusual statement. Not only were statements about the end couched with a fallback position in case later events proved prophetic expectation unfounded, but *Presbyterian Journal* was unlikely to draw lines in the eschatological sand to begin with. A possible explanation is that the writers and editors at the magazine could have as strong views on the end as anyone, but, coming from a Reformed perspective, it was simply not something they talked about much. Another likely contributing factor was that the world events since 1948 simply overwhelmed any hesitation or skepticism that otherwise would keep such enthusiasm in check.

The Yom Kippur War

For the second time in just over five years, evangelical commentators were treated to a major war in the Middle East. The brief October 1973 Yom Kippur War came upon both Israeli forces and evangelical minds without warning. In a fortuitous example of a marketable coincidence, the editors at *Moody* managed to speak of potential tumultuous wars just as a new one was breaking out. Declaring that the capture of Jerusalem by the Israelis a few years earlier was a key moment in eschatology history, one author wrote, "If the view presented here is correct, then we are living tremendous days. Perhaps the present distress and perplexity of nation is the beginning of that which Christ spoke. Perhaps the times of the Gentiles are soon to close. If, as many believe, the events mentioned by our Lord in Luke 21 have already begun to take place, then the kingdom of God is at hand."[84] Taylor had a similar comment when the fighting had broken out. He argued that

---

83. Charles Malik, "It's Cosmic," *PJ*, October 21, 1970, 1. Malik was a Lebanese diplomat to the UN and the US as well as an evangelical whose writings appeared regularly in *CT*.

84. S. Maxwell Coder, "Jerusalem: Key to the Future," *MM*, October 1973, 87. The Yom Kippur War was fought between October 6 and October 25, 1973, so this issue would have been arriving in subscribers' mailboxes just before or as the conflict erupted.

the Bible told its readers that international tensions would rise until the final war arrived. "By the time these words appear in print the situation may once again have simmered down—or it may have escalated unbear-ably. Either possibility seems quite likely as new reports tell of direct and increasing involvement by both the Soviet Union and the United States."[85] Later, when its editors were able to pull together articles about the now-realized conflict, articles in *Moody* shared the dramatic words from a regular contributor: "Simultaneously attacked by Egypt and Syria, Israel was at war for the fourth time in twenty-five years, struggling again for its very existence. Israel's Chief of Staff David Elazar called this Yom Kippur war, the 'War of the Day of Judgment,' an ominous reminder to Bible students of future conditions here in the Middle East." He later brought Cold War concerns into the discussion of the world's end, saying, "The Soviet Union's involvement creates a north-south power axis through the Middle East. Never before in his-tory has there been such a thrust. The time will come when the Soviet Union will ultimately be drawn into the very land of Israel (Ezek. 38: 39) [sic]."[86] Unfortunately for those expecting 1973 to bring in the end, but fortunately for those hoping to avoid World War III, the Russians and Americans kept their involvement to being background players and stayed out of each other's way.[87]

---

85. Taylor, "Is It Armageddon?" *PJ*, October 31, 1973, 12.

86. Goldberg, "Yom Kippur in Perspective," *MM*, December 1973, 8–9. Given that there is no Ezekiel 38:39 and there is an extra space before the 39, this biblical reference is likely a typo which is supposed to read "Ezek. 38, 39."

87. Yet again, the plight of the Arab Christian population found voice in these magazines. Sweeting asked his readers to consider their fellow Christians on the other side of this war. "At a time like this believers ought especially to remember in prayer the minority of Arab Christians—often overlooked by evangelicals sympa-thetic to Israel. ... Only a common bond in Jesus Christ can bridge such differences between the two peoples and bring some kind of harmony out of chaos." He did end with the hint that conclusion of history could be being written in that day. "As the Mideast again becomes the focus of world attention, the prophetic Scriptures remind us once more of the lateness of the hour. God's clock continues to wind down toward the hour 'which no man knoweth.' Such events—and many others around us today—suggest we are living in an unusual time in history. Let us not miss its meaning—nor its opportunities." Sweeting, "War Again in the Mid-East," *MM*, December 1973, 21.

ABSENT AMERICA

One curiosity for many end-times thinkers was the absence of any mention of the America from any biblical prophecy. If the US were the leading power in the world of the day, and this day was the last day, then why were there no biblical references to the land of the free? As Donald Barnhouse Jr., the son of the founder of *ET*, put it, "One of the perennial puzzles facing Bible students who try to make a detailed correspondence between current events and biblical prophecies is the difficulty of fitting the United States into the picture. References to the United States are either embarrassingly indirect and contrived, or it is admitted that no clear references exist." Barnhouse's conclusion did little to assuage American egos, as his point was that perhaps the US was not as important as its denizens would like. "In terms of people, and God has indicated that He cares for people, we are only 6% of the world's population, and dropping. Perhaps the American perspective on America has been somewhat distorted, and we may not really be worth much more than a vague footnote in the biblical view of the future."[88] Another writer did not exactly disagree, but he did suggest that the American people would play a role in the end, even if the United States did not endure. He admitted that the few theories finding a place for the US in an end-times scheme did not find support among conservative theologians, but he argued that the specific silence of the Bible did not mean a general statement of America's absence. "It is evident that any prophecy which speaks of all nations speaks of the United States and any other country in existence in the end time. We must look at these Scriptures, rather than at a few doubtful texts, for whatever God may have been pleased to reveal about the destiny of our own country or people." He said that certainly some nations would disappear from the time of the Bible's writing before the end came, but then he added, "However, if the end of the present order is at hand, as many students believe, then we may put the name of the USA. In passages dealing with all nations in the last days, just as any individual may put his name in place of the word 'whosoever' in gospel texts." Given his understanding

---

88. Donald Barnhouse Jr., "Worldview," *ET*, June 1973, 37.

of the closing days of human history, then the laid out several things he thought would inevitably happen to the US. These included the loss of its entire Christian population in the rapture, the end of domestic liberty and the rise of a foreign dictatorship, a renewal of Christianity within some Americans, great plagues across the land, a great judgment by God, and all this followed by its finding a place among all nations as part of God's kingdom on earth. None of these put America at the center of world-ending events, but neither did they exclude it as one among many participants in humanity's final act.[89] A professor at MBI offered his opinion of the presence or absence of the Americans from the end-times plans in the Bible, arguing that the US was indeed mentioned but only indirectly. His theory was that since the majority of the US population was descended from areas once in the Roman Empire, that its prophetic identity was subsumed within references to Rome. He later went on to suggest that America's absence was only a matter of perspective, and, in a move that was unlikely to endear him to the hearts of those wanting to have America be God's special nation, that US troops would be a part of the armies of the Antichrist.[90]

IMMORAL AMERICA

Culbertson painted a dark picture of American society, one which hardly fit with expectations of the US as God's eschatological handmaid. "For the thoughtful Christian, recent weeks have probably strengthened the impression that he lives in a time of grave deterioration. … Week after week the headlines of his daily paper have strengthened the impression that our nation—and, indeed, the world—is moving down a one-way road." While these points may have been written off as the regular evangelical critique for American immorality, he wondered whether they suggested another purpose.

> Viewed from the standpoint of prophetic revelation, what is happening before his eyes in 1970? Are the problems he sees, as some would argue, merely more ups and downs of history?

---

89. S. Maxwell Coder, "The Destiny of America," *MM*, January 1973, 30, 57–58.
90. Louis Barbieri, "Curious About the Future?" *MM*, November 1973, 114. Italics in original.

> Or are they, perhaps, the omens of impending judgment on his
> nation? Could they even be signs of the approaching end of the
> age—a world being made ready for the coming of the Antichrist
> and the catching away of the church?

Whatever the reality, whether random historical downtrend or the end
of history itself, he called on his readers to take hope in God, because
their ultimate trust was not in the power of America but in the determination of God. "Judged in terms of human attitudes and the course
of events, the outlook is hopeless, but if prophecy says anything it says
that God is not giving up. He will carry out His purposes." They might
not be successful in their self-identified missions, but so long as they
followed the lead of Christ and his Word, they could be confident of
winning the battle that mattered.[91]

The role of eschatology in evangelical opinions of this era was somewhat mixed. There certainly was plenty of material for anyone prone to
see the future in the present. Between moral decay in the United States
and war in the Middle East, the signs of the end continued to show up,
just as they had for decades. Some periodicals were as intent as ever that
the final days were upon them to the point that they found it hard to
conceive that anyone could think otherwise. Others, on the other hand,
found that the drumbeat of the end of the world was one that they had
heard too many times over the years. A simple explanation would be
that there were those authors and magazines which found eschatology
compelling and who wrote about it accordingly. In contrast to these
would be those who looked with suspicion at such predictions and who
then dismissed any such thought in print. However, this comforting

---

91. Culbertson, "What Do We Do at The End of The Age?" *MM*, May 1970, 22.
Some were more optimistic about the then-present. Another contributor to *MM*
came to similar conclusions about it being the end of the world, but he did so, in
part, from very different reasons. Rather than reciting a litany of all the things
going wrong in the world, he pointed to a great number of Christian conversions
in North America. "All across America and Canada the Spirit of God is working. A
new sense of excitement and urgency hangs in the air. The stories of conversion
are endless. I am only a layman, but as we weigh the material we have collected
and begin to write, we are overwhelmed by the movement of God in these days.
The time is short. The day of Jesus Christ's return has to be close! We are privileged
to live in the most exciting times, I believe, since the birth of our Lord." Bernard
Palmer, "The Spirit of '72," *MM*, July-August 1972, 29.

simplicity did not hold true in the writings in question. Russell Hitt could cynically comment that confidence about the nearness of the end had been equally high for some time now, but he could also note that a great many of the predictions of Barnhouse had indeed come to fruition. In much the same way, the staff at *Presbyterian Journal* had veered away from eschatological comment, but it was in their magazine that some of the strongest statements of confidence had been printed. Over the course of this period of time, evangelicals held varying degrees of confidence about the end of the world while maintaining varying degrees of skepticism about the same.

10

Conclusions

OVERVIEW

In the period between 1937 and 1973, American evangelicals witnessed one of the most tumultuous eras of human history. America had been one of several great powers in the 1920s, and, in fact, before returning to isolationism, it was poised to become the dominant player in world affairs as all other contenders lay debilitated by the First World War. By the end of the Second, however, it had become a superpower, equaled, if at all, by a single rival. The United States found that it could not retreat behind its oceanic barriers as easily as it had earlier. The default non-interventionism of American foreign policy failed when confronted with the prospect of long-range bombers and a self-identifying expansionist ideology holding sway over a third of the world.

This postwar period was ironically defined by war, either hot, in places like Korea, or cold, with the nuclear arms race and what Eisenhower called the "Military-Industrial Complex." Rarely did it escape Americans' attention in the 1950s that a new and greater war seemed always in the offing, ready to be ignited by the slightest movement or misstep in a highly contentious world. The fertile combination of globe-embracing geopolitical alliances, the existence of world-ending nuclear weapons, and the emotionally-charged emergence of the State of Israel created a perfect storm which threatened peace, prosperity, and civilization itself.

The late 1960s seemed to bring all of these elements together for evangelicals—cultural ferment at home, Communist assertiveness abroad, and end-times expectations apparently fulfilled before their very eyes. To a country which often defined itself by quick marches for liberty, the hard slog of fighting in Southeast Asia was a far less obvious candidate for heroic emulation. The clarity and confidence which had invigorated the entire nation a generation earlier now seemed little more than a memory. Any sense of moral superiority plummeted in the wake of Selma, My Lai, and Watergate. The perplexity of a never-ending fight for unspecified goals in Vietnam's "bad war" could never measure up to the "good war" days of pushing the Nazis back to Berlin.

Evangelical thinkers took to editorial pages, radio broadcasts, and personal communications to shape the response of their audiences to the ongoing global crises. These analyses of the situations confronting their nation and their church were no idle musings. Instead, they were intentional efforts to encourage the laity to think in a certain way and to act accordingly. Through the material and analysis of the chapters above, something of an answer can now be given to the initial question of this dissertation: In what ways did American evangelical leaders comment upon the United States involvement in the global crises from the beginnings of the Second World War through the end of American combat operations in Vietnam?

One component of the answer is that they responded to these crises by embracing both a continuity with past principles and a recognition of the complexity of the present. Over the course of several decades they reacted to distinct conflicts with various nations with the same basic comment, that great injustices warranted strong interventions. Evangelical objections to Soviet tanks in Prague in 1968 were nearly identical to their response to Nazi panzers thirty years earlier. They advocated certain alliances, nations, and geopolitical postures through-out the era, but they often did so with hesitancy and with particular attention to religious persecution. They were more concerned about the health and security of the worldwide church of Jesus Christ than they were with the position of the United States in the world. Further, they applied many of these same condemnations to aspects of their own country and were quite willing to rebuke United States policy and the immorality of its society. Or, to use biblical language, their trust was not in princes—even American ones.

ENEMIES

When commenting on the enemies of the United States, evangelical writers were emphatic about the relative superiority of their nation over against its foes. In researching this book, there was never an example of an evangelical leader suggesting that Nazi Germany, Soviet Russia, or any of its Communist allies were better than the United States. There were those who asked whether America's sins made it slouch to the level of these others, but they emphasized significant moral failings by rival powers. This, in their minds, made the United States the better of the competing options. Even so, this superiority was only relative. Merely being better than genocidal tyrants like Hitler, Stalin, and Mao allowed plenty of room for American sins.

Since supporting the war against Fascism has never been controversial, little needs to be noted here except that evangelicals were generally careful to distinguish the kingdom of God from the American republic. The counsel given by evangelical leaders during World War II generally focused on the oppressive and expansionist nature of the Axis regimes. Articles highlighted the persecutions and oppressions enacted by German, Italian, and Japanese governments against their own people and against their neighbors. During the same period these same authors made similar denunciations of Soviet actions within Russia and against Finland. While America and the Allies were clearly shown as the "good guys" in that war, American societal sins came under harsh, if only occasional, review. Further, even as evangelical magazines openly encouraged their readers to aid the war effort, writers warned against harboring hatred for the enemy and challenged the expectation that God was somehow on America's side.

With Communism's spread across much of the globe in the wake of the Second World War, many evangelicals amplified their habit of describing it as an enemy in and of itself and not merely as the political party controlling certain nations. While Communism was often portrayed as a dangerous system to rival that of the United States, much in the same way that an enemy monarchy might be described, evangelical commentators went beyond this. It was not a government which just happened to be tyrannical, but, rather, its oppressive and totalitarian habits were intrinsic. There could be no moral Communist state. In fact, E. Schuyler English had characterized Communism as being just as horrible as Nazism, while many of his fellow evangelicals spoke of it as inherently hostile to Christianity. They called upon Christians to oppose Communism just as they would a false and antagonistic religious faith and not merely as an alternative political party.

This point is more important than it might at first seem. Evangelical commentators, Henry and Schaeffer most prominently, regularly noted that they did not see Christianity as "religious" in the sense of being set off from everyday existence. Instead, it was an explanatory belief system for every aspect of life and not simply a collection of mutable rituals on the level of a hobby or sports affiliation. In the same way, they did not see Communism as a purely political and economic faction. Both Christianity and Communism were worldviews, explanations for the nature of the cosmos and humanity. Each of these systems provided a totalizing understanding of life. Even though they had very different answers for the world, they were equally self-defined as ultimate interpretations of the nature of human beings, the problems they faced, the meaning behind morality, and accompanied by a promise of an eschaton when all would be made right. To many of these writers, Communism was mutually exclusive and antithetical to Christianity in a way distinct from other forms of government.

This trend for evangelical writers to see Communism as a primary enemy often pushed individual nation-states like Russia and China into the background. It was not that such countries did not cause problems, but their governments were considered merely particular manifestations of the greater threat posed by their ideology. The animosity of Henry, Barnhouse, and Poling toward America's national enemies in this period had less to do with their patriotism than with their Christian humanism. They saw Communism not only as being against their specific nation but as against the well-being of the people of all nations. Their fears were not assuaged by seeing this opponent grow over the course of their lifetimes. As several of them noted, Communism had grown from the dream of a few Russian malcontents in the wake of World War I to the dominating nightmare for a third of humanity in the aftermath of World War II. Evangelical observers writing in the mid-twentieth century lacked the comfort of distance from this threat. They did not know that just decades later the bulk of the Communist edifice would come crashing down with the Berlin Wall. Communism was no benign growth in distant lands but an ever-growing cancer which grew nearer each day. Poling, English, and the others did not see themselves as going after Communism but that Communism was coming after them and after all others who refused to follow the party line.

That being said, these writers were not simplistic in their perception of their nemesis. Specifically, in the days after Castro's rise, evangelical commentary alternated between neutrality and outright support of the new power in Havana. Condemnations followed quickly, but many writers withheld judgment for some time. So long as Castro's regime worked for systemic reforms, he retained a measure of evangelical favor. It was only when he clearly joined in with the USSR that they turned against him. Similarly, when it came to the possibility of a Sino-Soviet split, many found the rift between Moscow and Beijing to be nothing more than a Red subterfuge. Others considered it to be a real phenomenon, but perhaps one that would not endure were conflict with the West to break out in earnest. There was a difference of opinion even among those who thought it was a real divergence. Some looked at it as a positive thing, as would the Nixon White House by the early 1970s. Others, on the other hand, had such a poor opinion of Mao's regime that they worried what China would do were it cut loose from its Russian partner. The implication here is that there was no singular view among evangelicals about this important geopolitical issue. They did not know quite what to make of it all, but they clearly recognized that Communism was a complex entity rather than a monolithic conspiracy directed by some sinister cabal in Moscow.

The attitude of Barnhouse is a good example of this nuanced understanding. Throughout his writings, he maintained a far higher opinion of Maoist China than any of these other thinkers. He was quite willing to praise, with some clear qualifications, the efforts of Mao Zedong to restore China's infrastructure, security situation, and general well-being. Further, long before President Carter did so in the late 1970s, Barnhouse favored the US granting diplomatic recognition to the People's Republic of China, even if this downgraded the role of Taiwan's Republic of China. This is interesting in and of itself. Left alone these facts could suggest only a softer stance on his part vis-à-vis Communism in general. However, this is not the case. When it came to European issues, Barnhouse could be just as hard-lined as anyone else. This was no open-minded liberal, ready to thaw the Cold War, whatever the cost. Nor was this a wild-eyed conservative, heedlessly pursuing any deviation from the American way of life. This was a man of strong opinions who evaluated a host of circumstances and counseled others accordingly.

The Communist world may have been a complex entity, but it was still a deeply flawed tyranny. Whatever differences they had with one another, each of these commentators shared a belief in Communism's consistently immoral and oppressive nature. While they had spoken similarly about the threats of Nazism and Fascism in the 1940s, these writers spent the following decades raging against the dangers of the supposedly more humane Communism. Despite the claim by Communists that they were working for the good of all people, evangelical writers saw them merely as a different form of the same tyrannical menace seen in Germany and Italy in the 1930s and 1940s.

The evangelicals studied here did not write about instances of Soviet oppression as though these were aberrations of Communist governance. Rather, they portrayed them as times when the mask came off and its reality was clear for all to see. This was not an irrational observation. After all, from the time of its imposition outside Russia in the late 1940s, Communism faced a major internal uprising roughly once a decade. With Hungary in 1956, Prague in 1968, Poland in 1981, and finally everywhere from Berlin to Tiananmen Square in 1989, the party of "the people" was found to be decidedly unacceptable by those very same people. The supposed beneficiaries of the workers' paradise regularly chose to be cast from their atheistic Eden.

AMERICA

Yet, evangelicals had not found their own Eden along the Potomac. On the contrary, they consistently maintained their focus on America's moral decline, even during the heightened religious activity of the 1950s. If any period could prove that evangelicals had mixed the cross and the flag, this would be it. With "In God We Trust" on US coins and Charlton Heston's *The Ten Commandments* in American theaters, mainstream society offered tantalizing hints of Christian nationalism and a nascent governmental theism. Indeed, there was some support by evangelical writers for this Christianizing of the Land of the Free, but only some. Some pointed to the increasing prominence of God in government as a positive move, but others questioned how constructive it was to alter the Pledge of Allegiance when the beliefs of the people remained the same. Rather than full-throated endorsement, many evangelical commentators were as likely, if not more so, to critique these activities as shallow. Instead of encouraging readers to gloss over any distinctions between their Christianity and their Americanness, editors and authors in evangelical magazines were prone to insist that there was a great difference between an increase in a general religious interest and a growth of genuine Christianity and, one step further, that the US was earning God's judgment.

This is where the evangelical emphasis on conversion comes into play. Their understanding of a true, biblical faith was not consistent with any civil religion worthy of the name. If all they were about was having a polite and political Christianity, then their ambivalent response to the civil religion of the Eisenhower years made no sense. They were pleased with some of the religious trappings brought out in the 1950s, and they certainly liked Ike, but they also thought 1950s religion was insufficient to halt the downward spiral of American moral life. True, they, along with many of their fellow Americans, saw the US as increasingly religious, but they did not see it as increasingly Christian. America was not being converted to biblical Christianity, as they saw it. A holistic and personal conversion was an intrinsic aspect of their Christianity. It was not just about going to church, adhering to an ethical or political platform, or finding a sense of identity in a confusing world. Conversion was about a real change, a real reorientation, away from the things of this world to him who was above the world. It was one thing to say "In God We Trust." It was quite another actually to trust him and his word. As the culture of the 1950s faded and its civil religion bared its shallow roots, what little expectation they had for a Christian America slipped away accordingly.

Undoubtedly, there were moments when God and country seemed inseparable in the pages of these magazines. However, far from being a product of the Cold War, this kind of thing reached its high point during the Second World War when the entire nation was galvanized against the Fascist threat. Once the guns fell silent in 1945, evangelical responses became increasingly complicated. However, even clear instances of nationalism need to be seen in a greater context. Taken by themselves, poems conflating Christian missionaries and American soldiers provide ample ammunition for the argument that simple nationalism was a key element in evangelical attitudes. However, doing this would be to take such articles out of context. Even were such examples to be fully representative of the individuals who wrote them, they cannot also be representative of other individuals who were very keen on condemning the nation as deeply immoral. As it turns out, even those praising America at one moment were among those condemning it at another. William Houghton, for example, both praised his own institution for declaring its loyalty to the nation in the midst of the Second World War and critiqued America for its many sins during the same period. He, and others like him, may have expressed too high an opinion of the United States at times, but this is a far cry from suggesting that this support was somehow uncritical. Support accompanied by criticism is critical by definition.

Certainly, like the rest of America in the period, and any other nation in the midst of a war, writers could get carried away in the moment, but this was hardly something unique to American evangelicals. How different was the impulse to clothe the nation's military endeavors in the robes of divine sovereignty from any other group within any other nation throughout history? Others have done much the same when seeing Marduk, Ra, Jupiter, Allah, the Pope, history, the people, or the race, as so ennobling their adventures. That evangelicals did so is hardly remarkable. What is remarkable, however, is that they tempered their accolades with regular warnings against the deification of the nation and state.

Far from calling for governmental theism, evangelical writers during this time expressed a deep and abiding suspicion of the state, as such. They believed that due to the ongoing effects of Adam's fall, humanity's flaws were so ingrained in people that any governmental attempt to solve its condition was as effective as rearranging chairs on the *Titanic*. No human government, even that of the US, could heal humanity's woes. America might have been a wonderful place in many ways, and its democratic government was far better in evangelical eyes than some of its international rivals, but such praise always came in a context which included condemnation. Neither governmental theism nor unconditional nationalism, then, were driving factors in evangelical assessments of US foreign policy.

What kept patriotism in check for the likes of Henry, Gaebelein, and Hitt was their orientation toward a biblically derived morality. This allowed them to speak ambiguously about their nation, championing it in some ways and accusing it in others. For example, while Poling praised American-style capitalism, he also condemned its decadence and corruption. Schaeffer went so far as to say that there was a sense in which there was nothing better about free market materialism over against Communist materialism. Graham gave an implicitly favorable comparison of Soviet morality when he spoke of the lack of sexually explicit material and behavior evident in Moscow, and several authors noted that even the atheistic Russians were shocked by the sheer lewdness of American popular culture. Yes, Hitt rebuked those who prioritized their status as Americans ahead of their identity as Christians, and this confirms that many were letting their nationalism overwhelm their Christian faith. However, his criticism entails that at least for some evangelicals, this was completely unacceptable.

WAR

While moral beliefs of L. Nelson Bell, Carl F. H. Henry, and the pseudonymous Gabriel Courier played a crucial role in shaping evangelical counsel during this period, the more basic circumstances of their historical context made their own indelible impression, too. One of the central issues forming the attitudes of these writers toward war in the 1950s and early 1960s was the experience of the 1930s and early 1940s. Many of those surveyed here had been born in the 1910s or 1920s, meaning that their minds were shaped significantly by the Second World War. Even those like Poling, Barnhouse, and Bell who were older would have been greatly shaken by that conflict.

Along with a great many other Americans during the era, many evangelicals came to the conclusion that World War II could have been prevented had the Western powers been more assertive in reaction to the early moves of Italy in Africa, Japan in East Asia, and Germany in Central Europe. Then they had seen the devastating results of war as nearly everything from the Pyrenees to the Volga and the Aleutians to Thailand was wrecked by the conflagration. Having just seen such destruction following the bellicose statements of Tojo, Mussolini, and Hitler, it would not have taken a great leap of imagination to believe that a similar danger was posed by Stalin, Khrushchev, and Mao, particularly when this latter trio spoke of encouraging worldwide violent revolution and built up enormous armies accordingly.

Another key aspect of evangelicals' reaction to war in this period was the way they responded to the development and danger of atomic weapons. While they shared the relief of the nation at the unexpectedly swift end to the Second World War brought about, in part, by the atomic bomb, evangelicals like Wilbur Smith and Henry quickly asked some uncomfortable questions. Instead of simplistically promoting the American cause and the ingenuity by which their nation had achieved such technological devastation, evangelicals were among those expressing concern about what atomic weaponry meant for the future. The pseudonymous Gabriel Courier was the most disturbed about the implications of the bomb, as he along with the rest of the staff at *CH* questioned the wisdom of collecting a nuclear stockpile as seen in his news reports and their regular editorial cartoons. Henry, too, worried about consequences of this new American prowess, going so far as to ask about the ethics of the Hiroshima and Nagasaki attacks. Even with the less-than-ideal statements by Bell, the overall evangelical reaction to the bomb was characterized by a cautious and uncertain support of America's possession of such devices, accompanied by a great fear of what would happen if they were ever used again. This hesitant advocacy was made even as they often wrote about what a nuclear war could look like and without even a semblance of eschatologically induced glee.

The attitude of evangelical toward their country's wars underwent changes during the period of study, just as it did for many of their fellow Americans. In the four years of US involvement in the Second World War and the three years in Korea, a fairly high degree of unanimity of support existed among evangelical commentators for

American policies. In terms of the enemy faced, it was quite clear that the evil and expansionism of both Nazism and Japanese militarism in the 1940s and Communism in the early 1950s warranted a strong military response. This remained true up through the late 1960s, as the objections to totalitarianism were the same as they had been thirty years earlier regardless of the specific international threat. To evangelical commentators in 1943, 1953, or 1963, the respective conflicts were the result of Fascist or Communist forces imposing their will through violence in an ever-expanding sphere.

In most of these conflicts, evangelical writers could hope that the horrors of war were worthwhile as there was progress toward victory. The lack of clarity over Vietnam—its questionable morality, its ambiguous purpose, its absence of battle lines—made these sacrifices and compromises harder to evaluate and perhaps even to justify. Evangelicals had a longstanding distrust of the state and a low opinion of American morality, yet the bulk of evangelical commentary maintained a strong support of the US as the less-bad combatant. However, within this support came questions, and some of these questions began to challenge just how less-bad the United States had become. The sheer vagueness of the government regarding the aims and methods employed by the military in the Vietnam War encouraged a diversity of opinions regarding the conflict. A war with no frontlines and with no end in sight did not lend itself to anyone's confidence in the government's plans.

In a way, this was something new. Yet, in another sense it was not. It was not new for evangelicals to have significant moral qualms about the behavior of the United States in general. The prevalence of regular and substantive condemnations of America in these periodicals could as easily make a case for evangelicals being anti-American as their being nationalistic. If these intellectuals could describe their society and government as corrupt and even oppressive at home, there was little reason to think they would not see it being so abroad. Neither was it unique in terms of suggestions that American military tactics had potentially violated the laws of war. Such evaluations were not common in the 1940s and 1950s, yet neither were they unknown. Henry's concern noted above, about the responsibility for the atomic attacks on Japan included the possibility of moral guilt for America if these actions were not taken justly. Bell's callous remarks that no fundamental difference existed between atomic and conventional weapons was rooted in the utter destructiveness of non-nuclear attacks against Japanese cities. What was different in this period was that what had once been largely theoretical criticisms of American military actions became realized condemnations. Several evangelical voices were overtly calling attention to morally questionable actions and even atrocities perpetrated by US forces. Both psychologically and morally, the destructiveness inherent in warfare could be justified, or at least stomached, were it to have some visible progress or even a clear goal. However, rallying around the flag held out little promise when years of bloodshed brought the war no closer to ending.

After a fashion this hesitant support exemplifies the entirety of evangelical reactions to American foreign policy. Many evangelical thinkers were comfortable acknowledging and rebuking the immorality and foolishness of the United States government and its society, yet they continued to offer it their solid and, all else being equal, outspoken support. One could construe this as hypocritical whitewashing or willful myopia, but only by ignoring their estimation of the nature of totalitarianism. While they confessed that their own nation's actions were despicable in many substantive ways, they also maintained that the failings of America's enemies were worse. They did not support their nation out of some misguided rose-colored view of the country. They supported it because, when compared to the policies of other governments, the US was relatively speaking the better choice.

END TIMES

The general consensus of evangelicals regarding the end times suggests that eschatological fascination led to a hardline support of the Israeli government in its actions. However, the reality was not quite so Manichean. Many writers offered strong support to both the US effort in Vietnam and to the Israeli claim to a unified Jerusalem and beyond. However, there were others who could strongly back one but not the other. For instance, while CT regularly championed the American effort in Vietnam, some authors, in that same periodical, argued that the atrocities of the Viet Cong in Southeast Asia had their origins in the tactics used by Jewish guerillas against British and Arab targets a generation earlier. On the other hand, writers at ET could be among the most likely to criticize the American actions in Southeast Asia, yet they openly expected that one day the Israeli state would encompass much of the territories of Syria, Iraq, Jordan, and Egypt. Indeed, this resurrection of a Jewish state in its ancestral homeland was too great a confirmation of long-held expectations to pass unnoticed in evangelical foreign policy discussions. Those studied above by and large saw the rise of the new nation as a positive development in world affairs and as the specific fulfillment of ancient prophecies. Nevertheless, this fascination was neither uniform nor unconditional. Interspersed within the great many pro-Israeli statements were strong denunciations of particular immoral actions by Israeli forces and even challenges to the fundamental legitimacy of the State of Israel.

While the place of the Israelis in the evangelical eschatological imagination was fairly certain, there was precious little confidence as to the fate of the United States. This uncertainty arose from the simple problem that, while many evangelicals were passionate about getting America to center its life on the Bible, there was no clear reference in the Bible to America. This led to an inconsistency in evangelical counsel regarding American wars by those most interested in end times. On the one hand there was the call by Donald Barnhouse Sr. for the US to support the Israelis since this was the only way to guarantee God's blessing in the standoff with Russia. On the other hand, in the few times that evangelical writers specified a place for America in the time of the final battle of Armageddon, the United States was a vassal of the Antichrist. Donald Barnhouse Jr. said that perhaps the US was merely a footnote in God's final plan. These hardly made for a ringing endorsement of American sanctity and significance before Christ.

Of the four issues under review in this dissertation, it was only the evangelical comments on end times which came close to the perception of recent scholarship. It did not dominate their thinking to the extent that some of these contemporary works have suggested but it is clear that eschatology played a significant role in evangelical analysis of world affairs. It did not play an exclusive one. A great many of these writers went out of their way to caution about reading too much into world events. Perhaps more importantly, many times they wrote of eschatology and foreign policy quite independently of one another. The most that can be said is that these evangelicals often spoke about the end of the world and they also often spoke about world events. Further, they often analyzed the latter in terms of the former. However, like a Venn diagram in which the circles only overlap at certain points, the vast majority of their commentary on the place of their nation in the world or its ongoing wars made no mention whatsoever of eschatology. The dominant portion of counsel on war by these writers was rooted in the circumstances of the then-present and not in the expectations of some anticipated future.

There was, indeed, a particular focus on the end of the world in those difficult times that was somewhat unique to evangelicals, but this focus did not necessarily have escapist motivation for these writers that is attributed to them. As strange as it might seem to non-evangelicals, part of the reason they thought the world was coming to an end was because they saw it as a matter of truth. They thought this was the end of the world, or at least the beginning of the end. They believed that everything around them pointed in that direction: the growth of a Russian-led confederation challenged by an alliance comprised of former provinces of the Roman Empire concurrent with a revived Jewish state in Palestine and the introduction of weapons powered by elemental fire. When so much that was supposed to happen according to their eschatological formulations actually came to pass, it would be difficult not to jump to conclusions.

In addition to this, there was also a personal connection, a connection they held in common with the authors and recipients of apocalyptic literature from ancient Israel and the early church. Part of the appeal and the reasoning behind these end-times pieces was the hope afforded to the reader in an otherwise confusing and frightening world. The dangers faced in the 1950s and 1960s were, in many ways, more dramatic than anyone had ever faced. Many of the people writing then had been adolescents or young adults during the horrors of World War II. They had seen destruction like no other generation had ever witnessed, and now it was worse. In their day the possibility of nuclear missiles raining down on any point on earth with little or no warning was not theoretical. This was a real threat. Eschatology was not about escaping from danger but knowing that the danger would one day end and that it had a meaning. This was the benefit of the biblical prophets explaining the fates of nations during the time of Judah's exile and for those reading the book of Revelation in the face of increasing Roman oppression. The world might be in chaos, but God was on his throne. Some suggested that there was an inconsistency with the way evangelical were interested in present-day affairs and in light of fascination with the end of all things. However, for these evangelicals, there was no contradiction. It was by looking to this promised future that they sought a better way to understand and to live in the present.

CONCLUSION

Evangelicals' discourse on American military affairs in the middle of the twentieth century tended to favor the efforts of their nation. However, the suggestion put forward by recent scholarship that this support was uncritical or nationalistic is untenable, given the consistent, substantive qualifications and outright rebukes offered by evangelical writers for their country's policies. The likes of Henry, Houghton, Culbertson, and Barnhouse supported the United States conditionally because they saw it as the flawed but better alternative compared to its totalitarian opponents. Their opposition to these national enemies was not rooted in xenophobia but in the behavior of Fascist and Communist governments. They did love the beauties of their native land of America and considered that it had been uniquely blessed by God. This blessing, however, was not intrinsic but flowed from the influence of Christianity in American history and in the potential of its continuing worthy moral behavior. Much to their chagrin, this necessary morality seemed to be disappearing. Longstanding issues, like racial injustice and newer manifestations of sin, such as increasing sexual immorality, combined to elicit from evangelical intellectuals regular notes of condemnation for their homeland. Rather than uncritical acceptance of governmental authority, they were more likely to see an encroaching state power, not as a cure for, but as a key part of, America's cultural malady. Wars, whether the world-encompassing struggles of the 1940s or the limited engagements immediately thereafter, were seen as regretfully necessary. The potential of nuclear weaponry terrified these writers so that they wrote of it almost exclusively as a horrifying deterrent, at best. The end of the world held a place of fascination for nearly all evangelical commentators. Yet this interest was itself checked by regular hesitation and openness to criticism with which so many thinkers discussed such matters.

The example of evangelical conversations about their nation in the world brings the discussion full circle, back to the question of what makes an evangelical. When we look back to Bebbington's fourfold definition of evangelicalism—activism, biblicism, conversionism, and crucicentrism, along with Sweeney's Protestant doctrinal focus as mediated by the Great Awakenings of the 1700s, we find that those very principles characterized evangelical discourse on American foreign policy in this period.

The authority of God and his word overruled any temporal power held by the United States and granted these writers the justification to avoid moral relativism when comparing the ethical merits of their nation and its foes. They could support their government in some aspects while refusing to grant it their full trust since they believed that humanity would always remain flawed without the divine intervention of conversion and revival. They could complain about American immorality while pleading for support of their fellow Christians on the other side of an international frontier because they saw their ultimate identity as those transformed by the work of Christ on the cross and not as the citizens of a local nation-state.

Perhaps the best summary of evangelical beliefs about their nation during this time comes from one of their number. In November 1979, just a few short years after this period of study, Carl Henry addressed a church conference in Arkansas on the topic of "Priorities for the Eighties." As a part of his discourse, he challenged the current academic narrative concerning evangelicalism and its relationship to the United States. He said, "I'm bullish on America, too, compared to some of the alternatives. But I'm also bearish when I read the Word of God and measure it to the contemporary drift."[1] Evangelical loyalty to their earthly citizenship was tempered by their reliance on divinely established standards of human morality and trumped by their abiding fealty to their heavenly citizenship.

---

1. Henry, "Priorities for the Eighties," sermon given at First Baptist Church, Conway, AR, November 14, 1979.

Bibliography

Adeney, David H. "Communism and Christianity." *Eternity*, September 1955.

"All Bible Graded Series." "Advertisement." *Christian Herald*, July 1941.

Aldrich, Roy L. "A Just and Enduring Peace." *Moody Monthly*, July 1944.

Allis, Oswald T. "Israel's Transgression in Palestine." *Christianity Today*, December 24, 1956.

The American Board of Missions to the Jews. "Advertisement." *Moody Monthly*, June 1937.

The American-European Fellowship. "Advertisement." *Moody Monthly*, April 1938.

The American Prophetic League, Inc. "Advertisement." *Moody Monthly*, November 1939.

Anderson, Henry E. "The Book of Revelation Has a Message of Comfort." *Moody Monthly*, March 1941.

Anderson, Ken. "My Son Went to Vietnam." *Moody Monthly*, October 1969.

Anderson, Mary Helen. "A Mother's Gift." *Moody Monthly*, October 1942.

———. "For God and Country." *Moody Monthly*, July 1942.

———. "Miracle at Hue." *Presbyterian Journal*, April 17, 1968.

———. "Quench Not the Smoking Flax." *Southern Presbyterian Journal*, February 4, 1953.

———. "Reaction to President's Trip Varies." *Presbyterian Journal*, August 4, 1971.

———. "They Don't Want It." *Southern Presbyterian Journal*, July 7, 1954.

———. "What About Kennedy?" *Eternity*, February 1958.

———. "What Will Happen in The Mid-East?" *Moody Monthly*, November 1970.

Armstrong, O. K. "But don't call him General." *Christian Herald*, April 1942.

Appelman, Hyman J. "Can Eisenhower Stop Malenkov?" *Moody Monthly*, August 1953.

Arms, George W. "Born That Way." *Presbyterian Journal*, January 31, 1968.

Arnett, Wendell. Editorial Cartoon, *Christian Herald*, April 1949.

Atkinson, J. A. Letter to the Editor, *Eternity*, June 1964.

Ayer, William Ward. "Should the Jew or the Arab Have the Land of Palestine?" *Our Hope*, April 1946.

Baker Book House-Publishers. "Advertisement." *Eternity*, November 1973.

Barbieri, Louis. "Curious About the Future?" *Moody Monthly*, November 1973.

Barnette, Henlee H. "The Church in Soviet Russia." *Christianity Today*, December 23, 1957.

Barnhouse, Donald G. "1950." *Eternity*, January 1951.

———. "1952." *Eternity*, January 1953.

———. "Adlai's Religion." *Eternity*, March 1956.

———. "After the Summit—What?" *Eternity*, July 1960.

———. "Arab Against Arab." *Eternity*, October 1951.

———. "British Israel Discredited." *Eternity*, January 1954.

———. "Che Guevara and the Social Gospel." *Eternity*, October 1960.

———. "China and the Western Powers." *Eternity*, September 1952.

———. "Fatima and Russia." *Eternity*, August 1951.

———. "For Whom to Vote." *Eternity*, November 1952.

———. "How Evangelize the World?" *Eternity*, July 1951.

———. "Integration and Segregation." *Eternity*, September 1956.

———. "Israel Returns to Her Land." *Eternity*, March 1959.

———. "Korean Debacle." *Eternity*, August 1953.

———. "Methodists for Segregation." *Eternity*, July 1955.

———. "NAACP." *Eternity*, June 1958.

———. "National Lying." *Eternity*, August 1956.

———. "National Predicament." *Eternity*, February 1951.

———. "The Nature of Our Danger." *Eternity*, March 1954.

———. "Negroes Unwelcome in Africa." *Eternity*, June 1953.

———. "Nineteen Fifty-Three." *Eternity*, January 1954.

———. "Nuclear Tests." *Eternity*, April 1959.

———. "Pastor Fired on Segregation Issue." *Eternity*, February 1955.

———. "Perils of Christian Amendment." *Eternity*, July 1954.

———. "Persecution in China." *Eternity*, October 1956.

———. "Policy Toward Israel." *Eternity*, November 1954.

———. "Postscript on Korea." *Eternity*, March 1951.

———. "The President's Speech." *Eternity*, April 1957.

———. "Race." *Eternity*, August 1956.

———. "Race Relations and the Church." *Eternity*, November 1961.

———. "Red China Increases Pressures." *Eternity*, January 1959.

———. "Reds Push Anti-God Campaign." *Eternity*, October 1954.

———. "Religion in Cuba." *Eternity*, July 1959.

———. "Repercussions Against Christianity." *Eternity*, December 1954.

———. "Right or Left." *Eternity*, July 1951.

———. "The Roman Empire Again." *Eternity*, June 1953.

———. "The Roman Empire is Revived." *Eternity*, April 1959.

———. "Russia Moves to Take Persia." *Eternity*, August 1951.

———. "Russian Liberty." *Eternity*, October 1955.

———. "Segregation." *Eternity*, August 1951.

———. "Sputnik's Year." *Eternity*, January 1958.

———. "Survey of the Year." *Eternity*, January 1959.

———. "A Survey of 1954." *Eternity*, January 1955.

———. "A Survey of 1955." *Eternity*, January 1956.

———. "The Tragic Year." *Eternity*, January 1957.

———. "Wang Ming Tao in Peking." *Eternity*, February 1957.

———. "Western European Unity." *Eternity*, May 1952.

———. "When Russia Descends on Israel." *Eternity*, June 1959.

Barnhouse, Donald, Jr. "Worldview." *Eternity*, June 1973.

Baxter, David M. "What About the John Birch Society?" *Eternity*, December 1961.

Bayly, Joseph T. "God or Caesar? Caesar is Posing New Threats." *Eternity*, May 1970.

———. "If Whites Were Blacks and … ." *Eternity*, February 1969.

———. "A Northern Christian Looks at the Race Question." *Eternity*, October 1956.

———. "Resolutions, But Never Any Revolutions." *Eternity*, July 1969.

———. "We Have Blundered Badly." *Eternity*, March 1963.

———. "Who Cares About Tomorrow?" *Eternity*, October 1972.

Bebbington, David W. *Evangelicals in Modern Britain: A History from the 1730s to the 1980s.* Grand Rapids, MI: Baker Book House, 1989.

Becker, Jasper. *Hungry Ghosts: Mao's Secret Famine.* New York: Henry Hold and Company, 1996.

Bell, A. Editorial Cartoon, *Moody Monthly*, July 1939.

———. Editorial Cartoon, *Moody Monthly*, July 1947.

———. Editorial Cartoon, *Moody Monthly*, January 1948.

———. "The Problem Child." *Moody Monthly*, November 1945.

Bell, L. Nelson. "The Arab Nations and Israel." *Southern Presbyterian Journal*, July 11, 1956.

———. "The Atom Bomb." *Southern Presbyterian Journal*, December 13, 1950.

———. "Before America There Lies a Choice and It Must Be Made Soon." *Southern Presbyterian Journal*, October 24, 1951.

———. "Blood, Sweat, and Tears." *Southern Presbyterian Journal*, December 27, 1950.

———. "Bombing Raid Described in the Book of Isaiah." *Southern Presbyterian Journal*, May 1942.

———. "Britain's Tragedy." *Southern Presbyterian Journal*, May 1, 1947.

———. "Can It Be? America, a Second-Rate Power!!" *Southern Presbyterian Journal*, May 16, 1956.

———. "Challenge to What?" *Southern Presbyterian Journal*, February 15, 1950.

———. "Chiang—Hated by Whom?" *Southern Presbyterian Journal*, February 23, 1955.

———. "China Today." *Presbyterian Journal*, August 4, 1971.

———. "The *Christian Beacon* and the Communists Attack Billy Graham." *Southern Presbyterian Journal*, April 6, 1955.

———. "Christian Race Relations Must Be Natural, Not Forced." *Southern Presbyterian Journal*, August 17, 1955.

———. "Christian Realism." *Southern Presbyterian Journal*, January 1, 1948.

———. "The Church and Nuclear Weapons." *Southern Presbyterian Journal*, September 15, 1954.

———. "The Church in China." *Southern Presbyterian Journal*, January 28, 1959.

———. "The Church in China Further Developments." *Southern Presbyterian Journal*, February 25, 1959.

———. "Communist China and the U.N." *Southern Presbyterian Journal*, September 2, 1953.

———. "A Deadly Peril." *Southern Presbyterian Journal*, April 8, 1953.

———. "Destiny at Stake." *Presbyterian Journal*, July 27, 1960.

———. "Eternal Vigilance." *Southern Presbyterian Journal*, July 1, 1947.

———. "The Evangelical Faith vs. 'Fundamentalism,'" *Southern Presbyterian Journal*, July 27, 1955.

———. "Evanston and the Lord's Return." *Southern Presbyterian Journal*, December 16, 1953.

———. "The Federal Council and National Policy." *Southern Presbyterian Journal*, November 15, 1946.

———. "The Forgotten Ones." *Presbyterian Journal*, July 16, 1969.

———. "Forward—On Our Knees." *Southern Presbyterian Journal*, June 6, 1951.

———. "Is Patriotism Wrong?" *Southern Presbyterian Journal*, August 1, 1956.

———. "It Is Not 'Cynical' to Face the Facts." *Southern Presbyterian Journal*, January 20, 1954.

———. "Juvenile Delinquency." *Southern Presbyterian Journal*, February 17, 1954.

———. " 'Knowest Thou Not Yet' (Exodus 10:7)." *Southern Presbyterian Journal*, August 15, 1950.

———. "Korea." *Southern Presbyterian Journal*, July 15, 1950.

———. "Korean Missions: Triumph and Shadow." *Christianity Today*, February 18, 1957.

———. "The Kremlin Smiles." *Presbyterian Journal*, April 13, 1960.

———. "Lest We Forget." *Christianity Today*, June 23, 1958.

———. Letter to Carl F. H. Henry, May 9, 1958, Box 1958 1, File Correspondence, L. Nelson Bell, Carl F. H. Henry Collection, Rolfing Library, Trinity International University, Deerfield, Illinois.

———. Letter to Carl F. H. Henry, February 11, 1964, Box 1964 2, File Pew Correspondence 1964–1965, Carl F. H. Henry Collection, Rolfing Library, Trinity International University, Deerfield, Illinois.

———. "Making Democracy Safe for the World." *Southern Presbyterian Journal*, March 1944.

———. "Missions and Our China Policy." *Southern Presbyterian Journal*, February 15, 1946.

———. "Needed—A New Policy!" *Southern Presbyterian Journal*, January 11, 1956.

———. "A Neglected Doctrine." *Southern Presbyterian Journal*, August 3, 1955.

———. "No Time for Pacifism." *Southern Presbyterian Journal*, September 13, 1950.

———. "Not If But When?" *Southern Presbyterian Journal*, October 28, 1953.

———. "Not Peace but a Sword." *Southern Presbyterian Journal*, January 6, 1954.

———. "Open Sewers." *Presbyterian Journal*, January 26, 1966.

———. "Our China Policy." *Southern Presbyterian Journal*, December 1, 1948.

———. "Our China Policy." *Southern Presbyterian Journal*, May 1, 1950.

———. "Our 'Spokesman' Again." *Southern Presbyterian Journal*, May 16, 1949.

———. "Pacifism Is Not Dead." *Southern Presbyterian Journal*, November 1, 1946.

———. "Pacifists Versus Peace Makers." *Southern Presbyterian Journal*, February 16, 1948.

———. "Paralyzed." *Southern Presbyterian Journal*, November 26, 1952.

———. "Peace in 1971." *Presbyterian Journal*, December 30, 1970.

———. "Peace Cannot Be Bought." *Southern Presbyterian Journal*, August 1, 1950.

———. " 'Peaceful Co-Existence' The Road to Ultimate Tragedy." *Southern Presbyterian Journal*, December 22, 1954.

———. "Policies—Not Personalities." *Southern Presbyterian Journal*, April 25, 1951.

———. "Pollyanna in the U.N." *Southern Presbyterian Journal*, October 7, 1953.

———. "Postwar Planning." *Southern Presbyterian Journal*, January 1945.

———. "Praying for Peace." *Presbyterian Journal,* January 13, 1971.

———. "Quemoy—A Principle." *Southern Presbyterian Journal,* October 8, 1958.

———. "Race Relations and Montreat." *Southern Presbyterian Journal,* June 15, 1950.

———. "Race Relations at Montreat." *Southern Presbyterian Journal,* July 15, 1950.

———. "The Red Guards." *Southern Presbyterian Journal,* November 2, 1966.

———. "Riding a Tiger." *Southern Presbyterian Journal,* August 1, 1946.

———. "A Rude Awakening ... It Is *Much* Later than We Thought." *Southern Presbyterian Journal,* October 16, 1957.

———. "Russia." *Southern Presbyterian Journal,* June 1944.

———. "Seeing Jesus." *Southern Presbyterian Journal,* September 12, 1951.

———. "Shall We Promote Freedom, etc." *Southern Presbyterian Journal,* January 21, 1959.

———. "Shall We Recognize Communist China?" *Southern Presbyterian Journal,* October 11, 1950.

———. "Shall We Recognize Communist China?" *Southern Presbyterian Journal,* February 24, 1954.

———. "Some Fruits of Pacifism." *Southern Presbyterian Journal,* August 1942.

———. "A Strange Pronouncement." *Southern Presbyterian Journal,* November 18, 1953.

———. "Syria and Egypt." *Southern Presbyterian Journal,* February 12, 1958.

———. "There Is But One Road from the Summit—Down!" *Southern Presbyterian Journal,* April 15, 1959.

———. "Thoughts about Fundamentalism." *Presbyterian Journal,* March 31, 1971.

———. "Tolerance and Communism." *Southern Presbyterian Journal,* October 15, 1946.

———. "A Tragic Victim." *Presbyterian Journal,* August 22, 1962.

———. "Watching a Nation Die." *Presbyterian Journal,* February 12, 1964.

———. "The Way Out." *Southern Presbyterian Journal,* May 30, 1951.

———. "We *Must* Change Our China Policy—And Quickly." *Southern Presbyterian Journal,* February 14, 1951.

———. "While Men Slept." *Southern Presbyterian Journal,* August 16, 1948.

———. "While Rome Burns." *Southern Presbyterian Journal,* April 4, 1951.

———. "A World in Agony and Some Things We Forget." *Southern Presbyterian Journal,* November 14, 1956.

———. "The Year Ahead." *Southern Presbyterian Journal,* January 1, 1958.

———. "You Don't Temporize with Cancer—Or Do You?" *Southern Presbyterian Journal,* December 16, 1959.

Benedict, Leonard. "Youth of America, Beware!" *Moody Monthly,* November 1938.

Benson, Clarence H. "16,291,000 Jews." *Moody Monthly,* May 1937.

———. "Christians and Fighting." *Moody Monthly,* August 1937.

———. "The Meaning of the Present War." *Moody Monthly,* February 1941.

———. "The Nazi Church." *Moody Monthly,* July 1940.

———. "Peace by Preparedness." *Moody Monthly,* July 1938.

———. "Restoring the Roman Empire." *Moody Monthly,* August 1939.

———. "Seeking World Peace." *Moody Monthly,* May 1937.

———. "War in the Plans of God." *Moody Monthly,* September 1940.

———. "Who Wants War?" *Moody Monthly,* March 1939.

———. "Why Does God Allow War?" *Moody Monthly*, September 1940.

Berkouwer, G. C. "The Church in the Last Days." *Christianity Today*, April 14, 1958.

Berg, R.O. Editorial Cartoon, *Christian Herald*, January 1941.

———. Editorial Cartoon, *Christian Herald*, March 1941.

The Biblical Research Society. "Advertisement." *Moody Monthly*, June 1941.

Bligh, David. "Red Guards Sweep Albania." *Eternity*, August 1969.

Boice, James M. "Are We Back in the Days of Noah?" *Eternity*, October 1972.

———. "Are We Nearing the Last Holocaust?" *Eternity*, December 1972.

———. "Will There Really Be a Golden Age?" *Eternity*, September 1972.

Bouscaren, Anthony T. "The War We Are In." *Presbyterian Journal*, July 3, 1963.

Bowlsby, Betty Burrell. "On Your Knees, America! Back to God!" *Moody Monthly*, July 1937.

Britan, Joseph Taylor. "An Appeal for Persecuted Israel." *Moody Monthly*, February 1939.

———. "God in a World at War." *Moody Monthly*, April 1944.

Brother Andrew, "Behind the Czech Curtain." *Moody Monthly*, December 1968.

Browne, Michael. "Red Guards: China's Mini-Mao Revivalists." *Christianity Today*, February 3, 1967.

Burnham, George. "Report from Israel." *Christianity Today*, December 10, 1956.

Campbell Robert F. "Christ's Words on War and Peace." *Southern Presbyterian Journal*, May 1942.

Carter, Christ, and Kim Newton. "Revelations." *The X-Files*, Season 3, Episode 11. Aired on December 15, 1995, on Fox.

Chambers, D. Glenn. "We Encountered the Japs, *and Not a Shot Was Fired.*" *Moody Monthly*, August 1943.

Christie, Ernest D. "Those Un-comic Comic Books." *Moody Monthly*, January 1954.

Christ's Mission, Inc. "Advertisement." *Eternity*, May 1954.

Christiansen, Avis B. "The Service Flag." *Moody Monthly*, July 1942.

Christiansen, Frederick W. "A Report from Italy." *Moody Monthly*, October 1944.

Coder, S. Maxwell "The Destiny of America." *Moody Monthly*, January 1973, 30.

———. "The Future of Russia." *Moody Monthly*, September 1963.

———. "Jerusalem: Key to the Future." *Moody Monthly*, October 1973.

Cohen, Gary G. "The Bible and the War in Viet Nam." *Moody Monthly*, May 1967. 30.

Cook, Harold R. "From the Fields." *Moody Monthly*, May 1951.

Cook, Robert A. "Twenty Minutes After." *Moody Monthly*, April 1962.

———. "Why Do You Want to Live Through?" *Moody Monthly*, February 1962.

Coote, Robert. "Russian Evangelicals: American Dilemma." *Eternity*, August 1969.

Courier, Gabriel. "Aggressors." *Christian Herald*, December 1956.

———. "Aliens." *Christian Herald*, April 1942.

———. "Atom." *Christian Herald*, August, 1946.

———. "Balloons." *Christian Herald*, March 1946.

———. "Berlin." *Christian Herald*, March 1942.

———. "Berlin." *Christian Herald*, January 1959.

———. "Birmingham." *Christian Herald*, July 1963.

———. "Blood." *Christian Herald*, June 1959.

———. "Bomb." *Christian Herald*, October 1945.

———. "Bomb." *Christian Herald*, September 1946.

———. "The Bombs." *Christian Herald*, January 1956.

———. "Burned." *Christian Herald*, November 1941.

———. "Castro." *Christian Herald*, June 1959.

———. "China." *Christian Herald*, April 1941.

———. "China." *Christian Herald*, April 1946.

———. "China." *Christian Herald*, January 1949.

———. "China." *Christian Herald*, March 1949.

———. "China." *Christian Herald*, October 1949.

———. "Churchill." *Christian Herald*, May 1946.

———. "Civil Rights." *Christian Herald*, August 1964.

———. "Civil War." *Christian Herald*, January 1946.

———. "Closer." *Christian Herald*, August 1942.

———. "Coming Candidates." *Christian Herald*, September 1963.

———. "Corroded Conscience." *Christian Herald*, May 1965.

———. "Cuba." *Christian Herald*, March 1961.

———. "Cuba." *Christian Herald*, June 1961.

———. "Defense." *Christian Herald*, January 1941.

———. "Democracy." *Christian Herald*, November 1942.

———. "Disarmament." *Christian Herald*, January 1952.

———. "Draft." *Christian Herald*, February 1942.

———. "East." *Christian Herald*, March 1942.

———. "The East." *Christian Herald*, February 1942.

———. "The East." *Christian Herald*, January 1949.

———. "End?" *Christian Herald*, November 1943.

———. "FBI." *Christian Herald*, July 1949.

———. "Failure." *Christian Herald*, December 1946.

———. "Family." *Christian Herald*, September 1959.

———. "Finis." *Christian Herald*, February 1949.

———. "Future." *Christian Herald*, June 1946.

———. "Greeks." *Christian Herald*, January 1941.

———. "Ike." *Christian Herald*, January 1952.

———. "Information." *Christian Herald*, May 1946.

———. "Internees." *Christian Herald*, August 1942.

———. "Invocation." *Christian Herald*, March 1953.

———. "Italy." *Christian Herald*, January 1942.

———. "John Birch." *Christian Herald*, July 1961.

———. "League." *Christian Herald*, January 1946.

———. "Japan." *Christian Herald*, January 1941.

———. "Khrushchev." *Christian Herald*, July 1959.

———. "Klan." *Christian Herald*, February 1949.

———. "Klan." *Christian Herald*, September 1949.

———. "Laos." *Christian Herald*, July 1962.

———. "Loyalty." *Christian Herald*, August 1949.

————. "Lynchings Still Decreasing." *Christian Herald*, September 1942.

————. "Missionaries." *Christian Herald*, February 1946.

————. "Moscow." *Christian Herald*, March 1941.

————. "Negotiations." *Christian Herald*, September 1965.

————. "Out." *Christian Herald*, October 1945.

————. "Peace." *Christian Herald*, May 1942.

————. "Peace." *Christian Herald*, April 1943.

————. "Pigs is Pigs." *Christian Herald*, August 1959.

————. "Powers." *Christian Herald*, July 1946.

————. "Race." *Christian Herald*, June 1964.

————. "Rift?" *Christian Herald*, March 1962.

————. "Separation." *Christian Herald*, January 1946.

————. "Soapbox." *Christian Herald*, November 1959.

————. "Spies." *Christian Herald*, October 1942.

————. "Spies." *Christian Herald*, February 1949.

————. "Test." *Christian Herald*, January 1959.

————. "Tito." *Christian Herald*, October 1949.

————. "Titoism." *Christian Herald*, June 1949.

————. "To Have and to Have Not." *Christian Herald*, September 1946.

————. "Tour." *Christian Herald*, January 1960.

————. "Tours." *Christian Herald*, February 1960.

————. "U-2." *Christian Herald*, August 1960.

————. "U-2, Brutus." *Christian Herald*, July 1960.

————. "Un-American." *Christian Herald*, February 1949.

————. "U. N. O." *Christian Herald*, March 1946.

————. "Viet Nam." *Christian Herald*, August 1963.

————. "Viet Nam." *Christian Herald*, September 1963.

————. "Viet Nam." *Christian Herald*, November 1963.

————. "Viet Nam." *Christian Herald*, April 1965.

————. "Viet Nam." *Christian Herald*, July 1965.

————. "Viet Nam." *Christian Herald*, October 1965.

————. "Winner Castro." *Christian Herald*, March 1959.

————. "War!" *Christian Herald*, January 1942.

————. "War." *Christian Herald*, June 1965.

————. "Washington." *Christian Herald*, February 1941.

————. "Without Hamlet." *Christian Herald*, November 1946.

Cowperthwaite, Irving A. "The Marvels of God's Atoms." *Moody Monthly*, December 1945.

Crawford. Editorial Cartoon, *Christian Herald*, October 1945.

Crouch, Malcom. "When Will the Jews Rebuild Their Temple?" *Moody Monthly*, December 1973.

Crowell, Grace Noll. "America, my country." *Christian Herald*, February 1942. 2.

Culbertson, William. "1952: A Sequel." *Moody Monthly*, March 1951. 442.

————. "A-Bomb Tests Opposed by National Churches." *Moody Monthly*, June 1957.

————. "After the Inauguration—What?" *Moody Monthly*, January 1969.

———. "Backtrack in Palestine." *Moody Monthly*, May 1948.

———. "Call for Mobilization." *Moody Monthly*, September 1950.

———. "The Christian and His Times." *Moody Monthly*, June 1954.

———. "Communism Chooses Weapons." *Moody Monthly*, December 1950.

———. "Communism in Israel." *Moody Monthly*, August 1948.

———. "Communist Printed Bibles Reach Canada and US." *Moody Monthly*, March 1957.

———. "Do You Want Real Freedom?" *Moody Monthly*, July 1948.

———. "The Downward Path." *Moody Monthly*, September 1955.

———. "Historical Perspective." *Moody Monthly*, May 1960.

———. "In Wake of the TV Hearings." *Moody Monthly*, January 1960.

———. "Is It Later Than We Think?" *Moody Monthly*, November 1961.

———. "Israel and Prophecy—1964." *Moody Monthly*, May 1965.

———. "Lest We Forget." *Moody Monthly*, December 1965.

———. "A Look at the World." *Moody Monthly*, August 1963.

———. "More Important Than Peace." *Moody Monthly*, June 1948.

———. "Movies Unlimited." *Moody Monthly*, March 1954.

———. "Nation Under God." *Moody Monthly*, July 1954.

———. "A New Coat for the Wall." *Moody Monthly*, March 1954.

———. "The Night is Far Spent." *Moody Monthly*, February 1950.

———. "No Room for Frustration." *Moody Monthly*, April 1965.

———. "Peace at any Price?" *Moody Monthly*, June 1966.

———. "Perspective of Arab-Israeli Tension." *Christianity Today*, June 7, 1968.

———. "Prelude to Prophecy." *Moody Monthly*, February 1948.

———. "Preparation for Last Things." *Moody Monthly*, March 1951.

———. "The President's Death." *Moody Monthly*, January 1964.

———. "Prophetic Trends." *Moody Monthly*, January 1963.

———. "A Roman Catholic for President?" *Moody Monthly*, March 1960.

———. "The Significance of 'Sing-Out'—'66." *Moody Monthly*, September 1966.

———. "The Spirit of the Age." *Moody Monthly*, January 1958.

———. "Sputnik and Perspective." *Moody Monthly*, December 1957.

———. "That Same Subtle Weapon." *Moody Monthly*, January 1957.

———. "Thoughts for Armistice Day, 1951." *Moody Monthly*, November 1951.

———. "The Time and the Place." *Moody Monthly*, September 1961.

———. "Two Years to Work?" *Moody Monthly*, March 1950.

———. "The United Arab Republic." *Moody Monthly*, June 1963.

———. "War is Not Always Evil." *Moody Monthly*, November 1954.

———. "What Do We Do at The End of The Age?" *Moody Monthly*, May 1970.

———. "Where Communism Has Failed." *Moody Monthly*, June 1953.

———. "Whose Face is Red?" *Moody Monthly*, February 1957.

Cummings, Emery J. "My Country: Right or Wrong?" *Eternity*, June 1967.

Dean, Horace F. "Revival Must Come." *Moody Monthly*, March 1948.

DeKoster, Lester. "Communism." *Eternity*, January 1964.

Dorsett, Lyle W. *Serving God and Country: US Military Chaplains in World War II*. New York: The Berkley Publishing Group, 2012.

Dowdy, Homer. "Chaplain for Cuba's Army." *Eternity*, June 1960.

Drescher, John. "Is This How to Teach the Christmas Message?" *Eternity*, December 1969.

Duryee, Spencer. "Candles or Thunderbolts: An Interview with Congressman Charles A. Eaton." *Christian Herald*, March 1946.

Edel, William W. "We Stand." *Christian Herald*, August 1942.

The Editors. "About This Issue." *Moody Monthly*, October 1958.

———. Announcement, *Moody Monthly*, October 1950.

———. "Around The World." *Moody Monthly*, November 1970.

———. "Arson in Jerusalem: No Way to Fulfill Prophecy." *Eternity*, December 1969. 32.

———. "Behind the Iron Curtain." *Moody Monthly*, December 1950.

———. "Berlin Prayers Asked." *Presbyterian Journal*, August 30, 1961.

———. "But Why?" *Moody Monthly*, July-August 1964.

———. "China." *Moody Monthly*, June 1948.

———. "China's Massacre." *Moody Monthly*, October 1968.

———. " 'Closed Door' Countries—Are They Really Open?" *Moody Monthly*, May 1965.

———. "Communist Move Against Church Groups." *Moody Monthly*, May 1949.

———. "Conceded to Be Lost." *Christianity Today*, March 30, 1962.

———. Cover, *Moody Monthly*, September 1942.

———. Cover, *Eternity*, January 1956.

———. Cover, *Southern Presbyterian Journal*, May 12, 1954.

———. Cover, *Southern Presbyterian Journal*, April 4, 1956.

———. Cover, *Eternity*, January 1960.

———. Cover, *Christian Herald*, July 1960.

———. Cover, *Moody Monthly*, February 1962.

———. Cover, *Presbyterian Journal*, May 17, 1972.

———. "Confusion in Red China." *Moody Monthly*, September 1966.

———. "Cubans Release Two Baptist Missionaries." *Eternity*, March 1969.

———. "Czech Churchmen Start Speaking Out." *Presbyterian Journal*, May 22, 1968.

———. "Czech Invasion Prompts Measured Statements." *Presbyterian Journal*, September 4, 1968.

———. Editorial Cartoon, *Christian Herald*, May 1946.

———. Editorial Cartoon, *Christian Herald*, August 1946.

———. Editorial Cartoon, *Moody Monthly*, July 1949.

———. "First Church of Jackson, Miss. Declares Itself on Segregation." *Southern Presbyterian Journal*, July 7, 1954.

———. "Flight to Freedom." *Presbyterian Journal*, May 24, 1967.

———. "French Indo-China." *Moody Monthly*, May 1948.

———. "From the Fields." *Moody Monthly*, December 1950.

———. "Getting Hotter." *Moody Monthly*, April 1964.

———. "Hate in Hungary." *Christianity Today*, November 12, 1956.

———. "Israel—The Fulfillment of Prophecy?" *Christianity Today*, May 26, 1958.

———. "Israelis Organize to Combat Missions." *Presbyterian Journal*, February 6, 1963.

———. "Korea." *Moody Monthly*, February 1949.

———. "Lincoln's Legacy." *Christian Herald*, February 1949.

————. "Mechanized March by Children of Israel." *Christianity Today*, November 12, 1956.

————. "Missionaries Bombed in Viet Nam." *Eternity*, April 1964.

————. "The Most Segregated Hour." *Eternity*, July 1953.

————. "News Report." *Moody Monthly*, September 1951.

————. "News Report." *Moody Monthly*, October 1951.

————. "Nigeria." *Moody Monthly*, May 1948.

————. "No Room for Them." *Eternity*, February 1968.

————. Photo Caption, *Christian Herald*, January 1946.

————. Photo Caption, "War's Harvest." *Christian Herald*, May 1946.

————. Photo Caption, *Christian Herald*, September 1949.

————. Photo Caption, *Eternity*, September 1954.

————. "President Inspired by Prayers." *Moody Monthly*, May 1969.

————. "Problem in the Middle East." *Moody Monthly*, December 1967.

————. "Racial Barriers." *Eternity*, February 1952.

————. "Reds Block Church Official's Re-Entry." *Presbyterian Journal*, September 27, 1961.

————. "Report from Russia." *Moody Monthly*, March 1967.

————. "South Africa Race Tensions." *Christianity Today*, September 1, 1958.

————. "Stronger Stand Urged Against Vietnam Bias." *Presbyterian Journal*, August 21, 1963.

————. "These Were the Big Stories in 1963." *Moody Monthly*, January 1964.

————. "Victory! Peace!" *Moody Monthly*, September 1945.

————. "We Open our Mail." *Christian Herald*, November 1942.

————. "Where is 'L.N.B'?" *Southern Presbyterian Journal*, March 11, 1953.

————. "White House Gets Bibles in 78 Tongues." *Eternity*, January 1954.

————. "A Window on the World." *Eternity*, January 1951.

————. "A Window on the World." *Eternity*, February 1951.

————. "A Window on the World." *Eternity*, April 1951.

————. "World News in Brief." *Moody Monthly*, July 1950.

————. "Yugoslavia to Have First Protestant Seminary." *Moody Monthly*, June 1949.

The Editors and Donald A. Barnhouse. "Should We Acknowledge Red China?" *Eternity*, September 1971.

Ehrenstein, Herbert Henry. "Fulfilled Prophecy." *Eternity*, July 1966.

Elliot, Delber H. "God in the Constitutional Convention." *Christianity Today*, July 8, 1957.

Elson, Edward L. R. "Worship in the Life of the Nation." *Christianity Today*, November 12, 1956.

English, E. Schuyler. "All Present and Accounted For." *Our Hope*, September 1943.

————. "All They That Take the Sword … ." *Our Hope*, June 1945.

————. "And in the North." *Our Hope*, September 1943.

————. "And Speaking of Russia." *Our Hope*, March 1946.

————. "Anti-Anti-Semitism." *Our Hope*, March 1944.

————. "The Atlantic Pact." *Our Hope*, May 1949.

————. "Better Understanding at Moscow Conference." *Our Hope*, February 1946.

———. "Blindfold Removed." *Our Hope*, May 1947.

———. "Building with Blocs." *Our Hope*, May 1946.

———. " ... But the End Is Not Yet." *Our Hope*, June 1949.

———. "The Chief Menace to Peace in the World." *Our Hope*, November 1948.

———. "Cold War." *Our Hope*, January 1948.

———. "The Collapse of China." *Our Hope*, March 1949.

———. "Communism vs. Christendom?" *Our Hope*, October 1944.

———. "A Date With Destiny." *Our Hope*, May 1947.

———. "Did Anyone Win the War?" *Our Hope*, September 1946.

———. "Extra! Extra!" *Our Hope*, September 1945.

———. "First Cast the Beam Out of Thine Own Eye." *Our Hope*, September 1943.

———. "Finis." *Our Hope*, October 1945.

———. "The Great Enigma." *Our Hope*, September 1944.

———. "A Hook in the Jaws of the Bear." *Our Hope*, September 1949.

———. "An Interesting Prophecy." *Our Hope*, January 1944.

———. "Little Change." *Our Hope*, April 1944.

———. "Looking Eastward." *Our Hope*, January 1949.

———. "Manchuria's Future." *Our Hope*, February 1948.

———. "The Menace of Moscow." *Our Hope*, December 1946.

———. "The Molotov Plan." *Our Hope*, September 1947.

———. "The Moscow Menace." *Our Hope*, October 1948.

———. "No Peace in China." *Our Hope*, September 1946.

———. "On the Other Side of the World." *Our Hope*, July 1944.

———. "Only More of the Same Things." *Our Hope*, January 1946.

———. "Operation Crossroads." *Our Hope*, August 1946.

———. "Polygamous America." *Our Hope*, November 1947.

———. "Recapitulation." *Our Hope*, March 1944.

———. "Review of the Month." *Our Hope*, December 1943.

———. "September 23, 1949." *Our Hope*, November 1949.

———. "Shrunken Caesar." *Our Hope*, September 1943.

———. "Stalin's Dilemma." *Our Hope*, December 1949.

———. "Strange Actions." *Our Hope*, April 1946.

———. "There Is No Defense." *Our Hope*, June 1946.

———. "The Truman Doctrine." *Our Hope*, July 1947.

———. "Weapons for World War III?" *Our Hope*, September 1944.

———. "What About the Atom Bomb?" *Our Hope*, October 1945.

———. "Where Lies the Answer?" *Our Hope*, February 1949.

———. "World Conflict, 1946 Variety." *Our Hope*, July 1946.

———. "World War III?" *Our Hope*, May 1948.

English, James W. "Could Racism Be Hereditary ... ?" *Eternity*, September 1970.

Engstrom, Ted W. "A New Wind Blowing in Vietnam: Missions, Servant to a Growing Church." *Moody Monthly*, February 1973.

Enloe, Winton. "Twenty Years Later." *Presbyterian Journal*, August 4, 1965.

Erdman, Frederick. "Jewish and Gentile Paradoxes." *Moody Monthly*, September 1946.

Erickson, S. M. "A Holy War." *Southern Presbyterian Journal*, November 1942.

Evans, B. Hoyt. "The American Way of Life." *Presbyterian Journal*, January 20, 1960.

———. " 'But We are a Christian Nation,' " *Southern Presbyterian Journal*, October 3, 1956.

———. "Scholarships for Arab Refugees." *Southern Presbyterian Journal*, March 26, 1958.

Fischer, Robert B. "The Message of the Atomic Bomb to the Church." *Moody Monthly*, March 1946.

Filkin, Warren. "Allegiance." *Moody Monthly*, July 1947.

Fisher, Dorothy Canfield. "Exiles in America." *Christian Herald*, April 1943.

Flood, Robert. "Israel: Land of Return." *Moody Monthly*, March 1973.

Flow, J. E. "The Second Coming of Christ." *Southern Presbyterian Journal*, March 1943.

Forrest, A. C. "The Arabs." *Eternity*, April 1969.

Foster, Dave. "Czechoslovakia, One Year Later." *Eternity*, August 1969.

———. "How to Stop Communism." *Moody Monthly*, March 1964.

Foster, W. G. "America The Beautiful?" *Southern Presbyterian Journal*, June 20, 1951.

Frazer, William H. "The Social Separation of the Races." *Southern Presbyterian Journal*, July 15, 1950.

Freed, Paul E. "Seven Days Behind the Iron Curtain." *Moody Monthly*, May 1957.

The Friends of Israel Refugee Relief Committee, Inc. "Advertisement." *Moody Monthly*, September 1940.

———. "Advertisement." *Moody Monthly*, April 1944.

Fuller, Carlos Greenleaf. "A Church Powered for an Atomic Age." *Christianity Today*, January 6, 1958.

Fulton, C. Darby. "A Deceitful 'Peace.' " *Presbyterian Journal*, June 21, 1972.

Gaebelein, Arno C. "Be Aware." *Our Hope*, July 1938.

———. "The Beastly Wholesale Murder, Called War, Glorified." *Our Hope*, January 1938.

———. "The Bible is our Mandate. A Better Note in Zionism." *Our Hope*, June 1937.

———. "Britain Has Turned Out Nine Million Gas Masks." *Our Hope*, September 1937.

———. "The Coming Worldwide Anti-Red Pact." *Our Hope*, January 1938.

———. "Diabolical Hypocrisy." *Our Hope*, January 1937.

———. "The End of German Capitalism." *Our Hope*, December 1937.

———. "The Fight against Religion in the United States." *Our Hope*, March 1937.

———. "The German Reich Takes over Austria." *Our Hope*, May 1938.

———. "Germany's Favorable Attitude." *Our Hope*, April 1937.

———. The Hitler Regime Outdoes Red Blasphemies." *Our Hope*, January 1939.

———. "Imperial Rome Reborn." *Our Hope*, June 1937.

———. "The Internal Chaos of the United States." *Our Hope*, July 1938.

———. "Is the Final North-Eastern Confederacy Looming up on the Political Horizon?" *Our Hope*, July 1937.

———. "Is the Revival of the Great Roman Empire in Europe at Hand?" *Our Hope*, April 1938.

———. "Left-Wing Religionists Organize in Ohio." *Our Hope*, March 1937.

———. "Japan's Vicious Warfare—China's Sufferings." *Our Hope*, September 1938.

———. "Menaces." *Our Hope*, June 1939.

———. "More Evidence as to Russia and Germany." *Our Hope*, August 1937.

———. "Mussolini Speaks of Peace." *Our Hope*, February 1937.

———. "Mussolini's Attitude Towards the New Testament." *Our Hope*, June 1934.

———. "The New Great World Crisis XXIV." *Our Hope*, July 1943.

———. "The New Great World Crisis XXV." *Our Hope*, August 1943.

———. "The New Great World Crisis XXVI." *Our Hope*, September 1943.

———. "Observations and Experiences." *Our Hope*, November 1937.

———. "Observations and Experiences." *Our Hope*, December 1937.

———. "Observations and Experiences." *Our Hope*, January 1938.

———. "Pacifists and Radicals Oppose 'Neutrality' and Defense Acts," *Our Hope*, August 1937.

———. "Radical Preachers Fight Criticism of Radicalism." *Our Hope*, July 1937.

———. "The Soviet Military Budget." *Our Hope*, March 1937.

———. "The Tower of Babel for the Paris Exposition." *Our Hope*, April 1937.

———. "A True Statement from Secretary Eden." *Our Hope*, April 1937.

———. "What About the United States?" *Our Hope*, December 1938.

———. "What is the Population of Palestine?" *Our Hope*, April 1937.

———. "What Will Happen in 1937?" *Our Hope*, January 1937.

———. "Where is Pacifism These Days?" *Our Hope*, November 1937.

Gartenhaus, Jacob. "The Resurrection of Israel." *Presbyterian Journal*, November 19, 1969.

Gibson, Alan. "Behind the Berlin Barrier." *Eternity*, March 1963.

Gillespie, Guy T. "A Southerner Looks at the Race Question." *Eternity*, July 1957.

———. "A Southern Christian Looks at the Race Problem." *Southern Presbyterian Journal*, June 5, 1957.

Glasgow, Samuel McPheeters. "Why Go On?" *Southern Presbyterian Journal*, May 1942.

Glasgow, Tom. "The Bible—A Christian and War." *Southern Presbyterian Journal*, October 1942.

Glasser, Arthur F. "Red China." *Eternity*, January 1972.

Gotaas, David S. "If You Want to Save Your Freedom." *Moody Monthly*, July-August 1969.

Goldberg, Louis. "The Goldbergs Discover Israel: I. Around the Land in Eight Days." *Moody Monthly*, September 1968.

———. "Religious Thought in Israel." *Moody Monthly*, October 1971.

———. "Yom Kippur in Perspective." *Moody Monthly*, December 1973.

Goldwater, Barry. "Hate and Debate." *Presbyterian Journal*, June 3, 1964.

Goodwin, John. "Survey of the Year." *Eternity*, January 1966.

Gordon, A. Culver. "Theistic or Secular Government?" *Christianity Today*, April 26, 1963.

Graham, Billy. "Christ Demands No Less." *Eternity*, June 1958.

———. "Facing the Anti-God Colossus." *Christianity Today*, December 21, 1962.

———. "Impressions of Moscow." *Christianity Today*, July 20, 1959.

———. Letter to Carl F. H. Henry, December 22, 1955, Box 1956, File 1956 Correspondence—Graham, Billy, Carl F. H. Henry Collection, Rolfing Library, Trinity International University, Deerfield, Illinois.

Gray, James M. "Why Germany Cannot Rule the World." *Moody Monthly*, September 1942.

Gray, Richard W. "God, America and Sputnik." *Christianity Today*, December 9, 1957.

Gribble, Robert F. "Column Left: March!" *Southern Presbyterian Journal*, July 15, 1948.

Gunn, T. Jeremy. *Spiritual Weapons: The Cold War and the Forging of an American National Religion*. Westport, CT: Praeger Publishers, 2009.

Haberski, Raymond, Jr. *God and War: American Civil Religion Since 1945*. New Brunswick, NJ: Rutgers University Press, 2012.

Hallen, E. A. "World Peace—When and How?" *Moody Monthly*, June 1939.

Hansen, Wolfe. "What's Going on in Cuba?" *Eternity*, March 1971.

Hanson, Oscar C. "Are They Dying in Vain?" *Moody Monthly*, January 1945.

Harcus, George A. "Some Very American Heresies." *Eternity*, July 1970.

Hardesty, Nancy. "Are We Selling Out Czechoslovakia." *Eternity*, November 1968.

Harris, J. E. "Hitler Will Fail—But When?" *Moody Monthly*, July 1943.

Harrison, William K. "The Christian in Military Service." *Presbyterian Journal*, May 18, 1966.

———. "Christianity and Peace in Our Day." *Christianity Today*, October 29, 1956.

———. "I Faced the Communists at Panmunjon." *Eternity*, December 1953.

———. "Is the United States Right in Bombing North Viet Nam?" *Christianity Today*, January 7, 1966.

———. "Reminiscences and a Prophecy." *Christianity Today*, March 4, 1957.

———. "The Search for Peace on Earth." *Christianity Today*, April 13, 1963.

Hatfield, Mark. "What Has Happened to Our Values?" *Eternity*, August 1968.

Hefley, James C. "Facing Their New World of Freedom." *Moody Monthly*, September 1973.

Henley, Wallace B. "The Danger of Messianic Politics." *Eternity*, September 1973.

Henry, Carl F. H. October 17, 1952, Carl F. H. Henry Papers, Box "Let the Chips Fall." Rolfing Library Archives, Trinity Evangelical Divinity School, Deerfield, Illinois.

———. November 2, 1952, Carl F. H. Henry Papers, Box "Let the Chips Fall." Rolfing Library Archives, Trinity Evangelical Divinity School, Deerfield, Illinois.

———. November 4, 1952, Carl F. H. Henry Papers, Box "Let the Chips Fall." Rolfing Library Archives, Trinity Evangelical Divinity School, Deerfield, Illinois.

———. November 5, 1952, Carl F. H. Henry Papers, Box "Let the Chips Fall." Rolfing Library Archives, Trinity Evangelical Divinity School, Deerfield, Illinois.

———. November 7, 1952, Carl F. H. Henry Papers, Box "Let the Chips Fall." Rolfing Library Archives, Trinity Evangelical Divinity School, Deerfield, Illinois.

———. November 9, 1952, Carl F. H. Henry Papers, Box "Let the Chips Fall." Rolfing Library Archives, Trinity Evangelical Divinity School, Deerfield, Illinois.

———. November 17, 1952, Carl F. H. Henry Papers, Box "Let the Chips Fall." Rolfing Library Archives, Trinity Evangelical Divinity School, Deerfield, Illinois.

———. December 1, 1952, Carl F. H. Henry Papers, Box "Let the Chips Fall." File dated Sep-Apr alphabetical by first word A-F, Rolfing Library Archives, Trinity Evangelical Divinity School, Deerfield, Illinois.

———. Address to a luncheon sponsored by Campus Crusade, July 30, 1965, Box 1965 2, Loose, Carl F. H. Henry Collection, Rolfing Library, Trinity International University, Deerfield, Illinois.

———. Address to the National Association of Evangelicals, November 27, 1954, Box 1954, File Public Education and Catholicism, Variety—Paper by Henry, Newspaper clippings and other misc., Rolfing Library Archives, Trinity International University, Deerfield, Illinois.

———. "All the King's Horses." *Christianity Today*, February 16, 1968.

———. "Another Exposure of US Morals." *Christianity Today*, February 14, 1964.

———. "The Assassination of the President." *Christianity Today*, December 6, 1963.

———. "Beware That Smile." *Christianity Today*, December 3, 1965.

———. "Can We Salvage the Republic?" *Christianity Today*, March 3, 1958.

———. "Christ and the Atom Bomb." *Christianity Today*, September 2, 1957.

———. "Christ and the Human Dilemma." *Lebanon Valley College Bulletin*, July 1965.

———. "Christian Education and Our American Schools." *United Evangelical Action*, December 1, 1955.

———. "Christian Faith and National Power." *Christianity Today*, July 2, 1965.

———. "Christian Responsibility and Communist Brutality." *Christianity Today*, November 26, 1956.

———. "The Christian's Duty in the Present Crisis." *Christianity Today*, January 5, 1959. 22.

———. "Christianity and the American Heritage." *United Evangelical Action*, July 1, 1954.

———. "Christianity and the Economic Crisis." *Eternity*, June 1955.

———. "The Church and Red China." *Christianity Today*, March 17, 1958.

———. "Civil Rights and Christian Concern." *Christianity Today*, May 8, 1964.

———. "Color is Skin Deep, Evil as Deep as the Heart." *Christianity Today*, May 24, 1963.

———. *Confessions of a Theologian: An Autobiography.* Waco: Word Books, 1986.

———. "Cuba Situation Becomes a Battle for the Hemisphere." *Christianity Today*, August 1, 1960.

———. "The Cuban Crisis and Pacifist Reaction." *Christianity Today*, March 1, 1963.

———. "Daniel A. Poling." *Christianity Today*, March 1, 1968.

———. "Desegregation and Regeneration." *Christianity Today*, September 29, 1958.

———. "The Dignity of Work: The Christian Concept." *Vital Speeches of the Day*, August 15, 1954.

———. "Dissent by Violence." *Christianity Today*, November 10, 1967.

———. "Eastern Europe's 'Congress on Evangelism.'" *Eternity*, November 1969.

———. "Eisenhower, Khurshchev Talks Shadowed by a Red Moon." *Christianity Today*, September 28, 1959.

———. "The Fiasco in Cuba and Freedom's Supports." *Christianity Today*, May 8, 1961.

———. "A Firm Reliance on Providence." *Christianity Today*, June 23, 1958.

———. "Footnote on Glory: Who is Mr. K?" *Christianity Today*, March 29, 1963.

———. "The Forgotten American." *Christianity Today*, May 22, 1964.

———. "The Fragility of Freedom in the West." *Christianity Today*, October 15, 1956.

———. "A Future Big with Hope." *Christianity Today*, November 20, 1964.

———. "God Makes Us Great." *Christianity Today*, June 22, 1962.

———. *God, Revelation and Authority Volume VI: God Who Stands and Stays Part Two.* Wheaton, IL: Crossway Books, 1999.

———. "God's Countdown: 1960." *Christianity Today*, December 21, 1959.

———. "God's Judgment on the Summit." *Christianity Today*, June 6, 1960.

———. "The Gospel in Modern Asia." *Christianity Today*, September 28, 1959.

———. "The Ground of Freedom." *Christianity Today*, July 3, 1964.

———. "Halting Red Aggression in Viet Nam." *Christianity Today*, April 23, 1965.

———. "His Coming Draws Near." *Eternity*, August 1971.

———. "Hopeful Developments in Birmingham." *Christianity Today*, April 24, 1964.

———. "A Hopeful Sign." *Christianity Today*, May 8, 1964.

———. "Human Rights in an Age of Tyranny." *Christianity Today*, February 4, 1957.

———. "Human Tragedy at Year-End." *Christianity Today*, January 5, 1968.

———. "Ignorance Often Has a Loud Voice." *Christianity Today*, February 12, 1965.

———. "International Crisis on the Sandy Wastes of Sinai." *Christianity Today*, November 12, 1956.

———. "Is Life Ever Cheap?" *Eternity*, February 1971.

———. "Is Modernity Worth Saving?" *Christianity Today*, January 7, 1957.

———. "Is There Hope for Palestine?" *Christianity Today*, June 7, 1968.

———. "Israel: Marvel Among the Nations." *Christianity Today*, September 11, 1961.

———. "It is Not Too Late." Address given at Berlin Conference, Box 1966, File Berlin Conference Background, Carl F. H. Henry Collection, Rolfing Library, Trinity International University, Deerfield, Illinois.

———. "Joint Moscow-Peking Threat Calls for Christian Realism." *Christianity Today*, March 4, 1957.

———. "Johnson, King, and Ho Chi Minh." *Christianity Today*, April 26, 1968.

———. "The Last Battle in Asia?" *Christianity Today*, June 19, 1964.

———. "Left Wing Attacks on FBI and House Un-American Activities Group." *Christianity Today*, March 30, 1959.

———. Letter to Billy Graham, August 1, 1970, Box 1970 3, File Correspondence, Graham, Billy, Carl F. H. Henry Collection, Rolfing Library, Trinity International University, Deerfield, Illinois.

———. Letter to the Editor of *Pasadena Star-News*, November 7, 1951, Carl F. H. Henry Papers, Box 1951 1, File Protestants and other Americans for the Separation of Church and State, Rolfing Library Archives, Trinity Evangelical Divinity School, Deerfield, Illinois.

———. Letter to Franklin Littrell, December 10, 1970, Box 1971 1, File Arab-Israeli, Carl F. H. Henry Collection, Rolfing Library, Trinity International University, Deerfield, Illinois.

———. Letter to Nelson Dilworth, Carl F. H. Henry Papers, Box 1953, File Correspondence to Senator Nelson Dilworth, Rofling Library Archives, Trinity Evangelical Divinity School, Deerfield, IL.

———. Letter to Stephen Olford, May 15, 1968, Box 1963 2, File Correspondence, Olford, Carl F. H. Henry Collection, Rolfing Library, Trinity International University, Deerfield, Illinois.

———. Letter to T. W. Wilson, September 2, 1965, Box 1965 2, File Correspondence, Billy Graham, Carl F. H. Henry Collection, Rolfing Library, Trinity International University, Deerfield, Illinois.

———. Letter to T. W. Wilson, September 10, 1965, Box 1965 2, File Correspondence, Billy Graham, Carl F. H. Henry Collection, Rolfing Library, Trinity International University, Deerfield, Illinois.

———. Letter to unknown recipient, February 1965, Box 1964 2, File Pew Correspondence 1964–1965, Carl F. H. Henry Collection, Rolfing Library, Trinity International University, Deerfield, Illinois.

———. "Like a Russian Ballot." *Christianity Today*, April 23, 1965.

———. Manuscript, Carl F. H. Henry Papers, Box 1960, File Correspondence, Writings, Rolfing Library Archives, Trinity Evangelical Divinity School, Deerfield, IL.

———. "Megaton or Manger?" *Christianity Today*, December 8, 1961.

———. "Modern Education and the Secularistic Tide." *The Watchman Examiner*, October 11, 1951.

———. "Moral Dilemmas, Dual Standards Widen in a Self-Righteous Age." *Christianity Today*, April 27, 1962.

———. "Moral Values in Public Education." *Eternity*, September 1954.

———. "Murder is Murder—Anywhere." *Christianity Today*, August 28, 1964.

———. "Newspaper Contribution to Modern Pornography." *Christianity Today*, March 16, 1959.

———. "On the Lord's Side." *Christianity Today*, June 4, 1965.

———. "Persecution in Russia." *Christianity Today*, January 1, 1965.

———. "Plight of the Korean Christians." *Christianity Today*, September 25, 1961.

———. "The Political Tightrope." *Christianity Today*, September 30, 1966.

———. "The Price of Peace." *Christianity Today*, April 23, 1965.

———. "Priorities for the Eighties." Sermon given at First Baptist Church, Conway, AR, November 14, 1979.

———. "Red China and World Morality." *Christianity Today*, December 10, 1956.

———. "Red Guards Spur Attack on Christian Remnant in Communist China." *Christianity Today*, September 16, 1966.

———. "Religion in Review: Outstanding Events in the Religious World During 1955." *Evangelical Beacon and Evangelist*, December 27, 1955.

———. "The Road to Freedom." *Christianity Today*, February 28, 1964.

———. Sermon at Southwestern Baptist Theological Seminary, September 19, 1961, Carl F. H. Henry Papers, Box 1961 2, File Speech "The Legacy of Christ," Rolfing Library Archives, Trinity Evangelical Divinity School, Deerfield, IL.

———. "Seven Minutes to Midnight?" *Christianity Today*, February 2, 1968.

———. "Shattering the American Image." *Christianity Today*, October 23, 1964.

———. "Signs of Vitality." *Christianity Today*, December 23, 1957.

———. "The Sins of Sodom—1963." *Christianity Today*, September 13, 1963.

———. "Space Cooperation May Prove to Be an Earthly Trap." *Christianity Today*, April 27, 1962.

———. "Summer of Racial Discontent." *Christianity Today*, July 21, 1967.

———. *Theology in the Present World Crisis*, Carl F. H. Henry Papers, Box 1964, Rolfing Library Archives, Trinity Evangelical Divinity School, Deerfield, Illinois.

———. "A Time for Moral Indignation." *Christianity Today*, March 12, 1965.

———. "Troubled Waters." *Christianity Today*, July 17, 1964.

———. "The Trumpet of the Lord." *Christianity Today*, June 10, 1957.

———. "The U.N. Falters in Debate While Dagger Diplomacy Widens." *Christianity Today*, October 13, 1961.

———. *The Uneasy Conscience of Modern Fundamentalism*. Grand Rapids, MI: Wm. B. Eerdmans Publishing Company, 1947.

———. "Viet Nam: A Moral Dilemma." *Christianity Today*, January 20, 1967.

———. "Viet Nam: Where Do We Go from Here?" *Christianity Today*, January 7, 1966.

———. "The Violent New Breed." *Christianity Today*, November 24, 1967.

———. "War and Peace at Winona." *Christianity Today*, September 27, 1963.

———. "War Sweeps the Bible Lands." *Christianity Today*, June 23, 1967.

———. "We Are in the Last Days." *Eternity*, July 1971.

———. "Western Tension Mounts as Reds Seal East Berlin Border." *Christianity Today*, August 28, 1961.

———. "What is the Target: Communism or Anti-Communism." *Christianity Today*, May 22, 1961.

———. "What of Tomorrow?" *Christianity Today*, March 3, 1958.

———. "What's Next?" *Eternity*, January 1970.

———. "Where is America Going?" *Christianity Today*, June 21, 1968.

———. "The White Conscience and the Negro Vote." *Christianity Today*, March 28, 1960.

———. "World Arms Race and the Moralizing of Power." *Christianity Today*, September 11, 1961.

Herring, Dallas. "Democracy and the Church." *Presbyterian Journal*, April 20, 1966.

Herzog, Jonathan P. *The Spiritual Industrial Complex: America's Religious Battle against Communism in the Early Cold War*. New York: Oxford University Press, 2011.

Hill, Bob. "From the Nation's Capital." *Moody Monthly*, October 1970.

———. "Graham Leads 'Honor America Day.'" *Moody Monthly*, September 1970.

———. "Nixon Visits Graham Crusade." *Moody Monthly*, July-August 1970.

Hitt, Russell T. "The Abortion Ruling: Christian Citizen's Dilemma." *Eternity*, April 1973.

———. "Americans First and Christians Second." *Eternity*, August 1961.

———. "Cuba's Christians Need Prayer." *Eternity*, April 1962.

———. "Crime: What Are You Doing About It?" *Eternity*, March 1969.

———. "Does Corruption Matter." *Eternity*, June 1973.

———. "Fifteen Minutes Over the Brink." *Eternity*, January 1963.

———. "Hope for the '70s." *Eternity*, January 1971.

———. "How to Perish in a Nuclear Attack." *Eternity*, March 1962.

———. "Is Government Control Next for Hollywood?" *Eternity*, June 1961.

———. "The Government's Right to Lie." *Eternity*, May 1963.

———. "Martyred for Their Faith by Communists." *Eternity*, February 1961.

———. "Our Epidemic of Violence: Is There a Cure?" *Eternity*, January 1970.

———. "Politics." *Eternity*, January 1973.

———. "The POW Story: Seven Years of Prison and Prayer." *Eternity*, June 1973.

———. "Reflections on Israel's Birthday." *Eternity*, May 1973.

———. "Translators Slain in Viet Nam." *Eternity*, April 1963.

———. "Twenty Trends." *Eternity*, January 1970.

———. "Vietnam Closes Doors." *Eternity*, June 1961.

———. "What Ike's Pastor Believes." *Eternity*, February 1954.

———. "Who Hears Ecclesiastical Pronouncements?" *Eternity*, January 1966.

———. "Who Is The True Servant of God?" *Eternity*, August 1969.

———. "Why Do We Have a Propensity for Violence?" *Eternity*, September 1969.

———. "World Peace, and Drama at the U.N." *Eternity*, December 1971.

———. "Wrongs Do Not Make Civil Rights." *Eternity*, June 1964.

Hockman, William H. "Missionary Department." *Moody Monthly*, January 1938.

———. "No Escape from Terror." *Moody Monthly*, April 1937.

———. "Family Prayers in the White House." *Moody Monthly*, December 1938.

Holbrook, Donald J. "What about the Atomic Bomb?" *Moody Monthly*, November 1945.

Holcomb, Luther J. "Christian America's Contribution to World Peace." *Moody Monthly*, October 1946.

Hoover, J. Edgar. "The Challenge of the Future." *Christianity Today*, May 26, 1958.

———. "The Communist Menace: Red Goals and Christian Ideals." *Christianity Today*, October 10, 1960.

———. "Let's Fight Communism Sanely!" *Christian Herald*, January 1962.

———. "We Must Defend America." *Moody Monthly*, July 1955.

Houghton, William H. "An Afflicted World." *Moody Monthly*, December 1942.

———. "America Helping Japan?" *Moody Monthly*, January 1939.

———. "American Missions Fields—Wake and Midway Islands." *Moody Monthly*, November 1941.

———. "The Atomic Bomb." *Moody Monthly*, October 1945.

———. "The Christian War." *Moody Monthly*, October 1942.

———. "Concerning the War." *Moody Monthly*, February 1942.

———. "The Editors to Those Who Run." *Moody Monthly*, June 1942.

———. "Europe Starving." *Moody Monthly*, July 1946.

———. "Fighting or Hating?" *Moody Monthly*, February 1943.

———. "God and Human Folly." *Moody Monthly*, November 1942. 124.

———. "God, Time, and Russia Are on Our Side ... or Are They?" *Moody Monthly*, March 1943.

———. "Good News." *Moody Monthly*, April 1944.

———. "Government and Peace." *Moody Monthly*, October 1943.

———. "How Slaves Are Made." *Moody Monthly*, March 1945.

———. "In a World of Tragic Need." *Moody Monthly*, May 1945.

———. "Is America Facing Sunrise or Sunset?" *Moody Monthly*, April 1944.

———. "Japanese Cruelty." *Moody Monthly*, March 1938.

———. "A Joke on Hitler?" *Moody Monthly*, October 1945.

———. "Liberty." *Moody Monthly*, July 1937.

———. "Love Your Enemies." *Moody Monthly*, August 1944.

———. "A Loyalty Pledge." *Moody Monthly*, September 1940.

———. "The New Armistice." *Moody Monthly*, November 1938.

———. "Pagan America." *Moody Monthly*, February 1945.

———. "Pessimism and Despair." *Moody Monthly*, May 1938.

———. "The Plight of the Jews." *Moody Monthly*, June 1941.

———. "Prayer and Victory." *Moody Monthly*, June 1944.

———. "A Question Often Asked." *Moody Monthly*, September 1942.

———. "Revolution Everywhere." *Moody Monthly*, May 1946.

———. "Russia and Prophecy." *Moody Monthly*, February 1940.

———. "Sinning Children." *Moody Monthly*, March 1944.

———. "The Spirit of Hitler." *Moody Monthly*, January 1944.

———. "Thanksgiving." *Moody Monthly*, November 1945.

———. "This Thing Called Civilization, No. 10." *Moody Monthly*, November 1939.

———. "Wanted—A New Americansim?" *Moody Monthly*, July 1940.

———. "War." *Moody Monthly*, April 1937.

———. "What Shall It Profit a Nation?" *Moody Monthly*, August 1943.

———. "Wonderful!" *Moody Monthly*, December 1945.

———. "The Year Closes." *Moody Monthly*, December 1938.

Hudson, George A. "Five Point Program for the Far East." *Southern Presbyterian Journal*, August 1944.

Huffman, J. "About Those POW's." *Moody Monthly*, November 1973.

Inboden, William. *Religion and American Foreign Policy, 1945–1960: The Soul of Containment*. New York: Cambridge University Press, 2008.

Jackson, Douglas. "Communism: Will the China-Russia Rift Grow Bigger?" *Eternity*, January 1963.

Johnson, Glenn. "The Face of the Enemy." *Moody Monthly*, June 1969.

Johnson, Jimmie. "What is Behind that Curtain?" *Moody Monthly*, August 1951.

———. "What is Behind that Curtain?" *Moody Monthly*, September 1951.

Jones, Joseph S. "The Ku Klux Klan, the NAACP, and the Presbyterian Church." *Southern Presbyterian Journal*, July 31, 1957.

Judd, Walter H. "What Should United States Policy in China Be?" *Southern Presbyterian Journal*, July 1, 1950.

———. "World Issues and the Christian." *Christianity Today*, June 23, 1958.

Kamm, S. Richey. "The American Revolution: Revolutionary or Liberative?" *Christianity Today*, July 3, 1964.

Kane, J. Herbert. "The Future of Missions in Red China." *Moody Monthly*, January 1951.

———. "Will China Re-Open to Missions?" *Moody Monthly*, November 1971.

Kelso, James L. "Perspective of Arab-Israeli Tension." *Christianity Today*, June 7, 1968.

Kennedy, David H. "New Glory for Old Glory." *Presbyterian Journal*, July 1, 1970. 9.

King, Louis L. "Asia." *Eternity*, January 1964.

———. "Report from Viet Nam." *Eternity*, February 1962.

Kligerman, Aaron J. "Palestine—Jewish Homeland." *Southern Presbyterian Journal*, June 1, 1948.

Knowland, William F. "Admit Red China?" *Christianity Today*, October 29, 1956.

Konrad, Arthur. "Guns in Albania." *Moody Monthly*, October 1939.

Kucharsky, David E. "Clergy Press Role in Peace Talks." *Christianity Today*, February 18, 1966.

———. "Compassion for the Cubans." *Christianity Today*, January 18, 1963.

———. "Compassion Gap in Viet Nam." *Christianity Today*, April 14, 1967.

———. "Did Khrushchev See America?" *Christianity Today*, October 12, 1959.

———. "East Germany: Church Losing Ground to Reds." *Christianity Today*, February 13, 1961.

———. "A Plea for Soviet Churches." *Christianity Today*, September 25, 1964.

———. "Race Showdown—An Unlikely Site." *Christianity Today*, July 21, 1958.

———. "Report from Cuba." *Christianity Today*, January 4, 1960.

———. "Special Report: Is 'News Management' Ethical?" *Christianity Today*, April 12, 1963.

———. "Southern Travellers." *Christianity Today*, January 5, 1962.

———. "The Unsettling War." *Christianity Today*, August 27, 1965.

———. "Viet Nam: Bullets and Brickbats." *Christianity Today*, July 30, 1965.

———. "Viet Nam Circuit Riders." *Christianity Today*, December 3, 1965.

———. "Viet Nam: The Spiritual War." *Christianity Today*, September 25, 1964.

———. "Viet Nam: The Vulnerable Ones." *Christianity Today*, March 1, 1968.

Kuhn, Harold. "Christian Surrender to Communism." *Christianity Today*, March 2, 1959.

Lahr, Angela M. *Millennial Dreams and Apocalyptic Nightmares: The Cold War Origins of Political Evangelicalism.* New York: Oxford University Press, 2007.

LaSor, William Sanford. "Have the 'Times of the Gentiles' Been Fulfilled?" *Eternity*, August 1967.

Lampman, Charles T. "Baptists in Russia Said to Enjoy Full Freedom." *Moody Monthly*, October 1955.

———. "Chinese Youth Steals Mission Funds for Reds." *Moody Monthly*, January 1954.

———. "Christian Persecution in China Increasing." *Moody Monthly*, June 1954.

———. "Desegregation in Capital Seen as Most Dramatic Success." *Moody Monthly*, December 1955.

———. "FBI Employees Attend Special Vespers Service." *Moody Monthly*, August 1954.

———. "God to be Honored in Flag Pledge Change." *Moody Monthly*, July 1954.

———. "New Clean Comic Book Code Seen to Lack Teeth." *Moody Monthly*, January 1955.

———. "President Accepts Bibles for White House." *Moody Monthly*, January 1954.

———. "President Praises Ministry of Christian Businessmen." *Moody Monthly*, January 1957.

———. "President's Pastor Scores Inadequate Giving." *Moody Monthly*, January 1954.

———. "Seaton's Statement as Later Related for Publication." *Moody Monthly*, August 1955.

———. "US Currency Motto to Honor God Urged." *Moody Monthly*, February 1954.

Landrum, Phil. "Martyrdom in Vietnam." *Moody Monthly*, May 1963.

Lane, Mortimer B. "The World's Richest Man." *Moody Monthly*, November 1939.

Larson, Robert. "China: Open Door to What?" *Christianity Today*, August 27, 1971.

Lawrence, David. "No Longer Treason?" *Presbyterian Journal*, December 6, 1967.

Lawrence, John. "Here are the Facts about Russian Protestants." *Eternity*, November 1955.

LeCraw, Roy. "A Message for Presbyterians." *Southern Presbyterian Journal*, July 4, 1951.

Lee, Davis. "Segregation." *Southern Presbyterian Journal*, July 7, 1954.

Lee, Robert G. "Weighed and Found Worthy." *Moody Monthly*, November 1950.

Lewis, C. S. "The Christian Hope." *Eternity*, March 1954.

Lewis, Norman. "America's Creeping Peril of Plenty." *Moody Monthly*, November 1964.

Lewis. Editorial Cartoon, *Christian Herald*, November 1945.

Lindsell, Harold. "30,000 Dead." *Christianity Today*, January 3, 1969.

———. "America on Its Knees?" *Christianity Today*, June 19, 1970.

———. "Arson in Jerusalem." *Christianity Today*, September 12, 1969.

———. "The Bible and Race Relations." *Eternity*, August 1956.

———. "The Calley Verdict." *Christianity Today*, April 23, 1971.

———. "The China Vote." *Christianity Today*, November 19, 1971.

———. "A Cordial Welcome—If You're White." *Christianity Today*, February 27, 1970.

———. "The Czech Caterpillar Keeps Stirring." *Christianity Today*, August 16, 1968.

———. "The Czech Quest for Freedom." *Christianity Today*, February 14, 1969.

———. "Farewell to Mr. Johnson." *Christianity Today*, January 31, 1969.

———. "Hooray for Ho?" *Christianity Today*, October 10, 1969.

———. "Is Patriotism Dead?" *Christianity Today*, July 4, 1969.

———. "The Options of Modern Man." *Christianity Today*, November 6, 1969.

———. "The Peking Gambit." *Christianity Today*, August 6, 1971.

———. "The President's Viet Nam Policy." *Christianity Today*, November 21, 1969.

———. "Radicals on the Rampage." *Christianity Today*, November 6, 1970.

———. "Refining Czech Communism." *Christianity Today*, September 13, 1968.

———. "A Sobering Outlook for President-elect Nixon." *Christianity Today*, November 22, 1968.

———. "Speeding Up Desegregation." *Christianity Today*, November 21, 1969.

———. "Viet Nam—Continuing Impasse." *Christianity Today*, August 6, 1971.

Lindsey, Samuel M. "Thank God for the United States of America." *Moody Monthly*, July 1946.

Lippincott, H. H. "World Government and Christianity." *Christianity Today*, February 3, 1958.

Little, Robert J. "Current Events and the Blessed Hope." *Moody Monthly*, February 1970.

———. "Good News from China." *Moody Monthly*, May 1969.

———. "The Mid-East Crisis." *Moody Monthly*, July-August 1967.

Lockerbie, D. Bruce. "Now that Kennedy is President." *Eternity*, January 1961.

Lundquist, Harold L. "Can a Soldier be a Christian?" *Moody Monthly*, May 1944.

———. "The Bible Made America." *Moody Monthly*, July 1946.

———. "Is the Stage Being Set?" *Moody Monthly*, August 1946.

———. "The Sins of the Church." *Moody Monthly*, March 1945.

Long, Egerton C. "Some Things War Cannot Touch." *Moody Monthly*, September 1945.

Love, H. Lawrence. "Roots of Prejudice." *Southern Presbyterian Journal*, July 8, 1953.

Madeira, Eugene. "God is Still in Charge." *Eternity*, January 1967.

Malefyt, Calvin S. "Watergate: A Question of Values." *Eternity*, July 1973.

Malik, Charles. "It's Cosmic." *Presbyterian Journal*, October 21, 1970.

Mardsen, George M. *Understanding Fundamentalism and Evangelicalism*. Grand Rapids, MI: Wm. B. Eerdmans, 1991.

Matson, G. Eric. "Whitewash for Zionism?" *Moody Monthly*, August 1950.

McCallie, J. P. "Resolution in Behalf of America and Victory." *Southern Presbyterian Journal*, September 1942.

———. "The Signs of the Times." *Southern Presbyterian Journal*, June 4, 1958.

McLauchlin, W. C. "Sailing Back." *Southern Presbyterian Journal*, January 15, 1946.

Mead, Frank. "Adam Can't Help Us Now." *Christian Herald*, May 1946.

Meadowcroft, Ralph Sadler. "What My Church is Doing to Maintain Morale." *Christian Herald*, September 1942.

Metcalf, Robert M. "Is the Night Inevitable?" *Presbyterian Journal*, September 1, 1965.

Moffett, Samuel H. "Can Communism Kill the Church." *Eternity*, May 1954.

Moberg, David O. "A Victory for Religious Liberty." *Eternity*, February 1961.

Moody Bible Institute. "Advertisement." *Christian Herald*, October 1942.

———. "Advertisement." *Moody Monthly*, May 1950.

———. "Advertisement." *Moody Monthly*, November 1951.

Morsell, John A. "NAACP Answers Charge." *Eternity*, November 1958.

Needham, William. "On Duty for Christ." *Moody Monthly*, November 1969.

Nelson, Wesley W. "Living in Apostate Days." *Moody Monthly*, November 1949.

Nottage, B. M. "You've Neglected My People." *Eternity*, December 1957.

Odell, Don C. "Answers from Israel." *Christianity Today*, November 12, 1956.

Olford, Stephen. "A Communist War." *Moody Monthly*, February 1969.

Oliver, C. Herbert. "The Christian Negro." *Eternity*, November 1960.

Olsen, Erling C. "The Gospel in the Postwar World." *Moody Monthly*, February 1945.

Oliver, Kay. "Graham Meetings Challenge Apartheid." *Moody Monthly*, June 1973.

Olsson, Karl A. "We Remember Brave Men." *Presbyterian Journal*, July 2, 1969.

Osterhaven, M. Eugene. "Pathos of Hungarian Protestantism." *Christianity Today*, November 26, 1956.

Ostling, Joan K. "Abortion: Time for a Hard, New Look." *Eternity*, May 1972.

Ostling, Richard N. "Inauguration Amid Religious Trappings." *Moody Monthly*, February 14, 1969.

———. "Czech Church Thaw." *Christianity Today*, August 30, 1968.

Painter, T. A. "Helping Forward the Affliction?" *Southern Presbyterian Journal*, October 1, 1945.

Palmer, Bernard. "The Spirit of '72." *Moody Monthly*, July-August 1972.

Parker, J. Kenton. "Jesus Teaches About the End of the Age." *Southern Presbyterian Journal*, February 4, 1959.

———. "Peace, Peace, When There is No Peace." *Southern Presbyterian Journal*, December 15, 1945.

Patterson, Vernon W. "Bases of a Just and Durable Peace: As Proposed by the Federal Council of Churches." *Southern Presbyterian Journal*, June 1942.

———. "The Principles and Objectives of the Federal Council." *Southern Presbyterian Journal*, October 1944.

Sam Paxton, "Attacking Smut." *Moody Monthly*, February 1953.

———. "News Report." *Moody Monthly*, April 1953.

———. "Faith, Government and Sense." *Moody Monthly*, April 1953.

Petersen, William. "Dueling with Gigantic Windmills: United States." *Eternity*, January 1961.

Peterson, Walfred. "Is Anti-Communist Foreign Policy Christian?" *Eternity*, August 1962.

———. "The Case Against Civil Religion." *Eternity*, October 1973.

———. "Must We Obey Our Country." *Eternity*, March 1964.

Phillips, John McCandlish. "Will the Christian Please Stand Up!" *Moody Monthly*, April 1971.

Pierard, Richard V. "New Look Over the Wall." *Eternity*, August 1969.

Pippert, Wesley G. "The Four-Star General Who Calls Men to the Lord." *Moody Monthly*, November 1972.

Poling, Daniel A. "The Atlantic Charter." *Christian Herald*, January 1942.

———. "Catholic F.B.I.?" *Christian Herald*, September 1959.

———. "A Correction." *Christian Herald*, March 1941.

———. "Doctor Polling Answers." *Christian Herald*, November 1941.

———. "Doctor Poling Answers." *Christian Herald*, March 1942.

———. "Doctor Poling Answers." *Christian Herald*, June 1942.

———. "Doctor Poling Answers." *Christian Herald*, October 1942.

———. "Doctor Poling Answers." *Christian Herald*, April 1943.

———. "Does Pacifism Become Activism?" *Christian Herald*, October 1965.

———. "Epic Hour." *Christian Herald*, October 1945.

———. "Fourth of July Meditations." *Christian Herald*, July 1941.

———. "It is Not Too Late." *Christian Herald*, October 1942.

———. "Lyndon B. Johnson, 36th President of the United States." *Christian Herald*, January 1964.

———. "Open Palestine Immediately." *Christian Herald*, January 1946.

———. "Out of My Mail." *Christian Herald*, January 1941.

———. "The Peace." *Christian Herald*, July 1944.

———. " 'People's Capitalism.' " *Christian Herald*, January 1959.

———. "We Choose Our Alternative." *Christian Herald*, February 1941.

———. "Well Done, Mr. President." *Christian Herald*, April 1961.

———. "What Jesus Christ Has to Say." *Christian Herald*, February 1942.

———. "World Freedom is Our Real Objective." *Christian Herald*, June 1961.

Price, Oliver. "America There is an Absolute!" *Moody Monthly*, July-August 1971.

Pugmire, Herbert J. "Chaplain to a Revolution." *Moody Monthly*, June 1959.

The Presbyterian Educational Association of the South. "Advertisement." *Southern Presbyterian Journal*, July 1, 1953.

Preston, Andrew. *Sword of the Spirit, Shield of Faith*. New York: Alfred A. Knopf, 2012.

Prophecy Monthly. "Advertisement." *Moody Monthly*, May 1938.

Ramm, Bernard. "Behind the Turmoil and Terror in the Mid-East." *Eternity*, September 1967.

Raney, Klahr. "Of War and Such." *Presbyterian Journal*, September 30, 1970.

Reinke, Manfred E. "Christ is Coming! ... Soon!" *Christianity Today*, November 10, 1961.

Reynolds, Arthur T. F. "The Missionary in China Looks Ahead." *Eternity*, January 1951.

Richardson, John R. "The Fearful Night That Has Fallen on Our World." *Southern Presbyterian Journal*, August 1942.

Roberts, Andrew. *Masters and Commanders: How Four Titans Won the War in the West, 1941–1945*. New York: HarperCollins, 2009.

Roberts, Ralph. Letter to the Editor, *Eternity*, October 1956.

Robinson, William C. "From King David to President David." *Southern Presbyterian Journal*, January 29, 1958.

———. "A Good Soldier of Jesus Christ." *Southern Presbyterian Journal*, January 1944.

———. "Pray for Victory!" *Presbyterian Journal*, August 17, 1966.

———. "Sparrow—Soldier—Sailor." *Southern Presbyterian Journal*, June 1943.

———. "V-E: A Day for Thanksgiving." *Southern Presbyterian Journal*, June 1945.

Rose, Ben L. "A Call to Humility." *Southern Presbyterian Journal*, June 1943.

Ross, Ed. "The Real Lesson of the Calley Trial." *Presbyterian Journal*, May 19, 1971.

Ryrie, Charles C. "Perspective on Palestine." *Christianity Today*, May 23, 1969.

Sale-Harrison, L. "The Combination of Nations and God's Great Prophetic Word." *Moody Monthly*, June 1940.

Sayegh, Fayez. "The Arab View." *Moody Monthly*, July 1955.

Schaeffer, Francis A. "Christian Compassion: Have We Lost Our Touch?" *Eternity*, December 1970.

———. Letter to Derek Sangster, June 13, 1968, Francis A. Schaeffer Collection, Box 49, File 26, The Library, Southeastern Baptist Theological Seminary, Wake Forest, North Carolina.

———. Letter to J. O. Buswell, April 16, 1952, Francis A. Schaeffer Collection, Box 57, File 22, The Library, Southeastern Baptist Theological Seminary, Wake Forest, North Carolina.

———. Letter to J. O. Buswell, May 30, 1952, Francis A. Schaeffer Collection, Southeastern Baptist Theological Seminary, Wake Forest, North Carolina.

———. Letter to J. O. Buswell, July 7, 1952, Francis A. Schaeffer Collection, Box 57, File 22, The Library, Southeastern Baptist Theological Seminary, Wake Forest, North Carolina.

————. Letter to George Smith, December 15, 1947, Francis A. Schaeffer Collection, Box 57, File 22, The Library, Southeastern Baptist Theological Seminary, Wake Forest, North Carolina.

————. Letter to Kenneth A. Kantzer, June 5, 1982, Francis A. Schaeffer Collection, Box 78, File 14, The Library, Southeastern Baptist Theological Seminary, Wake Forest, North Carolina.

————. Letter to Kenneth de Courcy, September 15, 1956, Francis A. Schaeffer Collection, Box 57, File 22, The Library, Southeastern Baptist Theological Seminary, Wake Forest, North Carolina.

————. Letter to Molly Holt, February 23, 1952, Francis A. Schaeffer Collection, Southeastern Baptist Theological Seminary, Wake Forest, North Carolina.

————. Letter to President Harry S. Truman, November 19, 1951, Francis A. Schaeffer Collection, Box 57, File 23, The Library, Southeastern Baptist Theological Seminary, Wake Forest, North Carolina.

————. Letter to Robert G. Rayburn, July 16, 1951, Francis A. Schaeffer Collection, Box 57, File 22, The Library, Southeastern Baptist Theological Seminary, Wake Forest, North Carolina.

————. Letter to Robert Rayburn, July 17, 1955, Francis A. Schaeffer Collection, Box 57, File 22, The Library, Southeastern Baptist Theological Seminary, Wake Forest, North Carolina.

————. Letter to Robert Rayburn, January 9, 1956, Francis A. Schaeffer Collection, Box 57, File 22, The Library, Southeastern Baptist Theological Seminary, Wake Forest, North Carolina.

————. Letter to Ted Noe, December 1957, Francis A. Schaeffer Collection, Box 57, File 22, The Library, Southeastern Baptist Theological Seminary, Wake Forest, North Carolina.

————. "The Modern Drift: Is Nobody Home in this World?" *Christianity Today*, June 20, 1960.

Scharlemann, Martin H. "The Church Must Be Color-Blind." *Eternity*, July 1957.

Schwarz, Frederick C. "Can We Meet the Red Challenge?" *Christianity Today*, April 13, 1959.

Scripture Press. "Advertisement." *Moody Monthly*, August 1951.

Seelye, Todd, Robert J. Little, Louis Goldberg, and Alan Johnson. "Bible Prophecy and The Mid-East Crisis." *Moody Monthly*, July-August 1967.

Semenchuck, Ken. "We Toured the Ukraine … and Found God." *Eternity*, August 1969.

Settje, David. *Faith and War: How Christians Debated the Cold and Vietnam Wars*. New York: New York University Press, 2011.

Shepherd, Coulson. "The Unholy Holy Land." *Moody Monthly*, July 1951.

Shepley, Reginald. "Can God Meet America's Need in the Present Crisis?" *Moody Monthly*, July 1938.

Shields, Jane Smith. "Our Soldiers and Foreign Missions." *Southern Presbyterian Journal*, February 1944.

Sigrist, Helen. "Prejudice: The Respectable Sin." *Eternity*, October 1953.

Simpson, J. David. "Non-Segregation Means Eventual Inter-Marriage." *Southern Presbyterian Journal*, March 15, 1948.

Singer, C. Gregg. "Are We Forgetting Our Government?" *Moody Monthly*, July 1947.

Silver Publishing Society. "Advertisement." *Moody Monthly*, May 1938.

Skinner, Tom. "Why We Must Win the American Negro." *Moody Monthly*, April 1968.

Slocum, Stephen E. "A Just and Durable Peace." *Moody Monthly*, November 1943.

———. "While We Watch for the Sunrise." *Moody Monthly*, February 1947.

Smith, Wilbur M. *The Atomic Bomb and the Word of God*. Chicago: Moody Press, 1945.

———. "The Church, the Tribulation and the Rapture." *Moody Monthly*, March 1957.

———. "How Antichrist Will Rule." *Moody Monthly*, February 1948.

———. "Israel in Her Promised Land." *Christianity Today*, December 24, 1956.

———. "Jerusalem in Prophecy, Part VI: Prophecies That Relate to This Age." *Moody Monthly*, October 1960.

———. "Religion in the White House." *Moody Monthly*, May 1953.

———. "The Significance of the Mediterranean Sea in the Old and New Testaments." *Moody Monthly*, May 1938.

———. *Studies in Faith and Hope: The Gospel of Mark for Men in Service*. Moody Press: Chicago, 1944.

———. "The Testimony of Bible Prophecy." *Moody Monthly*, September 1949.

———. "This Serious Hour." *Moody Monthly*, November 1954.

———. "What Christ Actually Taught about War." *Moody Monthly*, March 1942.

———. "What Christ Actually Taught about War." *Moody Monthly*, April 1942.

———. "What Christ Actually Taught about War." *Moody Monthly*, May 1942.

———. "What Christ Actually Taught about War." *Moody Monthly*, June 1942.

———. "World Crises and the Prophetic Scriptures, Part I." *Moody Monthly*, June 1950.

———. "World Government at the End of This Age: Part Iron and Part Clay." *Moody Monthly*, February 1939.

Solberg, Carl. "The Lutheran Church Ministers to its Men Under Arms." *Christian Herald*, August 1942.

Soltau, Eleanor. "Spotlight on Koreans." *Moody Monthly*, November 1950.

St. Clair, Robert J. "The Muddle of Viet Nam." *Eternity*, September 1965.

Stacey, Alexander. "Will Russia Stay with the Allies?" *Christian Herald*, August 1942.

Stacy, C. I. "The Other Side." *Moody Monthly*, April 1942.

Stegall, Carroll R. "God and the USA in Vietnam." *Eternity*, March 1968.

Stevens, Jason. *God Fearing and Free: A Spiritual History of America's Cold War*. Cambridge, MA: Harvard University Press, 2010.

Stob, Henry. "Calley Affair." *Eternity*, January 1972.

Stone, Nathan J. "Practical and Perplexing Questions." *Moody Monthly*, August 1946.

Stroh, Grant. "Hitler as the Antichrist." *Moody Monthly*, August 1940.

———. "Practical and Perplexing Questions." *Moody Monthly*, November 1939.

Strong, Robert. "The Second Coming of Christ." *Presbyterian Journal*, November 30, 1966.

Suekane, Toshio. "Report on Red China." *Christianity Today*, November 25, 1957.

The Sunday School Times. "Advertisement." *Moody Monthly*, November 1939.

Sutton, Matthew Avery. *American Apocalypse: A History of Modern Evangelicalism*. Cambridge, MA: Belknap Press, 2014.

Sweeney, Douglas. *The American Evangelical Story: The History of the Movement.* Grand Rapids, MI: Baker Academic, 2005.

Sweeting, George. "A New Surge in Prophecy." *Moody Monthly*, March 1973.

———. "Peace for All Time." *Moody Monthly*, November 1972.

———. "Thanksgiving: More Than a Holiday." *Moody Monthly*, November 1972.

———. "War Again in the Mid-East." *Moody Monthly*, December 1973.

Taylor, G. Aiken. "Across the Editor's Desk." *Presbyterian Journal*, May 17, 1972.

———. "Clergy Not Pacifists—Fellowship Finds." *Presbyterian Journal*, October 30, 1963.

———. "In the Wake of the Cease Fire." *Presbyterian Journal*, February 17, 1973.

———. "Is It Armageddon?" *Presbyterian Journal*, October 31, 1973.

———. "It's a Sort of Insanity." *Presbyterian Journal*, September 10, 1969.

———. "Not Attacking 'Institutions,' " *Presbyterian Journal*, February 14, 1962.

———. "Prayer Breakfast Most Impressive Ever." *Presbyterian Journal*, February 19, 1964.

———. "The Real War-Mongers." *Presbyterian Journal*, June 2, 1965.

———. "See 'Watergate.' " *Presbyterian Journal*, June 6, 1973.

———. "This is Not the Way to Justice." *Presbyterian Journal*, April 17, 1968.

———. "Two Black Men Went to Montreat." *Presbyterian Journal*, August 27, 1969.

———. "Why Communism Is Godless." *Christianity Today*, December 22, 1958.

Thompson, Robert N. "Mao's China." *Presbyterian Journal*, September 5, 1973.

Thompson, Willis. "How Will Jesus Return?" *Southern Presbyterian Journal*, June 1, 1949.

Thornton, Zeda. "Appeal to Castro." *Moody Monthly*, January 1970.

Tong, Hollington K. "Christians Are Still Being Martyred in Red China." *Moody Monthly*, October 1957.

Tyndale House Publishers. "Advertisement." *Moody Monthly*, September 1972.

Unger, J. Kelly. "The Great Delusion." *Southern Presbyterian Journal*, August 1945.

Vajda, Jaroslav. " 'We Will Not Give Up,' Czech People Vow." *Eternity*, October 1968.

Van Arnam, G. M. "What is Wrong with America?" *Moody Monthly*, July 1937.

Van Ryn, August. "Is Jesus Coming Soon?" *Moody Monthly*, April 1949.

Vassady, Bela. "Marginal Notes on the Tragedy of Hungary." *Christianity Today*, December 10, 1956.

Walvoord, John F. "Is the Lord's Coming Imminent?" *Eternity*, January 1954.

———. "Russia and the Middle East in Prophecy." *Moody Monthly*, December 1959.

———. "What is the Future of Communism?" *Eternity*, March 1955.

Warner Bros. "Advertisement." *Christian Herald*, July 1944.

Watson, Tom, Jr. "Three-Star General Under Higher Orders." *Moody Monthly*, November 1969.

Weber, Timothy P. *On the Road to Armageddon: How Evangelicals Became Israel's Best Friend.* Grand Rapids: Baker Academic, 2004.

Weinstein Michael L., and Davin Seay. *With God on Our Side: One Man's War against an Evangelical Coup in America's Military.* New York: Thomas Dunne Books, 2006.

Welch, Estelle Lovelle. "He's Home Tonight." *Moody Monthly*, September 1945.

Whaley, Howard. "The America of Today and Yesteryear." *Moody Monthly*, July–August 1972.

Williams, W. Twyman. "Christ And Caesar." *Southern Presbyterian Journal*, January 1943.

Woodbridge, Charles J. "Half Mast." *Southern Presbyterian Journal*, February 15, 1946.

———. "The Second Coming of Christ." *Moody Monthly*, May 1962.

Young, G. Douglas. "At East in Zion." *Eternity*, April 1969.

Zepp, Fred R. "Filth Threatens Your Home." *Christian Herald*, May 1965.

———. "Integration and You." *Christian Herald*, November 1964.

Author Index

Barnhouse, Donald Grey
4n, 16n, 18, 143n, 148, 150-151, 151n, 155,
156n, 160, 163n, 172n, 175, 175n, 178-
179, 179n, 180, 182, 184n, 188n-189n,
191, 193n, 196, 198, 198n, 200, 204,
210n-211n, 211, 214-215n, 219, 219n,
225-226, 225n-226n, 229-231, 230n, 235,
235n, 237n, 240n, 245, 246n, 255, 258n,
263n, 278, 279n, 319, 347n, 363, 363n,
365, 378-380, 383, 387, 389

Bell, L. Nelson
4n, 18, 56, 71, 81-82, 84, 104-105, 110,
116n, 119n, 122-123, 126, 126n, 130,
130-131n, 147n, 149, 149n, 151, 155n,
159-160, 160n, 164n, 166n, 167, 169,
170n, 173, 173-174n, 175-176, 178n-179n,
187n, 189, 189n, 191, 193, 193n, 197-199,
202n, 206n-207n, 212n-213n, 216-217,
216n-217n, 218-221, 224n, 230n, 234,
244, 244n, 251n, 255, 255n, 260, 287,
288n, 295, 298n, 327, 328n, 337n, 338n,
350n, 352, 352n-353n, 383-384, 386

Culbertson, William
18, 115, 123, 132, 133n, 140, 140n, 145,
145n, 148-149, 165, 176-177, 193n, 195,
196n, 204, 206, 206n, 208n, 217n,
219-220, 219n, 242, 257, 257n-258n,
276, 276n, 295, 297, 299, 306, 313n, 319,
320n, 322, 340, 372, 389

English, E. Schuyler
18, 57n-58n, 58, 62, 70, 72, 76, 82-84,
89, 89n, 91, 94-95, 94n-95n, 101, 104,
104n, 107-110, 110n, 117, 119, 122, 122n,
124-126, 129-130, 133n-136n, 134-135,
138, 178, 182, 377, 379

Henry, Carl F. H.
6, 17n, 18, 52n, 96, 144n, 146-147, 149,
156n, 157-159, 159n, 165-167, 169-180,
169n, 174, 181n, 184n, 187, 187n, 190-
192, 194n, 196-197, 203, 203n, 205,
206n, 208, 208-209n, 212, 212n, 217-
218, 220-222, 222-223n, 227, 227n-229n,
233, 236, 239, 242, 244n, 246, 249, 251,
251n, 253, 255-256, 260-261, 261n-262n,
264-269, 269n, 270n-271n, 277, 279-
280, 282, 282n-283n, 285, 288, 292-294,
294n, 295-296, 296n, 297, 298n, 300,
302-304, 305n-307n, 308, 308n-309n,
314, 315n, 316-320, 324, 325n, 335, 339,
342, 344, 348, 359, 360n, 366, 378, 383-
385, 389-390

Gaebelein, Arno C.
22-23, 26-30, 28n-29n, 33, 37, 37n-38n,
40-41, 44, 48n, 49-51, 53, 57-58, 58n, 63,
77, 78n, 94n-95n, 98, 134n, 135, 178-180,
182, 383

Graham, Billy
2n, 5n, 6, 9, 12, 17n, 18, 116n, 142, 142n,
187, 187n, 190, 190n-202n, 200, 239,
242, 243n, 248-249, 248n, 258, 258n,
272, 300n, 305n, 337, 341, 343, 351n, 383

Harrison, William K.
7, 19, 147-148, 191, 215-216, 215n-216n,
221, 228n-229n, 245n-246n, 279, 299n,
315n-316n, 355n

Hitt, Russell T.
16n, 18, 201, 237, 237n, 242, 253, 259-
260, 264, 271, 301, 301n-302n, 327, 330-
331, 331n, 335-336, 342-343, 345n-346n,
349n, 354-355, 361, 363, 363n, 365,
373-374, 383

Houghton, William H.
18, 21n, 24, 31, 31n, 35-39, 42-44, 49,
62-66, 65n, 66, 69-70, 72-75, 79, 84, 89,
89n, 91, 96, 112n, 113, 117, 382, 389

Kucharsky, David E.
57, 239-240, 239n-240n, 249, 259, 269,
285, 286n, 293n, 309n, 314n-315n

Lampman, Charles T.
   193n, 198n, 201n, 201, 201n-203n, 204,
   207n, 210-211
Lindsell, Harold
   213, 213n, 289-290, 290n, 294n,
   328, 329n, 332, 334, 336, 338-339,
   338n-339n, 340, 350, 352, 354, 356-358,
   367n-368n
Schaeffer, Francis A.
   19, 114, 143n-144n, 156n, 161-162, 162n,
   165-166, 186, 186n-187n, 197n, 208-
   209, 254, 282n, 351, 378, 383

Smith, Wilbur M.
   5n, 11n, 18, 31n, 51-52, 80n-81n, 87n,
   88, 97, 115-116, 133, 133n, 136, 137n, 155-
   156, 177, 182, 222n, 226, 226n, 230-231,
   275, 276-277, 321, 384
Sweeting, George
   339-340, 353, 362, 370n,
Taylor, G. Aiken
   187-188, 188n, 250, 267, 299-300, 306,
   309-310, 332-333, 343, 350n, 358-359,
   369-370

Subject Index

America as Christian Nation
  24, 40, 114-115, 159, 188n, 201n, 204,
  207, 293, 297, 346, 380
Atomic or Nuclear Weapons and War
  5, 5n, 7, 11, 14, 55, 84, 87-90, 88-90n,
  92, 97-98, 101, 108-109, 126-131, 128n,
  130n-131n, 136-137, 141, 154n, 167-172,
  169n, 172, 175-177, 180-181, 181n, 184-
  185, 185n, 217-221, 219n, 221n, 232-233,
  245, 245n, 249, 254, 258, 264-266, 270-
  271, 270n-271n, 274-275, 281-283, 290n,
  307n, 318-319, 355n, 364n, 375, 384-386,
  388, 390
Castro, Fidel
  239-242, 240n, 253, 269, 284, 333, 379
China
  20-21, 23-25, 23n, 58, 78n, 83, 94-95,
  100-101, 103-106, 104n, 121, 142, 147n,
  150-153, 151n-152n, 173n, 174-175, 175n,
  192-194, 192n-194n, 217, 234-236,
  235n-236n, 243, 243n, 253, 287-288,
  287n-288n, 292n, 302n, 327-330,
  328n-329n, 347n, 379
Cuba
  7, 69, 103, 232, 239, 240-242, 240n,
  243n, 253, 259, 269-270, 284, 333-334
East Germany; Berlin
  144, 160n, 238-239, 239n, 243-244,
  243n, 264, 268-269, 335, 378, 380
Europe; New Roman Empire
  25-27, 28n, 32, 48, 57, 94, 135, 141, 179-
  180, 182, 229n, 230, 272-273, 275, 278,
  279n, 318, 320, 362, 364n, 372, 388
Germany
  20-25, 27-33, 28n, 35-36, 46-51, 54, 55,
  57, 59-64, 71, 78, 80n, 83, 89n-90n, 92-
  94, 101, 107, 109, 111, 113, 122, 128n, 144n,
  148n, 150, 163n, 169, 230, 290-291, 298,
  303, 348, 351, 362, 377, 384

Hitler, Adolf
  21-24, 27-30, 28n, 31, 33-34, 42, 44, 46,
  48-49, 51, 52, 57, 61-63, 72, 75, 79n, 82,
  89, 93-94, 95n, 97, 109, 111, 122, 127, 133,
  336, 348, 377, 384
Hoover, J. Edgar
  7, 120n, 153, 202n-203n, 234n, 251, 251n
Hungary, 1956
  7, 101, 184n, 195-199, 195n, 197n, 268,
  288-290, 380
Italy
  21-27, 28n, 47, 50, 57, 57n, 62, 274
Japan
  5, 21n, 23-25, 23n, 25n, 31-33, 36, 36n,
  54-55, 57-65, 59n, 65n-66n, 77-78, 78n,
  92-93, 95, 101
Khrushchev, Nikita
  185n, 198, 235, 242-243, 245n-247n, 246,
  249, 255n, 259, 265, 268, 281, 291-292,
  384
Korea
  7, 19, 102, 110, 142-143, 145n, 147, 160-
  161, 160n, 165, 170-175, 172n-174n, 181,
  184, 189, 191-192, 192n, 218, 236-237,
  237n, 261, 296n, 315n, 359, 375, 384
Mao, Zedong
  23n, 103-104, 106, 142, 151, 151n-152n,
  182, 192-194, 192n-193n, 234-235, 236n,
  243, 287, 287n, 327-329, 328n, 347n, 377,
  379, 384
Mussolini, Benito
  22, 25-27, 26n, 33, 41-42, 44, 48, 50-51,
  57, 57n-58n, 62, 95n, 97, 133, 384
Pacifism
  4, 5n, 38n, 43-47, 45n, 84-87, 86n-87n,
  122-123, 166-167, 166n, 216-217,
  216n-217n, 267-268, 270n-271n, 308-
  310, 308n-310n, 315n-316n, 355n-356n
Prague, 1968
  290-291, 325, 328n, 334, 376, 380

Race; Segregation; Racism
42, 61, 65-66, 65n-66n, 74, 117-118,
146, 162-164, 163n-165n, 210-214,
210n-214n, 261-263, 261n-263n, 295,
300-306, 301n-306n, 346n, 349-352,
349n-351n
Red Scare; House Committee on
Un-American Activities; Joseph Mc-
Carthy
119-120, 119n-120n, 153, 186-188,
188n-189n, 251, 251n
Roman Catholicism
110, 143n-144n, 188n-189n, 203n, 211n,
237, 237n, 239, 251n, 257, 257n, 285,
286n, 309n, 314n, 363
Russia; USSR; Soviet Union
6-7, 9, 12, 20-23, 23n, 25-26, 28n, 29-
30, 30n, 32-33, 41-42, 44, 47-49, 55-57,
56n, 62-63, 75, 83, 92-95, 100-104,
104n, 106-111, 107n, 110n, 112, 116,
119n, 122-126, 124n, 126n, 128-132,
131n, 134-135, 135n, 141, 143-146,
143n-144n, 148-150, 149n, 152n, 153,
155n, 157, 159-160, 160n, 163n, 165, 170,
174-175, 175n, 177, 179-182, 184-185,
184n-185n, 189-191, 195-198, 195n,
197n-199n, 209-210, 209n, 216-220,
217n, 219n, 224n-225n, 225, 229n, 230,
230n, 232-233, 235n, 236, 242-249,
243n-245n, 248n, 254-256, 255n-256n,
263n, 265-267, 269n, 270, 273-275, 278,
279n, 281-282, 283n, 288n, 289-293,
290n-293n, 307n, 318-319, 321n, 323,
325-326, 328n, 329, 331-332, 334-337,
348, 361-362, 364, 364n, 367n, 370,
376-380, 383, 387-388
Stalin, Joseph
21, 23, 23n, 28n, 31, 49, 94, 107, 176,
189, 199, 245, 291, 318, 329, 377, 384
State of Israel
10-11, 11n, 137-141, 139n, 176-179, 179n,
182-183, 184n, 222-228, 223n-229n,
230-231, 272-273-278, 279n, 317, 319-
326, 321n, 323n-325n, 353, 362-370,
364n-368n, 370n, 375, 386-388

Totalitarianism
Nazism
4, 5n, 6, 27, 28n, 29-31, 33-34, 53, 57,
60, 62-64, 70, 73, 75, 79n-80n, 84,
89, 109-110, 132, 148, 212n, 222n,
236, 262n, 288n, 336, 348, 351, 376-
377, 380, 385
Fascism
5, 26, 29, 44, 57, 92, 110n, 252n, 377,
380,
Communism
6-8, 12-13, 22, 23n, 28n, 29, 32-34,
38n, 42, 52, 56, 69, 75, 92, 100-
112, 110n 104n 101n, 112, 119-120,
119n-120, 124-125, 130, 131n, 139,
142-153, 143n-148n, 152n, 157-159,
161, 165, 167, 171, 172n-174n, 174-175,
177, 181-182, 185-192, 187n-189n,
192n-195n, 193-194, 196, 197n-199n,
198, 201n-203n, 204, 208-209,
211n, 215n-216n, 216, 218, 228n,
230, 230n, 232-234, 234n, 235-254,
236n-237n, 239n-240n, 245n-246n,
250n-253n, 259, 263-266, 268, 271n,
273, 281-292, 282n-283n, 286n,
288n, 291n, 297-298, 302n, 308n,
309-312, 313n-316n, 314, 318, 328-
330, 328n-329n, 332, 332n, 335-336,
347n, 352, 355n, 356, 358, 366n, 375,
377-380, 383, 385, 389
United Nations
95, 126, 129, 132, 138, 140, 143, 147, 157,
175, 177, 184, 192, 192n, 209n, 211n,
221n, 225, 265, 302n, 327, 329n
U. S. Presidents
President Roosevelt
1, 35-36, 35n, 53, 114, 162,
President Truman
6, 12, 101n, 125, 130n, 134n, 135,
143n-144n, 156n, 173n, 184,
President Eisenhower
6, 12, 153, 155-157, 156n, 184n-185n,
185, 200-202, 200n-202n, 217, 232,
245, 247, 252n, 255-256, 255n-256n,
342, 344, 375, 381,

President Kennedy
  189n, 242, 257-259, 257n-258n,
  261n, 268, 281, 295, 306n, 358
President Johnson
  232, 281, 299-300, 308, 314, 354, 358
President Nixon; Watergate
  1, 202n, 288n, 294n, 300n, 326-327,
  340-344, 344n, 355, 358, 376, 379

Vietnam
  1, 4, 7-8, 14, 102, 218, 232, 237-238,
  237n, 285-286, 286n, 297, 302n, 308-
  317, 308n, 312n-315n, 325-326, 330-333,
  331n-332n, 337n, 340, 349, 354-358,
  355n, 376, 385-386,
Zionism
  28n, 53, 138-139, 178, 223n, 323, 367n